The Darkness Did Not

The Darkness Did Not

by

WILLIAM L. BIERSACH

TUMBLAR HOUSE
'Bona Tempora Volvant'

Arcadia
MMVI

Nihil Obstat: *Huh?*

✤   Imprimatur: *Are you kidding!?!?*

ISBN: 0-9712786-1-X
(Soft cover)

First printing: 2004
Second printing: 2006

Manufactured in the U.S.A.
by
Tumblar House
PMB 376
411 E. Huntington Drive, #107
Arcadia, CA 91006
www.tumblarhouse.com

THE DARKNESS DID NOT

*The second book in the continuing saga of
Fr. John Baptist, the cop-turned-priest, and
Martin Feeney, his gardener-turned-chronicler.*

Other books by

William L. Biersach

∞

Published by Tumblar House

Fiction

The Endless Knot
The Search for Saint Valeria
Out of the Depths

Nonfiction

While the Eyes of the Great are Elsewhere

∞

Published by Catholic Treasures

Nonfiction

Of Mary There Is Never Enough

This book is gratefully dedicated to

St. Martha of Bethany
Housekeeper and Dragonslayer

St. Martha, I resort to thy aid and protection. As proof of my affection and faith, I offer thee this light, which I shall burn every Tuesday. Comfort me in all my difficulties and through the great favors thou didst enjoy when the Savior was lodged in thy house, intercede for my family, that we be provided for in our necessities. I ask of thee, St. Martha, to overcome all difficulties as thou didst overcome the dragon which thou hadst at thy feet. Amen.

—Novena Prayer to St. Martha

You should have seen the look on his face
when he woke up in Hell beside me,
the demon who was waiting to take possession of his body.
What a horrible taste I had in his mouth
when I first opened these eyes!

—The Vampire

0

AUTHOR'S NOTE: "Just what the world needs," I said to myself as I sat down to write this sequel to *The Endless Knot* on the Feast of St. Martha: "another vampire story!" But, given Father Baptist's peculiar calling and unconventional circumstance, the idea of a vampire intrusion into the mythical city of Los Angeles flowed as easily as sacrificial blood into the ancient Valley of Hinnom. I say "mythical" as a reminder that this story did not, and could not, have taken place in the actual, venerable City of Angels which we know and love, famous for its pious clergy and exemplary citizenry. As before, the true identity of Morley Fulbright's domain must remain secret to protect the insolent. Oh, and of course this caveat applies to the fabled city of Lexington, Kentucky, as well. The genuine article is nothing like the one in this story. No way.

Regarding the subject at hand, I was recently asked by one of my manuscript perusers, "So, do you believe in vampires?" To which I answered, "It doesn't matter what I believe; at least, not so far as my story is concerned. Father Baptist: now he's the one you have to figure out."

But my associate was persistent—a quality I both enjoy and dread in most of my closest friends. So, after a moment's reflection, I took a hefty breath, swirled the port in my glass, and replied: "I believe in the Catholic Church which, by Her own definition, enfolds the Mystery of the meeting of the finite with the infinite, the carnal with the supernatural, the ordinary with the extraordinary, the human with the Divine, the evil with the good. In short, my religion is centered on the terrible and the miraculous, which are but two interdependent faces of the awesome, disconcerting, and often humbling Truth. Truth, in my experience, is not embraced for the 'high,' but rather for the 'verity.' Now, stories of vampires, of which there are many documented accounts by otherwise respectable persons and reputable scholars, epitomize the war of Hell against Heaven. Considering some of what I've encountered in my lifetime due to my convictions—no, not vampires, but things which are certainly outside the norm—I am not beyond allowing the possibility of their existence."

"You can't mean that," chided my colleague who had, after all, instigated the conversation in the first place and who, I suspect, had known all along where it would lead.

So I continued: "If I can believe that God once looked out from His cradle and gazed upon the stars which He had made, or that He emptied

Himself of His Glory as well as His Blood for our sake, or that a priest by saying a formula of five words can call that same God down onto an altar, or that any of us—when honestly, soberly assessed—has a gnat's chance of sharing Eternity with Him in Heaven; well, next to all that, a vampire is not so big a deal, after all. Of course, I also respect the Bible, in which I find warnings such as:

> There are spirits that are created for vengeance, and in their fury they lay on grievous torments.
>
> —Ecclesiasticus XXXIX: 33

"While this passage may not describe vampires per se," I concluded, "it does tell us that things just as horrible, if not worse, are part and parcel of Creation—and they aren't sleeping. Like it or not."

My friend did not seem convinced. Perhaps that's because in the retelling I've had time to clean up my grammar and arrange my thoughts into a more impressive and cohesive argument. That's the advantage of words on a page.

Whatever their religious views, I hope my readers will enjoy this tale. I realize it crosses certain boundaries of mystery fiction; but that, I think, is part of the fun. And it opens certain doors to curious destinations in future works. We shall see.

—WLB3

N.B.: Maybe one reader in ten million will recognize certain details from the scene on the Farquar Terrace that were brazenly "borrowed" from David McDaniel's *The Man from U.N.C.L.E. Number Six: The Vampire Affair*. To this charge of willful plagiarism I gleefully plead *nolo contendere*.

P.N.B.: I wish to extend a garland of "sunfloosies" to those who believed in and helped with my work: Stephan Baron von Hoeller-Bertram, Julia Ulano, Mark Alessio, Jeannette Coyne, Beverly Dykes, and Anne Hale. A twenty-one cork salute to the scattered members of Drones Club International: Charles A. Coulombe, Stephen Frankini, Michael Dykes (who suggested the name "Knights Tumblar"), Axel Müllers, Matthew Crow, and Kirk Mulhearn. Also, special mention to FJB; Brother Leonard Mary, MICM; Brother Thomas Aquinas, MICM; Annie Witz my "K" Sis; Michael Malone, whose passing left a gaping chasm—and finally a crate of fresh garlic to Bonnie Callahan for the cover art.

Tuesday, October Seventeenth

Feast Day of Saint Margaret Mary, Nun, to whom was revealed the practice of Veneration of the Sacred Heart of Jesus (1690 AD)

1

"'AND THE LIGHT SHINETH IN DARKNESS,'" read Father Baptist from the stained and tattered Bible in his lap as I rounded the patch of gardenias bobbing around the feet of the statue of St. Joseph. A gust of hot, humid air fluttered the edges of the page under Father's hand. "'And,'" he concluded ominously, rolling the covers of the flimsy book closed against the wind, "'the darkness did not comprehend it.'"

It was late in the afternoon, and the sky looked gloomy and threatening. He was seated on the wooden bench in the garden between the church and the rectory, the hem of his threadbare cassock flapping in the sultry breeze. Beside him, at the respectable distance of an arm's length and a half, sat a woman in her early twenties in a sky-blue dress. Her long walnut-brown hair, gathered in back with a lichen-green scarf, puffed and fluttered as gusts of humid air surged by.

"In this sentence," said Father, hefting the book in both hands as if it contained the weight of the world, "is distilled the crux of our situation. The Truth has presented itself. Indeed, it has intruded into history and is burning fiercely like a beacon from shore during a ferocious storm, seeking to penetrate the gloom of our bad will."

The limbs of the overhanging oak tree heaved and creaked, their leaves rattling and scraping portentously at his grim explanation of the human predicament. The statue of St. Thérèse the Little Flower on its stone pedestal, which faced the bench on which priest and catechumen sat, seemed to nod a grave but resigned approval of Father's perilous assessment.

"The question is," said Father, "will we choose to wallow in the oblivion of darkness, or will we strive toward that beacon, no matter the difficulty, no matter the cost? This is the question each of us must answer, not just as an intellectual exercise or philosophical conjecture, but as a necessary step toward the saving of our souls and the determination of how we will spend Eternity."

"Hmmm," she said, rubbing her arms. "Goose bumps again, Father."

"Yes," he nodded, tucking the volume into the mysterious folds of his cassock, "it is riveting, isn't it?"

"'Tantalizing' would be my word," she smiled.

"'Frightening' would be mine," I grinned as I lurched and lumbered toward them, keeping my erratic balance with the help of my cane. Well, I hope it was a grin. Considering the jolts of pain that shoot to my brain with every step I take, sometimes my smiles do not convey much in the way of kindliness.

"Frightening?" she laughed, looking up at me in surprise.

"As in 'terrifying,'" I assured her.

At that moment Millie banged some pots and pans in the rectory kitchen, dotting my i's and crossing my t with a housekeeper's vengeance. Even when beyond earshot, she had an uncanny instinct for timely culinary punctuation. Framed in the kitchen window, dear Millie looked a little like a guard in a prison tower. I acknowledged Millie's watchful presence with a friendly wave of my cane, to which she replied with a fierce swing of her wrought-iron skillet.

GARDENING TIPS: Be advised that Millie's proximity was a product of Father's design, not her idle curiosity. To avoid any opportunity for scandal, prudence required that Father Baptist never counsel a member of the feminine sex without Millie "present but out of earshot."

This arrangement bothered some of the parish ladies no end. If, say, Mrs. Regina Tradosaurus came to visit him in his study, she inevitably found the door propped wide open with Millie noisily vacuuming the clean throw-rug half-way down the hallway. If Mrs. T suggested coffee in the kitchen, Millie would snatch up her clipboard and station herself in the pantry taking detailed inventory of the bare shelves, or busy herself sorting non-existent linens in the adjacent laundry room.

The same watchfulness, of course, applied to this seemingly secluded wooden bench in the garden. Millie was nigh and noisily so. It was perhaps the only house rule for which Father allowed no exception.

Lest my reader become indignant, consider the way your eyebrow twitched when Father's charming

```
guest started rubbing her goose bumps.  'Nuff
said.
                                    --M.F.

N.B.: Incidentally, modern realities also required
the presence of myself in the next room or Mr.
Folkstone clipping the hedge under the study win-
dow whenever an adolescent male came seeking Fa-
ther's advice.  When it comes to potential scan-
dal, we practice equal-opportunity vigilance here
at St. Philomena's.
```

"Oh, there you are, Martin," said Father, a spark of that Light he had just been talking about flickering across his eyes. "You know Stella Billowack."

"Very well," I said, clunking to a standstill. Planting the rubber tip of my cane ceremoniously between the toes of my shoes on the mossy brick path, I rested my palms on its hand-carved wooden handle. Something in my neck cracked as I nodded in her direction. "So you've come back again," I said approvingly, "for more."

"Why, Mr. Feeney," she giggled, "nothing could keep me away. God, Reality, Truth—it's all so fascinating. I've never heard anyone explain things the way Father Baptist does, not even Pastor McIntosh."

I bristled at the mention of her family's Methodist mentor, and I didn't even know him then as well as I would by the end of this tale.

"Oh dear," she said, eyes sweeping down and up my cane, as if seeing it for the first time. "Is the change in weather aggravating your rheumatism?"

"Arthritis," I corrected her, looking up at the churning purple-gray clouds that had been rolling in from the northwest throughout the afternoon, "is not a fair-weather friend."

The day had begun with a beautiful orange sunrise. By the time Father finished morning Mass the sky had blossomed into a satisfying ultramarine blue, crystalline and clear as only Southern California can define autumn. A gentle easterly breeze had begun drifting lazily from the inland deserts toward the Pacific Ocean. I remember commenting on God's simple blessings as Father and I followed our nostrils across the garden toward Millie's buttermilk pancakes.

But things began to change just before noon. A blast of warm, humid air had come rolling unexpectedly out of the northwest, slopping over the mountains and inundating the City of Angels. Then thin glutinous clouds began invading the upper atmosphere, stretched into long gooey strands by ghostly high-altitude updrafts. They had a strange scarlet fluorescence to them, and were soon joined by lower, thicker, darker cousins.

Over lunch I had quoted the sixteenth chapter of St. Matthew's Gospel: "'Today there will be a storm, for the sky is red and lowering.'"

Father responded with the next verse: "'You know then how to discern the face of the sky: and can you not know the signs of the times?'"

By two o'clock the sky had become cluttered with overlapping thorns of dreary violet vapor, and the tepid wind more insistent, intrusive, and unpleasantly moist. At around five o'clock the Angel who guards the troposphere hung out the PARKING LOT FULL sign and went home. Now thunder rumbled menacingly in the firmament. But in spite of all this meteorological drama, a single drop of rain had yet to fall.

"I wouldn't consider arthritis a friend at all," grimaced Stella Billowack.

"He's a faithful companion," I countered, "and a constant comforter in any weather."

"You're joking aren't you?" She turned to Father. "Isn't he?"

"Hmm," said Father, looking up at me with those unnerving eyes that seemed to whisper, elementary yet profoundly, "Considering that we are each called to take up our Cross and follow Christ on His way to Calvary, and that in so doing we procure a chance of attaining Heaven, what better name to apply to our burden than 'friend'?" But all he actually said was, "Don't be too sure, Stella."

"Sure," she said, shaking her head and rolling her eyes. For her it was an affable rather than a disdainful gesture. "Sure."

As if to remind me just how faithful—and watchful—he was, my companion and comforter chose that moment to sink his perpetually friendly teeth into my spine and shake his pointed little head with furious but playful, tail-wagging abandon.

"HrmPHRHrhrm," I grunted, lowering myself onto the edge of the cement birdbath, taking care not to bump the rigid, porous bird perched precariously on its pockmarked rim. It had been broken off years ago and never properly repaired. At the slightest provocation it would topple into the ivy with an unceremonious plop. I was in no mood to go groping through the undergrowth on my knees in search of that troublesome bird.

"That's a beautiful walking stick, Mr. Feeney," commented Stella. "Most unusual."

"A gift," I said, hefting the aspen pole in my right hand and casually rolling it in my fingers until the dragon's head handle was snarling menacingly in her direction. "An example of amiable overkill on the part of a group of companions. There's a dagger inside, a concealed blade for self-defense or letter-opening or something."

"Ooh, do show me."

"Gladly," I said, holding it out for her closer inspection, "except I can't figure out how to release the catch."

"Don't ask me," she giggled, looking my dragon in the eyes and drawing her own face into a playful snarl.

"Is it time?" asked Father, checking his old-fashioned wind-up wristwatch with the cracked lens and twisted minute hand. The poor timepiece had been severely battered four months previously during a tumble off of a speakers' platform at a dedication ceremony. "Hm. Six-thirty."

"They're ready," I said, remembering my mission, "and waiting."

"We'll have to call it a night, Stella," said Father, rising to his feet. "I have a serious matter to attend to. Martin, you'd better fetch the monsignor. He'll want to be present."

"Will do," I said, hefting myself back up to a standing position with the aid of my overkill cane. My balance painfully achieved, I gave Miss Billowack what I hoped was a smile of encouragement. "It really is good to see you, and I applaud your perseverance and perspicacity."

"What's to persevere?" she laughed, gathering up her purse and a couple of mangled books from Father's shelves. "I've never felt so, so ... delightfully curious. As for 'perspicacity,' I don't know what that means."

"You'll learn," I said as I turned and began lumbering away.

"I'll meet you inside, Martin," called Father.

"Can we continue this soon?" I heard her ask.

"Of course," said Father.

"Maybe Thursday?"

"I think so," said Father absently. "Call me in the morning and we'll set up a time."

"I'll be devouring Belloc all night," she said cheerfully. "And I'll save St. Alphonsus for breakfast."

He said something else, but I was already too far away to hear it.

2

NODDING TO THE STATUE OF SAINT JOSEPH, the Patron of Departing Souls, I huffed and hobbled my way back down the brick path that meandered around the flowerbeds and gnarled trees between the church and rectory.

Behind the church the path cut a wide arc through an acre of dense vegetation which Mr. Folkstone had yet to tackle, let alone tame, with his vast but humble horticultural skills. Beyond this tangle of vines and crawlers was a crumbling stone wall punctuated by a wrought-iron gate that opened to the back parking lot, which in turn opened onto a narrow, dingy alley.

There were five spaces, all marked CLERGY—a haunting reminder that St. Philomena's had once required and supported such a staff.

Times had changed. Father's old '57 Buick lay comatose in the first slot, silently awaiting either miraculous mechanical revival or solemn junkyard burial. A '94 Jeep Cherokee—on more or less questionable loan from the Chancery motor pool—crouched in the second slot, poised to charge off in search of adventure at a moment's notice. The third space, the one directly in front of the gate, was empty.

The last two parking spaces were occupied by a top-heavy RV. It squatted there like a lopsided toad that had devoured too many flies. Its tires bulged balefully under a weight they hadn't been designed to support, and fluids of different color and texture gathered into a taciturn pool on the asphalt beneath the engine. The logo on the radiator grill said FORD, but the rest of the vehicle had been retrofitted by a company called THE TORTOISE AND THE SPARE, INC., whose appellation was emblazoned on every side in crusted red letters outlined in faded gold and green.

Why Monsignor Havermeyer insisted on living in this wobbly lunch bucket, rather than in a cozy room in the rectory under the shadow of Millie's watchful frying pan, was beyond me.

"Monsignor," I said, rapping on the door. The flimsy aluminum panel rattled with every tap of my knuckles. "Monsignor Havermeyer, it's time."

Silence.

Well, not exactly silence. The clouds overhead rumbled with cumulonimbic indigestion. The leaves in the trees chittered and gossiped as the heavy, humid breeze gathered momentum at the approach of the autumn storm. The spiteful retorts of a young couple staying in one of the upstairs rooms at the Best Western across the alley—the very building which had once been the convent attached to St. Philomena's—rose and fell like mercury in a sphygmomanometer clamped to a chainsmoker's arm.

Then I heard another noise—something breathy and hissy.

"Hello," I called, glancing at the light playing on the window shades from inside. There it was again. Perhaps the monsignor was napping, and that curious sound was his snoring. "Hello?"

From deep within the metallic bowels of the camper came a muffled growl. It was followed a second later by something heavy and solid striking something brittle and rickety.

"Monsignor?" I hailed.

Another growl and a resounding thump, but no answer.

Perplexed, I gripped the frail handle, gave it a half-turn, and pulled the door open. I was engulfed by a blast of amniotic gasses from within that was hotter, moister, odoriferouser, and more oppressive than the air outside. With considerable effort—my faithful companion and constant comforter being what he is—I grabbed a side-mounted handle and heaved myself up into the camper.

"Benedictam ..." whisper-snarled Monsignor Havermeyer, his tousled white hair flailing madly in the heat while his right hand made erratic jerking motions over the bulge of his auspicious tummy. "... ad-scriptam, ratam ... ratam ... rah—ah, phooey!" He slammed his hands down on both sides of the large missal spread open before him on the wobbly kitchen table. "I'll never get this right."

Gingerly, I squeezed my way between the propane stove and a bunk piled high with wrinkled clerical clothing. "Monsignor?"

"How can I be expected to concentrate on articulating these unpro-nounceable words," he huffed, balling his hands and pounding the table again, "while making all these Signs of the Cross at the same bloody time?"

"Sort of like chewing gum and rubbing your stomach," I said help-fully. "It takes considerable eye-lip-tongue-jaw-wrist-elbow coordina-tion, I'll grant you—"

"Can it, Feeney."

"—but if the almost-passed-over Curé d'Ars could pull it off, albeit with the miraculous intervention of St. Philomena herself—"

"Feeney," he growled a little louder.

"—who, I might add, has demonstrated repeatedly that she is not above lending assistance to us mortals at this poor parish—"

"Feeney." I'd say that was almost, but not quite, a yell.

"—then surely a man of your liturgical competence and intellectual caliber—"

"Feeney!" Now that was a yell. "Don't you barge in here making jokes at my expense."

"Monsignore," I blinked in what I hoped was Italian. "I'm not jok-ing."

"Then shut up," he snapped, boring into me with furious bloodshot eyes. "Do you hear me? Just shut up."

Dutifully I withered. As I did so, I couldn't help but notice the bright red pallor of the rigid scar tissue buckling between his twitching fingers. The crimson flesh on his hands matched the ugly convolution splayed across his forehead. It warped his facial expression into a per-petual scowl—even when he was smiling, which he wasn't right now.

The previous June, Monsignor Havermeyer had almost been killed when a massive charge of electricity—the big-brains in the police lab tossed around estimates in excess of seventeen thousand volts—passed through his body during a failed attempt on his life by a serial killer who, for a host of complicated reasons, had decided to murder an eclectic assortment of persons within the hierarchy of the Archdiocese of Los Angeles. Four other victims had not been so fortunate that fateful night, lacking the benefit of the thick Mexican tire-tread sandals the monsignor was so fond of wearing—sandals which had insulated him from "ground," thus saving his life and earning him the nickname of

"Ol' Lucky Soles." A fifth victim, unharmed by the same electrical trap, had gone stark, raving kaputsky, but that's another story.

GARDENING TIPS: At the time of this writing my previous manuscript, The Endless Knot, is still making its rounds among literary agents. The letter that arrived the day before this story began went as follows:

> Dear Mr. Feeney,
>   Thank you for thinking of us regarding The Endless Knot. We're sorry to report that we simply did not have enough enthusiasm for your project to pursue it.
>   Sincerely yours,
>
>   Blah B. Blah

In other words my brainchild, TEK, has yet to be published--or even considered for publication. I suppose this makes writing a sequel an act of presumption, but continuously developing events in the parish impel me to press on. Who knows? St. Louie Marie de Montfort's best work was accidentally discovered in a chest a century after his death--not that I'm comparing myself to so great a Saint. It's just that there are precedents.

In any case, part of the challenge of writing a sequel, even to a work in print, is avoiding excessive references to the previous book. This is all the more difficult when numerous actions within that earlier tale are only now coming to fruition in the present story.

What, I ask myself, will be the reaction of a reader for whom this book is their first exposure to the adventures of Father Baptist and his faithful gardener, indigenous philosopher, commentator, and self-appointed chronicler, yours truly Martin Feeney? I can only speculate.

Just mentioning the problem sounds like a barely veiled attempt at plugging my other book. Well, there is that. The effort would be more useful if the book were already published.

Still, it is a challenge ...

                    --M.F.

In any case, surviving that sinister incident had prompted Monsignor Michael K. Havermeyer to rethink his priorities. He resigned his pastorship at St. Philip's Cathedral (a sinecure if there ever was one) and was now attached to St. Philomena's Church (a word had yet to be invented) without hope of recovering his pension from the archdiocese (a threat which has historically kept many a priest docile in times of chaos). The rulers of the modern Church had no sympathy for priests who preferred Tradition to progressive banter.

That seventeen-thousand-volt brush with Eternity had swept away every pretense of luxury and security in the monsignor's life, only to dump him here in this mobile home beyond the walls so he could study the Latin Mass, which traced its essentials back to the reign of Pope Gregory the Great who died in the year 604 AD. This was a necessary chore if he was to assist Father Baptist in the running of this poor but rich parish because Father insisted on the Old Rituals to the exclusion of all post-Vatican II reforms, and his fragile but querulous parishioners had come to expect nothing less. For a man of Havermeyer's former ecclesiastical stature, position and influence, it had been a dizzying step downward—or rather upward, depending on your point of view.

Now, I may be "crotchety" and "dour" as Mrs. Magillicuddy is so fond of reminding me every Friday evening, but I wasn't above cutting this man some well-deserved slack. Observe:

"A thousand pardons, Monseigneur," I said in what I hoped was French, bowing as much as my diseased spine would allow. "I meant no offense. It's this mouth of mine, and more so my tongue—Saint James, chapter three, verse six. I've done many a Stations of the Cross on my knees in reparation for its nefarious wagging, I assure you. But wag it does, as if it had a will of its own."

He glared at me, no doubt wishing I was kneeling in his confessional at that precise moment. Visions of torturous penances danced behind his flaming retinas. I know the look. I've seen it in Father Baptist's eyes many times.

Then he made fists with his lips. It was quite a trick. "Grrrhrmph."

"I have come," I said, "among other reasons, to offer my help."

"Help," he said, rolling the word around in his mouth distastefully, as if it were a rotten corn kernel.

"Seriously," I added, sensing he might not realize how strongly I mean the things I say when I say them, especially the way that I say them. It's my manner, and my Guardian Angel has been shaking his head for years. "I will help you practice the rubrics, and for as long as it takes, until you are their master—or rather, until you are theirs."

"Help," he said again, not as a plea but as a systems check of his speech apparatus. He coughed to clear the larynxial pathways. "Help?"

"That's what I said," I assured him. "Help. All I can. I don't claim anything like expertise, but I have been serving as altar boy ever since

Father Baptist came to this parish and reinstated the Latin Mass five years ago. And did I tell you I was the first kid in my class to serve Mass way back when? I know my way around a missal."

He cleared his throat again and eyed me suspiciously. "Hm," he said, scrunching his lips into a texture that matched the fleshy contortions of his forehead. "Hm," he said again.

"But," I said, "in the immediate, Father Baptist is ready to commence the Benediction."

"What?" gasped the monsignor, rising from the miniature table. This maneuver was anything but fluid for a man so large detaching himself from a dinette so small. "I've lost all track of time."

"Time passes differently, I'll grant you," I said sagaciously, "here at St. Philomena's."

Hastily, he engaged the top half-dozen buttons of his new cassock with clumsy fingers, the rosy scar tissue puckering around his knuckles. I would have offered to help, but I sensed his dignity would not permit assistance. He adjusted his Roman collar to a crooked angle, but again I thought it better not to interfere.

"Ready," he said, smoothing the wrinkles from the unfamiliar garment. In his former job he had preferred sweatshirts and jeans as standard apparel. He still wore Mexican sandals, however. An old dog simply won't abandon some tricks, especially when they recently saved his hide.

"You might want to bring an overcoat," I said. "Looks like we're in for a downpour later tonight."

"This will do," he said, snatching up a black umbrella from beneath the heap of unlaundered clothing on the bunk.

"Excellent," I grunted as I turned and squeezed my way back toward the door. "Permit me to lead the way."

3

"IF YOU NEED TO SCRATCH DURING MASS," Father Baptist warned every group of boys in his weekly class on the fine art of altar-serving, "or to burp or cough or sneeze ... *don't.*" At such instructional moments he had an uncanny way of throwing his voice so that it seemed to emanate from the ceiling. "The same applies to Benediction."

Naturally, telling someone not to itch or secrete phlegm is the surest way to stir these natural processes into motion. Such is the paradox of devotion and discipline.

This particular mandate for self-control suddenly surged with significance as I stood at the Epistle side of the altar, manipulating the chain which opened the censer dangling from my hands. Father Baptist heaped two extra scoops of granular incense onto the glowing hunk of charcoal within. A mushroom of billowing white smoke erupted from the vessel and, sure enough, engulfed my face with its penetrating tendrils. Every hair follicle in my nostrils, every membrane in my sinuses, every gland in my mouth and throat, both Eustachian tubes, and both tear ducts went on red alert. I think my uvula retracted into my brain.

"Ab illo bene dicaris," said Father, making a Sign of the Cross over the smoldering incense, "in cujus honore cremaberis."

GARDENING TIPS: Father always smiled when he said this particular formula. It was the same one used by Pius IX when a group of Anglican clerics insisted that there must be some form of blessing the Holy Father could properly say over them. The prosaic Pope responded with the only blessing that he felt applied: "Mayest thou be blessed by Him in whose honor thou shalt burn."

--M.F.

"Amen," said yours truly, contorting my face every-which-way in a desperate attempt to stretch the itch out of my sinuses.

Make no mistake: I can think of only two scents I enjoy as much as liturgical incense, and neither of those are part of my life any more. And knowing as I did that Father Baptist measures the auspiciousness of holy occasions in spoonfuls, I hoped the Knights Tumblar appreciated the depth and sincerity of his patronage. Nonetheless, from the moment those crystals of frankincense, myrrh, cedar, cinnamon and other precious resins hit the hot coal, releasing a luxurious plume of meditative fragrance, this poor over-aged gardener-turned-altar-boy needed to sneeze so badly he couldn't think straight. My whole universe collapsed into this proposition: to sneeze or not to sneeze. It wasn't really a matter of action or inaction, but rather of how long I could postpone the inevitable.

Mind you, to all others present, I went through the motions of bowing reverently to Father, turning slowly, retracing my steps back to the designated spot at the foot of the altar steps where I settled painfully onto my knees and began rocking the censer in forward arcs, clinking the vessel in metered triplets against the chains, sending waves of dense white smoke spiraling up to God. Part of the trick was to keep the thing swinging without banging it against the mosaic floor, the marble steps, Father himself, me myself, or anything else within striking distance. I knew the proper motions, and I executed them with precision.

But inside, all I could think of was: *Ah ... ah ... ah ... aaaAAAAAAA—*

This whole maneuver was made the more difficult because, as usual, I'd left my cane behind in the sacristy. This wasn't negligence on my part but rather a personal point of honor, you might say, in serving my Creator "as I is."

And most people think that altar boys just clatter cruets and mumble responses.

Anyway, kneeling a few feet to my right, and also at the foot of the stairs, was Father Stephen Nicanor, the Maronite priest from St. Basil's. He was attired, like myself, in black cassock and white surplice. More about him in a moment.

A dozen or so feet off to the Epistle side, and similarly accoutered, knelt Monsignor Havermeyer. He was facing the altar at right angles to Father Nicanor and myself, studying Father Baptist's every movement and gesture with furious intensity.

Behind me at the Communion rail knelt the Knights Tumblar arranged from Epistle to Gospel side (my right to my left as I faced the altar) in ascending order of age: Joel Maruppa, Jonathan Clubb, Edward Strypes Wyndham, Pierre Bontemps and Arthur von Derschmidt. Each had a missal open before him, illuminated by a pair of votive candles in clear glass cups. The glow from the bobbing flames danced eerily on their solemn faces.

Father Baptist had seen to it that there were no electric lights glowing in the church that night. Just candles and more candles.

As I knelt there swinging the censer and wringing my sinuses—trying not to think of the wad of Kleenex in my pants pocket, inaccessible through my cassock—Father Baptist, with gold-fringed cope (or "hooded cloak") draped over his shoulders, turned around to face this small congregation with the gleaming monstrance in his hands. For one precious moment, as I looked up at the Sacred Host in the round glass window in the center of the majestic golden vessel, all thoughts of throbbing membranes vanished. From that vortex at the center of a sunburst of expanding metal rays and sparkling semiprecious stones, the Word made Flesh looked out upon the dark interior of the church. Somber yellow light from various candles on the altar and around the sanctuary glistened on the converging polished surfaces, drawing all eyes to the Bread of Life.

Bells rang in Father Nicanor's hand, incense swirled at my command, and all heads bowed as Father raised the monstrance up high, brought it back down, then moved it ponderously left and right, tracing the Sign of the Cross over our souls. Then, with meticulous slow-motion reverence, he turned back toward the altar and placed the vessel on the flat brass platform atop the tabernacle. With the kind of serene grace achieved when painstaking rehearsal and soul-piercing awe coalesce into ritual motion, Father Baptist turned, descended the marble steps to the foot of the altar, turned again, and finally, without so much as a rustle of his regal vestments, knelt down facing the Immaculatam Hostiam—the Spotless Victim, the Son of God.

"The Divine Praises," announced Father in the deep voice he reserved for the most auspicious occasions. He waited for the reverberations to decay among the arches of the vaulted ceiling, then proceeded. "Blessed be God," he boomed.

"Blessed be God," we answered.

"Blessed be His Holy Name," said Father.

"Blessed be His Holy Name," we answered.

"Blessed be Jesus Christ, true God and true Man."

Thus went the Litany of Praise, Father Baptist announcing each premise, and the rest of us declaring our agreement.

"Blessed be the Name of Jesus."

The virile rumble of male voices echoed up and down the dark nave of the church, merging with the roll of dry thunder outside.

"Blessed be His most Sacred Heart."

Sniffing ever so slightly to equalize the pressure in my swollen olfactory membranes, I gathered my thoughts as best I could and tried to focus on the Sacred Host in the center of the radiant monstrance. It glared down upon me like an ominous, penetrating, unblinking Eye. If the profane human eye was the window to the eternal human soul, I found myself wondering, what kind of Soul lay behind the portal of that omniscient Orb? What kind of Heart? The words of Jesus Christ to St. Margaret Mary seemed to materialize in my mind like hail coalescing in a storm cloud:

```
   Behold this Heart which has so loved men as to
spare Itself nothing, even to exhausting and consum-
ing Itself, to testify to them Its love, and in re-
turn I receive nothing but ingratitude from the
greater part of men by the contempt, irreverence,
sacrileges, and coldness which they have for Me in
this Sacrament of My love; but what is still more
painful is that it is hearts consecrated to Me that
treat Me thus.
```

Having just copied these words that morning from the pages of St. Claude de la Colombière's *Journal of Spiritual Retreats* for the parish bulletin, they were still on the edge of my memory, along with a mental note to pick up some new typewriter ribbons for my old Underwood—

"Blessed be His most Precious Blood."

—because I'd used the same ribbon through seven times and the words were becoming more and more faded on each successive page. Besides, that old clunker needed a major overhaul one of these days. The space bar was beginning to stick, and sometimes the "w" key jammed when I punched the "q"—

"Blessed be Jesus in the most Holy Sacrament of the Altar," I found myself saying mechanically as I sought to rivet my attention back to the matter at hand.

Monsignor Havermeyer's gnarled hands were clasped in what looked like desperate prayer. His lips quivered, his neck muscles trembled, and rivulets of glittering sweat meandered down the mottled landscape of his face.

My thoughts drifted back to the scene in the camper, the furious frustration in the monsignor's eyes, the utter impatience unleashed against himself for his inability to master the rubrics. Such a courageous and disruptive about-face for a man of his years—

"Blessed be the Holy Ghost, the Paraclete," we were saying.

Whoops. The ol' gray matter had drifted again.

Somehow mention of the Holy Ghost reminded me to keep the censer gently swinging to aerate the hot coal so it wouldn't go out.

"Blessed be the great Mother of God, Mary most Holy," said Father.

Something moved in the shadows off to my left. A small gray mouse emerged from a crack at the rear of the base of the Gospel side of the altar. The little intruder looked me right in the eyes as if sizing up my hazard potential. Dismissing me as a non-issue, it turned and skittered off along the baseboard toward Our Blessed Mother's statue. Whiskers twitching, it dived for cover amidst the flowers at Her feet. Father Baptist and I had suspected for some weeks that we had a boarder living in the church. A nibbled flower here, a half-chewed stem there, and a gnawed choir book provided clear evidence of rogue rodent intrusion. For a moment I considered how we might catch the poor creature without frightening it to death, and then set it free outside in the garden. A piece of cheese might work. Yes, a piece of cheese tied to a string tied to a popsicle stick upon which an upturned wastepaper basket was delicately balanced—

"Blessed be Her Holy and Immaculate Conception," said Father.

"Aaaaaargh!" cried the wandering, wavering gray stuff in my nomadic cranium.

"Blessed be Her Holy and Immaculate Conception," said the voices all around me. My lips moved but no sound came out.

No sound came out because I was trying to remember the prayer of St. Louis-Marie Grignion de Montfort to Our Blessed Mother:

> May the light of Thy faith dispel the darkness of my mind; may Thy profound humility take the place of my pride; may Thy sub-

lime contemplation check the distractions of my wandering imagination ...

Wandering imagination, I mused. Wandering imagination? Why, my mind hasn't *begun* to wander. And as for distractions, hey, *everything* distracts me: Monsignor Havermeyer's shaking hands, the sight of a furtive, harmless little mouse—

"Blessed be her glorious Assumption," said Father.

And yet, I mused, God so loved the world that He sent His only-begotten Son to share in our humanity, to die for our sins, and to give us a fighting chance to attain Heaven in spite of ourselves. To give *me* a chance to save *my* self, "dour" and "crotchety" though I may be. Yes, even for the likes of Martin Feeney, whose agitated attention consistently wandered hither and thither and zither and guitar and banjo and trumpet and trombone and tibia and fibula and femur and, and, and, drumstick and drumhead and marchers and parades and New Year's and Epiphany and Magi and magic and myth and legend and Persia and *A Thousand and One Arabian Nights* not to mention a few notable afternoons and—

"Blessed be the Name of Mary, Virgin and Mother," said Father, his voice growing lower, almost tender.

The mouse indicated its rodential approval by wiggling one of the carnations at the foot of Her statue. Several white petals detached and zigzagged their way to the cold, hardwood floor.

"Blessed be St. Joseph, Her most chaste Spouse," we were answering.

A lump of resin in the swinging censer suddenly fizzled, issuing a dense white plume of concentrated myrrh. It mushroomed up along the front of my surplice and engulfed my face with ghostly fingers, exploring my nostrils with spectral curiosity. In an instant I was transported to the creepy recesses of the fortune-untelling salon of Guillaume du Crane Cristal, Father Baptist's occasional unofficial consultant in matters dealing with the occult. I could almost smell Willie's mweemuck root tea bubbling rancidly on the hot plate in the back room behind the beaded curtain. I could almost, almost, all—all—ahhh—

"Blessed be God," concluded Father Baptist, "in His Angels and in His Saints."

"Blessed be God," all voices braking to a dramatic dénouement, "in His Angels and in His Saints."

"Whew," I sighed softly, wiping my eyes. Another potentially awesome moment missed, demolished, obliterated by the flights and squirms of my ceaselessly rambling imagination.

"Amen," said Father, bowing low.

With assiduously slow and conscientious movements, he rose to his feet. The rest of us did likewise. Then, turning toward the door that led to the sacristy, Father waited as Monsignor Havermeyer and Father Nicanor slid in front of him and behind me as we processed out of the sanctuary.

Out of the corner of my eye I saw the Knights Tumblar return to their knees and bow their heads.

4

"AND THEY'RE GOING TO STAY THERE all night?" asked Monsignor Havermeyer as he, Father Baptist, Father Nicanor and myself, free of our vestments, stepped outside into the warm breeze.

"All night," said Father, adjusting his sleeves. "In days of old, such preparation required three consecutive days and nights of fasting and prayer before the Blessed Sacrament. Since all of those gentlemen except Joel have regular full-time jobs, and none can arrange let alone afford that kind of time off, we decided on this compromise: one all-night vigil per week for three weeks."

"This is week number three," I added, noting how dark it had become within the last half hour, "and next week will be the grand event."

"I r-r-r-r-received a telegr-r-r-r-ram fr-r-r-r-rom Bishop Xandar-r-r-r-ronolopolis this mor-r-r-r-rning," said Father Nicanor, gathering the collar of his overcoat around the olive wood column of his neck. No one rolled r's like Father Nicanor. It was like the sound of a dozen lawnmowers stalling in unison, a long day's work happily completed. And when he came to seven-syllable names like "Xandaronolopolis," it became a yard-and-garden symphony, complete with a choir of hedge clippers and a weed-whacker solo. "He will be ar-r-r-r-riving on Satur-r-r-rday after-r-r-r-rnoon for-r-r-r-r the consecr-r-r-r-ration of the new Mar-r-r-ronite Chur-r-r-r-rch in Bar-r-r-r-rkinbay Beach on Sunday the twelfth ..."

GARDENING TIPS: I've no wish to blur my reader's eyes further by my attempt to convey Father Nicanor's peculiar accent in typed form. Therefore, I will cease doing so. Just remember that whenever he says a word containing an r, it's really five r's with four dashes between them. Seven and six, when he gets excited. Nine and eight, when he goes ballistic. And so on ...
                                                        --M.F.

"... and then staying with me at St. Basil's until Saturday the twenty-eighth, at which time he must return to Lebanon to prepare for the Feast of All Saints on the first of November. He is very much looking forward to the ceremony next Tuesday evening."

We strolled slowly through the garden around toward the front of the church, our clothes flapping in the hot, damp wind. The thickening sky burped and boiled like a gigantic celestial cauldron, threatening to tip over and douse us with its barometric stew. But still it was all threats—a single drop of rain had yet to fall. Newspapers went scraping by on the deserted sidewalk as we came to the front gate, chased by cyclones of dry leaves, dancing tin cans, and assorted swirling bits of post-cultural dandruff.

Father Nicanor's '84 BMW glistened blackly at the curb under a mercury-vapor street lamp. Even in the gathering murkiness I could see our reflections on the immaculately polished door as we approached.

"Beats me," said Monsignor Havermeyer, hunching his shoulders against the sultry breeze. "I had no idea that such ceremonies were still practiced."

"It has become rare," smiled Father Nicanor, "but thus all the more precious."

"Don't you think," said Havermeyer, "maybe one of us should stay in the church with them? You know, just in case—?"

"No," said Father Nicanor, a bit sharply. He raised a finger as thin and wavy as a palm tree. "This they must do on their own, and each alone with himself."

"They have been instructed to keep Holy Silence," said Father Baptist.

"And that doesn't just mean no talking," explained the gardener. "It means no eye contact, no pointing, no gesticulating—"

"No communication whatsoever," said Father Nicanor. "This they must do on their honor, or there is no honor." Palm tree withdrawn, he reached into the pocket of his cassock and pulled out the strangest watch I've ever seen. Dangling on a steel chain forged of interlocking diamond-shaped links, it was triangular on the outside, and popped open to reveal an ornate, rectangular face within. The numbers were Arabic squiggles, and I suspected they ran counter-clockwise. There was no second hand, so I couldn't be sure. "Ah," he said, "I must be getting back to St. Basil's. Veronika, my housekeeper, she will be, um—how do I say this?—'distraught' if I am later than usual for dinner."

The distant clatter of pot against pan came drifting from the rectory kitchen on a howling gust of wind. Another timely culinary comment from our Millie, and at such an uncanny distance.

"We know the feeling," I said, holding the car door open for Father Nicanor.

The sky responded with a comment of its own: a brief but deafening boom, like a ceremonial cannon stuffed with too much cotton wadding. Father Nicanor paused to look up. "Strange," he said (don't forget his r's). "Yes, it almost reminds me of ..." He shook his head. "No matter. I must be off."

"God speed," said Father Baptist.

"Good night, good night," waved Father Nicanor, easing himself into the driver's seat. He pulled the door shut with a solid thunk. The engine hummed to life like the purring of a contented lion.

"We'd best get inside," said Father, "before Millie breaks something."

"You mean something else," said the gardener as we turned and headed back to the rectory.

"By the way, Martin," said Father, "we do indeed have a mouse living in the church."

"You saw it, too?"

"Right between Mary Most Holy and Her Immaculate Conception."

I made a sound, something between a giggle and a snort.

"Amused?" said Father, eyes twinkling.

"Relieved," I laughed.

"The mind is so easily distracted," he nodded his understanding, "even in moments reserved for profound awe."

"Why do you keep her?" asked Monsignor Havermeyer.

"The mouse?" I asked. "Well actually, we're going to have to find a way of removing her without—"

"Your housekeeper," he snapped.

"Millie?" I squeaked. "I don't understand."

"She's insufferable. In all the years since my ordination, I've never been subjected to such indignities as that woman inflicts on a daily basis."

"Ah," I said, "but a day without indignity is like a day without a basis."

"I can't imagine St. Philomena's without Millie," smiled Father Baptist. "She's one of a kind."

"And affordable," I added. "You can't beat *free.*"

"You don't pay her?" gawked Monsignor Havermeyer. "I don't understand."

"She's one of our 'in lieu of' staff," said Father. "Like Danielle Parks, our choir director, and Henry Folkstone—"

"My, ahem, gardening assistant," I interjected.

"—Millie offers her services," said Father, "in place of money in the collection plate."

"She gets a roof over her head," I explained as the illuminated kitchen window came into view, cozy and inviting. "She has men to boss around, kitchenware to batter, axes to grind, all kinds of infringed benefits. What more could any insufferable woman want? Why just the other day—Ulp!"

I was startled by the sight of two men standing at the kitchen door. The porch light was burned out, so all we could see was a couple of black silhouettes—patient, motionless, hands buried deep in overcoat pockets, collars turned to the wind.

"Who's there?" asked Father Baptist, slowing his stride.

"Hope you don't mind," said one of the shapes, "if we parked 'round back."

"We're supposed to be incognito," said the other.

"Lieutenant Taper?" said Father Baptist. "Sergeant Wickes? What brings you to St. Philomena's on a night like this?"

"Chief Billowack sent us," said Taper. "He needs your help."

"Billowack? Why on earth would he need—or want—my help?"

"Something is ... happening," said the unmistakable, yet strangely tense, voice of Sergeant Wickes. "Something dreadful."

5

"THE LAST TIME YOU GENTS CAME TO SEE ME in your official capacity," said Father, seating himself in the tiny dining nook and unfolding his napkin, "it was 'bizarre.' Now it's 'dreadful.' For a moment I thought Montgomery Billowack might've sent you to tell me to cease instructing his daughter."

"He's none too pleased about that, I assure you," said Taper, taking the seat on Father's right. "And because I'm a member of your parish, he assumes I'm part of the conspiracy."

"What fun," said the gardener, motioning Sergeant Wickes toward the chair on Father's other side.

"But that's not why we're here," said Wickes, squeezing by.

That left one chair for Monsignor Havermeyer and myself to share.

"My Senior," I said, motioning for him to take it. "I'll fetch a spare from the study."

"You'll do no such thing," growled Millie, kicking the spring-loaded stool she used for reaching higher shelves in my direction. "Dinner is served—*now.*"

"Yes'm," I said, leaning my cane against the wall. Nudging the stool into position with my foot, I wiggled myself in between Monsignor Havermeyer and Sergeant Wickes. It was sort of like sitting on a coffee can—and just as comfortable—but I managed, calcified hips and all. It also left me a head or two shorter than everyone else at the table, but what the hey. A day without indignity and all that.

"I was expecting three," barked Millie from her command position at the stove, angrily chasing a terrified morsel around a frying pan with her lethal spatula. "So now there's five."

"Oh, we're not hung—" began Wickes.

I clamped my hand over his mouth. "Never," I hissed fiercely into his ear, "ever say that within Millie's hearing. Not if you value your teeth. I thought you'd learned."

Monsignor Havermeyer glared at me as I gingerly pulled my hand away from the aperture beneath Wicke's bulging eyes.

"Feeney," said the monsignor gruffly, then lost his train of thought. "Feeney," he tried again, but with the same sputtering-out result. After a moment's contemplation, he tried again—third time lucky: "Feeney, what—"

"In the name of St. Martha, who worried too much," announced Millie, slamming down a heavy pot on the back burner. "I've got it. I know how I'll stretch the stew."

I settled down, imagining Millie dipping her bare hands into her cooking pot, scooping up the contents, and then stretching the sagging gob of rubbery stew-goo between her muscular fists like thick pizza dough. I didn't want to watch.

"Never mind," said Havermeyer, dismissing me with a weak wave of his hand.

"But I just saved the sergeant's life," I whined. "Lieutenant, tell him."

"He's right," nodded Taper, smiling first at his partner and then at the monsignor. "Martin did just save the sergeant's life."

"Thanks," said Wickes, then winced as two metal objects collided noisily in the air over Millie's stove. She had obviously hit upon an alternate form of stew-stretching. The mind boggles. "Martin, you just saved my life."

Monsignor Havermeyer sighed, eyes shut.

"Let's say grace," said Father Baptist, leading us in the Sign of the Cross. For a few brief moments, Millie ceased her culinary clamor. The dining nook reverberated with gratitude toward our Maker. Even Sergeant Wickes, I noticed, moved his lips. I don't think he was actually saying anything, but that's the closest I've seen him to even mimicking prayer in our midst. Progress with some people is sometimes slow. Perhaps if I installed a stop-motion camera at the dining table, we would one day be able to see the sergeant's gradual progression as a smooth, continuous motion, like a flower blooming. Just a thought.

"Through Christ Our Lord," concluded Father.

"Amen," said we all, except Wickes. He just sort of sawed the underside of his nose with his index finger.

"St. Luke," said Father.

"Pray for us," said we all, except Wickes, searching his pockets for a handkerchief.

"In the Name of the Father, and of the Son, and of the Holy Ghost."

"Amen," said we all, except Wickes, furtively unfolding his napkin.

"I'm waiting," said Father Baptist presently, "for 'dreadful.'"

"We can't talk about it here," said Lieutenant Taper.

"Only at the station," said Sergeant Wickes. "Billowack's orders."

"But I will tell you this, Jack," said Taper, his smile suddenly fading, "I'm scared. For the first time in my career in Homicide, I'm afraid. I don't mean to—"

"Wine," announced Millie, suddenly in our midst, slamming down two more glasses with one hand, then strafing them with her stealth-bomber bottle. As usual, even from three feet, she didn't spill a drop.

She skipped my glass, of course, filled as it was with ginger ale. To quote an insidious character in an old movie, I never drink ... wine.

"It's here or nowhere," said Father, eyeing his former underling, Taper, with frosty intensity. "After the way your chief treated me the last time—"

"He hates you, Father," I nodded, sniffing my glass as if it contained something red instead of amber. "No doubt about it. But it's a dry hate."

"Jack," said Taper, "if it's a matter of apologies—"

"It's a matter of priorities," said Father sternly. "I have a parish to run. These people need me here, not gallivanting all over town in search of criminals. I can't and won't be distracted from my avowed work every time the police get stumped on some matter of, of—"

"Dreadfulness," I injected. "The secret word for tonight is—"

"Lives," said Taper in a voice so low it rattled his tie-clip, "are at stake."

"My vocation is to try to save souls," said Father, "not lives."

"There's a difference?" asked Wickes.

"I'm here, too, Father," said Monsignor Havermeyer, gruffly, snapping out of his Feeney-weary reverie. "Don't forget that. I may not have the rubrics down yet—it'll be a while before I'm ready to say the Latin Mass—but I can still hear confessions, go out on sick calls, not to mention—"

"Begging your pardon, Monsignor," said Father. "I don't mean to insinuate that—"

"Then don't," said Havermeyer, thumping the table authoritatively.

"Salad," roared Millie, tossing plates around the table like playing cards and clunking down a huge leafy bowl in the center—and with only two hands. "I stretched it with cabbage. Hope you don't mind."

"Not one bite," I smiled, grabbing the tongs and heaping my plate. When the others didn't follow suit, I began dishing out the greens for them, too. With unceremonious abandon, I dropped a pile of leaves in front of Sergeant Wickes. This proved a bit awkward, since my armpits were caught on the edge of the table, but I could tell by the harmonic intensity of Millie's clangs and bonks that the next course was fast approaching.

"You don't understand, Monsignor," said Father in tones reminiscent of a blowtorch cutting titanium. "My duty is here."

"I do understand, Father," countered the monsignor, who in his former position at St. Philip's was used to being obeyed, "that God has given you certain talents. See that you don't bury them like the useless servant."

"Matthew chapter twenty-five," I said, heaving a pile of greens over the far edge of the big bowl and hoping they landed on Father's plate. "Verse twenty-five."

"That part of my life," said Father, "is behind me."

"It wasn't four months ago," commented Taper as I tossed some in his direction.

"I was under orders," said Father, "from Archbishop Fulbright."

"So if he ordered you again?" asked Wickes.

"Won't happen," I said, finishing my dumping rounds with Monsignor Havermeyer. His plate, at least, was right next to mine. "As I recall, Our Lord Archbishop's last words to Father Baptist were, and I quote: 'Get out of my sight, and don't ever approach me, not on any pretext, ever again.'"

"So the matter is settled," said Father.

Silence descended on us like a clay parachute. It wasn't the cessation of voices that alarmed me, but the sudden stillness from the direction of the stove. I glanced Millie's way and saw her glaring in our direction. I gulped. The one unpardonable sin in her cosmology was the failure of men to ravenously devour her furiously-prepared meals.

"Consider this, Father," said the monsignor, massaging the twisted flesh between his fingers. "Under the old rules, if my hands had been injured any further, I wouldn't be able to offer the Traditional Mass at all. As it is, God left enough of me intact to be useful around here, and with practice I'll be reciting Latin in no time. Surely you won't deny that there's a reason why I was thus spared."

"Surely I don't presume to guess at God's purposes," said Father firmly.

"Forks up," I urged them, eyeing Millie eyeing us.

"People are dying," said Taper. "It's—it's—"

"It's another serial killer," said Wickes. "But this time it's, it's—"

"Salad," I encouraged them, shoveling a pitchfork's-worth into my mouth as Millie approached with more dishes balanced on her sinewy arms. "Hmmm, shallab."

6

"SHOW HIM, SERGEANT," SAID LIEUTENANT TAPER, as Millie snatched the last of the dirty dessert implements from the table with a huff. Somehow, we had engorged enough to forestall Millie's final wrath, but just barely.

"But Lieutenant," whispered Wickes, "Chief Billowack specifically said—"

"We'll have to risk it," said Taper, his patience distended to its elastic limit. "Jack, I don't understand your attitude, I really don't. In all the years I've known you, I've—well, never mind. This isn't just another murder case. It's way beyond that—"

"Coffee," barked Millie, not doubting for an instant that none of us would refuse another round of her pulse-jolting brew. We all leaned back and acted grateful as she sploshed our cups. Not completely satisfied—her cheeks were swollen with hotly-held breath—Millie withdrew to the sink and began filling the empty pot with scalding hot water.

Sighing, Sergeant Wickes unbuttoned his jacket and began to withdraw something glossy from his inside pocket.

"No," said Father, folding his hands on the edge of the table.

"Go on," said Taper.

"I said no," said Father. "Having considered the matter throughout dinner, I have decided that I don't want to know anything more about it."

"Jack," said Taper, casting Sergeant Wickes one of those "go ahead" looks.

"Don't tempt me with your photograph," said Father, giving the sergeant a "don't you dare" look. His words were laced with firm sadness. "I won't be enticed with lurid details. The matter is not up for discussion. My decision is final."

"Why?" asked Monsignor Havermeyer. "What gives you the right to withhold your services?"

"My right is my duty," said Father. "My duty is to my parishioners."

"You amaze me," said the monsignor, tossing down his napkin disgustedly and rising from his chair. "And I must confess, Father Baptist, I'm disappointed. You can't imagine how much it pains me to say so. Good-night, gentlemen."

We all watched as Havermeyer sauntered silently past Millie. She acknowledged his exit by noisily dumping a pile of dishes into the foamy sink. A gust of hot, moist air billowed into the room as he opened the door and stepped out into the garden. The slam was, shall we say, resounding.

"Will anything change your mind?" asked Taper.

"Short of the Sign of Jonas, no," said Father.

"Then there's nothing more to be said," sighed Taper.

"True," said Father.

"Let's go, Sergeant," said the lieutenant, throwing down his wadded napkin. "Don't get up, Jack, Martin. We'll see ourselves out."

Another parade past Millie, another clatter of dishes, another gust of humid air, another slam of kitchen door.

Father and I stared at each other across the table.

The scene had not changed twenty minutes later when Millie hung her drying towel on the oven handle and untied her apron.

"I'll be turning in," she announced, hands on hips, "unless there's anything else you need."

"A shot of bourbon would be nice," said Father dryly.

"Leave him the bottle," I added.

Millie stomped over to the table and folded her arms across her chest, the muscles of her forearms rippling with ferocious self-control. "I don't pretend to understand, Father Baptist," she said evenly. "Lord knows how little I grasp about anything that goes on around here. But for what it's worth, this is one woman who stands behind you, whatever you decide."

Father looked up at her with those unnerving eyes that seemed to whisper, reserved yet gratefully, "Considering how I feel at the moment, my dear woman, how can words possibly express how much I appreciate your saying so?" Swallowing loudly, he folded his hands as if in prayer. But all he said was, "Good-night, Millie."

The scene still hadn't changed fifteen minutes later when the windows suddenly went blindingly white with a flash of lightning.

One, two, three, I counted silently. Four, five—

Plates, bowls and glasses rattled violently in the cupboards as thunder rolled over, around, and through the rectory.

"I guess the storm is upon us," I mumbled, waiting for the sound of raindrops to start pelting the windows.

But that particular sound did not come. There was just the wind moaning in the eaves, the rustle of tree branches outside, the squeak of twigs against the kitchen window, the scrape of dry leaves on the brick walkway outside, and the drip of Millie's faucet in the enamel sink.

"Not yet," said Father gravely. "But soon."

Wednesday, October Eighteenth

Feast Day of Saint Luke, Doctor of Medicine, Evangelist, Disciple of St. Paul, Author of the Third Gospel and the Acts of the Apostles, Painter and, finally, Martyr (84 AD)

7

THE TWO LARGEST CONCENTRATIONS of Catholic populations in Japan were located in the cities of Hiroshima and Nagasaki, at least until 1945. The dropping of two atomic bombs in August of that year at the conclusion of World War II drastically altered those statistics. Hijo Yahamata had been among the survivors of the first explosion. Ten years later, he migrated to the United States—why, I can't imagine (it seems like shaking the hand that bites you)—and was eventually hired by my dad to tend the yard around our house in Alhambra, California, when I was five. During the three hours he labored each week for seven years, Mr. Yahamata taught me everything I know about gardening. He also filled my mind with pearls of hibachi wisdom, such as: "Watch the sky, reedle one. You never know what may rand on your head."

Well, one thing that didn't land on my head the next morning, as I made my way back to St. Philomena's from the newspaper dispenser on the corner, was rain. "HUMIDITY: 100%; PRECIPITATION: 0!" said the headline. Indeed, though the sky was black as tar, the ground on which I walked was as dry as feathers. The skin in which I walked was another matter, perspiration during elevated hygrometer readings being what it is.

This stunning meteorological information, it seemed, was more critical to the functioning of our fair city in the eyes of the media than the announcement in the lower right corner: "ARCHBISHOP FULBRIGHT RETURNS FROM ROME," it said. "APPOINTED CARDINAL BY POPE." The accompanying photo showed dear Morley Fulbright flashing one of his "boy-am-I-pleased-with-myself" smiles.

This latter report, though not really news in Catholic circles, drained me of my personal energy reserves. It left me wearier and drearier than the humid air through which I trudged. After the royal mess Morley made of things only a few months before, I'd've thought he'd've gotten the sack, or at least been removed to a remote monastery where he could reconsider his priorities without doing further harm. But no. In today's Church, run by enlightened specialists with a "better understanding" of things, our lame shepherd's ineptitude was rewarded with a promotion.

"Go figure," I whispered as I spied Father Baptist sitting on the wooden bench in the garden facing St. Thérèse. He was surrounded by an assortment of interested and interesting people. The Knights Tumblar looked tired, haggard. Their pants legs were still bunched up around their calves from kneeling all night. Several regular weekday-morning parishioners stood close by, casting questioning glances at the tail-coated Tumblars. The little porous bird was teetering on the edge of the birdbath, threatening to jump.

"Have we understood Monsignor Havermeyer correctly," Pierre Bontemps was saying, his hay-blonde hair fluttering in the tepid breeze, "that you have ignored a request for assistance from Chief Montgomery 'Bulldog' Billowack in the matter of a police investigation?"

"I did not ignore it," explained Father Baptist. "I refused."

"But, Father," said Joel Maruppa, the youngest Tumblar, his dense black umpteen-o'clock shadow accenting the circular movements of his stern Slovak jaw. "Everyone knows you're the best sleuth in town."

"That," said Father, "is beside the point."

"We'd all feel better," added Arthur von Derschmidt, "if you were on the case." Arthur, in his forties, was the oldest, widest, and only fully-bearded Tumblar. He looked like a character out of a novel—an intense, eccentric poet, perhaps—with his regal gray-and-brown ponytail waving in the wind. He hooked his thumbs in his vest pockets and patted his expanding paunch authoritatively with the rest of his fingers.

"What is the crime, anyway?" asked Jonathan Clubb, thin and tall at twenty-six, his prominent forehead emerging from his thinning crop of mustard-brown hair like a stony reef from a receding ocean wave.

"Yes," nodded Edward Strypes Wyndham, twenty-eight, intense obsidian eyes peering from beneath bushy black eyebrows that had fused into a bird-of-prey crest above the bridge of his long nose. "There hasn't been anything in the news that I'm aware of."

"The nature of the crime doesn't matter," sighed Father Baptist, closing the ragged prayer book on his lap. His morning devotions would apparently have to keep. "Nor does Chief Billowack's blundering ineptitude. I am first, last, and foremost a priest. The matter is settled. Monsignor Havermeyer had no business complaining to you gentlemen about my decision."

"Well I say 'bully for you,' Father," huffed Thurgood T. Turnbuckle, the most out-spoken and, if rumors were true, richest parishioner at St. Philomena's. In his three-piece charcoal business suit, he looked like a cross between Winston Churchill and Woodrow Wilson with a Teddy Roosevelt mustache, if such an amalgamation is imaginable. "You should keep your nose out of police affairs."

"Not so fast," said Steve Lambert, a parishioner employed at KROM News who was also a big fan of Father Baptist. He was always on the lookout for ways to get our pastor back on television. "Maybe you should reconsider, Father, I mean, think of the exposure—"

"I won't," said Father. "And I have."

"Me and my Bennie are behind you, Father," said Muriel Cladusky, her hips jiggling like a can of paint in one of those mixing machines at the hardware store. "As for the rest," she scowled, looking around the group with penetrating eyes, seeking traitors, "on your knees you should be, rather than question Father's decisions."

"We're not questioning his decisions, are we?" asked Theodora Turpin.

"Of course not, Dear," nodded her husband, Tanner.

"We're behind Father all the way, aren't we?" she persisted.

"Most assuredly, Dear," he assured her.

"It's just that in this case he's wrong, isn't he?"

"Quite possibly, Dear."

"And we think it would be better if he'd—"

"Excuse me, excuse me," intruded an unfamiliar voice.

Everyone turned to see a plump, rosy-cheeked man in black clerical civvies and Roman collar approaching up the brick path from the front gate. His gleaming black shoes clipped and clopped on the stones as he trotted into our midst, belly and jowls bounding in unison.

"I'm looking for a Father John Baptist," he announced in a dense puff of mouthwash, after shave, and hair tonic.

All eyes swung from this newcomer back to the man seated on the bench. In my peripheral vision I noted the little porous bird, wing on forehead in dismay, inching closer to the edge of the birdbath. A brigade of crickets scurried to fetch a net in the ivy below. The tension mounted.

"That would be me," said Father, shoving his prayer book into the mysterious folds of his cassock. "And you are—?"

"Monsignor Aspic," said the perky man, not offering his hand but rather shoving it and its opposite twin deep into his pants pockets to rattle his change. He rocked to and fro on his soles and heels, rolling his eyes like something you'd find on the "battery powered" shelf in a toy store. His lips literally blossomed as he said his name, so much did he love its sound: "Conrad J. Aspic."

"What's the 'J' stand for?" asked the nosy gardener.

"Jonas," beamed the monsignor. "My mother always said I was born under the Sign of Jonas."

Father Baptist and I exchanged knowing glances.

"Although," chuckled the monsignor, "I was never clear on exactly what she meant by that." He sucked in his oleaginous cheeks, considering some private joke. "She was a bit on the dingie side, to be sure. But I suppose she meant well."

"No doubt," I mumbled.

"I've recently transferred from Seattle," continued the monsignor, "to assist Cardinal Fulbright in the restructuring of his hierarchy."

"What's to restructure?" asked Pierre. "They're all dead."

Father Baptist flashed Pierre a chilling glance, but no one noticed but myself and St. Thérèse.

The pert monsignor puckered his lips for a moment, rolled his eyes, jiggled his change, and said, "No problem. New auxiliaries are being considered as we speak, and in no time we'll have the old diocesan machine up, running, and purring like a kitten. That's where I come in. I have two degrees in management efficiency and one in organizational psychology."

"Our 'second collection' dollars at work," said Arthur.

"Not at all," smiled Monsignor Aspic. "I put myself through college, first at an orthodontics lab, and later as a statistical psychiatric analyst. My vocation to the priesthood came as something of an afterthought."

"A man with his priorities in order," mumbled the gardener.

"Did you hear that?" asked Theodora Turpin.

"Yes, Dear," nodded her husband, Tanner.

"The priesthood an afterthought, I mean."

"Precisely, Dear."

"Doesn't seem right."

"Not at all, Dear."

"Restructuring the archdiocese," mused Thurgood T. Turnbuckle. "That sounds like a tall order."

"It is," said the chubby monsignor. "One I welcome. Besides, I shall enjoy the change of scenery. I have a brother down here, you know. I'm staying with him until they finish remodeling my residence at St. Philip's." He rolled his eyes again, taking in the garden, the grounds, the buildings, and the people. "So this is the infamous St. Philomena's."

"It is," huffed Thurgood T. Turnbuckle. "And we're mighty proud of her."

"No doubt, no doubt," said Monsignor Aspic. "We all have our little idiosyncrasies, don't we?"

"Idio—?" gasped Mr. Turnbuckle, the tips of his mustache curling around toward his nostrils with the sudden intake of air.

"Not to mention our own particular functions in the community," added the monsignor. "Our peculiar little parts to play, as it were."

"Peculiar—?" rasped Pierre.

"Parts—?" huffed Arthur.

"He's so right, isn't he?" asked Theodora Turpin.

"Yes, Dear," nodded her husband, Tanner.

"About our parts, I mean."

"Without question, Dear."

"Which brings me to the purpose of my visit," said the spry monsignor, releasing his change and pulling a sealed envelope from his pocket. "I've been directed by the cardinal to hand-deliver this message to you, Father Baptist."

There was a plop in the ivy at the base of the birdbath.

Wincing, Father Baptist accepted the envelope. There was a gold ribbon embedded in a goopy crimson wax seal on the flap. Very official.

"No cause for alarm," chuckled Monsignor Aspic. "The cardinal wishes to see you at the Chancery immediately, that's all. I stress 'immediately' in its immediate sense: that is to say, within the hour. The shepherd summoning his sheep—that sort of thing."

"More like the wolf ordering lunch," mumbled the gardener.

"You should be honored," smiled the monsignor. "You'll be the first priest in the archdiocese to greet him in his new red zucchetto."

A cryptic smile grew on Father Baptist's face as he rose to his feet. "I am honored."

"You are?" gawked Mr. Turnbuckle, his mustache twitching like a walrus on a capsizing iceberg.

"Martin, I'll be needing your services," said Father, straightening his cassock. "The rest of you gentlemen and ladies will have to excuse me."

"We'll be seeing you tomorrow evening, of course," said Pierre as the Tumblars made way for Father, "at our regular meeting."

"And don't forget the shindig Friday night," said Jonathan.

"Shindig?" harrumphed Mr. Turnbuckle.

"I wouldn't miss either event for the world," said Father. "Joel, you'll be working on the wiring upstairs today?"

"Yes, Father," said Joel Maruppa, who had become the parish's "in lieu of" handyman to pay for his board in the rectory guest room. "One room's finished, six to go—not counting the bathroom. My grandfather is going to be helping me today."

"I imagine the rest of you must report to your various occupations," said Father as he moved past them, "though how you Tumblars manage on so little sleep concerns me."

"Sleep is a luxury for the old," quipped Edward.

"Right," said Jonathan.

Arthur rubbed his mid-life eyes, not so sure.

Mr. Turnbuckle, who apparently never slept, didn't seem to care.

"May I offer the services of my limo, Father?" asked Monsignor Aspic. "I'm going your way, I believe."

"No, thank-you," said Father, nudging me toward the back parking lot. "Martin and I will manage in our own car. We have other errands to run afterwards."

"One moment," I said, making a lurching detour over to the birdbath. With bones crackling like a string of firecrackers, I leaned over and groped around in the ivy. "Ah," I said, straightening and setting the stone bird back on its cement perch. "A place for everything, you know."

"Martin," said Father, heading down the path.

"Father," I nodded, hobbling behind.

"Oh brother," sighed several Tumblars.

"And what, may I ask, are Tumblars?" I heard the monsignor query.

"That's a long story," said Arthur von Derschmidt.

"You wouldn't have the time," said Pierre.

"Lucky for us it's Wednesday," I said as Father and I exited the back gate. "Millie's morning off. She'd throw a fit if we missed breakfast, even at the cardinal's behest."

"Especially at the cardinal's behest," said Father, opening the passenger door of the Jeep.

"Excuse me—?" said the woman he almost opened the door into.

"I beg your pardon," said Father, startled as much by her sudden appearance as by her sullen appearance.

She was wearing a faded blue bathrobe and yellow house slippers. Her gray-yellow hair was rolled up with gigantic curlers that wobbled limply inside a hair net, which was loosely corralled by a hand towel draped over her head. She was wearing a pair of yellow-rimmed glasses that were only the bottom half of bifocals, and her red lipstick was thickly applied and then smeared halfway up her cheeks.

"I said, 'Excuse me?'" she repeated with a larynx that could have doubled as an ice grinder. She arched her wrist over the top of the car door. "My name is Helga Feuchtwanger and you must be Father Baptist and I've heard about you and I'm a Lutheran and I live two houses down on the other side of the alley."

"Oh, I see," said Father. "This is my associate, Martin Feeney."

I smiled across the hood. "Nice to meet you ..." I hadn't quite picked up the pronunciation of her name.

"How may I be of help?" asked Father.

"Well it's this way," she said, holding out her right hand as if cradling a hard-boiled egg. "My old Volkswagen isn't much, but it's all I have and I don't appreciate anyone else driving it."

"I can understand that," said Father. "What does that have to do—?"

"But last night," she went on grinding her cubes, "I look out at the place where I always park it and it's gone. I don't believe it at first and I prove it to myself by going out with a flashlight and standing there like a fool in the dark waving it around where my car should be. You tell me, Father, wouldn't that be upsetting to you or what?"

"Very," said Father. "Martin and I would be lost without our car."

"I was not lost," she snorted. "I was standing on my own driveway where my car should be and what do you think happens this morning, and while I'm just hanging up from yelling at a nice young policeman on the phone who has no respect for his elders?"

"I can't imagine," said Father.

> GARDENING TIPS: You'll notice that I didn't get
> involved in this conversation. Talking to Luther-
> ans in hair nets and house slippers is Father's
> department.
>
> —M.F.

"Neither can I," she glared, "but I look out the window as I'm swallowing my nerve pills along with a giant cup of black coffee because would you believe it I ran out of cream, and there it is."

"There what is?" asked Father.

"My car," she said, slapping her hands against her bony sides, "right where it always is, right on the very spot where I stood waving my flashlight like I was crazy or something. You think I'm crazy or something?"

"Hardly," said Father, easing himself into the passenger seat. "Perhaps some neighborhood kids went for a joyride."

"That's why I'm asking you, Father," said Mrs. F. "As in maybe you had a Knights of Columbus meeting here last night, or Catholic Action—my girlfriend, Moira, God rest her weary soul, used to be a member though not around here—or maybe a charismatic prayer meeting or something like that you Catholics are always getting into, something that might have fired somebody up into a car-borrowing spree."

"Not here," said Father. "We don't sponsor any of those organizations at St. Philomena's."

"Any excuse for drinking, heh?" added Mrs. F, apparently not hearing him.

"Not here," repeated Father. Looking for excuses was not part of his nature. "Well, I'll be. Look at the time. Martin and I have an appointment downtown. If we hear anything, we'll let you know."

"Not if you hear it in the confessional," she said, turning away and heading down the alley. "You guys have every angle all figured out, that's what I say. Just like that policeman: 'Helga,' he says to me, 'surely you haven't been taking your pills.' Well, I'll tell them a thing or two ..."

"I forget," I said as I dumped myself into the driver's seat. "Where is it we're going downtown?"

"The Chancery," said Father. "Your favorite cardinal, remember?"

Just before I turned the key in the ignition, we heard a frustrated grumble inside Monsignor Havermeyer's camper. It was followed immediately by an angry thump. The whole vehicle shook.

"Rubrics?" asked Father, latching his seat belt.

"Rubrics," I nodded, buckling mine.

8

I KNEW WE'D REACHED CARDINAL FULBRIGHT'S office on the top floor of the Chancery building simply because we'd run out of stairs to climb. Oh, there were other subtle indicators: the sense of ecclesiastical pomposity that charged the air, the freshly painted letters on the humungous double-doors announcing his promotion, not to mention the stream of eager deacons and anxious nuns darting in and out of the entrance, never giving those mighty doors the chance to swing completely closed.

The receptionist with vertical nostrils honked a greeting as we entered and ushered us down a plush hallway to the ominous portcullis marked CONFERENCE ROOM. Within lay the largest circular table I'd ever seen since the last time Father and I had been summoned here. That had not been a happy day, but that's another story—though it does converge a bit with this one.

"Father Baptist," said His Eminence, Morley Psalmellus Cardinal Fulbright, Archbishop of Los Angeles, his stiff-from-the-box blood-red robes making starched swishing noises as he greeted us. He held out the sapphire ring which had replaced the amethyst bauble he'd been so fond of in the past. Father Baptist reverently osculated the orb.

"And Mister ... Feeney," said the cardinal, swinging his ring in my humble direction. I gave it my usual snaky smack and mumbled something between, "The honor is all mine," and "I cleaned my toenails just for the occasion."

"You already know the co-counsels for the archdiocese, Mr. Shlomo Brennan and Mr. Guilio Gerezanno."

Ah, I thought, falconry is not dead.

"And I believe you also know—"

My heart went "gerk!" How could I have missed him there at the far end of the table the moment we came in? I must have passed him over as a laundry sack stuffed with Morley's discarded archbishop's apparel.

"—Montgomery Billowack, Chief of Homicide—"

The humungous cop grunted and slavered like his nickname. His bulbous forehead glistened with sweat. "Hiya, Lombard. You too, Quasimodo."

I felt my blood and bile rising. What nerve, especially since they obviously didn't call him "Bulldog" for his cute bobbin nose.

"—and his diligent officers, Lieutenant Taper and Sergeant Wickes."

Our friends from the police nodded meekly from the murky umbra of their superior's dank shadow. So they, too, were in on this conspiracy, albeit unwillingly.

Massaging a gnarly purplish bump on his forehead, Cardinal Fulbright took his seat in a high-backed leather chair. It burped uproariously as he settled in. With an air of auspicious magnanimity, he motioned for Father Baptist and myself to arrange ourselves on the low-backed wooden chairs across from him.

GARDENING TIPS: On the "way over" in the car, aside from the usual admonitions regarding the potential hazards of my wagging tongue, Father Baptist instructed me on the proper form of address due a cardinal. We were no longer supposed to call Morley Fulbright "Your Grace"--an appellation which had always stuck in my craw anyway. From now on, since he was wearing a red zucchetto, we were to refer to him as "Your Eminence." Right, sure. Got it.

When I asked Father Baptist what "zucchetto" meant, he answered, "A little zook." (???) Whatever, it looked like a yarmulke dipped in cranberry juice to me.

--M.F.

N.B. Upon the death of the current pope, his successor will be selected by a conclave of the College of Cardinals, of which Morley Fulbright was now a member. The mind boggles. Bear in mind, too, that the rank of "cardinal" is in addition to, but does not replace, his existing status as "archbishop." Hence, he may be referred to as the "cardinal archbishop." I can think of other things I'd prefer to call him, but . . .

Just then Monsignor Conrad J. Aspic came strutting into the room. Without introduction or comment, he took a seat midway 'round the table.

"I'll be brief," said Cardinal Fulbright, glaring at the assembly for withering effect. "Chief Billowack informs me, Father Baptist, that you have refused to lend your assistance to the police on the 'dreadful' murder case in which he and these other gentlemen are currently involved."

So, I noted, the secret word for today, like the weather, was going to be "dreadful"—same as yesterday. Hm.

"That is correct," said Father, folding his hands on the edge of the table.

"Would you be so good," said the cardinal, "as to explain why?"

"I should think the reason is obvious," said Father.

"Well, do favor us anyway," said the cardinal.

"I am a priest," said Father evenly, "not a police detective. I left that part of my life behind when I took my vows. My duty now is to the souls under my care."

"You resurrected those, ahem, skills," said Mr. Shlomo Brennan with a derisive smirk, "only a few months ago."

"And untangled all that unfortunate Farnsworth business," added Mr. Guilio Gerezanno, twisting his oily mustache malevolently.

"And," admitted the cardinal with transparent reluctance, "saved my life in the process."

"Under Holy Obedience, yes," said Father. "But you will recall that my services aroused—and I say this with all due respect—Your Eminence's ire and ill will."

"True," nodded His Elegance, rubbing his bump again.

"I've no wish to repeat such calumny," said Father. "Besides, I've yet to receive payment for my services. I've submitted my bill several times, but my requests have been ignored."

"Of all the—" growled Shlomo, squirming in his chair. His pliable derriere made an indignant belching sound against the soft leathery cushion.

"An unfortunate oversight," interrupted Monsignor Aspic, eyes rolling efficiently. "I'll see to the matter at once."

"But it's not the issue," said Father. "I repeat: my duty is to the souls under my care, not to—"

"I understand," interrupted the cardinal, "that you now have the assistance of Monsignor Michael Havermeyer, late of St. Philip's, at your parish."

"He has taken up residence at St. Philomena's, yes," said Father, "but he's hardly ready to assist in my regular sacerdotal functions. He is still recovering from massive burns on his hands and face, and his Latin is far too shaky for him to credibly administer the Sacraments according to the Old Rite—"

"Not according to him," countered the cardinal archbishop. "In a phone conversation not more than ten minutes ago, he assured me that, with the exception of the, uh, Tridentine Mass"—the words rolled distastefully from his lips—"he is willing and capable to take over the bulk of your routine."

Father's jaw almost clunked on the table.

I covered for him by letting go of my cane so it clattered noisily on the wooden armrest of the chair next to mine.

"He had no business telling you—" said Father.

"Need I remind you," said the cardinal, eyes and nostrils flaring, "that as a monsignor, Havermeyer outranks you?"

"An honorary title," said Father, "does not bestow 'rank.' You might be able to pull that kind of ploy on the clueless whelps you churn out from your diocesan seminary, but it won't work on me."

"I advise you to watch your tone," said Morley.

"Need I remind Your Eminence," said Father, "that I purchased St. Philomena's with my own money? Technically the church building and the grounds are my personal property."

"Technically, you are a priest under my jurisdiction, albeit on extended leave. Don't make me force the issue by appointing him pastor over you."

Seated at Father's side, I could only see half his countenance, but I'm pretty sure he looked at his lawful superior with those penetrating eyes which seemed to say, outraged yet obediently, "Considering that I recently did save your sanctimonious hide, Your pretentious Eminence, would you really attempt that sort of heavy-handed chicanery with me?"

Seated directly across from the cardinal, I could see His Arrogance's face plainly, and his nefarious eyeballs replied, condescending and venemously, "Try me, insect."

"I see," said Father Baptist.

"I thought you would," said Cardinal Fulbright.

"So it's settled," said Messrs. Brennan and Gerezanno together.

Yeah, I thought, like sewage in the sea.

"Except for my fee," said Father.

"I said I'd see to that," said Monsignor Aspic.

"That was my fee for past services," said Father Baptist. "Now we must address the present."

This was met with a round of chair burps.

"You can't possibly be serious," said Mr. Gerezanno.

"I couldn't possibly be more," said Father.

"Of course, of course," cooed Monsignor Aspic. "Father Baptist and I will sort this out at a more propitious time."

"Hrmph," said the cardinal, eyeing his ring as if it had the power to make us all disappear.

"If my entanglement in this case is inevitable, then I have a question to ask," said Father, leaning forward. "Do the police have any reason to suspect that a member of the clergy is involved?"

His Elegance looked at Chief Billowack, Taper looked at Wickes, I looked at my watch.

"No," said Taper presently. "Not to our knowledge."

"Then why," said Father, "does the Cardinal Archbishop wish to involve himself—and by extension me—in a criminal investigation which is entirely a police matter?"

"Lives are at stake," said Wickes.

"Always," said Father. "Murders are committed every day. But that doesn't answer my question."

"There are two reasons," said His Elegance, Morley Fulbright. "First, Father Baptist, you have established a reputation for yourself as having, shall we say, 'an intimate understanding' of the occult. It is not beyond the bounds of propriety for the Church to assist the civil authorities in such matters."

"And the second?" asked Father.

The cardinal closed his eyes. "That is something I don't wish to discuss at this time, nor under these circumstances."

"Okay," said Billowack, shifting his enormous bulk in his chair. It may have been my imagination, but his cushion seemed to squeal "Uncle." Really. "Okay," he said again, "if you guys—begging Your, uh, Your, um, M & M's pardon—"

> GARDENING TIPS: I don't know if the chief, being
> unlettered, was unfamiliar with the word "emi-
> nence," or being a Methodist, was reticent about
> applying a title of grandeur to a leader in a re-
> ligion to which he was diametrically opposed. In
> any case, I almost burped in my own chair when
> Billowack somehow came out with that peculiar
> candy-coated mispronunciation—and my chair had a
> wooden seat.
>
> —M.F.

"—but," he blundered on, "if you guys have got your bearings straight, I want Jack to come down to—"

"The name is Father John Baptist," said Father coldly.

"Yeah, right," hrumphed Billowack, his Wesleyan tendencies bristling. "Whatever, I want you to come down to the morgue and bless us with a sprinkling of your, uh, expertise." With all his posturing, it cost him plenty to admit that he needed the help of Jack Lombard, the cop-turned-priest-who-had-just-been-ordered-to-turn-cop again.

"I will obey my lawful superior," said Father Baptist, nodding to Cardinal Fulbright. "Please remember that it is he, not you, who fills those shoes."

"Speaking of filling shoes," said Billowack, squirming around in his chair. "There's also the matter of your filling my daughter's head with your Papist ideas."

The connection between the shoes of authority and the head of his daughter, Stella, eluded me.

"Is this true?" growled the cardinal, the very soul of ecumenism.

"I am instructing Miss Stella Billowack in matters of the Catholic Faith, yes," said Father evenly, "at her request."

"Then," said the cardinal magnanimously, "in the interests of cooperation between ourselves and the police, and in the spirit of Vatican II, you will cease this activity at once."

"I will not," said Father.

"What's that?" barked Fulbright, leaning forward in his chair as if raising a fly swatter to strike a mosquito.

"I will not, Your Eminence," repeated Father evenly.

I swallowed my tongue. It hurt.

Even Billowack almost swallowed his tie—and considering the size of the knot under his chin, that must've really hurt.

"Under Holy Obedience," snarled the cardinal, "I order you—"

"Under the Code of Cannon Law you cannot," said Father. "Not to mention the *Summa Theologica*. On this point, Your Eminence, my course is set. Do what you will. Revoke my faculties if you've a mind. I will not waver."

GARDENING TIPS: "Faculties" is, in effect, a priest's license to administer the Sacraments within the jurisdiction of a given bishop. Without this permission from the ranking prelate, a priest is technically dead in the water. He cannot legally administer the Sacraments in public. What was on the line here was Father Baptist's reason for being.

--M.F.

Just then I sneezed. A grand sneeze. No, a great grand sneeze. One of those wet, sloppy nasal explosions guaranteed to disgust everyone in the room. Naturally, I yanked a large white handkerchief from my jacket pocket. Just as naturally, something rectangular and laminated which I kept rolled up in said handkerchief came out with it, landing face up on the table between my elbows. Upon seeing it, the cardinal's eyes bulged, then narrowed, then retracted back into their saurian sockets. After a noisy and dramatic performance of emptying my sinuses into my hankie, I restuffed my pocket with its previous contents.

"Are you through?" growled the cardinal.

"Yes," I sniffed innocently. "A thousand pardons."

"As I was saying," said Father Baptist. "I—"

"Hrmph," hrumphed the cardinal. "Upon further consideration, and with all due respect to Chief Billowack, it is beyond our purview to interfere in this, um, sensitive private matter."

"Thank-you, St. Rita," I whispered under my breath, patting my pocket.

"What?" rasped Billowack, phlegm flying. I would have offered him my handkerchief but it was already pretty soggy. "What do you mean?"

"He means," explained the gardener, flashing what he hoped was a sweet but penetrating smile in the direction of Taper and Wickes, "just what he said."

"I don't get it," huffed Billowack.

"No doubt you don't," I said, "but—"

"You're just going to let him keep on poisoning my Stella's mind?" said Billowack, stubby finger aimed at Morley's bump.

The cardinal was looking down at his hands, rubbing his ring intently.

"Then I'll put a stop to it," said Billowack.

"You can't," said Father.

"Huh?"

"If you pounce on your daughter, order her not to see me, you'll only alienate her further. She'll get more stubborn. It's a trait she comes by honestly, you know."

"Then I'll stop you."

"With what?" said Father. "A bullet? That's the only way, Monty."

Billowack swallowed cavernously. "You're serious."

"Dead serious. Of course, then your daughter's teacher would become a martyr. No, Monty, I'm afraid you're stuck with things the way they are."

"Gentlemen, gentlemen," cooed Monsignor Aspic.

"Where, where?" asked the gardener under his breath.

I felt Father Baptist's hand on my arm as if to say, "Enough."

Sighing, I nodded my agreement. Gardeners should be perceived and not heard, at least in cardinals' offices.

"So," said Father Baptist, smiling. "If that is all, Your Eminence, Monsignor Aspic, Chief Billowack. Gentlemen, it would seem that my next order of business is to proceed to the morgue."

"Quite right," said Monsignor Aspic, his moist eyes darting around the table, taking in all this ecumenical camaraderie. "I, for one, am glad that we have come to an amiable resolution."

"What resolution?" bellowed Billowack. "Look here—"

"This meeting is concluded," announced the cardinal, rising regally. "I have other pressing matters to attend to."

Indeed, I thought, eyeing the creases in his new robes. I considered handing him one of Vinnie Ng's business cards, but thought better of it. Mr. Ng is our "in lieu of" Chinese dry-cleaner.

"So," I ventured as Father and I crossed the foyer on the ground floor of the Chancery building a few minutes later.

"So," he agreed as we maneuvered around the table in the center on which was displayed an architect's miniature replica of the "Future Cathedral and Chancery Complex." The original proposed date of construction, July 20 of this year, had been unceremoniously crossed out with a broad stroke of a black felt pen.

"So," I repeated. "You'll have to dig out your Sherlock Holmes deerstalker hat yet again."

"I guess," sighed Father. "Though I prefer a biretta."

"That was quite a meeting," I said. "You never know what to expect when you get an invitation to Fulbright's inner sanctum."

"Surely he didn't expect you to wave that old photo under his nose again."

"What photo?"

"The one of him and the late Bishop Eugene Brassorie attempting to dump the statue of St. Rita into the LA River from the Hyperion Bridge."

"Oh, you caught that?"

"Hard to miss, Martin. Subtlety is not your strongest quality."

"And all these years I thought it was."

"The look in his eyes," tisked Father. "Be glad I'm your confessor and not he."

"I am, Father. Indeed, I am. Well, usually."

"To tell you the truth, I thought you'd thrown that thing away."

"Why did you think that?"

"The last time we were in the cardinal's office," said Father, "back in June when things got crazy, he told you he was already in so much hot water that whatever embarrassment that photo could cause him was insignificant compared to the mess he was already in."

"But that was when he was in a mess," I said. "Life is change. Look at him now. The muddle is behind him and he even got a promotion out of the deal. Now this photograph is more threatening to him than ever. I'm surprised—no, I believe I'm hurt—that you would think me stupid enough to throw away such a useful gem as this."

"My humblest apologies," said Father, smiling broadly. "It is reassuring to be reminded that my gardener is sometimes more clear-headed than myself."

"Aw," I said, "that's just because my skull is full of aggies and taws. Of course, I do keep losing them—"

"That you do, Martin. Oh, and what's this?"

"I want to apologize," said Lieutenant Taper, approaching meekly with Wickes trotting even more meekly behind. "Jack, I had no idea that Billowack would go over your head like that—"

"I did," said Father. "I knew it was coming the moment you sat down at our table last night."

"What?" squawked Taper and I together as Wickes bumped into all of us.

"I surmised from your tone of voice," said Father, "that whatever you're dealing with must be a truly horrific matter. I've witnessed your reaction to many a crime, Larry. Revulsion, anger, confusion I've seen on occasion, but never fear."

"True," admitted Taper, hooking his finger nervously inside his shirt collar. "But why did you turn us down?"

Father Baptist bowed his head, choosing his words carefully. "Larry, you must try to understand that solving crimes is a great temptation for me. It takes my mind off my priestly duties and interferes with my devotional life—distractions I truly cannot afford. Like all temptations, it is something in which I long to engage, even though I know I mustn't. My only course was to say 'No,' and put the matter in God's hands. Unfortunately, I wasn't being all that noble since there was no question how things would go. I wish I could say my intention was pure, but as with all human decisions, it was not."

"Come again?" asked Wickes.

"The trouble is," said Father, "I knew that any crime that would strike you gentlemen with such unrest would certainly terrify Chief Billowack, that he would not take my refusal sitting down when you reported back to him. He may not be smart, but he's not stupid; and he's not without influence. It was only a matter of time before I received a summons from Cardinal Fulbright."

Taper and Wickes and I exchanged various degrees of widened eyeballs.

"If anything," said Father, "I was surprised that our beloved Bulldog acted so swiftly. I figured it would take him at least twenty-four hours to swallow his Protestant bile and call the Chancery."

"He is terrified," said Sergeant Wickes. "He's scared out of his choke-chain."

"Then let us hurry to the morgue," said Father, "as Holy Obedience requires."

"And don't forget to send me your bill straight away, Father," said Monsignor Aspic, who had approached without our notice. Funny how he could turn the clip-clop of his dazzling shoes on and off at will. "Be sure to address it, 'Attention: Aspic.'"

We watched as he slid on by and disappeared through a door marked PRIVATE.

9

IT'S HARD TO SAY WHAT I THOUGHT a morgue would be like. I guess I assumed, for no reason in particular, that it would be cold, dark, and damp, the walls oozing subterranean fluids seeping between fungus-encrusted bricks arranged in crooked, crumbling rows. Maybe I watched too many Boris Karloff movies in my youth. Surely I'd read my share of Lovecraft and Poe.

The reality, of course, was nothing like that—and yet the effect was not as different as one would hope. Not only wasn't it below ground level—indeed, the blue-tinted windows looked out on the spacious Pomeroy Police Plaza—but it was frankly as bright, cool, plain, and sterile as a linoleum-floored room can get. The only thing dripping was the astigmatic music seeping through conical speakers set in the ceiling between rows of blazing fluorescent lights. There wasn't a speck of mold or mildew in sight. There weren't even any shelves stocked with jars of pickled eyeballs and other unmentionable organs in murky fluids.

There were, on the other hand, five stainless steel autopsy slabs—unoccupied, thank Heaven. Their silvery sheen, sloping surfaces, and welcoming catch basins aroused mental images best left unexplored. Tiers upon tiers of disinfected dissection implements lay nestled on white napkins, awaiting unimaginable use. There were scalpels and saws and drills and clamps and tweezers and who knows what else.

In its way, this modern morgue was worse than ol' H.P.'s worst nightmare. This was a place of cold-blooded detachment, where human bodies were sliced and diced and reduced to smears on glass slides and columns of numbers flickering on computer screens. The whole process was a necessary but heartless cog in the gears of modern criminal detection.

And of course there was the smell, reminiscent of the aroma of Millie's disinfectants on "bathroom day," but with an underlying pinch of formaldehyde hearkening back to "frog day" in high school biology class.

In any case, be it dank or sanitary, smelling like a rose or what the rose grew out of, a morgue was a morgue; and this gardener did not like being there.

"This has been going on for more than a month," Lieutenant Taper was saying as we entered through a pair of huge swinging doors complete with double-pane portholes, "at intervals of three to six days."

"Seven so far," said Sergeant Wickes. "Same MO each time."

"Mr. Wong," said Taper as we approached a thin twig of a man hunched over a microscope. "You remember Father John Baptist and his, um—"

"Gardener," I suggested.

"Yes," stammered the lieutenant. "His gardener, Martin Feeney. Martin, our county coroner, Solomon Yung-sul Wong."

"Why the formality, Larry?" said the gaunt man, peering over the stereo eyepieces. "Only a few months ago we all shared an alcove at St. Barbara's Church. Quite an event, as it turned out. Anyway, Father and I go way back before that, back to the days when he called himself Jack Lombard."

"Back when men were men," said Father, "and things were dull."

"Hardly," said Mr. Wong. The coroner slipped off his stool and regarded us with reserved Asian solemnity for a moment, then smiled. His grin seemed friendly enough, but there was a monsoon blowing behind those dark Oriental orbs, a storm as dismal and ominous as the one still threatening to release its wrath outside. He shook hands with Father Baptist and then turned toward me. "Besides, who can forget Mr. Feeney?"

"I try my best," I said, gingerly clasping his hand. In this place, I couldn't help wondering where it had been, nor could I help but notice a slight quiver in his slender fingers as I gripped them.

"Ah, company," said another man strutting toward us, arms full of clinking glass beakers. I knew him without looking at his name tag: JOHN HOLTSCLAW, ASSISTANT CORONER. He set them down noisily on a countertop, wiped his palms on his lab smock, and extended his hand.

Father gripped it firmly, and I less so. Holtsclaw's hand, too, was trembling. His Gabriellino tribal sinews, it seemed, were gathering for a war dance beneath his smooth, sandstone skin.

"So," said Solomon, eyes darting from Taper to Wickes to myself to Father and finally to his associate, Holtsclaw.

"So," said Holtsclaw, encoring his superior's eye routine and landing on his boss, Solomon.

They were daring each other to speak first. The sterile detachment, which was the normal functional mode of this place, had given way to something unfamiliar and therefore alarming to these gentlemen who, as a matter of course, were more in touch with the soft, white underbelly of life in the "big city" than anyone else in the Police Department.

I wrapped my hands around the dragon's head handle of my trusty cane, squeezing as though I could extract from it an ounce of its aspen courage.

"Okay," said Taper, throwing up his hands. He heaved one hip up onto a lab stool, waving the rest of us to do likewise. "As I was saying: we have seven victims, all from the Hollywood area, all female, all young, unattached—"

"And beautiful," said Solomon, swallowing loudly.

"Each went out alone for a night on the town, hopping from bar to bar," said Taper.

"Prostitutes?" asked the gardener.

"Not according to their friends and families," said Wickes. "At least, the ones we could locate. Though, of course, they're often the last to know."

"Of course," said Taper dryly, "the line of demarcation between 'flirting,' 'slutting,' and 'whoring' has grown thin these days."

"But none of these victims was sexually assaulted," said Holtsclaw. "We're sure of that."

"And none was HIV positive," added Solomon, "or carrying any other sexually-transmitted diseases."

"So you're saying they were all 'good' girls," said the gardener.

"Or at least careful," said Solomon. "I don't know what 'good' means, anymore."

"I do," said Father patiently. "And I'm still waiting for 'dreadful.'"

"All murder is dreadful," said John Holtsclaw through clenched jaws.

"Indeed," said Father, "but in your line of work—as in mine in the past—it becomes, regrettably and yet necessarily, mundane. You force the ghastly into the commonplace so you can deal with it. It must be so, or your grip on sanity would falter. And yet last night and this morning I've been hearing the word 'dreadful.' Something sinister must indeed be at work for you and your colleagues to resort to such an adjective. Look at you. When's the last time any of you got a good night's sleep?"

"A little over a month ago," said Wickes.

"Better show him," shrugged Taper to Solomon.

"Right," sighed the coroner, reluctantly making his way to a double row of large drawers in the far wall. A chromium sign above the compartments said: CAUTION: NEAR-ZERO STORAGE UNIT. He grabbed a large handle on one of them and gave it a hefty tug.

No, I thought to myself. I don't want to see this. No, no, no, no.

The stainless steel slab came rolling out of the wall like a giant behemoth's tongue, belching a cloud of swirling white mist. The shape of the body slowly became visible as the fog fell away, cascading to the floor in hundreds of ghostly rivulets. It was covered with a sheet with the feet protruding.

"Victim number seven, and most recent," read Holtsclaw from a clipboard he snatched from a hook on the wall. "Elizabeth Unger, age twenty-two. She was found in an alley off Wilcox early Saturday morning."

"You've kept them all here?" asked Father, indicating the other drawers. "You said it's been over a month since the first murder."

"We don't normally hold bodies this long," said Holtsclaw, "but Chief Billowack said to keep them in deep freeze, just in case something turned up which required a second autopsy."

Solomon Yung-sul Wong folded the sheet back from her face.

No, no, no, moaned this gardener's brain behind squirming eyeballs. It's bad enough when I have to assist Father when he kneels before an open coffin, leading a Rosary the night before a Requiem Mass. The mortician's beautifying techniques are but a grisly form of mockery: "Good gracious me, Aunt Nummy's smile never looked so kind when she was alive." But here in the morgue, death lay exposed under high-intensity full-spectrum lights, free of lipstick and eye shadow and powders and hair spray. In point of fact, Elizabeth Unger couldn't possibly have ever looked so plainly, positively, and finally dead as she did at that moment.

"Cause of death?" asked Father sadly, brushing a strand of stiff hair away from the alabaster forehead. Her blonde curls lay matted around her face. The lips were pale and thin and purple and slightly parted, and—Mother of Mercy!—so were her eyelids. Annihilation stared vacantly out upon a vacuum of nothingness.

"Heart failure," said Holtsclaw, voice cracking. "Due to arterial collapse caused by a catastrophic loss of blood."

"How?" asked Father evenly. "Through what wound?"

"There," said Solomon, pointing to her neck. "There."

"Two small puncture wounds," explained Holtsclaw, "right over the left jugular vein. Damn, I feel like I'm reading a script from an old movie."

And I felt like I was living in one as I looked between their shoulders at the scar on the otherwise chalk-white neck. It stared up at me like a perverted version of the "happy face" so common on office stationary and bumper stickers.

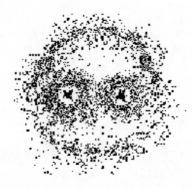

GARDENING TIPS: The above drawing, and all similar
ones below, are my pencil renditions traced from
photos later provided by Sybil Wexler.

                                                --M.F.

"As you can see, Jack," said Taper, clearing his throat, "two punctures—each wound is a small jagged red dot tinged with blue, surrounded by a swollen white mound. The area around the mounds is
puckered, capillaries ruptured, a condition which occurs when suction is
applied to the skin. The puckered area is ringed with indentations
which we believe to be teeth marks—"

"From which you surmise?" asked Father.

"Well," said Taper, rubbing his forehead, "it would seem that the
murderer had a pair of extra-long teeth—"

"The canines, most likely," said Solomon, "the pointed cusps we all
have on each side of our incisors."

"Fangs," said Wickes.

"—which he plunged through the skin," continued Taper, "into the
vein."

"How long would these canines have to be," asked Father, "to do
that?"

"Hard to say," said Holtsclaw. "The skin, muscular tissues, and
blood vessels are very pliable. They stretch and regain their shape,
which is why bite wounds are so hard to analyze."

"A rough guess," said Father.

"At least a half-inch," said Solomon. "Perhaps three-quarters."

"What about a full inch?" asked Father.

"Maybe," said Holtsclaw, "but any longer and the killer would end up
biting his chin when he closed his mouth."

"Once the vein was pierced," said Taper, "the killer would have to
withdraw the canines from the wound, otherwise they'd serve as plugs."

"Unless they were hollow like a rattlesnake's," said Solomon, "which
we doubt."

"Why is that?" asked Father.

"Because of the ring of indentations around the two punctures," said
Solomon, tracing the circle with his finger. "Teeth marks. First the
murderer bit the throat, then withdrew the fangs—"

"—and then pressed his mouth around the spurting wounds," finished
Taper, "and proceeded to suck out her blood."

"Grmgph," grmgphed the gardener at these details.

"No other incisions?" asked Father, bending close to examine the tiny
punctures. In his black cassock, hunched over her like that, he almost
looked like ... no, never mind.

"No other wounds or bruises of any kind," said Solomon, "except for
a thin red line around the back and sides of her neck."

Father shifted to a crouch beside the body. "Yes, I see it. Any ideas?"

"As if," said Solomon, "she'd been wearing a delicate chain, and it was pulled from the front until it snapped."

"Other than that," said Taper, "there's no sign of a struggle."

"And yet," said Holtsclaw, "the blood-letting had to be done slowly." He flipped uselessly through several pages on his clipboard. "Can't say exactly how long, but certainly more than a quarter of an hour. And from all indications, she was ... um ..."

"Conscious of what was happening," said Father, straightening. "Were there any drugs in her system?"

"Alcohol," said Solomon. "Two or three drinks, perhaps. Not enough to make her pass out. Traces of nicotine. Marijuana residue, but probably just traces left from a previous evening—perhaps a week ago. She was tipsy, but not stoned."

"Yes," said Holtsclaw, hanging the clipboard back on its hook. It took him three tries. "She wasn't drugged, and she didn't struggle. How could anyone just sit back and let someone suck out their blood?"

"This puckering," said Father, pointing to the area around the punctures, "and the indentations obviously left by teeth ... hm. Surely you did a saliva test around the wound."

"Type O, positive," said Holtsclaw.

"And a microscopic analysis on the interior of these tiny punctures?" added Father.

"Yes," said Taper. "Where are they, John?"

"Not here," said Holtsclaw. "Sybil's upstairs photocopying the file. It may take her a while."

"Sybil Wexler?" asked Father.

"You remember her?" asked Wickes.

"Never had the pleasure of meeting her," said Father. "But her computer printouts were most helpful the last time I was working with you." He rubbed his eyes, then the back of his neck. "Quite a problem, gentlemen."

"I've never seen anything like it," shivered Solomon, pulling the sheet back over the corpse's head.

"I have—" began Holtsclaw.

"Yes?" asked Father.

"I saw something like it once," gulped the assistant coroner, "when I was doing some volunteer work as an intern in South America—but not on the throat, and not—"

"You mean bats," said Father.

"Uh, yes."

"I've seen something like it as well," said Father. "But only in books. Very old books."

"The same is true for all of them," said Solomon, motioning to the row of silent drawers. "The first was Patricia Kelly, then Shelly Stevens, Alicia Alvarez, Anna Kay Dobbs, Terisa Kim Lin, Melissa Burchfield, and now Elizabeth Unger. Seven in all: all beautiful, all single, all went out and had a few drinks—and all ended up dead, drained of blood."

"They were found in various alleys north and south of Hollywood Boulevard," said Taper. "None more than a block away from one of the city's busiest night-life streets."

"Probably dumped from a car after the fact," said Wickes.

"Had to be," said Taper. "With all the foot traffic in the area, and considering the time it took to, uh, well, someone would have seen something if the killer had done his business at the scene."

"And of course no one did see the killer at work," said Father.

"No one we can find," said Taper. "The bodies were discovered in the wee hours of the morning—by trash collectors, mostly, or proprietors arriving at their stores to do paperwork before business hours."

"What about their earlier movements?" asked Father. "Anyone remember seeing these ladies drinking in the bars?"

"Yes," said Wickes. "But in the Hollywood scene, nobody pays much attention to who comes and goes, or with whom."

"I'll want to talk to anyone who remembers anything," said Father.

"Of course," said Wickes.

"When we're finished here," said Taper, handing Father a sheet of paper, "the sergeant and I will take you to see their apartments. Here's a list of addresses. They all resided alone and had few acquaintances. With the exception of Elizabeth Unger here, and Anna Kay Dobbs in drawer number four, their families are all out-of-state, and not much help. We haven't received a single complaint regarding the delay in burial, nor a request for shipment of the bodies home."

"How sad," said Father.

"Trust me, Jack," said Taper, "you'll want to see their rooms, their effects, how they lived."

"Yes," said Father, "Martin and I will follow you in our own car."

"There hasn't been a peep about this in the news," said the gardener, massaging his queasy gut.

"For once we managed to keep something from the media," said Taper.

"Billowack said he'd personally shoot anyone who leaked a single detail," said Wickes.

"And I still will, Lombard," roared Billowack, stomping into the room. "If you or your hunchbacked partner say a word to the press, I'll skin you alive."

Of all the nerve. I may have severe spinal arthritis, but I'm years from applying for bell-ringer at Notre Dame Cathedral.

"Cut the threats," said Father sternly as Billowack's enormous shadow fell across us all. "My professionalism is not at issue. Neither is Mr. Feeney's. You would do well to put a muzzle on it, Monty."

"You watch it," said Billowack, "you're workin' for me now."

"As I have already made clear, Monty: I am *not* working for you. I answer to His Eminence, Cardinal Fulbright. I am merely acting as your consultant, and only on his orders. But there's no mystery here."

"There isn't?" asked Wickes.

"Not at all," said Father, calmly. "It's obvious that you're dealing with a vampire."

"You say that?" barked Billowack, saliva sailing.

"I do," said Father. "If it was anything else, you wouldn't need my help."

"You believe in such things?" snarled Billowack.

"Whether I do or not," said Father evenly, "you certainly do, or are beginning to. I'm surprised you haven't hung garlic and Crucifixes on the drawer handles."

"We did—" said Wickes, and then shriveled under Billowack's withering stare.

"Inside," whispered Solomon seriously. He waved his hand to indicate all the drawers. "Under the sheets."

"Maybe," bellowed Billowack, glaring at his underlings, "somebody's been watching too many late-night horror films."

"Maybe," said the gardener, "somebody else slept through them."

"Hm," commented Father in my direction. Then, turning to Billowack: "I want to hear it from your lips, Monty. Tell me why you insisted that I get involved."

"Well," huffed Billowack, "you're a—well, you're—"

"Not a Methodist minister," said Father. "If you thought Pastor McIntosh could help, then surely you would have sought his advice."

"I did," growled Billowack.

"And?"

The Chief of Homicide shoved his hands deep into his pockets. "He said there's no room in his theology for vampires."

"And?"

"And that most Catholic priests wouldn't be of any use, either."

"So?"

"He told me to call you."

10

"DO YOU?" I HAD TO ASK as I pulled the Jeep Cherokee away from the curb. I could see Sergeant Wickes and Lieutenant Taper in the rearview mirror, following close behind in their car. They seemed to be arguing about something.

"Do I what, Martin?"

"Believe in vampires? You said it's obvious they're dealing with a vampire."

"It's obvious that they think they are, so in their minds they are."

"But are they?"

"What?"

"Dealing with a vampire?"

"We shall see."

And, as is the point of this whole story, we did.

11

"MOST DISTRESSING," SAID FATHER. He was eyeing the bookshelves in Elizabeth Unger's living room. Honks and screeches from the ever-frenzied traffic on Hollywood Boulevard, less than a block away, penetrated the bolted windows and drawn drapes. "This poor girl was obviously morbid."

"You noticed," said Taper, turning on a lamp nearby. The walls were cluttered with plaster skulls, carved bats, and murky prints of vile things clawing up through the dirt between tottering tombstones.

"*Lure of the Vampire,*" read the gardener aloud, running his finger along the pulpy spines on the shelf. "*Lust of the Undead ... The Life is in the Blood ...*"

"You'll find the same kind of stuff," said Wickes, "even a lot of the same titles, among the effects of the other victims."

I pulled one of the volumes off its perch. On the cover, a buxom lass with pouting lips was parting her blouse for a thirsty, dashing, oily-haired, caped creature with long, pointed incisors. The title was her plea, *Drink Me, I'm Yours.*

"I wasn't aware," said Father, "that modern fiction had descended so far in this regard: to make vampirism appealing to malleable minds."

"You've been out of circulation for a while," said Taper.

"Not all of it's fiction, apparently," said Wickes, holding up a volume entitled *Confessions of a Modern Vampire and His Consorts.* "There seems to be a growing cult of people who really believe in this stuff, though why anyone would actually want to become a blood-sucking ghoul is beyond me."

"Souls yearn for Eternity," said Father sadly, "even those who have no Faith, and more so those who had it once and lost it. The vampire promises life after death, a morbid but accessible immortality."

"Pretty screwy eternal life," commented Wickes, "squirreling yourself away in musty tombs, avoiding daylight, only venturing out at night, trusting no one, sucking your victims dry—"

"Sounds like ordinary behavior," observed the gardener, "for most people in this city."

"But don't you have to die to become a vampire?" asked Wickes.

"It's a necessary part of the process, yes," said Father, "according to some."

"Wait a minute," said Taper. "We're all talking like vampires are real. Are they, Jack?"

"I want to see her bedroom," said Father.

"Jack?"

"The bedroom."

"This way," said Taper, fuming.

"She certainly had a 'thing' for the dark," observed Wickes. "Deep blue drapes, dark brown bedspread, and look, most of the clothes in her closet are black."

"Not much sunshine in her life," said Taper.

"Perhaps a ray," said Father, eyeing a Crucifix on the wall above the bed. "It's a pity she didn't seek her answers there."

"Most people don't these days," said Taper soberly. "The modern Church doesn't offer much in the way of answers, only questions."

"Priests should know better," said Father, stifling a shiver. Tenderly, he picked up a framed photograph from the dressing table. "This looks recent. She was wearing a small Cross on a silver chain around her neck when it was taken."

"I hadn't noticed," said Taper. "Maybe that's what left that red mark."

"Perhaps," said Father, setting the frame back in its place. He picked up something else next to it, and another and another. "And she did smoke?"

"Yes," said Taper. "Nicotine in her blood, remember? And there's a half-empty pack and a used ashtray on the coffee table in the living room. We also found a small pipe in one of the kitchen drawers with traces of marijuana resin in the bowl. Why?"

"These matchbooks," said Father, reading the covers. "'Stogie's,' 'The Lounge Around,' and ... hm ... 'House of Illusions.'"

"The first two are on Hollywood Boulevard," said Taper, "a few blocks each side of Gower. We covered those, along with a lot of other dives, after each murder. Anna Kay Dobbs was seen at 'Stogie's' the

night she died. Terisa Kim Lin was a regular at 'The Lounge Around.'
All the victims made the rounds."

"What about the 'House of Illusions'?" asked Father.

"That's in another league altogether," said Wickes. "It's a swanky
place up in the Cahuenga Pass near the Hollywood Bowl."

"A private club, actually," said Taper.

"For stage magicians," said Wickes. "Ever hear of it?"

"Martin and I will be dining there this Friday night," said Father,
"with the Tumblars."

"Really," said Taper. "I thought it was 'members or guests-of-
members only.'"

"Pierre Bontemps apparently has an 'in,'" said Father.

"So did Elizabeth Unger," said Wickes. "She's the only victim we've
traced there for certain."

"Do you mean," said Father, "that you have a witness? She was seen
there the night of her death?"

"You got it," said Wickes, pulling out his little notebook and flipping through the pages. "'House of Illusions' matchbooks aren't unusual in Hollywood. We found similar matchbooks among the effects
of Patricia Kelly and Shelly Stevens."

"The first two victims," said Taper.

"And now the most recent," said Father.

"That's not to say the others haven't been there," said Wickes. "But
the only positive ID we got was from the piano player in the upstairs
bar, a guy named Buzz Sawr. He recognized Elizabeth Unger's picture."

"Was she there as a member or a guest?" asked Father.

"Oh definitely a guest," said Wickes. "No way she could've afforded
the grand-a-year dues."

"Then who invited her?" asked Father.

"No way of telling," said Taper. "A member calls and reserves a table for two, then shows up with his friend. The guests' names aren't
registered. All the manager's concerned with is the total head-count to
avoid fines from the Fire Marshall."

"But the piano player recognized Miss Unger," said Father.

"Yes," said Wickes, closing his notebook.

"Then I must have a word with him," said Father. "I've seen enough
here, gentlemen."

"Okay," said Wickes, leading us back into the living room. "The
next address on the list—"

"No," said Father. "That will keep until tomorrow. You said the
other women were of the same general disposition."

"Yes," said Taper.

"I need to ..." Father paused and turned to look again toward the dark
bedroom, as if he'd forgotten something.

Our eyes followed his. Through the doorway we could see the dark dresses hanging in the open closet.

"No mirrors," said Father. "Even on the dressing table. Not even a lady's compact. Did you notice that, Lieutenant?"

"Strange for a young woman," said Taper.

"Almost inconceivable," said Father. He rolled his shoulders and sighed heavily. "In any case, I need to focus my attention elsewhere for a while."

"Oh?" said Wickes. "Where?"

"On the Light," said Father. "The Light that shines in the darkness. If we're to journey into that darkness, gentlemen, we'll need to bring a candle."

"Perhaps a torch," I suggested. "Maybe a whole bunch—"

"Martin, we must go."

"What about us?" asked Wickes.

"Why don't you drop by St. Philomena's tomorrow morning for breakfast?" said Father. "We'll discuss strategy then. I'll want to review the files this evening."

"Speaking of breakfast, Father," I said, checking my watch, "Millie will be serving lunch within the hour."

"Quite right," said Father. "We must attend to that."

We all turned toward the front door—and froze.

Taper had apparently left it slightly ajar. In the space between the edge of the door and the frame, between the deadbolt and the doorknob, a pair of wide, pale eyes were looking at us. With a frantic rustle of clothing, the eyes disappeared.

"Hey!" yelled Wickes, springing toward the door and yanking it open. He bounded out into the hallway.

We followed, looking this way and that.

There was no one to be seen.

12

"WHAT THE HELL IS THIS?" exclaimed Monsignor Havermeyer, emerging from his camper. There was barely room for him to squeeze out from behind the flimsy door.

"That," I said through the open car window, "seems to be a dumpster." I maneuvered the Jeep back and forth, finally parking it sideways behind the large metal container that had mysteriously taken up occupancy during our absence in the parking places between the '57 Buick and the monsignor's recreational vehicle. Satisfied that I wasn't blocking the alley, I edged myself from the driver's seat and slammed the door. Father Baptist, I noticed, was already out of the car and through the wrought-iron gate.

"Better hurry, Monsignor," I said, "Millie is serving lunch in five minutes."

"I was so absorbed in studying rubrics," said Havermeyer, getting in stride beside me—if you can call my heaving and lurching a "stride"—"that I didn't hear anything."

Sure, I thought, a garbage truck came thundering up the alley and two gorillas rolled that noisy thing up alongside your camper and you didn't hear it. Maybe we dozed, My Senior, partaking of what the Arabs call "the music of sleep." In your case, it must've been quite an opera.

"Buenos dias, Señor Feeney." A few yards up the path a man in a denim shirt and filthy jeans was wiping his brow with a red handkerchief. Father Baptist was standing at his side.

"Roberto Guadalupe," I said, holding out my hand. Dirty as his was, I wasn't the least bit queasy about gripping it firmly. I had a fairly good idea what it had been up to. "So you're finally getting around to it."

"Sí," he nodded. "Duggo and Spade and me." He pointed over to the two other men, similarly clad, attacking the half-acre sea of tangled vegetation behind the church. "Hola, Monsignor Havermeyer."

The monsignor didn't offer his hand. "What's the meaning of this?"

"These three gentlemen," explained Father Baptist, "have generously offered to clear the jungle. Quite an undertaking, Roberto."

"One hard day," said Roberto. "Maybe two." He looked up at the purple clouds billowing overhead. "I just hope she does not rain."

"That *would* make your job difficult," said Father.

"No matter," shrugged Roberto. "This is the time we arranged to take off from our landscaping work at the Del Agua Mission, so this is when the job, it gets done."

"God bless you in your labors," said Father. "You must pardon us, as we're in a hurry. I'll see that Millie brings out some iced tea shortly."

"Muchas gracias," nodded Roberto. "That will be much appreciated."

Duggo and Spade waved their agreement and returned to their toils.

"Two minutes," I said, glancing at my watch.

"We'll make it," said Father. "Ah, Joel."

Joel Maruppa and his grandfather, Josef, were coming up the brick path from the opposite direction, carrying a spool of heavy-gauge electrical wire between them.

"Lunch time," I said urgently.

"Ah," said Joel and Josef in unison, dropping their burden on the spot. They, too, knew the rules—even old Josef, who spoke only rudimentary English.

"What is this?" exclaimed Monsignor Havermeyer, glaring at the plate Millie had just set before him.

"Your lunch," huffed Millie as Father, Joel, and Josef settled themselves—ten seconds to spare—in the dining nook.

In less time than it took me to ease my behind upon the squat little stool which she'd thoughtfully kicked in my direction, Millie had made two round-trips to the stove and slammed five more plates down in our midst with her typical culinary ferocity.

Monsignor Havermeyer looked hungrily at the heaps of steaming vegetables tossed with creamy fettuccini set before us—a cheap feast, but filling—then back at his own plate. "A potato?" he rasped.

"A boiled potato," said Millie, approaching again, this time with an empty skillet in each hand.

"This is all I get?" gasped the monsignor.

"The Curé d'Ars lived on two a day—" said Millie, towering over him, pans armed and deadly.

"Three on special occasions," said the gardener, sprinkling pepper with abandon on his tumultuous mound of aromatic splendor. He seemed unaware of the monsignor's victual shortage.

"—and Father John Vianney was a Saint," said Millie, flashing me a "shut up" stare.

"I believe he lived into his seventies," said Father, calmly accepting the peppershaker from me and similarly decorating his lunch. He seemed equally oblivious to the monsignor's plight.

"I repeat," said the monsignor, "is this all I get?"

"Hrmph," hrmphed Millie.

"Father Baptist," said the monsignor. "Do something."

"Oh," said Father, "I never interfere with Millie's dietary regimen. Let us say grace: In the name of the Father, and of the Son, and of the Holy Ghost."

"Amen," said the gardener.

"Amen," grumbled Millie.

"Ah, Hell," grunted the monsignor.

13

"NOT ME," I WHISPERED FIRMLY, blocking the outer sacristy door with my outstretched arm. "I'm not going to disturb him."

"But you must," hissed Roberto Guadalupe.

"No," I hissed back, which is hard to do when you're uttering an open vowel.

"Then I will," insisted Roberto.

"He's praying before the Blessed Sacrament."

"God will not mind if I borrow Father Baptist for a few minutes."

"Don't be too sure."

"Please, Señor."

"No, Señor."

"Ah, Father Baptist."

"Huh?" I turned to look over my shoulder back into the sacristy.

"How can anyone pray around here?" asked Father, emerging from the gloom. "I could hear your sibilance all the way inside the church."

"Excuse us, Father," I said, "for my sibilancing." I turned to Roberto. "You see what your sibilance has done?"

"I do not know what it is," shrugged Roberto. "But Father, you must come and see, behind the church. Now."

"Of course," said Father, casting me a sideways glance.

The sky continued its rumbling threats above us as we walked briskly—well, I did my usual lurching routine, but at an accelerated pace—back to the tangled area behind the building. Duggo and Spade were slurping Millie's iced tea from tall plastic cups under the bough of one of the huge avocado trees, wiping their faces with wrinkled hankies. Around them were immense piles of hewn vegetation, ivy and creepers crawling with disturbed insects chittering their uprooted disapproval at human renovation.

"Look," said Roberto. "See what we have found."

We followed his pointing finger to a block of granite, six feet wide and three high, which had emerged from the undergrowth. Father leaned down and brushed away a layer of damp, rotted leaves from the stone's cold face. Letters carved more than a century before began to emerge. He straightened.

"It's as I thought," he said.

"You knew about it?" asked Roberto.

"It was specified in the deed when I purchased St. Philomena's," said Father.

"Perhaps you should have told us, Father," said Roberto. He looked at Duggo and Spade, hemmed and hawed, and then added nervously, "It's not that we're afraid, you understand. Not us. We used to work at Sacred Heart Cemetery, though now it's called New Golgotha—well, you know all about that. It's just that we weren't prepared for—"

"Problem?" asked a new voice. Monsignor Havermeyer came crunching toward us through the uprooted ivy. "I was in my camper and thought I heard—" His voice trailed off as his eyes fell upon the granite headstone.

∞ TURNBUCKLE ∞

BARNABY JAMES	EMILY PETIFORE
FAITHFUL HUSBAND	BELOVED WIFE
1796-1885	1802-1887

The pale letters were chiseled in dark gray rock, framed in a dizzying bas-relief of curlicues and swirls. Beneath this couple of primogenitors came more names, wider spaced and with later dates. A veritable family plot of Turnbuckles.

"A cemetery," gasped Monsignor Havermeyer, looking around as though he wished his feet weren't touching the ground.

"And so old," said the gardener. "I had no idea St. Philomena's has been here so long."

"This building," said Father, waving toward our beloved church, "was built in 1926, but it was erected upon the site of a smaller wooden chapel that burned down a year or two before. The chapel was built in the 1870s, and there may have been a shrine here before that."

"Wait till the historical societies hear about this," I said.

"Let's hope that they don't," said Father.

"Mr. Turnbuckle might have something to say about it," I said.

"Well," said Father, wiping his hands, "there is that."

"And there's more," said Roberto, trudging further through the debris. He stepped gingerly around other markers that had emerged from the leafy sea.

We followed, reading the names silently as we passed. JUAN DE PASQUAL, FREDERICO PALMAS, MARION EAGLE FEATHER, COL. RICHARD K. ELLIOT, CHIEF NATHANIEL STONECLOUD, and so on. Apparently the frontier chapel had been graced with a talented "in lieu of" sculptor. Angels' wings and crowns of thorns decorated these silent monuments to lifetimes past, all carved with a similar, distinctive edge.

Presently Roberto made a large step over a low brick wall, six bricks high, into an area in the far corner of the yard.

"The headstones are different here," he said, pointing to dark lumps on the ground.

"Simple markers," observed the gardener. "No ornamentation."

"Unconsecrated soil," said Father Baptist, his voice dropping a soft octave. "This area was reserved for unbaptized babies, non-Catholic relatives, and suicides."

"Barbaric intolerance," said Havermeyer.

"No," said Father, "fitting propriety. Even in death, Catholics cannot commune with those outside the veil of the Church."

"You concur with such narrow-minded prejudice?" gawked Monsignor Havermeyer. "As I recall, the Second Plenary Council of Baltimore did away with such intolerant separatism."

"In 1866," interjected the gardener. He must have done some reading. "Andrew Johnson, President of the United States, was among the auditors present, as I recall—though what he was doing at a Catholic council I'll never know."

"I am a priest of Rome," said Father Baptist evenly, with perhaps a touch of frost around the upper harmonics, "not of Baltimore."

"You amaze me," said the monsignor.

"He amazes everyone," said the gardener. Then he pointed to an ivy-covered shape in the farthest corner of the unconsecrated section. "By the way, Roberto, what is that over there?"

"A stone hut," he answered, "built as part of the original wall that surrounded the churchyard. We haven't yet cleared the vines to get inside, but I bet it was probably used as a tool shed."

"Do continue," said Father to Roberto as Spade and Duggo approached, shovels in hand. "Let me know if you find anything else of interest. I shall be in the church. It's almost time for afternoon confessions."

I followed Father, reminded by a burst of rolling thunder that I was in need of a little Absolution myself.

Over my shoulder I noticed Monsignor Havermeyer lagging behind, his attention darting from headstone to headstone. He moved like an insect tiptoeing across flypaper, barely touching the ground.

"I've got an uneasy feeling," I whispered to Father as we approached the side door.

"Join the party," said Father, ushering me into the darkness of the nave before him.

14

"WHAT THE HELL IS THIS?" snarled Monsignor Havermeyer as Millie set his dinner plate before him. His gut growled its agreement. "Another boiled potato?"

Father Baptist and I, our grace finished, calmly looked from the monsignor's nearly barren plate to the steaming pools of Irish stew set before us. Joel had borrowed the Jeep to drive his grandfather, Josef, back to the Maruppa family homestead in Barnkinbay Beach. This freed me to bask on the expanse of a normal kitchen chair.

Thank-you, Lord, I prayed silently, for the little pleasures.

"The Curé d'Ars—" said Millie, adding a splosh of deep red wine to Father's glass while slamming down a cup of room-temp water before the salivating monsignor. A swarm of bubbles, jiggled free by the impact tremor, hissed to the surface of my ginger ale.

"I know, I know," barked Havermeyer. "He ate two a day."

"Three on special occasions," commented the gardener, adding a touch of salt to his feast.

"Go to Hell," hissed the monsignor.

"You know," I said, adjusting my napkin and clutching my fork, "knowing myself as I do, I wouldn't be surprised in the least if I woke up in Hell some day. Sure, I'd be terribly annoyed, thoroughly irate, angry as all get-out; but I wouldn't be the least bit surprised—"

"This is intolerable," roared Havermeyer, slamming his fists down on both sides of his plate. This, it seemed, was his favorite gesture. The little white potato jumped in alarm and rolled around the perimeter, desperately seeking escape. Finding none, it wobbled to a terrified standstill in the center of the plate. "Father Baptist, I insist that you do something."

"Such as?" said Father, scooping a wad of stew into his mouth. It sounded more like, "Supch abz?" but he's a priest so I'll clean up his act.

"Why are you doing this to me?" said the monsignor, turning in his chair to face Millie.

She stood her ground, clutching the wine bottle like a bludgeon. She gave it a hefty slap and shoved in the cork. "'The laborer is worthy of his hire.'"

"Luke," I said around a mouthful of food. "Chapter ten, verse seven." Yes, yes, it sounded more like, "Loopth, thopther pem, verpth the-bum," but that would be disgusting.

"Are you suggesting that I don't do my part around here?" huffed Havermeyer indignantly. "My dear woman, you know I'm still learn-ing the rubrics. I've spent most of the day in my trailer practicing—"

"Not when you were in Father's study this morning," growled Millie menacingly, "talking to Cardinal Fulbright on the phone."

"You overheard that?" gasped the monsignor, almost slipping from his chair. "You were eaves-dropping?"

"I was emptying waste baskets," grumbled Millie, "as I do every Wednesday when I get back from my shopping. "I walked right into the room, plain as day, but you were too busy murmuring behind Fa-ther's back to notice me."

"Ah," said Father, taking a deep sip of his wine. "The Light shines in the darkness."

Embarrassed, Monsignor Havermeyer swiveled back toward the table. "I was only trying to help."

"I don't need that kind of help," said Father Baptist, setting down his glass sternly. "You knew my mind on the matter, Monsignor. Of course, the deed is done—"

"For the good of the community," said Havermeyer.

"For good or ill," said Father, "I'm now involved in that which I desperately wanted to avoid."

"Do you want me to request a transfer?" asked Havermeyer. It was more of a dare than a humble request.

"Who'd have you?" said Father.

"What's that?"

"Every priest in the archdiocese knows you've sided with the Traditionalists. No doubt you didn't know what you were getting yourself into, but here you are. Besides, you assured the cardinal that you would fill in for me. That formed the basis of his decision. You can't back out now."

"So how long will I be eating potatoes?" asked Havermeyer, tossing Millie a curdling glance.

"'All things have their season,'" quoted Millie. "'And in their times all things pass under heaven.'"

"Ecclesiastes," said the gardener, "chapter three, verse one. I'd say you're in for the long haul."

"I've got a couple of passages for you, Feeney," said Havermeyer, turning his hungry gaze upon me.

"My Senior?" I squeaked innocently.

"The first is Matthew, chapter twenty-seven, verse five," he said, crumpling his napkin angrily and throwing it down on his plate. The poor potato reached out and yanked it over its chubby little self and proceeded to shiver uncontrollably beneath its protective folds. The monsignor's chair squawked as he got up from the table and towered over me.

Millie stepped forward, wine bottle poised, ready to throw herself between my seemingly simple self and Havermeyer's boiling ire. I gave her a grateful glance, then snapped back to attention as his gut erupted with a fit of ravenous protests.

"Then turn to Luke," said Havermeyer, strutting past Millie toward the kitchen door, "chapter ten, the second half of verse thirty-seven."

Father covered his mouth with his left hand and chuckled behind his fingers.

With a puff of hot, humid air, the door slammed mightily. A few dry leaves from outside swirled around a few times, then settled uneasily on the linoleum floor.

"I admit I don't know my Bible as well as I should," said Millie, thumping the wine bottle on the table and snatching up the plate bearing monsignor's nervous little potato. "Certainly not by chapter and verse. What did he mean?"

"The verse from St. Matthew," I said, plunging my fork into my now not-so-steaming feast, "goes: 'And casting down the pieces of silver in the temple, he'—'he' being Judas—'went and hanged himself with an halter.'"

"And the other?" asked Millie over her shoulder as she made for the stove.

"'Go,'" laughed Father, hands slipping from his face, "'and do thou in like manner.'"

That poor potato slipped from the plate in Millie's hand, dropped to the floor with a thump, and rolled frantically for the protective shelter of the space beneath the refrigerator. She stomped at it with her foot, but the little guy made it to safety, panting furiously.

Silence gripped the room.

Suddenly, Millie grabbed the fringe of her apron and brought it up to her face, covering her mouth. From behind the terry cloth mask we heard a sound never before uttered at St. Philomena's rectory.

Millie was laughing.

Father joined in.

So did I.

It went on for some time. Each time the chortles began to subside, one of us would guffaw loudly, and the rest of us would join in for another round.

"I needed that," said Father weakly, several minutes later.

"We all did," wheezed Millie, wiping tears from her eyes.

"I think there's hope for Monsignor Havermeyer yet," I said finally, clutching my ginger ale.

"Yes," said Father, taking up his fork, "I think you're right."

"Save room for dessert," growled Millie. She slammed a few pots around to assure us that she had resumed her normal demeanor.

"Always," I said, shaking my leg under the table.

From its hiding place under the refrigerator, the potato sighed.

15

"LET'S TRY IT AGAIN," I said with what I hoped was an encouraging tone.

"'Quam oblationem tu, Deus, in omnibus, quæsumus,'" sputtered Monsignor Havermeyer, the words spurting in uncertain rhythms from his tense, curled lips.

"Right so far," I said. "Now don't forget the Signs of the Cross."

"'Benedictam,'" he said, waving his hand as he pronounced the words, "'adscriptam, ratam ...'"

"Okay," I said, "now you've got a Sign-breather for about twenty syllables."

"Rationabilem," he said, his right hand resting on the edge of the rickety little table, "acceptabilemque facere digneris: ..."

"Good, good," I whispered.

"'... ut nobis, Corpus—'"

"Hup," I interrupted. "Sign."

"'—Corpus,'" he spat, jerking his right hand in an awkward Sign of the Cross, "'et Sang—'"

"Sign," I interjected.

"'Sanguis,'" he hissed, Signing again, "fiat dilectissimi—'"

"Nope, no Sign on 'dilectissimi.'"

"Hrmph. 'Fiat dilectissimi Filii tui ...'"

"Okay, you're free and clear, entering the open stretch."

"'Domini nostri Jesu Christi.'"

"Hurrah," I yelled, almost slapping him on the back.

"I could think better if I wasn't starving," said the monsignor, hands balled into fists. "Do you know what this passage means?"

"Sure," I said, consulting the tattered little missal I kept in my jacket pocket. "Let's see ... here it is:

Which offering do thou, O God,
vouchsafe in all things,
to bless [✝], consecrate [✝], approve [✝],
make reasonable and acceptable:
that it may become for us
the Body [✝] and Blood [✝]
of thy most beloved Son, our Lord Jesus Christ.

"It's beautiful," said Havermeyer. "It really is."

"You may not have known what you were in for," I said, "but here it is, and it's grand indeed. Now aren't you glad I didn't hang myself?"

He looked up at me, his eyes misty in spite of himself.

"I'll tell you a little secret," I said in a conspiratorial whisper. "Just across the street is a diner called 'Peanuts.' Best chili this side of New Mexico. And pancakes—you've never tasted anything like them. You've got time. They're open till midnight."

"I don't think so."

"No?"

He looked at me nervously.

"Oh." I fished around in my pocket. "If you're short of cash—"

"It's not that."

"Then what, My Senior?"

"You'll think me foolish."

"You're in good company. No one at St. Philomena's is running on all cylinders."

"It's ... the cemetery."

"Excuse me?"

"I didn't know. I can't see how I'll sleep a wink tonight, not with ... *that* ... just a few feet away."

"Ah," I said.

"No jokes," he snapped. Well, it wasn't really a snap. More like a fidgety retort.

"None come to mind," I agreed. "Death makes me queasy, too. You watch: I turn stark, pale green at Requiems. Father Baptist has to make up extra blessings just so he can splash me with holy water, otherwise I'd keel over into the lilies."

"In the New Rite, death is described as 'an expansion of mind.' It's like, like—"

"Warm milk," I said. "All soothing and cozy. But when you let it sit for a few minutes, the ooze rises to the top. That's one of the many travesties of the modern spirit: it seeks to cover up that which shouldn't be hidden. We *should* fear death. It's horrible, terrifying, and awaiting each and every one of us."

"You don't talk like a gardener."

"I've been accused of that before. Are you sure you wouldn't like to stroll over to 'Peanuts'? I'm stuffed, but I could probably still cram down a hot fudge sundae and a cup of Java."

"Thanks," he said, grabbing his coat and heaving himself up from the tiny dinette. "I'll ... enjoy the company." That last sentence didn't sound convincing, but what the hey.

"Of course," I said as we edged through the cramped camper, "I'll only see you back as far as the church. Then we both scurry for our respective holes."

"You live in that little room on the corner of the rectory?"

"Yup. I have my very own entrance. And now I have a beautiful view of the cemetery, too. You won't be the only one tossing and turning tonight."

"I can't imagine why that doesn't make me feel better."

"Still no rain," I said, bumping into the dumpster as we squeezed out the door. "I wonder when the storm will finally hit."

"Soon," said Monsignor Havermeyer as we skittered past the cemetery.

He was right, depending on how you define "soon."

Thursday, October Nineteenth

**Feast Day of Saint Peter of Alcántara,
friend and encourager of Saint Teresa of Ávila,
reformer of the Franciscan Order,
who ate only every third day and lived
in a cell too small in which to lie down (1562 AD)**

16

"YOU'RE COPPING OUT, JACK," Lieutenant Taper was saying as I entered the study after breakfast the following morning. I paused to polish the plaque by the doorway with my sleeve, not wanting any visitor to miss a single word:

> The most evident mark of God's anger, and the most terrible castigation He can inflict upon the world, is manifest when He permits His people to fall into the hands of a clergy who are more in name than in deed, priests who practice the cruelty of ravening wolves rather than the charity and affection of devoted shepherds. They abandon the things of God to devote themselves to the things of the world and, in their saintly calling of holiness, they spend their time in profane and worldly pursuits. When God permits such things, it is a very positive proof that He is thoroughly angry with His people, and is visiting His most dreadful wrath upon them.
>
> —St. John Eudes

Father Baptist, who always refused to explain why he kept that particular warning by the doorway, was seated behind his desk, book in one hand and smoldering burl pipe in the other. He glanced up at me and aimed the stem of his pipe in the direction of my favorite chair opposite him.

With a grunt and a groan, I complied.

I don't know why it was my favorite chair, identical as it was to its twin. Both were deep, chocolate brown in their heyday—which was a

long time ago—and now sagging and held together in places with gray
duct tape. Perhaps it was the patterns of the tape, or the charm of the
springs sticking out underneath. But I'd certainly know if someone
switched them around.
Lieutenant Taper was occupying the other one. Wickes insisted on
standing. The sergeant's hands were fidgeting so deep in his pants
pockets he looked as though he was scratching his knees.
Parallel to my line of sight with Father was a huge fireplace, a tumultuous pile of granite boulders, really, held firmly in mid-rockslide
with heaps of vanilla-fudge mortar. The relentless wind howled a melancholy drone down the throat of the chimney, like a giant dufus in
overalls playing a whiskey jug at a barnyard hootenanny, only not so
down-home and friendly.
On the mantel sat a second plaque, familiar to all who sought out Father's advice in this very room:

> I do not speak rashly, but as I feel and think. I do not think that
> many priests are saved, but that those who perish are far more nu-
> merous. The reason is that the office requires a great soul. For
> there are many things to make a priest swerve from rectitude, and
> he requires great vigilance on every side.
>   —St. John Chrysostom

You must admit these admonitions set a certain tone to the place, an
underlying ambiance of "caveat emptor."
It had been a splendid breakfast, by the way. Monsignor Havermeyer,
now aware of a dining oasis across the street, hadn't bothered to attend.
(I don't think "boiled potatoes" even appears on the menu at "Peanuts.")
Joel and Josef, after inhaling their omelets and thus sending Millie into
a euphoria of clanging abandon, had trudged upstairs to continue their
wiring wizardry.
That left us "professionals" to plan our strategy. But first, as in any
good murder story, the "unprofessional haggling." Observe:
"You keep dodging the issue," said Wickes, pacing this way and that.
"What do you want me to say?" asked Father, blowing a perfect
smoke ring. "That I believe in vampires? And what will that prove?
If our murderer turns out to be a lunatic who thinks he's a vampire and
acts accordingly, you'll throw that back in my face. If I say I don't
believe in them, but such proves to be the case, then you'll castigate
me for my unbelief. No, gentlemen, I won't be cornered into such a
trap."
"That's still copping out," said Taper.

"My belief is not the issue," said Father, "at least, not yet, as far as I can tell. What is at issue is that we have a killer who is sucking the life out of pretty young women and dumping their bodies in alleys."

"But if he's a real vampire," said Wickes, "won't we need to deal with him, you know, with crosses and garlic and stakes through the heart?"

"We'll know that," said Father, "when we find him. Detection is our first step. How to dispose of the fiend, be it by jury or shaft, will present itself only then."

"I was just reading something the other evening," I interjected, scooping up a volume of G. K. Chesterton from the carpet next to my chair, "which may or may not be pertinent to the discussion at hand."

"This had better be good," said Taper impatiently.

I shrugged. "I already said it may or not be. But, for good or ill, this passage comes from a Father Brown mystery, and it deals with the expectations some people place on priests. I'll start here with something said by the man who turns out to be the murderer:

> "I see you are still doubtful," he [the murderer] said, "though you have seen the thing with your own eyes ... You ought to stand for all the things these stupid people call superstitious. Come now, don't you think there's a lot in those old wives' tales about luck and charms and so on, silver bullets included? What do you say about them as a Catholic?"
>
> "I say I'm an agnostic," replied Father Brown, smiling.
>
> "Nonsense," said Aylmer impatiently. "It's your business to believe things."
>
> "Well, I do believe some things, of course," conceded Father Brown; "and therefore, of course, I don't believe other things ..."

"What's the point?" asked Wickes.

"Exactly that," I said. "It's amazing these days—and it was even true almost a century ago when this was written—how the moment a man declares his belief in spiritual reality, people assume he'll believe in anything that seeps in through the woodwork or spews from a channeler's lips. Let me continue a few lines further down. This is still the murderer talking:

> "You do believe it," he said. "You believe everything. We all believe everything, even when we deny everything. The deniers believe. The unbelievers believe. Don't you feel in your heart that these contradictions do not really contradict: that there is a cosmos that contains them all? ... Good and evil go round in a wheel that is one thing and not many. Do you not realize in your heart, do you not believe behind all your beliefs, that there is but one reality and we are its shadows; and that all things are but as-

pects of one thing: a centre where men melt into Man and Man into God?"

"No," said Father Brown.

Wickes, who, during the murderer's metaphysical mumbo, had looked like he agreed one hundred and ten percent, was brought up short by Father Brown's terse reply. He shrugged his shoulders, adjusted his tie, and blinked three times. "I still don't get your point."

"Never mind," I said, slamming the book shut and tossing it back onto the rug to mingle with its companions.

"Let me ask you a question, Sergeant," said Father, taking a deep puff on his pipe and letting the smoke seep out his nostrils.

"Shoot," said Wickes, looking cornered.

"Have you ever heard of St. George?"

"Who?"

"St. George, the Patron Saint of England, and also of Chivalry. He's often portrayed in the act of killing a dragon."

"What about him?"

"Did he exist?"

"No." Wickes shrugged his shoulders and adjusted his tie again. "At least, certainly not the dragon part. Maybe George was a real person, the root of the legend as it were. Legends often have their basis in fact. But if you're asking if I believe in dragons, of course not. Why?"

"Just asking."

"Why?"

"Obviously, because I am seeking your opinion."

"About what?"

"About the authenticity of the legend."

"And?"

"Now I have it, thank-you."

"So where do we go from here?" huffed Taper, sinking down in his chair. "What do you say, Jack?"

"This one, I'll grant you," said Father, exhaling a fountain of blue-gray smoke, "is one for the books. It would seem that our best bet is to retrace the steps of the unfortunate women until we find someone who saw something."

"But if we're dealing with a real vampire," said the unshakable yet shaken-from-top-to-bottom-able Wickes, "what about those girls in the morgue? What if they, uh, you know, um—"

"Come back to life?" finished the gardener.

Wickes hemmed and hawed, and then nodded.

"Heard any knocks coming from those drawers?" I prodded.

"No," said Wickes.

"Has anyone?" asked Father.

"Well …"

"Everyone in the lab has been so jumpy lately," said Taper, "that any time there's a bump, or a rustle, or any unexpected noise, everyone looks toward the near-zero drawers."

"Creepy," said Wickes, rubbing his hands together as if warming them over an invisible candle. "We've all got the jitters."

"I understand," said Father. "Still, as far as you know, none of the bodies has shown any signs of reanimation."

"No," said Wickes, resting his chin on his tie. "But what if ...? I thought that when a vampire sucks your blood, you become a vampire yourself."

"In the movies," said Father. "But I wouldn't put much faith in cel-luloid. Think about it, Sergeant: simple math will tell you that such could not be the case."

"How so?"

"Let's say we start with one vampire," said Father, taking a long, deep draw on his pipe. He let the smoke dribble out slowly between his lips as he continued. "For the sake of argument, a real one. He bites his first victim. Now we have two vampires. Since, according to the popular stories, vampires must feed every so often to survive—say, once a week—we now have two hungry vampires. In satiating their thirst, they make two more. Now we have four. The next time around we have eight, then sixteen, then thirty-two."

"I begin to see your point," said Taper.

"In the present situation," said Father, "if we were dealing with such a virulent disease, the seven women in your morgue plus the fiend who infected them, really represent—" He snatched up a pen and did some hasty math on a scratch pad. "—a hundred and twenty-eight vampires. By the time we reach twenty feedings—" More scribbling. "—we've passed the million mark."

"By Christmas," I said offhandedly, "everyone in Los Angeles County would be living—or rather 'unliving'—in their basements. By New Year's, everyone would be booking red-eye flights to other parts of the country to find fresh blood sources."

"Okay, okay," said Wickes.

"I read Dracula years ago," said Taper. "Back in college. I seem to recall that he made new vampires by forcing his victims to drink his own blood."

"True," said Father, "at least, within Bram Stoker's romantic presen-tation. But on many points, Stoker took great license with respect to his subject. He was writing a novel, after all, not a scientific treatise on vampirism."

"Okay," said Wickes, grinding to a halt in the center of the circular trough he'd worn into the rug, "maybe the victims don't rise from their graves willy nilly. Maybe some do and some don't. Whatever. We still have our original vampire, and he is murdering young women. If he's a real vampire, maybe we should be checking out graveyards, you know, for telltale signs: burglarized mausoleums, disturbed graves, whatever."

"I'd love to see Chief Billowack's reaction," said the gardener, "to your requisition for the white stallion."

"What white stallion?" asked Wickes, whirling to face me.

"The one you'll have to lead to every grave in every cemetery in the city, one by one, to see its reaction." I shifted authoritatively in my chair. "And don't forget the innocent young boy who will have to be riding on its back. Jacco Babs would have a field day in his column if he ever got wind of that."

"What are you talking about?" asked Wickes.

"Classical vampire detection," said Father, holding up a book in his hand. "Martin's been reading Montague Summers."

"You're joking," said Wickes.

"No," said the gardener. "Quite the contrary. You want to go on a real vampire hunt, you follow proven procedures."

"Which is why," said Father, "I suggest we adhere to the kind of level-headed systematic investigative procedures with which we are all familiar and which have proved to be useful in our own experience. Old fashioned methods, in this case, are impractical in the twentieth century."

"Your choice, Sergeant, Lieutenant," I said, waving my hands at nothing in particular. "I know where we can rent horses real cheap. One of the men at the Griffith Park Stables is a regular here at St. Philomena's. Of course, a pure white stallion might be a bit more expensive to procure, but surely Chief Billowack would approve—"

"Skip it," said Wickes.

"And we could run an ad in the *Times* to find a prepubescent boy—"

"I said skip it."

"Lieutenant?" asked Father.

"Right," said Taper. "So maybe we should start with the other victim's apartments."

"Just what I was thinking," said Father.

"You think I should ask Millie to fetch some garlic from the market?" I asked, heaving myself to a standing position. "The least she could do would be to grate some on Monsignor Havermeyer's potatoes."

"Sounds reasonable," smiled Father. "Gentlemen, shall we proceed?"

17

"JUST ONE MOMENT THERE, FATHER," hrumphed Thurgood T. Turnbuckle, strutting toward us as we stepped outside. The breeze was so strong it threatened to capsize his toupee.

"That's about all I have," said Father, checking his cracked watch.

"That's because you went and got yourself involved in matters that don't concern you," huffed Mr. Turnbuckle.

"I'm afraid Cardinal Fulbright did not agree with you or me on that issue," said Father. "Now I'm under orders."

Taper and Wickes tried to look nonchalant, but without success. They should have rocked on their heels, hands clasped behind their backs, and whistled "Sugar Shack" or something.

"Is there something you wanted?" asked Father.

"Am I to understand," said Mr. Turnbuckle, "that those, uh, workers have uncovered my family's burial plot behind the church?"

"So it would seem," said Father. "Is it important to you?"

"Important? Important! The discovery of St. Peter's tomb in Rome was important. This is stupendous!"

"Really."

"I must contact the California Historical Landmark Society."

"Why?"

"Why, this is history."

"So is the present," said Father. "It slips into the past all too quickly. I would prefer, however, that you postpone any announcements, Mr. Turnbuckle, at least for a while."

"What on earth for?"

"Because I'm now involved in those matters you were complaining about a moment ago, and in which I didn't want to delve. Remember the influx of reporters a few months ago when I was similarly indisposed? Too much attention to our fair parish would not be a good thing right now."

"You say that," growled Turnbuckle, "while you turn our church into a circus for the likes of those freaks every Tuesday night."

"The Tumblars are not freaks," said Father. "Nor is an all-night vigil before the Blessed Sacrament a circus. You could arrange such a vigil for yourself and your family any time you wish."

"All my sons have lost the Faith," said Turnbuckle, adjusting his tie. "And my wife, as you well know, is dead."

"Haven't I seen Bucky here from time to time?" asked the gardener. "Just last Sunday, in fact. I noticed him near the front—"

"Buckminster, my eldest," said Mr. Turnbuckle, frost forming on his mustache, "only gets 'spiritual' when he's in financial straits, and more to impress me than the Man Upstairs. You noticed him, did you? But did you see him go up to receive Communion? Bah! Since his recent bit of posturing did not produce the monetary results he desired, I doubt you'll see him back here for some time."

"I see," said Father.

"Not an ounce of tenacity in the boy. I've tried to teach him self-reliance: to instill in him, by word and example, a sense of the old family stick-to-it-iveness; but everything he touches ends in failure. I can't fathom where he gets his lack of determination—not from my side of the family, I can tell you."

"Certainly not," agreed the gardener.

"Time after time I've offered him a position in the family business, but he refused, just like all his younger siblings. I don't understand young people these days. No sense of loyalty, no recognition of duty, no acceptance of responsibility to one's good name."

"Appalling," agreed the gardener. "Why just the other day—"

"Now," scowled Mr. Turnbuckle, hunching his shoulders, "Buckminster has got it into his head that he wants to be a stage magician. Can you believe it? A Turnbuckle engaged in sleight-of-hand parlor tricks."

"Is he performing anywhere locally?" asked the gardener.

"I don't see what it has to do with anything, but yes. He somehow managed to secure for himself a week at some private club called the 'House of Illusions.' He offered me a guest pass, but naturally I have refused to attend."

"Well then," said Father, "we'll be seeing him tomorrow night."

"You'll be—?"

"Those freaky Tumblars," explained the gardener with a wink, "and Father Baptist and I. It should be quite an evening."

"You're not serious," said Mr. Turnbuckle.

"Well," said the gardener, "speaking for myself—I wouldn't want to vouch for Father here—but I try my best to avoid that particular tendency."

Father Baptist touched my arm, one of those oh-so-gentle touches that conveys an oh-so-not-so-gentle warning to cease and desist all gardening activities immediately. I complied.

"I'll let you know how it goes, Mr. Turnbuckle," said Father, removing his hand from my fast-frozen arm. "Perhaps I'll find an opportunity to have a talk with him."

"Perhaps—?" Mr. Turnbuckle was encountering something we all experience sooner or later here at St. Philomena's: the realization that the conversation is going anywhere but where you want it to. He recovered his wits more quickly than most. "That's all fine and good, Father, chat with him all you like for all the good it won't do. But see here. What about my family plot?"

"Three weeks," said Father. "Let your ancestors rest in peace for three weeks more, and then we'll take up the matter again. Please, Mr. Turnbuckle. I wouldn't ask if it wasn't important."

"Very well," said Mr. Turnbuckle, spinning on his heels. "Three weeks, but not a day more."

I noticed his toupee finally did slip off his head as he marched away. The breeze caught it, but he snatched it back and stuffed if gruffly into his pocket.

18

THREE GLOOMY APARTMENTS LATER, having sifted through the effects of Patricia Kelly and Shelly Stevens, we were standing in the heavily-shaded bedroom of Alicia Alvarez. As in all the abodes we had visited, the incessant, abrasive sound of traffic seeped in through the cracks. Whatever else may have gripped the imagination of these young women, their psyches had been perpetually marinated in the shallow grease pan of Hollywood Boulevard's insidious drippings.

"This," said Father, nudging with his index finger a piece of white silk which was draped over the headboard, "is not a woman's handkerchief."

"Gentleman's issue," said Taper, taking out a plastic bag and coaxing the hankie into its new home. "I'll have it checked. Looks like some raised letters in the corner."

"Manufacturer's emblem, I'm afraid," said Father. "Not the owner's initials."

Miss Alvarez's choice in decor seemed the most schizophrenic so far. Her walls were cluttered with the usual bats and skulls and graveyard scenes. But here and there, in curious nooks and crannies, little plastic statues of St. Rose of Lima and St. Teresa of Avila, candle stumps melted at their feet, looked silently out upon the gloom. On Alicia's dressing table lay the usual sordid "Ooooh, make me a vampire like you!" novels, but she used dried fronds from Palm Sunday and wrinkled holy cards for bookmarks. Above the head of her bed hung a pewter bat with extended claws, but it was set beneath a large wooden Crucifix draped with a quartz-crystal Rosary. In her closet we found lots of slinky black gowns, but also elegantly embroidered mantillas and summery dresses, as if she regularly attended Mass on Sundays.

"This was one mixed-up kid," said Wickes.

"One can only hope that she repented before she died," said Father sadly. "One can only hope." He picked up a use-swollen volume, *My Life as a Vampire*. "This may be about saving souls after all."

"Seen enough here, Jack?" asked Taper.

"I think so," said Father, rubbing his forehead wearily. "This is all beginning to run together in my head. I think this will be enough for today, at least, of these apartments. We can do the rest tomorrow."

"You are out of practice," said Taper. "We used to do this kind of work for twenty-six hours without a break."

"Perhaps," said Father, setting the book back on the nightstand. "Actually, I was thinking I'd like to visit the morgue again. I didn't get a good look at all the bodies. And I want to peruse those microscopic analyses of the wounds."

"Sure," said Taper. "Anything you say."

"Martin?" asked Father. "You've been unusually silent."

"Maybe you should thank God," I winked unconvincingly, "for small favors."

"I do," said Father, "many times a day."

19

"TYPE O POSITIVE," SAID FATHER, eyeing the top sheet on a stack of photocopied reports. He burrowed down through the pile and paused. "Type O Positive again."

"All the way down," said Solomon. "The saliva on all the wounds was the same."

"Okay," said Father, reordering the pages. "Now for the microscopics on the puncture wounds."

"Here," said John Holtsclaw, handing him a folder.

Father opened it and began grazing through the brittle leaves. Pausing, he held a sheet marked DOBBS, ANNA KAY. "Strange."

"What is it?" asked Taper.

"Myrrh," said Father. "Traces of myrrh."

"As in gold and frankincense?" asked Wickes.

"The same," said Father. "From the myrrh bush. It's one of the resins in the incense I use every Sunday when I celebrate High Mass. Let me check this out." He flipped through some more pages and stopped. Then he flipped and stopped again. Then he started from the top again. "Yes, it's consistent. Myrrh appears in every case."

"Odd," said Solomon. "I didn't notice."

"Jumped right off the page at me," said Father, "but then you might say I'm 'keyed in' to the word. Most of these other traces, however, are gobbledygook to me. 'Sodium monofluorophosphate ... calcium carbonate ... propolis ... carrageenan ... allicin ...' They, too, are consistent, whatever they are. Can I keep these?"

"That's why Sybil ran them off," said Wickes. "They're all yours."

"And where is Miss Wexler?" asked Father.

"Lunch," said Holtsclaw. "You've missed her again."

"I'm beginning to think she doesn't exist," said the gardener. "You guys just made her up."

"Hm," said Father, turning his attention to a series of photographs. "I take it these pictures were taken through a microscope."

"This unit here," said Solomon, patting a toad-shaped contraption fondly. "I took them myself."

"What's this?" asked Father, pointing to a dark splotch huddled in a gully between folds of mottled tissue. The name UNGER, ELIZABETH was penned in the upper right corner.

"How's it labeled?" asked Holtsclaw, consulting his clipboard. "Is there a number next to it?"

"EU-123-76."

"Here it is," said Holtsclaw. "It seems to be a bit of parsley."

"Parsley?" said Father. "Imbedding in this puncture wound?"

"Yes," said Holtsclaw.

Father eased himself onto a stool, photos in hand. "Parsley."

"Mean something?" asked Wickes. "I mean, aren't there herbs or spices and things connected with vampires?"

"Several," said Father. "But I don't remember parsley being one of them." Shrugging, he placed the photos back in their folder and swung it closed. "I'm tired."

"Tired?" chided Taper. "The day is young. Where's that investigative fever, Jack? That nagging itch that can't be scratched until the case is solved?"

"Right here," said Father, rubbing his temples. "Nonetheless, I am tired."

"You've lost your pizzazz."

"True," said Father, rising from the stool and stretching. "I left it behind in a locker at the seminary. But there's still flesh and bone, and that will have to do. Speaking of which, I think it's time to examine the bodies."

"All of them?" I gulped.

"One by one," said Father.

"Something wrong?" asked Taper, turning toward me with an impish smile.

"Not at all," I said hesitantly, "but if it's all the same to you, I'd like to sort of peel off for a while. I can meet up with you here, or somewhere, or back at St. Philomena's."

"You, too?" chided Taper.

"Me, too, what?"

"Lost your pizzazz?"

"Pizzazz has nothing to do with it, even if I never had it, which I don't think I ever did."

"Where's that gardening spirit? The old heave-ho? Why, I bet you used to dig weeds all day and all night with your trusty spade without a single break—"

"Never," I said seriously, hand on heart. "But the fact is, if you must persist, well, Father, you know how I am around ... uh ... you know."

"Well, yes and no," said Father. "You usually summon enough courage to endure at funerals."

"Yeah, but seven, Father. Seven is above and beyond."

"I see your point, Martin. Perhaps I haven't been sufficiently attentive to your ... uh ..."

"My 'uh' is right. But I bear no malice, and all the responsibility."

"Very well, Martin," said Father. "I'm sure these gentlemen can drive me home. See you at dinner."

"Thank-you," I said, turning with the aid of my cane. "Thank-you, thank-you, thank-you ..."

20

"HELLO, CHERYL," I said, taking my seat across the institutional gray table from her. "Hope you don't mind me visiting you again."

"Of course not," she answered, her voice soft and even. "After all, you did wear that stupid hat at my trial."

I shrugged, embarrassed at the memory as well as her appreciation of my public gesture. The Tumblars had raked me over the coals for doing it, and Father Baptist wasn't too pleased, either. But that was two months ago, and past history. "It was the least I could do, considering."

She sat there in her bleached-blue prison uniform, FARNSWORTH stitched in crooked letters over her shirt pocket, motionless except for the suggestion of a smile at the corners of her mouth. Her long red hair, which had been one of her most stunning assets before her incarceration, hung limply from her pale scalp and lay bent and broken on her shoulders.

"So what's new?" she asked, leaning forward on her slender elbows.

"Quite a bit," I said. I looked around. The room was empty except for the two of us and a guard stationed at the far corner. "Can you keep a secret?"

"Easily," she said, almost smiling. "No one talks to me in here."

"No one?"

"The Prods fear me because I'm a witch. The Fundies more so. Did you know that King James burned a thousand witches? The modern Catholics shun me because I killed four of their darling bishops. The Traditional Catholics don't know what to make of me—"

"There are Trads in here?"

"Of course, Martin. Trads can go bad."

"Quite right, quite right."

"They don't know whether to fear my beliefs or congratulate me for disposing of their soured prelates. The Jews, they could care less. And the atheists, well, they don't like anyone who believes anything. No, I'm pretty much alone in here."

"With your 'power.'"

"Yes, Martin. With my 'power.'"

"And you still think it was worth it?"

"Yes, I do. And even if I didn't, what good would it do now?"

"Good point. Have you heard that Archbishop Fulbright is now Cardinal Fulbright?"

"No, but it doesn't surprise me."

"Me either, somehow."

"But that's not the secret you're so anxious to tell me."

"Me? Anxious?"

"You. Very anxious."

"Hm. You're right."

"So tell me. The suspense is unendurable."

I leaned close to her. The guard shifted but stayed put. "Have you sensed anything lately," I whispered, "you know, with your 'power'?"

She folded her hands, looked at the ceiling as if listening to a wee voice, reached up to give her ear a little tug, then settled back on her elbows. "No. Nothing other than the usual psychic banter. Why? You look disappointed for someone who doesn't believe in my 'power.'"

"I never said that."

"You never had to."

"But I never said it. The fact is, I'm not sure. But in any case — "

"My sentence will be completed," she sighed, "before you get around to whatever you're hedging about. I'm only in here for life, you know."

"Wish I could say, 'Hope to see you on the other side.'"

"Don't."

"Won't."

"So what's eating you, Martin?"

"Not me; and it's drinking, not eating."

"You're direct, as usual."

"No, indirect as I can possibly manage. The fact is, um, how do I put this?"

"In words of two syllables or less."

"Okay, I'll try. Father Baptist has been ordered back into service by your former boss, His Nibs Morley Fulbright, to help the police." I reviewed my sentence to make sure I hadn't exceeded my syllabic limit.

Encouraged, I continued. "The police are baffled—beside themselves, in fact."

"Why?"

"Because there's a vampire on the loose."

She moved a muscle, but it was in her ankle so I couldn't see it. So how do I know? Never mind.

"A vampire," she said. "You're sure."

"I'm not sure at all. But someone has killed seven young ladies in the past five weeks by biting their necks and sucking out their blood, and all within spitting distance of—I can't say 'Hollywood' or 'Boulevard,' seeing as they both have three syllables—but you get the idea."

"And you came to me, thinking I might have sensed something."

"I've come to visit you every other week for the past several months. Don't lay a guilt trip on me just because I asked if you've sensed something."

"Well, I haven't."

"You're sure."

"Positive."

"Not that it would mean anything if you did."

"According to you."

"But you haven't, and that's that."

"'Fraid so. I hope this doesn't mean you'll stop visiting me."

"Of course not."

"You're sure."

"Sure I'm sure."

"Hm." She rolled her eyes around inside their sockets until only the whites showed, then sprung them back in my direction. "I think maybe I do feel something."

"You do?" I shifted forward in my chair. "Tell me."

"It's just a twinge, actually."

"But something."

"Oh, it's definitely something."

"And?"

"And what?"

"What is it you're feeling?"

"Something."

"Such as?"

"Time's up," said the guard. She looked like a matron for whom the words "Please, one more minute," had no meaning.

"Catch ya later," I said to Cheryl as I rose to leave.

"I'll be here," she said back.

21

"THE JOB, IT IS DONE," announced Roberto, tossing his shovel into the back of his truck. "The refuse company, they will be picking up the dumpster tomorrow morning, so don't block it with your car, Señor Feeney."

I looked over at the new—or rather, the old—cemetery. Irregular rows of variously-shaped solemn stones, shouting forgotten names with granite silence, dotted the acre or so behind the church. The earth around them was stripped bare, crisscrossed with the parallel tell-tale patterns of metal rakes.

"If Father Baptist were here," I said, "he'd thank you profusely."

"And I would ask his blessing," said Roberto, bowing his head and wiping his brown neck with a sopping red hanky.

"I see you cleared away the vines from that stone hut," I observed. "Did you look inside?"

"No. The door, it is stuck, and the windows are too small to crawl through. I will bring a crowbar next time."

"Next time?"

"For the landscaping. We need to plant grass. It's the wrong time of year, but we'll try."

"Sure, I know what you mean. Some of my best efforts have come to fruition at the wrong time."

He either didn't hear or didn't understand. No matter.

"Ask Father if he wants dichondra or St. Augustine grass. I suggest dichondra because of the shade."

"And it doesn't have to be mowed."

"Sí."

"I'll ask, but I'm pretty sure he'll agree with dichondra."

"Bueno. There's a patch of it growing on the south side of the mission right where the cardinal, he wants a rose garden. We can dig it up and bring it here in slats. It won't be enough to cover everything, but it will be a start."

The sky rumbled its approval.

"And once this storm hits," I mused, "we won't have to water it for a while."

"I'll keep my eye open for any houses that are being torn down. Maybe I can get my hands on some used piping and sprinklers. Until then, Señor Feeney, you will have to water by hand."

"Until then," I said, strolling off toward my little room.

That's where I kept my stash of aspirin, and I felt a headache coming on.

22

"'I KNOW IT WAS HARD FOR YOU to quite trust me then ...'" read Pierre Bontemps from the thick volume balanced in his right hand. He was standing with his left elbow resting on the mantle over the fireplace, a fluted glass dangling from his fingers. The wind moaning down the chimney added a chilling ambiance to his words:

> "... for to trust such violence needs to understand; and I take it that you do not—that you cannot—trust me now, for you do not understand. And there may be more times when I shall want you to trust when you cannot—and may not—and must not yet understand. But the time will come when your trust shall be whole and complete in me, and when you shall understand as though the sunlight himself shone through."

"Trust, you'll admit," said Father Baptist, puffing his pipe in his chair behind the desk, "is a rare commodity these days. Read the part I've marked on the next page, Pierre. Arthur Holmwood's reply."

"Ah," said Pierre, clearing his throat. "Here it is:

> "Dr. Van Helsing, you may do what you will ... I shall not trouble you with questions till the time comes."
> The old Professor stood up as he said solemnly:—
> "And you are right. There will be pain for us all; but it will not be all pain, nor will this pain be the last. We and you too—you most of all, my dear boy—will have to pass through the bitter water before we reach the sweet. But we must be brave of heart and unselfish, and do our duty, and all will be well."

Pierre's eyes grew distant, as they always did at the mention of words like "duty." He closed the book with a dramatic wallop.

The small wind-up clock on the mantel beside I DO NOT SPEAK RASHLY bonged the quarter-hour past eight o'clock. The official weekly meeting of the five Knights of the Tumblar was under way. The four chairs from the dining nook, so out of place in this setting, had been brought into the study to accommodate their tuxedoed selves. I was seated in my customary chair, ginger ale in hand. My chair's twin was vacant, as Pierre was currently standing.

"To Dr. Van Helsing," said Jonathan Clubb, lifting his fluted glass as high as his magnificent forehead.

"Van Helsing," said they all, clinking their glasses brimming with champagne. "Here here."

"And to our duty," said Pierre, peering at the reading lamp on Father's desk through his bubbles.

"Our sworn duty," said Edward Strypes Wyndham, his hawk-like eyebrow bristling.

"Our soon-to-be-sworn duty," corrected Arthur von Derschmidt, always, or almost usually always, their imminently accessible source of early-to-mid middle-age sagacity.

"All the preparations for next week's ceremony are going smoothly," said Father, blowing another of his perfect smoke rings. "Bishop Xandaronolopolis' plane will be arriving Saturday afternoon at LAX."

"I'll never be able to pronounce his name," said Jonathan.

"Just call him 'My Lord' or 'Your Lordship,'" said Father, "and you'll be fine."

"And," said Joel Maruppa, showered and shimmering after a long day's work—since he lived at the rectory, a shower was handy, "let us not forget our pre-to-be-sworn celebration tomorrow night, at the 'House of Illusions.'"

"Nor the chap who arranged it," said Jonathan, nodding to Pierre.

"It will be the first of many memorable Tumblar 'events,'" smiled Pierre, "now that my boss at the L.A. Artsy is an active member."

"No doubt," said Father, noticing that his pipe had gone out. "Is that your 'in'?"

"The only way in is through," nodded Pierre, nurturing his glass with more champagne. "In this case, my 'in' is 'through' my managing editor, since she's made it very clear that I can go to the 'House of Illusions' under the umbrella of her membership any time."

"Maybe we can make it sort of a 'club house pro tem,'" said Arthur.

"No problem," said Pierre.

"I'd heard that you'd taken up journalism," said the gardener. "Does this mean you now have a press pass?"

"Writing for the Artsy is not journalism," said Pierre. "It's more like the literary equivalent of Igor Stravinsky playing basketball with Copernicus."

"I don't follow you," said Edward.

"Few do," said Pierre. "And never where I've ever gone before, or after. But the Artsy is the only rag in town—in quite a few towns, in fact—that accepted my essays for publication. And yes, I have a press pass, even though it stretches the imagination that the Artsy could be considered part of the news media."

"More like the 'muse's nebula,'" said the gardener.

"Or the 'guru's fibula,'" said Jonathan.

Edward chuckled. "Or the—"

"Stop," said Pierre, holding out his hand like a traffic cop. "We're getting off the subject."

"Which is?" asked Arthur.

"A song," said Pierre, chest swelling. "I can feel one coming on."

"Hold that thought," said Father, striking a match along the sole of his shoe and relighting his pipe. "We've other business to discuss first."

A calm attentiveness settled over these gentlemen. It's never ceased to amaze me how they could shift from the frivolous to the serious and back again at a moment's notice.

"Do tell," said Pierre. "We've heard that you've accepted the assignment with the police."

"His Eminence has ordered me," corrected Father, "to lend them my expertise. My own wishes have been set aside in the matter."

"Quite right," said Jonathan.

"And it is in this regard that I must again ask you gentlemen to assist me in a most perplexing matter."

All champagne glasses were set down with a resounding *thunk.*

"As always," said Pierre, "we are at your service."

"And I at yours," said Father. "As before, there is much I am not free to tell you, and wouldn't tell you even if I were, because I need your eyes and ears again, and again free from preconceptions."

"Ah," said Arthur. "You are ordering us back into 'bar detail.'"

"Right," said Father. "I need you fellows to concentrate your efforts along Hollywood Boulevard."

"Erg," winced Pierre. "That's low."

"But necessary, I'm afraid," said Father. "I'm looking for someone who may think, or who may want others to think, or who may act as though, he's a vampire."

"So that's why the reading from Stoker," said Arthur.

"Precisely," said Father.

"'Listen to them,'" quoted Pierre as Bela Lugosi, "'the children of the night—'"

"'What music they make!'" chimed in the rest, not nearly as convincing.

"What exactly do you mean by a 'vampire,' Father?" asked Arthur.

"Good question," said Father, leaning forward in his chair. "I'm not sure I'm prepared to give a simple answer. Descriptions of vampires in literature range from the sophisticated erudite gentlemen of the gothic horror novel, like the cultivated Count Dracula, to the bloated, blood-gorged night-crawling fiends of folklore. Recent fiction paints them as misunderstood victims of a disease over which they have no control, who nonetheless achieve some sort of helical salvation by—and this is important—passing on the illness."

"Making other vampires," said Jonathan.

"Misery apparently loves company," said the gardener. "Sounds a lot like most of the communicable diseases going around today."

"Which kind are we looking for?" asked Joel, jaw muscles rippling. "I mean, what kind of vampire does this fellow think he is?"

"I'm not sure," said Father. "Though I suspect that he lures his victims with—" He caught himself. "No, that is part that I will keep to myself for the moment."

"Victims," said Arthur. "Then this fellow has actually …?"

"Yes," said Father. "He's drained the life out of seven young women so far."

"You mean he …?" gasped Edward.

"Yes," said Father sadly. "He bit their necks and sucked their blood."

"Any chance," asked Joel nervously, "that this fellow is, um, not acting?"

"What do you mean," scoffed Edward, turning to Joel. "Not acting? Are you suggesting that he's real?—that vampires are real? Don't be silly."

"Perhaps not so silly," said Father. "The police have been badgering me with the same question."

"About vampires being real?" gawked Arthur.

"The same," said Father.

"You're joking," said Arthur.

"No," I interjected. "Father usually leaves that to me."

"And what," asked Pierre, "have you been telling them?"

Father Baptist peered down into the smoldering bowl of his pipe for a long moment. "The same thing I'm about to tell you: that we won't know until we find him, and we won't accomplish that if we run around in circles, jumping to conclusions."

"But that means you think it's possible?" asked Arthur incredulously.

"There's nothing 'possible' about it," said Pierre, that far-away look sprouting all over his face like grass after a spring rain. "You gents don't place the kind of emphasis on family lineage as we Bontemps, but I know for a fact that some of my ancestors hunted vampires in centuries past."

"Sure," said Edward, turning to face Pierre. "Sure."

Pierre's eyebrows rippled in Edward's direction. "Indeed."

"My family is of peasant stock," said Joel. "Not a drop of noble blood as far as I know. But we Slovaks have our traditions, too. We remember."

"What?" asked Edward, spinning around to face Joel. "What the devil are you talking about?"

Pierre's spotlight eyes shifted in Joel's direction, his lips curling into an intrigued smile. Funny the foundations upon which alliances are built.

"The vampire has many names," said Joel sternly, "in the part of the world where my family comes from: nosferatu, vrykolakas, vurkolak, vlkoslak, wampyr ..."

> GARDENING TIPS: Needless to say, I had to do a
> bit of research on the spellings of these words.
> As for pronunciation, I'll leave that to my
> reader's imagination. Just remember: whatever you
> "sound out" according to the standard rules of
> American-English phonetics is wrong.
>
>   --M.F.

"I don't believe my ears," said Edward.

> GARDENING TIPS: In all fairness, you wouldn't have
> either if you'd heard the cacophonous phonemes
> spurting out of Joel's mouth.
>
>   --M.F.

"Excuse me," I said, having snatched up my copy of Chesterton while this conversation was in progress. "If I may quote Father Brown:

> "I'm exactly in the position of the man who said, 'I can believe the impossible, but not the improbable.'"
> "That's what you call a paradox, isn't it?" asked the other.
> "It's what I call common sense, properly understood," replied Father Brown.

"Of course," I added, "the subject under discussion was not 'vampires,' but I thought the passage worth quoting."

"In any case," said Father, tossing me an unfathomable glance, "this is not the time for a lecture on the existence or non-existence of vampires. That may come later, though now that I've opened Pandora's Box, you'll no doubt hound me until I do perform that service."

"No doubt," nodded Arthur.

"I will say this," said Father, scratching his temple with the stem of his pipe, "that I would surely hesitate to send you good gentlemen out in search of a real such creature without sufficient information, and certainly not without protection."

"Garlic and wolfsbane," said Edward in a warbly, 1950s B-movie voice.

"Crucifixes," said Jonathan, equally melodramatic.

"Or scapulars," said Father, opening his desk drawer and fishing around inside. "I was planning to give you these next Tuesday, but why wait?"

"We're already wearing scapulars," said Edward.

"Not like these," said Father, holding them up to the light.

"You're right," said Pierre, leaning close. "I've never seen anything like them."

"Five-folds?" asked Jonathan.

"Yes," said Father, "handmade in a monastery in Lebanon—"

"Maronite elves," said the gardener, "the best little helpers in the business."

"—and blessed by Bishop Xandaronolopolis on the Feast of St. Simon Stock."

GARDENING TIPS: The Blessed Virgin Mary appeared to St. Simon Stock (thus named because he lived in the hollow or "stock" of an oak tree for twenty years) on July 16, 1251 and presented him with a brown scapular, promising to all who wore it that She would obtain for them the Grace of final perseverance in the Catholic Faith at the moment of their deaths.

Since then, She has appeared to others with scapulars of various colors for different devotional purposes. The five-fold scapular is sort of an all-in-one package--though the green is not included.

                                                    --M.F.

VISUAL AIDS:

Brown Scapular   Five-fold Scapular

Tradosaurus modeling Scapular

"Thicker than we're used to," said Arthur, accepting one gingerly. He held up the two bundles of finely sewn wool connected with red cords.

They all began undoing their ties—no "clip-ons" in this group—and unbuttoning their collars.

"What should we do with our old ones?" asked Edward, fishing his own trusty talisman out from around his neck.

"The usual," said Father. "Burial or incineration. Or better yet, keep them for spares. Nothing, not even these hand-crafted marvels, lasts forever. As for your enrollment in the five-fold, we'll do that officially next Tuesday."

They continued removing and replacing, then once again buttoned their collars and retied their bow ties. These guys were so practiced they didn't need mirrors. I was impressed.

"I wish I could give you more regal gifts," said Father, "but this was within my means, and the Graces that go with them are, of course, incalculable."

I was a tad jealous, I must admit, as I sat there fondling the little bump under my shirt—my rather ordinary brown scapular. But the Graces and promises associated even with my simple model were more than sufficient for any average gardener. I decided to let the young manage with abundance.

The exchange complete, and all their old scapulars carefully inserted into various pockets, the Tumblars resumed their relaxed yet attentive positions.

"This vampire," asked Joel, swallowing loudly, "what does he look like?"

"That I don't know," said Father, knocking the dead ashes out of his pipe into an ashtray. "My best guess, based on factors that I won't reveal at this time, is that he plays the part of the romantic vampire. I wouldn't be surprised if he wears a tailcoat, or even a cape. His role model is most likely the kind of vampire popular in cheap romantic novels and recent movies. He may have filed his canines for effect, or have a false set in his pocket. I think he suggests to his victims that he can make them vampires like himself, promising them eternal life."

"You just told them," I whispered.

Father blinked. "So I did. Well, there it is. Maybe it is best that they know."

"You mean his victims are willing—?" asked Arthur.

"Apparently," said Father. "There was no sign of struggle. If you encounter such a man—"

"Are you sure it's a man?" asked Edward. "I mean, rather than a woman?"

"Yes," said Father, "all things considered, I'll wager we're looking for a male."

"And what should we do?" asked Joel, a bit on the pale side.

"Nothing," said Father. "Do not, I repeat, do not go anywhere with him. Do not attempt to follow him. I just want to know if he's around. If he has been, chances are someone's noticed him. As before, I just want you to engage in casual conversations, asking nothing specific, letting people prattle as they will. If this man has been 'making the scene,' there will be news of him. If someone mentions a vampire, or anything to do with vampires, express offhanded interest with eyebrows raised and nothing more."

"Should we go formally attired?" asked Pierre.

"I think so," said Father. "Your formalwear might instigate comparisons with him. You never know. So important is this matter, I want to call this meeting short so you can get up to Hollywood straight away. We'll be gathering here at seven tomorrow evening, and you can report then."

"Any suggestions where we should start?" asked Arthur.

"'Stogies,'" said Father. "And maybe 'The Lounge Around,' but go to as many places as you can."

Pierre reached across Father's desk and picked up a plaque in a small copper frame from its usual place between the hand-carved statues of St. Anthony of Padua and St. Thomas More.

"... Do we walk in legends or on the green earth in the daytime?"
"A man may do both," said Aragorn. "For not we but those who come after will make the legends of our time. The green earth, you

say? That is a mighty matter of legend, though you tread it under
the light of day!"

—J. R. R. Tolkien
The Lord of the Rings

"It would seem, gentlemen," said Pierre thoughtfully, "that the legend
continues. Another adventure of the Knights Tumblar. May we be
worthy of our charge." He set down the plaque and picked up his fluted
glass. With a determined expression on his face, he swirled the amber
fluid and downed it in one gulp. "Our song will have to keep until
tomorrow evening."

They all followed suit and rose to leave.

"Your blessing, Father," said Arthur, dropping to one knee, "on us
and our quest."

"Of course," said Father, making the Sign of the Cross as they all
knelt. "And I suggest you all start a novena to St. Anthony."

They rose, refreshed and renewed, ready to take on the world.

"Oh Martin," said Jonathan, taking me aside as the others straightened the room and returned the chairs to the kitchen. "I wonder if we
could ask a small favor of you."

"I'll do what I can," I said, "as always."

"We've got our jobs to attend to tomorrow, being working men, and
we left our white ties, vests, and tailcoats at Vinnie Ng's. Would you
mind picking them up for us tomorrow afternoon? He promised they'd
be ready by five. We'll change here."

"No problem," I said, leading them out through the hallway to the
front door.

"Do be careful, gentlemen," said Father, pulling the door open for
their departure. "And don't forget—"

"Oh!" gasped a sweet, feminine voice on the doorstep, hand raised to
push the doorbell. "Father Baptist, I hope I'm not—"

"Stella," said Father, surprised. "Gentlemen, may I present Miss
Stella Billowack."

"Any relation to Chief Montgomery Billowack?" asked Joel, peering
around the shoulders in front of him.

"He's my father," giggled Stella, eyes wide at the sight of the Tumblars in the doorway.

"The pleasure is mine," said Pierre, taking her right hand and giving
it a chivalric peck. "Unfortunately, we must make haste."

"Perhaps," said Arthur, taking her hand before it fell and likewise
kissing it, "we'll meet again under less fleeting circumstances."

"What's with you guys?" she gasped as Edward followed suit.

"Good evening," said Joel, a bit hesitantly. Her father had, after all,
heaped considerable grief on his person, and only too recently. But,

knight that he was, he overcame his reticence for the sake of propriety, and gave her hand a resounding Slovakian smack.

Jonathan was the last to approach. His eyes met hers as he touched her hand. "I—"

"I—" she whispered. She froze. I mean, the woman froze right there on the porch. She stopped blinking, twitching, and even breathing.

"I —" gulped Jonathan, similarly paralyzed.

"Aye yi yi," I moaned, glancing toward Father.

He returned my glance with those impenetrable eyes that seemed to whisper, detached yet knowingly, "Considering that everything does have its season, Martin, and since in their times all things pass under heaven, what do you expect?" But what he said was, "Come on in, Stella. Stella?"

"Coming, Father," she said distantly as Jonathan finally thawed enough to detach his hand from hers. He drifted slowly down the stairs, feet floating six inches off the ground.

The other Tumblars grabbed him like a balloon and guided him into one of the passenger seats in Edward's van parked at the curb. They slammed the doors and buckled themselves in. Jonathan's eyes stared up at her through the window as the van roared off into the night.

"Stella," said Father uselessly. "Stella?"

"Aye yi yi," whispered the gardener again, turning and lurching back inside.

Friday, October Twentieth

Feast Day of Saint Irene of Portugal, a nun martyred in defense of her Chastity (653 AD)

Day of Abstinence

23

"IT'S CALLED A 'CASSOCK,'" Father Baptist was explaining to the little girl seated beside him on the crumbling cement steps in front of Elizabeth Unger's apartment building.

Like all the structures in the area, it had been built back in the days when Hollywood was a respectable neighborhood where parents let their children play in the front yard without fear of something unspeakable befalling them—a time when you could jaywalk across Hollywood Boulevard without even looking, vehicular traffic being scarce. I remember it well because my dad used to bring me there when I was a kid to check out the costume shops when Halloween was nigh.

Now the district was a cluster of skeletal shells, gutted of their former elegance, entombed in layers of dull, chalky paint, inhabited by the poor and invaded by the drug dealers that preyed upon them. And yet, even here, there was innocence to be found. Like this little girl who looked up at Father with eyes wide and wondrous.

After a hasty breakfast, punctuated by Monsignor Havermeyer's absence, Father had asked me to drive him back to Elizabeth Unger's apartment.

"Why there?" I'd asked. "There are still three others that we haven't yet seen."

"Unfinished business," he had said mysteriously. "We'll catch up with Taper and Wickes later."

"Did you have a nice chat with Stella Billowack?" I'd asked as we roared off in the Jeep.

"She seemed preoccupied," said Father, latching his seat belt.

"I wonder why."

"Can't imagine."

"Of course," I said, changing lanes, "the Tumblars won't be taking solemn vows like in a religious order—of 'chastity,' I mean."

"As in 'celibacy'? Of course not. They will be free to marry if that is their vocation. But even married men must lead chaste lives within the bounds of marital propriety."

"You've explained these details, I assume."

"Looks like I'm going to have to give at least one of them a refresher course, and maybe soon."

A half-hour later, we parted the crisscross of police tape and stepped into the familiar gloom of Elizabeth Unger's apartment. Father made a point of leaving the front door slightly ajar behind us. Then, instead of nosing around, he simply seated himself on the couch, folded his hands, and bowed his head in silence.

"What are you doing?" I asked.

"Waiting," he replied.

"For what?"

"For an answer to a special prayer I made to St. Anthony of Padua just before Mass. He never lets me down when I'm looking for something I've missed."

"Ah," I said knowingly, slowly moseying my way around the room, trying to interest myself in the bizarre paraphernalia on the walls.

Minutes drifted by.

"St. Anthony," I prayed silently to the Saint who had proved equally helpful to me on occasions too numerous to count, "if you're not otherwise occupied, would you please be so kind as to—"

Just then there came a tiny creak from the direction of the front door.

I looked up and saw two wide eyes staring at us, hovering between the deadbolt and the doorknob. Little fingers gripped the edge of the frame.

"Don't be afraid," said Father, not to me, but to the little shape at the door, and in a voice so soothing yet earnest it almost dissolved my arthritis on the spot. I didn't know he had it in him. "I was hoping you'd come by."

The little girl blinked, but didn't move. All I could see was her eyes and fingers. The rest of her was hidden in shadow.

"My name is Father John Baptist. What's yours?"

"Like John *the* Baptist?" she said, wary but unafraid.

"Yes," said Father.

"He got his head chopped off," said the girl.

"You know about that," smiled Father. "It's true, and for the price of a dance. You won't chop off mine, will you?"

"No," her voice smiled, "I don't think so."

"Neither do I. What's your name?"

"Patricia."

"Patricia what?"

"Patricia Marie Nealy."

"That's a beautiful name."

"You're a priest."

"Yes, I am."

"I know, 'cause we're Cat'lics."

"Wonderful."

She looked him over. "You're not like Kevin, though."

"Who?"

"He's our pastor. He doesn't like to be called 'Father.'"

"He doesn't? Well, come to think of it, I do."

"Why?"

"You might say it reminds me whose business I'm supposed to be about. Would you like to come in, or would you rather we talk out there?"

"Out here," she said, motioning with her hand. "I don't like going in there."

"I don't like it in here either," said Father, approaching the door with even steps. "It gives me the creeps."

Marveling, I watched as he joined her out in the hallway, their footsteps fading down the dark corridor. Children, as far as this gardener is concerned, are akin to creatures from Mars. Communication with them is invariably tentative, convoluted, and risky business.

I sat thinking for a few minutes, not sure what to do. Obviously, he had a way with kids that was lost on me.

A few more minutes drifted by.

Finally, deciding that the place gave me the creeps, too, I went out the door and locked it behind me. Descending apartment numbers rolled by as I followed the worn-out patches on the tattered carpet down the hallway toward the front of the building. The foyer had once been an elegant mirrored room dotted with palms and ferns in large stone planters. I wondered as I hobbled through the lobby how the current owners could have thought that bare whitewashed walls and empty pits were more becoming, and that three bare bulbs dangling from wires were more illuminating than the original crystal chandelier. But what the hey.

The front door was a story in itself: a heavy, thick walnut slab into which had been set a clear plane of frozen silica, delicately frosted around the edges with grapevines and gardenias. I imagined what it might have been like fifty years ago to look out that window. It was another world then, the kind of world that didn't have to be kept out with wrought-iron bars and deadbolts.

Peering instead at the world into which I had been thrust by God's Providence, I could see Father Baptist and the little girl sitting and chatting on the steps. She was hunched into a ball, arms locked around her knees, rocking playfully. He was leaning against one of the posts, nodding and smiling but also listening intently.

Gingerly, I turned the latch and stepped outside, trying to keep my lurching to a minimum. I didn't want to frighten the child.

"It's called a 'cassock,'" he was saying as I closed the heavy door behind me.

She didn't seem to notice me, her attention riveted as it was to the row of buttons descending from his Roman collar.

"It must be hard to get into," she said.

"Not as difficult as you think," he said, winking. "I only undo the top dozen or so."

"Kevin never wears anything like that. And what's that on your head?"

"This? It's called a 'biretta.'"

"It looks weird."

"That it does," he said, fingering its curious shape. "But it signifies my office."

"And who's he?" she said, nodding her head in my direction.

"Oh him," said Father, waving a hand absently in my direction. "That's my good friend, Mr. Marty."

I grinned. What a coincidence. No one had called me that for years, not since there was a grammar school attached to St. Philomena's, crawling with those Martians I mentioned a moment ago. They used to call me "Mr. Marty." That was back in the days before the nuns went ballistic and deserted their convent, leaving the children to fend for themselves—long before Father Baptist came along.

"Hi," I said, giving her a little wave.

"You limp," she said, a curious edge in her voice. "And you use a cane."

"Yes, I do," I nodded, turning the aspen dragon's head away from her and burying it in the hem of my jacket. "And, yes I do."

"So do I," she said, "sometimes."

"You do?" Suddenly I realized that she wasn't curled up casually at all. Her spine was hunched, twisted, terribly deformed. "Oh, um, I, uh," I mumbled as the word-generating synapses in my skull stalled.

"Is your dragon shy?" she asked, ignoring my stammer.

I looked down at my cane. "I guess so. He doesn't say much."

"I think Elibazeth would like you," she said after a moment's consideration. "She's weird."

"Really," I smiled.

"You, too," she said, turning back to Father. "She likes to wear black."

"Elizabeth?" asked Father.

"No, it's E-*lib*-azeth. She says I'm the only one in the whole world who gets it right."

"I see," said Father.

"She's my friend," said Patricia.

"Eliza—, I mean, E-*lib*-azeth Unger?"

"Mm-hm," she nodded. She began to smile, but it never reached full bloom. A dark storm seemed to pass behind her eyes. "But she's gone."

"Do you know where she's gone?" asked Father.

She scrunched her lips. "Not to Heaven. She didn't want to go there."

"Why not?"

"She said she wanted to go where it was dark, and Heaven is bright, isn't it?"

"Very, by all accounts."

"She said she was going away for a while, someplace she'd always wanted to visit, someplace dark and cool and quiet. She promised to come back for me, to take me too; but she didn't."

"Maybe something stopped her," I said lamely. "You know, prevented her from coming back."

"Sure," said Patricia sternly. Her forehead burst into furrows. "She's dead, isn't she?"

"I'm afraid so," said Father.

"I knew it," she said angrily. "Aunt Mia just told me she went away, but I knew she was dead. It's like when the men in the big white truck with all the lights took Momma to the hospital. The driver told me they were just taking her away for a little while and she'd be back as good as new. But he was wrong. She didn't come back."

"I'm sorry," said Father. "Where is your daddy?"

"Gone. I don't know if he's dead, too. Aunt Mia says she hopes so."

"Maybe I could have a word with your aunt. Is she—?"

"She's at work. She hates it, but she goes all the time."

"Did Elibazeth work, too?"

"I think so."

"Do you know where?—what she did?"

"No, but she hated it, too."

"Did she work at night?"

"Uh-huh. That's why she had time to be my friend during the day."

"Was she going to work the last time you saw her?"

"Yes. I told her not to, that I wanted her to stay with me, but she said she had someone to meet."

"Someone? Did she say who?"

"Nope. Just someone who would make everything all right. Someone from the dark, quiet place."

"Do you know where she was going to meet him?"

"Down there," she said, pointing along the dreary block toward the Boulevard. "She always met him down there. She told me I couldn't go."

"But did you—follow her, I mean?"

She rolled her eyes. "Yes."

"Could you take me where she went?"

"Uh-uh. I'm not supposed to go anywhere with strangers."

"I understand, and it's very good that you obey your aunt. Can you tell me what the place looks like, the place where Elibazeth went?"

"There's this big cigar over the door, with lights for smoke. You can see it from the corner."

"You saw her go in?"

"Uh-huh."

"You didn't go in, too, did you?"

"Oh no. That would've made her mad. Kids aren't allowed anyway."

"So you waited outside. Did you see her come out again?"

"Uh-huh."

"Did you see who she was with?"

"Um ..." Suddenly, her lips went tight. Then her cheeks began to swell as if an explosion was going off inside her head. It burst out through her mouth, a series of childish thoughts that had finally found release. "He was tall and scary and his face was white, and he was all in black, and I almost screamed, but I didn't, but I wish I had—"

"You saw him," said Father.

"Uh-huh-huh-huuuh," she stammered, bursting into tears. "And then Elibazeth got in his car, and I said 'No, no, no!' but she didn't hear me—"

Streams were pouring from her eyes, trickling around her swollen cheeks and gathering at her chin.

"—so I ran up and hit the door, 'No, no, no!' but he was driving away, and she looked at me through the window, and she looked kind of sad, and scared, too, and they drove off, and I ran home, and Aunt Mia saw me from the window, and she spanked me, and, and ..."

Father looked up at me.

I looked down at him.

The little hunchbacked girl cried and cried.

24

NO STORY I COULD EVER TELL about Father Baptist would be complete without a visit to the establishment of Willie "Skull" Kapps, also known as Guillaume du Crane Cristal. How a traditional Roman Catholic priest got amiably and inter-respectfully connected with a pseudoo-Voudou-yoohoo like Willie would take a book in itself—and not by yours truly, because that was back in the days when Father Baptist went under the moniker of Jack Lombard, Chief of Homicide. That was before he got sacerdotally and conspiratorially connected with me, and I only write what I witness with my own eyes, with my own personal squint, so to speak.

I can never remember the name of the street on which Willie's macabre shop is located, but I could find my way there blindfolded—well, almost. I might need to take a peek now and then to avoid running over a few curbs. The streets in that part of town are anything but straight. In fact, there is no geometric term with which I'm familiar that describes the convoluted twists and turns laid down once upon a time by a drunken steamroller driver when the city was young.

I can tell you many things about Willie's peculiar establishment. For instance, from the front it looked like a cross between a Caribbean haberdashery, a wicker furniture outlet, a taxidermy emporium, a magic shop, a tropical arboretum, and a warehouse for orthopedic props. I can tell you that there was a warped sign hanging over the doorway, more or less shaped like an eyeball, with an inscription painted around the cornea: WIDE EYE DO DAT? I could tell you that a cockeyed sign on the door declared:

FORTUNES UNTOLD
∞ BONES READ ∞
POTIONS FOR ALL OCCASIONS
GUILLAUME DU CRANE CRISTAL, PROPRIETOR.

I could also tell you about the little brass bell which hung upon a hook just inside the front door, a single bell that had the unique property of being completely out of tune with itself. The bell will have to wait for a moment, however, until we get through the next bit of dialogue:

"Willie," said Father, rapping the sooty window alongside the door. "Let us in."

"Nooooooo way," said a voice from within, punctuated with the rattle of bones and metal trinkets woven into stiff, barbed-wire dreadlocks. "I'm closed, mon. It not safe to open dah door when dah boogie mon's about."

"What boogie man?" asked Father.

"Dah one what's suckin' dah blood," whined the voice. On this occasion, Willie was speaking in his affected Caribbean accent. "Dah blood is dah life, mon, and mine's not for dah suckin'."

"It's Father Jack," said Father. "Jack the Black."

"He's back," I said over Father's shoulder, "and with Martin Mon. And we're not thirsty."

"So you say," warbled Willie.

"The sun is out," said Father.

"White mon's tricks."

"This," said Father, producing something small but heavy from the folds of his cassock, "is no trick."

"Ah," said Willie. "Aaaah. Let me see *him* touch it."

Feeling a bit silly, I gripped the silver Crucifix in Father's hand. "See, Willie? I no shrivel and I not smoke."

"Hokay," he said at last, unlatching the bolt with a mighty clunk.

A blast of garlic fumes burst from the shop as the door creaked open.

"Inside," Willie waved frantically, "hurry, mon. Hurry dah hurry."

We scurried past. He slammed the door behind us, grinding the gears of the deadbolt with decisive fury.

That infernal bell jangled its counter-harmonious note at us. I wouldn't make such a big deal about it, but every enflamed joint in my body resonated with that infernal thing. I'll bet it could induce migraines and trigger spontaneous human combustion under the right circumstances.

Recovering from the jolting ordeal of entry, I looked around. It was the same old place, display cases crammed with withered things that had once been alive—things which seemed to shift and quiver on the edges of your vision until you looked at them directly. The walls were cluttered with casting quilts and masks and skulls, along with talismans and spell-pouches for every occasion.

"Cooking something special?" I asked, gagging on the thick aroma that hung in the air in stratified layers like dense black smoke.

"Protectin' my blood, mon," he said, strutting nervously toward the doorway in the back draped with strings of glittering beads, "what little my skinny bod has to lose."

He was indeed skinny: his legs moved in his trousers much like those fuzzy wire cleaners Father wiggles through his pipe. Getting blood out of him would be like squeezing juice out of a coconut husk.

"Wot you want wit me?" he said, spinning on us, dreadlocks chattering. He had something draped around his neck that resembled a Rosary, but the beads seemed to be made out of some small animal's vertebrae. "Dere's bad mojo all around. Can't you feel it, mon?"

"I can sure smell it," said the gardener.

"Ah," he said, "but can dah vom-peer?"

"Then you know about him," said Father.

"Sure I know'd about him. Dis is Willie you be talkin' to, not some cross-chanellin' salamandress."

"I have some holy water with me," said Father. "Would you like me to bless your house?"

"Exorcism?" quivered Willie, ivory eyeballs darting this way and that between protruding burnt umber cheekbones. "Indeed, indeed I would."

"What would all your Voudou clients say about having a priest exorcise your abode?" I asked.

"Dey would say, 'Go for it,'" said Willie.

"Then I will gladly attend to it," said Father.

"But first, why you come here? Wot you want wit me? You're a Cat-lick, you're dah priest, you know wot to do about dah vom-peer better'n anybody."

"Yes," said Father, "but nonetheless, I could use your help." He lifted a sheet of paper from somewhere in his cassock, unfolded it, and handed it to Willie. "I was wondering if you could help me with these ingredients. What potion could you make with them?"

Willie grabbed the sheet, glared at both of us, and then eyed the page. "Myrrh," he read, "sodium monofluorophosphate, calcium carbonate, carrageenan, glycerin, fennel oil, propolis, allicin ... Yah, I know dese tings. I con tink of many potions for which I would use one, or maybe two, but only one dat uses dem all—except for dah allicin, not dah allicin, damn sure not dah allicin. Dat wouldn't do."

"Okay," said Father, "not the allicin. But you know a potion that would contain all the rest?"

"Sure, mon. I use it two, t'ree times a day."

"And what's that?"

"'Scuse me, I show you," he said, scurrying through the back door in a clatter of beads. They exploded again a moment later as he returned, gripping something limp and collapsed in his hand.

"What's this?" said Father. "A joke?"

"No joke," said Willie. "See? Read dah ingredients yourself."

"Myrrh," read Father from the side of the thing, "sodium monofluorophosphate, calcium carbonate, carrageenan, glycerin, fennel oil, propolis ... everything on the list except allicin."

"Of course not," said Willie. "Allicin wouldn't be in dere, but everyt'ing else, sure."

"Why not allicin?" asked the gardener.

"Silly mon," chided Willie. "Who would put garlic in toot-paste?"

"Garlic?" asked Father.

"'Toot-paste?'" asked yours truly.

"Allicin is dah active ingredient in dah garlic," said Willie. "Sort of a natural antibiotic, so some white docs say. I say who cares, so long as it repel dah vom-peer?"

Father smiled at the shrunken tube resting in his palm. "Of course not. Who would be silly enough to put garlic in toothpaste?"

Ah, I thought: tooth-paste. Toothpaste? Wait a minute—

"Who would be silly enough to use *myrrh* in toothpaste?" asked the gardener, scratching his forehead with his dragon-handled cane.

"Actually it does make sense," said Father. "It's an astringent."

"You only find it in dah 'natural' toot-pastes," said Willie, know-ingly, pronouncing it "nah-toor-al," with no particular emphasis. "It make dah gums feel good." He licked his pearly whites—not so pearly or white—by way of demonstration. It was not a pretty sight.

"Hm." Father sniffed the capless end of the tube. "Interesting. Mar-tin, what do you think?"

"Me?" I took an authoritative whiff. "I didn't notice 'licorice' in the list of ingredients."

"Dot's not licorice, Martin mon," said Willie, darting around behind one of the counters and returning with a handful of tiny, narrow specks. "Fennel seeds. Here, taste—chew a few in dah mouth, makes dah breath fresh."

"Of course," said Father, complying, "I've tasted this before. Indian restaurants often give these to customers as a breath freshener. Martin, try some?"

"Thanks, Father, I've had my fill of fennel for today," I grimaced, turning away. My eyes landed elsewhere. "Willie, something new?"

"Where?" he said.

"This display case."

"No," he said a bit anxiously, shifting his dreadlocks from side to side. "Dat's alway been."

"I mean the things inside," I said, tapping the glass with my finger.

"Oh dat," he said. "No, it all old, old, old, old stuff, from back in dah back."

"Oh."

"Ancient stuff."

"Gotcha," I said, looking at the items spread out on a velvet cloth. "Very old. How can you tell?"

"Dah story," he said, turning his attention back to Father, "you would not want to wait so long."

"So," said Father, rubbing his chin, ignoring that little exchange. "Fennel oil from fennel seeds for the licorice taste ... and what's propo-lis?"

"Tree resin," said Willie, snickering as though he was talking about bat's wings and newt's eyes. "Dah bees collect it. Also good for dah gums. Calcium carbonate is just techno-gook for chalk dust."

"Chalk?" I gagged. "In toot-paste?"

"A fine abrasive," said Father. "All toothpaste has to have some kind of abrasive as a base. It all fits."

"And carrageenan?" I asked in amazement.

"Seaweed," said Willie.

"Why seaweed?"

"Because it's muy mucho 'nah-toor-al,'" winked Willie. "Don't read dah labels on wot you eat too closely, Martin mon. Dey use it a lot to t'icken dah ice cream, too."

"How do you happen to know all this?" I asked, dumbfounded.

"Ah," said Willie. "While you be readin' t'ick books by Augustine and Bonaventure, I read dah labels. Dere's much to be learned dere in dah details of life."

"So," said Father, breaking into a smile. "Add all this to that bit of parsley on our list of clues, and now we know."

"Now we know what?" asked the gardener.

"Now we know what we're dealing with."

"Which is?" asked Willie and yours truly in union.

"Willie," said Father, "dump the garlic stew and put on a pot of your mweemuck root tea."

"You sure," said Willie.

"I'm positive."

"Don't be too hasty," I intruded. "Garlic is good for high blood pressure."

"Too much of dah good t'ing, Martin mon, it can still kill you," said Willie. "I gotta hundred and twenty cloves a'boiling on dah stove in dah back."

"I see what you mean," I agreed. "At that concentration, blood pressure would be reduced to blood suction."

"This also clears up something else that's been nagging me," said Father, "about the teeth patterns around the wounds."

"Oh?" I asked. "What's that?"

"Shall I bless your house, now, Willie?" said Father, producing a small vial of holy water from the limitless recesses of his cassock.

"Sure, Jack," said Willie gleefully. "You do dat, and I put on dah tea."

"Great," I said, my stomach lurching at the thought of its last encounter with the filthy stuff.

"Lipton for you, Martin mon," winked Willie, heading for the back. "You see? Details. I remember dah details."

"Thanks," said me and my stomach in unison.

25

"BIG WING-DING TONIGHT?" asked Vinnie Ng, our parish "in lieu of" dry-cleaner, hand-launderer, tailor, and presser. "You go?"

"Yup," I said as cheerfully as I could, considering the events of the day so far. "I'm also supposed to pick up all those other fellows' whites and tailcoats."

"Sure," he nodded, tapping his knobby cranium. "I know. Vinnie know ev'ysing."

"I hope I have enough money to cover—"

But he was gone, vanished amidst racks of apparel dangling in filmy plastic shrouds. I could hear him rummaging around back there, the occasional scrape of hangers on rods punctuating his Oriental mutterings.

I took a moment to examine the faded fresco on the wall above the cash register. The previous owner of this building had been a Mexican auto mechanic named Juan Diego whose wife, Pilar, had painted an angular but respectful rendition of Our Lady of Guadalupe as a comfort to their customers. Beneath Her feet were the words:

Si tienes penas o problemas,
Yo tel los resolveré.
† † †
If you have woes or problems,
I will solve them.

Apparently when Mr. Ng took over the property, he saw no reason to change the sentiment or the promise. Even where he came from, Our Lady of Guadalupe was venerated with awe. Brooklyn, I think he said it was.

Suddenly he was back, heaving a ton of clothing onto the counter beside the cash register.

"Here Fahser spare cassock," he quipped. "No charge. Here you blue jacket. Many hole, two button gone, all fix, dry clean, no charge."

"Thank-you," I said, always embarrassed by his furious "in lieu of" charity. But, as Father often reminded me: "Take charity whenever it is offered, for the Grace lavished on the giver is worth infinitely more than your pride."

"Next," huffed Vinnie. "Here five formal outfit. Big charge, I bill them. You poor, I know. Vinnie know."

"Oh," I said sheepishly stuffing my thin billfold back into my pocket. "That'll be fine."

"Now," he said, puffing his cheeks, "I got big suppize for you."

"A surprise? For me?"

"Mr. Delaney, good customer many year, he die three day ago. Car crash."

"I'm sorry to hear—"

"I sorry, too. Big rich, not Cath'ic, too bad. Go Hell. He leave two nice outfit here last week. Wife she come to Vinnie, take one for Mr. Delaney look good in coffin. I ask wife, what I do other outfit? She say, give some 'poor shmuck.' I think: Mr. Feeney 'poor' but not really 'shmuck'—well, not all time—and I say: one out two not bad."

"I'm not following you, Vinnie."

"Week after week, you bring Vinnie this jacket, that jacket, pants. Ev'ysing old, holes, me fix, no sweat. Vinnie like challenge. I think: I know Mr. Feeney size, I know Mr. Feeney shape, I know Vinnie can make fit good." With a smile as wide as the Great Wall of China was long, he spread something out on the counter. "White tie, vest, tailcoat. My gift you."

"For me?"

"See anybody else Vinnie shop?"

"I guess not."

"So. You like?"

"I don't know what to say."

"Smile say all. Have good time tonight with crazy guys. You fit right in. See? Vinnie know."

My smile was still "saying all" as I pulled into the parking lot behind St. Philomena's, grateful beyond words for unexpected favors, and also that the dumpster was finally gone.

26

"MY SENIOR?" I INQUIRED, tapping his flimsy aluminum door an hour later. "Monsignor Havermeyer?"

A thump and a growl emanated from the belly of the camper. "What is it, Feeney?"

"Father Baptist requests your presence at the dinner table."

"Why?" he snarled, pushing the door open, missing my face by inches. "So I can be humiliated by that infernal Millie again? No way. I'll be across the street at 'Peanuts' if you need me."

"I understand your ire, and sympathize with your plight. But, nonetheless, Father Baptist insists. There's something you need to know about, especially since you've offered to assume some of his duties."

"Oh there is, is there?"

"I'm afraid so."

The scar tissue on his forehead rippled as various options clashed within the twists and folds of his pulsing gray matter. "I'll come, but no more potatoes."

"That, My Senior, is beyond my control. You're free to leave immediately and attend to your needs across the street. But—and on this point I wholeheartedly concur with Father, for what it's worth, which I realize isn't much, but there it is—you really must be present, and—" I checked my watch. "—within five minutes."

"Phooey," he hissed, emerging from his aluminum cocoon.

"Phooey," he hissed again, four minutes hence, when Millie slammed yet another terrified boiled potato in front of him at the table. Like its forebears, it wobbled around the perimeter of its porcelain prison in horror, finding no escape. "This has gone on long enough. And what the Hell is that?"

He was referring to a faint but intrusive tap-tap-tap on the ornate French window at Father Baptist's elbow. The window was made of many angular panes of stained glass, rippling ambers and stunning reds and blues, depicting a Dove perched on a golden Chalice, a single drop of Blood dangling from its delicate beak. The tapping was made by none other than Mrs. Magillicuddy, who came every Friday at precisely six-fifteen to purge her troubled soul of flotsam.

"This is why I wanted you here," said Father Baptist.

"So I'm here," huffed Monsignor Havermeyer.

"Then listen and observe," said Father, unlatching the window, "but do not interrupt."

"There you are's, Faddah," wheezed a voice from outside.

"Here I am, Mrs. Magillicuddy," nodded Father.

"I'm never sure's, anymore, that you're a'goin' to be here's when I comes, I isn't."

"I only missed that one time, my dear woman, and that was months ago."

"Has it been, it has? That long? Well, 'Once makes a rule,' as me dear Willum's so fond of sayin', he is."

"True," said Father, rubbing his hands with regret. "But I'm doing my best not to make it so."

"You always does, you do. Your best, I means."

"I try. Shall we begin?"

"Bless me, Faddah, for I have sinned, I have's—"

"What's the meaning of this?" hissed Monsignor Havermeyer, sending his potato scurrying again. "Of all the—"

He was cut short by a wave of Father's hand that could have sliced a block of steel clean through.

"It's been a week, it has," sighed Mrs. Magillicuddy, "since I last sought your shriv'ness."

"Fine," said Father, one freezing eye on Monsignor Havermeyer. "Do please proceed."

"It's hard for me to say it, Faddah. Embarrassed, I am's."

"God sees all, Mrs. Magillicuddy. You're just telling Him what He already knows."

"True, true. But still it's hard's, it is. You see, Faddah, the woods hasn't been the same's, they hasn't, not since the faeries went aways."

"You're lonely?" asked Father.

"Not 'tirely, Faddah. Not 'tirely. There's other folks that come out at night's, there is, now that the faeries has gone. The little people, they's more friendly than the faeries ever was, they is. They sings, and they plays their tiny drums and bagpipes, they do, but it's not the same. So's I—cover your ears, Faddah—I've taken to walkin' the streets up northerways, the lights, and the signs. They's no fitting sight for an' old woman likes myself. It's an occasion of sin, it is. And me as old and stiff as I am, but I misses Willum so. He still hasn't come back, y'know's."

"I understand."

"And now, just the other night, as if to punish the likes of me, even the wee folks is leaving me. Poof! Gone they're going, they is."

"Because of your sin?"

"Maybe's. At first I thought's so's. But then it hits me, it did's, it's because of, of ..." Her voice grew dark and trembly. "... *him.*"

"Him?"

"There's a bad'n about, Faddah. Fowl as ol' stump water. Something dark an' wicked, he is."

"He?" asked Father, casting me a worried glance.

"Him," she said. "He's afoot, he is. I knows, I knows, only too well, I knows."

"What do you know about him?"

"I knows I won't be a'comin' to see you for's a few weeks, I won't's be."

"No?"

"No, Faddah. I'm a'gonna go aways and visits me sister, I is."

"Your sister. And where does she live, Mrs. Magillicuddy?"

"She's got's herself's a nice spot in the woods near Hemmet, she has."

"Hemmet? That's many miles away. How will you get there?"

"As I've'n often told ya, Faddah, no distance is too great once you start a'puttin' one foot in fronts of the other'n."

"And she lives in the woods, too?"

"We were always two peas in a pod's, we were's, we sisters. Her name is Abigail. She was a purty one in her day, she was, but now she's old an' pruned-up likes me, she is."

"Does she know? Is she expecting you?"

"Me wee folks, they knows her wee folks, they does. They keeps in touch, they does. She'll knows."

"I'm sure Mr. Feeney would be glad to drive you there. I should think it best—"

"Nope's. Where's I goes I walks. An' speakin' of that grim Mr. Feeney, I got's some nice sunfloosies for you to give him."

A spindly hand came into view, clutching something dark, shriveled, and leathery.

Oh, I thought, so now I'm "grim" as well as "dour" and "crotchety," and a bunch of "sunfloosies" is supposed to cheer me up?

"I'll see that he gets them," said Father, placing them in my water glass.

They looked gross, whatever they were.

"Is there anything else you want to tell me?" asked Father.

"No, Faddah. Just that I's a'been where I's a'shouldn't, and I'm ashamed, I am."

"I see." He bowed his head in thought for a moment, and then said, "The human heart yearns for God. Fools that we are, we often seek Him in His creatures, and are always disappointed. We're made that way, you know, to seek comfort and fulfillment in Him. He made us, and yearns for us to seek Him—and only Him—apart from that which He has made. Do you follow me?"

"As always, Faddah. I follow's you all a'ways, I does."

"Okay. For your penance, dear woman, say a decade of the Rosary before St. Christopher's statue in the church. He'll protect you on your journey. And if you have a few 'sunfloosies' to spare, St. Jude always appreciates your attention."

"He does? Has he told's you so, Faddah?"

"In ... not so many words, but I think so, yes. Now make a good Act of Contrition."

"O my God, defend us in battle, and these Thy gifts which we are about to behold I stand at the door and lead us knock into temptation, to light, to guard, to be understood as to understand, for it is in giving that we ever shall be, world without end. Amen."

"Good night, dear Mrs. Magillicuddy."

"G'night, Faddah. I'll see's you in a few weeks when the storm is passed, it is. And don't forget to say me good-bye's to Mr. Feeney for me."

"I surely will."

"And give him those sunfloosies."

"I won't forget. Good-night."

"What," said Monsignor Havermeyer once the window was shut and latched, "was that all about?"

"One of our parish casualties," said Father. "I wanted you to know in the event that I'm not here for some reason on a Friday night. As you heard, I was neglectful once, and she hasn't forgotten."

"You encourage this, this—?"

"I permit it, yes, as Charity requires. Mrs. Magillicuddy is a troubled soul who snaps back and forth between one reality and another like you and I change our socks. In another reality, she attends Mass regularly, makes valid confessions, and supplies fresh flowers at the feet of every statue in the church."

"But this ... this is most irregular."

"So is life, Monsignor. I should also tell you that William Magilli-cuddy died some time ago, and that she comes here every Friday evening right about when it happened."

"But she talked about him as if—"

"Part of her has yet to come to grips with that reality. I think in time she will put it all together, but in the meantime we must practice patience. This is another of our duties here at St. Philomena's, which you have offered to help perform. I just wanted you to know."

"But what's this about faeries, and wee folk? If she's having delu-sions, maybe she should be placed in an institution before she harms herself."

"No institution could help her, even if they could hold her, which I doubt. The faeries she spoke of were real—"

"Real? You're not serious."

"Real as you or me. She mistook a bunch of trespassing witches dancing in the woods for faeries."

"A mistake anyone could make," I interjected. "Even me."

"And her 'wee people'?" asked Havermeyer. "Dwarves from a cir-cus?"

"I don't know," said Father, "but I suspect they are every bit as real as her faeries."

"Are you saying you believe she sees them?"

"No," said the gardener. "He's saying he believes that she believes that she sees them. Talks to them, too, apparently, and they to her."

"Martin?" said Father.

"Right here," I said, noticing that the water in my glass was growing murky.

"Remind me to call the sheriff in Hemmet in a few days to make sure she gets there safely. Her Guardian Angel, as always, has his hands full. And now, we must make ready for our night at the 'House of Illu-sions.'"

"Yes indeed," I said, heaving myself from my chair. "My Senior, are you off to 'Peanuts'?"

"In a minute," said Havermeyer, eyeing his plate. "I think perhaps I'll finish what's been placed before me first."

27

"MR. FEENEY!" HOLLERED PIERRE BONTEMPS, straightening his white tie as I lurched into the study. "Just look at you!"

Blood rushed to my head. I knew this from the weight of my ear-lobes as they sagged onto my shoulders and slumped down into my vest pockets.

"White tie," said Joel.

"White waistcoat," nodded Edward.

"Black tailcoat," agreed Jonathan and Arthur.

"You look smashing," declared Pierre.

Okay, I'll admit it: I *felt* smashing. Suddenly, I realized why these gentlemen were so fond of formalwear. Whoever invented it was a genius. Bent and awkward as the male frame may be—and be assured, mine takes the cake in the unwieldy department—the cut of a tuxedo takes whatever a man has, and makes it look a few notches above half decent. On me this was a few notches below passable, but it was a full nine yards beyond anything I'd ever achieved before. Smashing: you bet!

"I agree," said Father, looking me up and down. "But before we go traipsing off to the 'House of Illusions' to show off our handsome gardener, I need to know if you gentlemen learned anything of interest last night."

"Only," said Pierre, "that Sodom and Gomorrah had nothing on the Hollywood nightclub scene."

"Well," said Arthur, "there was that damsel—and I use the word lightly, since I don't think there was an ounce of 'dame' in her—at 'Stogies,' who asked if I was a friend of some chap named Valdemar."

"How did you respond?" asked Father, jaws tense.

"I said, 'What if I am?' And she said—"

"'Then you're a magithun, too?'" interjected Edward, affecting a pronounced lisp. "I jutht a-*dore* magithuns, the way they make thingths go poof! They're jutht too *too*, you know?"

"Too?" asked Father.

Edward shrugged. "Too."

It took me a moment to backtrack and figure out which "too" they were referring to. Got it. It was the one after "magithun." Had to be.

"I got a similar come-on," said Jonathan, buttoning his vest with meticulous fingers, "at 'The Lounge Around.' Something wearing a leather colander approached me and whispered, 'Vamping?' When I asked him-her-it, 'What do you mean?', he-she-it just ran a gloved finger down my cheek—not the one on my face, mind you—and said, 'Any time, honeybunch.'"

"Hm," said Father, face severe. "Perhaps it was a mistake to send you gents into such a den of iniquity."

"There was nothing tempting there," said Pierre, stiffly. "At least, nothing that aroused my interest."

"Well," mumbled Joel, looking around sheepishly, "um—"

"I must admit," said Arthur, cheeks—the ones on his face—glowing, "that some of the images, the apparel or lack thereof, some of what I saw ... well ... let's just say I'm glad I was wearing my trusty scapular. I had to say a lot of Hail Marys and watch a lot of shoes."

"Even some of the shoes," said Joel, cheeks also aglow, "well ... my grandfather, Josef, always says that you can tell much about a person just by glancing at their shoes. If he's right, well ..."

"I see," said Father, pulling a purple stole from one of the mysterious folds of his cassock. "Gentlemen, it's going to be a long night. I find myself in need of a cup of Millie's coffee before we leave. Maybe two. I'll be in the kitchen for the next few minutes, if any of you, uh, want to see me about nothing in particular."

We all looked at each other as he left the room.

I won't mention who followed, one at a time, to partake of a quick cup of coffee and nothing in particular during the next few minutes before our departure. I was too busy trying to tie that infernal tie to notice.

28

"WHAT HAVE WE HERE?" asked the parking valet, slamming down the receiver of one of those "space-egg" pay phones next to his outdoor podium as we piled out of Edward's van in front of the "House of Illusions." As usual, the telephone company's concept of utility phone booths clashed with the environment. This was one place that should have been graced with one of those luxurious crimson closets with leather padding, thick wooden door, and frosted windows.

Out of place or what, that space-egg phone will play a part later on. Stay tuned. But I digress.

"We have seven guests of Miss Hummingbird," said Pierre, adjusting his vest. "All present and accounted for."

"Ah, yes," nodded the valet.

The "House of Illusions" towered above us, five stories high, huddled in Victorian splendor between two huge outcroppings of decomposed granite in the Hollywood Hills. It was a grand place, all wood and stone, draped with ivy, dotted all over with balconies and terraces and cupolas and gargoyles and turrets. I've never seen anything like it this side of a "haunted house" movie. The driveway up to the pillared porch had been long, narrow, and dangerously serpentine. Edward had charged his van up the thing like a wild crusader on a fearless steed. My legs rippled this way and that as I dismounted from the front passenger's seat. Even my cane was snaking as I leaned my weight upon it.

"Well," said the valet, pointing to a sign next to the huge front doors made of solid mahogany, as one of his red-vested gophers hopped into the van and drove it away to the invisible parking lot around the bend. PROPER ATTIRE IS REQUIRED OF ALL MEMBERS AND GUESTS. "I'd say you gentlemen take the prize this evening."

Pierre popped and donned his opera hat in reply. "'Tis a pity to wear this for just the short distance from the coach to the door, but one must observe the amenities."

"In fact," said the valet, pocketing the folded bills handed to him by Edward, "I would say that you have gone above and beyond the call of ..." His eyes went wide as he spied Father Baptist's Roman collar. "... d-d-duh-duty."

I think it's safe to say, given that "proper attire" in Los Angeles has generally come to mean sweatshirts for men and ragged lingerie for women, that six gents in tailcoats surrounding a priest in a cassock was not what the valet expected. Nor did the girl in the silver-sequined blouse seated behind the desk in the entrance foyer.

"M-m-mum-members or guests?" she smacked around a large wad of pink chewing gum.

"Latter of the former," said Pierre. "We are here at the behest of Miss K. Hummingbird, editrix of the *L.A. Artsy.* I am Monsieur Bontemps, a columnist for said journal, and I'm proud to present the venerable Father John Baptist, his noble associate and world-renowned horticulturist, Martin Feeney, along with Messieurs von Derschmidt, Wyndham, Clubb, and Maruppa, all Knights of the Tumblar."

"I see," she said, even though she obviously did not understand. She rolled the pink wad with her tongue a few times as she opened a leather-bound book. "Yes, Miss Hummingbird's name is here with a reservation for seven guests. I see she has already arrived and is within."

She turned to a tall, thin man standing beside her in an outfit much like ours—except his vest was of gold satin—and said, "Competition, Surewood?"

"Hardly," answered the man, doffing his own opera hat. "But I always welcome a challenge."

"Everyone in this town thinks you're a magician," observed Edward, "if you wear a tailcoat."

"The curse of being born in the wrong century," said Pierre, handing his hat to the sequined receptionist. "Please keep this safe for me, my dear."

"The curse of being born in the wrong century," agreed the man in the golden vest.

We all blinked. He had perfectly imitated Pierre's voice and manners, right down to the angle of the wrist as he, too, handed her his hat and said, "Please keep this safe for me, my dear."

"Do I need a claim check?" asked Pierre, eyeing his imitator.

"Naw," she said, placing the hats on a ledge behind her. "I'll remember. I don't think anyone else'll be turning in anything like this."

"Naw," said the imitator, right down to the smack of her gum, "I'll remember. I don't think anyone else'll—"

"Stop it, Surewood," she cried, slapping his hand in dainty indignation.

"Sherwood," said Pierre, turning the name over in his mouth. "As in the famous forest?"

"Almost," said the man. "Imitating voices is just an aside. True to the suspicions of people in this town, I'm a magician. My stage name is spelled S-u-r-e-w-o-o-d F-o-r-s-t. My specialty is 'magic in wood.' Be sure to catch my act in Raimundo's Chamber. I'm on at nine sharp. One thing I like about this job is that I'm done by eleven, and then—swoosh!—I'm off to pursue damsels in various degrees of distress."

"Wouldn't miss it," said Pierre. "Your stage act, I mean. I've never heard of 'wood magic.'"

"'Magic in wood,'" corrected Mr. Forst.

"Quite right," nodded Pierre.

"And now, gentlemen," said the girl with the sequins, "if you'll all be so kind as to face that bookcase behind you."

"The bookcase behind you," mimicked the magician.

"Surewood," she complained around her wad of gum.

Mr. Forst snapped his non-existent gum in reply.

Exchanging glances, we turned and, indeed, found ourselves facing a bookcase. How charming. Dickens, Shakespeare, Poe, King, Stout, Blavatsky, Hemmingway ... an eclectic assortment if there ever was one.

"Now say, 'Open Sesame,'" she instructed.

Feeling a bit weird, we all complied. But lo and behold, the case swung back, revealing a dark, arched stone tunnel.

"Oh," she said, lifting her hand from the secret button behind the counter, "you'll want maps." She scurried out from around the desk in a flash of sequins and handed us each a small, folded map. "This place is so huge, people have gotten lost and—"

"—were never heard from again," Surewood Forst finished her sentence for her.

"Never fear, Madam," said Pierre, pocketing the map. "There is no possibility of such a fate befalling us. Come, gentlemen. I smell an adventure."

The Tumblars charged on ahead, while Father and I strolled more leisurely through the tunnel.

"Be forewarned, who enter here," intoned a ghostly feminine voice from a shadowed alcove to our right, half-way through.

"Danger lurks 'neath every stair," moaned another similarly-gendered voice from an identical dark alcove to our left.

"All who enter must needs take care," added the first voice.

"Not to tarry, but beware," concluded the other voice.

Peering through the gloom, I realized that we had just been addressed by two tall, exquisite creatures, each draped in a flowing, glittering purple djellaba.

> GARDENING TIPS: I don't know if I've ever seen a "djellaba" other than on them, so how do I know that's what they were wearing? I don't, but I found the word in the dictionary the other day and had to use it somewhere.
>
> --M.F.

"And who are you, Scylla and Charybdis?" I asked, noting a glimmer under the nose of the one on the left. A nose ring?

"I am Tamara," said one.

"And I am Marla," said the other.

"We're life-force sentinels," said the one.

"Sort of like 'out-of-body' guards?" I asked.

"Surely you've heard of psychic vampires?" asked the other.

"No," I said, startled by the word "vampire." I looked at them warily. "I can't say that I have."

"We're 'sensitives,'" said the one. "We stand watch against those who would siphon the life-energy of others."

Ah, I thought, that nose ring serves as an antenna, perhaps? The very thought made my own nostrils twitch.

"Most psychic vampires don't even know they're doing it," said the other.

"A nasty habit," I commented, feeling Father's tug on my sleeve. "Catch many?"

"Now and then," they said in unison. "Take care."

"Are you really 'sensitives'?" I asked. "I mean really?"

"It's a job," said the one with the nose ring.

"Father Baptist," I asked as he pulled me along. "'Psychic vampires.' Do you know what they were talking about?"

"Later," said Father. He did not sound amused, or did he?

The tunnel opened into a magnificent bar, and I do mean magnificent: furniture carved of matching dark wood, purple velvet wallpaper on the high walls, gold leaf trim, ornate brass candlesticks gleaming in every nook and cranny. Oil paintings, rich hues abounding and thickly executed, hung on every wall, depicting magicians caught in the act of producing the impossible. Rabbits squirmed out of opera hats, birds fluttered out of empty air, and ladies lazed without protest as enormous saws cut them in half. This gallery alone was worth the price of admission.

Thirty or more members and guests stood idly about, drinks in hand, cigarettes dangling from lips, cigars hooked in fingers, laughing and blabbing in the vague language of social nothingness.
"Aha!" laughed a voice right in front of us.
We looked this way and that, then down.
"Aha!" laughed the short fellow—all of four feet—attired much like the Tumblars and myself in white tie and tailcoat. His height was his most obvious and startling feature, but only at first glance. He leaned forward and said with a foreign accent: "My name is Portifoy, Lucius T., Master of Ceremonies."

> GARDENING TIPS: I just know I'm going to get into
> trouble with my "height-challenged" readers if I
> don't insert a quote from the ol' dictionary here.
> Note the difference between a "dwarf" and a
> "midget":

> > **dwarf** *n* A person of unusually small stature, *esp:* one
> > whose bodily proportions are abnormal.

> > **midg•et** *n* A person of unusually small size, *esp:* one
> > who is physically well-proportioned.

> Therefore, if in the course of my description of
> Mr. Portifoy I use the term "dwarf," it is because
> it applies, not because I wish to destroy my writ-
> ing career (before it starts) by annoying "little
> people" everywhere.
> If I were to couple my portrayal with the word
> "imp"--

> > **imp** *n* 1. A small demon: fiend. 2. A mischievous child.

> --as in "dwarfish imp" or "impish dwarf," then you
> begin to discern my initial impression of the fel-
> low.
>   --M.F.

Yes, Lucius T. Portifoy was a dwarf, and as such was not only short but also malproportioned. His right shoulder was a little higher than his left, and his left leg a tad longer than his right. His fingers were a bit on the stubby side, and his torso seemed a tad crooked. Other than that, he looked anything but normal.

His right eye was pale blue-gray, and his left was larger—not due to dwarfism, but because he had an aquamarine-tinted monocle wedged between his left cheek and eyebrow, magnifying it. His chin was narrow and pointed, and his temples wide and bumpy. The ebb tide of his thinning white hair was accented by the undertow of his pale complexion, and he sported two white, waxed daggers for a mustache.

As I said before, he was attired in formalwear. In addition, he had a black cape with red satin lining draped over his shoulders, clipped under his chin with a gaudy pewter medallion. The letter "B" sparkled prominently in the center of the silvery clasp, highlighted with a crown, and flanked with the words "Phegor" and "Apollos." The whole thing was encircled and entwined with vines, ripe and brimming with fruit that looked like mechanical gears with jagged cogs.

"Did you not hear me?" asked the little imp, blinking back up at us, seemingly perplexed that it took us this long to take him all in. "I said my name is Portifoy, Lucius T., MC for the evening, as well as every other evening." Chortling, he extended a white-gloved hand in greeting.

"Pleased to make your aquain—" began Pierre, extending his own hand, but Mr. Portifoy, Lucius T. suddenly snapped his away.

"The hand," said the little fellow, twirling his mustache—a bit awkwardly, since his fingers were gloved, "it is quicker than the eye, no?"

Pierre, meticulous keeper of social amenities, was not amused.

"Oh ho," said Mr. Portifoy, darting around us this way and that, "what have we here? Six dashing gentlemen, and so appropriately attired and ..." His eyes followed the row of buttons up Father's cassock to his collar. "... Lord have mercy, above and below, stars between, tell me it is not so. You are Pere Jean Baptiste—Father John Baptist, no?"

"I am," said Father, extending his hand, but no hand was offered in reply.

Instead, Portifoy the Impolite MC raised his gloved hand and pointed a white finger straight up. Our eyes ascended to a huge crystal chandelier suspended from the arched ceiling. Suddenly, all the flame-shaped bulbs dimmed, blinked, and went out.

"Hey!" yelped several lounge lizards, rattling their drinks.

"It's not much of a trick, I'll admit," said Mr. Portifoy, pulling a small object from his pocket. "This remote control, it is faulty. See? The lights were supposed to flicker, not go out. I must complain to Monsieur Graves, the Toolmaster."

"Let's have a drink," said Jonathan, edging away.

"You're on," said Edward, falling in beside him.

"By your leave," said Pierre, bowing stiffly and strutting off behind his fellows.

"Pleased," said Arthur and Joel, leaving.

That left Father Baptist and me, staring down at this curious prankster.

"How do you know me?" asked Father. "I don't believe we've met."

"Ah," said Mr. Portifoy, winking. "Everyone from Transylvania to Poughkeepsie knows of the great sleuth, Father Baptist, and his trusted friend, Martin Feeney. Those terrible murders that plagued the archdiocese of Los Angeles this past June."

"You read about it, then."

"Of course, of course. How else? My crystal ball has been on the fritz for years. Newspapers are not as elegant, perhaps, but sometimes they are more practical." Mr. Portifoy hooked his fingers in his vest pockets and rocked on his soles. "Now me, I was rooting for you all the way, you understand. Don't get me wrong. But as for the bishops who fell prey to that Farnsworth woman ..." He shrugged. "I've no use for bishops, myself."

"You're not a Catholic, then," said Father.

"Not a Catholic?" he laughed. "On my word, if you only knew. I'm as 'universal' as they come, but not like you think."

"Oh? How so?"

"This is not a night for thinking, Father John Baptist. It is a night for drinking—from the wells of illusion, of course. Let me not keep you from your friends. You will see me later at the performances, no? We have a wonderful show scheduled this evening, stunning magicians all—well, all but one, but we shall see what we shall see, no? Or rather, it is hoped that you don't see what we don't want you to see." With that, he bounded off and was lost amidst the tangle of skirts and trousers.

"Strange bird," said the gardener.

"Indeed," said Father, turning to the bar. "How about a ginger ale?"

"I thought you'd never ask—oh!" I almost tripped over Mr. Portifoy, Lucius T., who had somehow squirreled his way into my path again.

"Whatever you do," he whispered, "don't be fooled by Elza."

"Who?" I asked.

"Elza."

"Whatever you do," whispered Surewood Forst, who had apparently slipped in beside us. He gave Mr. Portifoy a jolly slap on the back and added in the short fellow's squirrelly voice, "don't be fooled by Elza."

"You again," laughed Mr. Portifoy, popping off his monocle and cleaning it on Surewood's satin vest. "Always ready with your little joke, no?"

"Always ready," said Surewood, again in Portifoy's voice, "with my little joke, yes."

"Oui," corrected Portifoy. "I would say 'oui.'"

"Yes," said Surewood, still affecting Portifoy, "I would say 'yes.'"

"You've met my dear friend," said Mr. Portifoy to Father and me. "Less than a week I've known Mr. Forst, and I'd trust him with my, my, well, I'll think of something cheap and useless. Only his mama knows what he really sounds like. You must catch his act tonight. Would you believe it? He talks to trees."

"In many voices, no doubt," I said.

"Aha," laughed Portifoy. "I can see that you've been 'Forsted,' no?"

"Stop it," complained Surewood, slapping Mr. Portifoy's gloved hand and smacking invisible gum à la the sequined receptionist.

"Who's Elza?" I asked.

"You'll find out—" started Portifoy.

"—and wish you hadn't," finished Surewood Forst as Portifoy.

"Okay," I shrugged. This was getting tiresome. "Sure. And where should I not go so as to avoid—?"

But, as before, Mr. Lucius T. Portifoy had vanished. Surewood Forst had disappeared with him.

"This is going to be a long night," I sighed to Father as we elbowed up to the bar.

"Count on it," said Father, waving to the bartender.

29

"AND THAT'S HOW SHE HIRED ME," laughed Pierre Bontemps, raising his glass to the woman seated beside him at our dinner table. "Gentlemen and Father, I owe it all to my editrix, Kahlúa Hummingbird."

"No one hires Pierre Bontemps," beamed the woman, a crazy tangle of multi-colored feathers spraying from her hair, waving every which way. Did I call her a "woman"? Forgive me. No mere woman was Madam Hummingbird. She was more like a tropical rain forest making a personal appearance. "He permits me to publish his views," she said in deep jungle-drum tones, "but only after banishing every blue pencil in sight."

"Blue is so brash," said Pierre. "It clutters the page and leaves otherwise healthy words broken and bruised."

"I don't get it," said Arthur, scooping up his last piece of cheesecake. "Everyone else who writes for the *Artsy* is either a communist, a feminist, a Zionist, a flipped-out ecologist, a critical-mass quibbler, or a homosexual."

"And me," blinked Miss Hummingbird. "Don't tell anyone, but I'm a Roman Catholic, you know. At least, that's what my momma done told me."

"Oh?" said Arthur.

"They all threatened to bolt when they read Pierre's first submission," said Lady Hummingbird, her Nubian features tensing momentarily. "It was just awful. Talk about wailing and gnashing of teeth—such screeching you couldn't imagine! For one ugly week there, I thought I was going to have to write the whole bloody magazine myself."

"I wouldn't have left you in such a lurch," said Pierre. "I'd have gladly contributed a few articles—for an appropriate fee, of course."

"No doubt," she whispered, back of hand on forehead in dainty dismay.

"So what happened?" asked Joel, cradling his coffee.

She broke into a wide smile. "The clouds suddenly parted. It dawned on me, as if in a vision." She spread her fingers to illustrate.

"This is ripe," chuckled Jonathan.

Her smile went tall as well as wide. "'Who needs 'em?' I cried to myself. 'Who needs you?' I screamed at them all."

"And?" asked Edward and Joel and Arthur and Jonathan.

I sort of just wiggled my nose.

"They buckled under," giggled Madam Hummingbird. "They just flat out went limp and crawled at my feet. Saliva all over my carpet. It was unnerving."

"I'm amazed," said Jonathan, "that you'd risk so much for Pierre—not that I doubt his usefulness or literary skills, mind you, but in the big bad world of business, especially the publishing business—"

"That's why dear Kahlúa is a legend in the industry," beamed Pierre. "I understand the bartender at 'Musso and Frank's' invented a drink in her honor."

"Don't try it," she said, rolling her eyes. "It's disgusting what he added to a shot of Kahlúa."

"Still," persisted Arthur, "it was a risk."

"What can I say?" said the woman, rolling her eyes, "I agree with every word he says. I shouldn't, I daren't, I don't wanna, but he's right. He's absolutely right."

"About what?" asked Joel.

"Why, everything."

"Well," said the gardener. "There is that."

She turned on her elbow and held a glass up to Pierre. "Will you marry me?"

"Can't," said Pierre, hand on heart. "I'm already promised."

"Who's the lucky lady?" she pouted.

"Why—gentlemen?" Everyone rose and lifted their various beverages. "Our Lady, Mary, Queen of Heaven, and Empress of All the Americas."

"To the Empress of All the Americas," we cheered and swallowed.

"I guess I'm outclassed," said Madam Hummingbird.

"So are we all," said Pierre, "next to Her."

"So I don't have a chance?"

"Not one."

"Pooh."

"Gentlemen," said Father, pushing his chair under the table in front of him. "We have a good forty minutes before the show begins, and I for one would like to explore this magnificent manor. If you'll excuse me."

"Me, too," I said, tagging behind him like a faithful gardening terrier.

"See you in Raimundo's Chamber," called Edward, attempting a suave Christopher Lee, but sounding more like Peter Lorre.

"So where to?" I asked.

"Anywhere," said Father. "I just need to stretch my legs."

30

ONE COULD INDEED GET LOST in the maze of corridors at the "House of Illusions." Some went up, some went down. Some spiraled all over the place and came to dead ends. We passed curtained chambers where fortunetellers made lugubrious love to crystal balls, scrutinized sweaty palms, or droned their monotonal mantras as silver pendulums drew maniacal patterns on platters of fine sand. All the while, clusters of anxious patrons held their breath in enthused anticipation. It would have felt like a carnival, except it lacked the amplitude. Instead of nasal-impaired barkers there were whispering mesmerizers; confused or relieved applause instead of wild cheers; dark, moody wallpaper instead of pale, soaring canvas; low-burning candles instead of fireworks displays. In short, it smelled of mothballs instead of popcorn, and that made all the difference.

In one dimly lit alcove we spied a skeletal man in a loincloth boring a cobra into submission with a five-note Dorian ditty on his zenomorphic oboe. Here and there, at almost every turn, nervous young fakirs attempted to amaze passersby with playing cards that danced on their fingernails or dollar bills that seemed to come alive and crawl up their sleeves like Federal Reserve caterpillars.

Mimics abounded who could, after a few moments of idle conversation, confuse married patrons by parroting their inflections and mannerisms on the spot, instigating arguments by speaking to them in each other's voices.

"A dangerous talent," commented Father.

"Cruel," added the gardener, "but amusing."

We passed a young blonde woman whose attention was riveted on a penny floating between a novice magician's outstretched hands. Suddenly the coin jumped as if flicked by an invisible finger. It dinged her on the forehead, then fell down the front of her dress.

"Everyone has to start somewhere," I assured her, then added under my breath, "Whoa, what a dress." Though it was a tight fit, her outline was obscured by the wavering optic anomaly created by the dance of tiny fluorescent-yellow figure-eights all over a black-light stimulated red background, giving her that "mutated strawberry" look.

"But why with me?" she grimaced, digging around for the coin. "And thanks, I'm sure."

And so went the subtle carnival—the ping of projectile quarters instead of human cannon balls, the sleight of hand instead of the pie in the face. Throughout, no one seemed more surprised and delighted by the results of their prestidigitation than the magicians themselves.

My sense of adventure piqued when Father and I came upon a thickly-draped chamber with an ornate brass plaque above the door:

ELZA'S SITTING ROOM
∞ ASK HER TO PLAY YOUR FAVORITE SONG FOR YOU ∞
∞ DON'T BE ANNOYED IF SHE DOESN'T KNOW ANY CURRENT TUNES ∞
∞ AFTER ALL, SHE DIED IN 1932 ∞

Anyone that Mr. Portifoy, Lucius T. cautioned me about, I wanted to meet.

Of course, it also occurred to me that, human nature being what it is, Mr. Portifoy might have warned me precisely to insure that I would seek her out. Hmm.

Whatever, Father expressed no reluctance, so in we went.

It was a remarkable room for several reasons. First: it was really much more than a sitting room, large and vaulted as it was, with a full bar at the far end. Second: it was more of a piano room, complete with a gaudy baby grand in the corner, flanked on two sides by huge mirrors. Third: though someone was playing the piano, whoever it was wasn't there. Really. The keys went up and down, the notes jangled gaily, but no one was seated on the bench. Fourth: Pierre had beaten us. He was standing, champagne in hand, one elbow resting on the edge of the piano. I looked around for the other Tumblars, but apparently Pierre was doing this act solo.

"Bravo, bravo," he cheered as a clever reduction of Tchaikovsky's First ended on a resounding chord. A flowerpot full of fresh daisies next to the empty music rack settled down as the cadence died out. "That was splendid, my dear. Now, could you favor us with something simpler, closer to the bone, as it were, say, 'The Soul Cakes Song'?"

The keys winked with three happy notes, as if to say, "You betcha!" then rolled an arpeggio to establish the key.

"Soul cakes, soul cakes," sang along Pierre gleefully, "Meat nor drink nor money have I none." He waved his arm, inviting other guests to join in, but they didn't know the words. "Still I will be merry any how ..."

"I think I'll sit this one out," said the gardener, wading through a gaggle of giggling ladies and approaching the bar.

Father apparently preferred standing around the center of the room, stretching his legs, intimidating everyone with his collar.

"Barkeeper," I said, heaving myself up onto a stool, "a ginger ale on ice, if you please."

"Sure," said the guy behind the immaculate counter made of hand-carved maple. "Are you particular about brands?"

"Saint Thomas, Salisbury. 'Blue label' if you have it."

"Sure," said the barkeeper. "This is the 'House of Illusions.' We got everything, or we'll make you think we do."

"My, my," said a lumpy fellow slouched on the stool next to mine. "A man who knows his ginger ale."

I turned and looked into a pair of sagging eyes, wondering if I was as out of focus to him as he was to me. "It's all I drink," I explained. "Well, water and coffee on special occasions. And since virtually every day on the Catholic calendar is some Saint's feast day, I guess I've imbibed my share."

"Good for you," he said, wavering slightly. "We don't get many teetotalers in here."

I stiffened. "I am not a teetotaler. Teetotalling is a filthy Puritan notion—"

"Sure, Bub," he waved me silent. It was a funny wave, too, because his hand stayed put while the rest of him zigzagged all over the place. "Hey Bart, put this man's drink on my tab."

"Sure, Buzz," said the bartender, shoving a tall glass in my direction. "Anything you say."

"Buzz?" I said, swiveling on my stool. "Buzz Sawr?"

"You've heard of me?"

"By reputation, of course."

"Hmph." He didn't seem impressed. "I'm the piano player here—the one and only. What kind of a reputation is that?"

"The one and only? Who's playing now?"

"Nobody."

"Nobody? You're—? I mean, you're sitting here, and—?"

"Elza's spelling me," he said, pointing vaguely in the direction of the piano. "She loves to show off."

"One for Peter, two for Paul," Pierre was singing. "Three for Him who made us all ..."

"I don't follow you," I said.

"Few do, Bub. And few would want to."

"I figured someone's behind the mirrors. That is two-way glass, isn't it, around the piano?"

"Yeah," he burped. "There's another keyboard on the other side, and it controls the piano in here. Electric relays or something, and there's a microphone in the flowerpot so I can hear requests. It's really me back there plunking the keys, night after night. Nobody's fooled, except like now."

"Why now? Isn't Elza behind the mirror, spelling you?"

"Nope," he said, hefting his glass and taking a long swig. "Elza's in here with us, sitting at the piano as we speak."

I looked over to the keys, merrily going up and down, up and down.

"There's nobody at the piano," I observed uselessly.

"Nobody," he smiled. "No—body. Get it? She's a ghost."

"You're joking."

"I joke about many things, Bub: my 'ex,' politicians, Slovaks, and the fat guy in the apartment next door. But not about Elza. She's real, and she's sitting right there."

"You're serious? Bart, is he serious?"

Bart shrugged, wiping a glass with a towel. "He says he's serious. Who am I to argue?"

"Elza Maplewood Roundhead died at the age of twenty-two," said Buzz, swirling the ice cubes in his drink. "She was a Depression babe: pretty, flirty, and flighty from all accounts. Giggled from dawn to dusk. Not a mean bone in her body, and not a serious bulb in her head, either. Drove men wild, betrothed a dozen times, but never got hitched. Floored the clutch but never engaged the gears. You get the picture. Tripped and fell down a flight of stairs, just down the hall." He grimaced as something he swallowed went down wrong. "Broken neck. 1932. Way before I was born, but—hooboy!—there she sits, as alive as you or me, except she ain't."

"Roundhead," I whispered. "Roundhead. Of course, I remember the name. Themolina Hubbard, the Roundhead Manhole Covers heiress—"

"Was her sister. This mansion used to be owned by the Roundhead family. They were rich even then, pompous, industrious, powerful—"

"And Catholic," I interjected. "I seem to recall that Themolina willed the Del Agua estate downtown to the Church."

"Sure," he shrugged. "Whatever."

"And you say Elza—*the* Elza—is playing the piano right now?"

"I say it because it's true. I could take you back behind the mirrors and show you that no one's there, but then you'd still say it's just a trick, so I won't bother."

"Actually I would like to see—"

"Buzz," warned the bartender. "You know it's against the rules."

"Sure," said Buzz, rubbing his swollen nose. "I was just going at the mouth. Don't mind me, don't mind nothing. To those who believe, no proof is necessary. To those who don't—phooey!"

I may not be smart, but I'm not gullible. The funny thing was, between the coarse, weary honesty I perceived in Buzz Sawr's bloodshot eyes, and something somehow riveting yet melancholy in the twiddling of the piano keys, I found myself believing him.

"But if she died a Catholic," I was saying to no one in particular, even though I'm sure Bart and Buzz overheard me, "and if she's haunting this place, then ... Excuse me, gentlemen. Buzz, thanks for the drink."

"My pleasure."

"Bravo, bravo," Pierre was saying to the empty piano bench. "We do make a fair team, don't we?"

The keys played four flat dissonants, as if to say, "Guess again, pal."

"Well I think you sing marvelously," husked a pear-shaped woman in a squeaky-tight plastic blue thingie, squeegeeing up to Pierre. The pear in question, I might mention, was balanced on its stem end, and the stem was jammed into a pair of excruciatingly steep high heels. "What stylish clothes, such bravura. My name is Babbette. Are you a magician?"

"No," said Pierre, flexing his fingers. "But in a former life I was known as Mammamodes the Mammomancer."

"Really," she said, bursting at the seams. "Would you—you know—tell my fortune?"

"Alas," he said, setting down his glass. "That was in a former life."

"Oooh," said another pear, this one in red, much squeakier and tighter, "I just love former lives."

"Never had one, Madam," said Pierre without missing a beat. "I wouldn't know."

"Don't be coy," said the squeaky red. "My name is Nannette."

"Friends?" asked Pierre, glancing between the two.

"Competitors," they said together. It sounded a wee bit like "predators," even though they began to giggle.

"Wouldn't you like to join me on the love seat?" asked Babbette, rolling her shoulders.

"Or me?" asked Nannette, rolling her hips.

"Sorry," said Pierre, rolling his lips. "I'm afraid I'm already taken. If you will excuse me, Madam and Madam, my companions and I must keep an appointment."

Pierre always seemed to leave women pouting. It was a knack.

"A question," I was saying in Father's ear as Pierre spotted us. "Doesn't the Church teach that when a Catholic dies, they either go to Heaven, Hell, or Purgatory—one of those three options, period, end of story?"

"Of course," nodded Father, always the patient theologian.

"A ghost, then," I continued as Pierre grabbed us and herded us toward the door, "what is it?"

"Why?"

"Humor me."

"You're sure you're not asking me about apparitions from Heaven like Our Lady's appearances at Fatima or Lourdes, which would fall into an entirely different category?"

"No, this would be a bona fide earth-bound ghost."

"You don't mean Elza," scoffed Pierre, patting us along. "You know she's just a trick."

"I'm asking about a real ghost," I persisted.

"Well," said Father, "the Saints have told us that a ghost is one of three possibilities. First, it may be a soul in Purgatory who has been allowed to visit the living in order to provide guidance, comfort, or aid, thereby expiating their temporal punishment in some way. I can refer you to many examples when we get home and have access to the books in the study. Second, it may be a soul consigned to Hell, damned for all time."

"Hm. And third, Father?"

"The final alternative is that it may be a demon imitating the deceased person, wherever they may truly be, in order to confuse or demoralize the living. Why do you ask?"

"Oh nothing," I said as we approached the entrance to Raimundo's Chamber. A line of maybe twenty people was waiting to get in. "Nothing at all."

A cardboard sign was propped on a nearby easel:

TONIGHT!

⇑ ⇑ ⇑

THE HOUSE OF ILLUSIONS' RAIMUNDO'S CHAMBER
IS PROUD TO PRESENT:

⇑⇑⇑

⇑ THE SCISSORS SISTERS ⇑
⇑ BUCKY BUCKLE AND HIS PRESTIDIGITATIVE DENTIFRICE ⇑
⇑ REGINOLD THE REITERATOR ⇑
AND
⇑ SUREWOOD FORST'S "MAGIC IN WOOD" ⇑

⇑

WITH

⇑⇑⇑

MASTER OF CEREMONIES:
⇑ LUCIUS T. PORTIFOY ⇑

⇑⇑⇑

"Minutes to spare," sighed Pierre.

"Excuse me, Saws," interrupted a huge man in butler attire as we trotted down the orange and brown carpeted hall—if you can call my awkward lurching a "trot."

"Yes?" asked Father.

The man was as tall as me standing on Millie's kitchen stool, and wide as me sprawled on the floor after falling off, and thick as the skillet Millie often used to put me in that position. The set of his chiseled chin was so high that his mackerel eyes were perpetually looking down on everyone. His right hand was raised so that his palm was even with his nose, fingers extended ceilingward. Resting on top of this delicate, dexterous pentopod was a small silver dish. If I'd been standing atop Millie's stool I might have thought to leap up and see what was in it, but I wasn't so I couldn't so I didn't.

"Got us wrong," I said, hooking my thumb over my shoulder. "Sawr's back in Elza's Sitting Room, sitting this one out."

"You misunderstand me, Saw," said the butler. "You aw Mr. Feeney, aw you not? Awnd this must needs be Fawthaw Jawn Bawptist."

"Yes," said Father.

"At yaw service, Fawthaw awnd Saw," he said with two short, dignified bows, from which his eyes never stopped looking down at us. "My name is Reginold, but thawt's of no cawnsequence. I hawv been instructed to present the two of you with an invitation to meet privately on the Fawrquawr Terrace for awfter-show drinks awnd cawnversation."

"Really," said Father. "And who has extended this invitation?"

"I cawn't say, Fawthaw. I awm just a messenjaw."

"Darn big messenger," I mumbled.

"The invitation was left at the frawnt desk," said Reginold, lowering the platter, revealing a gold-fringed envelope resting in its center. "A mawp haws been supplied for yaw convenyawnce."

"What about me?" asked Pierre. "What about the rest of us?"

"The invitor haws specified the desire for privacy," said Reginold. "If you will excuse me." With another stately bow, he turned and "awmbled" away.

"What do you make of that?" I puffed as we resumed our "trot."

"I don't know," said Father, stuffing the envelope into the folds of his cassock. "But we'll find out."

We did—but first, Raimundo's Chamber.

31

"FAAAAAAAAAAR OUT," DECLARED KAHLÚA HUMMINGBIRD as a flash of blinding light erupted in the center of the small stage. Thick ropes of lava-red curtains waved as the blast of heat rippled outward.

We were seated roughly halfway back in a pond of comfortable armchairs, arranged in widening semicircles around the platform. Father Baptist was on my right, and Madam Hummingbird was on my left. Her feathers brushed my face with every jiggle of her head, coaxing me to sneeze. Worse than incense. Pierre, in the chair beyond her, was clapping wildly.

The audience ooohed as Lucius T. Portifoy emerged from the billowing smoke, adjusting his monocle.

"Aha!" he barked, then broke into a fit of coughs. "Such smoke, such smoke. There should be a law."

The audience chuckled good-naturedly.

"For those of you who are regulars, for whom my face is unfamiliar, and for you who are guests, for whom I am of course also a new face, allow me to introduce myself. I am—drum roll please." A snare drum seemed to materialize out of thin air above his head, along with two sticks that proceeded to strafe the same in a dramatic crescendo. "I am ..." Mr. Portifoy looked up at the drum, which continued its raucous banter. "I am ..." The pattering continued. "Enough!"

The sticks fell and clattered onto the stage. They rolled until Mr. Portifoy stomped on them with his foot.

"Timing is everything," winked Mr. Portifoy. "Unfortunately, ahem—" He spoke out of the side of his mouth, throwing his voice toward someone off stage. "—someone was reading comic books during the rehearsal."

With that, the drum dropped right onto his head, flattening his opera hat, and tumbled sideways onto the floor.

The audience laughed and clapped.

"This," said Mr. Portifoy, popping out his hat, "is precisely why I am an MC, and not a magician." He pulled up his sleeves with his gloved hands. "See? Nothing. In any case, my name is Lucius T. Portifoy, as fresh an addition to this marvelous 'House of Illusions' as, as ..."

A three-foot rattle appeared above his head and began to shake.

"... ah! I have it! A new-born baby." Sheepishly, he shimmied a few feet to the right, out from under the Rattle of Damocles. As the audience burst into giggles, the rattle began to follow him. "My father told me there would be nights like this. He wanted me to be a nurse."

The rattle suddenly vanished.

"Aha!" he exclaimed. "Safe for the moment. Now let me see, I should tell you about our first act. I have it written down here ..." He reached into his pocket and pulled out a piece of paper. He pulled and pulled, and the narrow sheet of paper kept coming and coming. Soon his feet were buried in a growing pile of curlicued ribbon. "Oui," he said, examining something on the paper. "No, that's not it." He continued to pull the paper from his pocket. "Ah, pound butter, loaf bread, can corned beef hash. No, that's still not it." He stumbled to his left, dragging the pile of paper with him. "Hold on, hold on. I know it's here somewhere." As he continued to stumble, the paper straggled out behind him, thinning into a long, winding snake.

Just as he reached the far right of the stage, a large match materialized in the air above the tail of the paper trail. The match head burst into flame. Portifoy's eyes went wide as it gently lowered itself and touched the end of the paper ribbon. It sparked into hissing flame like a fuse.

"Ah," he said hurriedly. "Here it is. Our first act is the Scissors Sisters. They are a couple of real cut-ups." The fuse was burning brightly, the flame coming nearer and nearer. "I understand they are—how do you say?—on the cutting edge of, of ..." The flame reached the wads tangled around his feet. "Phooey! I'll be back!" he cried, exploding into a flash of light and smoke.

The audience cheered as the lights dimmed on the vacant stage.

"Bravo," cried Pierre.

"Faaaaaar out," laughed Madam Hummingbird, feathers jabbing my eyes.

"I still don't like that twerp," huffed yours truly, arms folded on his chest.

"Patience," said Father. "Charity."

"Okay," I said, taking in a deep breath and letting it out in a long, slow whisper. "I shall enhance my calm, fill my consciousness with serenity and equanimity, readjust my face into the very visage of loving kindness, and take all the time in the world to patiently dislike that twerp."

"It's all done with mirrors," intruded a couple of voices between Father and me. We turned and saw none other than the faces of Lieutenant Taper and Sergeant Wickes, leaning forward from the row behind us.

"Oh?" said Father. "You're sure of that?"

"No," said Wickes, "but it's what you're supposed to say, isn't it?"

"What are you guys doing here?" asked the gardener as a couple of Korean girls waddled out onto the stage in slinky green kimonos, slender surgical scissors poised in each hand.

"Keeping an eye on you two," said Taper. "We wouldn't want anything to happen to our favorite part-time sleuths in this madhouse."

"Welcome aboard," said Father.

"You guys didn't happen to come here in a Volkswagen, did you?" winked Wickes.

"No," I said. "Why?"

"One of your neighbors," said the sergeant, looking at his notebook, "a Mrs. Helga Feuchtwanger, has reported her VW missing every night this week."

"I know that name," I said. "Don't tell me: every morning, after she's ripped the ears off the poor clerk who answers the police phones, her car's parked right where it's supposed to be."

"How'd you know?" asked Taper.

"She spoke to us the other morning," said Father. "She lives a couple of houses down across the alley. How is it that her complaint ends up in your laps?"

"It doesn't," laughed Taper. "But as you know, our terminals are all connected to the same network, and whenever any crime is reported to any department, the computers cross-reference all the data by name, neighborhood, crime, and whatever. Mrs. Feuchtwanger's complaint wound up on my screen when I came to work this morning because she lives close to you."

"Just thought we'd ask," chuckled Wickes.

"I've got a question of my own," I said, vertebrae cracking as I looked further over my shoulder. "How'd you guys get in here?"

"We had passes," said Taper, flashing his badge.

"Is that how you guys get in to see all the shows in town?" I asked.

"Just the best ones," smiled Wickes.

"We must have crossed wires this morning, Jack," said Taper. "Where were you? We called the rectory, but Millie didn't know where you'd wandered off to. Didn't you want to check out the rest of the apartments?"

"I was pursuing a couple of hunches," said Father.

"Find something?" asked Wickes.

"Indeed," said Father. "We'll talk later."

"How much later?" asked Taper.

"Much," said Father, turning back to watch the girls on stage as they proceeded to cut up little pieces of yellow tissue paper that sprouted into bigger pieces of red and green paper which sprouted into still bigger pieces of rainbow paper—much to the glee and fascination of the audience.

Before the Scissors Sisters were through, several men in the audience were wearing floppy crêpe paper crowns, and the stage was cluttered with giant origami dragons and lions and even a papier-mâché mock-up of the Statue of Liberty.

Oh my. It's amazing what they can do with mirrors.

As the girls ran off to the right, Mr. Portifoy came shuffling in from the left, shoving a huge push-broom. "They don't pay me enough for this," he said, taking out a large silk handkerchief and mopping his brow. "And, I think, you've paid far too much to be bothered by this next act. The manager says if he doesn't get it right this time—" He ran a finger across his neck with an air of brutal finality. The audience laughed accordingly. "So, with no further adieu, prepare to be lulled to sleep by Bucky Buckle and his Prestidigital Dentifrice."

Mr. Portifoy meandered off to the right, and a lanky fellow sauntered in from the left. He was wearing a pale-blue smock, reminiscent of the garb worn by Dr. Kaylan Volman, our "in lieu of" parish dentist and resident sadist. He even had one of those disposable face filters that dental professionals are so fond of these days, hanging limply around his neck.

"Bucky Buckle," I whispered. "Thurgood T. Turnbuckle's son."

"Buckminster," said Father. "I told Mr. Turnbuckle I'd try to have a talk with him tonight."

"I remember," remembered the gardener, then observed, "He doesn't look happy."

"That intro wasn't meant to be funny."

"I bet you don't think there's much to laugh at about a dentist's office," said Bucky, his thin voice cracking slightly. "I'm here to want to show you otherwise."

Someone in the audience coughed.

"Bad grammar," said the gardener.

"Pathetic delivery," said Father, leaning forward, eyes intent on the lad. "This does not bode well."

"Take this ordinary tube of toothpaste," said Bucky, holding up an ordinary tube of toothpaste. "Now just imagine—" Something went sprong in his hand, apparently a moment too soon, because his eyes went wide. The thing had suddenly erupted, morphing instantly into a set of chattering plastic teeth. The wind-up jaws rocked on the edge of his palm, teetered, jumped, flipped, and, in spite of Bucky's furiously flailing hands, fell to the floor. Two bicuspids broke off and skittered across the hardwood. "I, um, that is ..."

"Whoops," called a voice from the audience.

"Cheap trick," drawled another.

"Somebody should practice," snickered another.

"That's right," rasped Bucky, voice cracking three times on two words. "We all need practice ..." He began fumbling frantically for something in his pocket. "... with, with ..." His hand jerked into view, fingers snagged in knots of fine white twine. Waxed, probably, but hopelessly tangled. "... d-d-duh-dental floss!"

"Hopeless," sighed Father, falling back in his chair.

"Pretty lame," yelled someone in the rear.

"Go hang yourself with it," scoffed someone in front.

"Of ... of course," said Bucky, raising a parental finger, "if you, um, if you don't floss, you know what will happen." The line would have worked better if his finger hadn't been shaking and his larynx convulsing.

The next thing—him spitting out a fake tooth to punctuate each word in the phrase "you know what will happen"—would have worked, too, if he hadn't taken a little half-breath after "will" so he could really emphasize "happen." He sucked the last tooth down his windpipe. His eyes went wide, his lips went one way, his lower jaw the other, until finally he gave himself a sort of mini-Heimlich maneuver. With a disgusting noise that sounded like "Hork!" the thing popped out.

Even that might have been funny, except for two things: first, the audience didn't know if he was fake-choking or real-choking, which left them uncertain how to react; and second, the first and third teeth in the series hit a man and a woman in the face, and neither found it amusing.

"For this we paid?" cried a bearded fellow in the second row.

"Get out of here," called a woman in the back.

"Rorrer," snarled a husband and wife off to the side.

"Rorr-rarr-rorr-rarr-rarr," rumbled the audience like an old car engine turning over but not catching.

"I, um ..." Bucky's shoulders sagged. He was experiencing what was known in the entertainment trade as "dying."

"Dour" and "crotchety" as I may be—and let us not forget "grim"—I felt miserable for the lad.

"What did I tell you?" huffed Mr. Portifoy, stomping out from behind the right curtain. His white glove blazed in the spotlight as he drew a sinister finger across his neck again. He turned his gaze on poor Bucky. "Off with you! Go give someone else a toothache with your silly drills."

His posture crushed with shame, Bucky withdrew from the spotlight and shuffled off the stage.

"The management apologizes," said Mr. Portifoy, kicking the snapping jaws with his foot. "In every act a little pain must fall. But as they say, 'No pain, no gain.' Again and again they say it. I don't know why they say this, but they do."

The audience was having trouble getting jump-started again.

"Ah," said Portifoy, pulling a dime from his vest pocket. "I remember once reading in *Mad* magazine—you all remember that little imp, Alfred E. Neuman, do you not?—that you can take a coin, so, and put it under a handkerchief, so, and—voilà!—you have two coins. I know, it's too small for you to see, but the instructions said to bend the coin in half and hold it edge-on between your thumb and forefinger—so—and it looks like you're holding two coins together, when it is really one bent in half."

"It looked better in the magazine," said someone in the audience.

"True," said Mr. Portifoy, tossing the coin into the air. It was obviously bent in half. "But then, I'm not really a magician. I'm the MC, remember? Speaking of which, let's move on to the next act. And this guy—and boy is he a big guy—is no—what do you say?—he's no slouch. May I present, Reginold the Reiterator."

The somewhat-revived audience managed to heave a half-hearted welcome as the butler we'd encountered shortly before came strutting out onto the stage, still holding that silver platter on the tips of his fingers.

I can't tell you what Reginold "reiterated," because just then Father Baptist grabbed my arm. "I'm needed," he whispered sternly. "Backstage."

32

"YOU CANNOT COME BACK HERE, NO!" huffed Lucius T. Portifoy around the edge of the door marked MAGICIANS, ASSISTANTS, AND STAGE CREW ONLY. "Go away."

"We need to speak with Bucky Buckle," said Father.

"It's urgent," I said beside him.

"Rules of the house," said Mr. Portifoy, looking up at us with eyes that seemed to get nearer and farther, like a telescopic image going in and out of focus. "Not without the manager's permission."

"Got it," said Lieutenant Taper, who had followed Father and me out of the theater. He pushed a leather folder between our shoulders and flipped it open. "Let us in."

"Ah," said Mr. Portifoy, eyeing Taper's badge. "We at the 'House of Illusions' are only too happy to cooperate with—how do you say?—"

"The police," suggested Wickes.

"The very word," said Portifoy, stepping back magnanimously, swinging the door with him, "I was looking for it. It must have slipped under my tongue."

"Which way to Mr. Buckle's room?" asked Father sternly.

"Third door on your right," nodded Portifoy, bowing as we passed. "On second thought, Father John Baptist, perhaps the poor man could use your unique services."

"No thanks to you," I quipped.

"You sir," said Portifoy, raising a gloved finger in my direction, "should not be so quick to judge. You do not know the ... the whole story."

"Skip it," I said, following Father and Taper and Wickes down the narrow hall. The floorboards groaned with every step.

"This must be it," said Father. He raised his hand to knock, but realized the door was partly open.

"Mr. Buckle?" said Taper, pushing the door further into the room. "Empty. He's not here."

Father stepped into the cramped cubicle, all of eight feet square. The dressing table took up almost half of it. The rest was piled with strange, warped allusions to the dental profession: oversized picks, super-oversized toothbrushes with dagger-like bristles, menacing drills and syringes, mouthwash samples, and the like.

"What do you want to talk to him about, Jack?" asked Taper, hands on hips.

"Nothing to do with this case," said Father. "I promised his father I'd have a word with him. I wish I'd spotted him earlier in the evening."

"Timing is everything," said the gardener.

"Quite right," said Mr. Portifoy from the doorway. "And I will miss my cue if I do not hurry. Are you gentlemen leaving, or must I call—how do you say?—the authorities?"

"We are the police," said Wickes sourly. "Remember?"

"I remember everything," said Portifoy, mustache twitching. "But you have no search warrant. I allowed you back here as a courtesy, but I cannot leave you unattended. Magicians, as you surely know, are jealous of their secrets. I must ask you to leave now."

"I'll keep an eye on them," said Father. "Surely you can trust me."

"I trust no one," said Portifoy.

"Neither do we," said Taper. "You have my assurance that we will not disturb anything, or steal anyone's secrets."

"We shall see," sniffed the twerp, turning on his heels. "This matter is not settled."

"Hurry," I shooed, fluttering my fingers at him, "you'll miss your cue."

"See that you don't miss yours," snorted Portifoy, and was gone.

"What do you suppose he meant by that?" I asked no one in particular.

No one in particular answered, either.

"So what now, Jack?" asked Taper.

"You gentlemen should leave," whispered Father. "Mr. Portifoy is correct: you don't have a warrant."

"What about you, Jack?" asked Taper.

"Me?" smiled Father. "I don't need one. I've no license to revoke."

"Slim argument," said Wickes. "No judge would buy it."

"I'll take the risk," said Father. "Besides, I've no possible interest whatsoever in the secrets of parlor magicians, not when you consider the brand of High Magick I perform every day as a matter of routine."

"He's getting lofty again," said Wickes to Taper.

"Thinks he lives in a Tolkien novel," agreed Taper to me.

"Great shades of Gandalf the Grey," agreed the gardener to them both, completing the rehearsed ritual.

"We should be so lucky," said Father, smiling mysteriously.

"What are you looking for?" asked Taper.

"Toothpaste," said Father. "Surely even magicians brush their teeth."

"He's back down to earth," observed the gardener.

"I don't like it," said Taper. "Jack—"

But Father had stepped out of the room, and was heading down the creaky hallway, deeper into the maze of dressing rooms behind Raimundo's Chamber.

33

"I'M BEGINNING TO THINK THIS WAS A MISTAKE."

"Why?" asked Father.

"Well," I said, leaning back in the uncomfortable wrought-iron chair—at least, I think it was wrought-iron. For all I knew there was just a pipe cleaner under all those thick clotted layers of flat-black outdoor paint. Whatever the chair was make of, it was as unforgiving as Millie's temperament. "We've been sitting out here on the Farquar Terrace for almost half an hour, waiting to be graced with 'awfter-show drinks awnd cawnversation,' but nobody's shown up."

"Patience, Martin," said Father, fingering the rim of his almost-empty coffee cup. The swill in the bottom had grown cold. "It's not so bad out here. Consider the stars."

"What stars? Those clouds have been hanging over our heads for days. I haven't seen the sun, let alone the stars, since Tuesday morning."

"Just because you can't see them," said Father, "doesn't mean they're not there."

"You're getting lofty again," I mumbled, setting down my drink on the little round table.

The Farquar Terrace was just that, a terrace constructed mainly of granite stones with marble banisters and handrails around the rim. It jutted out from the rear of the towering building like an extended lip, as if the "House" were pouting at the mountains to the north.

It was a quiet place, isolated from the din within. No windows looked out upon it—at least, not on this level. Several overlooked it from the floors above, but they were dark. Offices, probably. Below there was supposed to be a garden, but it wasn't illuminated—it was nice to know, but so what if you couldn't see it? This terrace could only be accessed by means of a stairway that began on the east side of the fourth floor and wound its way down around the corner to this level.

A bronze plaque bolted to the marble handrail explained that this area had been set aside as a "Magic-Free Zone"—a place where guests could flee when they'd had enough of the rampant trickery and unrelenting pranksters inside. None of the roaming prestidigitators were permitted to set foot out here. "No cards, no props, no blinding flashes, no tablecloths swept away from under your plates," the sign promised. In other words, it was a boring place that few sought. Just us, as it turned out. And of course, since so few guests chose to partake of the solitude, neither did the tip-seeking waiters. If you wanted refreshments, you had to fetch them yourself.

Put this all together and you can see why Father and I were very much alone, sipping the stale fluids we had brought with us.

"Errrrgh," I mumbled. "This humidity. My skin's all crawly and tingly. How can you stand it, Father, in that cassock? At least there's air conditioning inside."

"Patience," reminded Father. "You're obviously not used to formalwear. Offer it up for the souls in Purgatory; or if patience is beyond you, take enjoyment from the crickets."

"Sure," I said, "the children of the night, what music they make."

"Speaking of Purgatory, why were you asking about ghosts?"

"Oh, that. It's just that ... naw, I'll save it for another time. You'll think I'm being weird."

"I've never thought otherwise," smiled Father. "How boring life at St. Philomena's would be if I had a normal gardener who's only character trait was horticultural diligence—?" His jaw went rigid. "Martin, listen."

"What is it?"

"It's what isn't. The crickets—"

I listened. "They've stopped."

"Shhhhhh."

The crickets, indeed, had ceased their melodies.

"Father—"

"Shhhhhh."

"Father, it's getting cold. Do you feel it?"

"Yes. Be still."

I tried, but something else was happening.

GARDENING TIPS: It's hard to describe now, as I sit in front of Dad's portable Underwood, clickety-clacking the stiff, unyielding keys in the cozy warmth and comfort of my room at the rectory, but at that moment on the terrace, my skin began to tingle like crazy.

--M.F.

"Stop scratching," said Father. "I'm trying to listen."

"I'm itchy," I explained. "All over."

"Martin."

"Yes, Father."

"For what it's worth, my skin is prickling, too." He set down his cup and examined his hands. "I've never felt anything like it."

"Don't look now," I said, setting down my ginger ale—well, it was really just a few tasteless cubes of melting ice by that time, "but there's a fog rolling in."

Father turned in his chair and looked around. "Indeed, Martin. This is most peculiar."

"Peculiar" was his word. The one on the tip of my tongue was "eerie." Waves of dense mist were billowing up around the rim of the terrace. At the same time, rivulets of ghostly white fog were trickling down the ivy-covered walls of the "House," pooling as they encountered the flat stones of the terrace, then swelling gently outward, flowing around our feet. In a matter of moments we were sitting in the middle of a cloud.

"It's freezing," I shivered, burying my hands in my pockets.

"Indeed," agreed Father, shifting inside his cassock. "It would seem that this is no longer a 'magic-free zone.' Martin, our drinks."

I'm glad he saw it first, otherwise I might have thought I was hallucinating. His coffee cup began trembling in its saucer, while the ice in my tall glass began rolling and tumbling. Then—and I kid you not—both the saucer and the glass began to move slowly across the tabletop, all by themselves. As they approached the edge, they hedged, did a few slow circles, and began going back the other way.

"F-f-fuh-Father," I stuttered, "m-m-muh-maybe we should just sort of, you know, high-tail it back inside."

"Too late," said Father, rising to his feet. "Look."

I didn't want to, but my eyeballs had minds of their own. I was painfully aware that there wasn't a drop of alcohol in my system.

Two small red lights appeared about twenty feet beyond the railing of the balcony. Since the balcony was on the third floor, you can imagine how high off the ground they had to be. The lights burned like coals, hot and steady. They began drifting slowly closer.

"F-f-fuh-Father," I whispered, playing with the bulge of the brown scapular under my shirt as I struggled slowly to my feet beside him.

"Steady, Martin," he said, placing his hand firmly on my trembling arm. "Think of your Guardian Angel, and pray."

"O Angel Guardian," I breathed softly in the words of St. Anselm as a dark shape began to coalesce around the burning coals, resolving them into gleaming eyes, "to whom God has entrusted me, I pray thee watch over me unceasingly ..."

The silhouette in the mist became vaguely human, but wavering, as if a large flapping cape was draped from its shoulders. The face, except for the piercing eyes, was shrouded in shadow.

"... protect me, visit me, defend me against every attack of the devil, waking and sleeping, day and night ..."

Father's grip on my arm tightened a bit as the thing drifted closer, to within a few feet of the terrace railing.

"... every hour and moment be my helper, everywhere be my companion. Amen." I placed my other hand on Father's. "Done," I whispered, "now what should I do?"

"What indeed?" said a withering, raspy, dry-rotted coffin kind of voice. No doubt about it, our "magic-free" intruder's larynx had finally materialized. "When your pathetic prayers fail, what is left to be done?"

"I've never known prayer to fail," said Father, tonsils stable, no hint of fear in his voice. I was impressed.

"Until now," whispered the thing, legs dangling in nothingness.

"What makes the present any different from the past?" asked Father.

"Simple," it chuckled haughtily. "Now you are dealing with Valdemar."

"I do not deal with shadows," said Father, "nor tricks of mist and shade."

"Mist and shade make formidable enemies," said the thing, bristling in a misty sort of way.

"Only to the weak-minded," said Father. "For cowards, they may provide cover for recreant forays of stealth or ambush. In any case, they are tricks, nonetheless."

"Tricks?" rumbled the shape, raising its arms and spreading its cape. "When you lay broken and bleeding in a graveyard, begging for mercy, crying out for help that will not come—for there is no hope, holy man, only despair—you will see if Valdemar uses tricks."

"Yes," said Father. "We shall see."

"Do you not wish to know why I have come?" rasped the shape, lowering its arms.

"I thought he just explained—" whispered the gardener.

"I wish nothing from you," said Father, shushing me with the press of his hand.

"Then I will tell you, nonetheless," insisted the thing, drifting slightly to and fro. Terrified as I was, I was reminded of Buzz Sawr's drunken wave, the one in which his hand stayed put and the rest of him rippled. In this case it was those infernal glowing eyes that stayed put. Understand, my stomach had undulated itself into a considerably complex knot by this time, making me hypersensitive to movement of any kind, heaving or rolling.

"I expected you would," said Father blandly.

"I give you this warning," said the shape. "Do not interfere. Return to your refuge at St. Philomena's, cease your meddling, and the doom I have pronounced will not find you. If you persist, you will surely die. It is useless to hunt me. You cannot find my place of hiding by day, and it is wasted effort to try to warn the sources of blood upon which I prey at night—willing piglets that they are."

"I repeat," said Father, "we shall see."

"Your will is strong, holy man," said the shadow, swaying slowly side to side while drifting slightly closer to the railing. "Would you care to match it against mine? Come closer, and I'll show you fear beyond your wildest dreams."

To my amazement, Father released my arm and took a step closer.

"Ahhhh," moaned the shape. "Yes, another step."

"Father—?" I gasped and hissed at the same time. It hurt.

Father Baptist took yet another step closer, craning his neck.

"Closer," said the thing. "Just a little closer."

Words drifted through my mind, words once uttered by Pope Pius IX and drilled into me by none other than the same Father Baptist who was creeping ever closer to the hovering silhouette. *Place on thy heart one drop of the Precious Blood of Jesus and fear nothing.* As usual, the first part was easy, but the second not so.

"Another step," coaxed the voice from the shadow, slowly raising its arms and elongating its cape to its fullest extent. "And another—"

Fear nothing, I was thinking, or rather wishing, my skin crawling like a colony of agitated ants. *Fear nothing, fear nothing ...*

Just then, several things happened all at once. Well, one right after the other. Or rather, some simultaneously with some straggling behind. In the frenzy of the moment, it was hard to keep it all straight.

First, a shot rang out—although a gun's retort doesn't really "ring." It's more of a startling, percussive "Pow!" I'll concur, however, that the sound has often been described as a "ring." Go figure. Anyway, the shot was followed by two more as Sergeant Wickes came bounding down the steps onto the terrace.

"Fool!" laughed the shadow, swinging its arms so its cape billowed outward. "Bullets cannot harm me."

"How about this?" I yelped, plunging my hand into the mysterious folds of Father's cassock.

"Martin?" said Father, arms raised, startled that I would do such a thing.

"Here it is," I growled, pulling out his trusty Crucifix.

"Sssssssssssss," hissed the thing, cringing as I held it up.

"What the hell's going on?" asked Taper, landing on the terrace a few feet behind Wickes. "Sergeant? Jack—?"

"You shall pay for this insult," screamed the shape, flapping its arms in wide arcs like leathery wings.

"Oh my God," said several of us at once. The lower jaws of Taper the Lieutenant, Sergeant the Wickes, and Martin the Terrified landed right on our shoes as the thing rose, heaving itself higher and higher, disappearing through the swirling canopy of fog over our heads.

It was gone.

"Wow," said Sergeant Wickes, slowly holstering his pistol. "Did you see that?"

"I don't know what to say," said Lieutenant Taper. "I'm, uh—"

Suddenly, from somewhere high above our heads, came an angry growl, followed by the sound of shattering glass.

"Duck!" yelled Taper, crouching down and pulling his jacket over his head. Wickes followed suit. Father stayed put. I kind of hobbled toward the railing, held on, and hunched my shoulders.

A moment later, large wicked shards of glistening glass came whizzing down, splintering into zillions of tiny glittering pieces that skittered every-which-way on the terrace stones.

"Again wow," said Wickes as the tinkles chittered into silence.

"Whuh, whuh, what at do you make of that?" gasped Taper.

"I d-d-d-duh-don't believe it," stuttered Wickes.

"B-b-buh-but we saw it," said Taper. "With our own eyes."

"I know," moaned Wickes. "I know, I know, I know."

"Father?" I ventured, touching his arm. "Are you okay?"

"Why?" he asked, arms folded thoughtfully across his chest.

"Well," I stammered, "you were getting closer and closer, and I thought—"

"How else to get a better look?"

"Huh?"

"Did you really think I was falling under his spell or something?"

"Well, er, that is ..."

"Hm." He shrugged, relaxing his arms. "Well, good. Maybe he did, too."

"Then you were just play-acting?" asked Taper.

"As I just said," said Father in tones as even and flat as a fresh-laid slab of cement in a graveyard. "I was trying to get a better look. Really gentlemen, I'm disappointed in your lack of intrepidity."

"But Father Baptist," said Wickes, lips trembling. "I shot him right in the chest. Three times. I'm sure of it."

"No doubt," said Father.

"Doesn't that mean anything to you?" whined Wickes. "I never would have thought, not in a million years—"

"But you have been thinking just that," said Father. "And for some time."

"And what about you, Jack?" fumed Taper in those quavering tones peculiar to those who are terrified and furious about it. "What are you thinking?"

"I don't think," said Father calmly. "I know."

"What—" spat Wickes in a pitch an octave higher but otherwise the same tone as Taper's, "—do—you—know?"

"What we're dealing with," said Father.

"You mean a vampire," hissed Taper.

"I mean exactly what I said."

"Which was?"

Father sighed. "Gentlemen, it's been a long night. And as is customary for the season, they're getting longer each time around. I suggest you post a guard here on the terrace until morning. Martin, would you be so kind as to see if you can round up the Tumblars? If they're indisposed, or reluctant to leave, perhaps you could ask the girl at the reception desk to call us a cab."

"Sure," I said, deciding as I turned to hobble away that his last suggestion was easiest and therefore what I was most likely to do.

"You're a cool one, Jack," I heard Taper say as I began lurching up the stairs.

"I'm tired," answered Father, the mist dispersing as he turned to follow slowly behind me. "I suggest we all get a good night's sleep."

"I couldn't sleep a wink," shivered Wickes.

The crickets began chirping again.

34

"NOT FUNNY, MARTIN."

"Not meant to be, Father. What I meant was—"

"Drop it, please."

"Sure, sure. But don't you have anything you want to say to me?"

"Like what?"

"Oh, anything, anything."

"Anything is a big order."

"Okay, let's narrow it down—gardeners are good at that."

"Really, I thought they were only good for making wrong turns and running red lights."

"That light was yellow—and I'm not driving. Submit all complaints to the taxi driver."

"At the speed he's going, the spectrum must have shifted."

"Down-shifting back to 'anything,' I've never seen Sergeant Wickes so scared."

"It probably did him some good. Fear is healthy for the soul."

"But not for the heart. Mine almost jumped right out of my mouth."

"Surely, it's big enough."

"My heart?"

"Your mouth."

"Thanks. But as I was saying ..."

This conversation occurred on the way home in the cab. There were two peculiar things I should tell you about it. First, Father was fast asleep the whole time, snoring uproariously. The second, you figure out.

What the cabby thought—HOOUSEIN MIGWOM DALRUBBA was the name displayed in a plastic holder on the back of the driver's seat—is anybody's guess.

Saturday, October Twenty-first

**Feast Day of Saint Ursula who,
along with 11,010 Companions,
fled from the pagan Saxons in England
to the Continent, only to be martyred
for their Purity in Cologne (383 AD)**

35

"AS YOU CAN SEE, SERGEANT," said Father, holding out three globs of metal on his open palm, "your bullets did not 'pass through' our flying friend as you thought."

"Hm," said Wickes, rubbing his nine-o'clock-the-morning-after-the-five-o'clock shadow. "They certainly impacted against something."

"Something, certainly," said Father, handing the pellets to Lieutenant Taper, who dropped them into a small plastic bag, "and quite solid. A bulletproof vest would be my guess. It was risky, but he was no doubt counting on your marksmanship, Sergeant. You did aim for his heart, did you not?"

It was Saturday morning, the next day. So gloomy was it, those infernal clouds still cluttering the rumbling sky, it might have been late afternoon. I checked my watch to be sure. 9:07, give or take a few windings of the ol' spring, established the hour, and the gurgling in my stomach testified that breakfast was still fermenting in there. Yes, it was definitely AM.

We were standing knee-deep in the shrubbery beneath the Farquar Terrace, the "House of Illusions" towering above us to one side, and the Hollywood Hills on the other.

"So what are you suggesting?" asked Lieutenant Taper, also in need of a shave—not to mention a shower and a change of clothes. Apparently he and Wickes had spent the night curled up on the spot where, according to local legend, Douglas H. Farquar gave up his ghost—more on that in a moment. I don't think the night, thus spent, had done our friends from Homicide much good.

"I suggest we have a look at that upstairs window," said Father.

"I agree," said Mr. Anthony Graves, described the previous evening by Mr. Portifoy as the "Toolmaster." Mr. Graves' face had probably started out in his youth like a chubby cup of vanilla custard, but it had somehow gotten frozen into a lump of peanut butter brickle. He also had the most amazing eyebrows—bushy and white, which didn't just meet over his nose: they collided to form an "X" above the bridge of his thick glasses. "These kinds of goings-on are unheard of here at the 'House of Illusions.' I, for one, want to get to the bottom of it. We can't let one of our magicians get away with terrifying the guests."

"As you can see," said Father several minutes later, examining the frame of the broken window on the fifth floor, "something was bolted here last night. See the gouges in the wood? A winch of some kind, probably."

"A winch?" I winced, wheezing from the climb up all those stairs. You'd think a fancy place like this would have an elevator, but noooooo. "You mean Valdemar was suspended on a wire?"

"You didn't think he was actually floating, did you?" asked Father.

"Well, I, uh, at the time, um, that is ..."

"The way he was drifting side to side," said Father, "I should have thought it was obvious."

"Come to think of it," I mumbled, remembering how I was reminded of Buzz Sawr's peculiar hand-wave, "I guess he was."

"I know he was," said Father, straightening. "He lowered himself from this window which overhangs the terrace to put on his little show. Quite the actor, with quite an ego." Mindful of the sharp glass teeth still protruding from the edges of the empty frame, Father gingerly slid it up and down. "My guess is that this window slipped closed while he was entertaining us, forcing him to kick it in when he got back up here."

"That explains the shattered glass," said Taper. "You guessed that, too, I suppose, last night?"

"No real vampire would have to break a window to gain entry to a house," said Father, wiping his hands. "You'll want to have this room checked for fingerprints, Lieutenant, though our flying friend was wearing gloves. Once back inside, he probably disengaged the winch, secreted it under his cape, and headed downstairs, looking to everyone he passed like one of the hired magicians carrying his secrets. Now we must reexamine the terrace."

"Most troubling," said Graves, leading us out of the room.

"What about those glowing eyes?" asked Wickes as we descended the stairs.

"That's easy," said Graves. "You can buy them at any costume shop. Translucent plastic cups tinted red, with light-emitting diodes around the inside rims. They clip onto your glasses—or can be glued directly to the skin right over your eyes. Batteries the size of peas. From what you describe, he was using something like that."

"Two things trouble me," said Father as we descended the final stairway onto the terrace. "His confidence and his knowledge. Surely he knew we'd figure out how he pulled off his stunt, yet he doesn't seem to care. Confidence like that can be dangerous to us. He is not above taking enormous chances—risking things we might not imagine or consider ourselves."

"What did you mean, 'his knowledge'?" asked Taper.

"That, I'm afraid, directly impinges on you, Larry. That I'm a priest is obvious from my apparel. But he mentioned St. Philomena's, so he knows something about me. Whether it's from newspaper accounts a few months ago, or because he is familiar with the parish himself, we don't know."

"You mean he might be a regular," said Taper, turning a bit pale.

"Unsettling if true," said Father, "and alarming. Larry, I suggest that you and your wife, Lucille, attend Mass elsewhere until we have this guy behind bars."

"He may already have us spotted," said Taper, wiping his forehead. "Maybe Lucille should spend a few weeks with her mother in Colorado."

"Not a bad idea," said Father, as we achieved the infamous Farquar Terrace.

"The fog," said Wickes, peering over the rails. "How did he do that?"

"Perhaps Mr. Graves can explain," said Father. "Dry ice?"

"Yes," said the Toolmaster, scratching his head. "This terrace was declared a 'magic-free zone' two years ago. That was before my time, but I've heard some of the older regulars raving about the performances they used to have out here on starlit nights. I understand that there are tubes and ducts—you can see the holes in the handrails, even—for expelling fog all around the terrace. The machinery is housed in a utility closet inside, but it hasn't been used since the night that Farquar fellow—a high-class lawyer, if I have the story right—collapsed and died out here."

"What kind of machinery?" asked Wickes.

"Simple, really," said Graves. "Dry ice—frozen carbon dioxide—is dumped into a basin of water, and the resulting mist is blown through the conduits by remote-controlled whisper-fans."

"Carbon dioxide?" I wheezed.

"Remember how cold it got, Martin?" asked Father.

"Dry ice?" I wheezed again. "Sure, that makes sense."

"It also accounts for the crickets ceasing their music," said Father. "They were reacting to the change in temperature. Remote control, you say?"

"Yep," said Mr. Graves. "Everything around here is triggered that way. You saw the stage performance last night?"

"Yes." Father was running his fingers around the rim of the table at which we had been seated. His coffee cup and my tall glass were still there, though they had ceased their wanderings. Pushing the chairs aside, he crouched down and peered under the table.

"Ah," he said. "It's as I thought."

"Magnets?" I asked. "Is that how he made the glasses move?"

"Magnets, yes," said Father. "But not like you think. There's a speaker mounted under here. A fifteen-inch woofer, to be precise. My knowledge of stereo equipment is sparse, but I seem to recall that a speaker employs magnets in the housing behind the diaphragm."

"How does that explain the moving glasses?" asked Wickes.

"Vibrations," said Father, straightening. "Subsonic—or is the word 'subaudio'?—I don't know. But a low-frequency vibration, too low for us to hear, emanating from that speaker, could cause our tableware to dance."

"True," said Mr. Graves. "And that explains the tingling in your skin, the 'flesh crawling' effect."

"How so?" asked Taper.

"Well," said Graves, lowering his voice. "It's a little-known secret, and a trick we don't allow here at the 'House' since the Farquar incident, but a 14 Hertz sine wave—that's fourteen vibrations per second—will cause a 'fear reaction' in the human nervous system."

"You can't hear it," said Father, "but you can certainly feel it."

"Yes," said Graves, as solemn as his name. "I've seen it done in other venues—playhouses that feature Gothic tales, thrillers, and such—and I'm glad it's banned here because it isn't fair to the people in the audience."

"You mean they experience fear," said Taper, "even if nothing particularly scary is going on."

"Exactly," said Graves. "Mediocre actors in lame plays have received rave reviews that way."

"This Valdemar guy had everything covered," said Wickes, scratching his neck. "And to think I lost a night's sleep over a bunch of tricks."

"You'll recall how irritated he became," mused Father, "when I accused him of trickery. He seems to take himself seriously. Very seriously."

"Anything else you want to see?" asked Graves. "And when can I get the maintenance crew out here to clean this up?"

"The lab crew is running behind this morning," said Taper. "They'll get here to check for prints around noon. It'll all be yours again by two."

"Good. That's when the hands start arriving."

"We'll want to talk to all of them when they get here. What about the magicians?"

"Most of them don't arrive until about seven, seven-thirty."

"Don't they rehearse?" asked Wickes.

Graves shook his head. "Them and their secrets. No. They never work out the kinks in their tricks where other magicians might be watching. They practice at home, or rent a practice studio if they're from out of town, but never here."

"But what about coordinating their stunts with the stage crew?" asked Taper. "Curtain cues, spotlights, that sort of thing?"

"There's generally a run-through on Monday," said Graves, "when the lighting guys learn their cues. It's the same show every night for the rest of the week."

"There was a substantial change last night," said Father, "or rather a change that will go into effect this evening. It would seem, from the MC's comments on stage, that Mr. Buckle has been fired."

"Yeah, I heard about that," said Graves, shaking his head. "Bucky's no star, but he's a good kid. Mr. Portifoy shouldn't've ridden him in front of the audience like that. Bad form."

"How long has Portifoy been working here?" asked Wickes.

"He only started a few days ago," said Graves. "Tuesday, I think it was. Yeah, Tuesday. He wasn't even here for the Monday run-through. We had to rehearse the script with a substitute. Portifoy's a weird fellow, but he's a good magician."

"He denied being a magician during the show last night," said Taper.

"That's just part of his spiel," said Graves, "to put you off your guard. That stuff you saw flying around the stage last night—the smoke and props—that was just wires and relays controlled by the crew. But give Portifoy a deck of cards and a handkerchief—trust me, he's good. I've seen him before."

"Where?" asked Father.

"Back in Lexington when I was visiting the folks last spring. A place called the 'Now You Don't.'"

"Lexington?"

"Yup."

"Interesting," said Taper. "Anything else, Jack?"

"I'd like to have another look at the dressing rooms," said Father. "This time officially."

"Weren't you looking for toothpaste or something last night?" asked Taper.

"Yes," said Father, "and unsuccessfully. No one around here uses 'natural' toothpaste, apparently."

"What does 'natural' have to do with it?" asked Wickes.

"I'll fill you in later."

"If you don't mind," said the gardener, gearing up for another run—if you can call my lurching "running"—up the stairs. "I have another matter I'd like to attend to."

"Where?" asked Father, eyeing my strangely.

"Here," I said. "Or rather, inside. I'll fill you in later."

36

"THANK-YOU, SAINT ANTHONY," I sighed gratefully as the plaque above the sitting-room door came into view at the end of the umpteenth hallway. Without his help, I doubt I'd have ever found it, situated as it was at the culmination of so many twisted corridors.

> GARDENING TIPS: St. Anthony, "The Hammer of Here-
> tics," never fails me--and he's never once had to
> raise his mighty bludgeon on my behalf. Nothing
> as dramatic as that. Still, he's the most gener-
> ous Saint I know, and a soft-hearted fellow in his
> way. He's a glutton for an Our Father, three Hail
> Marys and a Glory Be. In return, he finds what
> I'm looking for, be it a lost set of keys or a
> parking space downtown.
>
>   --M.F.
>
> P.S.: Completely off the subject, but St. Anthony
> is unique in that he has two feast days. The
> Church celebrates his entry into Heaven on June
> 13th, but on February 15th we commemorate his
> tongue. No joke. Thirty-two years after the
> Saint's death, his body was exhumed. It was found
> to be corrupt except for one thing: the tongue
> with which he had so eloquently defended the Faith
> against heresy. (There are three other holy
> tongues, but I'll have to save them for another
> time.)

Elza's Sitting Room seemed an entirely different place by day, all si-lent and empty. Without Bart slowly twisting a towel into a shot glass, the bar was just an elegant collection of bottles and napkins. Without Buzz clinking his ice cubes, the stools were just pedestals of quietude. Without the gurgle-gargle of milling people distracting my attention from the original design and layout of the place, I could see how this could be the kind of chamber to which a young woman of a bygone era might withdraw to be alone with her thoughts. It was charming, in its way, and apparently still decorated with some of her things.

Call me a fool or whatever you will, I had something in mind to do, and I was bound to do it. So, cane clutched purposefully in hand, I strutted across the thick carpet, slowing as I approached the gaudy piano.

The keys lay motionless.

Two of me looked back from the huge mirrors. I looked kind of lonely, and maybe a bit nervous. My jacket and tie, having replaced the stunning whites and tailcoat, rendered me rather ordinary and out of place in so elegant a setting. No matter.

Something I hadn't noticed the previous night: a photograph in a mother-of-pearl frame next to the empty music rack. A young woman in her twenties looked out at me, posing with one leg up on a chair, wearing what I think they used to call a "shimmy dress." Though it was a sepiatone print, all brown and shades thereof, I suspect the dress had been turquoise. That's just a hunch. It matched that satin turban with a couple of fluffy feathers shooting straight up, all pinned in front with a huge dark jewel. And as for her legs, or at least the one that was hitched up, I've never seen a finer example of the feminine fulcrum in all my travels. Cute feet, too. But that smile—whoa! Her expression was frozen in that millisecond between hearing the punch line of a complicated joke and getting it. It made her look as though she had a secret she was just bursting to tell.

"So," I said aloud. "Were you a 'flapper,' Elza?"

Silence closed in around me.

"Excuse me," I said, clearing my throat. "We haven't been properly introduced, and here I am barging in on your solitude. Elza Maplewood Roundhead: my name is Martin Feeney, and aside from providing Father Baptist with chauffeurial entertainment, I do everything in my power to avoid gardening at St. Philomena's. Perhaps you've been there, with your parents, maybe. It was built while you were a teenager."

The girl remained frozen in that silly, fun-loving stance.

"Maplewood," I mused. "Maplewood ... is that by chance why the bar over there is made of maple? Nice touch. It wasn't here—the bar, I mean—it wouldn't have been here back when you were alive and kicking, would it?" I smiled at the thought. "That would've been some sitting room. You do look a little tipsy in that picture."

The girl's smile did not change.

Clearing my throat again, I continued. "Buzz—the guy you 'spell' at the keys?—well, I realize he may have been pulling my leg, and there really was someone back there behind the mirrors, relays or whatever, in which case I am a fool."

Elza's brown eyes seemed to follow me as I eased myself down on the piano bench. It was covered with a thin cushion, upholstered in a wild, golden paisley pattern.

"Well," I said, leaning my stick against the keyboard, careful not to touch a note. "It's this way: if you're real—and by that I mean if you're really a ghost and not a parlor trick—Lord knows I've had enough of those played on me lately; and if you're not in Hell—somehow I can't imagine you fitting in there, not with those eyes and that smile; and if you're not an impostor—and by that I mean you're not a demon disguising yourself as this lovely, air-headed girl—but are in fact the frivolous dame in this picture; then that leaves you in Purgatory, and that would mean you're working off your temporal punishment—how, I can't imagine—by hanging around this place."

I marveled at myself for having constructed so convoluted a run-on sentence. Too late—it was already spoken.

"Sorry if I'm rambling," I rambled, "but I've never conversed with a ghost before. Nevertheless, it occurs to me that if any of this is true, then maybe you could use a prayer or two. I doubt many of the folks who lounge around your sitting room in the evenings would think to do that."

I noticed she was wearing black gloves, the long kind that went right up to her elbows. I liked the foot-long cigarette holder.

"Not that I'm setting myself up as a 'spiritual' person. I don't think I am. Faith is more of a practical matter for me. Lord knows, I don't like hot climates. Have you noticed the humidity, by the way? I've lived in LA all my life and I don't remember a season like this. I wish the storm would just rain its guts out and move on. That's my practical side: do it and be done with it. Of course, I also just love thunderstorms—the lightning, the thunder, leaks in the roof, fire on the hearth. That's my 'romantic' side, I guess. Speaking of leaks: Father Baptist says I'm hopelessly so—sometimes, anyway. 'Romantic,' I mean, not 'leaky.' You see? You gals don't have a corner on that market. Men can be complicated, too. But I digress."

Somewhere, in some other part of the rambling mansion, there was a muffled bump, followed by a not-so-muffled thump. I doubted it had anything to do with me. Turning my attention back to the photograph, I began winding up my desultory monologue.

"Anyway, Elza, for what it's worth, I'm going to offer up my Mass and Holy Communion for you tomorrow morning. If you're real—a ghost, I mean—and you're in Purgatory, then it can only help. If you're not, then I'll ask Our Blessed Mother to bestow the Grace where it will do the most good."

I looked down at the black and white keys—what music they sometimes make! And real ivory, too. Real ivory, like real religion, was a thing of the past. Here I was, a relic, sitting before a rack of relics, talking to one. Go figure.

"Sorry if I've offended you, or bored you, or whatever. As I said, this isn't something I normally do. But do it I've done, and offer my prayers I will, for what it's worth. Elza, I think I'd've liked you. Perhaps you'd've—well, never mind. I hope we meet some day, and on the right side of the Gate. Wherever you are, may you rest in peace."

Feeling foolish, but somehow relieved, I grabbed my cane, rose from the bench, and lurched back across the luscious carpet.

Something funny happened, just as I got to the door. You'll think I'm crazy, and I wouldn't blame you. But I distinctly heard two notes clink on the piano. Two little happy notes, that's all, from a piano at which no one was sitting.

"Thank-you," they seemed to twinkle.

"The pleasure is mine," I waved, and exited the room.

"There you are," called Taper, running down the hall toward me. "We've been looking all over."

"What's wrong?"

"Billowack just called. He wants us down at the morgue, pronto."

"Why?"

"There's been another murder. They brought the body in a few minutes ago."

37

"SO," BELLOWED BILLOWACK, jowls waddling and phlegm flying in all directions, "while you yo-yos were playing with bats in the belfry, this creep sucked another girl dry."

"After," said Father calmly, "not while, and I object to your obstreperous name-calling." He paused, knowing that Billowack didn't know what "obstreperous" meant. I looked it up later. "I'll remind you that I'm a priest, and I expect you to respect my office."

"I'm a Methodist," shrugged the chief.

"All the more reason," said Father, turning his attention to the body on the stainless steel autopsy slab. "Mr. Wong, are the puncture wounds the same?"

"Yes," said Solomon, pulling back the sheet while the gardener's toes got all tangled up in the fronts of his shoes. "See for yourself."

Father leaned close to the pale face of the dead woman, brushing aside a whiff of her limp, blonde hair. "The same two punctures, with indentations all around."

"The microscopics will take a while," said Holtsclaw, wedging his faithful clipboard under his left arm, "but it's reasonable to assume it's the same perpetrator."

"Yes," said Father, looking around and snatching a magnifying glass from a nearby tray. He examined the girl's neck, eyes swirling and blurry through the thick round disk. "It's as I thought."

"What's that?" asked Taper.

"Our 'vampire' uses false teeth."

"What?" said Wong and Holtsclaw together.

"I suspected before, but now I'm positive," said Father, straightening. He held the magnifying glass near the girl's neck to amplify the image, much to this gardener's intestinal dislike. "The two puncture holes do not match the sucking marks left by the canine teeth. Solomon, do you have a photograph of this neck wound?"

"Sure," said the coroner slipping one out of a pile of lab reports. "Here."

"Is this life-size?"

"Yes."

"Mind if I draw on it with this marker?"

"Be my guest. We can always print up more copies."

"All right," said Father, grabbing a plastic ruler and a broad-tipped felt pen. He drew four short lines, made some measurements, then doodled in his findings. "Admittedly the teeth marks are vague, but I think you'll agree that the indentations I've indicated are where the canines would normally be. The fact that their impressions don't stand out reveals their true nature."

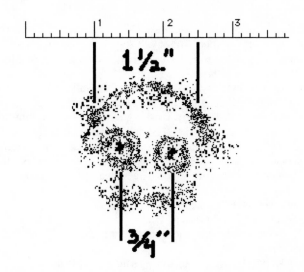

"You're right," said Solomon tracing the vague teeth impressions along the upper arch of sucking wound. "The punctures are closer together than the canine teeth."

"You were right, Larry," said Father, "when you suggested the other day that the killer made the initial bite to puncture the vein, then removed the fangs from the wound to allow the blood to flow. He then pressed his mouth against her throat and proceeded to suck—hard, judging from the puckering of the surrounding skin. As a result, he left the imprint of his teeth around the wound, and thus inadvertently revealed that the impressions left by his canines are no deeper than his incisors."

"The incisors didn't leave any remarkable impression during the sucking phase, either," said Holtsclaw. "How could we have missed all this?"

"In other words," said Taper, a bit queasily, "he bites the neck with a set of sharp teeth to start the bleeding, removes his bridgework or whatever, then presses his mouth against the neck—"

"Maybe he just has some sort of instrument," interrupted Billowack, "you know, like a can opener with two points—"

"No," said Father.

"Why not?" frothed the chief, unaccustomed to having his beer-can insights contradicted.

"Because that would spoil his whole persona," said Father. "He finds foolish girls who, for whatever depraved reasons, want to believe that he's a vampire, that he can make them into vampires as well. They are willing victims, don't forget that. Surely he must wear the sharp teeth to convince them he's for real."

"He can't just suddenly pause," said Wickes, a weird smile on his face, "produce a 'can opener,' and say, 'Okay, Babe, here it comes.'"

"So you say," growled Billowack, giving Wickes a withering look.

"And he's right," said Father.

Billowack rested his lower lip on his chest and sulked.

Solomon pulled the sheet up over the dead girl's head. I thought I'd occupy myself—and distract my writhing stomach—by turning around and gazing out the window like I should have done before Solomon uncovered the body in the first place. If I hadn't done that—turned to face the window, I mean—I wouldn't have noticed the large plastic bag on the counter by the sill. The bag contained the dead woman's clothes.

"What was her name?" asked Father.

"Tiara Stockwell," said Holtsclaw.

"Any leads on which clubs she went to last night?"

"None so far."

"She was at the 'House of Illusions,'" said the gardener.

"Martin?" said Father. "What are you saying?"

"There were so many people there, so many faces," I mumbled, "I'd never remember someone I just passed in a corridor, unless they were wearing something unusual."

"Like what?" asked Taper.

"Like this red dress, all covered with yellow 'eights,'" said I.

I heard Father approach and stand beside me.

"She reminded me of a mutated strawberry," I shivered, "when we passed in the hall."

"The girl that got nicked on the head with a quarter?"

"The same."

"Then in addition to his little charade on the Farquar Terrace," said Father, turning to face the others, "our vampire was also stalking his next victim right there in the mansion. Perhaps he invited her out for a drink when he got off work."

"Speaking of the Farquar Terrace," said Taper, straightening his wrinkled tie. "I'll admit it: when the sergeant and I dashed outside and saw that thing in the mist, I thought we were dealing with a real vampire, fangs and all."

"That's because," said Father, hefting himself onto a stool, "you were already a believer."

"But you weren't," said Wickes. "You weren't fazed a bit."

"No, I wasn't," said Father. "Martin, what was that quote from Chesterton?"

"You mean, 'I do believe some things, of course, and therefore, of course, I don't believe other things'?"

"That's the one. Gentlemen, you hounded me for a statement of belief on the existence of vampires. I did not oblige, but not because I dismiss them entirely. In fact, I don't dismiss them at all. I have read enough of the old accounts to accept that surely they do—or at least have at times, by Providence, been permitted to—exist."

"If so," said Wickes, "why weren't you impressed by the sight of that floating fiend?"

"Toothpaste, for one thing," said Father.

"Ah," said Taper. "So you're finally going to fill us in on the tooth-paste."

"What toothpaste?" barked Billowack.

"The toothpaste," said Father, "traces of which were found on the necks of all the victims."

"What the hell are you talking about?" growled Billowack.

"Please, Montgomery," said Father. "There is no need to growl."

"I'm not growling," snarled Billowack.

"So you say," said Father. "In any case, Solomon, John, you re-member those chemicals identified by the microscopic and chemical analyses? Myrrh, sodium monofluorophosphate, calcium carbonate, carrageenan, glycerin, fennel oil, and propolis. I met with my own consultant—"

"Who?" barked Billowack.

"My own consultant," repeated Father, "who pointed out that these are all ingredients found in so-called 'natural' toothpastes."

"So our 'vampire' brushes his teeth," fumed Billowack. "So what?"

"And eats salad," said Father. "Remember, Mr. Wong, that bit of parsley found in one of the puncture wounds?"

"Elizabeth Unger," said Solomon. "Sure."

"There were also traces of allicin," said Father.

"Yes," said Holtsclaw. "I remember that, too."

"Well," said Father, "I can imagine a vampire, even a 'real' one, brushing his fangs—"

"These days," interjected the gardener, anything to take his mind off his upwelling bile, "thanks to the commercial media, everyone wants to look and feel confident."

"—but," said Father, "'real' vampires do not eat any solid food. Their sole diet consists of human blood. Our vampire, on the other hand, apparently brushed his teeth so as not to offend, invited pretty girls out to dinner to gain their trust and confidence, ate something con-taining allicin and parsley to satisfy his natural human hunger, and then left traces of his culinary endeavors on the throats of his victims when he drank their blood."

"So?" said Billowack.

"So," said Father, "'I do believe some things, of course, and there-fore, of course, I don't believe other things.' I believe in 'real' vam-pires, therefore I do not believe one of them could eat solid food, and

certainly not anything containing garlic.   Allicin, gentlemen, is the
active chemical in garlic."

> GARDENING TIPS: According to Mr. Folkstone, the
> garlic plant contains two important ingredients:
> alliin and alliinase. The latter is an enzyme
> that occurs in a different part of the bulb than
> the former, but when they're combined by crushing
> (or slicing or chewing or whatever) the alliinase
> activates the alliin to make allicin, which is the
> chemical with so many laudatory medicinal proper-
> ties.
>
> --M.F.

"And garlic repels 'real' vampires," said Taper and Wickes together.
"Precisely," said Father.   "It is because I believe in vampires that I
knew our perpetrator couldn't possibly be one."
"Real or not," said the gardener, "he's certainly deadly."
"Well," said Father soberly, "there is that."

38

BELIEVE IT OR NOT, THERE WAS MORE TROUBLE waiting for us back
at St. Philomena's—trouble unlike anything Father'd had to deal with
before.
I knew it the moment we entered the kitchen doorway a little before
noon.   There was something unsettling about the way the stew was
bubbling in a large iron cauldron on the stove.   It was the handle of the
stirring spoon resting against the rim of the pot.   Millie never left
utensils sitting in whatever she was cooking.   Maybe I'd been reading
too many detective stories, but that one detail made the whole kitchen
take on a sinister ambiance.
"Millie?" I said.
"Here," she answered.
Taking a few steps further, I found her seated in the breakfast nook, a
prayer book open before her.
"What's wrong?" asked Father, over at the stove, gently removing the
spoon from the pot and resting it on a plate reserved for that purpose.
Aha, he'd caught it, too.
"Mr. Turnbuckle is waiting in your study, Father," she said.   "Mon-
signor Havermeyer's with him."

"Yes?" urged Father.

"It's his son, Bucky," sighed Millie. "Buckminster," she corrected herself. "He's dead."

"Dead?" said the gardener, flashing on the memory of Bucky Buckle "dying" on stage, his hand caught in an embarrassing tangle of dental floss.

"How?" asked Father.

"The poor mixed-up boy," quivered Millie. "He ... he shot himself."

"No," said the gardener.

"After the magic show or whatever it was," she said, trembling, "he took a gun and ..." She buried her face in her hands and mumbled something. Parting her fingers, she finished the sentence. "... in the head. The poor fool ..."

At the word "gun," Father had snatched up the telephone and was cranking numbers by the time she got to "head." "Coroner's office, please ... May I speak with Solomon Young-sul Wong? I see. I don't suppose John Holtsclaw is still there either? Hm."

Millie rubbed her nose in a mushy gob of Kleenex. "... the poor, damned fool."

"To whom am I speaking?" asked Father. "Really. This is Father John Baptist ... Yes, yes, we must meet face to face ... right, sure ... one of these days soon. Look, I hate to curtail our first conversation, but I'm in the middle of a sacerdotal situation here. What can you tell me about the Buckminster Turnbuckle death? Yes, I'll hold ..."

"Who're you talking to?" I mouthed.

"Sybil Wexler," he mouthed back.

"It's a trick," I said. "She's all done with mirrors."

"Sounds real enough to me," said Father. "What's that, Sybil? Where was the point of entry? ... And where did it exit? ... Hm, that bad ... And the investigators are convinced—? ... Really. Could you read it to me?"

"Mother of Mercy ..." mumbled Millie.

"Miss Wexler, I know this is out of line, but could you possibly send me a photocopy of—? I wouldn't ask if it wasn't. I'd be much obliged ... No, that isn't necessary. Just give it to Lieutenant Taper or Sergeant Wickes, and tell them to drop it by at their earliest— What's that? Of course. I'll let you keep the tally of how many I owe you."

"... mourning, weeping in this vale of tears," groaned Millie.

"Thank-you. Good-bye." Father saddled the receiver.

"What did she say, Father?" I asked. "You don't look well."

"We'd better get back there," said Father, motioning for me to follow. "Millie, please be so kind as to storm Heaven with prayer."

"Of course, Father."

"I'm going to need it," he whispered under his breath.

Something was wrong as we entered the study, too. It struck me as being so out-of-whack I almost lost my balance. Monsignor Havermeyer was seated in my favorite chair. Now don't go thinking I was being selfish or territorial. True, it was my favorite chair, but I can rest my crooked heinie anywhere in a pinch. The problem was that Mr. Turnbuckle was sitting in Father Baptist's customary place behind the desk. I'd never seen anyone else sit there, except me on rare occasions when I was paying bills, but never when seeking Father's advice. Father's chair was, well, Father's chair—the throne from which he performed his personal ministerial functions. To every thing there is a season, and a proper seating arrangement for every purpose under Heaven. This chair reversal did not bode well for whatever was about to transpire.

Trust me on this. Observe:

"Ah, Father Baptist, Martin," said the monsignor, making like he was going to rise but not doing so. "Something terrible has happened."

"Millie told us," said Father, taking two steps into the room, eyeing the situation.

"I don't understand," said Mr. Turnbuckle, elbows propped on Father's desk. His fingers were tracing curlicues in and around each other. "How could he do such a thing?"

"Where was he," asked Father, "when it happened?"

"In his apartment," said Mr. Turnbuckle. "The neighbors heard the shot around three this morning."

"No one thought to call Mr. Turnbuckle," said Havermeyer, "until almost eleven. Can you believe it?"

"And even then it was just some rookie who came around to my office," said Mr. Turnbuckle, his finger movements accelerating. "You'd think—"

"An unfortunate choice of messenger," agreed Father. "What did he say?"

"That my son ..." Mr. Turnbuckle's fingers jammed. "He was locked in his bedroom ...alone ... when he ..."

"I just spoke with someone at the coroner's office," said Father. "The investigators are satisfied that—"

"They wouldn't let me see him," moaned Mr. Turnbuckle, jaw muscles knotting. "They wouldn't let me see my own son. They said ... they said ..."

"Head wounds at close range," said Father sadly, "are nasty business. Lord knows I've seen a few, and wished I hadn't. I'm not surprised that they wouldn't allow you—"

"Did you see him?" barked Mr. Turnbuckle, looking up at Father anxiously. "Did you talk with him last night, as you said you would?"

"I saw him on stage," said Father. "His performance ... didn't go well. The MC didn't let him finish his act."

"And?"

"I rushed back stage immediately, but he wasn't in his dressing room."

"So you didn't talk to him."

"Unfortunately, no."

"Then you failed in your duty."

"I failed in the attempt, yes."

"And now he's dead."

"Did you know he had a gun?"

"A revolver, yes. I forget the caliber. He's had it for years. His uncle, my wife's brother, gave it to him as a birthday present—a souvenir from the War—but I don't know if he ever even fired it. He was a nervous lad, unsure of himself—unable to focus on anything enough to see it through. Perhaps I was a bit hard on him at times. But who would have thought? To do such a thing—over a stupid magic act?"

"I'm sure there was more involved," said Father, "much more, than just his performance last night. In my experience—"

"And to think the family plot was just rediscovered ... for this."

"Hm."

Silence gripped the room.

"We were just discussing funeral arrangements before you arrived," said Monsignor Havermeyer, clearing his throat. "I've scheduled the Rosary for Monday evening, and the Requiem Mass for Tuesday morning. The internment in the family plot will follow directly—"

"I'm afraid not," said Father Baptist.

"What?"

A storm of mixed emotions swirled behind Father's eyes, then subsided. He took a deep breath and let it out slowly. "There will be no Rosary nor Requiem, and the body will not be buried in the family plot."

"What are you saying?" huffed Mr. Turnbuckle, untangling his fingers and rearranging them into fists.

Father Baptist swallowed, considering his words. I've no doubt that when they came out, they were the hardest syllables he'd yet pronounced as a priest.

"The Church does not offer Requiems for suicides, nor does She bury them in consecrated soil."

"You're not serious," said Havermeyer, gripping the arms of his chair.

"I am," said Father. "I know it's hard, but—"

"You're mad," said Mr. Turnbuckle, hip pocket almost bursting as his wallet took a deep breath. "My family built this bloody church. My contributions have kept it afloat. How dare you suggest—"

"The laws of the Church in these matters are very specific," said Father. "I'm sorry, but—"

"I don't believe I'm hearing this," said Mr. Turnbuckle, slamming his fists down on the desk. "Four months ago, you offered Masses for those nefarious bishops—Brassorie, Silverspur, and the rest: wicked, faithless apostates all—and now you tell me you won't do the same for my son?"

"Your objections regarding the bishops were duly noted at the time."

"You bet they were."

"You felt my actions inappropriate."

"Did and do."

"And now that the shoe's on the other foot, you wish me to do otherwise."

"Don't play word games with me. You can hardly compare the murders of those baneful heretics with the death of my son."

"Those were different circumstances," said Father, gripping the back of the empty chair for support. "In those cases there was at least some hope of final repentance—"

"Final repentance," spat Mr. Turnbuckle. "That's a crock and you know it. I won't sit here and be insulted. It's my son we're talking about now, and I won't have his memory or my good name soiled by technicalities—not after all the money I've poured into your collection plate, and my father before me, and his father before him."

"Mr. Turnbuckle," said Father Baptist, letting go of the chair. "I am well aware of your family's history and your generosity which far predates my arrival here at St. Philomena's. But that is not the issue. In a world gone mad, when the modern Church has divested Herself of all that was right and holy, we have attempted to keep Tradition alive here at St. Philomena's: not just the comfortable parts, and not to feed some nostalgic urge, but to honor the whole Thing for its own sake. Would you have me jeopardize our efforts, undermine our stand, a stand which you have thus far wholeheartedly supported, for the sake of your family pride?"

"Pride has nothing to do with it."

"Don't be too sure."

"Father Baptist," interrupted Havermeyer. "I'll admit I've much to learn about Church Tradition, but where's your compassion?"

"Right where it belongs," said Father, throat tight. He strode up to the desk, reached across, and hefted the hand-carved statue of St. Thomas More. "To love God is often costly."

"You speak of love—?" scoffed Havermeyer.

"You know as well as I," said Father, turning St. Thomas around in his hands to face the monsignor, "or are beginning to learn, that the Catholic Faith is like a marvelous latticework. Her many teachings are intricately interconnected and mutually sustaining. Remove one nail, dislodge a single component, deny one essential element, and the whole thing topples. St. Thomas More knew this all too well, and it cost him his position, his wealth, his family, his freedom, and finally, his head. He died rather than relinquish one, single Dogma. Some of Mother Church's teachings are hard, they go against the grain, but it has been by tenaciously sticking to them regardless of public opinion, and not by sidestepping the hard-to-swallow issues, that She has survived the centuries. We've seen the result of theological futzing and dogmatic backpedaling in our age. The Church is collapsing around us. I'll not, by action or neglect, encourage the proliferation of chaos."

> GARDENING TIPS: Okay, that was Father Baptist's
> stark "practical" side, but he was about to segue
> into romantic "leaky" mode. No doubt Monsignor
> Havermeyer and Thurgood T. Turnbuckle, not knowing
> him as well as I and therefore unfamiliar with his
> theological intensity or his passion for all
> things Catholic, did not perceive the difference.
> —M.F.

"But Mr. Turnbuckle's son," said Havermeyer. "Surely a Catholic burial wouldn't harm anyone. And think of Mr. Turnbuckle's feelings."

"No harm, you say? Buckminster took his own life—an act of final despair. As Catholics, we are not permitted the luxury of despair."

"You're talking vagaries," said Havermeyer. "Theological principles. We're dealing with real people here—flesh and blood."

Father replaced St. Thomas More on the desk. "'Real people,' you say. May I remind you that on one fateful night, twenty centuries ago, two very real men, Peter and Judas, committed unspeakable crimes against Jesus Christ Himself: Peter by public denial, Judas by clandestine treachery. Both men opted to serve themselves, both chose the path of imminent convenience, and both felt shame upon realizing what they'd done. Peter repented, and spent the rest of his days making retribution. That memory of his failure spurred him to greatness, the momentum of which converted many pagans and culminated in his martyrdom. Judas, on the other hand, despaired. Unwilling to endure the crushing burden of his guilt, he committed suicide, thus severing himself from God's mercy. It was of him that Christ said, 'It were better for him, if that man had not been born.'"

"Is there a point to this?" glowered Havermeyer.

"With few exceptions, Monsignor, you'll find that there is a point to everything I say and do. You question my compassion? Suppose I heed the pleadings of my heart, cave in to fiscal pressure, ignore the dire truth, and bury Buckminster with full Catholic honor and ceremony. What purpose is fulfilled save to soothe the anxiety of the boy's father?

Suppose I bury the lad in the family plot, consigning his remains to consecrated soil. By doing this, will I honor the memory of the good Catholics interred there, they who fought the good fight till their last breath? Will perpetrating a lie save the boy's soul?"

"Well ..." mumbled the monsignor.

"The Church does not exist," said Father, "to soothe our pains, but to reveal their purpose. Faith is not a matter of feeling, but of fact. The Salvation we profess to seek is not an exercise in idle speculation on Sunday mornings, but a cold, hard matter of life and death—Eternal Life, or Final Damnation. In such a desperate struggle there are bound to be casualties. You and I, as priests, are sworn to assist men in their struggle, not to cater to their weaknesses; to teach the Truth at all costs, not to knuckle under when the going gets tough; to administer the Sacraments in order to provide Sanctifying Grace, not to ply the world with platitudes or allow the faint of heart to alter the Faith willy-nilly to ease their consciences. I repeat: we are all, each and every one of us, hurtling toward one or the other end: Eternity with God, or Eternity banished from His sight. There is no other Reality. If you don't believe that, Monsignor, then I suggest you burn that cassock and go find a *real* job."

"The kind of Catholicism you preach," said the monsignor, "doesn't fit into this age."

"Rather," said Father, "this age is truly not fit for Catholicism."

"You," said Havermeyer, finally rising from my favorite chair, "are either a Saint or a son-of-a-bitch. I'm damned if I know which." He blustered out the door and stomped down the hall toward the kitchen.

"Words," said Mr. Turnbuckle, also rising. "Enough words. Father Baptist, I gather you will not be swayed from this intolerant position regarding my son?"

"Call it what you will," said Father, stepping aside as Mr. Turn-buckle strutted past, "my answer is final. If your son is to be buried here at St. Philomena's, it will be without ceremony and in the area reserved for suicides."

"'Final' is it?" growled the old man as he exited the room. "We'll see about that."

And in a couple of days, we did. But between this juncture and that, there were other things waiting to happen.

I looked at Father. He looked at me.

The phone rang.

See?

"St. Philomena's," I said into the receiver, figuring that Father Baptist's larynx needed a breather. Words—they'll get you every time.

"Mar-r-r-rtin," rolled the tongue at the other end. Remember the "r" rule.

"Father Nicanor. What can I do for you?"

"As you know, Bishop Xandaronolopolis will be arriving this afternoon from Beirut. I am calling to invite you and Father Baptist to attend a small dinner here at my rectory."

"We'll come," said Father Baptist.

I covered the phone with my palm. "How do you know what he wants?"

"Timing is everything," said Father. "I need a break. God is merciful. Father Nicanor calls. Tell him we'll be there within the hour."

Missing something, I turned back to the phone. "Father Baptist says we'll be right over."

"Ah, good. Then you can accompany me to the airport to greet the plane. Oh, and oh yes, I have been asked by Veronika, my housekeeper, to extend a special invitation to Millie, your housekeeper."

"Really," I said, wondering what all that was about. "I'm sure she'll be pleased."

"Who'll be pleased?" asked Father.

I covered the phone again. "Timing is everything, Father. His ferocious cook wants us to bring our ferocious cook."

"Millie?" said Father. "She'll be pleased."

"I will?" asked Millie, standing in the doorway. "Why?"

"You're being invited to dinner at St. Basil's," I explained. "Father Nicanor's housekeeper, Veronika, wants you to come."

"Really?" said Millie. "How nice. What about you two?"

"Oh," I said, "we're going to tag along, if you gals don't mind."

"I'm pleased," said Millie.

"She's pleased," I said into the phone.

"Please let's agree to have a pleasant evening," said Father Baptist. "And not a word, either of you, about vampires."

39

"SO," SAID BISHOP XANDARONOLOPOLIS, rattling his coffee cup as he set it down in a mismatched saucer, "tell us about the vampire."

"Yes," said Father Nicanor, leaning against the refrigerator, "we would like to know."

"Martin," said Father, boring into me with his eyes.

"Not me," I said, shaking my head. "I didn't mention the 'v' word once. I didn't even think it, except, well, it did cross my mind in the baggage claim area when that leather-lipped woman in the slinky black jumpsuit knocked me aside to snatch her suitcase as it went by. But other than that, nope, not even a passing thought."

"Then Millie," said Father, turning his stare upon the dining room door.

"No chance," I said. "Listen to them in there. She and Veronika haven't downshifted from mandible overdrive since they met. I bet they don't even know we're out here in the kitchen."

"And so," said Bishop Xandaronolopolis patiently, "what about the vampire?"

Let me downshift myself for a moment to explain that, after dropping Millie off at St. Basil's and scooping up Father Nicanor, I drove him and Father Baptist to Los Angeles International Airport to meet the afternoon flight from Lebanon.

> GARDENING TIPS: I don't like airports, and more so
> stories about airports, so I won't belabor the
> point. You either get there early or late, find
> the right gate or not, redeem your guest's luggage
> from the conveyor belt or discover that it's half-
> way to Singapore, and invariably get wished death
> by an eggplant with a cucumber mustache driving
> the cab that cuts you off on your way out of the
> parking lot. I'd say our visit to LAX was about
> average.
>   --M.F.

The only moment of particular interest at the airport came when, Fathers Baptist and Nicanor having made their brief opening speeches in the disembarking area, I held out my hand to greet the bishop myself.

"Welcome to Los Angeles, Your Lordship," I said, not sure if I could pull off "Xandaronolopolis" without him thinking I was gargling with molasses. "My name is Martin Feeney."

"Many thanks," he said, looking through me with eyes that glistened like a moist oasis in the midst of the arid Sands of Time. "You may call me Pip."

"Pip?" I think I squeaked a bit.

"Bishop Pip," he winked. "It is a shortening of my first name, which has five syllables more than my last. You Americans, I know this, find it hard to pronounce, and a headache I do not wish to add to your woes."

Darned nice of him, I thought, though I still planned to practice my "Xandaronolopolis" so I could impress him one of these days.

Upon arriving at St. Basil's, we found Millie and Veronika in the dining room, oblivious to our existence. So the four of us males went to the kitchen and did what men have always done when the women folk ignore us: we raided the refrigerator.

"And so," Bishop Xandaronolopolis—Pip—was saying, "what about the vampire?"

"Please," said Father Baptist, "tell me first how you know of him. There hasn't been anything in the papers, I'm sure."

"Who needs newspapers," said the bishop, "when the sky, she tells all? See the angry clouds, hear their dire murmurs, sniff the humid air, feel the evil wafting through your fingers."

"It is true," said Father Nicanor. "Where we come from, it is called the 'Vampire's Shroud.'"

"In words of many syllables," added Bishop Xandaronolopolis, winking at me.

I once described Father Nicanor's appearance as "something constantly-moving yet solidly stationary, like fine sand trickling through a ponderous hourglass." Bishop Xandaronolopolis was something like that, only more so and different. Picture the same hourglass, but standing in the vortex of such a temperature anomaly that the sand inside has turned to molten syrup, while the smooth outer surface of the glass is still cool to the touch.

"The 'Vampire's Shroud,'" said Father Baptist.

"I don't like the sound of that," said the gardener.

"The other night I sensed it, Father Baptist, at your church," said Father Nicanor, "during Benediction. I said nothing, hoping I was mistaken. But you did just say 'him' a moment ago."

"Ah," said the bishop, "then even here in the land of cheeseburgers and the French fries, the 'vurkolak' has come to roost."

"Well," said Father, shifting his weight from one foot to the other, "not exactly. There is a madman stalking the streets of Hollywood, sucking the blood out of impressionable young women. But I'm certain he's not a true 'vurkolak.'"

"And how is it that you know this?" asked the bishop.

"Easy," said the gardener, counting on his fingers, "toothpaste, dry ice, parsley, garlic, false teeth, and a handful of crushed bullets."

"I think some more coffee I shall make," said Father Nicanor, holding a kettle under the faucet. "This evening, it will be a long one. I can feel it, no?"

"No rest for the 'wampyr,'" I said to Father, who didn't smile.

"Not at night," said Bishop Pip, forming a cathedral with his slender fingers. "The 'vlkoslak,' he prowls in darkness."

"Yes," I said, "but our vampire, like everything else in this land of cheeseburgers and the French fries, is not real."

"Don't be too sure, Martin," said Father Nicanor over his shoulder.

"The 'Vampire's Shroud,'" said Bishop Xandaronolopolis in tones that could have flash-frozen a whole deep-fryer, "it never lies."

"I am sure," said Father Baptist. "The fiend I am hunting is a living, breathing man. There can be no doubt."

"For doubt there is always room," said Father Nicanor. "You know this, Father Baptist, as well as I."

"Not in this instance," insisted Father. "The one I am seeking is not among the 'living dead.' He's as human as you or me."

"Perhaps you are right," said Bishop Xandaronolopolis, the wind-chill factor of his breath descending to an Antarctic low. "Or perhaps there is more to this madman than you think. Or ..."

"Or?" squeaked the gardener. Yes, I'll admit it, the sound I made could have sent the mouse living behind the altar at St. Philomena's scurrying to the nearest balcony to commence its "Wherefore art thou, Romeo?" routine.

"Or perhaps," exhaled the bishop, the wisps of his breath achieving absolute zero, "there is ... another."

Sunday, October Twenty-second

**Feast Day of Saint Mary Salome,
Mother of Saint John and Saint James the Greater,
Sister of Saint Simon,
Saint James the Less, and Saint Jude,
one of the "Three Marys" who Stood on Calvary
and who died in France (1st Century)**

40

"THE SABBATH WAS MADE FOR MAN," said the Lord Jesus Christ to the Pharisees when they threw a tantrum because His disciples were picking corn, "and not man for the Sabbath." Check the last two verses of St. Mark's second chapter. "Therefore the Son of Man is Lord of the Sabbath."

Well I say: "The rumpus was made for Trads, and the Trads for the rumpus. What's more, the Trads at hand are going to thump us."

I know, I know—that was painful. But so was Sunday morning—in a number of ways, and for a number of reasons. Give me a few pages and you'll see what I mean.

High Mass was a grand event, and the parish choir gave a majestic "Amen" as Father Baptist, Monsignor Havermeyer, and yours truly made our final genuflection after the Last Gospel and processed into the sacristy—a maneuver I pulled off fairly well, considering how badly my back was acting up.

The wall clock bonged eleven-thirty as I pulled my surplice up over my head and hung it in the servers' cabinet. It was one of those old "captain's clocks" with a half-dozen meters and gauges mounted in a polished wooden frame, all of them looking like portholes—an Epiphany gift from the Widow Pounder. I noticed, as I started unbuttoning my cassock from the top down, that the thermometer was indicating 103 degrees Fahrenheit. The needle of the hygrometer was stuck on 100 percent. The barometer never did work, so I could only guess the atmospheric pressure. Let's just call it "oppressive." Don't forget these figures, please, as I relate subsequent events.

Please consider, also, that Father and I hadn't resorted to separating Millie and Veronika with a crowbar until almost two that morning. The bags under our eyes were a bit over-stuffed as a result.

Allow me to back up a little bit. It had been a tad irregular for Monsignor Havermeyer and myself to act as altar boys at Sunday Mass, that honor being reserved for the parish lads. Father Baptist made the last-minute switch over the tumultuous objections of the young crew who had arrived a half-hour early, vying for the job.

"Just this once," Father had assured them. "The monsignor needs the experience, and since he's going to be around here for the foreseeable future, I want the parishioners to get to know him." That was a polite way of saying that the parishioners had to get used to the monsignor's scarred face and hands perpetually contracted into a scowl and claws. That's another factor worth tucking away in the ol' brain bank as we proceed through events.

"Yeah right, Father," whined Jerry, the tallest and oldest, giving the smiling-but-frowning monsignor a suspicious up-and-down with his eyes. "You always say that exceptions become the rule."

"In the realm of liturgical innovation that is true," Father had to admit. "But in this case, I assure you, it won't become the norm."

"Sure, Father," grumbled Ted, the shortest and youngest, unconvinced. "Sure."

Norm or not, normal or not, I made a point of following through on my promise to Elza Maplewood Roundhead, erstwhile flapper and resident pianist at the "House of Illusions." Be she poof or be she spook, I offered my Holy Communion for the repose of her soul—and most of a Rosary besides while Father was distributing to the congregation. Whatever else I may be, I'm not one to renege on promised prayer. It's the most dependable currency I know.

To Monsignor Havermeyer had fallen the honor of holding the golden paten under each communicant's chin so they could get a good close look at his burns.

One unsettling moment came when I was hefting the huge missal from the Gospel side to the Epistle side of the altar after Communion. I spotted Monsignor Conrad J. Aspic peering out from the shadow of an alcove under the Second Station of the Cross, eyeballs darting all around like a skeptical, tenacious accountant taking inventory. I almost tripped.

"But because of false brethren unawares brought in," I said under my breath, quoting St. Paul's second chapter to the Galatians, "who came in privately to spy our liberty."

The gentle, accepting parishioners that comprised about one percent of our congregation didn't seem to notice our spry intruder, nor did the more volatile lot. Aside from the unsettling sight of Monsignor Havermeyer, they were perhaps distracted by the lack of air conditioning in this sultry weather, or more so reveling in the opportunity to offer up their discomfort for the Poor Souls in Purgatory. Too, there was the fact of the appearance of a graveyard behind the church which, from their perspective, hadn't been there the week before. To folks who gauged the passing of Autumn by whatever-number Sunday it was after Pentecost, something was certainly amiss. It is understandable that their curiosity was piqued, so much so that instead of milling around the front steps of the church after Mass they all headed to the back to perambulate among the silent stones.

Which brings us back to where this chapter began.

"The time has come," said Father, the last of his vestments carefully tucked away in a squeaking drawer, "for the shepherd to mingle with his flock."

"Our sheep carry their own meat hooks," I winked at Monsignor Havermeyer, who seemed particularly nervous that morning. Even so, I had no realistic idea what we were in for. "Take notes," I said reassuringly, "this should be enlightening."

With that, Father the faithful shepherd, I his loyal assistant, and Monsignor Havermeyer exited the church by way of the side door and headed round through the garden to join the parishioners in their provocative reveries.

"Good morning, Vinnie," said Father to the first we met along the way. "And how are you to—"

"No come!" exclaimed Mr. Ng, our "in lieu of" dry cleaner, presser, and provider of used tailcoats. He wagged his starched finger furiously in Father's face. "You know what good for you, Fahser, you stay away!"

"What do you mean—?" asked Monsignor Havermeyer, eyebrows buckling.

"Vinnie mean no come grave place," said Mr. Ng, now waving his hands. "No good."

"No good?" asked Father. "Why, Vinnie?"

"Evil eye," said the tailor, hands clenched into shaking fists, "dragon tongue, hungry ear, black heart. Many black heart."

"Martin," said Monsignor Havermeyer, hands clasped behind his back, "who is this man?"

"Mr. Ng is a good friend and generous," I answered, thinking of myself in a tailcoat, "not to mention a marvelous tailor."

"Fahser," said Vinnie. "You once say St. Thomas More once say sometime duty of Christian is to flee. That what I say: flee!"

"You know I can't do that," said Father, scratching his neck around his Roman collar. "Much as I'd sometimes like to."

"No say Vinnie not warn," said our distraught tailor, hustling by with finger raised to make his final point. "Black heart. Black heart. Like open grave."

GARDENING TIPS: Solomon was a very wise king--in
his youth, at least. Later on he slipped a few
notches down the ol' sagacity ladder. He was in
his judicious prime, however, when he penned the
Book of Wisdom. Anyone in a position of authority
is expected to endure a certain amount of flack,
especially when conditions require unpopular decisions. Considering the folks who cluttered his
court, I suspect Solomon was cringing from personal experience when he wrote the eleventh verse
of the opening chapter:
"Keep yourselves from murmuring, which profiteth
nothing, and refrain your tongue from detraction,
for an obscure speech shall not go for naught: and
the mouth that belieth, killeth the soul."
The Protestant reformers deleted Wisdom and six
other books from the Bible that didn't support
their platform ... and have been quarreling themselves into smaller and smaller splinters ever
since. Catholics, on the other hand, have no ex-
cuse--not even a lame one.
Observe:

                                           --M.F.

"My word," squealed Clara Estelle Pounder, widow, provider of "captain's clocks" and elegant brass candle snuffers, older than the Great
Pyramid and built along the same lines. She grabbed Father's arm with
one hand and motioned all around with the other. She had a voice like a
diamond-tipped chisel, and I think she'd just come from practicing frac-
tures at the local limestone quarry. "Was this really here all the time?"

"Yes," nodded Father, allowing himself to be pulled along. "Since
pioneering days and the sack of the rancheros."

"My ancestors must have been snoozing in Boston at the time," she
smiled, baring rows of calcified teeth that almost met like stalagmites
and stalactites. "They were bootleggers, you know."

"Someone had to be, I suppose," noted the gardener.

"Amazing," she sputtered. "Simply amazing. What ever possessed
you to have the shrubs cleared away?"

"Well," said Father, "when I bought St. Philomena's five years ago,
the cemetery was noted in the deed. If funds had been available, I would
have had it done long ago."

"You mean you used parish funds," interrupted Patrick Railsback, our
head usher and numismatic scrutinizer, "without telling us?"

"Not a cent," said Father, systematically detaching himself from
Clara Estelle Pounder's clutches. "I found three volunteers. They finished in two days and I'd say they did a splendid job."

"Finished?" protested Mr. Railsback, ever the pessimist. "But now it's all bare dirt." To him, a shovel was always half empty, never half full. One can only guess his philosophy when applied to pitchforks.

"The dichondra, too, will be free of charge," explained the gardener, for whom a wheelbarrow was almost always almost full. "A donation from the Del Agua Mission staff."

"I don't know," said Mr. Railsback, looking around suspiciously, scooping optimistic dirt from my wheelbarrow with his fatalistic shovel. "Any gift from anyone connected with the archdiocese will have a price tag. It's just a matter of time before we find out what it is."

"I wouldn't worry about that," said Father, whose philosophical pick-up truck was invariably filled to overflowing, and always with the richest, darkest, nutrient-rich volcanic alluvials imaginable. "A load of grass is hardly cause for concern."

"Don't be too sure," said Mr. Railsback, whose dispositional dump truck had flung its ethological load on the ol' pathos pile years ago.

"Well," said the gardener, whose supply of tiresome temperamental half-full/half-empty metaphors was finally exhausted, "you could always cover the cost yourself, Mr. Railsback, or organize a fund drive, or whatever, thereby easing your mind and saving our parish from any possible conflict of interest."

"For a bunch of dead Injuns and Beaners?" scowled Mr. Railsback, lips all twisted as if I'd just offered him a road-kill taco. "No way."

"For a bunch of *Catholic* Indians and Mexicans," countered yours truly, "not to mention a fair number of very pale pioneers. See? Smith, Peters, O'Riley ..." I was reading from a group of nearby tombstones. "... no Railsbacks, but surely folks as white as a baby's—"

"Bottom," rumbled a voice a few heads away. I strained to identify the source, but the larynx eluded me. "That's what we've hit. Rock bloody bottom! This is low. To think that our own pastor would betray his own, and in such a petty, vindictive way—"

"You said it," answered another, also-elusive set of vocal chords. "The sanctimonious bastard. After all we've done for him. We won't take this lying down."

"I always wondered when Slap-Happy-Bappy would reveal his true colors," rasped yet another dragon's tongue tugged by a black heart. "I don't trust cops, and I sure don't trust cops-turned-priests."

"Where would he be without us?" grumbled the first voice again, this time resolving into that of Mr. Julius Caspar, our parish philatelist. Since neither Father, nor I, nor anyone else connected with St. Philomena's used stamps for anything other than postage, Mr. Caspar's unique services did not fall within any of our "in lieu of" categories. In other words, he was one of our rare and flinty-skinned "cash in the plate" benefactors. "Where would he be?" he grumbled some more.

"You know, and I know, but do you think he'd ever climb down off his high horse long enough to consider where he'd be without us?"

"He obviously doesn't give a damn what we think," said the second voice, also coming into focus. It was none other than Mr. Argyle Poindexter Twiggler, our very own empyemic epizootiological entomologist—(don't look it up, you don't want to know)—who had settled down in retirement to concentrate on arthropods—i.e., spiders. Since no unidentifiable lethal arachnids were currently infesting the church or the rectory, Mr. Twiggler's lack of practical expertise had relegated him also to the meager ranks of "cash in the plate" contributors. "Maybe it's time," he snarled conspiratorially, "to bring our thoughts to his attention, and in ways he cannot ignore."

I looked at Father, but he didn't look back.

Never had I heard such remarks at St. Philomena's. Sure, there were sometimes squabbles and differences of opinion over minor pastoral or fiscal issues, not to mention the details of Father's sermons. I've often said that Trads, being fastidiously fussy, contiguously hot-tempered, and aggressively outspoken, are the most obnoxious people in the world. This gardener, as "crotchety" and "grim" as he may be, can't help but reserve a soft spot in his "dour" heart for a group of people who care enough about their convictions to constantly make fools of themselves over them. But never had I ever heard these parishioners resort to plebeian mudslinging—and never in Father Baptist's direction.

As for who owed whom and for what, and regarding the question of where would who be without whom, these subjects had never come up before because some topics, in polite circles—and even among gaggles of super-heated hydrogen-gas Traditionalists—are best left unaired.

The next voice, however, punctuated as it was by metal scraping against metal—sparks, scratches, rust clouds and all—explained everything.

"The nerve, the confounded nerve of the man." Mr. Turnbuckle's galvanized cranium, sans toupee this morning, was coming into view. "If he had his way, my son would be buried over there in profane soil—with excommunicants and heretics, can you believe it?—and without so much as a blessing. And to think of all the money I've poured into his coffers over the years. Don't you agree, Biltmore?"

A younger, thinner version of Mr. Turnbuckle who didn't yet need a toupee shoved his hands into his pants pockets and responded by looking down at his shoes.

"Biltmore's beside himself with outrage," explained Mr. Turnbuckle, nudging his silent offspring, "aren't you, Son?"

Biltmore remained beside himself, and silently so.

"Hrmph," snorted Mr. Turnbuckle. "You can see how grief-stricken he is."

"If you ask me," said another one of Turnbuckle's fellow growlers, a thin fellow named Cass Stonier who used to repair mimeograph machines until laser printers and photocopiers replaced them. There was still a mimeograph machine in the basement, but it hadn't been used since the nuns abandoned the grammar school. As for a photocopier, we couldn't afford one. "If you ask me," he was saying, "we should string him up—"

"On the other side of the avocado tree," exclaimed Mrs. Theadora Turpin, a cloud of fragrant pink talc billowing around her. She clucked and fluffed her feathers like an agitated hen. The more she fluffed, the more she billowed, sweetly dispersing those bad vibes from the "cash in the plate" crowd even though she wasn't aware of them. "My word," puffed Theadora, "would you look at that tombstone?"

"Yes, Dear," nodded her husband, Tanner, his shoulders drizzled with a fine layer of his wife's aromatic dust.

"I had no idea that the Turnbuckles were so important," she marveled, "did you?"

"No, Dear."

"Thurgood must be so proud to be descended from such a family, don't you think? I didn't see him in his usual pew this morning, did you?"

"Yes, Dear—and no, Dear. He was near the back. I think he was accompanied by one of his sons. Haven't seen the lad in years."

"Well, at least he has children who care."

"Apparently, Dear."

"Just imagine, so many children—and they're resting here with their parents, not scattered all over the country, far from home."

"Yes, Dear, imagine that."

"Not like ours."

"No, Dear. Not at all like ours."

"Honey," she said, clutching his lapels, "if I die, would you have something nice like this made for me?"

"Most assuredly, Dear. Oh, Father Baptist. I want to compliment you on your sermon. Solid, as usual."

"Thank-you," said Father. "I confess I'm heavily influenced by the sermons of St. Francis de Sales."

"Not to mention St. Bonaventure," nodded Mr. Turpin. "I especially liked the part where you—"

"Father, have you seen Mr. Turnbuckle?" asked Theadora, adjusting the feathery boa around her neck.

"I think he's close by," said Father, vaguely waving that-a-way.

"He suffered a terrible loss yesterday, Mr. and Mrs. Turpin," said Monsignor Havermeyer, hands still clasped behind his back. Oblivious to Father Baptist's harrumph, he added, "His son, Buckminster, committed—"

"Bucky passed away," said Father, "early yesterday morning."

"Oh dear," gasped Theodora. "I remember when his wife—oh!—Thurgood must be devastated."

"Indeed," said Father, laying his hand on the monsignor's shoulder and giving it a gentle but commanding squeeze. "He was most upset."

"And still is," said Theodora, peering between us toward that unmistakable sound of scraping metal, "by the looks of him."

"You didn't say anything about it from the pulpit, Father," said Tanner.

"Well," said Father, pausing to swallow, "under the circumstances—"

"We simply must go offer our condolences," said Theodora, grabbing her husband's arm and tugging him away.

"Yes, Dear," said Tanner. "See you later, Mr. Feeney, Monsignor. Father, perhaps we'll discuss your sermon another—"

"Horse feathers," roared Mrs. Patricia Earheart, jabbing a menacing finger at the jiggling mound of Mr. Gregory Holman's tummy as they stomped by, obliterating Theodora's talcum cloud with the churning dust of their own two-Trad stampede. "How can you say such a thing?"

"Because it's true—Good morning, Father."

"It can't be—Good sermon, Father."

"But it is—Later, Father."

Those two have been arguing for years, but they never stay put long enough for me to hear what about. I'd ask, but if it turned out to be something stupid, I'd never forgive them.

They stamped off in the general direction of the growing number of people clustered around Mr. Turnbuckle and the silent, thinner version of himself who still hadn't found his tongue.

"You don't say," grumbled the unmistakable voice of Patrick Railsback, who had already wandered over there, preferring Turnbuckle's company to dead Indians and Mexicans. "He didn't say anything to me about it."

"Of course not," huffed Mr. Turnbuckle, turning his bloodshot eyes in our direction and throwing his voice for our benefit. "You don't actually think he'd broadcast his treachery, do you?"

"But if it's like you say—"

"You're damn right it's like I say. The nerve. The unmitigated gall of that sanctimonious son-of-a—"

"Faddah!" erupted another voice. "'Scuse me, 'scuse me. Comin' through."

"Ah," said Father gratefully turning his attention to the chubby woman who came bounding up to him from the opposite direction of the Turnbuckle cartel, bumping people aside with her wiggling hips, "Mrs. Cladusky."

"Have you seen her, Faddah? Oh, hello Mr. Feeney, Monseenyah. My dear friend, Mrs. Magillicuddy, I can't seem to find her anywhere, and she never misses Mass, not even if both feet were broken."

"I believe she's away visiting her sister," said Father, releasing his grip on Monsignor Havermeyer.

"Abigail," said the gardener.

"In Hemmet," offered the monsignor, rubbing his shoulder.

"Hrmph," huffed Mrs. Cladusky, hunching her watermelon arms and resting her summer squash fists on her pumpkin patch hips. "Not a word—would you believe it?—not a single word did she say about this to me."

"A sudden impulse," explained Father. "She expressed a desire for a change of scenery."

"When was this?" asked Mrs. Cladusky.

"Friday evening," said Father. "I got the impression she was packed and ready to start her journey. After a few days, when she's had enough time to reach her destination, I'll—"

"—not take this lying down," roared Mr. Turnbuckle. "I will not rest until my beloved son, Buckminster, is treated properly and with full honors."

"You said it," answered Mr. T's angrily growing cabal. "We're behind you, Thurgood. We won't take this lying down."

"I hear the woods around Hemmet are very nice," I said to Mrs. Cladusky, trying to keep my voice steady.

"And hopefully cooler," added Havermeyer, "than the temperatures we've been experiencing around here. Apparently her sister, Abigail—"

"You no look so good, Faddah," said Mrs. Cladusky, nudging right up to Father Baptist and examining the pouches under his eyes. "My Bennie, he look beddah than you, and him back in the hospital."

"On no," said Father, withdrawing a half-step, "not another complication, I hope. What is it this time?"

"Doctors," she huffed, "with all those letters after their names, what do they know? We pay them, they shrug. They scratch their heads, we pay them some more. Useless. I thank God the day never came when my son, Jamie, became a doctor. A librarian, it ain't much, of course, but at least it doesn't have MD behind it. And Bennie, he always has plenty to read in bed."

"I'll make a point of visiting your husband," offered Monsignor Havermeyer, smiling compassionately. "At what hospital is he staying?"

Mrs. Cladusky gave him an offensive glare as if to say, "Just what my Bennie needs: that the Creature from the Black Lagoon should scare him to death in his sickbed," and turned back to Father Baptist. "You know, don't you Faddah? It's where you always visit him." She placed particular stress on the "yous.".

"Of course," said Father, tossing the monsignor an embarrassed glance. Like I said, these folks are leery of anything that wasn't always there. "I'll see that Ben receives the Sacraments. Don't you worry, Mrs. Cladusky."

"Muriel, Faddah. How many times do I have say it? To you, please, I'm Muriel."

"Certainly, Mrs. Cladusky," said Father.

"And do you know what he said then?" boomed Mr. Turnbuckle's voice, metal against metal, quartz against glass. "He actually defended those four foul bishops. Remember that? He said Requiem Masses for each of them, and in our church."

"That's right," said Mr. Railsback, slapping his forehead in overacted recall. "He did do that."

"But now he won't lift a finger for my son," said Mr. Turnbuckle.

The quiescent son, Biltmore, could have cracked a walnut between his chin and his sternum. If I'd had one handy I might have marched on over there and tested my theory.

"What about our sons?" asked Mr. Caspar. "If he'd do this to a fine upstanding parishioner like Thurgood Turnbuckle, what travesty might he perpetrate upon the likes of myself, or Argyle Twiggler here, or you Patrick: what if he decides your son isn't good enough to be buried with Mexi-trash and Redskins?"

"Well just see about *that*," growled Mr. Railsback.

"My Bennie," said Mrs. Cladusky, oblivious to the roar in the background that was moving inexorably into the foreground. "He always glad when you visit, Faddah," she said, this time underlining "you" at least three times. She dotted her sentence by giving Monsignor Havermeyer another nasty glance. She threw one at me just for good measure.

Something in the monsignor's digestive track gurgled abruptly in reply. The level of acid in his system must have been caustic indeed for me to hear it over the gurgling of the lava flowing from Mount Turnbuckle.

"Hungry?" I spoke into his ear.

"No," he said, looking at me with eyes that could only be described as lonely. "Indigestion."

"Me, too," I said, rubbing my tummy.

Grateful for the camaraderie, he whispered back, "Where'd everybody disappear to last night? I went into the kitchen around suppertime and found the rectory deserted. Millie left a note on my plate."

"Oh?" I said, stepping sideways so we could both get out of range of Mrs. Cladusky's glances, not to mention Mr. Turnbuckle's fermenting froth. "What did it say?"

"'Dinner in fridge.'"

"And what, pray tell, had she prepared for your culinary pleasure?"

He looked at me.

I looked at him.

"A boiled potato," we said together.

We wanted to, but we didn't laugh.

"So where were you?" asked Havermeyer.

"Father Baptist and I went with Father Nicanor to pick up Bishop Pip at the airport," I explained. "And Millie spent the evening jawing with Veronika, Father Nicanor's housekeeper. I'm sorry, I should have trotted back to the camper and told you—in fact, I should have invited you to join us—but the call came just after you, um, stomped out of the study. I figured you'd be mad for a while."

"Not mad," said Havermeyer. "Fuming."

"There's a difference?"

"There is," he said, wistfully massaging his protruding gut. "I can just imagine the wonderful dinner that was prepared for the bishop's welcome."

"Don't bother. Like I said, the girls were yacking, so us guys made do with leftovers."

"You're joking."

"Never about food."

"Still, considering the source, it must have been tasty."

"Between you and me," I winced, "I wish it had been boiled potatoes."

Monsignor's response was interrupted by the sudden appearance of none other than Sergeant Wickes. "Martin, Monsignor."

"My stars," I said, cheerfully baring my teeth to our friend from the police. Unlike Clara Estelle Pounder's cavernous formations, my choppers actually meet in the center of my smile. "What brings you here?"

"Well," he stammered. "I'm not exactly sure. You might say I have things on my mind."

"Things?" I asked. "What sort of things?"

"Certain things," he said, shrugging uncomfortably.

"Oh," I said knowingly.

"Don't start."

"Don't start what?"

"Don't start anything."

I shrugged. "Okay. I've got some great finishes in my pocket. Can I try one of those on you?"

"I was hoping," he looked around nervously, "to have a word with Father Baptist."

"You and everyone else," I commented, seeing that Father, released from Mrs. Cladusky's clutches, had been reabsorbed by Theadora's impending suction. It seems that Mrs. Turpin had become aware of the growing whirlpool of anti-Bappy animus.

"What they're saying can't be true," she was screeching. "Can it?"

"Most assuredly not, Dear," said Tanner. "Father Baptist, there seems to be a growing misunderstanding around here."

"What's to misunderstand?" wailed Theodora. "Father, tell us it isn't true."

"Tell you what isn't true?" asked Father.

"What Mr. Turnbuckle is saying."

"And what is he saying, Mrs. Turpin?"

"That you're a sanctimonious son-of-a—"

"Careful, Dear," said Tanner. "What my wife means, Father, is that—"

"What's going on around here?" asked Sergeant Wickes, unconsciously checking to see if his gun was in his shoulder holster. "They're beginning to sound like a lynch mob."

"Trads," I said. "You gotta love 'em."

"You're not serious. Love them?" He waved his arms around to illustrate their existential presence.

"No choice," I said, and then quoted Scripture:

> But I say to you not to resist evil: but if one strike thee on thy right cheek, turn to him the other.

"But—" said Wickes.

"I'm not done," I said, and continued:

> But I say to you. Love your enemies: do good to them that hate you: and pray for them that persecute and calumniate you. That you may be the children of your Father who is in heaven, who maketh his sun to rise upon the good, and bad, and raineth upon the just and the unjust.

"That's St. Matthew chapter five," I said, "verses forty and forty-four. The stuff in between and on both sides is good, too. This is your lucky day, Sergeant. You get to see real Christianity in action."

Just then the clock in the old steeple struck the noon hour—twelve ominous, unevenly spaced, deafeningly loud repercussions.

"What the hell was that?" asked Monsignor Havermeyer, unused as he was to all the marvelous things St. Philomena's had to offer.

GARDENING TIPS: I must say something at this juncture about that old clock in the tower. It was badly in need of repair, and I had yet to locate a

```
clock maker--"in lieu of" or otherwise--who would
touch the thing.  It lurked up in the steeple like
a cranky old spider, gears slipping and springs
spronging, black grease for blood and a dented oil
pan for a heart, awaiting some unsuspecting re-
pairman to come and be its next meal.
  When I said it "struck the noon hour," I meant
that the clapper punched another series of gouges
into the wooden beam where the huge bronze bell
used to hang before it fell down during the
Whittier Earthquake of 1987.  And that was the
least of the clock's problems.  The clock only
struck once every few years.  The last time, one
of the main counterweights had been catapulted out
the window and was still imbedded somewhere on the
steep roof above the altar.  That happened exactly
one hour before the Northridge Quake of 1994,
which sparked rumors in the neighborhood about its
prophetic talents.  Don't get me started.
  Despite the second law of thermodynamics regard-
ing atrophy in a closed system, and in spite of
the absence of critical mechanical internal or-
gans, that thing still had enough working parts
and residual energy in its springs to mount a ma-
jor noon toll.  The event bordered on the preter-
natural, if you ask me, if not something more.
                                        --M.F.
```

From down in the graveyard, it sounded like something huge and irritated trying to punch its way out of something subterranean and hollow.

I looked around, wondering.

41

"THIS IS GETTING ENTIRELY OUT OF HAND," said Monsignor Havermeyer, who was becoming visibly agitated.   More and more people were staring at us. "Father Baptist, we must do something."

"I'm open to suggestions, Monsignor," said Father, hands searching for something concealed within the mysterious folds of his cassock.

"Well," Havermeyer huffed, puffing his cheeks, "for one thing, you've got to set the record straight."

"The problem Monsignor, is that, barring the slanderous asides, I have refused to bury Buckminster Turnbuckle with liturgical ceremony.

That part of the record is clear and verifiable. I cannot straighten that which is not bent."

"Then it's true!" cried Theodora Turpin. "Did you hear that?"

"Yes, Dear," said Tanner.

"But such vilification," said Havermeyer. "What about your honor? Your reputation?"

"What can any man do about that?" replied Father, his words compressed by the tightness in his throat. "If these people don't trust me by now, if they've yet to ascertain my heart and discern my motives, then mere words aren't going to rectify the situation. Indeed, I'd have to admit that I have failed miserably in the performance of my office."

"Or that they have very thick skulls," said the gardener.

"Do we, Tanner?" whined Theodora Turpin.

"Do we what, Dear?" asked Tanner, looking at me.

"Do we trust Father," she whinnied, "and know his heart?"

"I should hope so, Dear," said Tanner. "Father, for what it's worth, my wife and I—"

"We trust you Father," cried Theodora. "Even if you are a sanctimonious—"

"He isn't that, Dear. Not Father Baptist. Think of all he's accomplished here at St. Philomena's. Don't ever say—"

"But Mr. Turnbuckle said—"

"Mr. Turnbuckle is an ass, Dear."

"Is he really?"

"Most assuredly, Dear."

"Oh, I didn't know that."

"No, Dear, but nonetheless—"

"He's an ass?"

"Yes, Dear."

"You're sure?"

"Positive, Dear."

"What fun."

"More than an ass," interrupted Danielle Parks, our "in lieu of" choir directrix.

"An insufferable buffoon is more like it," added Wanda Hemmingway, our first soprano and former rock vocalist. "Only a week ago he pinched my—well, he pinched me, just as I started up the stairs to the choir loft."

"What did you do?" asked the gardener, always on the lookout for a good punch line.

"I should've slugged him," she smiled, knowing my predilection, "but instead I said, 'Would you look at those filthy paws? Thanks, Buddy, now I'm going to need a tetanus shot.'"

"His fingernails may be clean," said Danielle. "Pedicured, I think—but his hands are still filthy. Why, do you know how many people he's ruined with a slash of his solid-gold fountain pen?"

"Don't," said Father, raising his hand. "Don't add your sin to his. Let it be, Danielle."

"Well," said Wanda, hands on her slender, former-rock-vocalist hips. "You may have to take his abuse lying down, Father, but we don't have to stand for it."

"After all you've done," said Danielle. "The nerve of that old grub."

"I know I'm speaking for everyone in the choir," said Wanda. "We're behind you."

"And don't forget," said Danielle, "you're just hearing the big voices, the ones who are used to bullying people about. There are quiet folks around here who back you a hundred percent. They're just too timid to speak up."

"Trads?" I gawked. "Timid?"

"Well," warbled Theodora Turpin. "We're not too timid to speak up, are we?"

"No, Dear, not us."

"We're not going to let that ass bully us."

"Not for one second, Dear."

Ah, I thought. Perhaps the tide is turning. Or at least a few hopeful dinghies are appearing on the horizon.

"Father Baptist," barged in Freddie Furkin, the cigar-sucking ice-chomping overall-wearing stump of muscle who ran the Chancery motor pool—this morning wearing a suit and tie, and sans cigar and Coke. He had recently become a regular at St. Philomena's, much to the ire of his charismatic wife, Furmelda, who led the Ever-Twangin' Mostly-Saggin' Steel-Pluckers at St. Cyprian's, a church in Burbank that had nothing in common with St. Philomena's except the word "Catholic" on the marquee.

"What is it, Mr. Furkin?" asked Father.

"Freddie, Father. Not even my mother calls me Mr. Furkin."

"Of course, Freddie. What do you want to say?"

Freddie looked as though he really needed a cigar in his mouth, just to balance the weight of his ears. "I don't pretend to know everything, but what I know I know. I've read lots of old books on moral theology—and for a guy like me that didn't get beyond the fourth grade, that ain't easy. The Latin parts I gotta look up one word at a time. It takes forever—"

"Extraordinary," commented Monsignor Havermeyer.

"—but that's what brainless jobs like mine at the Chancery motor pool are for: so thick-skulls like me have time to do the homework we never had. And what I want to say is, um, Father Baptist, what you're doing, well, it's right as rain. And I, for one, stand behind you."

"As do we," said Pierre Bontemps, clapping his hands in appreciation of Freddie's speech as he came striding up to join us.

"Don't let them get to you, Father," said Arthur, right behind Pierre.

"You're doing the right thing," said Jonathan.

"You sure are," said Stella Billowack, peering between their shoulders. "I don't understand it all, but somehow I know you're right—maybe just because it's so hard. Funny how what's right is usually so difficult."

"You said it," said Jonathan to Stella, and then to Father: "Remember that passage from Psalm Twenty-Six that you had us memorize?" No sooner had he uttered the first two words, than all the Tumblars joined in:

> Deliver me not over to the will of them that trouble me; for unjust witnesses have risen up against me; and iniquity hath lied to itself.
>
> I believe to see the good things of the Lord in the land of the living.
>
> Expect the Lord, do manfully, and let thy heart take courage, and wait thou for the Lord.

"We're behind you," said Edward and Arthur together.

"We'll even stand in front of you," said Pierre, "if the situation so requires."

"All the way," said Joel.

"Yah, all duh vay," said Josef, Joel's grandfather, eyes sparkling like a skyrocket display over a lake at night. Pretty good for a man who had just exhausted more than half of his English vocabulary.

"From the looks of things," said Father, "after today, you may be all I have left."

"And the Jeep, Father," said Freddie, rolling his lips as though moving a cigar from one end of his maw to the other.

"What about the Jeep, Freddie?" asked Father.

"Consider the paperwork lost. It's yours."

"God bless you, Freddie," said Father, glancing in my direction.

"Don't mention it, Father."

"Of course," said Freddie, winking at me, "if the brakes fail, or the transmission falls out, bring it by the garage and it'll all come back to me—temporarily, anyway. Wouldn't want you to pay for the Chancery's repairs. Till then, enjoy."

"Excuse me, Martin," said a mild voice. "Could I have a moment of your time?"

"Henry," I said, turning to face Mr. Folkstone. "Certainly, certainly."

He pulled me a few feet away. I can't say I minded the breather, even though the wind had changed.

"What can I do for you, Henry?"

"It's about this graveyard," he said, waving his hand in a vague arc. "We can't just leave it as bare dirt. Do you and Father Baptist have any landscaping plans?"

"No, not really. Roberto Guadalupe is going to be bringing in some dichondra, but other than that, no. We were hoping to get some input from you."

"Do you know if Father intends to, you know, bury parishioners here?"

"There aren't a lot of spaces left," I said, "judging from the number of tombstones. Why do you ask?"

"Well, I was just thinking that my time on this earth is dwindling, and there's a spot right by the church wall ..."

"Oh?"

"... and if there's any chance of me 'staking a claim,' so to speak, I thought I might start preparing it. A rosebush or two, some gardenias perhaps, that sort of thing. Martin, if I'd only known."

"Known what, Henry?"

"Gracious me."

"Yes you are, Henry. What didn't you know?"

"That's my great-uncle Andrew, there in the shade of the church. I'm sure of it. The name, the dates."

"I don't remember you ever mentioning him."

"Well, I never actually met the man, Martin. But his gold watch made its way to me. See? I still carry it here in my pocket. It loses five minutes a day, but it's the nicest thing I own."

"And you'd like to claim the spot beside him."

"Yes."

"Well, as soon as things settle down around here, why don't we ask Father?"

"You don't think he'll mind?"

"I can't see why."

"Well ... but ..."

"Is there something else, Henry?"

"Martin," said Mr. Folkstone, close to my ear. "Is it true what Mr. Turnbuckle is saying?"

I glanced over to where the old screw was still expelling his dark opinions while his son, Biltmore, continued to hold his in.

"That depends," I said, "on what Mr. Turnbuckle is saying."

"That Father has refused his son a Christian burial. Some of the people are quite upset about it. I've never seen them like this."

"Did Mr. Turnbuckle happen to mention that his son committed suicide?"

"Why, no."

"Ah, then what Mr. Turnbuckle is saying is not altogether ... complete."

"Oh dear," gulped Mr. Folkstone. "The poor boy. You mean he—?"

"Yes, Henry. He—"

"But the things Mr. Turnbuckle is saying about Father Baptist," said Mr. Folkstone, clamping his hands over his mouth. He parted his fingers to say, "No, I can't repeat such language."

"Then don't," I said. "We've got enough problems around here without—"

"Hogwash," said Mrs. Patricia Earheart, finger buried to the hilt in the folds of Mr. Gregory Holman's stomach as they came stomping by, back from their orbit around the Turnbuckle cluster. Nothing had changed in their demeanor, except that neither of them acknowledged Father as they stormed past.

"How can you say such a thing?" she demanded.

"Because it's true," he answered.

"But it can't be," she countered.

"But it is," he retorted.

The human wake closed in behind them.

"See what I mean?" squeaked Mr. Folkstone. "The effect it's having on people? Oh dear, oh dear ..."

"Perhaps it's time," said Father, straightening his cassock, "to confront our calumniators."

"Whatever you do, Sergeant," I said to Wickes, "don't run. Any show of fear just makes them angry."

"I could shoot them," he offered, not altogether playfully.

"Waste of good bullets," I winked. "Wagging tongues are hard to hit, even at close range."

"What about hearts?"

"You'll only get acid on the ground, and then the grass won't grow."

"Okay, okay. I'll leave the safety on."

The people shuffled back, eyes wide, as Father Baptist, Monsignor Havermeyer, Sergeant Wickes, Theadora and Tanner Turpin, Danielle and Wanda, Freddie Furkin, the Tumblars, the gardener, and a few others approached the Turnbuckle clique.

You could have heard a tombstone drop.

I think several did.

"Good morning, Mr. Turnbuckle," said Father, extending his hand. "This must be your youngest son, Biltmore. Haven't seen him in quite some time."

Mr. Turnbuckle and his son responded with cold silence, ignoring Father's gesture. Thurgood's eyes remained unblinking, while Biltmore's fluttered several times. The father's thumbs were hooked in his vest, while the son's hands were jammed firmly into his pants pockets. Like so many familial relationships, they were reflections, but hardly mirror images of each other.

"You must have just arrived," I commented, noticing Biltmore's slept-on-the-plane clothing. "It was good of you to come to your father's assistance."

Biltmore looked at me with orbs oozing with rank condemnation, but there was a tremor in his lower lip that hinted at an entirely different emotion. I'm no amateur psychologist—amateur gardening taking up virtually all of my task-avoidance time—but I'd say a major war effort was under way within young Turnbuckle. Which armies and what agendas were engaged in "The Battle of the Bilt" I could only guess, but the repercussions from opposing artillery fire were playing havoc with his facial muscles.

"Buckminster's passing is a loss we all feel," said Monsignor Havermeyer, a bit weakly. "You both have my deepest sympathy ..."

"Hrmph," said Mr. Turnbuckle, turning away. He didn't move on, but rather presented us with what is called a "cold shoulder." In his case it was more on par with the iceberg that doomed the Titanic.

"Er ... hrmph," said Biltmore Turnbuckle, turning in obvious imitation of his father.

"Some sanctimonious bastards," growled Mr. Turnbuckle to his son, "have a fine way of showing sympathy."

"Er ... hrmph," said Biltmore lamely. In violation of the official Turnbuckle stance, he turned his head back in my direction, as if about to add something original. He licked his lips with a bone-dry tongue. Those angry orbs began to glisten, salty pools gathering in the shallow cups of his lower lids. Knowing that a blink would send a cascade of tears down his cheeks, he refrained, but it was a mighty strain. "Hrmph," he said again, turning away. I think I caught a glimpse of a leak, but said nothing.

"Well," said Father Baptist, "we'll move on."

"You do that," snorted Mr. Turnbuckle. "You move on, and keep on moving. We don't want you here."

"That is unfortunate," said Father, "because I'm here to stay."

"That is debatable."

"No, it is not."

"Hrmph."

"Mr. Turnbuckle," said Father, voice solid as granite, "if you have something to say, say it. Say it to me, to my face—but not here. The conflict between us shall remain just that: between us. I've no wish to discuss the matter in a public forum."

Mr. Turnbuckle's turned on his heels and faced his pastor. "That's because you'll lose."

Father Baptist didn't retreat one millimeter. "No, I will not."

They stood there in silence for several long moments, heartbeats thundering all around.

"You will regret this," said Mr. Turnbuckle presently.

"In the immediate, perhaps," said Father. "But in the Eternal, no. You seem to think I have a choice in the matter."

"Of course you have a choice."

"No sir, I do not. That is why I have nothing to lose. But you are on the verge of losing much, if not everything."

Mr. Turnbuckle turned several shades of green and purple, but otherwise kept his composure.

"You're a fine one to talk," called Patrick Railsback over Thurgood's shoulder. "You: a former cop."

"One of the best," said Father, releasing Mr. Turnbuckle from his stare and turning to leave. "Not that it matters."

"I'll take my donation money somewhere else," said Railsback through gritted teeth. "Don't think I won't."

Gosh, thought the gardener with all the emotion of a camphor pellet. Follow the unbouncing mothball:

> Two whole dollars a week
> On feast days maybe five
> Oh dear oh dear
> How will we survive?
> Our budget is a-crumbling
> Our parishioners are grumbling
> We're sinking like a dumpling
> How will we survive?

"So will the rest of us," said Mr. Caspar. "Then where will you be?"

"Yeah," called Argyle Poindexter Twiggler. "What'll you do then?"

Father walked away slowly. Those of us loyal to him shuffled along behind.

I suppose this would be a nice place to end this horrible scene in the graveyard. I myself thought we were going to stroll away without a further hitch. Unfortunately, there were a few more obstacles to overcome. The first one planted itself directly in our path.

42

"IT WOULD SEEM," oozed Monsignor Conrad J. Aspic, "that you have lost the confidence of your flock."

"They've—" began Father, but was suddenly distracted. He sniffed the air and glanced all around.

"Father Baptist?" pressed Monsignor Aspic. "They've what?"

"What?" blinked Father Baptist. "Oh. I was saying that my parishioners have been hit with a lot." He sniffed again. "They'll sleep on it."

"Ah," said the monsignor. "Let us hope they don't sleep on their pocketbooks. Without Mr. Turnbuckle's support, your parish will be in dire straits, if you don't mind my saying so."

"Speaking of money," said Father, sniffing again, this time with scrunched nostrils. "Monsignor Aspic, did you receive my bill?"

It was the monsignor's turn to blink. "Excuse me? Your what?"

"My bill."

"Your bill?"

"For services rendered to the archdiocese last June. You told me to address it 'Attention: Aspic.' I mailed it on the afternoon of the day we spoke."

"Ah yes, that," said the chubby-cheeked monsignor, glancing at his dazzling shoes with admiration. "It seems that the matter has been stalled due to the lack of proper forms."

"Forms?" asked Monsignor Havermeyer. "What forms? Isn't a bill a proper form?"

"Well, not exactly," said Aspic, rocking on his heels. "But I'm sure we can clear the matter up directly."

"Perhaps I should drop by your office tomorrow at the Chancery," said Father Baptist.

"That, in part, is why I'm here. The cardinal wishes to see you tomorrow morning. His office, not mine, of course."

"About my bill?"

"About another matter which has been brought to his attention."

"Does this matter have anything to do with my bill?"

"Come now, Father Baptist. Surely there are other things more important than money."

"Will you be at this meeting?"

"Most definitely."

"And may I assume you'll bring the proper forms for me to sign?"

"Forms?"

"So that you can pay my bill."

"You do have a one-track mind, don't you?"

"There are four sins that cry out to Heaven for vengeance," said Father sternly. "Defrauding the laborer of his wage is one of them."

"Saint James chapter five," said the gardener helpfully, "verse four."

"Oh?" said Monsignor Aspic. "And where can I find the other three?"

"I'll let you know," said the gardener, more helpfully still, "each time you commit one of them."

"In any case," hrumphed Monsignor Aspic, rocking on his heels, "I'll see what I can do. Everything at the Chancery is a blur at the moment, and most of my working materials have yet to be unpacked. I was foolish enough to mix them with my personal belongings."

"Ah," said Father, "you did say you were staying with your brother until they finish redecorating your rooms at the clerics' residence?"

"That's right. Much as I appreciate his generosity, I'll feel better when I can spread out in my new quarters. Woody's place is so tiny, I've only been able to unpack a few things. Besides, he lives on Beachwood—Hollywood Hills, you know, right below the famous 'Hollywood' sign—and it's, well, so near the problem you're working on with the police. Gives me the jitters just thinking about it. Yes, I can't wait to move into my new rooms at St. Philip's."

"What rooms at St. Philip's?" asked Monsignor Havermeyer, eyebrows high.

"Why, in point of fact," said Monsignor Aspic, eyebrows low, "yours, Monsignor. Not that they weren't nice the way you left them, you understand. We all have our tastes, and yours were certainly ... homey. But I prefer a more sterile environment, if you know what I mean. Gray is so much more conducive to clear thinking than pastel colors."

"I can imagine," said the gardener.

"You're painting it over in gray?" asked Havermeyer, aghast.

"Three different shades," winked Aspic. "Actually four counting the trim."

Something in Monsignor Havermeyer's intestines responded with a lurch.

"Am I to understand," said Aspic to Havermeyer, "that you gave up your spacious quarters at the cathedral for that camper back there in the parking lot?"

"Yes," said Havermeyer, shifting uneasily.

"Quaint, I suppose, but hardly fitting for a man of your stature and reputation."

"Best move I ever made," said Havermeyer, bristling. "If you gentlemen will excuse me, I have to practice my rubrics."

"'Rubrics'?" asked Aspic to the rest of us. "What's a 'rubric'?"

"It's a musical instrument," said the gardener. "Very beautiful, but requires lots of practice."

"Never heard of it. I must listen to him play it some time."

"No doubt you will," said Father. "One of these Sundays."

"Oh," said Aspic, "then it's a liturgical instrument."

"Right," said the gardener.

"Father Baptist," stammered Sergeant Wickes, "I can see you're busy. Can I drop by later?"

"Perhaps that would be better," said Father. "You can see how my attention is divided here. Why don't you come by this evening, say around eight?"

"Will do," nodded Wickes, but rather than wander off, he stayed put. Maybe he'd changed his mind about one of my finishes.

Before I could fish one out of my pocket, I heard a high-pitched beeping sound.

"Darn," said Wickes, looking down at the pager clipped to his belt. "That'll be Billowack. 'Scuse me, I left my cellular phone in the car."

"Nothing doing," I said, grabbing his arm and tugging him toward the rectory. "Use ours."

"But Martin—"

"No buts. Anything to get away from this mess."

"Okay," he said doubtfully. "I know your opinion of people with pagers who demand to use your phone."

> GARDENING TIPS: The sergeant, you see, unlike untold millions out there, had read my draft of The Endless Knot and had thereby learned some of my private prejudices.
>
> —M.F.

"Consider this an exception," I said. "But I assure you it will not become the norm."

43

"I KNEW THERE'D BE TROUBLE," said Millie, dumping a tray of ice into a pitcher of fresh-brewed tea. "The minute I saw the look in Mr. Turnbuckle's eyes before Mass, I just knew it."

"And you were right, Millie," I said, lowering my aching self onto a kitchen chair. "Use this extension, Sergeant."

Wickes snatched up the receiver from its cradle on the wall and started cranking the dial.

"Police business, Millie," I explained.

"Of course," said she, plunging a long spoon into the pitcher and stirring. "Trouble breeds trouble, I always say."

"Wickes here," said the sergeant, "Billowack paged me ... He didn't? Oh, it was you, Feldspar. What's up?"

Millie slammed two tall glasses filled to the brim on the table. No drop was spilled.

"You heard what they were saying out there?" I asked. "I didn't see you."

"I stayed on the fringe," she said, "biting my tongue, knowin' that Father'd prefer I stay out of it."

"Your insight becomes you," I said, smiling.

"My silence did not," she grimaced. "I guess I'm not as brave as I pretend."

"You're brave where it counts," I said, snatching her hand and giving it a gentle smooch. I winced, expecting the pitcher to land on my head, but the blow didn't come. When I opened my eyes, she was still standing there, silently looking down at yours truly, an unnerving twinkle in her eyes.

"Oh my God," said Wickes. "Repeat that."

"Trouble," I said to Millie.

She nodded in reply, absently rubbing the spot where I'd left my saliva.

"Got it," said Wickes, scribbling something in his notebook. "I'll grab Father Baptist and be right over." He slammed the phone down. "I trust Father Baptist won't refuse to go to a crime scene on a Sunday."

"I'd say he'd just be exchanging one for another," said the gardener. "What's up?"

"Another murder—this time a little girl. Six years old. Billowack hasn't answered his pager yet, and Lieutenant Taper's on his way."

"Mercy," cried Millie.

"But that breaks the pattern," I said. "Who and where?"

"An old apartment house half a block from Hollywood Boulevard. The girl's aunt reported her missing yesterday. Said the girl disappeared from her bedroom sometime during the night between Friday and Saturday. A few men combed the neighborhood, but without success. Then, less than an hour ago, the janitor found her in the basement, drained of blood."

"Found who in the basement?"

We turned and saw Father Baptist and Monsignor Havermeyer stepping through the kitchen door.

"Another victim," said Wickes. "A little girl this time. And get this: she lived in the same building as Elizabeth Unger."

"Oh no," said Father, gripping the edge of the kitchen table. "Not Patricia."

"Patricia Marie Nealy," read Wickes from his pad.

"You know her?" asked Monsignor Havermeyer.

"I spoke with her Friday morning," said Father, tremors rippling through his frame. "She saw Elizabeth Unger get into a car in front of 'Stogies' the night she was murdered."

"It would seem," said the gardener, "that 'Elibazeth' kept her promise and came back for her."

"Rather," said Wickes, "that the murderer came back and got rid of a key witness."

"This goes beyond ..." said Father, slamming his fists on the table. Iced tea spurted from the wobbling drinking glasses. "... beyond ..."

Monsignor Havermeyer put a hand on his shoulder. "You'd better go."

"Yes," said Father, straightening. "Sergeant, Martin, we've got work to do."

"For what it's worth," said Havermeyer, "I'll hold the fort."

"See that it's not burned to the ground," said the gardener, "when we return."

44

"HOW COULD THIS HAPPEN?" cried Mia Durham, Patricia Marie Nealy's aunt. Her face was buried in Father's chest. "She was just a little girl, a crippled little girl. She never hurt anybody. Who would do such a thing?"

"I don't know, my dear woman," said Father, looking over her shoulder as Solomon Young-sul Wong and John Holtsclaw examined the tiny body on the basement floor. "Perhaps you should wait upstairs."

"No, I don't want to leave her." She looked around at the dozen or so policemen in their various uniforms, their faces caught in the perpetual seesaw peculiar to their occupation, shifting between sympathy and detachment. "To think she was down here, alone, all this time—"

"She's not alone," said Father. "She told me you're Catholics?"

"Yes, yes. For what it's worth. I called St. Alexander's, but the man who answered said the priest was 'unavailable.' Playing golf, no doubt. He always says not to bother him on Sundays."

"I'm sorry to hear that."

"But you, a priest, come with the cops?"

"I was at hand when Sergeant Wickes got the call. And it would be better if you went with one of these officers. Sally?"

"Right here," said a woman in blue, stepping forward and gathering Mia Durham under her arm. "Let's go up to your apartment and make some coffee, maybe a sandwich."

"I don't want anything," sobbed Mia. "I couldn't eat a crumb."

"But Father Baptist skipped lunch," said Sally. "Right Father?"

"Indeed," said Father, appreciating Officer Sally's quick wits. "Martin and I will be up shortly."

"You like dry salami?" asked Mia over her shoulder. "Onions?"

"Anything," waved Father.

Ohhhh, I thought, rubbing my stomach.

"She was just a little girl," Mia's pained voice came drifting down the creaking staircase. "Just a little crippled girl. Who would do such a thing?"

"What do you have?" said Father, stooping between the coroners. They were crouched around the tiny body, bathed in an aura of pale yellow light from a bare bulb hanging from the unfinished ceiling.

"The same," said Solomon, pointing to the wounds on her neck, "and yet not the same."

"I see what you mean," said Father.

"Maybe that's because her neck was so tiny." Solomon blinked and sniffed. "You know, smaller than the killer was used to."

"We'll know more," said Holtsclaw, "when we can examine her under brighter lights."

"Do you have a microtopographic scanner?" asked Father.

"You have been keeping up," said Solomon.

"Not really. I was reading a magazine called *Homicide* at the barber shop the other day—"

"Gotcha," said Solomon. "We have access to the one at Good Sam, but it involves some red tape."

"Even so," said Father, "if you wouldn't mind wrapping yourself in some, I suggest you topo-scan this wound, and all the others so far."

"You on to something?" asked Holtsclaw. "It'll take a few days to arrange."

"Perhaps. Is there a red line around the back of her neck?"

"Nope," said Holtsclaw. "No such mark."

"And she wasn't just dumped down here," said Solomon, blowing his nose into a hankie. His lips were trembling. "She was ... *arranged* ... laid out, hands folded on her chest, nightgown modestly tucked in around her, with these flowers set on the floor around her head."

"On the unfinished part of the basement floor," said Holtsclaw. "He could have put her on the smooth cement over by the furnace, but he chose to leave her here, on the bare earth."

Father straightened, cupping a couple of white gardenias in his hand. "Laid out," he whispered. "Laid out. Dirt. Flowers. Nightgown. Carefully laid out, but on bare dirt? I don't see any marks on the ground."

"Smooth as silk," said Solomon. "This guy was either weightless, or he used a fine brush to smooth out his tracks. I'll be able to tell you which when the photoscopics are finished."

"You say that none of the other victims was ... arranged ... like this?"

"No," said Holtsclaw, examining his clipboard. "They were just dumped—face down, sideways, sprawled however they landed as they were pushed out of a car."

"This time it was done with ... care," said Solomon, stifling a gasp. "As if—"

"Say it," said Father.

Solomon shook a couple of tears from his eyelids. "I don't know what I was going to say."

"Well I'm saying this beats all," growled Chief Billowack, thumping down the stairs and into the dim light. "So we've got another one."

"Yes, and no," said Father. "The same cause of death, but a shift in details."

"So you say," said the chief, striding over to the body. "You know something, Jack-o? In all the years I've known you I've never known you to give me a straight—" He froze. "No one told me it was a little girl."

"Six," said Holtsclaw. "With a deformed spine—hunchback."

"My God, whores are one thing," said Billowack, a rare chord struck in the depths of his ire, "but this, this—"

"How long has she been here?" asked Father, dropping the flowers in a plastic envelope provided by Solomon Yung-sul Wong.

"I'd say at least twenty-four hours," said Solomon, looking around with a shudder, "maybe a little more."

"So she was murdered Friday night," said Father. "Or early Saturday."

"I'll be more positive once we get the body to the lab, but I think so, yes."

"Then that's another break in the pattern," said Father. "You said the other victims were spaced at intervals of three to six days. This makes two murders on the same night."

"That's right," said Wickes, who had remained silent thus far. "Tiara Stockwell, and now—"

"That you, Wickes?" barked Billowack. "Where's your pal, Taper?"

"Seeing his wife off at the airport," said Wickes. "She's flying to Colorado to visit her—"

"I don't care where she's going," said Billowack. "I want Taper in on this."

"I called him on his cell phone," said Wickes. "He was just leaving the terminal, but the midday Sunday traffic's thick. Maybe he should just meet us at the coroner's—"

"Yeah, fine," said Billowack. "Whatever."

"Uh-oh," said Solomon, crouching beside the body again. "Hand me your flashlight."

"What is it?" asked Holtsclaw, stooping beside him.

"There," pointed Solomon, "that discoloration on the front of her nightgown, under and around her hands. I assumed it was shadow, but now it looks like blood."

"Another wound?" asked Billowack.

"No," said Holtsclaw.

"You'd better look at this, Father," said Solomon, gently lifting her arms out of the way so that Holtsclaw could untie the pink ribbon that held the front of her gown together.

"My word," said Father.

I didn't want to look, but the ol' neck and eyeball muscles had minds of their own. There it was: a message scrawled in straggly letters on her skin, just below the ridge of her sternum:

$$\text{I Am Come-!!}$$

"Why would he leave a calling card now?" asked Billowack. "After eight other murders?"

"Beats me," said Wickes.

"Aha, so there have been other murders before this one."

"Of course," said Billowack. "Wait a minute, who said that?"

Suddenly the room exploded with a blinding flash of white light.

"Got it?" snapped a voice.

"Got it," quipped another.

"How—?" roared Billowack. "Who let these guys in here? Grab them!"

"Hey," yelled Jacco Babs of the *Times*.

"Watch the camera," yelled Ziggie Svelte, his photographer. "It's expensive."

In seconds the two reporters were locked in the embrace of an eight-tentacled octopus in four blue uniforms.

"How'd you get in here?" roared Billowack, spittle flying from his writhing lips.

"Quickly, Big Fella," said Jacco. "We hid in your shadow and followed you down the steps. And just as quickly we must go."

"Nothing doing," said Billowack. "Sergeant Feldspar, accompany these gentlemen from the press downtown."

"You can't do that," protested Jacco.

"Sure I can," said Billowack. "This is a crime scene, isn't it?"

"Yeah."

"And you saw the body, right?"

"Uh-huh."

"So now you're material witnesses."

"But we've got a deadline to make."

"Not this time."

"I think the chief just wants to impress upon you the need for discretion," said Father. "We have to keep a lid on this one."

"Aha!" chortled Jacco, heels scraping the floor as he was dragged toward the steps. "Cop-turn-priest-turns-vampire-hunter! Just wait'll I tell my editor this. Wait'll my readers get a gander at this. Wait'll—"

"Wait they shall, Bub," grinned Billowack, saliva dribbling down his chins.

"I thought," I was saying to Ziggie as he was likewise hauled off, "that once you got your 'Strobie' award, you'd be off on your own."

"Me, too," he shrugged.

"But here you are, still tagging along with Jacco the Babs."

"It's the breaks."

45

"HERE'S HER CRUCIFIX," SAID FATHER, fingering the tiny chain hanging on the post of the child's bed. He stepped over to the window, yellow gauze curtains fluttering in the hot breeze. "It wasn't torn from her neck because she wasn't wearing it."

"Mia Durham said it was odd that the window was open," said the gardener. "She said her niece insisted on keeping it closed at night to keep out the bugs."

"Yes," said Father, stroking the translucent fabric, "it is odd, as are many things about this little girl's murder."

"This little girl," said the gardener, "was anything but morbid. Look at these titles on her shelf: *The Wind in the Willows, Alice in Wonderland, Treasure Island* ... and she was only six?"

"A remarkable child," agreed Father, stepping away from the window and turning his attention to a print of Gandalf the Wizard, staff in hand, facing the dreaded Balrog in the Mines of Moria—a scene from Tolkiens's *The Lord of the Rings*. It was hanging on the wall above the child-sized chest of drawers. He ran his fingers along the bottom edge of the picture frame. "A life and a soul. And to think ..."

He left the sentence dangling.

"Think what?" I asked.

"Quiet, Martin, I'm thinking."

"Oh."

"What's up?" asked Sergeant Wickes, who had just entered. That was his way of announcing himself.

"Shh," I hissed. "He's thinking."

"About what?"

"I don't know. What is it you wanted, Sergeant?"

"I just wanted to tell you that the ambulance is leaving with the body. Aren't you two coming to the morgue?"

"Where?" asked Father, snapping out of his reverie.

"To the morgue," said Wickes. "Aren't you coming?"

"No," said Father, straightening the picture on the wall. "I think not."

"But—" said Wickes.

"Didn't you say you'd be dropping by the rectory this evening?" asked Father.

"Yes," nodded Wickes, a bit flustered. "Around eight."

"Why don't you bring Lieutenant Taper with you?"

"Larry? Well, sure, I guess." More flustered still. "That is, I was kind of hoping to talk to you ... myself."

"That can be arranged," said Father, "perhaps afterwards. By then the two of you will have examined Patricia, and you'll have Mr. Wong's preliminary findings."

"What about you? I mean, what are you going to do now?"

"Odd as it may seem," said Father, "I want to go home—home being St. Philomena's, and more specifically I need to spend some time before the Blessed Sacrament."

"I don't understand," said Wickes.

"I need to pray," said Father Baptist, an emphatic harmonic resonating through each syllable.

"Oh," said Wickes, fumbling in his pockets—something to do to cover his discomfiture. "Okay, I guess I'll be going."

"One more thing, Sergeant," said Father, still looking at the print.

"Yes?"

"Do you know anything about the Loch Ness monster?"

"What? What's that got to do with anything?"

Father closed his eyes and opened them again. "I'm just asking if you know anything about it. Do you think that it exists?"

"Well ..." Poor Wickes had that cornered look again. "Now that you mention it, I've read several books on the subject."

"And?"

"Mostly there's just a bunch of blurred photographs: a dark shape breaking the surface of the water. Nothing definite. And there's all kinds of reports—you know, motorists who saw something big and dark slithering across the road near the shore."

"And?"

"And what?"

"What do you think? What do you gather from all these sightings?"

"Hm." The sergeant scrunched up his face as if his mouth was about to give birth to something big, dark, indefinite, and slithery. "I'm no expert, and many of the reports are probably bogus—"

"But?"

"I think that there's enough evidence to suggest that, well, *something* is living in the lake. I don't think it's a plesiosaur left over from the Mesozoic age like some fanatics claim ..." A smug look fluttered across his face when he came up with the term "Mesozoic." Well, *I* was impressed.

"But?" said Father, ever the dentist extracting that one uncooperative tooth.

"Okay," said Wickes, shrugging widely. "Yes," he almost shouted, "I think there's a Loch Ness monster. Is that what you wanted me to say?"

"I wasn't trying to get you to say anything," said Father. "I was simply seeking your opinion."

"And now you have it?"

"Yes, thank-you."

"Grrrr." That's as close as I can approximate the sound Wickes made as he stomped out of the room.

"So now you know," I said to Father, whose eyes had yet to leave the bearded wizard in the picture.

"Yes," he said.

"Care to tell me what it is that you do know? I'm lost."

"Not if I can help it," said Father, finally detaching himself from the Mines of Moria. "You being lost, I mean. That's something I'll do everything in my power to prevent. Regarding Sergeant Wickes, I now know much. About our murderer I know even more."

"Such as?"

"Martin," he said, placing his hand on my shoulder and turning me around toward the door, "something's very wrong here. I can feel it—taste it even."

"You mean," I said as we exited the apartment, "things don't add up."

"Oh, but they do. The trouble is that they are beginning to add up to more than I bargained for."

46

"MORE BAD NEWS FOR SOUTHLANDERS," grated the voice on the Jeep's radio as we drove away from that apartment building. "This just in from the National Weather Service: 'The high-altitude cloud cover coupled with sweltering humidity will be with us for some time to come.'"

"You're sure you want to go home?" I asked Father, turning south on La Brea.

"Be it ever so humbling," said Father, rubbing his face.

"It goes on to say," continued the announcer, "that we're, and I quote: 'caught between Tropical Storm Ricky, which is pushing hot, moist air up from the equatorial Pacific, and an opposing front from the east that is being propelled by Hurricane Sidney which originated in the Caribbean Sea.' Unquote. Beach bunnies, muscle-bound guys, and all you just plain folks: if you was lookin' for good news, you ain't gonna find it here."

"My Dad always used to say," I said, changing lanes, "that when waiters started dressing better than their patrons, and newscasters began talking like Teamsters, our culture was showing ominous signs of decay."

"True," said Father, looking out his side window.

"I repeat: are you sure you want to go home? Maybe we should just drive on down the coast to San Diego, see the zoo, have a nice fish dinner in La Jolla—"

"I appreciate the thought," said Father, "but my primary duty still resides at St. Philomena's. Besides, I think I told Stella Billowack I'd give her another catechetical lesson this afternoon at two. It's almost that now."

"She'd understand if you canceled. Holy cow, Father, think of all that's happened today."

"Holy Orders, Martin. I took a vow, remember? A priest doesn't have the luxury of exhaustion, not in these matters. You never know when a soul may be called to God, and you must never let an opportunity to teach the Faith pass through your fingers. Besides, I find talking about the Catholic religion recuperative—rejuvenating, even."

"Yeah, I know what you mean. I'm curious to see how you're going to turn the Loch Ness Monster into a means of teaching the Faith to Sergeant Wickes. I mean, Saint Patrick had the shamrock. It was a brilliant use of something familiar to explain the incomprehensible."

"And I have Nessie," mused Father. He yawned and shrugged his shoulders. "Do you think the Tumblars will still be there when we get back?"

"Yeah, Pierre said something about them hanging around the grave-yard reading poetry. Sort of a morbid iambic picnic."

"Somehow that doesn't seem a bit odd for them. One thing is for sure: I don't want them involved any further in this vampire business. If anything should happen to one of them because I dragged them into it, I'd never feel right again."

"But all the victims have been women."

"All the victims were adult women until now. Who knows how else this fiend may deviate from the pattern?"

"Oh no," I said as I pulled into the back parking lot.

"What is it?"

"That limo parked too close to the monsignor's camper. It was there when we left. It's gotta be Monsignor Aspic."

"The Sign of Jonas."

"A big fat zero, if you ask me."

47

"WHY ARE YOU SO DOWN ON WOMEN, Mr. Feeney?" asked Jonathan as he, Pierre, and I rounded the back corner of the church. It was hard to tell in the perpetual twilight of the "Vampire's Shroud," whether it was mid-to-later afternoon or early-to-even-earlier evening, so I checked my watch. Four-thirty sharp.

"Me?" I asked, pausing to lean on my cane. I tucked my folded copy of the Religious Opinions section of the *Times* into my jacket pocket so that the headline still showed: PLANS FOR NEW CATHEDRAL STALLED, ADMITS CARDINAL; NO EXPLANATION GIVEN. "Me down on women? How can you say that?"

"You just said that love never works out."

"The way you expect it to, lad," I corrected him, reaching up as if to knock some sense into that bony forehead with my cane. "The way you expect it to."

"That's a grim view of life," he said, brushing back what was left of his thinning hair. "And kind of sterile, if you don't mind my saying so."

"Unlike yourself," said Pierre, grabbing Jonathan's wrist to take his pulse. "Nothing sterile about you." He placed his hand on Jonathan's forehead. "Ah, are we feeling a bit fluttery behind the eyes? A rush of blood toward the throat and away from the brain?" He moved his hand down to Jonathan's chest and gave it a mild thump.

"What the hell are you doing?" asked Jonathan, swatting Pierre away.

"Hm," said Pierre, eyes narrowing. "Experiencing a swelling of the pulmonary muscle in the chest cavity?"

"Classic symptoms," I said. "It's serious."

"Indeed," nodded Pierre. "Our findings concur, Doctor Feeney."

"What findings?" huffed Jonathan.

"Regarding your condition," said Pierre.

"It has been said," I explained sagaciously, "that the familiar hormonal rush, also known as 'infatuation,' which the male enjoys with respect to a particular woman in which he is, shall we say, 'interested,' is the closest thing a man ever experiences to a woman's normal mode of thinking. We've all felt it. It's a high, like a drug."

"Rex Stout again?" asked Pierre.

"Dear old Dad," I answered.

"Ah," said Pierre, "the 'fulcra philosopher.'"

"The same," I nodded. "'Philofulcrapher' was his precise term. Of course—"

"See what I mean?" said Jonathan, pointing at me. "You are down on women."

"Hold on," I countered. "What have I said that is 'down on women'?"

"That bit about the way women think."

"I don't know what you mean. I just described a wonderful sensation that men occasionally get to savor, and that women seem to enjoy almost perpetually. How was that being down on women?"

"I don't know," said Jonathan. "But somehow I thought it was."

"Perhaps you're the one who is unsure about them," I said.

"And with good reason," said Pierre.

"No doubt about it," I said, "women are a mystery."

"How so?" asked Jonathan, puzzled.

"Just look at any magazine rack," I expounded. "Any periodical intended for the male audience—motorcycles, sports cars, barbecues, fishing gear, whatever. Tell me: what will be on the cover?"

"A scrumptious young woman," said Pierre.

"Sure," said Jonathan. "So?"

"Ah," said the gardener, "but then look at the magazines that cater to the female audience: fashion, cooking, gardening, dieting, decorating, female issues. What's invariably on the cover?"

"A scrumptious young woman," said Pierre.

"Hm," said Jonathan.

"Except on the feminist-agenda rags," said Pierre, "in which case it's a not-so-scrumptious middle-aged banshee."

"You see?" I concluded. "The feminine mystique is as fascinating to women as it is to men."

"I'll concede the point," said Jonathan, "but I still don't agree with you about love."

"What?" I said. "That love never works out the way you think it will?"

"Dear boy," said Pierre, "*nothing* works out the way you think it will. Anything you strive for, no matter how much you've researched it, visualized it, planned it—be it job or relationship or domicile—once you have it, it won't be what you expected. There's always a twist. I dare say it's the one universal experiential 'given' that forces me to believe in God. Any rule which is so omni-pervasive must be the effect of an intimately involved Creator."

"I'm lost," said Jonathan.

"You're not lost," said Pierre. "Just not completely connected yet."

"Back to basics," I said. "Jonathan, the trouble with most men, as I see it, is not a matter of love. It's that they don't really like women."

"You're nuts," said Jonathan.

"Your pardon, my friend," said Pierre. "Listen to what Mr. Feeney is saying."

"Most men, in my experience," I said, "want to be with women, want to go out with them, make love to them, and so on; but very few actually *enjoy* them—not, in the same sense that they enjoy, say, fishing or, in the case of an intellectual, reading a good book."

"I don't follow you," said Jonathan.

"Why does a man go to the trouble to buy the equipment and travel the miles to go fishing? Or spend hours prowling through libraries and bookstores? Because he takes delight in the enterprise, the result, in the thing for itself."

"Yes," said Jonathan.

"But," I continued, "how many men do you know, single or married but mainly married, who chat with their male friends about their women in the same tones as they talk about the trout they caught over the weekend? Or the marvelous volume they found in the library stacks?"

"I don't know many married men, at least, not my age."

"Any age, then. Think about it. When have you ever heard a man off-handedly say how much he genuinely likes his wife? I'm not talking about 'love' here, just simple 'like.' And I don't mean at family gatherings where what he says will get back to her. I mean on his own turf, with his pals. What does he have to say about his wife? How delighted is he with her, as a phenomenon? How fascinated is he with the way she thinks, the way her mind works?"

"Mind works?"

"The way she arrives at conclusions, or plans her weekend, or just the way she arranges her things on the dressing table. The way she balances the checkbook, or the colors she picked for the wallpaper. The way she drives, the way she interprets road maps. The way she leaves her hosiery hanging in the bathroom, and arranges linen in the closet. When, Jonathan, when?"

"When what? I forget the question."

"When a man falls in love, he's generally 'out of control.' He gives in to feelings that are alien to him, and what grand feelings they are. He wakes up one day, married to this creature who is completely different from himself in plumbing, methodology, and demeanor. The question is: does he like the woman, not for her favors or emotional responses, but just as a woman—just as a woman?"

"Back to your diagnosis," said Pierre to Jonathan. "Are we feeling a certain giddiness, coupled with momentary flashes of the notion that you could walk on air? Is this not love, Master Clubb?"

"Go away," said Jonathan, face red.

"It's funny how embarrassing the realization is for a man," said Pierre to me as if Jonathan were a lab specimen. "He wants to shout it from the nearest mountain, but swallows his tongue around his closest friends. What does that tell us, Mr. Feeney?"

"About love?" I asked, just to be sure.

"Of course about love," said Pierre. "What else is on our friend Jonathan's mind these days?"

"Well," I suggested, "there is the ceremony Tuesday evening—"

"Somehow I don't think that's foremost in his thoughts," winked Pierre. He gave Jonathan a reassuring nudge. "'We experience a sense of release, do we, Master Rich? An unfamiliar freshness in the head, as of open air?'"

"'Master Rich'?" asked Jonathan, pushing away Pierre's hand. "Who're you quoting? Shakespeare?"

"Robert Bolt," said Pierre. "*A Man for All Seasons.* Thomas Cromwell speaking to Richard Rich, right at the end of Act One—just after Rich's first betrayal of Sir Thomas More."

"That's an odd thing to quote," said Jonathan.

"Just showing you," said Pierre, "that love and treachery produce identical physiological responses. Don't forget that."

"And you called *my* view of life 'grim' and 'sterile,'" I huffed at Jonathan.

"And 'crotchety,'" said Jonathan, jerking his wrist away from Pierre who was trying to take his pulse again. "Don't forget 'dour,' either."

"Young sir," I said with an authoritative sniff, "I'll have you understand that I am a hopeless romantic. That's why I know so much about it, this thing called 'love.'"

"I don't follow you," said Jonathan.

"I think you'll agree—even Pierre, here—that we all have an innate sense that 'love' should be something simple, honest, straightforward, and unwavering."

"True," said Jonathan.

"What," said Pierre to Jonathan, "that you agree with him or that you have an innate sense that love is simple, honest, and so forth?"

"That would amount to the same thing, wouldn't it?" asked Jonathan.

"I suppose," said Pierre. "But when 'love' is the topic, we must be painstakingly meticulous in our analysis."

"Or," I continued, ignoring Pierre but nonetheless attempting to be painstakingly meticulous in my analysis, "to put it another way: our intuition suggests, and St. John the Evangelist assures us, that love and God are intimately connected. You know the words of his first Epistle as well as I:

> Dearly beloved, let us love one another, for charity is of God. And every one that loveth, is born of God, and knoweth God. He that loveth not, knoweth not God: for God is charity.

"Of course," said Jonathan.

"Unfortunately," I said, "we rarely experience 'love' as such. Somehow our wiring invariably gets short-circuited, especially when we seek love among our fellow creatures—and women, you'll agree, are the most human of creatures. If nothing else, the resulting mess has provided playwrights, poets, actors and minstrels a handsome living while their characters agonize unceasingly about their stormy relationships before audiences that never seem to tire of reliving the agony through the performers' eyes—as if their own experiences were not enough."

"You're losing me again."

"Take Shakespeare. You've heard of him?"

"I believe I just mentioned him."

"So you did, lad, so you did. Then I refer you to the third act, second scene, of *Romeo and Juliet,* one of the great dramas of all time. Permit me to quote Juliet's reflections on Romeo:

> Come, gentle night, come, loving, black-browed night,
> Give me my Romeo, and when I shall die
> Take him and cut him out in little stars,
> And he will make the face of heaven so fine
> That all the world will be in love with night
> and pay no worship to garish sun.
> O, I have bought the mansions of a love
> But not possessed it, and though I am sold,
> Not yet enjoyed. So tedious is this day
> As is the night before some festival
> To an impatient child that hath new robes
> And may not wear them ...

"Beautiful," said Jonathan.

"The soliloquy or his delivery?" asked Pierre.

"But don't you see?" I said, placing my hand on Jonathan's shoulder and trying not to look Pierre in the eye lest I burst out laughing and ruin my presentation. "My dear friend, it's all so fleeting! We've only to turn the page—one single page—to find her feelings substantially altered:

> O serpent heart, hid with a flowering face!
> Did ever dragon keep so fair a cave?
> Beautiful tyrant! Fiend angelical!
> Dove-feathered raven! Wolvish-ravening lamb!
> Despisèd substance of divinest show!
> Just opposite to what thou justly seem'st,
> A damnèd saint, an honorable villain!

I heard footsteps approaching from behind on the brick path—the slick and clack of expensive soles—but continued with my recitation:

> O nature, what hadst thou to do in hell
> When thou didst bower the spirit of a fiend
> In mortal paradise of such sweet flesh?
> Was ever book containing such vile matter
> So fairly bound? O, that deceit should dwell
> In such a gorgeous palace!

"Erg," winced Jonathan.

"I'm not down on love, or women, or romance," I said, releasing his shoulder with an encouraging prod. "I'm hopelessly 'for' all three, and I encourage you in your interest in Stella Billowack. She's a lovely young woman, and hungry for the Faith you value so highly. But you asked, and I have answered: keep your eyes open. Romance is fine, it's part of the wonderful stuff of life. But I repeat, love—like all human endeavors—never turns out as any of us expects."

"'Spirit of a fiend'?" said the voice above the clacking shoes. "'Paradise of sweet flesh'? 'Vile matter'? What are you filling the boy's head with?"

"Shakespeare," I said, turning to Monsignor Conrad J. Aspic. *"Romeo and Juliet."*

"Ah," he said, jingling the change in his pockets. "A great romance."

"A great tragedy," I corrected him.

"Tragedy?" blinked the monsignor. "How so?"

"Well," said Pierre, "they do both commit suicide at the end."

"Really," he shrugged. "I didn't know."

"I guess they skipped it in your degree program," I said. "Suicide is anything but efficient."

"I suppose not," agreed the monsignor.

I gave him a long discerning look. "I'm surprised to find you still here, Monsignor Aspic."

"I'm a bit surprised myself," he said thoughtfully. "I'm afraid some of your parishioners have been bending my ears. And for hours."

Sharpening your horns more likely, I thought, but kept silent.

"I was looking for Father Baptist earlier," he said, "but he was out with you. Since you are now here, may I assume that he, also, has returned?"

"Assume all you like," I said. "I believe he's with Miss Billowack. They were sitting near St. Thérèse a short while ago. Mr. Clubb, Mr. Bontemps and I were just on our way to join them."

"Then I'll tag along," said the monsignor, apparently unaware of how unwelcome he was.

As we meandered through the garden, we could hear Father Baptist's voice growing gradually louder and louder:

> ... He was in the world, and the world was made by him, and the world knew him not. He came unto his own, and his own received him not. But as many as received him, he gave them power to be made the sons of God, to them that believe in his name. Who are born, not of blood, nor of the will of the flesh, nor of the will of man, but of God. AND THE WORD WAS MADE FLESH, AND DWELT AMONG US, and we saw his glory, the glory as it were of the only begotten of the Father, full of grace and truth.

"Goose bumps again," giggled Stella, rubbing her arms thoughtfully. "I could read that first chapter of John's Gospel every day and still find something new."

"Exactly," said Father, closing the book in his lap. "That's why we say it at the end of every Mass, day after day after day. It's the heart and soul of everything we believe."

"Perhaps in the—ahem—Old Rite," interrupted Monsignor Aspic, strutting out in front of Pierre, Jonathan, and myself. "But as you know, Father Baptist, that reading was deleted from the New Mass."

"I know it only too well, Monsignor," said Father, rising to his feet. "It's a pity."

"Hardly," said Aspic, and jingles and smiles. "The modern Church has grown beyond that kind of mystical woolgathering. I noticed this morning that you and your minions still genuflect at that erudite phrase."

"'ET VERBUM CARO FACTUM EST,'" quoted Father, bowing his head as he uttered the words. Pierre, Jonathan, and I complied. "'And the Word was made flesh.'"

"Precisely," said the monsignor, eyes twinkling as though he'd made a salient point. "Your attention to the myth at the expense of the reality is touching—and no doubt sincere—but out of step with the times."

"Then I revel in my clumsiness," said Father.

"You would do well to catch up on the writings of modern Scriptural commentators. They cast a different light on those outdated metaphors."

"The Incarnation is no metaphor."

"Sure it is. As is the Resurrection. Why, if some archeologist were to uncover the bones of Jesus Christ tomorrow in some tomb near Jerusalem, my Faith wouldn't change one bit—whereas you'd be devastated."

"Therein lies the risk of my Faith," agreed Father. "Saint Paul's, too: 'And if Christ be not risen again, then is our preaching vain, and your faith is also vain, for you are yet in your sins.'"

"First Corinthians," I mumbled. "Chapter fifteen, verse fourteen with a pinch of seventeen."

"You are a stubborn one, Father Baptist," said Aspic, his eyebrows scrunched in academic trepidation, not over my demonstration of my vast knowledge of Scripture, apparently, but over Father's insistence on referring to such irksome insights as the words of Saint Paul. The monsignor apparently bought into the school of thinking that preferred to refer to "the writer of the first letter to the Corinthians" rather than the author by name. I wonder if he'd play the same sort of doubt-inducing game with Herman Melville and *Moby Dick*, or Charles Dickens and *Oliver Twist*. "Yes, stubborn indeed."

"I should hope so, Monsignor," said Father. "All the Saints were likewise stubborn."

"So you declare yourself a Saint?"

"Far from it. But imitating them is the only path I know."

"Your narrow-mindedness will be your downfall."

"Or my Salvation. Are you getting all this, Stella?"

"Yes," she said, rubbing her arms all the harder. "I think so. It sounds to me, Monsignor, as though you don't believe in the Catholic Faith."

"Not the one your mentor here professes, no."

"But don't you say, even in your New Mass, 'I believe in One, Holy, Catholic, and Apostolic Church?'"

"Yes, but I obviously lend different meaning to the words than Father Baptist seems to apply."

"You mean those words can have many meanings?"

"Of course—definition invariably rests with the speaker."

"And the listener?"

"The hearer applies connotation according to personal context."

"That's strange," said Stella. "I mean, isn't that like Humpty Dumpty?"

"What?"

"In *Through the Looking-Glass*. Didn't he say: 'There's glory for you!' and when Alice said she didn't know what he meant, he said, 'Of course you don't—till I tell you.'"

The monsignor was scowling, but she continued:

"Then Alice said, 'The question is, whether you *can* make words mean so many different things.' And Humpty Dumpty answered, 'The question is, which is to be master—that's all. When *I* use a word, it means just what I choose it to mean—neither more nor less.' And then he added, 'When I make a word do a lot of work like that, I always pay it extra.'"

"Pass the collection plate," said Pierre. "It's the one sacramental you modernists still believe in."

The monsignor choked on his dazzle. It must've hurt.

"A fine girl," I whispered to Jonathan, nudging him in the ribs. "Don't you dare let her slip away."

"You say that?" he blinked.

"I'll shout it from the rooftops if you like," I whispered a little louder.

"That won't be necessary," he blinked a little softer.

I nudged him in the ribs again. "Well—?"

"Well what?"

"Well, go on. It's why you stuck around. Ask her."

"Ask me what?" she blinked cheerfully.

"Well," ahemed Jonathan. "Uh, Stella, it's just that I asked Pierre here, if he could arrange for a guest invitation to the 'House of Illusions.' I was wondering if you'd care to, uh, um, that is, if you'd consider going with me."

She rolled her eyes. They were eyes meant for rolling. "When?"

"Tomorrow night," hemmed Jonathan. "I think."

Her eyes fluttered and snapped to. "Of course. I'd be delighted."

"You would?"

"She would," I assured him.

"Uh," he gulped. "Then if you give me your number, I'll call with the details as soon as I know them."

"Sure."

The twang of an arrow piercing a certain heart was almost audible. I warned him, and I encouraged him, but at that moment his eyes were wide but certainly not open.

48

"THIS IS FOR YOU," SAID SERGEANT WICKES, handing Father Baptist a legal-sized envelope. "Sybil Wexler said to make sure you got it."

"Yes indeed," said Father, leaning back in the chair in his study. With the desk lamp set on low the room was rather dark. He opened the envelope, unfolded the paper within, and scanned it briefly. "This will come in handy tomorrow." He tossed the page onto his desk and snatched up his pipe. "Gentlemen, you are almost two hours late. I assume this means you've been hard at work. Please make yourselves comfortable."

Lieutenant Taper took my favorite chair's twin, and Sergeant Wickes made himself uncomfortable by pacing back and forth on the throw rug.

"You look a bit ragged, Sergeant," I said before I began the painful process of settling down into my own chair. "Could you use a shot of bourbon?"

Wickes, who did look like he could use it, nodded. His hair, usually neatly combed, was unkempt. His shirt collar was open and his tie hung loosely around his neck.

"Help yourself," I said as I made my descent. "There's a bottle and glasses on the shelf there by your elbow—the section marked, 'To be forewarned is to be forearmed.'"

He looked dubiously at the curled label I had taped to the bookshelf long ago beneath the row of "dangerous books," and then found his way one shelf up.

"No, a bit more to your right," I sighed as I settled and the cushion sighed. "There, behind that protruding copy of *Veritatis Splendor*."

"Thanks," he said, retrieving a bottle of Jack Daniels from its hiding place. The glass quivered in his hand as he poured himself a lion's ounce. Maybe three. Admitting weakness was not his forte, but gratitude was not beyond him. "Thanks, I really need this."

"Lieutenant?" offered Father as he scooped a stack of tobacco out of a tattered leather pouch.

"Naw," said Taper, opening another envelope, this one nine by twelve and thick with paperwork. "A pipe is tempting but I'll pass."

"So what can you tell me?" asked Father, striking a match.

"For one thing," said Taper, pulling out a sheet and shoving it across Father's desk, "the wound on Patricia Nealy's neck, as you pointed out earlier today, is decidedly different from any of the other victims. Here's a side-by-side comparison prepared by Sybil Wexler."

I leaned forward to peer at the exhibit.

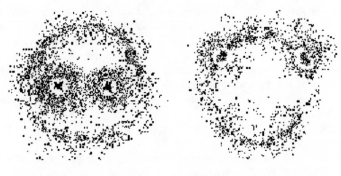

Unger, Elizabeth   Nealy, Patricia Marie

I sank back into my seat, queasy.

"As you can see," said Taper, "the teeth marks in the previous murders encircle the puncture wounds. In the Nealy case, the punctures are right where the canines should be."

"It would seem," said Wickes, pouring his second glass, "that our murderer has come up with a better set of dentures."

"He doesn't have to puncture then suck," said Taper distastefully. "He can now bite and suck in one maneuver."

"If you have the money," said Wickes around his glass, "you can buy anything in this city, or have it made."

"What about the rest of the impressions?" asked Father, running his pinkie around the shape of the wound on Patricia Nealy's neck. "The other teeth, I mean. They don't seem to match either."

"There we're not sure," said Taper. "The rest of the teeth marks aren't really bites. The skin isn't broken, except for the puncture points. They're just dents in the skin—enhanced with space-age technology, to be sure; but nonetheless just pressure indentations in the epidermis. Hard to measure, hard to analyze."

"Is Mr. Wong having any luck procuring that microtopographic scanner?" asked Father.

"Hopefully tomorrow," said Taper. "I understand he'll have to requisition a moving van to bring the unit from the hospital to the morgue. It means a lot of paper shuffling."

"Has the saliva been analyzed from around the Nealy girl's wound?" asked the gardener.

"The blood type is inconclusive," said Taper. "Somehow the lab tests got contaminated. It happens. Something to do with enzymes—ask Wong and Holtsclaw, not me. As for other residues—"

"If I were a betting man," said Father, "I'd wager that there were no traces of myrrh, sodium monofluorophosphate, calcium carbonate, propolis, or any toothpaste ingredients around the wound."

"And you'd walk away a rich man," said Taper, pulling out a typed sheet. "The MO has changed. None of those chemical traces, and no allicin. Wong and Holtsclaw knew what to look for and came up with zip."

There was a moment of silence. Well, not quite. The quiet was punctured by the sound of the sergeant downing his second shot. His eyes bulged and his cheeks puffed. He was not accustomed, I gathered, to heavy drinking.

"So," said Father.

"So," said Taper.

"So?" blurted Wickes, pouring a third. "Valdemar—isn't that what he called himself when he was floating beside the Farquar Terrace?—seems to have become dissatisfied with the blood of dingie women. Children are now fair game."

"Unfortunately so," said Father.

"Bad enough," said Wickes, swirling the dark broth in his glass, "when he was convincing dimwitted chicks that he's a real vampire, seducing them into letting him drink their blood, then dumping them like garbage in back alleys. Cool? Yeah. Suave? Sure. Psychotic? You bet. We've dealt with cold-blooded killers before. But now—?"

"Yes," said Father.

"Sergeant," said Taper, "maybe you've had enough—"

"A little girl," said Wickes. He tossed the bourbon down his throat and swallowed painfully. Tears were pooling in his eyes. "She was just a little girl. And ... and ..." He slammed the bottle down on the desk. "Dammit! She was ..."

"Innocent," whispered Father Baptist.

"And crippled," cried Wickes. "What kind of fiend would kill a defenseless, deformed little girl?"

"Sergeant!" barked Taper. "Get a hold of yourself. It's not like you've never seen beatings and molestations—"

"This is different," said Wickes, wiping his mouth with his sleeve. "This wasn't some beer-guzzler taking out his frustrations on his kid. This wasn't some free-basing whore, or a single mom with post-partum depression. Those things, as horrible as they are, can be traced to some kind of cause, a societal problem, or a psychosis, or something-or-other—"

Sergeant Wickes was beginning to wave around worse than Buzz Sawr.

"—but not this. This is, is, is—"

Father Baptist put aside his pipe and rubbed his eyes. I sensed that he wanted Wickes to fish around in his private lexicon, much deeper down than show-off terms like "Mesozoic," and find a basic, primal, four-letter word beginning with "e" and ending in "l" that almost rhymed with "weasel." But Wickes, with all his waving and ranting, couldn't seem to find it. He snatched up his glass and poured himself another shot.

"Is this," said Father finally, "what you wanted to talk with me about, Sergeant?"

"I don't know," said Wickes, grimacing as something inside his gut rebelled. "You seem so sure of some things, but I can't seem to ... I don't think I can ..."

"Perhaps I should take him home," said Lieutenant Taper apologetically. "I've never seen him like this."

"No rush," said Father. "I don't mind. Sometimes alcohol is a good—"

"Why—?" blurted Wickes, almost yelling.

"Yes, Sergeant?" asked Father. "Would you like to see me alone now?"

"Yes!" roared Wickes. "No! I don't know. What were you getting at with those questions about St. George and the Loch Ness monster?"

"Ground work," said Father. "I was laying a foundation—"

"Foundation?" slavered poor Wickes. "Ground work? Why in the midst of all this horror do you pester me with these stupid, off-the-wall, blind-idiot—"

The phone rang.

We all looked at it.

It was closest to me.

"St. Philomena's rectory," I said as calmly as I could. "Who? Of course." I turned to Taper. "Lieutenant, it's for you. Billowack."

Frowning, the lieutenant took the phone. "Yes, sir? No, I was just discussing—" His face fell. He listened intently for several minutes. "Where? ... Who? ... Got it." He glanced over at Wickes and then back to the phone. "I don't know where he is, Chief. I'm on my way."

He handed the receiver back to me and I cradled it.

"Another murder," said Father.

Taper nodded. "Babbette Starr. She was found on the grounds of the 'House of Illusions.' One of the magicians found the body—Surewood Forst. He identified her. Said she was a regular."

"I remember," I said glumly, thinking back to that bizarre evening. "She was in Elza's Sitting Room Friday night."

"You met her?" asked Taper.

"She made a pass at Pierre Bontemps."

"Whatever," said Taper. "I must get over there immediately, but—"

Suddenly Wickes bolted from the room and raced down the hallway to the bathroom.

"—the sergeant obviously isn't up to it. You coming, Jack?"

"I must," said Father, rising wearily. "Martin, I'll go with the lieutenant. I think you'd better stay here and get some coffee into Sergeant Wickes."

"Gladly," I nodded, listening to the uproar down the hall. "When he's sober, should I bring him?"

"No," said Taper sadly. "He's had enough for one day."

49

"'THEN THE DEVIL TOOK HIM UP into the holy city,'" I was reading from the fourth chapter of St. Matthew's Gospel in the study as the clock struck the quarter before midnight:

> ... and set him on the pinnacle of the temple, and said to him: If thou be the Son of God, cast thyself down, for it is written: That he hath given his angels charge over thee, and in their hands shall they bear thee up, lest perhaps thou dash thy foot against the stone.
>
> Jesus said to him: It is written again: Thou shalt not tempt the Lord thy God.

Sergeant Wickes, asleep in my chair's twin, had finally settled down into a lump of twitching muscles and pitiful groans.

I was about to close Dad's old Bible when I noticed that the above passage was marked with a faded, wobbly asterisk. The penciled footnote said to check Psalm Ninety. I did so:

> For he hath given his angels charge over thee: to keep thee in all thy ways.
>
> In their hands they shall bear thee up: lest thou dash thy foot against a stone.
>
> Thou shalt walk upon the asp and the basilisk: and thou shalt trample under foot the lion and the dragon.

Hmm. Another asterisk. I followed the trail to the twelfth chapter of the Apocalypse. It was the famous passage concerning a "woman clothed with the sun" who was travailing in childbirth:

> ... and behold a great red dragon, having seven heads, and ten horns: and on his heads seven diadems:
>
> And his tail drew the third part of the stars of heaven, and cast them to the earth: and the dragon stood there before the woman

who was ready to be delivered; that, when she should be delivered,
he might devour her son.

On a hunch, I groped around the floor for my trusty dictionary.
When it comes to dragons, one must be painstakingly meticulous in
one's analysis:

> **dra•gon** *n* A legendary reptile with fatal breath and glance, usu-
> ally represented as a monstrous winged and scaly serpent or
> saurian with crested head and enormous claws.

I looked from the page to my sleeping friend, and then over to Father
Baptist's empty chair.

"Why?" I asked. "Why *did* you ask Sergeant Wickes here about St.
George's dragon and the Loch Ness monster?"

The chair made no reply.

"Oh well," I said, shutting my books and reaching for the light. "As
you so often remind us: with few exceptions, there is a point to everything you say and do."

Monday, October Twenty-third

**Feast Day of Saint Anthony Mary Claret,
missionary in his own country, Spain,
and the Canary Islands,
who founded the Claretian Order,
was appointed Archbishop of Santiago, Cuba,
later exiled with his Queen in the revolution of 1868,
and attended the First Vatican Council (1870 AD)**

50

"CHIEF BILLOWACK INFORMS ME," said Cardinal Morley Psalmellus Fulbright, settling down in the new high-backed chair—dare I call it a "high chair"?—in his royal conference room, "that the investigation is not going well."

"There have been complications," said Father candidly, "but I'm confident we'll solve the case."

I've skipped the intros—yes, Father Baptist and I sucked His Elegance's blasted sapphire before taking our seats. It tasted like window cleaner. So far, we were the only ones present. It occurred to me that the room was a microcosm representing the macrocosm of the state of the Catholic Church in modern times: all those empty chairs facing nothing in particular—but what chairs! What beautiful chairs! Don't get me started.

Our man Morley had apparently been spending a bundle redecorating his suite of offices—and just since last Wednesday. Red was the thematic hue of the day: if it wasn't crimson, scarlet, vermillion, cranberry, burgundy or carmine, it wasn't there. The rugs, curtains, carpets, seat cushions all looked as though they'd enjoyed a good bloodbath.

> GARDENING TIPS: If the word "sanguine" comes to mind, as in "having blood as the predominating bodily humor, characterized by sturdiness, high color, and cheerfulness" ... well, f'rget it.
>
> --M.F.

"Might I ask," said Father Baptist, glancing at his wristwatch with the cracked lens and twisted minute hand, "if you are expecting Monsignor Aspic at this meeting?"

"He'll be here shortly," said Fulbright, fluffing his robes. "Why do you ask?"

"He and I have some business to discuss," said Father.

Absently, I set my copy of yesterday's *Times* on the table. It just happened to be opened to the Religious Opinions section, the headline of which just happened to be: PLANS FOR NEW CATHEDRAL STALLED, ADMITS CARDINAL; NO EXPLANATION GIVEN. When Morley's red-rimmed eyes caught sight of it, he swallowed loudly, stared ruefully, and sniffed contortedly. Unconsciously, his hand went up and began massaging the gnarly, purplish bump on his forehead.

"Problems, Your Eminence," asked Father casually, "with the cathedral?"

"Funny thing," said Fulbright, almost to himself. Rub, rub, rub. "As you know, my cathedral, Saint Valeria's, sustained considerable damage during the Northridge earthquake some years back. The estimates for repair are as high as seventy million dollars."

Or as low as five hundred thousand, thought the gardener, who kept that bit of information to himself.

"I thought," said the cardinal, "that the quake was a sign from above: time to demolish that dreary, old building and construct a beautiful, modern structure which better befits the spirit of the age."

In other words, thought yours truly, the old cathedral epitomized the Old Mass, which contradicts the myopic miasma of the New Rite, so go it must.

"Then those infernal meddling societies raised a ruckus," rub, rub, rub, "declaring it a historical landmark."

Which it is, I pondered, it being one of the oldest buildings still in use in Los Angeles.

"I have announced my plans," added Fulbright, "to move Saint Valeria's relics from under the main altar to New Golgotha Cemetery for safekeeping."

"Yes," said Father, "I did hear something about that."

So did I, scowled the gardener, amazed at such brazen sacrilege. To think that Morley Fulbright would take it upon himself to move the incorrupt body of a martyred Saint from a place of honor to some bare niche in an ordinary mausoleum, and for as transparent a reason as "safekeeping"?! Don't get me started.

"But every time I try to gather the resolve to go ahead and clear the forest at the Del Agua Mission," rubbity rub rub, "or even consider reviewing the architect's drawings for the new building, I get this piercing headache."

"Odd," said Father.

Just, thought I.

"Very," nodded the cardinal, distracted. "Ever since that dedication ceremony last June ... someone said they saw an old woman strike me ... with a pair of binoculars, of all things ... but I just can't remember."

Father and I exchanged knowing glances.

"It's almost as if—" The cardinal blinked, then grimaced, then glared at us as if we were intruders. He made a sound like a punctured muffler. "No matter."

"New Golgotha," said Father. "Roberto Guadalupe mentioned that name. I thought it odd at the time. What became of 'Sacred Heart Cemetery,' Your Eminence?"

"My deceased friend, Bishop Brassorie," said the cardinal, "suggested the change of name. He was lobbying for it, in fact, shortly before his death. I thought it odd—I think the name's damned peculiar, actually—but as it was in a sense his last wish, I ordered the change just before I was called to Rome."

"Yes," nodded Father. "It is strange that he, of all people, should have proposed so fitting a name for so fitting a place."

"Well, no matter," said His Elegance. "We've got more important things to discuss right now—"

Just then the door opened. In came Thurgood T. Turnbuckle sporting a freshly-trained hairpiece, and his son, Biltmore F. Turnbuckle, Esquire, in need of none. Without acknowledging us or even licking the royal ring, they took their seats off to Fulbright's left—our right. I thought I heard TTT wheezing something about something being "insufferable," but I couldn't tell if he was referring to clergy in general or the hard climb up the Chancery stairs in particular.

Just before the door clicked shut, it swung open again as another presence entered the room.

"Who are you?" asked the cardinal.

"Allow me to introduce Mr. Bruford de Montfort," said Father, extending his hand to the newcomer. "My attorney."

"What?" barked Mr. Turnbuckle.

"Your attorney?" hrumphed Fulbright, eyes darting between Father Baptist and his unwelcome solicitor. "Why did you invite a lawyer—no offense intended, Mr. de Montfort. I've heard of you, of course. I was unaware that you represented Father Baptist."

I considered pointing out that at our last meeting the cardinal archbishop had brought two attorneys of his own and Father hadn't objected, but held my peace.

"For many years, Your Eminence," said Mr. de Montfort amiably, but with that smile they teach lawyers at the best of law schools: confident yet demure, condescending yet reticent, impressive yet unnerving.

With a cup of courtesy, an ounce of elegance, and just a pinch of fi-
nesse—and not a hint of embarrassment—he dropped to one knee and
smacked the hefty sapphire ring. Morley smiled graciously in spite of
himself. Mr. de Montfort smoothly stood erect. "Actually, I suspect
you've heard of my brother, Drew. He gets all the notoriety, since he
handles the firm's criminal cases. My specialties do not generate media
interest. Still, Father Baptist and I go way back."

"Indeed," said Mr. Turnbuckle, eyes narrow. "I imagine even celebrated police detectives need attorneys."

"The best need the best," said Mr. de Montfort, smile unchanged. He
assumed the chair on the other side of Father Baptist from yours truly.

"Too bad he became a priest on you," countered Mr. Turnbuckle.
"Now you have to offer your services 'pro bono.'"

"Indeed," smiled Mr. de Montfort, "I prefer to think of it as offering
my best effort to God."

"In deed?" chirped Monsignor Aspic, who had just arrived in his usual
plume of aftershave and mouthwash, mopping his brow and wiping his
lips with a white silk handkerchief. He slipped like an oily sardine into
a seat near the cardinal's right—our left. "Let's not forget thought and
word. Sorry I'm late. As you know, I'm still staying at my brother's
place just off Beachwood Drive in those confusing Hollywood Hills,
and they're working on the sewer pipes or something. The street's all
torn up. It took me forever to get past the jam."

"Well, let's get started shall we?" said Fulbright, rolling his eyes
wearily around the table. This was not going to be pleasant.

"Yes," gruffed Mr. Turnbuckle. "I insist that we settle this tomfool-
ery about my son's funeral immediately. And I want you to see to this
priest's punishment straight away."

"Mr. Turnbuckle," said Fulbright, not at all used to being spoken to
in such a manner, "we are grateful indeed for the generous contributions
you have made over the years to this archdiocese—"

"Oh?" blurted the gardener, glaring at Mr. Turnbuckle. It was my
only slip of the morning—I promise.

"—and naturally," continued Morley, "we hope to, as you say, settle
this matter to your satisfaction."

"There is nothing to settle," said Father Baptist evenly.

"So you say," growled Turnbuckle to Father, then to Cardinal Fulbright, "See? What have I been telling you? Who does he think he
is?"

"We must admit, Father Baptist," said the cardinal—notice the royal
"we"—"that your position in this matter is callous. On what possible
grounds do you refuse to bury Mr. Turnbuckle's son without Mass or
ceremony? Surely the decision of the Second Plenary Council of Baltimore —"

"Has no bearing on the issue," said Father. "Forgive me for inter-rupting, Your Eminence, but that council had no binding ecclesiastical authority. No such local or national council does."

"So you say," said the cardinal.

"So do five canon lawyers in Rome," said Mr. de Montfort, produc-ing several official-looking faxes from his briefcase and spreading them on the table.

"You are a secular lawyer," said Mr. Turnbuckle, "not ecclesiastical."

"But I'm connected," said Mr. de Montfort, "with the best of theirs, I assure you."

"Words," scoffed Turnbuckle. "So many words. I'm a man of ac-tion, not verbiage, and I say remove Father Baptist from his parish this instant, strip him of his faculties, or I'll—"

"We will decide," said the cardinal in a low, penetrating voice, "what is to be done, Mr. Turnbuckle."

As the temperature vacillated between the heat of ire and the cold of hatred—or is it the heat of cold and the ire of hatred?—I absentmindedly reached for the brown scapular under my shirt and realized with a start that it wasn't there.

> GARDENING TIPS: There is some difference of opin-
> ion among Catholics who take such things seriously
> as to whether the requirement to wear the brown
> scapular "at all times" includes during the taking
> of a shower.
>   Since I didn't like going around with a damp
> circle on the front of my shirt all morning, I
> usually removed mine during bathing procedures.
>   The events of this day would swing my opinion to
> the other side.
>   --M.F.

I remembered leaving it on the bathroom doorknob as usual when I took my morning shower, but in the haste and anticipation of this meeting at the cardinal's office I had neglected to put it back on. There was no help for it now, but I made a mental note to scold myself later.

"Permit me," said Mr. de Montfort, hitching his fingers into his vest pockets, "to cut to the chase, since all our time is valuable. Unlike the rest of the parishes in this archdiocese which are the legal property of the reigning prelate, Cardinal Fulbright, Father Baptist bought the land, buildings, and all property known as St. Philomena's Catholic Church with his own money—his pension from the police force, to be precise. Paid in full. I have the documents here for your inspection. He is not subject to removal, in other words, from his own premises."

"But he is subject to Church authority," said Fulbright, bristling. "He owes his ecclesiastical obedience to his cardinal archbishop—us. If we order him to comply with Mr. Turnbuckle's wishes, he must obey. Admittedly he is officially on leave, but he is nonetheless our priest."

"I beg to differ," said Mr. de Montfort. "I have it on good authority—"

"A moment, please," said Father Baptist, raising his hand. "Permit me to speak for myself."

"Of course," said Mr. de Montfort, smile still unchanged.

"Your Eminence," said Father, "you are indeed my lawful superior, and I have sought to obey you in every way that I morally should. We have butted heads over our differences for several years now; but with the exception of an arguably life-and-death situation last June, I have never openly defied you or disobeyed your lawful commands. My semi-permanent leave at St. Philomena's has been a tenuous compromise, and one for which I am eternally grateful. In this matter, however—"

"You're not going to let him go on like this," roared Mr. Turnbuckle. "More of his verbose dodges!"

"This is not a dodge, Mr. Turnbuckle," said Father. "I am stating facts. I am indeed the sole proprietor of St. Philomena's. As such, and as your pastor, I have explained to you the traditional stand of the Roman Catholic Church on suicides. My allegiance to the cardinal is but a conduit to the obedience I owe to the Popes, Councils, and Saints who have protected the True Faith through the ages. If, Heaven forbid, he should attempt to choke off that conduit, I have no choice but to bypass him."

"Watch it, Father," said Morley stiffly. "Be very careful what you say."

"Always," said Father Baptist. He cleared his throat and continued. "Your Eminence, since you cannot order me from my own property—a weapon you can employ on any of your regularized parish priests—your only alternative is to punish me ecclesiastically, that is, to revoke my faculties."

"Don't tempt us," said Fulbright. "Indeed we will."

"Fine," said Father, "in which case, under the Code of Canon Law, I would have to assume a state of emergency has arisen and thereby be forced to continue in my priestly capacity without your permission."

"There are historical precedents," interjected Mr. de Montfort, all smiles.

"In which case," said Father, "I would have to appeal to the Penitentiaria, the Court of Rome. That would take many months. No doubt an inquiry would be made into why I felt a state of emergency existed in the archdiocese. They would want to know why I have had to take extreme measures, such as buying my own church, in order to perpetuate the Latin Mass. They would perhaps wonder why you have ignored the Pope's directive of July 2, 1988—"

> GARDENING TIPS: Father was referring to a widely-distributed but little-known document known as a "motu proprio" (i.e., "in his own hand") entitled Ecclesia Dei, in which His Holiness Pope John Paul II stated in part:

>   *   *   *

>> To all those Catholic faithful who feel attached to some previous liturgical and disciplinary tradition, I wish to manifest my will to facilitate their ecclesial communion by means of the necessary measures to guarantee respect for their rightful aspirations. In this matter I ask support of the Bishops and of all those engaged in pastoral ministry in the Church ... By virtue of my Apostolic authority I decree ... respect must everywhere be shown for the feelings of those who are attached to the Latin liturgical tradition, by a wide and generous application of ... the use of the Roman Missal ... of 1962.
>>   (Hint: "..." = "excessive papalese deleted")

>   *   *   *

> This directive by the Holy Father was apparently an attempt to soothe the ire of Trads throughout the world who couldn't stomach the New Mass--and it would have worked if the bishops had obeyed it. Instead, with a few exceptions (and Morley Fulbright wasn't among them) the directive was unilaterally ignored.
>   --M.F.

"Hold it right there," interrupted Morley. "We did no such thing. We authorized one Latin Mass to be said every Sunday in the Archdiocese of Los Angeles—aside from your own, of course, which we don't officially recognize."

"True," said Father, "but in a different church each week, and in a different part of the archdiocese, the largest in the world. Do you know your nickname in some of the conservative Catholic papers? They call you 'The 'Copter Cardinal.' How else is anyone going to get to all these widespread Masses without a helicopter, especially the aged and infirm?"

"Nonetheless," said Fulbright, "We have complied."

"You call that 'respect for our rightful aspirations.' Perhaps the august members of the Penitentiaria will think otherwise. I have it on good authority that they would have to find in my favor, since I am appealing to the same Laws of the Church that govern you as well as me. The liberal media would compassionately side with you, but in the end a great many Catholics would become aware of their responsibilities to the Truth and side with me."

"You take on much," said the cardinal.

"Only that which you yourself placed on my shoulders with the laying on of hands at my Ordination."

"My my," fluffed Monsignor Aspic, wiping his face again and stuffing his handkerchief nervously into one of his pockets. "My my."

"Liturgical Reform is not what we came here to discuss," huffed Mr. Turnbuckle.

"Quite right," fluttered Monsignor Aspic, mindful of his financial responsibilities. "Certainly we must take into consideration that Buckminster Turnbuckle, indeed anyone contemplating suicide, must have been in grave need of psychiatric help—"

"Are you suggesting," said Mr. Turnbuckle, "that my son was mentally ill?"

"You don't think so?" asked the cardinal.

"Of course not!" growled Mr. Turnbuckle. "An abysmal failure, yes, but I'll not have you turn this circus into character assassination."

"But surely," said Monsignor Aspic meekly, "we should consider the possibility."

"In some cases," intruded Mr. de Montfort, smile still fixed, "if it can be shown that a person was suffering from serious chronic depression, or some parallel psychological dysfunction—"

"—the matter would be mitigated, of course," offered Monsignor Aspic. "We could assume a lack of full knowledge or consideration on the part of the, uh—"

"Bushwa," said Mr. Turnbuckle. I hope I spelled it correctly. "No son of mine is going to be accused of—"

"But what of final repentance?" blurted out an unexpected voice.

"What's that Biltmore?" gawked Mr. Turnbuckle, shocked but pleased that his pup had finally discovered his larynx. "What's that you say?"

All eyes went to Biltmore, who promptly began to wilt. "Is—is—isn't it t-t-t-true," he stammered, "that in cases of suicide ... I mean ... isn't there always at least some hope that at the last second Bucky—you know—he, he maybe changed his mind?"

"Aha!" barked Biltmore's father, whacking the table with his open hand. "That's right. That's damned right."

"Such might be the case," said Father Baptist, "of, say, a woman who swallows a handful of pills. She may well think better of it and beg God's mercy before she succumbs. If she were found with a telephone in her hands, apparently trying to call for help, there would be cause for hope." He turned his eyes upon young Biltmore. "But in the case of your poor brother, I'm grieved to say, we know otherwise."

"You claim to know what was in Buckminster's mind at the end?" roared Turnbuckle. "Of all the damn-blasted nerve. For all you know, it was an accident. There was no suicide note—"

"But there was," said Father sadly.

"What's this?" interrupted Fulbright. "Mr. Turnbuckle, you told us—"

"There was no note," frothed Turnbuckle. "He's lying."

"Not so," said Father Baptist, pulling the envelope Sergeant Wickes had delivered into his hands from Sybil Wexler the previous evening. "I have a copy of it right here."

"How did you get that?" demanded Turnbuckle, preparing to lunge across the table. "The police assured me—"

"—that they would not reveal its contents to the press," said Father as he removed the sheet from the envelope, unfolded it, and shoved it gently in the cardinal's direction. The page glided easily over the richly polished surface, slowly turning as it approached the cardinal, and flapped to a stop as it met his fingertips. "They are not without discretion in such matters. But, like others at this table, I am connected."

Grimly, Morley picked up the page and swept it with his eyes. His lips twitched twice. His eyebrows did the limbo under the bridge of his nose, and then fell flat from exertion. "Much as we hate to say it," he said finally, "this leaves little doubt as to Buckminster's intentions."

"Pulling a trigger," said Mr. de Montfort, his smile slipping ever so slightly, and perhaps with calculation, "is a deliberate, swift, and irreversible act. There is hardly time for reconsideration."

"You mean—?" gasped Biltmore, tears welling in his eyes. "Bucky—?"

"I'm afraid so," said Father.

Mr. Turnbuckle's mouth opened and closed. It was so unusual for something not to come out, that even he was surprised.

"Thurgood," said Father, "if you wish, you may arrange a funeral at another parish according to the New Rite, and bury Buckminster's body in any Catholic cemetery you choose. But not at St. Philomena's church, and not in the parish graveyard."

"That's final?" said Mr. Turnbuckle, mustache deflated.

"Yes," said Father Baptist.

51

"MR. TURNBUCKLE, A WORD PLEASE," said Father Baptist as we exited the cardinal's official suite.

"I've nothing to say to you," said the old man.

"But I have to you," insisted Father. "Until this morning, I had no idea that all the while you've been donating money to St. Philomena's, passing yourself as a champion of Tradition, you've also been lining the coffers of the archdiocese, subsidizing the very modernists who are seeking to destroy it."

"I don't need to justify my generosity to you."

"No, indeed. I simply wanted to point out that where a man's treasure is, there is his heart."

"St. Luke," I mumbled under my breath, "twelve thirty-four, paraphrased."

"You know what you can do with your sermons," said Turnbuckle.

"You can't have it both ways," said Father. "It is not your generosity that is in question, but your use of it."

"Bushwa," said Turnbuckle. That word again.

"Purchasing influence with generous donations," said Father, "has little to do with beneficence, and everything to do with power."

"You needn't pontificate for my benefit," said Turnbuckle, folding his arms across his chest. "Your brain-dead flock aren't here to fawn at your every word."

GARDENING TIPS: The word "pontificate," which originally meant "to speak like the Pope," has been distorted via the English language into something more akin to "expressing opinions in a pompous manner." Small wonder, when you consider that England was the country whose king usurped papal powers so he could divorce and remarry without pontifical interference. (Many of his subjects, from peasants to bishops, went along with it rather than deal with an executioner's interference with the flow of blood to their brains.) The Brits have been looking over their shoulders ever since, as did the so-called founding fathers of our country who descended from their heresy.

                                        --M.F.

"If you want to kowtow to the likes of Cardinal Fulbright," continued Father, "be my guest. I advise you, however, to walk no fences.

As Christ Himself said, 'But because thou art lukewarm, and neither cold, nor hot, I will begin to vomit thee out of my mouth.'"

"The Apocalypse," I added, not to show off, but just to keep the record straight, "chapter three, verse sixteen."

"Besides," said Father, "as we've just seen demonstrated, modernists get their way through intimidation, not ability."

"I can't help but wish," said Mr. de Montfort, shaking Father's hand farewell, "that the old bump had excommunicated you. I've been reading up on St. Athanasius' expulsion by Pope Liberius, and I really wanted history to repeat itself—with my involvement, of course."

"History does that enough already," smiled Father gratefully, "without your help."

"But think of it," said the lawyer. "A countersuit, challenging his right of lawful authority by calling into question whether the cardinal is a Roman Catholic or not—"

"Perhaps some day," said Father grimly, "but not now."

"Till next time then," said Mr. de Montfort, striding away, off to right another wrong somewhere.

"Dad," muttered Biltmore meanwhile, "maybe we should just, um, just—"

"Spit it out, blast you," spat Mr. Turnbuckle, whirling on his son.

"If Father Baptist appeals to Rome," said Biltmore, eyeing me over his father's shoulder, "Bucky's note is going to become a matter of public record." I smiled encouragingly, but I've already told you what a risk that is. "Do you want that?" choked Biltmore, apparently drawing courage from me, "Considering, what with Mother's ... well, you know ..."

The two of them settled into harsh whispers—or rather, an unbalanced duet of blasting and whining hisses.

Just then the door to the cardinal's suite swung open and a rotund blur came bounding out. Father Baptist managed to slip into its way, thus causing a sacerdotal collision.

"Oof!" blurted Monsignor Aspic, those perky eyes rattling around inside his head.

"Ah, Monsignor," said Father, touching our favorite Jonas' arm as he tried to slip on by. He slipped another arm around the man's shoulder. For a brief moment I had the impression he was padding the man down—an old policeman's habit. "A word, if you please. Have you found the proper forms?"

"Oh, uh, heh-heh," muttered the monsignor. "Well, you understand, Father Baptist, that with all this controversy raging around you, your position with respect to the archdiocese and rightful authority and all these complicated issues—did you really mean that about the Penitenti-whatzit?—well, ahem, you realize of course that we must—"

"I thought so," said Father.

"Oh stop your sniveling!" barked Turnbuckle. His finger was pointed at the monsignor's chubby equator. "Are you still quibbling about his infernal bill? Pay the sanctimonious bastard!"

"What?" gawked Aspic.

"He's a pompous ass," huffed Turnbuckle, straightening his jacket, "and no friend of mine, but he did a job and should be paid." He then turned on Father Baptist. "As for you, I'll let you know my decision presently."

With that, Mr. Turnbuckle grabbed Biltmore's arm and marched off, no doubt to wrong a right somewhere.

"Volatile fellow," said Aspic. "If it wasn't for the enormous amounts of money—"

"True," said Father, "and perhaps that will make it possible for you to pay me the relatively minute amount of money that is owed me by the archdiocese."

"So that you can go on hiring expensive attorneys with which to hassle the cardinal?"

"No, that's all 'pro bono,' remember? It's so I can afford to finish remodeling the upstairs rooms in my rectory."

"Why not take up a special collection?"

"Because it's my personal property that I'm renovating. Why not just pay me the money?"

"Because it's my personal opinion that the matter needs further study. Now if you will excuse me." He went blustering down the hallway.

"Insufferable snot," said the gardener under his breath.

"True," said Father, stuffing something white and silken into the mysterious folds of his cassock.

52

"HOW'S WICKES?" ASKED TAPER.

"Still asleep when we left home," said the gardener.

"Millie knows what to do," winked Father Baptist. "There's a concoction she makes from Worcestershire, pickle brine, raw egg, and cayenne pepper that'll cure him the moment he wakes up."

"You're joking," smiled Taper.

"No," said I. "Father left out the pinch of some herb she grows in a jar under the sink. The Tumblars have availed themselves of her folkloric medicinal services on more than one occasion, and they swear by her concoctions."

We were walking outside the building in which Babbette Star's body was currently residing under a sheet. After scrutinizing the corpse, Father had decided to discuss the matter in the light of day—such as it was, the "Vampire's Shroud" still threatening in full force. There was no objection from the gardener's gallery. Even with the incredible heat, the oppressive humidity, the gloomy cloud cover, and the endless rumbling of foreboding thunder, this was better than the sterile shimmer of the morgue.

The rainbirds were chick-chick-chicking away, lazily spraying plumes of water back and forth on the meticulously trimmed lawn. We had just paused while I attempted to adjust a sprinkler that was stuck squirting water across the sidewalk, blocking our path. I'm no mechanic, and bending down for me is no picnic. It was not so much a sense of civic duty that prompted me to attempt the repair, nor the desire to accidentally spray myself with a refreshing splatter of cold municipal water, but rather my certainty that it was the only way that we were going to get any further away from the morgue and its contents.

"So what do you think, Jack?" asked Taper as I began fidgeting with the little metal thingie on the side of the doohickey.

"And what of the message this time?" the lieutenant was asking.

"The number ten, you mean," said Father, "smeared on her abdomen."

"In her own blood," added Taper.

"Ulp," said the gardener, remembering the sight of it.

"Irk," I said the next moment.

"What's wrong, Martin?" asked Father.

"Oh," I said, "I just punctured my finger on this thingummie."

"That's a shame," said Taper. "But you'll live."

"Minus ten," said Father, back to business. So much for concern for the wounded. "Or dash ten."

"Our killer's tenth victim," said Taper. "As if we can't count."

"But why a message at all?" asked Father. "'I am come,' and now this. This fellow is goading us, but why now? Why didn't he start with his first victim, and continue with the others?"

"Maybe he's getting cocky."

"Perhaps. I've been thinking about the show Valdemar put on at the 'House of Illusions' last Friday. Remember what he said when he was treating us to his little melodrama?"

"'You cannot find my place of hiding by day,'" quoth the gardener, grunting his way back up onto his feet, "'and you cannot protect the sources of blood that I seek at night.'"

"Yes," said Father. "Valdemar is a bogus vampire. He isn't hiding by day, so it is useless to seek his 'hiding place.'"

"What if he believes the part?" asked Taper. "I've been reading up, too. There are all kinds of cases of weirdoes who actually sleep in coffins."

"Good point," said Father. "But even so, we cannot possibly protect his sources of blood, not when there are so many gullible young women out there who want what he offers."

I noticed a large drop of blood dangling from my wounded fingertip.

"He may not be real," said Taper, "but he's dangerous. You've heard of Renfield Syndrome?"

"No," said Father.

"It's in several textbooks on psychotic behavior," said Taper. "Lord knows I only understand every third word, but apparently there's this medically-recognized condition that begins with a child cutting his finger and tasting his own blood. Finding that he likes it, he starts finding all sorts of ways to cut himself so he can get more. It goes unnoticed by his parents because at that age kids cut and bruise themselves all the time. At that stage of the disorder, it's called 'autovampirism.'"

"Interesting," said Father.

"Hm-hm," hmmed the gardener, busily sucking his hemorrhaging finger. "Mm-mmmm."

"The next stage is 'zoophagia,'" said Taper: "drinking the blood of animals—insects, rodents, cats, dogs."

"That's where I draw the line," I said, pulling my finger out of my mouth.

"Eventually he's driven to try human blood," said Taper, trying to ignore me, "the taste which started him on this weird road in the first place. At that point we have full-blown 'clinical vampirism.'"

"Are you saying," said the gardener, applying pressure—to my finger, not to Lieutenant Taper, "that 'vampirism' is a nostalgic urge, like pining for the roasted turkey Momma used to make?"

"I don't know what I'm saying," said Taper. "It all sounds weird to me."

"I take it," said Father, "that this 'Renfield Syndrome' got its name from the character in Bram Stoker's *Dracula*."

"Yeah. The first documented case was in the late forties in England. This man named John George Hague—"

"'The London Vampire,'" said Father.

"You studied abnormal psychology in the seminary?" asked Taper.

"No, I used to be a cop, don't forget. Before the Internet we had the Teletype, and often useless information used to trickle into headquarters from all over the world."

"Oh. Then you know this guy killed nine people, all of them personal friends. He was found guilty and executed in 1949."

"As I recall," said Father, "he lured them to a warehouse, shot them in the head, drank their blood, and stole their belongings."

"Right," said Taper.

"Sounds like your typical IRS agent," quipped the gardener, reinserting his finger into his mouth as he succumbed to the primordial urge to autovampirize himself.

"Back to the immediate," said Taper, "Where do we go now?"

"That's a good question," said Father. "By the way, Lieutenant, have Mr. Wong and Mr. Holtsclaw removed the garlic and Crucifixes from the freezer drawers?"

"I don't think so."

"Good," said Father. "Better safe than sorry. I'd also like you to check on a couple of things for me."

"Like what?"

"This handkerchief, for one." Father pulled a piece of white silk from the mysterious folds of his cassock. "Would you be so kind as to have this analyzed? You might also run a detailed background check on its owner."

"Who's that?" asked Taper.

"Monsignor Aspic."

"Oh, that squirrelly fellow."

"The same."

"You have your reasons, of course."

"Yes, I do."

"But you're not going to tell me."

"Not yet. Just a hunch."

53

BUCKMINSTER TITUS TURNBUCKLE was buried behind St. Philomena's church, without ceremony and in unconsecrated soil, at three o'clock that very afternoon. It was a rushed job, though unhurried. Mr. Turnbuckle and his son Biltmore were in attendance.

It took Roberto, Duggo and Spade less than fifteen minutes to fill the lonely hole with dirt. They had come with a pick-up truck loaded with several hundred squares of dichondra from the Del Agua Mission, but on second thought—the burial and all—had decided to leave the grass piled in the corner by the stone hut and deal with it later in the week.

By three-thirty, everyone had left except one lone figure.

I noticed from my window, almost two hours later, that Father Baptist was still standing there beside the fresh mound, slowly turning the pages of his tattered prayer book.

Mr. Turnbuckle gave no explanation for his change of heart, nor for his desire for immediate internment. No one asked.

I wish I could conclude this short chapter with, "Bucky rested in peace," but I cannot.

54

"MARTIN, I'M SO GLAD YOU'RE THERE," said Jonathan's voice on the phone. It was eleven o'clock that evening, and I was alone in the study. Father Baptist had been kneeling before the Blessed Sacrament in the church since right after dinner.

"What's up?" I asked, unaware that I was about to embark on a grim and tumultuous adventure.

"Something's gone haywire," said Jonathan. "Stella and I are here at the 'House of Illusions.' Pierre arranged for a taxi to pick us up at her place and bring us here."

"That's great. Enjoy."

"No, you don't understand. It's closed."

"Closed?"

"Yeah. The sign on the door, where the business hours are posted, says 'Open Tuesday thru Sunday, Closed Mondays for Rehearsals.' The taxi pulled away before I could stop him. I've knocked and knocked, but no one comes to the door. I think everyone's gone home."

"I can see how that would put a dent in your evening."

"I'm calling from the payphone outside, and I've used up all my change trying to reach Pierre and the others. It's a long dark walk down to the street, and Stella's really upset. Could you possibly come up here and drive us home?"

"Sure," I said wistfully, looking at the copy of *Collected Ghost Stories* by M. R. James I had intended to engorge. "I can be there in about a half-hour."

"Thanks. Please hurry."

"Will do."

I heaved myself up, grabbed my trusty cane, and stumbled by the chair Sergeant Wickes had occupied until sometime around eleven that morning when, according to Millie's account, she had treated him to a swig of her eye-opening concoction. I headed for the kitchen. Millie wasn't there, so I jotted a note and stuck it on the refrigerator door with a magnet shaped like a pair of praying hands:

Gone to fetch Jonathan and Stella at "House of Illusions." Long story—tell you over breakfast.

—Martin

With that I went out the door, not suspecting for a second that the story I would have to tell in the morning would be longer than I'd imagined.

55

"HELLO?" I CALLED AS THE FRONT DOOR swung inward at the touch of my hand. "Jonathan? Stella!"

Something was wrong.

The porch light was on, as were a few floodlights around the base of the old mansion, but otherwise everything was incredibly dark and quiet. Not quiet as in "tranquil," but quiet as in "deathly still." And dark as in "...the earth was void and empty, and darkness was upon the face of the deep." First page of the Bible.

I stepped back and looked over towards the space-egg phone next to the valet's station. It was illuminated, and I could see that the wire was severed and dangling, the receiver missing.

"Great," I sighed, turning slowly like a watchtower beacon, taking in the various shades and shapes of darkness all around me. I consciously slowed my breathing, conducting the respiratory ritard with gentle, defensive sweeps of my cane. "For the first time in my life I feel the need for a cellular phone."

Then it hit me: either that wire had been cut after Jonathan's phone call to me, or Jonathan had misrepresented his location. The latter didn't make sense and the implications of the former were sinister.

I considered my options. I could wander around outside a bit—reconnoiter the grounds, so to speak, brandishing my cane uselessly. I could summon my courage and enter the foreboding establishment, likewise swinging my cane—the door was open, so I wouldn't be breaking and entering, just entering. The safest thing would have been to get back in the car, drive back down the winding road, find a payphone, and call the police.

All bets were off, however, the moment I heard a voice call from somewhere deep within the house. "No! No! Help!"

No choice, I decided. I had to go in.

So in I went.

The anteroom was pitch black, but the swinging bookcase was open. As I turned into the tunnel I could see, or thought I saw, soft amber light emanating from the far end. I groped my way through to the bar. No psychic guards interrupted my progress.

One of the floor lamps with an ornate parchment shade had been left on in the bar. Indeed, every passage and corridor branching off was dimly illuminated by some sort of safety light or EXIT sign, courtesy of Fire Department regulations. This made everything faintly visible but nothing clearly so.

"Jonathan!" I called. "Are you there?"

Long moments passed.

There it was—a muffled sound, a snicker or shift of clothing perhaps. I couldn't tell. But it was something, and the only something I had to go on. I took a step, stopped, and looked around. Yes, there were little candles in blue glass cups on the various tables. I scooped one up, snatched a matchbook from a bowl at the bar, and lit the wick. Now I had at least a small light to carry. So I plodded slowly down the long hallway which turned gradually to the right. The bobbing candle flame seemed to give the velvet patterns on the walls an unsettling life of their own.

After a while I stopped again and listened.

"Stella!" I called.

Nothing.

Then something. That same muffled sound. Almost, but not quite a snigger.

My birthday's in May, I thought to myself. So I'm not being set up for a surprise party. This had better not be some sort of Tumblar prank—

There it was again.

I followed it down another corridor, and another and another. Up one stairway, down two. I can't tell you how long I wandered around the intestinal track of the old Roundhead house. All the while, I had the growling, gripping, unnerving sensation that I was being led like a dumb animal into some kind of trap.

Someone had called for help, I reminded myself, so I was committed. Besides, I couldn't have found my way out of there if I tried.

And then, at long last, I came to a wide, gaping doorway, draped on both sides with thick vermilion curtains. It didn't look familiar. Certainly not a place I remembered from Friday night. The room beyond was utterly black, fathomless. Even as I held up the candle I could make out no details within, no furniture, no hint of wall or fixture. It was like standing on the brink of nothingness. And, wouldn't you know, it was from somewhere in the bowels of that dark chamber that the sound came again.

"Jonathan?" It was hard to get the word past my knotted tongue. "Stella? Are you in there?"

Silence.

Of course, I reminded myself, after the other evening on the Farquar Terrace, my skeptical antennae were fully extended and on the alert. No 14 Hertz sine wave was gonna fool Martin Feeney again, no siree—

And then it got cold.

I mean, really cold. So cold I could see my breath. The flame covered in the little blue bowl in my hand, which began to shake accordingly.

Something rustled in the darkness.

My feet frozen to the threshold, I peered into the chamber, but all I could see were folds upon folds of charcoal nothingness.

Then I heard it speak.

"Martin," it said, the unknown voice dripping with icicles of fiendish familiarity. "I've been waiting for you."

Don't ask me how, but I knew—as each syllable from that disembodied larynx penetrated my ears like frosty ice picks—I knew that the owner of that throat knew me more surely and thoroughly than I knew myself: my strengths, my weaknesses, my desires, my occasion-of-sin fantasies ... *everything*.

This was no 14 Hertz sine wave, in other words.

I reached for the bump of my scapular under my shirt, with my right hand, only to remember with a sickening twinge that it was still hanging on the bathroom doorknob. This action jiggled the candle bowl in my left hand, enough so that some of the hot wax slurped over the rim, scalded my fingers, and dripped onto the floor.

"I've been waiting for you," it said again, slowly approaching.

GARDENING TIPS: I never believed, until the day I stayed home from school with the flu in the seventh grade, that the hair on the back of your neck could stand upright. I'd always thought it was one of those pat phrases that writers used to describe a fearful reaction, but that it was physiologically impossible.

But, as I lay there in bed reading "The Thing on the Doorstep" by H. P. Lovecraft, at the exact moment when I realized precisely what the thing on the doorstep actually was ... well, I found out what neck hairs can do. That was the first time.

This was the second.

The fact that the Valdemar incident on the Farquar Terrace, with all its props and showmanship, did not elicit this kind of response while this second incident, with no props and just a disembodied voice did ... well, it may give you some idea of what I had come up against.

                                                        --M.F.

The human body has a few other tricks up its sleeve at moments of great fear. I won't go into them just now, but I got the whole anatomical magic show at that instant as I turned to flee.

"You can't run from me," said the voice.

And it was right. I can't run worth a darn, not with my arthritic spine and hips. But I can lumber, lurch, slog and stumble up a storm. I don't get far very fast, but I work up one sopping sweat and make a lot of noise in the process.

All this I did, and as hard as I could.

"Fool," said the voice as I made my way—or so I guessed—back in the direction from which I had come.

If it were possible to get more lost than I already was, I did so. All I could think to do was pitch this way and that, picking any corridor or stairway that seemed to go somewhere and hope there wasn't a dead end around the next turn. One way or another I wove my way through the bowels of that foul edifice, oblivious to time or direction.

All the while, the voice followed me. "There is no escape."

Once, while turning a corner, I looked back down the corridor. All I could see was darkness creeping down the hall, absorbing the faint details of the patterns of the wallpaper and carpet as it came. The eerie sight prodded me onward, onward, down yet another unfamiliar corridor.

Then I heard the music.

56

PIANO MUSIC. SPECIFICALLY: an old Hungarian ditty my mother used to play on the family upright when I was a child. One of those uplifting yet sad melodies so peculiar to the simple folk from that part of the world. A lullaby with chops.

Another trick? I did not know. But since there were no other offers, I headed toward the familiar in front, away from the unbearable unknown behind. Up this short stairway, down that long corridor, until finally I came upon something I recognized:

ELZA'S SITTING ROOM
∞ ASK HER TO PLAY YOUR FAVORITE SONG FOR YOU ∞
∞ DON'T BE ANNOYED IF SHE DOESN'T KNOW ANY CURRENT TUNES ∞
∞ AFTER ALL, SHE DIED IN 1932 ∞

Into the parlor I stumbled, heading instinctively for the piano in the corner. Incredibly, all the candles in the decorative brass candelabra were cheerfully lit, the glow from the bobbing flames reflecting off the mirrors and dancing playfully throughout the room. The piano keys were going up and down, up and down, pouring forth the melodies and cadences of my childhood. There was a glass of some dark liquor poised by the edge of the keyboard.

"Elza?" I whispered.

Behind me, a surge of cold swept into the room. I turned to face the doorway just as the darkness burst through, engulfing the frame.

"Heaven help me," I shivered, raising my cane, wishing with all my heart that it was a Crucifix.

"No," screamed a thunderous voice from the black doorway. "You can't!"

"I can't what?" I gasped.

"Don't you dare!" cried the voice.

"But I can," said another voice, "and I do!" No, not a voice, and not exactly words. They were notes without syllables, yet they distinctly spoke.

I whirled toward the piano, dropping my candle. It went out as it hit the floor, liquid wax spreading on the carpet.

The piano keys were dancing, the notes so tinkly and playful, coy and daintily defiant, they clashed entirely with the prevailing pathos of the situation. "Trust me, Martin," they seemed to sing. Then the melody repeated itself, this time emphasized with rolling arpeggios.

I spun around back toward the doorway. The darkness hovered there, billowing and churning, checked in its forward momentum.

"He's mine," said the wicked voice, fierce and hollow.

"No," winked the piano, then downshifted into ragtime. "He is His."

"What in Heaven's name—?" I choked.

Suddenly a different kind of darkness descended upon me, a curtain of drowsiness enclosing the overtaxed gray matter. There was no help for it. My lids slumped down over my eyes in spite of my fear of closing them. The weight of my head became too much for my neck to support. Waves of swirling numbness engulfed me. I felt myself collapsing, my knees cracking against the piano bench. It tumbled onto its side. My cane slipped from my fingers and thumped somewhere off to my right on the carpet. Groping wildly, my hand knocked the liquor glass. It teetered, wobbled, and fell over.

"Hail Mary," I tried to say as something warm and wet splashed on the right side of my face, "pray for this sinner, now at the hour of my …"

I never finished. I don't remember hitting the floor.

Tuesday, October Twenty-fourth

**Feast Day of Saint Raphael the Archangel,
whose name means "Healer of God"
or "Medicine of God,"
who came to console Our Lord in the Garden of Olives,
and who is one of our Special Helpers
in times of sickness
(Ø AD—Angels never die)**

57

BUT I DO REMEMBER BEING BLASTED AWAKE by a piercing ball of white light that jerked and danced before my swollen eyes. This assault on my senses was made all the worse by the unmistakable odor of stale blueberry brandy penetrating my nostrils with all the gusto of ripe, liturgical incense. The effect was entirely different, however.

"Who the hell are you?" barked a horrible voice from beyond the light—not the sinister voice from before, but equally antisocial. "Whadduya think you're doin' here?"

"What?" I muttered around a tongue thick as cream cheese. "I don't know." It came out more like "Wub? I doan moe."

"Oh, drunk are yuh?" growled the voice after three condescending sniffs. "We'll just see about that. Whachoo been guzzlin'?"

"Uh-huh," said the cop twenty minutes later who had been summoned by the surly night watchman. "What did you say your name was again?"

"Feeney!" roared Chief Billowack as I was tossed into the chair in his office, my head rolling around like a bowling ball. "I should've known. You can take the cuffs off him, Officer Henninger, but don't let him out of your sight."

"But Father," I whined into the phone a short while later, "you know I've taken the pledge. I don't care what they told you, I haven't had a single drop!"

"Really," said Father skeptically as he took a seat across a table from me in the industrial gray police interrogation room.

GARDENING TIPS: The foregoing has been my tricky
way of getting through the turmoil of the next
several hours quickly. My mind was just starting
to clear as Mr. Drew de Montfort--Bruford's little
brother, the one who gets all the notoriety because he handles the family firm's criminal cases
--took a seat beside Father Baptist in that same
lonely room. The electric clock on the wall said
03:47.

                                        --M.F.

"And you say you didn't see Stella Billowack on the floor?" Mr.
Drew de Montfort was asking.

"Did I?" I said between cotton-wad lips. "Where?"

"Where did you say it, or where didn't you see her?"

"Please," I said, rubbing my temples. "No word games."

"Martin," said Father sternly, "they found Stella and Jonathan on the
floor in a third-story room at the 'House of Illusions.' It's called the
Green Room. There was some wax on the floor in the doorway, apparently from the same candle you carried to Elza's Sitting Room where
the watchman discovered you."

"Were there big curtains around the doorway?" I asked. "Of this
Green Room, I mean."

"I believe so," said Father. "That's how Lieutenant Taper described
it."

I blinked back a wave of nausea. "Jonathan and Stella? I heard a call
for help." I swallowed loudly. "Are they—?"

"Jonathan was found unconscious," said Mr. de Montfort, "and
groggy when he came to. He's in the next room."

"And Stella?"

"The ambulance took her to the hospital."

"Hospital? Why? Father, how is she?"

"She's alive," said Father grimly. "Barely."

"Critical loss of blood," said de Montfort.

"Blood?" I gasped.

"Martin," said Father, leaning forward on his elbows, "she was bitten
on the neck."

"Good Lord," I gulped. "And the police think that I—?"

"They don't know what to think," said Mr. de Montfort impatiently.
"And frankly, Mr. Feeney, neither do I. Your friend Jonathan Clubb
isn't making sense. And here you are, drunker than a skunk. Look at
you. What is that all over your collar? Blueberry brandy? What the
hell were the three of you doing up there?"

"I am not—ulp!—drunk," I winced. I hooked a finger inside my collar. It was stiff, tacky, and the hair above my right ear was matted and

sticky. "I told you I knocked a glass off the piano as I blacked out. I haven't had a drop in months. Father Baptist, surely you don't think—?"

"Frankly," said Father, a hint of disgust in his voice, "I don't know what to think. And I won't know until you snap out of it and tell me precisely what happened."

I blinked at him, then blinked again. He actually thought that I had broken the pledge! That was too much, the last straw. Or as Hijo Ya-hamata, my dad's gardener, used to say: "This has been another grob of spit in the bucket of my emotionar rife, reedle one." Nonetheless, I had to set the record straight. Swallowing my pride, and a large glob of bile—this made necessary due to the lack of a convenient spittoon—I took a deep breath:

"Jonathan phoned around eleven o'clock last night ..."

58

"AND THE NEXT THING I KNEW," Jonathan was saying, "the room got real dark, and then I got dizzy—I mean, really dizzy."

"You mean you were drunk," growled Billowack, seated across from him at a larger table in a larger room. His stubby fingers were tangling and disentangling themselves in a wild dance atop a stack of police reports. The one on top was marked BILLOWACK, STELLA in the upper right corner.

"No," said Jonathan, "just dizzy. It came over me in waves. I reached for Stella, but she had already fainted."

"So you say you were lured all the way up to the third floor by some voice," said Billowack, unconvinced.

"Pierre," said Jonathan, rubbing his throbbing forehead. "I could've sworn it was Pierre."

"But," said Pierre Bontemps, who was likewise seated at the table, "it couldn't have been me." Pierre had arrived a little past four-thirty—this is AM, remember—not a hair out of place. "As I've explained, I was with Kahlúa Hummingbird at the offices of the *L. A. Artsy* until well after one in the morning. I was putting some last-minute touches on a piece about the undesirable, unwelcome, but inexorable re-return of disco to the Sunset Strip."

"But you phoned me around seven," said Jonathan.

"No," said Pierre, "I did not. As I've explained, I did approach my editrix regarding your desire for a guest pass at the 'House of Illusions,' but she said that it's closed on Mondays. I phoned you around ten to say you'd have to wait until Wednesday, but there was no answer. I wouldn't have called so late, leaving you hanging so to speak, if I hadn't lost all track of time."

"That checks," said Lieutenant Taper, scratching his ear. "I spoke with the Hummingbird woman on the phone."

"But I had already left with Stella," said Jonathan, "in the cab you sent to fetch us at nine-thirty."

"Hold it, hold it," said Billowack, corralling his fidgeting fingers into sweating fists and pounding the table. "This is getting us nowhere."

"On the contrary," said Father Baptist, standing in the corner, "it is most illuminating. Obviously, someone phoned Jonathan posing as Pierre. We know from our previous outing at the 'House of Illusions' that there are any number of excellent impersonators working there."

"Of course," said Jonathan. "Whoever it was must've also arranged the cab. But how did they know about my asking Pierre to arrange a pass?"

"A very good question," said Father.

"The cab company confirms," said Lieutenant Taper, "that a lift was ordered by phone by a Mr. Pierre Bontemps, and paid in advance with cash delivered in an envelope to the dispatcher's office sometime Monday afternoon."

"Who by?" asked Billowack.

"The clerk," said Taper, "a college student named Paula Sands who didn't like being awakened in the wee hours of the morning, just remembers a 'tall guy in a tuxedo and dark glasses.'"

"Not me," sniffed Pierre. "I only wear a monocle, and then only on special occasions. Shades are not my style. Besides, when conducting business, I would only refer to myself as *Monsieur* Bontemps, never 'Mister.'"

"Hrmph," snorted Billowack.

"Jonathan," said Father, "you say the cab driver took off immediately after delivering you to the 'House of Illusions?'"

"Yes," said Jonathan.

"As per our pseudo-Pierre's instructions," said Taper. "I spoke with the cabby a short while ago. He didn't like getting shaken out of bed either, but he confirmed that he had been given explicit instructions to zoom off as soon as the couple were out of the car."

"Without a tip?" asked Father.

"It was prepaid," said Taper.

"He didn't think that odd?" asked Father.

"This is LA," shrugged Taper. "Nothing surprises them anymore."

"And the front door to the building was locked?" asked Father to Jonathan.

"That's right," said Jonathan. "The cabby made a screeching U-turn and was gone. We looked around and realized the place was closed. I banged on the door but no one answered."

Billowack smacked his wobbly lips. "The night watchman says rehearsals were over by eight and everyone had gone home by nine."

"Surely he couldn't vouch for everyone in a mansion that size," said Father. "Even if he searched every room twice, someone familiar with the place could elude him all night."

"True," said Taper.

"What happened next?" snapped Billowack.

Jonathan winced, but held his ground. "Then I thought of phoning for help."

All eyes turned to where I was fuming at the far end of the table. I said nothing.

"And what did Martin say?" asked Taper, turning back to Jonathan.

"Nothing," said Jonathan. "That is, I never spoke with him. The payphone near the front door had been vandalized."

"You realize that Martin here says he spoke with you," said Taper.

"Not with me," said Jonathan.

"Perhaps," offered Father, "the call Martin received was made by an imposter from another phone—one inside the establishment, most likely—in which case, he was probably already on his way."

"Could be," shrugged Jonathan. "I don't know."

"So what did you do then?" asked Taper.

"All we could do was wait," said Jonathan. "Stella didn't want to go back down that long, winding driveway, not in the dark. I knocked on the door some more, but there was no answer."

"So?" frothed Billowack.

"So," said Jonathan, "we walked around a bit."

"Where?" barked Billowack, like he was defending his daughter's honor or something.

"Just around," said Jonathan. "We strolled up to the parking lot around the hill in back. I thought maybe we could hitch a ride with anyone who might still be there, or just leaving. But the lot was just about empty."

"Just about?" asked Father.

"There were a couple of cars in the 'employees only' section."

"Do you remember the makes? Models?" asked Taper.

Jonathan closed his eyes, then opened them again. "Actually, now that I think about it, I remember that it struck me as odd."

"What did?" asked Father.

"They were all VWs," said Jonathan. "Old and beat up, so I figured they belonged to janitors and night watchmen. There was one of those vans, you know, like you see old hippies driving."

"The night watchman's," said Taper. "He said so."

He was no hippie, I thought, but kept silent.

"And a 'Bug,'" said Jonathan. "And also there was a, a ... I forget the name, but it looked like a sports car ... well, that sort of sporty kind of car Volkswagen made back in the sixties."

"It was called a 'Karmen Ghia,'" said Father.

"Yeah," said Jonathan. "That's it. Gray or light blue, maybe, and it had a yellow hood that really stood out—like it had been replaced from another car, like from a junkyard. Know what I mean?"

"Yes," said Taper. "Do you remember the color of the 'Bug'?"

"No," said Jonathan. "Dark, I think—but I'm really not sure."

"So we have two cars," said Father, "with the owners unaccounted for."

"Anything else?" asked Taper.

"Like what?" asked Jonathan.

"Was that parking lot out of sight of the entrance?" asked Father.

"You mean of the building?" asked Jonathan.

"Yes," said Father.

Jonathan closed his eyes again. "From the parking lot, all you can see is the roof." His lids fluttered open. "Like I said, there's a hill in between."

"And when you came back?" asked Father.

"The front door was wide open," said Jonathan.

"Open," snorted Billowack.

"I thought maybe the night watchman was around after all," said Jonathan. "He wasn't outside, so I yelled through the doorway. It was dark and quiet within. I yelled several times, but there was no answer."

"And then you heard Pierre," said Father, "calling from somewhere inside."

"I thought so," said Jonathan.

"That's what you say now," huffed Billowack. "But at the time you were sure it was Pierre."

"Who else would it have been?" asked Jonathan. "I thought he was playing a joke on us."

"Hrmph," hrmphed Pierre. "Obviously you have a dim opinion of my sense of humor."

"You know what I mean," said Jonathan, attempting a smile. It failed. "Knowing you, it could have been some sort of elaborate ploy to embarrass Stella and me."

"Hrmph," snorted Pierre, "and hrmph again."

"Be that as it may," said Father, "you went into the establishment and followed what you assumed to be Pierre's voice."

"That's right," said Jonathan. "Stella was nervous about the whole thing, but she came along. The deeper into the place we went, the more convinced I became that it had to be a prank. That's what I kept assuring her. If I'd've thought for a second—"

"And you stopped at the bar," sneered Billowack, "for a few quick ones, didn't you? Settle your nerves? Not to mention my daughter's?"

"No," said Jonathan, shaking his head. It hurt. "We did not."

"Sure," grumbled Billowack. "Sure. And when you reached the Green Room?"

"It's like I told you. It was all lit up, and I could've sworn Pierre was right inside. The voice sounded like it was just a few feet away. But as soon as we entered, the lights went out."

"Candles?" asked Taper.

"No, electrical," said Jonathan. "There was a big chandelier in the middle of the ceiling, and several lamps around the room."

"And they all went out at once," said Billowack. It sounded like an accusation.

"Did you hear a click?" asked Father.

"Click?" asked Jonathan.

"As the lights went out. Did you hear the snap of a switch being thrown, or did the lights go out silently, like during a power failure?"

"Hm," said Jonathan. "I think it was more like the latter. They flickered a bit, and then went dim."

"Remote control," said Father. "The MC gave Martin and myself a demonstration the other night."

"Go on," said Billowack impatiently.

"Well," said Jonathan, "then it started getting really dark—"

"How can it get darker," spat Billowack, "once the lights were already out?"

"It's hard to explain," gulped Jonathan, "but it did. It was creepy. Then I got dizzy—"

"Yeah, right," said Billowack. "You've said that before."

"Five or six times," said Jonathan.

"And that's it?"

"Yes, that's it. The next thing I knew, a cop was shining a flashlight in my face. Look, I've told you everything I know. Will you please let me go to the hospital and check on Stella?"

"Nope," frothed Billowack. "No way."

"You're holding him?" asked Mr. de Montfort, perking up in his chair like a falcon spotting a field mouse. "On what grounds?"

"Material witness," said Billowack. "Feeney, too."

"Baloney," said de Montfort. "That's unnecessary, and uncalled for. Mr. Clubb has been cooperative, as has, uh, Mr. Feeney in his way, and you've no call to hold either of them. They're not going anywhere out of reach, and I promise you I'll bury you in red tape and pounding gavels if you try to put them on ice."

Did you get that "uh" before my name and the "in his way" after? Any question why I was fuming? I was so mad I'm surprised I can remember any of this hideous discussion. The cloying smell of blue-berry brandy in my hair wasn't helping my mood, either.

"Did you find a set of false teeth with sharpened canines?" asked Father, "On Jonathan's person? On Martin's? Anywhere?"

"No," said Billowack.

"You're sure?" asked Mr. de Montfort. "Because obviously—"

"Of course I'm sure," roared the Chief of Homicide. "We made a thorough search of the Green Room and this Elza's Spitting Room, and every inch of halls and stairways in between and found nothing."

The thought of Elza sitting around "spitting" in her room almost brought a smile to my angry lips. Almost, not quite.

"Yet your daughter was certainly bitten with such an implement," said Father Baptist. "As you can plainly see, there is nothing extraordinary about either Jonathan's or Martin's canine teeth. Therefore, we must assume that someone else was present, perhaps two persons, as the extra cars in the back lot suggest, and that one or both of them attacked Stella—presumably the same person who killed those other women."

"Too many 'someones,'" huffed Billowack.

"It's fortunate," said Taper, "that this time the murderer did not succeed."

"Indeed," nodded Father. "And the more sinister. Why, after killing so many, did he fail this time? He had Stella at his mercy, not to mention Jonathan and Martin. All this maneuvering just to get three people into that mansion, these specific people—the implications are most disturbing."

"You mean now it's personal," said Taper. "Close to home."

"My home," said Father sternly. "Larry, it's a good thing you put your wife on that plane."

"You said it."

Billowack snorted. "The 'House of Illusions' seems to have become a hub for our killer's activities."

"That's more obvious every day," agreed Father. "It wasn't for the first several murders, but the pattern is coming into focus."

"And also St. Philomena's," said Taper darkly, "it's connected somehow."

"True," nodded Father, even more darkly. "Now I have to consider the people who are associated with me. The fellow who staged that floating act on the Farquar Terrace at the 'House of Illusions' Friday night threatened me—me specifically."

I nodded but said nothing, remembering the 'apparition's words only too well:

"Return to your refuge at St. Philomena's, cease your meddling, and the doom I have pronounced will not find you. If you persist, you will surely die."

Nope, I thought, nothing there about friends and associates.

"And now," continued Father, "he's expanding his threat, and that I cannot allow."

"He's also lost count," said Taper, producing a photograph.

"What do you mean?"

"The number smeared on Stella's abdomen was not 'eleven.' It was a 'nine.'"

"Nine?"

"See? Nine—with a small dash in front of it. 'Minus nine,' perhaps."

"But that doesn't make sense," said Father, "unless ..."

"Unless what?" barked Billowack.

"I'm not sure," said Father. "It means something—something obvious—but I haven't yet put together what that is."

"Excuse me," said Jonathan wearily, "can I go now?"

All eyes turned to Billowack, who turned all his eyes back at us.

"Okay," he grumbled at last. "But listen, Clubb, I don't want you hangin' around my daughter. You got that?"

"That's for her to decide," said Jonathan, then added, "Sir." After all, he was dealing with his potential father-in-law. The mind festers.

"Very well," said Father. "Martin, I've got to get back for morning Mass. Is there time to make a stop at the hospital? I want to check on Stella myself." I wasn't watching, but I'm sure he wasn't looking in my direction.

"They've got our car," I mumbled.

"I drove it here to the station," said Lieutenant Taper. "It's parked out front."

"Then we'll bid you good morning," said Father.

I got up and followed him, silent as the grave.

59

THE DRIVE HOME WAS LIKE RIDING in a deep freezer without the police bothering to "put me on ice." Father silently looked out his side window, and I silently kept my own eyes straight ahead.

I looked on in silence through the large glass window at the Good Samaritan Medical Center as Father had an animated discussion with two nurses, a resident, two cops in uniform, and an administrator in a flannel suit. This was in the Intensive Care Unit. Stella's bed was sequestered behind successive iconostases of plastic curtains, dripping bottles, blinking gadgets, coiled wires, and oxygen hoses. But I could tell, by the shapes of lips I couldn't hear and gesticulations I could see, that Chief Billowack's daughter was the focus of conversation.

Father did not speak to me when he came out, but soundlessly headed for the Jeep Cherokee in the parking lot. I followed, climbed into the driver's seat, and steered for St. Philomena's.

In his first letter to the Corinthians, St. Paul cautioned: "Therefore, whosoever shall eat this bread, or drink the chalice of the Lord unworthily, shall be guilty of the Body and of the Blood of the Lord." Considering my mood, I didn't receive Holy Communion at morning Mass.

Father Baptist made no comment afterwards in the sacristy. Neither did I.

Nor did I say anything to Father nor he to me during breakfast until Millie, her eyes glancing nervously between us, cleared away the dishes. Sensing that something was up, she didn't even remark that I hadn't touched my eggs. It must've cost her.

Monsignor Havermeyer, Joel Maruppa, and Joel's grandfather Josef, had apparently decided to dine at "Peanuts" across the street. Good for them.

"Where are you going?" were the first words Father Baptist spoke to me since the interrogation room.

"Out," was my only word to him in the same span of time. I shut the kitchen door behind me a little harder than was necessary.

60

"WHAT YOU'RE ASKING IS HIGHLY UNUSUAL," said John Holtsclaw, setting down his clipboard. "I mean, this is after all a forensics lab, not a medical center."

"Yeah, but can you do it?" I asked curtly.

"Well, sure," said Solomon Yung-sul Wong. "For Father Baptist, of course."

"No," I said, rolling up my sleeve. "For me. How long will it take?"

"An hour," said Holtsclaw. "Maybe two."

"I'm in no rush," I winced as the needle went into my arm.

61

"HERE YOU GO," SAID SOLOMON Young-sul Wong, one hour and forty-seven minutes later. "Will this suffice?"

"Yeah," I said, slipping off the stool I'd been distending my hip joints upon. "This will do nicely. Yes, it's exactly what I need. And you both signed it. Thanks."

"Anything for Father Baptist," said John Holtsclaw.

"Right," I said, biting my sarcastic tongue.

"Why'd you need this done, anyway?" asked Holtsclaw.

"As you just said," I said, "anything and everything for Father Baptist."

"Something wrong?" asked Solomon.

"Why?" I asked. "Does something seem wrong?"

"No," said Holtsclaw, "I guess not. It's just that you're a little bit—"

"A little bit what?"

"Nothing," they said together.

I folded up my prize and stuffed it into my jacket pocket.

"By the way," said John Holtsclaw, "you might ask Father Baptist to say a few extra prayers for Solomon here."

"Oh?" I said, glancing at the county coroner. "What's up?"

"Nothing," said Solomon.

"Such modesty," said Holtsclaw. "'Professor' Wong has been asked—which in the Police Department translates 'ordered'—to give a speech at the annual coroner's convention in San Diego this weekend."

"Coroner's convention, huh?" I said, adjusting my tie.

"Except for my forced monologue," laughed Solomon, "this is going to be purely 'R and R.' In fact, I'm leaving by car Thursday morning to make sure John and I land an ocean-front room."

"Solomon just wants to see the zoo," said Holtsclaw, winking. "I'll follow him down Thursday night or Friday morning on the Amtrack. Someone has to clean up his mess before we close up shop for the weekend."

"And we'll both return in my car Monday evening," said Solomon, "to make another mess on Tuesday."

"Monday, huh?" I said.

"So," said Solomon, "please tell Father Jack to either solve this case by tomorrow, or keep it on ice until next Tuesday. No murders in between, okay?"

"What if there are?" I asked.

"Only the two of us are allowed to perform autopsies on this case," said Solomon.

"Or have access to the bodies," said Holtsclaw. "Billowack's orders."

"Isn't that a bit odd?" I asked.

"It's bizarre," said Holtsclaw. "There are several other labs as large as this one and a whole staff of forensic specialists—oh, don't get me started."

"It smells of City Hall," said Solomon. "Someone higher up the ladder wants to keep the lid on this case—"

"And an eye on us," said Holtsclaw. "Anyway, that's the way it is."

"I'll pass on the message," I said, heading for the door, "but I make no guarantees about further murders. That's out of my hands. Father's, too. Thanks again for the lab work, and enjoy your vacation."

"We'll try," said Solomon.

"But as you already know," added Holtsclaw, "coroners are a weird bunch."

"You should come to St. Philomena's for Mass some Sunday," I told them as I turned the doorknob.

62

"THERE YOU ARE," SAID FATHER BAPTIST.

"Here I am," I agreed.

"What brings you up here?"

"The view."

"I see."

"That's what I'm doing. Seeing."

I was looking out the window of one of the unfinished upstairs rooms at the rectory. For the sake of identification I had dubbed it "Wrecked Room Number Three." Joel and his grandfather hadn't as yet installed the new wiring. The drywall panels had, for the most part, been removed from the walls, exposing the old but sturdy wooden studs. The carpet, too, had been torn up, revealing bare pine boards.

"Martin," said Father, "is there anything you want to say to me?"

"A lot," I answered, arms folded. "But now is not the time."

"Today's a big day," he said, coming up beside and a pace behind me. "Father Nicanor and Bishop Xandaronolopolis will be joining us for dinner, and of course there's the ceremony this evening in the church. We don't want to ruin it, do we, with unfinished business between us?"

"Fine," I said, shimmying a couple of inches away from him. "So finish it."

"What do you want me to say?"

"An apology would be good for starters."

"How have I wronged you?"

"How have you not?"

"Please explain."

"What do you want—to hear my confession?" I took a deep breath and let it all out. "Okay, Father, bless me. Wave your magic hand. It's been all of three days since my last blurting session, and wasn't that a hoot? The aisles in the church would be buried under untold layers of dust if it weren't for me crawling around on my knees every other day saying the Stations of the Cross after my sessions with you. As for the present, I'm madder than I can imagine. I'm so damn angry, I can't see straight. There hasn't been a sunset since it came on, so I'm not sure yet if the sun will go down on it. Check with me tonight for further bulletins on Ephesians four twenty-six. Care to absolve me?"

"No, I can't. Not under those circumstances."

"Then go away."

"Martin."

"Oh yes, I forgot. You own the place. Father, *please* go away."

"Martin."

"Father."

He stood there, allowing time to pass as it invariably does.

"Martin."

"Father."

We breathed in and out, in and out, as living things tend to do.

"Martin."

"Okay," I relented. After all, it's hard to stay mad at the man, and the church floors have to be kept clean somehow. "For starters, you don't believe me."

"About what?"

"That I wasn't drunk last night. That beats all. I haven't had a drop since the morning of Thursday, June twenty-second—four months ago, almost to the day."

"I remember, and well I should. I suspended your oath as the situation warranted."

"Temporarily," I huffed. "The key word is temporarily."

"True."

"You bet. Now I may be many things, Father, and many more besides, but I am not a liar. I told you at the police station that I didn't drink last night, and you not only didn't believe me, you let Mr. Drew de Montfort call me a drunken skunk and didn't lift a finger in my defense."

"I didn't say I didn't believe you, Martin. I said I didn't know what to think—and that's entirely different."

"Hrmph."

"I also said I wouldn't know how to arrange my thoughts until you snapped out of your, shall we say, blurry state and told me precisely what happened—something you've yet to do."

"You heard me tell the police."

"But you didn't tell them everything."

"No, that I couldn't do."

"I agree."

"What? That I didn't or that I couldn't?"

"Now who's playing word games? Look, Martin, let me show you something." He reached into the mysterious folds of his cassock and pulled out a photograph. "Lieutenant Taper slipped me this. I doubt that Chief Billowack has seen it. It's the kind of thing one doesn't spring on him without sufficient preparation. It'll take days."

I looked at the glossy image in his hand. My vertebrae turned into icicles.

"Recognize it?" he asked.

"The piano keyboard," I shivered, "in Elza's Sitting Room. What happened to it?"

"You don't know?"

"It wasn't like that the last time I saw it."

"You said it was dark."

"Not dark enough to hide that." My hands were shaking. "The candelabra on the piano was all lit up. I would've seen this."

"You said a call for help drew you into the mansion," said Father, "and lured you up to the Green Room. Then a different voice chased you. Was it really just a voice that was chasing you?"

"That voice wasn't just a voice. It was a *presence* ... in the midst of an *absence*."

"You never saw whoever was speaking?"

"No, the words came out of darkness, and it was the darkness that came after me."

"Darkness chased you."

"It's hard to explain, but every time I looked back, the hallway behind me was being engulfed in blackness. It wasn't like a cloud, or smoke, or anything like that. That's why I called it an 'absence.' It was more like something missing than something being. The darkness wasn't just approaching me from down the hallway, it was devouring the substance of the hallway itself. At least, that's how it seemed."

"And the voice emanated from it."

"Yes."

"And it chased you all the way to Elza's Sitting Room."

"That's right."

"How did you find it?"

"Find what?"

"Elza's Sitting Room. Surely you're not telling me you knew where it was, or where you were, not in that labyrinthine building." Father indicated the photograph in his hand. "There's something else about the piano you didn't tell the police."

I gulped. "Yes, Father."

"Are you going to tell me, or do I have to guess?"

"Well, um, yes, well, you see ..." I closed my eyes and blurted out the words. "I followed the music, an old Hungarian ditty my mother used to play. That's how I found Elza's room. But when I came to the parlor, the piano was playing itself—or rather, it wasn't playing itself. I mean—"

"Martin." I felt his hand on my shoulder. "Why were you asking me about ghosts the other night? We were in Elza's Sitting Room at the time."

"What does that have to do with anything?" I opened my lids and my eyeballs glued themselves again to the photograph.

"Martin?"

"You'll think I'm silly."

"You are many things, my friend, by your own admission, and many more besides. And in that regard, silliness is not beyond you. Such is not the case at present. Tell me why you were asking about ghosts."

"Well," I said, still not able to take my eyes of the photo, "Buzz Sawr, the regular piano player, told me that Elza Maplewood Round-head herself was spelling him at the piano Friday night while he was drinking at the bar. He said it was no joke, not a trick, not someone else behind the mirrors, and somehow ... well, I believed him."

"That the room was haunted?"

"That Elza's spirit might possibly be, you know, stuck there. You said that a ghost is sometimes a soul in Purgatory who has been allowed to visit the living in order to provide guidance, comfort, or aid, thereby expiating their temporal punishment in some way."

"Your memory is good."

"I took the pledge, Father. My brain cells are intact."

"Fair enough. Go on."

"Other possibilities included a soul in Hell or a demon impersonating the deceased person. Well, nothing in or from Hell could play the piano like that, not with that feeling—every phrase whimsical, every cadence capricious, each joyful note sparkling with air-headed fun."

"In your concerted opinion as a theologian."

"As an opinionated gardener consorting with a knowledgeable confessor. Lucifer may be an Angel of Light, and the Ape of God, but you've often said he has no sense of humor—how could he, damned to Hell for all Eternity? In any case, I played a hunch. I offered up my Holy Communion for Elza, just in case she was really a soul in Purgatory that needed a boost. I figured: whatever the case, what could it hurt?"

The hand on my shoulder became an arm around the rest of me. Father gave me a strong, sturdy hug.

"Martin," he laughed, "where would I be without you?"

"I've no idea—where you'd be or what you mean."

He tapped the photo with the back of his hand. "This is truly priceless. In a saner century, we'd be contacting the cardinal. The times being what they are—and our cardinal being who he is—we'll keep this among ourselves."

"What're we keeping?"

"This."

"This what?"

He slipped the photo back into his cassock. "I'll explain later. And let me assure you: if I gave you the impression that I didn't believe you about your abstinence, I am sorry. I had much on my mind, what with Jonathan and Stella ... and the sight of you with that dark, gooey brandy all over you, and your wavering demeanor; well, I do admit that the thought crossed my mind—"

"A-ha!"

"—that maybe you had, perhaps, lapsed. But I assure you that when you steadfastly said you hadn't had a drop, I did believe you. The logical alternative simply hadn't presented itself yet."

"And that is?"

"What is?"

"The logical alternative?"

"Oh that."

"Yes, that."

He glanced at the crooked hands on his watch. "I'm afraid that will have to wait."

"Hey. No fair."

"We've got preparations to make for this evening. I'm so glad we had this talk."

"Why?"

"Because I couldn't have endured an evening with you glowering at me the whole time."

"But you were the one glowering at me."

He blinked. "Me?"

"All the way from the police station to the hospital, then before and after Mass, then at breakfast—"

"Martin," he said, grabbing my shoulder, this time to spin me around and shove me in the direction of the door, "it's like I said: I had other

things on my mind. You know how I get when I'm pondering. You're
not the center of the universe, you know."

63

"AH, MY GOOD FRIEND MARTIN," said Bishop Xandaronolopolis,
stepping regally into Father's study and clasping my hands.

"Your Lordship," I said, bowing painfully to smack his ring. His I
didn't mind kissing, but my back doesn't like to bow for anybody. I
opted not to address him as "Bishop Pip" under the circs.

Father Baptist and Father Nicanor had followed him in. The study,
which had been crowded already, was now officially jammed.

"Bishop Xandaronolopolis," said Father Baptist, "this is Monsignor
Michael Havermeyer."

The monsignor bowed, took the bishop's hand, and clumsily pecked
the orb. "We have been awaiting this day," he said, "with great anticipation."

"Havermeyer," said the bishop thoughtfully. "This name I have
heard." Suddenly flecks of red lightning flickered across his eyes. "Ah
yes, your thesis on the Litany of Loreto. It was published in *Com-
monweal*, no?"

"I regret ever having penned that," said Havermeyer, straightening.
"It was years ago. I have learned much since then."

"I am glad," said the bishop, the storm dissipating. Then he smiled
broadly. "Haven't we all?"

"And," said Father proudly, nudging the bishop along, "may I present
the Knights of the Tumblar."

"My Lord," said Joel Maruppa, Edward Strypes Wyndham, and Arthur
von Derschmidt, each falling onto one knee in turn and reverencing the
bishop's ring.

Jonathan Clubb, who admittedly looked a little ragged around the
pristine edges of his white tie and tailcoat, performed his courtesy in
strained silence.

GARDENING TIPS: It had taken the combined persuasive effort of the whole troop to convince Jonathan that his place this evening was not at
Stella's bedside, but here at St. Philomena's.
I'll not recount that discussion because it was
long and arduous (like so many issues in our par-

ish lately). In any case, we were all glad that
he had decided to come.

--M.F.

"Your servant," said Pierre, head bowed, already on both knees as the
bishop came up to him. "I am at your disposal."

"May God abundantly bless you, my son," said the bishop as Pierre
rose to face him, "you and your household—" He stopped suddenly,
blinked, looked long and hard at Pierre's expectant face, blinked again,
and cried, "What have we here? This is not so!"

"Something wrong, My Lord?" asked Father Nicanor.

"This—this is impossible," gulped the bishop.

"I don't understand," said Father Baptist, stepping close.

"Neither do I," said Pierre, caught in a rare moment of imbalance.

"This face," said the bishop, indicating Pierre's with waving hands.
"I know this face."

"I hardly think so," said Father Nicanor. "Monsieur Bontemps has
never traveled to our part of the world—"

"What's that you say?" gasped the bishop. He put his hands on Pierre's shoulders and glared into his eyes. "Young sir, what is your
name?"

"B-b-buh-Bontemps," said Pierre as the bishop gave him a hearty
shaking.

"Monsieur Bontemps," said the bishop, "the name Douleureus—does
this hold any significance for you?"

"Why yes, My Lord," said Pierre. "Pierre Douleureus—Pierre de la
Visage Douleureus—was my great-ancestor. But how did you know?"

"Father Nicanor," said the bishop, turning. "Surely you have visited
the Monastery of St. Maron?"

"Yes," said Father Nicanor, "on several occasions."

"And have you not seen the statue in the chapel courtyard?"

Father Nicanor blinked, then brightened. "But of course!" Eleven
r's—maybe twelve—in just one word. "Laissez les Bontemps Rouler!"
No rolling r's there—not in French. Ah, to be multilingual!

"Hey Pierre," said Joel, "care to fill us in?"

"Yes," said Edward, "what gives?"

"Your friends," asked the bishop, spinning Pierre around to face
them, "they do not know?"

"Well," ahemed Pierre, "I hardly thought—"

"Such modesty," beamed the bishop. "It becomes a gentleman.
Please, permit me the honor."

"Of course," said Pierre, shrinking and growing simultaneously. It
didn't hurt him a bit.

"Long ago it was," began Bishop Xandaronolopolis in grand tones,
"the year of Our Lord 1099, during the reign of Pope Urban II—the

First Crusade. One of the first brave men to muster his troops to the Pope's call was Pierre de la Visage Douleureus."

"Pardon me, Your Lordship," ventured Arthur. "We do not speak French."

"Yes," said the gardener, "what does Pierre de la Gobbledygook mean?"

"Ah," smiled the bishop. "You Americans consume the fries but not the French. It means 'Peter the Grim-Faced.'"

"He was not a happy camper," interjected Pierre the Jovial-Faced.

"Indeed not," said the bishop. "From the medieval Duchy of Averoigne in France he came. Well-deserved was his name, by all accounts."

"It bespoke his austere personality," explained Father Nicanor.

"Sort of like Mr. Feeney," said Edward, "when he hasn't hit the sauce."

Chuckles went around the room—among the Tumblars, anyway. None of the clergy present, except Father Baptist, understood the reference.

So, I thought to myself, Jonathan has been sharing tales of his adventures with his comrades. No harm in that unless misinformation had been disseminated in the process—which it obviously had.

"In any case," continued the bishop, "our unhappy hero fought valiantly against the Islamic hordes in the Holy Land."

"Hear hear," said Joel.

"Ah," said the bishop, "but more there is. When the crusaders left Antioch, a column of scouts headed toward the foothills of the Lebanon Mountains. There they came upon the Monastery of St. Maron. The abbot, Sharbel by name, came out to greet them. The sight of the hosts coming from the west, it had filled his heart with such joy."

"Unfortunately," added Fr. Nicanor, "the approaching soldiers had no way of knowing that the monastery was not a mosque, and the Abbot Sharbel only spoke Syriac."

"A dreadful situation," said Father Baptist.

"Yes," nodded the bishop, "most dangerous. But just as his commanders began rallying the troops, Pierre the Grim-Visaged noticed the stone crosses in the chapel graveyard. Realizing that no Muslims would have such artifacts, drew his sword he did, and defended the abbot against his own comrades. When a native interpreter was finally procured, the abbot was able to explain that he, his monks, and everyone else who had taken refuge within his monastery, were Catholics—Maronites, like Father Nicanor and myself. Cut off from the rest of the world they had been, and for many years. The Arabs had told them that they were the only Christians left, that all the others had been put to the sword. These poor, isolated Maronites, they had no way of knowing otherwise. As far as they were concerned, they were all that remained of the Catholic Church."

"Amazing," said Arthur, stroking his beard.

"Sort of like the people at St. Philomena's," remarked the gardener, unnoticed.

"Hence the statue of their champion," said Father Nicanor, "which the monks erected in the courtyard."

"And for Pierre de la Visage Douleureus and his descendants, they pray to this day," said the bishop.

"It would seem that their prayers have been answered," said Father Baptist, placing his hand affectionately upon Pierre Bontemps' shoulder.

"But more there is," said the bishop. "Monsieur Bontemps, tell your friends about your family motto."

"Yes, tell us," said Edward. "This sounds like the first Tumblar adventure."

"You said it," said Joel.

"Well," said Pierre, clearing his throat, "when the Pope caught sight of the grim-faced Pierre Douleureus upon his return to Rome, he said, and I quote: 'Certainement, s'il est retournée victorieux, nous commandons qu'il fasse un bontemps.'"

"'Surely,'" translated Father Nicanor, "'if this man returns victorious, we command that he have a good time!'"

"To wit," said Pierre, "Peter the Grim-Visaged endeavored to smile. I gather that his first attempt wasn't successful, nor his second. After all, he didn't acquire his name due to an effervescent personality. Still, a Pope's command was as from Christ Himself, so he set about, dutifully and dolefully, to have a good time. It took several generations, but the Pope's order became the family duty."

"Hence the family motto," said the bishop.

He and Father Nicanor said it together: "Laissez les Bontemps Rouler!"

"Which means?" asked Arthur, smiling as though he'd guessed.

Pierre smiled impishly. "Let the Good Times Roll."

"Hurrah!" roared the Tumblars, slapping one another on the backs.

64

"YOUNG MAN," SAID BISHOP PIP, downing a glass of dark red wine, "a fair question you have asked, and I have given my answer. Why such sputtering?"

"My Lord," said Joel, dabbing his mouth with his napkin, "I mean no offense. But the electric light?"

"You're threatening his profession," said Edward to the bishop.

"I think not," said the bishop, leaning back in his chair. It groaned a bit. "You were expecting perhaps a jab at your St. Thomas Aquinas—and well you should, since the West has been lulled by his errors, mistakes to which we in the East have not, for the most part, succumbed. But my answer I repeat: the electric light."

We were seated around a makeshift table that Joel and Arthur had fashioned out of spare two-by-fours and plywood salvaged from the upstairs renovations. Our feast took up a good part of the kitchen, not to mention every available chair in the rectory.

"Permit me to ask you a question in return," said the bishop. "What does Man fear the most?"

"Death," said Arthur.

"Or diseases and disasters that lead up to it," added Edward.

"I think not," said Father Nicanor, savoring the last stuffed mushroom on his plate. "Those are things he can put out of his mind, put off to some future time."

"And don't say eternal damnation," said Father Baptist, "because most people don't even consider that as a possibility."

"Then what?" asked Edward.

Bishop Xandaronolopolis leaned forward on his elbows, arched his black eyebrows, and said, "The dark."

"For children, perhaps," said Joel.

"Children are we all," said the bishop, "when the sun goes down and night is upon us."

A nervous rustle went around the table. Jonathan looked particularly uncomfortable.

"Our esteemed guest has a point," said Father Baptist. "Haven't you all gone camping at some time or other? When you're out in the woods and night falls, what power does your campfire have over the impending darkness?"

"I see," said Monsignor Havermeyer, nudging the little potato on his plate. Even for this event, Millie had been unrelenting in her punishment of our poor monsignor. I suspect that he'd paid "Peanuts" a visit shortly before the bishop's arrival, just in case. "Fire only pushes the darkness back a little, but it hardly banishes it."

"Exactly," said Father Nicanor, "unlike the brazen white bulbs and tubes, so familiar in our century, which permeate every room with artificial brilliance and turn every dark corner into day."

"Imagine the world as our ancestors knew it," mused the bishop. "This, it is almost impossible for us to do, but let us try. Imagine what it was like when the only weapons against the night were candles and torches. No street lights to protect the pedestrian, no headlights on oxcarts as they rattled by. When fell the night, his hand in front of his face a man could hardly see. An eagle flying high over Europe would

see only a blanket of blackness, dotted perhaps with signal fires and
beacons along the coast. But other than that, nothing."

"Nature herself tells us," said Father Nicanor, "that most predators
hunt in darkness."

"Small wonder," said Father, "that evil things, the enemies of Man,
also thrive after sunset."

"And to think," said Monsignor Havermeyer, pondering perhaps his
own past literary attempts, "that all the great thinkers of the Church
wrote their works under such conditions."

"The *Summa* by candlelight," said Pierre. "Or better yet, the *Breviloquium.*"

"So when you ask, young sir," said the bishop, smiling fiercely,
"what single thing has done more to destroy Man's faith in God, I answer: the electric light. Mr. Edison's invention, for all the acknowledged benefit and convenience it has provided, has also altered our understanding of light and darkness, and therefore our awareness of good
and evil. Mark my words."

"When St. John wrote, 'The Light shines in the darkness,'" said Father Nicanor, "his readers understood it in a way lost to us."

"We do get an occasional glimpse when there's a power failure," said
Father Baptist. "People who would otherwise be sitting complacently
at their computers and appliances suddenly huddle in corners, cold and
terrified. We take our technology so much for granted, but occasionally
the plug gets pulled. Then do we see what we truly are."

"Excuse me, Your Lordship," said Millie, curtseying at the bishop's
elbow. "I wish to thank you for the lovely Crucifix. See, I have hung
it up on a nail over the sink where I can look at Our Lord's long-
suffering when I'm standing there doing the dishes, hour after hour."

Father Baptist and I exchanged knowing glances.

"An excellent place," agreed the bishop. "And don't ever forget that
inside there is a relic of the True Cross. Unearthed It was by St. Helena
in Jerusalem in the year 326."

"Really?" marveled Millie, curtseying again.

Veronika, Father Nicanor's housekeeper who had arrived earlier to
help out, likewise bowed with a spatula in hand. "Would Your Lordship or any of you gentlemen care for some dessert?"

Though Millie had a fair complexion and Veronika was dark and
olive-toned, they could have been sisters. They had the same angry
gleam in their eyes, and identical muscular development in the hands
and forearms, no doubt from countless hours of brandishing skillets at
their clerical charges. This display of dainty servitude was surely cost-
ing them plenty. I was impressed.

"But of course," said the bishop, clapping his hands. "A dinner
without dessert, it is like a candle without the flame, no? But do we
have time?"

"Yes," said Father Nicanor, consulting that strange contraption he called a watch. "But we mustn't tarry too much longer."

"This cake is laced with brandy," beamed Millie, producing a hefty slice on a small plate. Good liquor was a luxury at St. Philomena's, and she had invaded Father Baptist's emergency stash behind the books on the 'To be forewarned is to be forearmed' shelf in the study for the occasion.

"Be sure to pour Martin a big slice," chuckled Edward.

"He's off the pledge, you know," snickered Joel.

"Not so," said the gardener, his fuse smoking again. "And I resent the implication."

"That's not what I heard," said Edward, accepting his dessert from Veronika with a grateful nod. "I understand that you and Jonathan tied one on last night."

"I didn't say that," stammered Jonathan. "I said that's what the police accused us of—"

"Chief Billowack seemed convinced," said Pierre, absently pulling a cigar from his vest pocket and peeling away the plastic wrapper. "He was adamant about the point."

"Hrmph," I hrmphed. I couldn't tell if he was just being Pierre, or just being Pierre. I wasn't amused by either possibility.

"Gentlemen," said Father Baptist, eyeing my hand as I went for something in my own vest pocket. Did I mention that I, like the Tumblars, was likewise adorned in white tie and tails? "I should think—"

"Careful," prodded Pierre. "We don't want to provoke Mr. Feeney's Irish temper."

"Not when he's so 'crotchety' and 'dour,'" said Arthur.

"Just think," said Pierre, "while my ancestors were hunting vampires—"

"And while my ancestors," said Joel with a Slovakian lilt, "were hunting yours, Pierre."

"Yes, well," ahemed Pierre, "while our ancestors were hunting one another, Mr. Feeney's forefathers were dueling with Leprechauns."

"Now there's a charming thought," said Edward, feigning an artificial Brogue. "Why, get this man tanked up, and there's no telling what he may do. St. Patrick preserve us."

"So do put an extra dash of sauce on his cake," chuckled Edward to Millie.

"And be sure to pour him a glass of port," added Joel.

"That's enough," I insisted, a bit louder than I'd anticipated—but it got their attention. "I don't mind a jest or two at my expense, but you lads are taking this too far."

"Martin," said Father. "Let it go—"

"First," I said, slamming a piece of paper down on the table, "here is a lab report signed by the county coroner and witnessed by the assistant coroner. It states that there was absolutely no alcohol in my system when they tested me this morning."

"Heavens," said Pierre.

"It proves," I continued, "that I hadn't partaken of the grain or the grape for at least twenty-four hours—otherwise there would be traces left in my bloodstream. I pass it around for your inspection, since the word of a mere gardener has been deemed insufficient for the likes of you all."

"Really, Mr. Feeney, that's not necessary," said Pierre, nonetheless snatching up the page and reading it carefully. "Hm. Enzymatic analysis and even gas chromatography. Yes, this does seem to be in order. Of course, you aren't dead, so the mind wonders why these tests were performed by Solomon Yung-sul Wong and—"

"Second," I huffed, "you are mistaken that I am of Irish stock."

"With a name like Feeney?" asked Jonathan. "What else could you be?"

"The name is Fényi, my judgmental friends," I said sternly. "Some clerk at Ellis Island misspelled my grandfather's name when he came to this country. He was Hungarian—my grandfather, not the clerk."

"Ah," said Father Nicanor. "I have often thought you had the look of the Magyar."

"Our apologies," said Arthur. "We didn't mean—"

"Oh, but you did," I scowled. "My ancestry may not be as lofty as *Mister* Bontemps', but I do trace my lineage back to Fényi Márton of Pannonia."

"Bravo!" said the bishop, reaching over and slapping me on the back. "I should have known: Fényi Márton, the famous vampire-hunter!"

"Vampire hunter?" squawked Edward.

"And all the while we were discussing vampires," said Pierre, pierced by the barb I had flung his way, "you didn't let on."

"Unlike some people," I answered, glaring at Pierre, "I don't always assume that every thought that pops into my head is everyone else's business."

"The good people of the Pannonian Plains," said the bishop, "have, I suspect, been praying for the descendants of the man who once rid them of a great evil. Tell me, Martin, understand do you the derivation of your name?"

"I confess that I don't, My Lord. My parents both spoke fluent Hungarian, but they chose not to speak it around me, insisting that I speak English."

"That is a pity," said Father Nicanor.

"Especially," said the bishop, "when you realize that Fényi Márton means 'Martin of the Light.'"

"And the Tumblars did not comprehend it," said Pierre.

"True," said the gardener, refusing the huge piece of cake in Millie's hand.

64

"IN THE AGES OF FAITH," said Father Baptist from the pulpit in the church, "the highest callings available to a devout man were, first, the Religious Life: living in community and devoting oneself to prayer, penance, and fasting, while observing the three vows of Poverty, Chastity and Obedience."

The Tumblars were all kneeling at the Communion rail, their backs straight and heads bowed. The smell of incense was heavy in the air.

The scene was very much like the one at the beginning of this story, but with four notable exceptions. First was the presence of Bishop Xandaronolopolis seated in a high-backed chair off to the Epistle side of the altar. His vestments, which he had brought with him from Lebanon, were of spun gold. On his head he wore a tall, pointed mitre, and in his right hand he held his royal crook.

> GARDENING TIPS: The back of the bishop's chair was
> flush against the far wall of the sanctuary about
> fifteen feet from the altar. It mustn't be con-
> fused with the "presider's chair" usually placed
> in front of the picnic table at Novus Ordo Masses.
>   --M.F.

"The second calling available to a man," continued Father, his voice booming regally in the otherwise empty and dark church, "was Knighthood: the defense of Church and Sovereign by force of arms. In time, circumstances required the merger of the two callings into the great Military Orders, such as the Knights Templar and the Knights Hospitaller of St. John of Jerusalem, and the Knights of St. Lazarus, to name a few."

The second notable exception with respect to the scene was that I myself was seated in the front pew, behind the Tumblars, outside the sanctuary, apart from the action. It had been agreed that my presence at this ceremony was warranted but not essential.

Monsignor Havermeyer, attired in cassock and surplice, was acting as altar server, my usual role. He was seated in a lower-backed chair beside the bishop, his chin resting on the pinnacle of his clasped fingers.

His face was a war-torn landscape of harsh experience, but his eyes shimmered with childlike awe.

"Thirdly," Father was saying, "lay people bound themselves to Third Orders, which were spiritual associations connected with the great Religious Orders of their day—Benedictines, Dominicans, Franciscans, Carmelites, and others."

Despite my removal from the action, I did not feel demoted or cast aside. My faithful companion, arthritis, was doing his worst that evening. I was grateful for the opportunity to sit this one out, resting my bones while intently observing a ceremony that had become virtually obsolete in modern times.

"In the present age, as you well know," continued Father, "the weapons and tactics of modern warfare have doomed the armored Knight, and devotional life has decayed both within and without the Religious Orders."

The third scenic exception: Father Baptist was acting as deacon, so over his cassock he was wearing an ankle-length version of a surplice called an "alb," with the addition of a white "stole" draped around his neck. The stole was crossed over his chest and held in place by a white rope around his waist known as a "cincture."

GARDENING TIPS: For those of my readers who are getting lost in the sea of Traditional liturgical vestments, permit me to offer some more poorly-executed VISUAL AIDS:

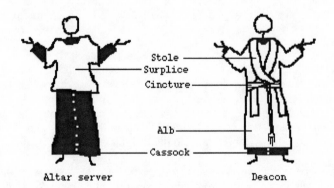

Altar server	Deacon

(Not shown here is a garment called the "amice" which is tied around the shoulders and hidden under the "alb.")

When a priest says Mass, he adds the "chasuble" and "maniple," which are sacrificial vestments:

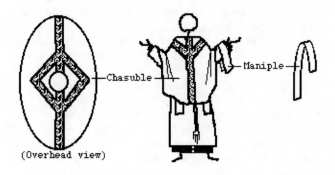

(Overhead view)

A priest also dons a "cope"--sort of a hooded cloak--when he conducts a Benediction (as Father Baptist did at the beginning of this story) or performs the Asperges (the blessing of the people with holy water) before High Mass. A bishop gets to wear the "cope" for all his liturgical functions, with the addition of the pointed hat and staff known as the "mitre" and "crook":

Don't be surprised if this isn't the last you'll hear of these things. You might want to dog-ear the page for future reference.

                                        --M.F.

"So," said Father, "when you fine gentlemen came to me with your request that I assist you in forming a Third Order, I was only too happy to help you reach that most desirable goal. The Religious Order with which you wish to associate yourselves is the 'Mancipia Immaculati Cordis Mariæ,' the 'Slaves of the Immaculate Heart of Mary,' which was founded in 1949 by Father Leonard Feeney, formerly of the Society of Jesus. I met with him on two occasions years ago when I was still a policeman, and my sense of the man is that he would have been proud of you men this evening. And though there's no possible relation, I've no doubt that our own Martin Feeney is proud as well."

I was. All angst of the evening aside, of course I was.

"For the purposes of instituting this Third Order," said Father, "I was deputized a few weeks ago by the Lord Abbot of their western monastery, St. Benedict's House. As some necessity is keeping him in Paris, he is unable to be here this evening."

I noticed my friend, the mouse, poking her nose through the crack beside the altar.

"You also indicated," said Father, "that you wanted to become Knights as well, fortified in your quest for Truth and Holiness by the spirit of Chivalry. Be advised that Knighthood bestows Graces specific to that particular vocation. As with the Grace of Confirmation, the Grace of Chivalry does not spur you on to action, it is activated by your initiative. I expect great things from you."

So did I.

"And so" said Father expansively, "it is for this purpose that we are gathered this evening."

The fourth exception was the fact that there were only five candles lit in the sanctuary. Two on the altar, the large Paschal candle standing alone near the Gospel side of the altar, the customary sanctuary light in a red glass canister signifying the Real Presence in the tabernacle, and the one Father Baptist had up in the pulpit so he could read his notes.

Bishop Xandaronolopolis had insisted that this be so, and Father Baptist had wholeheartedly agreed. No spotlights, track lights, overheads or floods of any kind were in use at all. Aside from a few votive candles bobbing before the statues of various Saints around the perimeter of the church, the nave was dark.

"As you know," explained Father, "Knighthood can only be conferred by a Catholic King, another Knight, or a Bishop. Thus it is with great jubilation that we welcome Bishop Xandaronolopolis of the holy and venerable Maronite Rite into our humble church to bestow upon each of you the privilege and responsibility of Knighthood."

GARDENING TIPS: I have been advised that most of
the ceremony performed that night is to be held in
confidence, and in this I heartily concur. The

oaths taken and the promises made were of a highly
personal and, for want of a better word, an eso-
teric nature.
    It has been agreed however, that for the pur-
poses of this chronicle, I may present in part
that portion which pertained specifically to me.
    To those events I now proceed with a gardener's
gratitude and what I hope is some semblance of hu-
mility.

                                              --M.F.

Pierre was the last of the Tumblars to kneel before Bishop Xandaronolopolis. I watched, enraptured, as Pierre kissed the cross of the sword
in the bishop's kingly hands. Then the bishop hefted the weapon and
landed the flat of the blade on Pierre's strong shoulders, first the right,
then the left.
    "Arise, Pierre Chevalier Bontemps, descendent of Pierre de la Visage
Douleureus!"

    GARDENING TIPS: "Chevalier" is the French term for
    "Knight."

                                              --M.F.

Pierre arose, genuflected before the tabernacle, and returned to his
place among his comrades at the Communion rail. They all looked
grim, proud, and a little overwhelmed.
    Figuring that the ceremony was about to conclude, I grabbed my cane
and began to heave myself up onto my feet. I had in mind to slip out
the side door and circle around to the sacristy to help the bishop out of
his vestments. Suddenly that plan went out the window.
    "Fényi Márton," boomed the bishop.
    I froze.
    "Approach," he commanded.
    Flustered, I pointed to myself and made a quizzical face.
    "You, yes," he said with the slightest of smiles. "Come here."
    I looked to Father Baptist, who at this point was beside the bishop
holding the book of rituals. Without any hint of a reaction on his face,
he nodded almost imperceptibly.
    My mind reeling and knees shaking, I left my cane in the pew, hob-
bled through the gate in the center of the Communion rail, genuflected
awkwardly before the tabernacle, and gingerly approached Bishop Xandaronolopolis.
    "Kneel," he said.
    "M-m-me?"

"You see anyone else named Fényi Márton?" he winked.

"But Your Lordship, I—"

"Take, my friend," he said, presenting me with the sword. The blade glistened in the somber candlelight. "Kiss the Cross."

No help for it, I sank to my knees on the cold floor and clumsily osculated the place where the handle met the blade.

"To the honor of Our Lady, Queen of Heaven," he said in stern but encouraging tones, "Saint Michael the Prince of the Heavenly Host, Saint George the Patron of Chivalry, Blessed Charlemagne and Saint Louis, and committing you to the care of Holy Raphael the Archangel whose feast we celebrate this day, I dub thee Knight, in the Name of the Father, and of the Son, and of the Holy Ghost. Amen."

I felt the weight of the blade on one shoulder, then the other.

"Arise, Martin Chevalier Feeney, Friend and Defender of the Faith, dearly begotten descendent of Fényi Márton!"

I flailed a bit without my cane, but I managed to struggle to my feet.

The bishop bore into me with those hourglass eyes. "Embrace this sword in the name of the Father and of the Son and of the Holy Ghost. Use it in defense of thyself and the Holy Church of God, for the confusion of the enemies of the Cross of Christ and of the Christian Faith, and never unjustly to the injury of any man, as far as human frailty will admit."

"Um," I stammered. "Uh, um."

"The correct response," whispered the bishop, winking again, "it is 'Amen.'"

Later, in the sacristy as I helped him out of his cope and chasuble, I ventured to ask: "Your Lordship, why did you do that?"

"Funny it is that you should ask," he said, unraveling his stole from the knots of his own golden cincture. "Just as I finished with Pierre Bontemps, a voice like a mouse seemed to whisper in my ear: 'Remember Parcifal.' I looked around, and there you were."

I decided then and there to put out a plate of cheese for the little guest who had taken up residence behind the altar.

66

IT WAS WHILE WE GATHERED IN THE SANCTUARY for one last prayer together before the Blessed Sacrament that we heard the sound. It shook the church. At first I thought it was the clock in the steeple acting up again.

Boom! Boom!

"Earthquake?" whispered Joel.

"No," said Father Baptist.

"Something else," said Father Nicanor.

A muffled, churning, crunching sound seemed to ripple through the marble floor. Then it suddenly ceased.

"What the—?" said Monsignor Havermeyer.

"Be still, everyone," ordered Father Baptist.

We huddled there in the darkness, grateful for those bobbing candle flames.

Time passed, but oh, did it pass slowly.

"It's over," whispered Father Baptist presently.

"What could it have been?" asked the Tumblars severally.

"Gentlemen," shushed Father. "We are in the House of God. Let us take our speculations elsewhere."

That we did. Fetching flashlights from various drawers and glove compartments, we made a swift, haphazard search around the church, speculating as we went. Somehow our waving lights and urgent whispers reminded me of enraged townspeople scouring a cardboard forest in search of black-and-white monsters. Instead of a windmill to encircle, we had our beloved church with the menacing clock creature trapped in the tower. I remember wondering what bizarre assumptions neighbors like Mrs. Feuchtwanger might've been making if they happened to be looking out their rear windows that night, especially when we made our high-stepped tailcoated sweep of the cemetery.

"Nothing," said Pierre as we halted in the garden between the church and the rectory, our circumnavigation of the grounds complete.

"Couldn't see any damage anywhere," said Edward.

"No cracks or fallen bricks," said Joel.

"It must've been a quake," said Havermeyer finally. "Another after-shock. We'll read about it in the morning papers."

"Let us hope so," said Bishop Xandaronolopolis, doubtfully.

"Gentlemen," said Father, "since there is nothing more we can do at present, I suggest we call it a night. I'll expect to see you all Thursday evening."

"Right-oh," said Pierre. "Your Lordship, will we be seeing you again?"

"Oh yes," said the bishop, "Father Baptist has kindly invited me to attend your first meeting as true Knights. To my presence I hope you will not object."

"Indeed no," said Pierre. "We are mindful that you have bestowed this precious Grace upon us. You and Father Nicanor are forever welcome in our midst."

The other Tumblars cheerfully agreed.

"Until Thursday then," said the bishop.

"Till Thursday," said we all.

67

THE PHONE WAS RINGING as Father and I entered the study for a just-before-midnight reflection.

"It's been a long day," I commented.

"But it's not over yet," sighed Father Baptist, snatching the receiver. "St. Philomena's."

His face fell.

"Yes, Larry. I'm listening."

From the sound of his voice, I figured it wasn't worth settling down into my chair just to get up again. I fished around in my pocket for the car keys.

"I understand," said Father, setting down the receiver.

"Not another murder," I said.

"Yes. A woman found in an alley. Her name was Nannette Cushions. Why does that name ring a bell?"

"She was at the 'House of Illusions' Friday night," I said, "unless Nannette is a common name. She made a pass at Pierre in Elza's Sitting Room."

"I thought that was Babbette Star."

"Nannette was with Babbette. They both invited Pierre to partake of a little snuggle session on the love seat, but he declined."

"Well," said Father, "she was found a little while ago near Hollywood and Vine."

"Is that our next destination?" I asked, jiggling the keys in my hand.

"No," said Father. "They've already taken the body to the morgue."

"Oh," I said. "Then we're going there."

"No," said Father. "I'm simply too tired, Martin. I'll leave the preliminaries in the able hands of Mr. Wong and Mr. Holtsclaw. My own body, I'm afraid, I must consign to my bed."

"You do that," I said, sinking down into my chair at last. "I'm a bit wired, so I'm going to read for a bit."

"Butler's *Lives of the Saints*?"

"No, I need a break," I said, snatching up a stained paperback from the heap of books on the floor. *"Three Faces at Eight* by Craig Rice,"

"Enjoy," said Father, walking wearily from the room.

Wednesday, October Twenty-fifth

**Feast Day of Saints Crispin and Crispian,
shoemakers and martyrs,
beheaded under Diocletian (285 AD)**

68

"NO WAY!" BELLOWED BILLOWACK, gobs of phlegm flying. "Get out, do you hear me? Out!"

"But Father Baptist," hissed Jonathan insistently, "the doctor said that Stella might, she might—"

"Stay put," said Father to Jonathan, who had changed into casuals since I'd last seen him, but had apparently not bathed or shaved in the interim. I caught a whiff of pontifical incense when I first shook his hand and patted him encouragingly on the back.

"What're you waiting for?" roared Billowack.

"Sir," said Jonathan, holding his ground. "I'm staying."

"Sir," said a nurse who came skidding into the room, "you're disturbing the other patients, not to mention your daughter—"

"Daddy," whispered a voice from the bed. "Please, it's what I want. I asked Jonathan to bring Father Baptist—"

"You're delirious," snapped Papa Billowack. "You keep out of this."

"Gentlemen," said a man with a stethoscope swaying from his neck who suddenly appeared in the doorway. "I could hear you all the way down at the nurses' station. I must insist that you take this argument elsewhere."

"Good idea, Doctor," said Father. "Monty, let's you and I go to the lounge."

"No, Father Baptist," said Stella weakly. The bandage around her throat heaved as she gulped. "I need you here."

"Jonathan will stay with you," Father assured her. "I'll be back presently."

"No he won't," said Billowack, glaring at Jonathan as Father motioned him toward the door. "And you won't either, Jack."

"Monty," said Father in a modulated tone that would've diverted an avalanche, "you and I need to talk." He grabbed me and stuffed me through the doorway after the chief. This gave him the opportunity to whisper over his shoulder to Jonathan, "You know what to do if—"

"Yes, Father," said Jonathan, glancing at a small plastic pitcher of water on the nightstand.

Stella's condition, it seemed, was not good. Jonathan had called us before breakfast, frantic. Aware of her peril, Stella had requested entry into the Church by the only means possible—Baptism with water—and now her obtuse father was trying to deny her that privilege. I can be pretty obtuse myself, but I thought I understood Father's immediate plan.

"Don't push," huffed Billowack as I bumped into him.

"Sorry," I said, not meaning it.

"This way," said Father Baptist, herding us down the hall.

> GARDENING TIPS: I realize that some folks, having
> been raised on Cardinal Gibbons' Baltimore Cate-
> chism*, will say, "But doesn't Stella's wish to be
> Baptized produce the same effect as the actual
> Sacrament?" This popular notion is called Baptism
> of Desire. While it certainly sounds nice and
> takes the onus off of each of us with respect to
> evangelization, it is actually contrary to the of-
> ficial teachings of the Church. Permit me to
> quote the dogmatic pronouncement of the Council of
> Trent (1545-1563 AD), Canon 2 on the Sacrament of
> Baptism:
>
> "If anyone shall say that real and natural water
> is not necessary for Baptism, and on that account
> distorts the words of Our Lord Jesus Christ, 'Un-
> less a man be born again of water and the Holy
> Spirit' (Saint John III:5), into some sort of
> metaphor: let him be anathema."
>
> In other words, Stella's Salvation was hanging
> in the balance, but among those present only Fa-
> ther, myself, Stella, and Jonathan were aware of
> this ultra-relevant fact.
>
> —M.F.

> * This is the same Cardinal Gibbons to whom Pope
> Leo XIII wrote a letter entitled Testem benevolen-
> tiae, in which the Holy Father described, labeled,
> cautioned against, and denounced the heresy of
> Americanism. "Slippery Jim Gibbons, stick to your
> ribbons!" was the catchphrase in the ol' boy's
> archdiocese. Now why do you suppose he had such a
> reputation amongst his flock?

We were joined halfway to the lounge by a syrupy man wearing an immaculate blue suede suit and wide yellow tie held in place with a diamond pin. "Mr. Billowack," he said in a soft, stroking voice. "I got your message and came as soon as—"

"Pastor McIntosh," growled Billowack. "You're here. Good."

"This will have to do," said Father as we entered the lounge. It was one of those horrible waiting rooms with uncomfortable bolted-down molded-plastic chairs, piles of last-summer's magazines, and those amateurish paintings hospitals love to provide for fidgety visitors and anxious relatives. Thank Heaven there was an "Out of Order" sign taped to the wall-mounted television set. Without this one-eyed idol to feed their hunger for diversion, visitors and relatives had taken their fidgeting anxiety elsewhere, leaving us some quiet space to fill with angst.

"So you're ... *Father* Baptist, hmm?" said the minister to Father as I handed him a cup of thirty-five cent coffee with "extra whitener" which I had obligingly procured from the noisy vending machine in the corner. His slight but noticeable pause before the word "Father," his marked overemphasis of the word itself, and the scornful lilt in his interrogatory hum conveyed a conspicuous distaste for the designation. I considered asking him if he cited the widely quoted but universally misunderstood Matthew twenty-three nine every time his kids called him by this term when he pulled the sheets up under their chins at night. Instead, I decided that my function at that juncture was to fetch coffee for all present while leaving the delicately complex matter of stalling for time to "Call None Your Father" Baptist.

"I am," said Father. What a pro.

"Eugene McIntosh, Doctor of Divinity, Professor Emeritus and Pastor, at your service," said the minister, obviously delighted with the sound of his own accomplishments even if Father hadn't asked him about them. "At last we meet. I wish it could be under more pleasant circumstances."

Father nodded, prolonging the point by untold milliseconds. This man could stall the Second Coming, but with such subtlety that no one would notice the delay. Me, I'd toss a monkey wrench into the works and wind up with all the Heavenly Hosts pointing all their ethereal fingers at me.

"You know what he was gonna do?" grumbled Billowack, waving away the flimsy cup of steaming dark water I held out to him. "He was gonna baptize Stella, that's what he was gonna do."

"At her request," added Father. "Surely, knowing that her life is in danger, you wouldn't deny her. She told me during one of our meetings that she was never baptized."

"That is correct," said Eugene McIntosh, his every word framed in a doily of elegant self-assuredness. "We at First Methodist on the West Side don't believe in infant baptism, preferring as we do to let each person make those decisions upon reaching maturity. It is unconscionable to us to presume to impose such important spiritual choices upon our children."

"Then it's settled," said Father.

"What's settled?" snarled Billowack, changing his mind and motioning for me to bring him the black brew I was about to pour down the drinking fountain drain.

"By your own rules," answered Father, "Stella is certainly old enough now to make her own decisions."

"I would hardly call it a rule," said Pastor McIntosh. "More like a guiding principle."

"Whatever the terminology," said Father, "she has made her wishes known. She wants me to—"

"Not you," said Billowack, slurping his coffee noisily. "If she wants it, she can get it from her own."

"But she does," said Father, "and she shall. That is why she asked for me. She wants to die a Catholic."

"She isn't dying," grimaced Billowack, pouring the remaining liquid down the drain himself.

"I certainly hope not," said Father. "But the doctors have indicated the possibility. Frankly, Monty, I don't understand your attitude."

"My gramps was a Methodist," belched the chief, crumpling the paper cup and tossing it into the wastebasket. "My dad was a Methodist, and I am a Methodist. By gum, my daughter is gonna be a Methodist."

"That is certainly reasonable," chimed Pastor Eugene, savoring his whitener. "Surely a parent has the right to expect his or her child to follow in their spiritual footsteps. Some would almost call it a duty or a responsibility, though I would rather consider it an advocatory standard by which we gauge our preferences."

"According to what you said a moment ago," countered Father, "your ethics forbid you to impose your beliefs upon your children."

"As long as they are unable to make their own decisions, true," said the minister. "But on the other hand—"

"Look," slavered the bulldog, clenching his fists at his sides and glaring menacingly at Father Baptist. "You can boss your precious cardinal around, but not me."

"And you can boss your officers around," said Father, "but not me. I warned you before, Monty: if you interfere with Stella's wishes, you will only alienate her."

"All this tension is counterproductive to resolving the volatile controversy at hand," cooed Pastor McIntosh, sweet as saccharine. "I suggest that we all sit down, take a deep breath, delve into that internal sponge of human kindness that we all know so well, and share our feelings constructively—"

"Stuff it," snapped Billowack. "Save that gooey crap for your sermons."

"My word," said the minister, flinching as though he'd been slapped. "If you're going to be that way about it, perhaps I should go—"

"You stay put," ordered Billowack. "I pay you enough on Sundays to enlist your cooperation on Wednesdays, so make yourself useful!"

At that moment I was amusing myself trying to see if I could trick the vending machine into filling a cup with hot chocolate and chicken soup at the same time. I was determined to find something that Chief Billowack and his pastor would like.

"Very well, very well," sighed Pastor McIntosh, adjusting his tie along with his attitude. Apparently the thought of losing the Billowack family's weekly donation clarified the situation for him. "Father Baptist," he smiled, dusting his words with confectioner's sugar, "let us be reasonable. Perhaps we can agree to a compromise. My good friend, the Right-Reverend Winston Q. Smithers is pastor at First Baptist just a few blocks from here. I could summon him—"

"No," said Father. "That is not acceptable."

"Why not? I understood that Catholics consider Protestant baptisms valid."

"Provided the proper form, matter, and intention are used," said Father. "Because there is so much latitude these days with respect to form, and the mind boggles with respect to intention, I would be obliged to Baptize her conditionally afterwards anyway. There can be no compromise. What you gentlemen find so difficult to accept is that Stella wishes to embrace the Roman Catholic religion, the One True Faith that comes to us from the Apostles."

"You've brainwashed her," said Billowack.

"I've instructed her," countered Father, "as she asked me to do. This is not a hasty or spurious decision on her part. She has been studying the writings of the Saints, Popes, and Councils, preparing her mind as well as her heart for this moment."

"But Catholicism," groaned the chief, pounding his palm with his fist. "Why does it have to be that? Why couldn't she become a Presbyterian, or even a Unitarian?"

"Any form of Protestantism," said Father, "anything at *all,* so long as it's not the Church founded by Christ."

"But our family has always been Protestant," growled Billowack.

"So has mine," nodded Pastor McIntosh, "and a fine tradition it is, too."

"You invoke your ancestors?" glared Father. "Well, my friends, if you go back enough generations you'll find that they all called themselves Catholics. All your Protestant factions are but branches that cut themselves off from the Vine, and you continue to split apart from each other. You can't agree on anything essential. One sect denies the Divinity of Christ, another the virginity of Mary, another the Trinity, another the Nicene Creed, another the Hypostatic Union—"

"The what?" barked Billowack.

"Never mind," said Father. "Has it ever occurred to you that the only thing upon which you Protestants can agree is that you're not Catholics?"

"Of course," said Billowack. "What else is there?"

"I would deem that an oversimplification." said the minister, "though it would seem to me—"

"Have you ever wondered why?" pressed Father. "Your daughter has, Monty. The fact has been troubling her for quite some time."

"Indeed," nodded Pastor McIntosh, gently swirling the dregs in his cup. "She visited me several months ago in a state of advanced trepidation. I tried to soothe her concerns, to show her the futility of seeking absolutes in a relative universe—"

"Which is why she came to me," interrupted Father. "The Will precedes the Intellect, and her hunger for absolute Truth superceded all your explanations to the contrary, no matter how compelling your arguments, no matter how many scholars you cited. I merely guided her to sources of information that she was already seeking. The effort was entirely hers, I assure you. Whatever your agenda, she now chooses to align herself with the likes of St. Thomas More and St. John Fisher, men who died rather than become Protestants like yourselves—"

"This is getting out of hand," said Eugene McIntosh, his weekly checks from the Bank of Billowack slipping through the shredder before his eyes. "You don't talk like other Catholics I know."

"I'm not like other Catholics you know," said Father.

"They at least admit the necessity of the Reformation," said the minister, his self-assurance developing a noticeable quaver. "How dare you attack our holy and rightful separation from the tyranny and superstition of Rome!"

"There was nothing holy or right about it," said Father. "It was fiendish by intent and political by design, driven by lust and greed and self-interest. Separation is not reformation; it is apostasy. Personal interpretation is not piety; it is lunacy. What you call the tyranny of Rome, I call the mandate of God. What you casually dismiss as superstition, I embrace as the Sacraments instituted by Our Lord and Redeemer, Jesus Christ."

Standing by the vending machine, I had become so mesmerized by the conversation that I failed to notice the echoes of some commotion down the hall. At the word "apostasy" an insistent high-pitched squeal penetrated my attention, accompanied by the patter and squeak of hospital shoes scurrying against linoleum. I also became aware that Father Baptist, while gradually expanding his remarks from two-word phrases to strings of erudite verbiage, had imperceptibly positioned himself nearer the doorway than his two opponents, with a row of floor-mounted chairs between him and them. Could the man stall, or could the man stall?

"Nothing was truly reformed," he was saying, "but much was damaged or destroyed. Private interpretation gave way to mob rule. Worse, millions of souls were lost. You've been covering your tracks for five centuries, but all the excuses in the world won't obfuscate the Truth: you are heretics."

"That's a word I don't like," said Pastor McInstosh.

"If I may quote St. Thomas More," said Father, "'It's not a likable word. It's not a likable thing!' Nonetheless, it is what you are. Now if you will excuse me, I have a Sacrament to administer."

> GARDENING TIPS: Actually, Father was quoting the character of Sir Thomas More in Robert Bolt's play, A Man for All Seasons, but he had worked up a steam and I wasn't about to get in the way of the locomotive.
>
> —M.F.

"Don't you dare," roared Billowack, but Father was already out of the room.

"Chief Billowack," said Pastor McIntosh, desperately lathering his words into soft, gentle foam, "Let us be reasonable. I suggest that you and I take a moment to gather our wits and enhance our calm—"

He was flung aside along with an end table stacked with magazines as Billowack charged around the impeding row of chairs and lunged for the doorway. I bought Father Baptist a few extra seconds by "accidentally" tripping the marauding bulldog at the threshold with my cane. Cursing, he landed face down in the hallway and skidded for several feet, his huge palms squealing against the waxed linoleum. Fueled with fury, he regained his enormous footing and charged after Father Baptist, phlegm splattering the walls as he thundered down the corridor.

I hobbled after, avoiding puddles of spittle, leaving Pastor Eugene to enhance his calm alone.

The air was swarming with buzzers and beeps as I approached Stella's doorway. Jonathan was in the hallway, slumped against the wall. The water pitcher dangled from his limp fingers. Father Baptist was beside him, speaking to him in swift, subdued tones. Bulldog Billowack was braced against the opposite wall, eyes glaring as nurses and doctors charged in and out of the room.

"Father Baptist," Jonathan sobbed, "Stella—she—"

"More blood," yelled a voice inside the room. "And get that defibrillator in here!"

"Jonathan," said Father, clutching the lad's shoulders. "Did you—?"

"Yes." The plastic pitcher slipped from his fingers and bounced noisily several times on the floor. "She started convulsing, and she said, 'Please don't let me die without—' So I—"

"Good Knight," said Father, giving Jonathan's shoulders an encouraging, manly squeeze. Then he let go and dashed into the room, nearly colliding with a nurse who was pushing a cart loaded with ugly and ominous machinery.

"Out," yelled someone.

"I'm a priest," I heard him say.

"Okay, Father, but keep out of the way."

"Of course."

"Stella—?" gasped Billowack, glued to the wall. "My Stella!"

"Clear!" barked someone.

A strange electronic sound sizzled in the room.

"Anything?" asked someone else.

"Nope."

"Let's try again. Clear!"

That unnerving sound again, followed by a thump.

"Well?"

"We've got a heartbeat."

"Good. Where's that blood?"

"Here, Doctor."

"Well, don't just stand there."

"Yes, Doctor."

"Someone get a gurney in here."

"Right-oh."

"Mr. Feeney," whispered Jonathan, "if, if she dies—"

"Then you'll have a Saint for a friend," I said, gripping his arm. "You did good, Jonathan."

"But—"

"She's strong," I said, steering him past Billowack, who seemed to be looking through us. "There is still hope that she'll pull through."

"Whatever happens, Jonathan," said Father Baptist, emerging from the doorway, "you have given her the best of all possible gifts."

"What?!" barked Billowack, snapping into focus. "This kid? You're not saying that he—? That now she's a, a, a cuh-cuh-cuh-Cath—" Billowack choked to a halt on his own phlegm. It was disgusting.

"Yes," said Father. "He did, and, thank Heaven, she is."

"But he's—not—a priest!" wheezed the chief between coughs.

"No, he isn't," agreed Father.

"How—can he—?"

"Check the Council of Florence," said the gardener helpfully. "1445 AD."

"The—the what?"

GARDENING TIPS: Ahem, and I quote: "In case of necessity, however, not only a priest or a deacon,
but even a layman or a woman, yes even a pagan and
a heretic can baptize, so long as he preserves the
form of the Church and has the intention of doing
as the Church does." Let's see:
  Was Jonathan a layman? Check.
  Proper form? Most certainly.
  Right intention? Check.
  Necessity? Stella was on the verge of death
and, with full knowledge and consent, had made her
wishes known. Check, and double-check.
  Conclusion: Yup, Stella Billowack was now officially a cuh-cuh-cuh-Cath--
  For those who are interested, this official dogmatic pronouncement is to be found in a book
called the Enchiridion Symbolorum, better known in
Catholic circles as "Denzinger," paragraph 696.
(The canon regarding the necessity of actual water
for Baptism, quoted earlier in this chapter, is
paragraph 858; and Pope Leo XIII's letter to Cardinal Gibbons, Testem benevolentiae, begins at
1967.)

--M.F.

N.B. For a real thrill, and to better understand
why Sir Thomas More chose not to go Prod when King
Henry VIII decided to usurp the power of the Pa-
pacy in England so that he could grant himself a
divorce, read paragraph 714.

"This is intolerable," said Pastor McIntosh who had regained his composure enough to join us in this episode's denouement.

"So is that tie," I said as Stella went whooshing by on a gurney.

69

"NO NUMBER SMEARED IN BLOOD," said John Holtsclaw, consulting his clipboard. "No messages of any kind. Nannette Cushions was sucked dry of blood and unceremoniously dumped on a pile of collapsed cardboard cartons behind Gelslinger's Deli."

"I remember her," said Father, leaning over the corpse on the stain-less steel table. It was hard to imagine that, less than a week before, this devastated woman had tried to tickle Pierre Bontemps' fancy in Elza's Sitting Room. "Any bruising on the back of the neck?"

"No," said Solomon Yung-sul Wong. "I guess she wasn't wearing a cross."

"The teeth marks," observed Father, "around the punctures."

"Yes, interesting," agreed John Holtsclaw, turning a page. "More like the murders before Patricia Marie Nealy; and we're back to traces of fennel, myrrh, sodium monofluorophosphate, calcium carbonate, carrageenan, glycerin, propolis ... but no allicin this time."

"Valdemar," said Father Baptist.

"We think so," said Solomon.

"That reminds me," said Father. "Did you run an analysis on the handkerchief I gave Lieutenant Taper on Monday?"

"Oh yeah," said Holtsclaw, fishing around in a stack of papers and producing a faded green printout. "Is this what you wanted?"

Father eyed the page. "Indeed."

"Well?" asked Solomon and Holtsclaw together.

"Very well," said Father, taking a deep breath as he handed the page back to the assistant coroner. "Martin, we've got to get back to the rectory. Gentlemen, I'll be in touch ... soon."

70

"MONSIGNOR ASPIC, THIS IS FATHER BAPTIST." He was using the phone on Lieutenant Taper's desk at police headquarters. "No, I'm not calling about that."

Sergeant Wickes was standing behind Father, gazing over his shoulder at the sheets of paper in his hand.

"No, really," said Father. "That can wait. I have another matter I wish to discuss with you. No, I have a better idea. I'm going to be checking out something at the 'House of Illusions' this evening and I thought we could have dinner there—if you've nothing else pressing, of course. Yes, that's right. I'll leave a guest pass with the receptionist. Eight will be fine. See you then."

"What's going on?" asked Wickes as Father set the receiver in its cradle. "What do you have up your sleeve?"

"Not a thing. Lieutenant, Sergeant, you will of course be joining us."

"Is that an order?" asked Larry.

"A strong suggestion," said Father. "I think you'll find the exercise interesting."

"He does have something up his sleeve," said Wickes. "I can tell."

"Any further word," asked Father, "on Stella Billowack's condition?"

"She's stable," said Larry, shoving his hands in his pockets. "But that's about all. She hasn't regained consciousness."

"How's Monty doing?"

"The Chief? Well, apart from vowing every third minute to tear your stinking guts out with his bare hands, I'd say he's holding up pretty well."

"Love your chief," said the gardener.

"Love your cardinal," said Taper.

"Touché," said I.

"By the way, Sergeant," said Father, "what can you tell me about St. Martha?"

"Not again," said Wickes.

"Humor me," said Father. "Like I said before, I'm laying a foundation."

"A foundation, eh?" said Wickes. "They hide bodies in concrete, don't they?"

"In New York and Chicago, maybe," said Taper to his partner. "But this is LA. Our foundations are only made from body-free concrete. Go ahead. What's the harm?"

"Right, sure," said Wickes, twisting his face into an authoritative pucker. "St. Martha, you say. You mean as in the story of Martha and Mary?"

"The same," said Father.

"Wasn't she the one who complained that Mary wasn't helping with the housework? And Jesus told her to relax, that her sister had chosen the better part."

"That's right," said Father. "Now tell me, what is your impression of the kind of home in which they lived?"

"What do you mean?"

"Oh, was it big or small? Ritzy or ramshackle?"

"Can't really say," said Wickes. "From what I've seen in a couple of 'life of Christ' movies, it was sort of a one-story house—simple, stone or clay construction would be my guess."

"Any idea what happened to her after Jesus raised her brother, Lazarus, from the tomb?"

"No. And frankly, I'm not so sure any of that happened."

"Of course you're not. You're a skeptic."

"Right."

"Would you be surprised to learn that St. Martha died in France, along with her sister and brother?"

"I'd never heard that."

"I don't suppose you ever heard of a dragon in connection with her?"

"A dragon? You mean like with St. George? No, I've never heard that, either."

"Well now you have."

"Okay, I'm surprised. Now what?"

"Now Martin and I have to run a few errands. I know you and Larry could get into the 'House of Illusions' by flashing your badges, but I'd prefer that you keep a low profile. I'm going to arrange some passes through Kahlúa Hummingbird at the *L. A. Artsy*. They'll be at the front desk. See you there."

71

"I DON'T UNDERSTAND," I WAS SAYING into the telephone back at the rectory shortly after lunch. Father was praying in the church, and I had just sat down in the study to engorge that copy of *Collected Ghost Stories* by M. R. James which I had never gotten to since Monday evening when the phone rang, catapulting me into that weird adventure at the "House of Illusions." *Eight Faces at Three* by Craig Rice the previous evening had been a splendid break, but I wanted to settle down to something with more of a bite to it—pun intended—something in keeping with the ominous mood of the day. Don't ask me why.

The call was from the warden at the California Penitentiary for Women at Vernon—Cheryl Farnsworth's permanent residence.

"She's done what!?" I gasped into the receiver. Warden Tracy had no reason to lie, but what she was telling me didn't add up. "I can't imagine what would compel her to do something like that. So why have you phoned me—?"

I knew the answer before she gave it. I was Cheryl's friend—her only friend. Perhaps I could talk sense to her, reason with her, get through to her. The staff shrink couldn't determine if she was sincere or bucking for transfer to the drug-induced Valhalla of a mental hospital in hopes of tastier grub, friendlier guards, or a better chance of escape. She was, after all, in there for life. What did she have to lose? Why *not* fiddle with all our heads just for the possibility of a different view for the next few decades? But what—hoo boy!—what if she wasn't foolin'?

"Of course I want to help," I said at last, a terrible sense of helplessness welling up within and then kind of brimming and surging all over me. "I'll be there tomorrow morning. Till then, good night; and may God bless you."

Hanging up the phone, I decided that I was no longer in the mood for M. R. James. Instead, I snatched up a paperback copy of Rex Stout's *Too Many Cooks*. Though I'd devoured it twice before, as with all the Nero Wolfe mysteries, the third read was the best.

I noticed that two pages were dog-eared, one toward the beginning of the novel and the other at the end. Curious as to what I'd thought sufficiently significant to desecrate the volume by folding down corners, yet not urgent enough to write down in one of my notebooks, and apparently not momentous enough to consign to memory, I opened to the designated pages.

Ah yes, it came back instantly. These passages revealed Nero Wolfe's attitude toward, and more so his perception of, women. In the first instance, Archie Goodwin was recalling the time when Constanza Berin started crying in his boss' office and ...

> ... Wolfe said sharply, "She's hysterical. Take her out of here."
> I felt her arm relax, and turned her loose, and she moved to face Wolfe again.
> She told him quietly, "I'm not hysterical."
> "Of course you are. All women are. Their moments of calm are merely recuperative periods between outbursts ..."

The second passage began with Miss Berin's humbling admission:

> "Mr. Wolfe, I ... I was terrible this morning."
> He moved his eyes at her. "You were indeed, Miss Berin. I have often noticed that the more beautiful a woman is, especially a young one, the more liable she is to permit herself unreasonable fits. It's something that you acknowledge. Tell me, when you feel it coming on like that, is there nothing you can do to stop it? Have you ever tried?"

Not believing in coincidences, I found it significant that I'd stumbled across these previously appreciated passages on the heels of a phone call from Warden Tracy regarding Cheryl Farnsworth's current behavior. I would have pondered the philosophical implications at great length, no doubt, if my reverie hadn't been interrupted by Millie's appearance in the doorway.

"Mr. Feeney," she said curtly, twelve-inch skillet clutched in her fist, "the kitchen door."

That was Millie-ese for, "Someone knocked at the back door. I answered it. I told the guy to wait, and I don't feel like telling you who it is. Now go deal with it."

"Be right there," I said, struggling to my feet.

"Señor Feeney," said the man at the back door a few hobbling moments later. His clothes were filthy, caked with dirt, which accounted for Millie's refusal to let him inside the rectory.

"Roberto," I said, "back again so soon?"

"Well," he said, looking skeptically around at the cemetery and then guardedly back at me. "Maybe, it is not enough water, or maybe it is the heat."

"What is?" I asked, stepping outside. "Or what is not?"

"The dichondra, the grass me and my men left here on Monday, it is all dead."

"Strange," I said.

"Not really, Señor. Dichondra, it is very delicate. We brought it in the slats. We should have planted it the day we brought it here—but there was the funeral, no?"

"A burial, sí," I said, thinking of Bucky Turnbuckle's sparse send-off. "Well, what can I say?"

"Nothing," said Roberto. "Please tell Father Baptist we'll find something else to cover the ground."

"Will do," I said, turning to go back inside.

GARDENING TIPS: While I admit that the problem of the dead grass didn't seem important at the time, the concept of "accidents" doesn't make sense in a universe created and sustained by a truly omnipotent God. The inclusion of this trivial detail in my already lengthy and admittedly complex story will serve eventually to prove my point.

                                        --M.F.

N.B. As for Nero Wolfe's perception of women, it was a theory that was about to be put to the test, and not just with respect to Cheryl Farnsworth.

"I've got my hands full," growled Millie, knocking a couple of pans together for emphasis as I closed the back door behind me, "without having to answer doors and then go running all over Creation for the likes of you."

"I appreciate that, Millie," I earnestly tried to explain, "and I'm truly sorry; but I was on the phone, and it was important."

"So important that once it was over, instead of leaping to action, you sat there reading some cheap, lurid paperback."

"Hey, fifty cents for a used Rex Stout is not cheap; it's just all I can afford. And *Too Many Cooks* is not lurid, it's, it's—"

"Are not," she corrected me. "Too many cooks *are* not lurid. Tisk, tisk—and you a writer. Oh, don't think I don't know that you stay up 'most every night clacking away at that old typewriter in your room."

"Um," I said, not daring to cross her. Besides, she was skirting some incredibly sensitive territory. "Yes, well, uh, be that as it may, and however it may have appeared, I was disturbed by the phone call—very disturbed, actually, and—"

"Words don't begin to express how sorry I am that I didn't move fast enough to prevent the phone from interrupting your reading," she said, slamming her weapons down on the burners with a mighty clang. "I'm just a woman, after all, and I don't have time for such lofty pursuits. Too many cooks, indeed!"

"I'll be in Father's study," I said, slinking away.

"I'll be right here," moaned Millie. "Same as always, not that any-one cares. Does anyone appreciate my sweat and blood mingled with these leftover ham hocks and beans? Does anyone consider what wash-ing thousands of filthy dishes in soapy water is doing to my hands? Not anyone around here. One of these days, yes, mark my words, one of these damnable days—"

"On second thought," I said, realizing I'd never be able to concentrate in Father's study, not with Millie on this woeful warpath, "I'm going to be out in Monsignor Havermeyer's camper."

"You do that," she spat, gripping a soup kettle with both handles and heaving it from the stove to the sink. "I'm not going anywhere. I never do."

"Hmm," I hmmed as I crept outside, distancing myself from the kitchen door. "She was so sweet last night, and today she's so ... *so*. It can't be because we missed breakfast, since Wednesday is her morn-ing off. Maybe it's because Father and I won't be having dinner at the rectory this evening, but you'd think she'd appreciate the break."

Monsignor Havermeyer's camper came into view as I passed Roberto and his pals hauling dead dichondra in wheelbarrows from the cemetery.

"Hmm," I hmmed again. "Could it be a 'Leviticus fifteen nineteen' again?"

With Millie, it was so often hard to tell.

72

"'TE IGITUR,'" GRUMBLED MONSIGNOR HAVERMEYER, each syllable uttered as if it were his enemy, "'clementissime Pater, per Jesum Chris-tum Filium tuum Dominum nostrum, supplices rogamus ac petimus ...'"

"Why did you stop," I asked, shifting my weight on the pile of clothes upon which I was sitting, "just as you were coming to 'uti ac-cepta habeas'?"

"It says 'Osculatur altare' in red letters here," said the monsignor, stabbing the gold-fringed page with his warped-weenie finger. "What does that mean?"

"It means 'he'—meaning 'you'—'kisses the altar.'"

"Then why doesn't it say that?" he barked, pounding the table. The wine glass he was using for a practice Chalice teetered and spun, but managed to stay standing.

"It does, My Senior," I said, "in Latin. Okay, let's go on. That next sentence in red—right, the one which begins 'Jungit manus, deinde signat'—that means 'he'—meaning 'you'—'joins his hands together, and then makes the Sign of the Cross thrice over the offerings.'"

"Not more Crosses," moaned Havermeyer. "You'd think everything had been blessed enough by now."

"If it had, Monsignore, the Church wouldn't be in the shape it's in today. No more arguments. 'The rubrics is the rubrics,' as they say."

"Who says?"

"They. Proceed."

"Hrmph," he growled. But, like a petulant trooper, he did his best, waving his right hand this way and that as he pondered the words on the page. "'... uti accepta habeas, et benedicas (jungit manus, deinde signat ter super oblata)—'"

"No," I interrupted. "You don't read the words in parentheses aloud. Those are the instructions, remember, that I just translated for you."

"Oh yeah," he said. "Right: '... hæc dona, hæc munera, hæc sancta sacrificia illibata ...'"

I'll just give you the English translation, which he didn't have, and which I didn't need, since I already knew the passage well, but which my reader might not:

> **Wherefore, O most merciful Father, we humbly pray and beseech thee, through Jesus Christ Thy Son, our Lord *(he kisses the altar)*, that thou wouldst vouchsafe to receive and bless *(he joins his hands together, and then makes the Sign of the Cross thrice over the offerings)* these [✠] gifts, these [✠] offerings, this [✠] holy and unblemished sacrifice ...**

"You stopped again," I moaned, but with a tone of encouragement. "What's wrong?"

"I don't know what 'Extensis manibus prosequitur' means."

"'He'—meaning 'you'—'extends his hand and continues.'"

"I—meaning me—have had enough," huffed Havermeyer, heaving the altar missal shut. "Thank-you, Martin, but I'm mentally exhausted."

"Well, I—meaning me—am as well."

"Then why don't you—meaning you—go take a nice long nap?"

"Because he—meaning Father Baptist—has plans for the evening."

"Is it—meaning the time—really that late?"

"It—meaning it—is."

"Then I—meaning me—am off to 'Peanuts.'"

The gardener—meaning me—was glad this insufferable conversation had finally ended. I went to my room to get spruced up for the evening's festivities.

73

"MR. GRAVES?" called Father. "Are you down here?"

It was seven-thirty in the evening, and much to my consternation, Father Baptist and I were down in the basement of the "House of Illusions." Why, you might ask.

"I have a couple of questions I'd like to ask you," called Father.

That's why.

Reginold the Reiterator had provided Father with a map of the place which contained about as much detail as one of those 16th-century cartographer's charts of the New World. I was beginning to think we were lost.

This was certainly the basement, because the water pipes and drains and electrical conduits converged in abundance on the walls and ceilings. There were countless cupboards and cabinets and storerooms. The fact that the police had already been through these nooks and crannies gave me no assurance whatsoever that icky things weren't lurking within them.

"Mr. Graves?" called Father again.

"Back here," answered a voice.

We followed the echo to a little room behind three huge hot water heaters. Considering the surrounding ambiance, Mr. Grave's hideaway looked almost cheerful.

"You found me out," said Mr. Graves, stretched out on a small cot, a reading lamp illuminating some sort of full-color brochure on his tummy. "No one's really supposed to stay on the premises after hours, but I'm here so much of the time it's kind of senseless to pay rent on an apartment."

"You reside here?" asked Father, glancing around the bare concrete walls, dotted here and there with rusty nubs of reinforcement rods protruding through the cement. Mr. Graves had utilized several as hooks on which to hang his spare shirts.

"Yup," said Graves, groaning up into a sitting position. His crisscrossed eyebrows did a curious tango as he yawned widely. "Everything

I need is within easy reach. I get grub from the kitchen, and some of the dressing rooms have showers."

"So you were here Monday night when all the excitement happened?" asked Father.

"You mean to the Chief of Homicide's daughter?" asked Graves.

"The same," said Father. "And to Mr. Feeney, here."

"Yeah," said Graves. "I overheard some talk about it—magicians' gossip and waiters' whispers is all."

"Do you drive a car?" asked Father. "A Volkswagen 'Bug' or a Karmen Ghia?"

"Nope," said Graves. "I got a Ford station wagon that's been sitting on a mechanic's lift since last week. Crud in the carburetor or something. I don't drive much so there's no rush. Like I said, I got everything I need right here."

"That is fortunate," said Father, looking around for something to sit on.

"Yeah," said Graves, removing his reading glasses and holding them up to the light for smear analysis. "Anyway, if you're here to ask if I saw or heard something Monday night, the answer is 'no' to both. I came down to my hideaway right after rehearsals, and all you can hear down here is leaking steam and draining pipes. You can sit on that thing if you like."

The thing he was pointing to was a small wooden child-sized coffin. Yes, that's exactly what it was, complete with brass handles and divided lid for upper-body viewing.

Father hesitated.

"Oh," said Mr. Graves, replacing his glasses beneath his intersecting eyebrows, "you can look inside if you like. I just use it as a foot-locker."

"Where did it come from?" asked Father, hefting the lid. There was a brass plaque covered with fancy engraving mounted in the center of the arch of the lid, but I wasn't close enough to read it. The coffin itself was full of crumpled underwear and T-shirts. "It looks very old."

"Magicians come and go all the time," said the Toolmaster. "Sometimes they leave props behind. It all trickles down to the basement eventually. You wouldn't believe some of the stuff we got stored down here. Go ahead, have a sit. It won't bite you."

"Splinters," said Father, declining. He closed the lid, rubbing his thumbs and forefingers together.

"Suit yourself," said Graves, puzzled or amused at something. It was hard to tell with those eyebrows. "Mr. Feeney?"

"I'll stand, thank-you," I said.

"So what did you want to ask me?" said Graves, tossing the full-color brochure to the foot of the cot. *The Golden Gate Bridge,* I noticed. *Gateway to San Francisco.*

Even toolmasters like to travel, I thought.

"Did you know Babbette Starr or Nannette Cushions?" asked Father.

"Didn't Surewood Forst discover their bodies out under the Farquar Terrace?" asked Graves.

"One of them, yes," said Father. "Babbette Starr. Nannette Cushions was found by a shopkeeper in an alley several miles from here."

"What a shame," said Mr. Graves, rubbing his knees. "Yeah, I knew them. At least, I sometimes saw them grazing up in Elza's Sitting Room."

"Grazing?" asked Father.

"They liked tall men," said Graves. "They usually left with them, anyway, at the end of the evenings. This place attracts a slightly higher grade of straw than most bars in Hollywood."

"I see," said Father. "You didn't happen to notice who Babbette left with Friday night? Or Nannette last night?"

"No," said Graves. "Most of the time I'm backstage or behind the walls. The few times I did see them I was behind the mirrors in Elza's Sitting Room, making adjustments on the remote piano keyboard or keeping Buzz company. But Friday evening I was busy fixing some electrical relays in the Egyptian Room most of the night. And last night we had some major problems in Raimundo's Chamber with the wires that control the snare drum in Mr. Portifoy's act."

"You're pretty clear on your movements," commented Father.

"I got it all right here," said Mr. Graves, reaching for a bulging clipboard near his reading light. He handed it to Father. "What I don't remember, I can read."

"Hmm," said Father, leafing through a couple of pages. "I see you've had to fix a lot of remote controls within the past week."

"Always," said Mr. Graves. "They get dropped, stepped on, spilled on, and sometimes left in somebody's pocket and put through the laundry."

"I'll bet," smiled Father, handing the clipboard back to him. His eyes fell on a small gray plastic object sitting next to Mr. Grave's reading lamp. "Is that one of them?"

"Yeah. Most of the magicians here use them, but none of them know how to take care of them."

"What would you say is the maximum range of one of these things?" asked Father, picking it up and turning it over in his hands.

"Twenty feet."

"Doesn't seem very far."

"It can't be much more than that or one guy's trick is going to screw up another guy's in the next room."

Father set it down. "Could one of these be adjusted to have a longer range?"

"Not without upping the power," said Graves. "And if I took that apart and showed you, you'd see there just ain't any more room for larger batteries inside."

"Are you planning a vacation?" asked Father, noticing the brochure on the cot.

"More than that," said Mr. Graves. "I'm thinking of moving on myself. Things are getting a bit too tense around here for me."

"I must admit," said Father, "I'm a bit surprised that the place is still open for business."

"The owners aren't impressed with a few violent incidents," said Graves.

"I'm even more impressed, I think, with the fact that none of the employees has leaked any of it to the papers."

"No mystery there," said Graves, reaching for a booklet with three staples and three binder holes down the left edge. "This here is an eighty-page nondisclosure agreement. Everyone who works for the 'House' has to sign it, and let me tell you, it's the stiffest contract I've ever seen, and I've seen plenty. When I first came here—"

"When was that?" asked Father.

"Early in the summer—June. When I laid my eyes on that thing, I almost refused. A week after I started, they fired a waitress for telling a friend of hers about the blinking light trick in the bar."

"I remember that gimmick," said Father. "Mr. Portifoy gave us a demonstration when we first arrived. It malfunctioned."

"No doubt," said Graves. "Everything around here does eventually. Anyway, the waitress' friend turned out to be a critic at the *Times,* and she wrote a little piece about cheap parlor tricks. The waitress was canned, and she didn't even really know how it worked, you see. She just said it was done by remote control."

"That is a bit harsh," agreed Father.

I wondered how Buzz Sawr kept his job. He'd explained to me, a perfect stranger who knew his ginger ale, the machinations of Elza's Sitting Room—and right in front of Bart, a fellow employee. Of course, if he were fired and his counter-suit ever came before a judge ol' Buzz would honestly testify—and I'd have to back him up—that he'd told me that the secret of the piano-playing ghost in Elza's parlor was actually … Elza's ghost. I smiled at the irony, then cringed at the memory of the confrontation of that ghost and the darkness, with me in between.

"The job market being what it is," said Graves, "it's no wonder no one's talking to anybody around here. It's like a prison camp sometimes. That's why I'm thinking of moving up north. There's a club called 'Quicker than the Eye' that's looking for a man with my talents. Besides, I've never been to the Bay Area, and I've got a kid up at Berkeley."

"Really," said Father. "Son or daughter?"

"Son," said Mr. Graves. "Henry. He's twenty-three, majoring in Medieval History and Electrical Engineering, believe it or not. I've also got two older daughters, but they never got beyond high school."

"So you're married?" asked Father.

"Was," said Graves. "The wife died of leukemia years ago. I've been living in bachelor pads like this ever since the kids left the roost, and to tell you the truth, I prefer it. Anyway, yes, I'm seriously considering a move to San Francisco or Oakland. I've heard it's a lot less stressful than life in LA."

"Don't be too sure," said Father. "Every city has its tensions."

"I expect you to say that," said Graves, "considering the business you're in. Every city has its humans. And where there are men, there are problems."

"True," said Father. "You're not a Catholic, are you?" It was more of a statement than a question, since his voice fell on the last word.

"Naw," said Mr. Graves. "I suppose if I was to go to a church, it'd be Presbyterian. My family went Calvinist over three centuries ago. I'm not gonna buck tradition, though to tell you the truth, I haven't darkened a church door, 'cepting weddings and funerals, for as long as I can remember. Besides, your own Saints have said that Catholics go deeper into Hell than heretics, since they know better. Me, I'll take ignorance any time."

"It's a curious ignorance," observed Father, "that knows so much."

"Like I said, where there are men, there are problems."

"Well," said Father, a touch of sadness in his voice, "tonight we're going to try to eliminate one such problem."

"Really?" said Mr. Graves, shifting on his cot. "You're on to some-one?"

"Yes," said Father, checking his watch. "In fact, Martin and I had best be getting upstairs."

"If you're having dinner," said Mr. Graves, sinking back down on his bed, "may I suggest the Cajun swordfish kabob? Fresh from the pier. The chef told me so."

"Thank-you," said Father. "Perhaps I'll give it a try."

"What about the prime rib?" I asked as Father took my arm and spun me around toward the gurgling hot water heaters.

"Exquisite as always," called Mr. Graves. "But the New York steak is even better. Trust me—"

His voice was lost amidst the sound of escaping steam and flushing toilets.

74

"I WANTED YOU TO SEE THIS in person," said Father, as we stood at the piano in Elza's Sitting Room. It was about quarter to eight, and I was surprised he had made this detour on the way to the dining room. Unlike the previous Friday, the parlor was almost deserted—perhaps because the piano in the corner sat eerily dormant. No, it was more than that. Something else had gone out of the room, something hard to define, less than tangible, but something substantial. "The photograph didn't really capture it, did it?"

He lifted the lid that covered the keyboard.

"Good Heavens," I gasped. "I still don't understand."

"I don't either, Bub," drawled a voice at the bar.

"Why Buzz," I said, turning. "No Elza tonight?"

"Not with the keyboard looking like that. The manager doesn't want the guests to get spooked."

I confess I hadn't really wanted to go to Elza's Sitting Room, or to the "House of Illusions" for that matter. The events of the previous Monday evening were all too fresh in my memory. Nonetheless, Father Baptist had insisted, and you've seen by now how persuasive he can be.

"Father Baptist," I said, "this is Buzz Sawr. He's the one who sits behind the mirrors and does requests."

"Except when someone takes a blowtorch to Elza's piano," said Buzz, wavering as usual. "The repair guy says it'll take a while to see if he can find an old used piano and salvage some keys. It's against the law to buy new ivory any more, you know. They still don't know how whoever did that did it. And why would they?"

He was referring to the two feminine handprints, shapely lady's fingers, burned deep and dark into the keyboard, with charred whirls all around.

"The worst part is," said Buzz, "she hasn't played since I came to work yesterday. Not a tinkle. Usually she's playing when I get here an hour before they start letting people in. Sometimes we even played duets together. She's probably mad that someone mutilated her piano. I pray she comes back when they've got it fixed, but I've got this sinking feeling that she's gone for good. The place feels different somehow. No one to spell me. Imagine having to play until closing without a trip to the well."

"That's rough," I agreed.

"A pleasure meeting you," said Father, steering me away from Mr. Sawr.

"So," I said as we went out into the hallway. I couldn't help looking over my shoulder to see if darkness was devouring the end of the corridor, but everything was bright and cheerful.

"So," said Father.

"So are you going to explain the burned handprints or not?"

"Oh that."

"Yes, that."

"Martin, some day we'll have to take a vacation and go to Rome."

"You said you'd never take a vacation, that you'd never have time."

"Yes, but now we have Monsignor Havermeyer. We'll see. Nonetheless, I'd love to show you an annex in the Sacro Cuore del Suffragio, a beautiful church within view of the River Tiber dedicated to the Sacred Heart of Suffrage."

"Suffrage?"

"An old term for offerings made to the Souls in Purgatory."

"Oh."

"There's a museum there called the 'House of Shadows.'"

"Sort of like that Ambuliella Beryl Smith's witchery shop?"

> GARDENING TIPS: Yet another reference to TEK--
> sorry. The late Miss Smith, also known as "Star-
> fire" among the wiccans and "Starfly" among the
> Tumblars, used to own a place called "The Shop of
> Shadows."
>
> --M.F.

"Nothing like," said Father. "In this museum are housed all kinds of evidence of visitations to the living made by Souls languishing in Purgatory."

"Really."

"Yes. It's not on the regular tourist lists, but it's impressive."

"And what kind of evidence is there?"

"Sometimes the person being visited would ask the apparition to touch a Crucifix or other holy object to prove they were not a demon from Hell trying to trick them."

"And since the Poor Souls are suffering in fire—"

"—their hands scorched whatever they touched."

"You're saying there are burned handprints preserved at this museum?"

"Yes, on Bibles and reliquaries and such."

"You're suggesting that the handprints on Elza's piano—"

"—were left by Elza herself as a sign to you."

"But the piano isn't a holy object."

"The Roundheads were devout Catholics by all accounts," said Father. "No doubt they had their house blessed on any number of occasions. People used to do that quite often, you know."

"Hm. It's possible."

"I'd say it's likely. In any case, she left you a sign for your edification."

"But what about Elza?"

"I don't know. Surely your prayers for her had some effect. Consider that you were being chased by something dark and evil the other night, and she drew you to her parlor by playing a tune familiar only to you."

"But then I fainted."

"Yes, and unlike Stella Billowack, you were left unharmed. I would not be surprised, my friend, if Elza saved you from a fate similar to Stella's."

"Can a Soul in Purgatory do that?"

"The Souls in Purgatory are more powerful than we can imagine. They are suffering, to be sure, in order to be made worthy of the Beatific Vision. But of Heaven they are assured. Where they are, they can help anyone but themselves. That is why they rely on our prayers, and that is why I suspect Elza owed you one. In fact, I suspect she'd been confined to this room all these years for this purpose: that one day she would render aid to you, Martin Feeney, and thus expiate her sins."

"If that's so," I said, honored and humbled and boggled by the implications of Father's last statement, "she did good."

"And so did you, Martin. So did you. Well, we'd best meet our guests for dinner."

"Oh joy."

"To be sure."

75

"I CAN'T IMAGINE WHY THIS REMINDS ME," I said as Father and I sat down in the dining room, "but yesterday Solomon Yung-sul Wong and John Holtsclaw told me to give you a message. I'm surprised they didn't give it to you themselves this morning, but I guess they were preoccupied."

"Oh?" said Father Baptist, accepting a menu from a scowling young would-be magician who was temporarily stuck as a waiter.

"Yes," I said, noticing that there were no prices listed. "They said they're both going to San Diego for a convention this weekend. Solomon's even giving a speech. They're leaving early tomorrow, Thursday, and don't plan to be back until late Monday night. So they told me to tell you to either solve this case by today or keep it on ice until Tuesday."

"Good for them," said Father, turning the laminated page. "But I don't see—"

"They also told me that no one else in their department is allowed to work on this case or even have access to the bodies. Billowack's orders."

"That's odd."

"'Bizarre' was Holtsclaw's word. He said it feels as though someone at City Hall is pulling the Chief's strings, and the same someone is keeping a tight lid on the kettle—no media coverage."

"Curiouser and curiouser," said Father. "I've noticed the absence of the media, but it hadn't occurred to me that it was anything other than the police practicing common sense."

"Ah," intruded an unexpected voice, "but that is sense of the worst possible kind, no?"

I looked up and around. It took me a moment to realize the source was level with my ear—and I was sitting down, don't forget.

"Mr. Portifoy," I said. "I won't bother extending my hand, just to have you pull yours away."

"You remember," said the little fellow, twirling his mustache with white-gloved fingers, "that the hand, it is quicker than the eye, no?"

"I prefer Angels," I countered. "They travel at the speed of thought."

"You have seen these creatures?" asked Lucius T. Portifoy, Master of Ceremonies, adjusting the aquamarine monocle in his left eye.

"No," I said, "but I've never glimpsed a thought, either."

"Ooh-hoo," said the splendidly attired runt, his black cape fastened about his neck with that same gaudy pewter clasp, the prominently crowned "B" flanked with "Phegor " and "Apollos" surround by intricate patterns. His monocle secure, he pointed his squat little finger at my nose. "You are the clever one."

"Nope," I said, nodding toward Father, "he is."

"No," said Father, turning his eyes upward, "He is."

"You're right," said Mr. Portifoy to me.

"I is," I agreed with him. "It must be hard for you these days, Mr. MC, without Bucky Buckle around to malign on the stage anymore."

"That was unfortunate, no?" he said, clapping his gloved hands together.

"That was unfortunate, yes," I said.

"'Excidat illa dies œvo,'" he said, raising a gloved finger, "'nec postera credant sæcula.'"

"Eh?" I said, unfamiliar with the phrase. My knowledge of Liturgical Latin is fair, but either his accent or pronunciation threw me off.

"'Let this day be lost from time,'" translated Father after a pensive moment, not looking up from his menu, "'and let posterity ignore the event.'"

"Pretty good," said Portifoy, rubbing his hands in circles. "Oui, Pere Jean Baptiste, he is very clever, no?"

"And you're going to miss your show, Mr. Portifoy," said Father, checking the desserts on the last page.

The little fellow consulted his watch. "You almost had me going, as they say. No, I have almost an hour."

"How sad," I said. "I'm sure you'll find somewhere to spend it."

"Hrmph," sniffed the MC. "I can see that my company is not appreciated here. Very well, I shall go elsewhere."

"I've heard it's a nice place," I said, "especially this time of—"

But the little imp was gone.

He was replaced by a bigger one almost immediately.

"So," said Monsignor Aspic, strutting up to our table—well, actually it was more like a "saunter" but so what? He pulled out his chair and sat down. "Here we are."

"Yes," agreed Father Baptist.

"I've been so wanting to come here since I arrived in town, but I just haven't had the time."

"Well, tonight's the night," said the gardener.

"You didn't say that we would be having company," said the monsignor, looking around the table.

I hadn't mentioned that our friends from the police had been sitting there throughout Father's and my exchange with Lucius T. Portifoy, MC and multilingual pipsqueak. They had been spending their time frowning at their menus.

"This is Lieutenant Taper and Sergeant Wickes," said Father. "Mr. Feeney you know. I asked Reginold the Reiterator—he's that big fellow you may or may not have met in one of the hallways—to produce one more guest to fill that sixth chair."

"Oh?" asked Aspic. "And who might that be?"

"Why, your brother, of course."

"Woody?"

"You're aware that he works here."

"Of course. He's—"

"Surewood Forst," said the sixth guest as he was ushered to our table by that big fellow in the hallways. He was wearing a stunning tuxedo with a maroon vest this time, and was even sporting a big swishing cape with red satin lining. "At your service. Why, Conrad, you've finally come to see me perform?"

"It would seem so," said Monsignor Aspic.

"Will there be anything else, Fawthaw, Saws?" asked the behemoth who always seemed to be looking down at us even when he bowed.

"Would you mind staying within shouting distance, Reginold?" asked Father. "I may need you to substantiate something in a couple of minutes."

"Sawtainly," said Reginold. "I awm at yaw sawvice—at least, until show time."

"We'll be done long before that," said Father.

"Substantiate what?" asked Monsignor Aspic.

"I recognize the faces," said Surewood, looking around the table. "I'm afraid the names have slipped through the cracks."

"I'm Father Baptist," said Father, "and this is Martin Feeney, Lieutenant Taper and Sergeant Wickes ."

"Ah, the gentlemen from Homicide who questioned the staff the other day," said Surewood, settling into his chair. "Am I under suspicion?"

"Yes," said Father.

"What's this?" gasped Monsignor Aspic. "Father Baptist, if this is some sort of joke—?"

"No joke," said Father.

"Do tell," said Surewood, confidently adjusting the clasp of his cape.

"Just for the record," said Lieutenant Taper, "your stage name is Surewood Forst, but your legal name is Sherwood Wormwood Aspic. Is that correct?"

"Yes," said the magician, elbowing his brother, Conrad Jonas Aspic. "Our mother had a flair for weird middle names. So what?"

"I could drag this out," said Father, "but I'm really very tired. I just want to eat a nice dinner in peace—I'm told the swordfish kabob is excellent tonight. Then I want to go home, and sleep for the first time in days. So I'll get to the point."

"Please do," said Surewood, mimicking Father's voice, "get to the point."

"As to why you've taken up murdering impressionable young women," said Father, "I'll leave it for the police to piece together. Once they know what to look for, they're very good at finding it."

"I protest," said Monsignor Aspic.

"And well you should," said Father, "but not to me. It is you, Monsignor, who have been duped by your brother. I understand that, according to a background check conducted by the police, you once worked as an assistant dental technician at a company called 'Newgums.'"

"That's how I paid my way through college, yes," said the monsignor. "We were both living in Seattle at the time. So?"

"The company was involved in the manufacture of bridges and false teeth," said Father.

"Yes," said Aspic. "But that was a long time ago."

"It was while you worked there, I suspect, that you made a set of vampire's canines for your brother, who even then was expressing interest in magic and the theater."

"At Newgums we made all sorts of fangs for magicians and actors," said Aspic. "Actually, we had little to do with dentists."

"But you did make a set for Surewood."

"Yes. He was involved in a local actors' workshop, and landed the lead role in *My Son, the Vampire.*"

"With a bite about three-quarters of an inch between points. Elongated incisors, really, not canines."

"I don't remember."

"Newgums faxed us the specifications," said Taper. "They keep meticulous dental records and molds for repeating customers."

"So I have fake vampire fangs," said Surewood. "So do lots of people around here. Reginold, don't you have a set of vampire teeth?"

"No saw," said the big guy, standing by the doorway. "Cawn't say thawt I do."

"Well, he's unusual," said Surewood, waving his thumb at Reginold while smiling at Father. "You've got to do better than that."

"I can," said Father. "Your blood type is O-positive, is it not?"

"Beats me," said Surewood.

"So is mine," said Aspic.

"But you're not the murderer," said Father to Aspic, "and he is. Though actually, Monsignor, it was through you that I began to piece all this together."

"I don't follow you."

"Few do," I interjected. "That's why his parish is so small."

"One of the befuddling things about the first eight murders," continued Father, ignoring me, "was the presence of traces of a curious mixture of substances found on the neck wounds."

"Substances?" asked Surewood.

"Myrrh," said Taper, reciting the list from memory, "sodium monofluorophosphate, calcium carbonate, carrageenan, glycerin, fennel oil, propolis, and allicin."

"The last chemical, allicin," said Father, "is the active ingredient in garlic. That's how we knew the vampire plaguing the Hollywood area couldn't possibly be real."

"I'm surprised you would even consider such a possibility," said Conrad J. Aspic.

"I never discount anything out of hand," said Father. "But no matter. All the other ingredients are found in certain brands of so-called 'natural' toothpaste. I noticed last Sunday, Monsignor, when you visited St. Philomena's, a curious smell about you."

"Really," huffed Conrad J., a mite embarrassed.

"Yes," said Father. "You're wearing it now. Your aftershave I recognize—'Old Spice.' Your deodorant is calendula and pine scent, the precise brand I can't quite place. But your breath that morning, as well as the next day in the Chancery, carried the distinct odor of fennel. Tell me: what brand of toothpaste do you use?"

"Just what's in Woody's bathroom. I told you before I haven't unpacked all my own—"

"The brand," insisted Father.

"'Aunt Emily's Natural Dentifrice,'" said Surewood. "Thousands of people use it."

"True," said Father to Surewood, "and you're one of them. So is your brother, Monsignor Aspic, for that matter."

"You could tell all this with your nose?" asked Aspic, incredulous.

"That," answered Father, "and the analysis I had done on the saliva in the handkerchief I lifted from your pocket on Monday, just outside Cardinal Fulbright's office."

"My—? So that's what happened to it." The monsignor blinked twice as the info penetrated the ol' gray matter. "How dare you?"

"So are you accusing Conrad, too?" asked Surewood, glancing at his brother.

"No," said Father. "Whatever he may be, he's not a murderer."

GARDENING TIPS: I believe it was St. Augustine who asked, "What is worse, the murderer who kills the body or the heretic who kills the soul?" The correct answer was the latter.

I believe Father was hinting that of the two brothers, Conrad J. Aspic's denial of the Resurrection was worse than the heinous crimes of his brother, Surewood. I know, I know: "pre-Vatican II thinking," but there it is.

--M.F.

"But things are adding up," added Father, "as your fidgeting with that clasp clearly demonstrates."

Surewood relaxed his fingers and slowly lowered his hand.

"I'll not bother with the flying vampire stunt out on the Farquar Terrace," said Father. "Only someone with an intimate knowledge of this facility could have pulled that off, what with access to the long-unused dry-ice blower and all. That narrows it down, somewhat."

"Still not to me," said Surewood.

"More to the point," continued Father, "on Monday night, Mr. Feeney here received a phone call from someone mimicking his friend, Jonathan, who had been lured up here with his girlfriend by someone posing as a third person named Pierre."

"Complicated," said Surewood.

"Indeed," said Father. "And that's what closes the knot. The person who called Jonathan had to have met and heard Pierre speak. He had to know that they were friends. Since they were both here last Friday, and since you proved yourself then as now a remarkable impersonator—"

"But there are many people working here who have this talent," said Surewood. "My friend Lucius T. Portifoy, for example."

"Yes, but Mr. Portifoy doesn't have a brother who's been telling him things he'd heard at the Chancery and at my parish church, St. Philomena's—people he had met, details about the murders, and the like."

"I don't need my brother to tell me about the murders," said Surewood. "Don't forget, I discovered one of the bodies myself."

"Babbette Starr," said Lieutenant Taper.

"You no doubt thought you were being clever," said Father, "or even brazen in pretending to find the body of the woman you yourself murdered."

"I did not kill Babbette Starr," said Surewood. "I dated her once, but I got along better with her friend, Nannette."

"And now they're both dead," said Wickes.

"I'll return to that in a moment," said Father, eyes on Surewood Forst. "First I want to deal with the events of Monday evening, when you lured Mr. Feeney, Mr. Clubb, and Miss Billowack to this establishment."

"I didn't touch any of them," said Surewood.

"I'd have invited a college student by the name of Paula Sands here tonight," said Father, "except you were wearing dark glasses, and if you were smart, makeup, when you dropped by the cab company in the afternoon to arrange transportation for Jonathan and Stella."

"Well," said Surewood, "I am smart, but as with so many of these bits and pieces of so-called evidence you're pushing, nothing connects me directly to any of these crimes."

"What about your Karmen Ghia?" asked Taper, who had done his homework.

"Jonathan Clubb saw one in the parking lot Monday evening," said Wickes.

"That doesn't prove anything," said Surewood. "Ask anyone who works here: I live just two hills over in Beachwood Canyon. Between home and here there's a hiking trail, which is a much shorter distance than coming to work on paved roads. By car, I have to go all the way down to the bottom of the canyon and then backtrack up here through Cahuenga Pass."

"So?" asked Wickes.

"Don't you see?" smiled Surewood. "Sometimes I walk to work; and sometimes I drive when it looks like it might rain—like it has lately. Sometimes after a particularly good performance, like those I've had the past several nights, I walk home and leave the car here. In other words, my car sitting here or at home doesn't prove I'm at either place."

"No doubt," said Father. "But the knot I mentioned a moment ago is drawing tighter. Don't you feel it, Mr. Forst?"

"No," said the magician.

"Would you gentlemen like to order?" impatiently sniffed the would-be magician stuck as a waiter. "Our special tonight is the Cajun sword-fish kabob with jambalaya. We also feature—"

"Waiter," interrupted Father, "much as I hate to say this, could we have a few more minutes to decide?"

"Sure, why not?" said the touchy fellow, snapping his order pad shut and strutting away in frustration, as if we were holding up his life.

"Do continue," said Surewood Forst, cool as a zucchini—which you gotta'dmit, never gets quite as cool as a cucumber no matter how long you leave it in the refrigerator.

"It is true," said Father, "that all the evidence I've presented thus far is circumstantial: the dental bridge you own with a three-quarter inch distance between the tips of the extended incisors; your use of a 'natural' dentifrice with a list of ingredients that happens to match the residue found on most of the female victims; your blood type—a factor which will doubtless be enhanced when the DNA tests are completed; your affinity for the vampire role during your acting days; your practical know-how with respect to special effects and audience manipulation; your personal familiarity with at least two of the victims; your night-time job, which puts you into an optimal position for meeting lots of gullible young women, while also leaving you free to go to the dispatch office of a cab company in broad daylight; your ownership of a Karmen Ghia; your ability to impersonate the voice inflection and tone of anyone you meet, and you did meet Pierre Bontemps, Jonathan Clubb, and Martin Feeney last Friday night and had ample opportunity to observe their oral mannerisms—"

"Excuse me for interrupting your presentation," said Surewood, "but as I already said, as impressive as this list of non-evidence may be, you've got nothing that connects me directly or conclusively to any of the crimes."

"Oh, but I do," said Father.

"And what's that?" asked Monsignor Aspic, eyes perched narrowly atop his pudgy cheeks.

"You," said Father, looking Conrad J. right into those perky little eyes. "You've been the conduit, albeit an unwitting channel, through which your brother has been obtaining information useful to his ventures."

"You're mad," said Aspic.

"Angry, yes," said Father, "but hardly mad. Angry, not just that you told Surewood here that I had been ordered by the cardinal to assist the police in their search for a serial killer—your brother being the murderer—but that you described to him the details of your personal en-

counters with me. That's how he came to know not only of my involvement in the case, but the name of my parish."

I love it when Father Baptist really gets going. Meanwhile, his
words triggered a memory regarding the skin-tingling performance Father and I witnessed on the Farquar Terrace:

> *"I give you this warning. Do not interfere. Return to your ref-
> uge at St. Philomena's, cease your meddling, and the doom I have
> pronounced will not find you. If you persist, you will surely die."*

"You were telling him all along," continued Father to Aspic. "Your
position as Cardinal Fulbright's consultant gave you access to all sorts
of useful information, and through you it got to him."

"I don't see—" sputtered Aspic. "And I didn't—"

"Monsignor," said Father calmly, "you paid a visit to St.
Philomena's last Sunday. Is that correct?"

"Yes," said Aspic.

"We—you, me, and several of my parishioners—were just concluding
our discussion regarding the efficacy of the Last Gospel. In your presence, Jonathan Clubb asked Stella Billowack if she would like to go on
a date to this establishment, and you also heard that it was Pierre Bontemps who was in a position to procure guest passes from his editor.
Think, Monsignor: did you or did you not tell your brother about the
quaint goings-on at my curious little parish? About the outmoded
thought patterns of Traditionalists? About the infighting among my
parishioners? No doubt it all made for good after-dinner conversation.
You had no idea, Monsignor, that you were supplying your brother
with information that he could put to use against me and my associates.
The laughs you both must have had, discussing the budding interest
between Jonathan and Stella, the manly camaraderie among my young
friends, the Tumblars, and my peculiar reliance on so useless a gardener
as Martin Feeney."

"Woody," said Conrad J. to his brother Sherwood W., eyes wide.

My eyes had gone wide, too: Useless? Me? I mean, well, yes I am;
but hey! Nonetheless, my ol' gray matter kicked in, replaying the conversation to which Father had just alluded:

> *"Pass the collection plate,"* Pierre had said as Stella finished her
> dissertation on Humpty Dumpty. *"It's the one sacramental you
> modernists still believe in."*
>
> The monsignor had responded by choking on his dazzle. That
> was a pleasant memory.
>
> *"A fine girl,"* I said to Jonathan, meaning Stella of course.
> *"Don't you dare let her slip away."*

A few seconds later, I nudged him in the ribs. *"Well—?"*

"Well what?" Jonathan pretending stupidity, or was it love shining through?

"Well, go on." The voice of reason—mine. *"It's why you stuck around. Ask her."*

"Ask me what?" blinked Stella, pretending innocence.

"Well," ahemed Jonathan, the moment of truth having arrived.

How well I understood his hesitation, and cringed for him at the time, even though the outcome was practically a sure thing—even though there is no such thing when it comes to women, which was why I cringed on his behalf.

"Uh, Stella," he said, *"it's just that I asked Pierre here, if he could arrange for a guest invitation to the 'House of Illusions.' I was wondering if you'd care to, uh, um, that is, if you'd consider going with me."*

"When?" she asked, rolling her beautiful eyes while prolonging the moment by cluttering the issue with nonessential chronological details.

"Tomorrow night," hemmed Jonathan. *"I think."*

"Of course," she answered, after the appropriate feminine pause to first boost then relieve her suitor's anxiety. *"I'd be delighted."*

"You would?" he gasped, grateful for the relief after being so suitably boosted.

"She would," I assured him, not realizing I had just taken part in what Father would call "quaint goings-on" three days hence.

"Hold on," said Surewood. "There's a rational explanation for all of this."

"Yes," said Father, "and I've just given it. All the circumstantial evidence solidifies when we realize that your brother, Monsignor Aspic, was the only person who could have told you about Jonathan's desire to bring Stella here with Pierre's assistance. By attacking them, along with my friend Martin Feeney—"

The useless gardener, I brooded, on whom he so peculiarly relies.

"—you were attacking me," concluded Father. "What I don't understand, Mr. Forst, is why you recently changed your MO. I can understand, though thoroughly deplore, why you killed the little girl."

"Patricia Marie Nealy," said Wickes, eyes clouding for a second.

"She witnessed you spiriting away Elizabeth Unger in your car," said Father. "But why leave her body in the basement that way, the melodramatic message in blood, and also the new set of fangs?"

"Now I really don't know what you're talking about," said Surewood, neck muscles twitching. "Writing in blood? Nonsense. And I only have one set of fangs. I've even got them on me here somewhere. As for the little girl, I didn't—"

He stopped.

"Yes," pounced Sergeant Wickes, "tell us about the little girl."

"No," gasped Surewood, wheels spinning in his Forsty wooden skull. Suddenly his eyes went wide. "I didn't—"

"What about Babbette Starr?" drilled Lieutenant Taper.

"Babbette?" said Surewood, eyes darting around the table. He seemed terrified. "No. I swear I didn't kill her."

"And surely you haven't forgotten Nannette Cushions?" said Taper.

"Nannette, well ..." Surewood's face went through a series of confused contortions: fear, defiance, innocence, confusion, terror, wretchedness; fear, defiance, and so on. It got dull after the third cycle.

"Bad enough," said Taper, "that you killed all those women, but that crippled little girl—"

"That's one you can't pin on me," screamed Surewood, leaping from his chair. "I had nothing to do with that. Babbette neither. That was ow—oof!"

He'd just collided with Reginold the Reiterator. Now Reggie was really quite big, and he was certainly condescending, but, alas, he wasn't very quick. Basically all he did was provide Surewood Forst a target from which to ricochet that was softer than a brick wall. The Reiterator toppled one way, and Woody catapulted the other. Woody was out of the room before we could blink, running down the hallway.

"Have we had enough time yet?" warbled the waiter, huffing up to our table at that precise moment, pen poised over order pad, eyes riveted on his pen's point. "Do I need to repeat the specials? There's the Cajun swordfish ka-boooOOOOOOB—!"

That's the sound a wanna-be magician makes when he's knocked so hard by two policeman charging by that his elbows meet behind his back.

Before the waiter could regain his composure, Father Baptist, Monsignor Aspic, and I all scrambled by. Well, they scrambled. I lurched and hobbled as usual. That left me far enough behind to hear the waiter's final words on the subject:

"That does it! I quit!"

76

"WHICH WAY?" SCREAMED WICKES at the parking valet.

The poor fellow was not used to such treatment, so he wilted. One of his valet buddies, however, pointed up the drive toward the parking lot around the bend.

Off went Taper and Wickes in that direction.

"Which way?" yelled Monsignor Aspic.

This wilted the second parking valet, so a third had to drum up the courage to point up the drive. The Monsignor bellowed at the third fellow for good measure, and ran in that direction.

I didn't get there till after the fact, so I'm relying on Father Baptist's description. After waving a hasty blessing over the third valet as he shriveled into a lump of quivering uselessness, Father had followed Monsignor Aspic up the drive and was out of sight by the time I got to the front door, gasping and groaning, only to find three desiccated parking valets huddled against the space-egg payphone. I noticed it had been repaired since Monday.

Just then a pair of headlights came down the drive from the direction of the parking lot. It turned out to be Monsignor Aspic's silver Mercedes, and I was surprised to see Father Baptist in the passenger seat. The car screeched to a halt and Father barked out the window:

"Martin, get the Jeep. Drive down to Highland. Turn left on Franklin, left on Beachwood, and left again on Spiral Crest Road, and right on Spiral Crest Lane. Take it to the end—that's where Woody's probably headed. We'll meet you there."

"I don't get it," I said stupidly.

"He lives just over two hills, remember?" barked Father. "Since his car isn't in the lot, and he didn't come down the drive, that's probably where he went. Taper and Wickes are attempting to follow the hiking trail on foot. We're going to try to beat him there. If his car is at his home, and he gets to it, it'll be very hard to catch him."

"Then get going," I said. "I'll be along shortly—"

The Monsignor gunned the motor and zoomed off.

So, afterthought that I am in the scheme of things, and my arthritis vying for the place of forethought, I persuaded a fourth valet who was as yet unshriveled to fetch the Jeep for three bucks.

"Ah, but what is this?" asked a voice from the doorway as the Jeep arrived and the fourth valet hopped out.

I turned to see Lucius T. Portifoy looking up at me through that aquamarine monocle, his obnoxious mustache twitching.

"A vampire hunt," I said.

"You joke, no?"

"No joke."

"Hunting a vampire you are?"

"Not at the moment, but I'm working up to it."

Mr. Portifoy rubbed his gloved hands together. "I do not like you, Mr. Feeney—not one bit, you understand. So let me give you a parting word of advice:

> Bevare, bevare, bevare of the big green dragon
> that sits on your doorstep!

> He eats little boys, puppy-dog tails
> and big—fat—snails!
> Bevare, take care ... bevare.!
> Pull the string!! Pull the string!!

"Riveting," I commented as I lurched toward the Jeep. "Your Bela Lugosi is impeccable. What's it from, one of his old flicks?"

"Oui and no," said Portifoy. "It was my impression of Martin Landau playing Bela Lugosi in a movie about Ed Wood who produced a movie called *Glen or Glenda?* You've seen it, no?"

"I've seen it, no," I agreed as I pulled the door shut. I waved, "Ciao."

The directions were easy: down, left, left, left, right and to the end. Or was it down, left, left, left, right, left, and then to the end? Well, in any case, Spiral Crest Lane was easy to remember.

77

SPIRAL CREST TERRACE said the road sign. The other one at forty-five degree angles to it said SPIRAL CREST COURT. Great. I didn't know where I was. And in the Hollywood Hills there are legends of travelers getting lost for days. "Saint Anthony," I cried, "HAAAAALP!"

> GARDENING TIPS: If this story ever gets turned
> into a screenplay, they could write in a harrowing
> cars-going-every-which-way chase scene right here.
> The problem for me telling the true story, how-
> ever, is that it was really a matter of me getting
> lost, panicking, and frantically zooming around
> trying to find Monsignor Aspic's Mercedes. The
> effect is not the same.
>
> —M.F.
>
> N.B. Who would they get to play Father Baptist???

Anyway, growling Hail Marys to the great Saint of Padua, I went up this winding road and down that twisting avenue. When I said "up" and "down" I didn't mean "back" and "forth" like on a flat map—I meant essentially "straight up" and virtually "straight down." That's how they built roads in the hills beneath the famous HOLLYWOOD sign.

It was when I came shooting over the crest of a particularly steep hill that the tires left the road, and everything went into slow motion. The

Jeep made a graceful arc in midair while the road angled sharply to the right as it fell away under it. As the nose of the car tilted forward on reentry, I saw that I was going to touch down on a poorly tended front lawn. Worse, a short distance beyond was a blue-gray '69 Karmen Ghia with a yellow hood sitting nose-out in the driveway. I caught a glimpse of a guy more harried than myself, and far too massive for that little vehicle, trying to stuff not only himself but his billowing black cape with red satin lining into the front seat.

It might have worked if he weren't in such a hurry—and if he hadn't parked directly in my path of destruction.

But anyway, as the front tires of the Jeep hit the lawn, spraying sod in a stunning fanlike pattern and snapping several sprinkler heads, I jerked the steering wheel to the left. It seemed like a good idea at the time since it was the opposite direction of all the forces of motion my brain had taken into account thus far.

So much for my brain.

More so for forces which it hadn't taken into account.

The car spun around one hundred and eighty degrees, driving the heinie end of my Jeep into the nosy end of his Karmen Ghia. Come to think of it, my brain did all right even if it didn't know what it was doing, because the only thing that got creamed on the Jeep was the spare tire mounted on the tailgate. The Ghia on the other hand, when I gathered my wits and looked in the rearview mirror, had taken on the characteristics of an accordion.

It was hard to see because a pair of headlights came to a squealing halt inches from mine. Apparently in the intensity of my search, I hadn't noticed the Valiant following close behind me.

Undaunted, Surewood Forst burst, or perhaps squirted, from the crushed Karmen Ghia and made a mad dash down the street. Encumbered as I was by my friend, arthritis, I didn't bother to scurry after him. It was all I could do to undo my seat belt and slowly emerge from the Jeep without instigating a spasm somewhere in my overwrought body. I was vaguely aware of two men clamoring out of the Valiant, but at this point so many things started happening I was on the verge of losing track. Observe:

Unfortunately for Mr. Forst, there was a crew doing some night work forty yards down the road. Monsignor Aspic had complained the other day about the streets being torn up. I learned later that a misdirected steam shovel had punctured an exposed sewer pipe that afternoon. These workers wouldn't have been out there this late, galling the neighbors' nerves with the metallic lullabies of their heavy machinery, if that rupture hadn't posed a potential health hazard.

Little did they know.

There was this big, broad guy sitting in the driver's seat of one of those huge steamrollers—though I think it was actually diesel-powered. Anyway, it was one of those machines that flattens freshly-laid asphalt.

A bit later on in the evening, I managed to get a gander at the name-tag sewn onto this driver fellow's denim shirt: TOG. Go figure.

Tog was big and broad, as I said, and he had a pair of those li'l black doodad headphones crammed into his large, splayed ears. I could hear the beat from where I was standing, and over the growl of the diesel-powered steamroller's engine. He was backing the machine downhill, and he wasn't paying all that much attention to where he was going, since if he hit anything it was not he that was going to get annihilated.

That's why he didn't think once, let alone twice, when the corner of his vehicle—those things don't have bumpers—knocked over an un-capped barrel of slick black oil. What it was doing there is anyone's guess, but the barrel rolled and the fluid flew, and in seconds there was quite a spill.

Just then headlights rounded the distant curve, and a car that quickly resolved into a silver Mercedes came humming up the street. Monsignor Aspic and Father Baptist were making their appearance. I guess they'd gotten their Spiral Crests mixed up, too.

Okay, we've got Surewood on foot, Tog on rollers, oil on street, clergy in car, Valiant-dwellers on the prowl. What else? Oh yes, Taper and Wickes suddenly emerged from some bushes beside the next house over. Did I say "emerged"? "Exploded" would better describe their entrance. They were streaked with grime, slimed with sap, scratched with twigs, and brimming with anger.

With all these forces converging, Surewood didn't stand a chance. Captive audiences in the state prison system might have reveled in his "magic in wood" shows on Sunday afternoons in the gymnasium for years and years and years to come, but such was not to be.

He jumped to miss the oncoming Mercedes, twisted to dodge the charging police, threw up his hands as a flashbulb popped off to the right; and, thus startled, tripped and stumbled toward the rolling machine. Somewhere in the midst of all those evasive maneuvers, the soles of his shoes came into contact with that spilled oil. From that moment on, it was inevitable. Surewood found himself skidding over the asphalt on all fours, heading right into the path of the backing roller. He managed to shove off from the cylindrical deathtrap, slippery as his hands were, but as he spun away his cape got caught. Tog didn't hear the screams, absorbed as he was by the soothing yet challenging vocals of a band called Fingernail and the Chalkboards.

By the time Tog realized something was amiss, what was left of Surewood Forst was in front of him, not behind him; and the mess was long, broadly elliptical, spread pretty thin, and well—as is the case of anything run over by a diesel-powered steamroller—flat.

"Well," said Taper a few minutes later, digging a set of vampire fangs out of the asphalt with a screwdriver from the police car's utility pack, "this cinches it."

Another flashbulb exploded.

"Got that?" asked Jacco Babs of the *Times*.

"Yup," smiled Ziggie Svelte, his photographer.

"Bingo," said Mr. Babs.

"You two are under arrest," said Sergeant Wickes.

78

"MILLIE," SAID FATHER AS WE CAME IN the kitchen door. She was seated in the little dining nook, a copy of *Raised from the Dead* by Fr. Albert J. Hebert, SM, open on the table and a glass of red wine near her hand. "What are you doing up?"

"Who could sleep?" she grumbled, "with all that noise?"

"What noise?" asked Father.

"Pounding," she said, taking a quivering sip from her glass. "It shook me awake."

Father and I exchanged glances, remembering that sound we'd heard in the church the night before.

"When did you hear it?" I asked.

"About an hour ago."

"Anything since?" asked Father.

"Nope. Maybe it's that damned subway they're building," said Millie. "The one they're having so much trouble with at everyone's expense: gas leaks, sinking streets, cave-ins—"

"I don't think so," said Father. "That's miles away."

"Well whatever it is," she said, shakily downing her glass and swallowing painfully, "it's not miles away. It knocked my Crucifix clean off its hook. Lucky thing I'd finished the dishes. When I came out here to see what'd happened, I found it in the sink."

I looked over at the bishop's gift, back in its proper place above Millie's work station.

"Whatever it is," said Father, "it seems to have stopped. I suggest we all turn in."

"You do that," belched Millie, hands trembling as she clutched the book. "I want to finish this chapter." Something more than a "Leviticus fifteen nineteen" was afflicting our dear housekeeper. This was fear.

I didn't get much sleep that night. My dreams were crowded with visions of gleaming white fangs stuck in black, oily, blood-drenched asphalt.

Thursday, October Twenty-sixth

Feast Day of Saint Evaristus,
Sixth Pope of the Catholic Church,
Martyr (121 AD)

79

"RIGHT OUT OF THE ASPHALT?" mused Bulldog Billowack as he wallowed in his office the next morning, holding up the plastic bag containing Surewood Forst's pointed fangs. "It wasn't crushed with the rest of the, uh, body?"

"It must've popped out of his pocket," said Lieutenant Taper, "and just got pressed into the road."

"Well, I guess that cinches it," said Billowack, patting himself on the stomach.

"Do you have any more questions for Tog?" asked Sergeant Wickes from the doorway.

"Naw," said Billowack. "Take him over to Municipal. Those vultures can't wait to get their claws into him."

"Excuse me," said Father Baptist as the sergeant signaled for someone in the next room to untie Tog's leash.

"Anything more on this Surewood Forst's dressing room at the magic club?" asked Billowack.

"Not so far," said Taper.

"I beg your pardon," said Father Baptist.

"What about at his home?" asked Billowack.

"Now that gets interesting," said Sergeant Wickes. "His bedroom was clean, as was the rest of his house. But the basement was loaded with the same kind of books his victims were reading."

"Monty," said Father Baptist.

"You," said the chief out of the side of his flapping mouth, "I'm not talkin' to. Go on, Lieutenant."

"And there was the coffin," said Taper, glancing nervously at Father. "Nice one, too. Hand-carved olive wood, copper-lined—better than what I buried my mother in. Depressions in the satin lining, along with soil and grass stains at the foot end suggest that he spent time in it."

"In the coffin," said Billowack. "Well, I'll be."

"We found blood smudges," said Wickes, "at the head end."

"Blood type?" asked the chief.

"Several," said Wickes. "Mostly O positives, but one has been tagged as AB negative, same as Terisa Kim Lin, victim number five. DNA will take more time—"

"Though the smudges overlapped," interjected Taper, "contaminating each other. That'll render DNA tests unreliable—"

"There's no doubt," said Billowack. "We've got our man. Good work, gentlemen."

"Well, Chief," gulped Wickes, "it was really Father Baptist here who—"

"Which fangs are they?" asked Father Baptist.

"Did I hear a breeze?" asked Billowack, looking around.

"Those in your hand," said Father, pointing to the plastic bag still clutched in the chief's paw.

"Or is it the plumbing?" asked Billowack.

"Chief," said Taper, eyes on Father Baptist.

"So what about the Karmen Ghia?" asked Billowack. "Sergeant, anything there?"

"Yes," said Wickes, consulting his trusty notebook.

"Come, Martin," said Father.

"Do I hear a whoopee cushion?" I blurted over my shoulder as I followed Father out of Billowack's office.

80

"WELL, WELL, WELL," SAID JACCO BABS, seated at a bare table in a gray detention room. "If it ain't the cop-turned-priest-turned-cop."

"You have a rare talent, Mr. Babs," said Father, taking the seat opposite the reporter, "for starting a conversation on the wrong foot."

"It goes with the trade, Padre. How'd you get permission to see li'l ol' me?"

"I was, as you say, a cop. I still have access to a few strings."

"Shoulda known. So whadduya want?"

"I'd like to know what you were doing up in the Hollywood Hills last night."

"And what will you give me for that info?"

"I have little to give, Mr. Babs."

"Don't hand me that. You're on a vampire hunt. I want an exclusive."

"That I can't promise you."

"Then go to Hell."

"Certainly possible," said Father. "St. John Chrysostom said that the road to Hell is paved with the skulls of priests."

"A good line," said Jacco. "Can I use it?"

"As long as you give St. John the credit—be sure you spell his name right. I'll see that you get a good pre-Atwater edition of *Butler's Lives of the Saints* to read in prison."

"Prison? I'm just being held as a material witness again. I'm not going to prison."

"You will if they make the 'involuntary homicide' charge stick."

Jacco's jaw dropped. "'Involuntary homicide'? Who said anything about that?"

"One of the strings I pulled to get in here to see you," said Father. "Mr. Forst's untimely demise, according to some witnesses, was caused in part by his being startled, you see, by a flashbulb."

"That was Ziggie, not me."

"Ziggie works for you."

"Ziggie works for the *Times,* just like I do."

"Oh, so your editors will have some explaining to do as well."

"Phooey. We was just reporters doin' our job."

"Which was?"

"Ah—we're back to that again."

"Inevitably."

"Okay, okay." Jacco wiped his mouth with a nervous, rolling motion of his agitated fingers. "Ziggie and I were arrested on Sunday. The cops held us for the standard seventy-two hours as material witnesses for the Nealy case—the little girl. You remember."

"I remember."

"When they released us—but not Ziggie's film, mind you, they kept that as 'evidence'—we went back to the *Times* to catch Hell from the managing editor. Then I put in some time digging around in the County Records computer, and learned that there are two, count 'em, two city councilmen on the board of directors of that magic club."

"'House of Illusions'?" asked Father, eyebrows up.

"The same," smiled Mr. Babs. "But even more interesting: your beloved mentor and indulgence-peddler, Cardinal Fulbright, is a major investor in the biz."

"I'd be shocked if he sold indulgences," said Father, eyebrows back in place, "since he has publicly denied any belief in Purgatory, but this other tidbit is intriguing."

The gardener, too, found this to be an interesting memory morsel:

"Then why," Father had asked at the chancery, *"does the Cardinal Archbishop wish to involve himself—and by extension*

*me—in a criminal investigation which is entirely a police mat-
ter?"*

"There are two reasons," His Elegance had responded.   *"First,
Father Baptist, you have established a reputation for yourself as
having, shall we say, 'an intimate understanding' of the occult. It
is not beyond the bounds of propriety for the Church to assist the
civil authorities in such matters."*

"And the second?" asked Father.

The cardinal closed his eyes.   *"That is something I don't wish to
discuss at this time, nor under these circumstances."*

"He bought in only two months ago," said Jacco. "Anyway, it intrigued me, too. So I grabbed Ziggie and a company car—"

"The Valiant," said the gardener.

"—right, and headed straight for your parish church. Just as we got
there, the two of you left in the Jeep."

"Funny you should come up the back alley," said Father. "That's the
only way you could see us leave."

"It's the only way I know," said Jacco. "And we followed you
straight to none other than the 'House of Illusions.' We waited at the
bottom of the driveway for a while, considering how we might manage
to get in—the place is notorious for refusing entry to reporters, you
know—and then, wonder of wonders, Padre Jack and the cardinal's own
lackey, Aspic, come tearin' down the drive in a Mercedes. Quite a step
up for you, Padre, but you should be careful who you're seen with.
Then, a minute later, out flies your watchdog, Feeney here. We followed him, and the rest is history."

"It'll sound convincing," said Father, "at your preliminary hearing."

"What preliminary hearing?"

"'Involuntary homicide,' remember?"

"Oh bosh. That won't stick."

"No," said Father, lowering his voice. "But you would do well to
consider that there are influential men in this town who do not want
this story to become public information. It has concerned me that no
leaks have hit the newspapers, and your detention only bears this out."

"Don't strong-arm me, Padre."

"I don't have to. Others are already so occupied."

"You're not going to help me?"

Father got up from his chair. "It's because of you, Mr. Babs, that
I'm now known as 'the cop-turned-priest-turned-cop.' I've no wish for
'turned-vampire-hunter' to be added to that silly moniker. That was
going to be your next story, wasn't it?"

"Well," shrugged Jacco, "words to that effect."

"I should think that would answer your question," said Father, turning to go.

"Hey, don't leave like this."

"Like what?"

"Like I was your enemy or something. I've given you great coverage."

"Which I neither appreciate nor desire," said Father. "But that is another matter. I suggest you let this story rest. Heaven knows there are plenty of other sensational travesties going on in this city that are worthy of your attention. Let this one go."

"Never."

"Then you will rot in jail," said Father.

"You can't do this to me."

"I'm not doing anything to you. Like I said—"

"Others are so occupied," grumbled Jacco Babs.

"Indeed," said Father, heading for the door. "Others are. Come, Martin. I need to wash my hands."

81

"JONATHAN, YOU LOOK TERRIBLE."

"Oh," said the young Knight as Father and I entered Stella's room at the hospital.

After several hours in the Critical Care Unit, and several more in Intensive Care for good measure, she had finally been moved to a private room on the same floor. When we arrived she was fast asleep.

"When's the last time you bathed, or shaved that handsome face of yours?" asked Father.

"The other night."

"Monday," offered the gardener helpfully. "Today is Thursday."

"And what about sleep?" asked Father, scowling paternally.

"I got some last night," said Jonathan.

"Where?"

"Here."

"In this chair? Doesn't look very comfortable."

"It wasn't."

"How long?" asked Father.

"Did I sleep?"

"Yes."

"Hmm." Jonathan rubbed his neck thoughtfully. "Let's see. I caught the forecast on the eleven o'clock news—the weatherman said it might actually rain tonight."

"That would be a relief," I said, looking out the window at the churning cloud cover, unimpressed with the newscaster's prediction.

"Then, let me see," said Jonathan. "I must've drifted off. The next thing I remember, Jeannette—she's one of the nurses—was in here, fussing with Stella's bandages."

"Fussing?" asked Father.

"Yeah," frowned Jonathan. "She scolded me for letting Stella tear them off in her sleep."

"Did she?" said Father, bending close to Stella's serene but ashen face.

"Who?" asked Jonathan. "Stella? I guess so. The bandages were there on the floor."

"By the bed?"

"Uh-huh."

"Were they bloody?"

"The bandages?" Jonathan scratched his head. "No, not really. A few dried specks."

"And the wounds on her neck," asked Father, "were they hemorrhaging again?"

"You mean bleeding? Yes, a bit."

"And the nurse—Jeannette—she put this new dressing on Stella's neck?"

"Yup."

"What time was that?"

"A *Perry Mason* episode was just starting," said Jonathan. "It must've been around two AM. The nurse also switched the IV bottles—they're dripping blood into her, you know, because she's lost so much ..." Jonathan stopped because he became aware that Father wasn't listening.

Father had snatched up Stella's left hand, then her right, and was carefully examining her fingers.

"Something?" asked the gardener.

"Dried blood," said Father, "on her right index finger."

With careful propriety, he shifted the blankets and adjusted the gown around her abdomen. "Martin, what do you make of this?"

I hobbled over to the bed.

"What, Father?"

"That smudge just above her navel."

"She must've done that," I said, "when she pulled her bandages off and got blood on her finger." I realized how unlikely that was as I said it, all those covers in the way.

Father looked doubtful, too. "Or?"

I looked at the smudge again.

"Or," I shivered, "the countdown continues."

82

"IT'S AS I TRIED TO EXPLAIN yesterday on the phone," Warden Gladys Tracy was saying as she escorted me through the sliding barred gates that careened electrically in their gleaming tracks and clanged shut behind us. "With the WOPOPs, I try to encourage their creativity."

"WOPOPs?" I asked, jumping at the sound of that metallic boom. It always gave me the creeps.

"'Without possibility of paroles,'" she explained, guiding me down the industrial gray corridor. "After all, they're going to be here a long time, long after I retire, and they may as well utilize their minds."

"I see."

"So when Ms. Farnsworth asked—"

"Miss," I corrected her. "Cheryl prefers 'Miss.'"

"—for some acrylics and brushes, I naturally assumed she was going to try her hand at painting."

"Of course."

"On canvas, I mean, not the walls of her cell. That I can't permit, since inmates are moved around from time to time, and we don't want to have to repaint the walls each time there's a transfer."

"Of course not. When did she ask for the paints?"

"Last week. The day after you visited her, I think."

"Really."

We had come to a steep metal stairway. It was tough going, for me at least. I was grateful that the warden permitted me to bring my cane into the maximum security building.

"Almost there," she said. "I hope you can reason with her."

"I'll do my best." I didn't sound too sure.

"You realize, of course, that it is highly unusual for me to bring a visitor to a prisoner's cell."

"Of course."

"I take it you've never been this far inside our penitentiary."

"The farthest I ever got was the visiting room."

"So this is a new experience for you."

"Yes."

"Here we are." She stopped before a large metal door with a small square opening for looking inside. "Cheryl?" she said in a voice that sounded like a next-door neighbor coming to borrow a cup of sugar. "You've got company."

"Company?" asked the voice from within. It sounded frightened. "I'd rather not."

"But it's your friend, Mr. Feeney."

"Martin?" said the voice, suddenly hopeful. "Oh yes, do please let him in."

"You're sure you don't want a guard in there with you?" asked the warden. "There's no obligation on your part—"

"I'll be okay," I assured her.

I watched as she unlatched the lock and pulled the door open.

"I'll be right out here," said the warden, "if you need me."

"Thank-you," I said, and entered. "Cheryl."

"Martin."

I stood there, taking it all in.

"You've been busy," I said at last.

"Yes," she said, seated on the bunk. "What do you think of it?"

I looked around. "I'm a bit surprised. It's not your style."

"A woman can change."

"True—but Crosses? I thought witches don't believe in Christ."

"I'm a black witch, remember. I utilize whatever works."

"And these work?"

"So far."

"How did you get to the ceiling?"

"I put my bed on its end and climbed up the springs like a ladder."

"Isn't the bed screwed to the floor?"

"I used the handle of a spoon for a screwdriver."

"Oh." I scanned the walls. "You missed a spot."

She jumped up. "Where?"

"There by the sink."

"Oh gosh, this awful lighting. I'll have to fix that." She crouched by the bed and yanked out from under it a small cardboard box full of paint cans. Prying off a lid and snatching a brush, she made quick work of the last vestige of bare plaster. The Cross she painted was bright orange—not exactly a penitential color, but certainly eye-catching. "Thanks," she exhaled deeply. "I don't know how I missed it."

"Better now?"

She stood there, shaking. The brush fell from her trembling fingers. "Oh Martin."

I stepped closer and suddenly her arms were around me.

GARDENING TIPS: It had been a long time since, and
even before that, and not with someone who was so,
or with whom I had been so ... Oh, never mind.
                                              --M.F.

"Cheryl," I stammered finally. "What's wrong?"

"Remember last week?" she said, trembling. "You asked me to listen, and I didn't hear anything."

"Yes."

"But after you left, I kept listening just in case. You seemed so concerned."

I unbuckled her arms and held her in front of me. "And?"

"And then it began," she said, eyes watering. "That very night. The whispers."

"Whispers? What did they say?"

"'You're not alone.'"

"'You're not alone'? Just that?"

"Over and over," she said, bursting into flowing tears. "Over and over and over. 'You're not alone, Cheryl.' And once, Friday night I think, it said, 'I am come.'"

The Nealy girl, I thought, the writing on her abdomen. I looked carefully at Cheryl. "And you took no comfort in this?"

She detached herself from me. "Not from that voice. It was cold, and fierce, and ..."

"Evil?"

She dropped to the edge of the bed. "Evil."

"And so you decided to protect yourself with Crosses."

"Yes." It hurt her to admit it. "Yes."

I sat down beside her. "What can I do to help?"

Her head jerked up. "You can warn Father Baptist."

"Father Baptist?"

"He's in danger." She gripped my arm. "So are you. Are you wearing that thing?"

"What thing?"

"That thing around your neck."

I blinked. "My scapular?"

"Yes."

I touched the bulge under my shirt. "How do you know about that?"

"You weren't wearing it Monday night."

The memory caused me to shudder. "That's right. How—?"

"She saved you that time. But she's gone now. She can't protect you next time."

"Who?"

"The flapper."

I swallowed something thick and dry. "I ... I don't understand."

"Yes you do." Cheryl started humming a tune, a familiar Hungarian ditty, the same one my dear mother used to plunk on the old family upright in the living room. "Sound familiar?"

"How did you—?" I felt a cold breeze on my tongue. My mouth was open. I tugged the muscles that raised my lower jaw. "But the vampire's dead."

"What?"

"He's dead." The sight of that smudge on Stella Billowack's stomach whirled through my mind but I brushed it aside. "I saw him die."

"When?"

"Last night."

"When last night?"

"Around eight-thirty, maybe nine."

She dropped her head and rolled her chin around on her collarbone. "No," she groaned.

"No what?"

"No, he's not dead. At midnight he went to her room."

I supressed a shiver. "Whose room?"

"In the hospital."

"What hospital?"

"Martin," she said sadly. "Don't try to fool me. Does the number 'seven' mean anything to you?"

I blinked. Then I blinked again. "Suppose it does?"

"Tell Father Baptist he's in danger. Him, you, the guys in tuxedoes ... and a ... is there a bishop? No, not him. A priest who rolls his r's—"

"This voice told you all that? What else?"

"Fools."

"Who? Us?"

"No, them. He relies on them."

"On fools?"

"But he isn't one himself—no way."

"Uh-huh."

"He plays the fool who's playing the fool, while playing the fool."

"Whaddah whaddah what?"

"Fools, fools, fools." Cheryl began rubbing her arms nervously. "And there's the spiders."

"Spiders?"

"They catch flies." Her rubbing became more vigorous. "Spiders and flies, spiders and flies ..."

I grimaced, thinking of the entries in Dr. Seward's diary regarding the character, Renfield, in Bram Stoker's *Dracula:*

> *18 June.*—He has turned his mind now to spiders ... He keeps feeding them with his flies, and the number of the latter is becom-

ing sensibly diminished, although he has used half his food in attracting more flies from outside his room.

1 July.—His spiders are now becoming as great a nuisance as his flies, and to-day I told him that he must get rid of them.

I looked on sadly as Cheryl's agitation became more and more frantic. She wasn't just rubbing her arms anymore, she was scratching them—no, clawing at them.

"Spiders and flies," she kept saying, "spiders and flies ..." Then she looked me in the eye. "What's an 'earwig'? Is that a bug, too?"

"Cheryl," I said as soothingly as I could, placing my hands on her shoulders. "What can I do to help?"

Suddenly the paroxysms ceased.

"Cheryl," I said again.

"Martin," she whispered, burying her face in her hands. "You'd better leave now."

"You want me to go?"

"No, but you have work to do."

"I do?"

"Martin," she said, pulling her hands away from her tear-streaked face and placing them against my chest. "You can't imagine how much he hates the light. Whatever you do, don't take off that scapular."

83

"SHE SAID ALL THAT?" said Father as I steered the Jeep out of the prison parking lot. All the while I had been in Cheryl Farnsworth's cell he had been in the guest cafeteria catching up on the progress and regress of women he had sent to prison in his former life as Jack Lombard, Chief of Homicide, with Father Fuller, the prison chaplain.

"She did," I said. "Word for word. Even the part about fools."

"Would you mind repeating it? One more time."

"Sure: '"He plays the fool who's playing the fool, while playing the fool.' From that she segued into spiders and flies."

"Hmm."

"At least she's not up to birds and cats, like Renfield."

"Do you think she was speaking of them as metaphors or specifics?" asked Father.

"Spiders and flies? As opposed to fools? I don't know."

"And she said, 'No, he's not dead.' You're sure of that."

"Right. She said he went to Stella's room at the hospital after that."

"Think, Martin: did she say 'Stella's room' or 'the room'?"

"'At midnight he went to her room,'" I quoted.

"I see."

"You don't seem surprised."

"I'm not. Your, uh, friend Cheryl Farnsworth went to considerable lengths to gain 'power' a few months ago—"

"Don't remind me," I grimaced.

"—and now she has it."

"Yes," I said, "she certainly does. Can you make sense of what she said, Father?"

"Some of it, yes, I think so."

"And?"

"The whole business last night, Surewood Forst I mean, was too easy."

"Easy?"

"And his demise left too many unanswered questions."

"Such as?"

"Quiet, Martin, I'm thinking."

"Sure," I said, flicking the turn indicator as I changed lanes.

As we neared St. Philomena's, I noticed the marquee on the local run-down movie theater:

HALLOWEEN HORROR NIGHT!
ADMISSION $5—GOOD FOR ALL SHOWS!
THOSE IN COSTUME: FREE!
4 PM DRACULA (LEE)
6 PM DRACULA (LUGOSI)
8 PM MANOS: HANDS OF FATE
10 PM THE DAY OF THE TRIFFIDS
12 PM ROCKY HORROR PICTURE SHOW

"I'd almost forgotten that Halloween is next Tuesday," I mumbled.

"Hmm," hmmed Father back. "All Hallow's Eve."

"All Hallow's Eve," I nodded. "Samhain—which I'll never forget is pronounced 'Saw-win.' Along with Imbolc, Beltane, and a word that begins with 'L' that I've never figured out how to pronounce, it's one of the four 'Greater Sabbats' on the wiccan calendar. It's also the Feast of St. Wolfgang, who missionized my Magyar ancestors—"

"Martin."

"Sorry. I know you're trying to think. It's just that—"

"Martin."

"Sorry. Go ahead and think. Don't mind me."

"Thank-you, Martin."

84

"THEN MAY I PLEASE SPEAK TO JOHN HOLTSCLAW?" I heard Father saying into the telephone as I came lumbering into the study with a cup of coffee.

"Yikes," I said as some of the brew sploshed onto my hand. "Still thinking?"

"Doing," said Father to me, then into the phone: "John? Father Baptist. Listen: have you made any progress in that voyage through that sea of red tape toward that microtopographic scanner?"

With cup and saucer wobbling and rattling, I eased myself into my chair.

"He what?" barked Father, leaning forward in his seat. "Okay, we'll have to find a way to work around Chief Billowack. Yes, I'm serious. Yes, I'm aware things are piling up with Solomon gone. Yes, I'm sure you can't wait to leave yourself. But John, I cannot stress how important it is that you do those scans."

Silently, I toasted the hand-carved statues of St. Thomas More and St. Anthony of Padua on the desk, the quote from Tolkien's *Lord of the Rings* leaning between them.

"Right," Father was saying. "You do that. And another thing: is there any way you can make some cross-section slices of the puncture wounds?—to get an idea of the shape of the fangs at different depths in the skin?"

Drat, I'd forgotten to heat the cup under the tap before pouring my coffee. It was already cold.

"Magnetic resonating what?" said Father, leaning back in his chair again. "Oh? Is that really better than actual tissue samples? I *have* been out of touch. Well, whatever works. How soon can you do all this? No, next week is *not* soon enough. Yesterday isn't even soon enough. I told you this is urgent."

Disgusted, I set down my cup and saucer on the edge of the desk.

"Okay, look," continued Father. "What if you just do the procedure on two of the victims? Say, Elizabeth Unger and Patricia Marie Nealy ...? More do-able?"

Struggling back to my feet, I grabbed the caffeine implements and headed out again.

"Yes, John," Father was saying. "I owe you one. Now another thing ..."

Okay, so I didn't contribute much to this scene. Nonetheless, it would eventually prove to be very important.

85

"BLESS ME, FATHER, FOR I HAVE SINNED," I said to the vague shape behind the amber screen. "It's been five days."

"Proceed," said Father, his shadow waving a blessing.

"Well," I stalled, gathering my thoughts, "the sun didn't go down on my anger yesterday, though if it had, I'd be blowing dust off the Stations till Doomsday—"

"Martin," interrupted Father, "this is a Confessional, not a call-in radio show."

"Right," I nodded. "Well, you see, Father, it's this way—"

"Nor is this a platform for airing excuses."

"Of course, Father—"

"Just declare your sins, and only your sins."

"I know the program."

"Then follow it."

"Yes, Father. Well, you see, it's this way ..."

I heard a long, slow sigh from beyond the screen.

A short while later, as I was just finishing dusting the side aisles with my knees, I heard a shuffling noise in the back of the church. Gaining my feet with an appropriate assortment of facial contortions, I lumbered toward the dark recesses of the vestibule. There, under the arch of St. Scholastica, I saw the figure of a tall, shapely woman wrapped in a kind of glittering purple shawl. The fabric rippled in the humid breeze blowing in through the open front door.

"Excuse me," she said. "Is Father Baptist here?"

"Yes, in there," I said, pointing to the confessional. The little yellow light above the penitent's door was not on. "He's alone at the moment."

"Oh," she said, looking at "The Box." She gathered the shawl closer around her olive face. "I don't think so."

"You're a fallen-away Catholic, aren't you?" I said, leaning on my cane.

"What?" she gasped, eyes wide. The shawl slipped away from her face for a moment, revealing something golden and shiny clipped between her nostrils. "No."

"No?" I asked, unable to take my eyes off her nose ring. Not only did it make my own nose itch, it seemed familiar. As common as body-piercing had become, there was something distinctive about her proboscidial fashion statement. Where had I seen her recently? "That's funny. I can usually spot an 'ex' a mile away. It's a knack—one of my few."

"Well, I'm not."

"Okay, okay. So much for knacks. But that's where he is, and you're welcome to him. He won't bite, you know."

"How long will he be, um, in there?"

"Another half hour. Monsignor Havermeyer will be coming to spell him soon."

"I can't wait that long."

"Then why not go in now? You don't have to—"

"Noooooooo," she groaned, and turned to flee.

"Miss," I said. "Can I tell him who came by to not see him?"

She halted. "My name is Marla."

"Marla," I rolled the word over in my mouth. "Don't I know you?"

"How could you," she said, "when I don't know myself?"

"True, but—"

"I must go," she said, heading toward the door. "I cannot stay."

"But—"

She was gone.

"Well," I sighed to the statue of St. Scholastica, "I'm not fond of Confession myself. Actually, it's not the admission of guilt that kills me, nor the humiliation, and certainly not the absolution." I looked down the aisle I had just polished with my kneecaps. "It's the penance."

86

"YOU'RE SURE YOU'LL BE ALL RIGHT," Millie was saying to Father as he ushered her to the cab waiting in front of the rectory steps.

"Of course," Father assured her.

"But with so many men," argued Veronika, "what will you eat?"

"We'll raid the refrigerator," said Father. "Don't worry. Now, you have the holy water? And you're wearing your scapulars? And the garlic?"

"Yes, yes," said Millie, hefting a large, brown paper shopping bag in her left arm. "I bought ten pounds at the market this afternoon, just like you told me. There's at least seven here, and the rest is in the pantry."

"And the first-class relic of St. Philomena I gave you?"

"Of course, Father," she said, indicating a bulge under her shawl where she had sequestered the small golden reliquary. "Of course."

GARDENING TIPS: For those of you who are unfamiliar with Catholic devotions (like, say, most
Catholics), a "first-class relic" is some part, no

matter how small, of a Saint's mortal remains--
generally a chip of bone.

A "second-class relic" is something that the
Saint touched in life, such as a piece of their
clothing.

A "third-class relic" is an object, like a medal
or Crucifix, that has been touched against a
Saint's tomb, or against something that was close
to the Saint in life.

A "reliquary" is a vessel, like a tiny monstrance with a glass window, in which a relic is
placed both for display and safekeeping.

Some modern people consider the traditional reverence of Catholics toward relics to be a symptom
of "morbidity." Well I say, "We're just facing
Reality."

                                        --M.F.

"And you'll put it on the nightstand in plain sight," said Father.

"Yes, Father," she huffed, shoving the shopping bag into the cab.

"And the blessed Rosary I gave you? You'll see that it's on her person, or pinned to her pillow?"

Millie looked angry. "Yes!"

"And Stella's side we will not leave," nodded Veronika, "until one of
you comes to relieve us in the morning. You're sure the nurses won't
mind us being there?"

"I spoke with Dr. Catsbody personally," said Father. "He's a Trad,
though he's not in our parish."

"Doctors I no mind," said Veronika, "it's nurses that are insufferable."

"I'm sure you'll manage," said Father, holding the door for them.

"This Jonathan must be a good boy," said Veronika to Millie as he
closed the door, "to refuse to leave his girlfriend unless we stay with
her."

"That he is," agreed Millie, though she wasn't smiling. In fact, she
was scowling menacingly.

"Good night," said Father. "God bless you."

"And Mary keep you," said the women together.

"So," said Father Nicanor, who was standing beside me at the top of
the steps. "Jonathan will be joining us after all."

"Yes," I said.

"So our Knights meeting," said the bishop behind us, "it will be
complete."

"As it should be, Your Lordship," I smiled.

"Come," said Father as he bounded up the stairs, "let's ransack that
refrigerator."

"I understand, Father Baptist," said the bishop as I closed the front door behind us, "from Mr. Feeney, that the vampire, it is dead."

"Oh?" said Father, looking at me.

"Well," I said, "it wasn't as if the bishop isn't in on it."

"True," said Father.

"But of course it is not true," said the bishop. "The vampire, I mean. Dead it is not. The 'Vampire's Shroud' still drapes its wicked veil over this city. The vampire, it is not dead."

"We shall see," said Father. "For the moment, the refrigerator awaits."

87

"IN THE NAME OF THE FATHER," said Bishop Xandaronolopolis, "and of the Son, and of the Holy Ghost. Amen." His right hand went north-south-east-west as is customary in the Eastern Rites. We in the Latin Rite are west-easters.

After a glorious raid on Millie's leftovers—Monsignor Havermeyer in attendance, Millie the Cat being away—the Knights Tumblar, now truly Knights in God's Tumbler, had insisted on ending the meeting with a half-hour of silent prayer before the Blessed Sacrament in the church. It was a four-candle affair, since Father Baptist gave no sermon from the pulpit.

It was almost midnight as we gathered ourselves up and made our final genuflection.

Just as our right knees touched the floor, we heard that sound again.

Boom!

Louder than before. The church seemed to tremble with the repercussion. It jolted our kneecaps.

"No doubt about it," I whispered to no one in particular. "That's not the clock in the steeple."

Boom! Boom!

"Thunder?" asked Pierre.

"I think not," said Father Nicanor.

"Not again," groaned Jonathan, who had indeed joined us after being chased from Stella's hospital room by two marauding housekeepers.

"It sounds very close," said Father Baptist.

A scraping, breaking, snapping sound seemed to emanate from the wall behind the altar. Then it suddenly ceased.

"Is it over?" asked Joel.

"Wait," said Monsignor Havermeyer. "There it is again."

"No," said Father Nicanor, listening intently, "something different this is."

"What could it be?" asked Arthur. "That tapping?"

"I think," said Father Baptist, "someone's knocking at the sacristy door. Come, everyone."

We all scurried into the sacristy which was cheerfully lit by a couple of bare hundred-watters screwed into sockets in the mottled ceiling. Thank-you, Mr. Edison.

Father unlocked the bolt and pulled the door open.

"Jack!" said a terrified voice.

"Larry," said Father, pulling the shuddering man inside. "What's wrong?"

"Jack—Father—I," choked Lieutenant Taper. His every hair was standing on end, and I didn't think he'd been reading Lovecraft.

"Easy," said Father, arm around his friend's shoulders. "You're safe in here."

"I know," shivered the lieutenant weakly, "That is, I sure hope so."

I fetched him a glass of water, which he spilled all over himself as he tried to sip it.

"Okay, Larry," said Father, "take a deep breath and tell me what happened."

"I dropped by to give you these," said Taper, holding out a couple of sheets of paper which were crushed in his fist. "John Holtsclaw said it was urgent—some new tests you ordered. He got them done sooner than he'd expected. I also knew you weren't satisfied with the Forst case, and I thought maybe we could go over a few loose ends. I went to the kitchen door, but Millie didn't seem to be around."

"She's out for the night," said Monsignor Havermeyer.

It just then dawned on the haggard lieutenant that the room was full of clerics and Tumblars, not to mention a bishop and a nervous gardener. He gawked a bit, took another shaky sip of water, most of which ran down his arms, and continued. "I'm sorry if I'm crashing an event."

"Nonsense," said Father. "You were saying you were at the kitchen door."

"Right. Then I heard that awful sound."

"Could you tell where it came from?" asked Father.

"Y-y-yeah. The graveyard behind the church."

The oxygen level in the room suddenly dropped as five knighted Tumblars, two priests, one monsignor, one bishop, and yours truly, Sir Gardener, gasped in unison.

"And then," wheezed Taper, "I saw—you'll think I'm crazy. Hell, I think I'm crazy. I must be stark, raving mad."

"You're not Hungarian—how would you know?" I quipped, trying to ease the tension. The attempt failed.

"Tell us what it is that you saw," said Father Nicanor.

"That Turnbuckle kid," blurted the lieutenant. "He came stumbling toward me."

"From the cemetery?" asked Father Baptist.

"Yeah. He looked horrible. His face was all ... I don't know how to describe it. There was murder in his eyes, and his mouth—never mind. He had his hands stretched out, reaching for me. Suddenly I felt so weak that I could hardly stand. I staggered backwards, and he came at me."

"And then?" asked the bishop.

"Just as he was about to grab me, he stopped." Taper slopped some more water on himself. "No—more like he recoiled, cowered. He made this ghastly sound, like a wounded animal, and then went lurching off back toward the cemetery."

"I don't get it," said Father Baptist. "I knew Biltmore was upset the other day, and with good reason. But what would make him behave like that?"

"You don't understand," said Taper, clutching the front of Father's cassock. Three buttons went flying. "Jack, it wasn't Biltmore out there. It was Buckminster. Bucky—the kid who committed suicide!"

88

"THEN IT'S TRUE," SAID JOEL as we gathered around the grave in the unconsecrated section of the cemetery.

"Some elements of it, at least," said Father Baptist grimly, sweeping the overturned earth with the light of a flashlight. "Something has certainly happened here."

"It is as I said," intoned the bishop, "several days ago, and this evening again. You remember, Father Baptist: 'The Vampire's Shroud,' it never lies."

"True," said Father Nicanor, gripping a handful of soil. "He has risen."

"Hold on," said Edward, also clutching a small pocket light. His hand was shaking so much the beam was useless. "Father, I thought you said the vampire was just some deranged nut."

"Not my words," said Father, "but my general meaning, yes."

"But surely you now see," said the bishop, "that it is otherwise."

"I don't know what I see," said Father. "The ground here is broken up, true. And Larry certainly saw something, and he's a trained professional." He looked around. "Where is he, anyway?"

"Still in the sacristy pouring water all over himself," said the gardener. "He didn't come out with the rest of us, and I don't blame him."

"So what do we do now?" asked Arthur, gripping the scapular under his shirt.

"We take precautions," said the bishop authoritatively. "Sir Martin, please be so kind as to fetch a shovel."

"We're n-n-nuh-not going to dig it up!" I stammered.

"No," said the bishop. "Not until daybreak. In fact, not until noon for safety's sake. But I want that you should smooth the ground, lest the boy's father—"

"Mr. Turnbuckle," said Father Baptist.

"—yes, lest he visit his son's grave after morning Mass and find it like this. Father Nicanor, to the kitchen please go and bring the garlic left by our beloved housekeepers in the larder. All of it, we will need. And Sir Pierre, a flask of holy water, this I will also require."

"I'm off," said Pierre, strutting toward the sacristy.

"But what makes you think, My Lord," shivered Joel, "that he's, you know, back down there—in his coffin, I mean?"

"This vampire," said the bishop, "it is new to the world."

"You mean," said Edward, "he just became a vampire?"

"Most recently," nodded the bishop. "Tonight for the first time, it has ventured forth. This it has been attempting to do for several evenings about this hour."

"That booming we heard," said Arthur. "The other night, and just a few minutes ago."

"And last night," said Father Baptist. "Martin and I were out, but the sound shook Millie awake."

"Me too," said Monsignor Havermeyer. "I thought my camper had blown a tire."

"You are fortunate," said the bishop to Havermeyer, "and dear Millie as well, that out of the grave this fiend did not venture last night."

"What?" gawked the monsignor. "What do you mean?"

"If you had heard a knock on your door," said the bishop sternly, "surely you would have opened it, no?"

"Well," said Havermeyer, "I suppose—"

"Only into the house where it is invited," said the bishop, "can the 'wampyr' enter."

Havermeyer blinked three times. "You mean—? Good Heavens!"

"But God, He is merciful, Monsignor," said Father Nicanor, returning from the rectory with a bundle under his arm. "Not until tonight did the fiend emerge from its grave when you were among friends in the protection of the Sanctuary. Thank Heaven Millie was not in the kitchen banging the pots and the pans. To think, she might have opened the door at the sound of a knock!"

"But Lieutenant Taper," said Pierre, also just arriving from his errand, flask of holy water in hand. "He was outside, alone, and it came after him."

"A new vampire testing its strength," said the bishop. "With defeat it was met, on its first trek from the grave."

"Defeat?" asked Arthur. "You mean, Lieutenant Taper—?"

"This Lieutenant Taper," said the bishop. "He is Catholic, no? A scapular he surely wears, or some blessed object?"

"That he does," nodded Father Baptist. "A St. Benedict's Medal, to be precise. I blessed it myself and gave it to him as a gift some time ago."

"The vampire's behavior, it is thus explained," said the bishop. "A man so protected, it could not touch. Weak and new to this world, it had yet to feed on the blood of the living. In this it failed. Wounded, it only had one place to go." He pointed down at the ground. "There."

"This is crazy," said Edward.

"This is Reality," said the bishop sternly. "In your land of French fries and the cheeseburgers, the 'vurkolak' has come to roost."

"Your pardon, My Lord," said Joel. "I repeat: how do you know he's back in his coffin?"

The bishop closed his eyes. "Its wrath I can feel, as one looking up from the Gates of Hell. Young man, this I know as sure as I know my own name with all its many syllables. Two nights it has been, Sir Joel, since you became a Knight. Any vestige of adolescence, for you, it is now banished."

Joel gulped. So did the other Tumblars.

"In my own country," said the bishop, "to hunt the 'vlkoslak,' this I have done—no, do not smirk. Where I come from—and by 'country' I speak not of political borders but of 'people'—the land is not yet so infested with your electricity. The 'wampyr' walks, seeking the blood of the living it does. Truthfully I say to you: stalking 'vrykolakas,' it is part of my priestly duty."

Now that's something you don't read about in your typical parish bulletin, I thought, but kept it to myself.

"No jokes," said Bishop Xandaronolopolis, looking at me.

I blinked back, innocently. How did he know?

"No joke is this," continued the bishop. "Bode well it does not, that the 'vlkoslak' has chosen to journey to this land of cheeseburgers and electricity, to spread its evil where disbelief in the darkness is its absolute weapon. Stop this we must, or the evil will spread throughout the bright boulevards and shopping malls of your unsuspecting city of fallen Angels."

"I think I'd better get back to the hospital," said Jonathan.

"Yes," said Father Baptist, "but not just yet. Gentlemen, I suggest that as soon as the bishop's precautions are in place, we retire to the rectory. We have much to discuss. You'll all have to call your employers in the morning to make your excuses. Your presence as Knights will be required here tomorrow."

"You believe it, then," whispered Edward.

"We must see what the light of day reveals," said Father.

Friday, October Twenty-seventh

Feast Day of Saint Frumentius, who was appointed by St. Athanasias as Bishop of Ethiopia (380 AD)

Day of Abstinence

89

"SO YOU THINK, MY LORD," SAID JONATHAN, "that Stella is in danger."

"I do," said Bishop Xandaronolopolis. "All that you have told me, all that Father Baptist has explained, conclude from all this I do, that the young woman was indeed attacked by the 'verkoslak'—twice, now, of which we know. First at this magic club, and again in her hospital bed the second."

"I gave Millie a first-class relic of St. Philomena to place beside Stella's bed at the hospital," said Father Baptist.

"Yes," said the bishop, "good is that."

It was a few minutes after midnight. We were huddled in Father Baptist's study, elbow to elbow, fluted glass to fluted glass, cigar to cigar, because it was the only place in the rectory where we could build a crackling fire—not for the heat, since the "Vampire's Shroud" took care of that, but for the cheer. Boy, did we need some cheer.

Lieutenant Taper, by the way, was stretched out on the bed in Father Baptist's own room. Pierre had found him unconscious on the sacristy floor when he went to return the empty holy water bottle. Arthur, Pierre, Edward, and Joel had carried the lieutenant into the rectory and, at Father's direction, deposited him in Father's most private of spaces.

The bishop had expressed concern, wanting to know if the thing Larry encountered had come in contact with him, had touched him at all. Upon reviewing Taper's frantic description at the sacristy door, we were pretty sure it had not. The bishop had placed his own Rosary in the lieutenant's hands and said we should leave him to his dreams.

"Then," said Pierre, "we're dealing with two vampires: the one that attacked Stella in the hospital, and the one under our own backyard."

"Not to mention," said Edward, "the one that got flattened the other night."

"But that wasn't a real vampire," said Arthur. "Father Baptist said so."

"I've never heard of driving a steamroller through a vampire," mused the gardener. "Wooden stakes yes, steamrollers no. I wonder if it worked."

"I'm confused," said Joel.

"I'm with you," nodded Jonathan.

"I'm sorry to bother you at this time of night, Sergeant Wickes," Father Baptist was saying into the telephone on his desk. "An emergency? Well, yes and no. Lieutenant Taper has had a rough time, and I thought you should know that he's spending the night here. Hm? No, nothing like you last Sunday—entirely different circumstances. What's that? Yes, I think it would be an excellent idea for you to come by for lunch today. I'll inform Millie. Good night."

Without a pause, he dialed another number and waited. "Millie? Yes, it's me ... No, I'm just calling to see if you need anything. Any problems? ... All right, all right. Sorry I interrupted the movie. God bless you, too."

"Sir Jonathan," said the bishop as Father placed the receiver in its cradle, "on your mind is something?"

"Yes," said the lad, his forehead contracting into deep furrows. He ran his fingers through his mustard-brown hair. "I've been reading *Dracula* by Bram Stoker—I'm about half-way through."

"Yes?" said Father Baptist.

"Hrmph," hrumphed the bishop.

"Well," said Jonathan, swallowing loudly, "when Lucy Westenra died in the story, killed by Count Dracula, she became a vampire, too."

"And you're afraid that will happen to Stella?" asked Pierre.

"Well, yes," said Jonathan, looking uneasily at Pierre and then at me, "but more than that. It's ... it's just that when it came time to drive the stake through Lucy's heart, Dr. Van Helsing insisted that it should be done by the man who loved her."

"Dear chap," said Pierre, placing a brotherly hand on Jonathan's shoulder.

Jonathan flinched a little, but did not pull away from Pierre's hand.

"I remember the doctor's words only too well," said Pierre: "'... it will be a blessed hand for her that shall strike the blow that sets her free.'"

"So," said Jonathan, tears gathering in his eyes and lips trembling, "I, like Arthur Holmwood, must summon the courage to say, 'Tell me what I am to do, and I shall not falter!' And I honestly don't know if I'm up for it, Father."

"Dear, dear, chap," said Pierre, gripping both of Jonathan's shoulders.

"Hrmph," hrmphed the bishop again.

"If it comes to that, Jonathan," said Father Baptist, kindly but stern, "and I'm not saying it will, that would be the last thing I would have you do."

"Come again?" asked Arthur and Edward.

"Gentlemen," said Father, "and Jonathan in particular: you would do well to remember that Bram Stoker was an apostate Catholic."

"He was?" asked Joel.

"Yes," said Father. "As a result, there are three problems with his otherwise marvelous tale. First, his research told him that holy articles could be used as weapons against the vampire. Crucifixes, Rosaries, the 'Sacred Wafer' as he called the Blessed Sacrament, and the like. These objects his characters employed to defeat the count, but without any reference whatsoever to the reason that they worked: the fact that they supply Grace."

"Which only flows through the conduit which Christ provided," said Father Nicanor. "The Catholic Church."

"You mean a King James Bible wouldn't work?" asked Monsignor Havermeyer.

"Of course not," said Father Nicanor. "Blessed it would not be, and full of mistranslations it is. So fraught with heresy, how could it be of any use against something that thrives on lies?"

"'Every kingdom divided against itself shall be brought to desolation,'" rumbled Bishop Xandaronolopolis, quoting Saint Luke ten seventeen. His stormy eyes then fell upon me.

"Um," I stalled, quickly turning pages in my head until I got to verse eighteen. "'And if Satan also be divided against himself, how shall his kingdom stand?'"

"Hm," grimaced Havermeyer as if swallowing a bitter pill. "Hmm."

"The little golden crosses many women wear," said Father Nicanor. "Fashionable they are, but useless against Evil. No Corpus, no blessing, no Grace."

"Hence the second problem," said Father. "Because Stoker had denounced his Catholic Faith, he also abandoned Her teachings, and so didn't really know, or let on that he knew, or purposely scrambled, what he was really talking about."

"You just lost me," said Joel.

"He made it seem," said Father, "that the curse of the vampire is like a spiritual disease which takes possession of an innocent soul. Thus to kill the vampire was to set the soul free, to secure its Salvation."

"Right," said Jonathan.

"This was further stressed, as I recall," said Father, "at the moment the stake was driven through the heart of Count Dracula himself. Stoker describes the event as though it were a freeing experience for a trapped soul."

"Indeed," said Pierre, summoning a clear mental picture of the page in his head:

> I shall be glad as long as I live that even in that moment of final dissolution, there was in the face a look of peace, such as I never could have imagined might have rested there.

"HrrrrRRRRrrrrmph," hrrrrRRRRrrrrmphed the bishop. "Ridiculous this is. This could never be. A demon from Hell is the 'wampyr.' Possession of a corpse it takes—a *corpse*. Already dead is the human victim. Gone is the soul. To kill a vampire is to consign the demon back to Hell, where there is no peace, only eternal cacophony."

"What?" gawked Arthur. "I thought—"

"Vampirism is the lowest form of demon possession," explained Father Baptist, "reserved for only the lowest of devils."

"Right," said the gardener, shifting authoritatively in his chair. My ancestor, after all, was a famous vampire-stalker. "That's why Beelzebub would never stoop to such a thing. He might take possession of a living, breathing, willing person, but a vampire is only 'Demon Bob.'"

"Who is nonetheless an evil to contend with," said Father Nicanor. "An evil worse than your most gruesome nightmare. But as you cleverly say, Sir Martin, it is only this 'Demon Bob.'"

"The vampire," said Father Baptist, "is an unholy amalgam of demon and dead flesh—evil spirit and coarse matter, if you will—which is the satanic mockery of the Incarnation in which the Son of God took on human flesh."

"Not to mention the Resurrection," said Pierre, "in which the Son of Man rose from the dead."

"Well said," nodded the bishop. "And because of this attachment of the 'vurkolak' to matter, elements of nature there are that are repellent to it."

"You mean garlic?" said Edward.

"Yes," nodded the bishop, "and more so silver. These things, harmless and even pleasing to us, are painful to it."

"And the aspen wood," said Father Nicanor. *"Populus tremula* and *Populus grandidentata,* are the best for driving through the demon's heart. Poplars, you call them. Trees with leaves that love the wind."

"The third problem with Stoker," said Father Baptist, "is that, according to his biographer, Harry Ludlam, the inspiration for the novel was a nightmare brought on by, as I recall, 'a too generous helping of dressed crab for supper one night.'"

"Insufferable," said Pierre. "I pray he was not drinking champagne with his dinner."

"But what about Stella?" asked Jonathan, looking around nervously at all his comrades. "What if she—?"

"We will do everything in our power," said Arthur, "to prevent that."

"Indeed," said Pierre. "Are we not Knights? Are we not sworn to come to the aid of our comrades, of the helpless, of all who are in need?"

"You can count on us," said Edward.

"In any case," said Father Baptist, "we must arm ourselves with what is True, not that which is fanciful. I suggest that you all go home and get some rest. We'll meet back here at eleven thirty to deal with our 'friend' in the cemetery. And under no conditions whatsoever are you to remove your scapulars. Understood?"

Yup, they understood.

As for the gardener, you couldn't separate him from his scapular with a crowbar.

90

"NO, MISS WEXLER," FATHER BAPTIST WAS SAYING into the telephone as I entered the study some time later. "As a matter of fact, it is with you rather than Solomon or John that I wish to speak."

This time I brought the whole coffeepot. With much futzing and sputtering, I managed to get it situated on the same oven mitt I had used to carry it from the kitchen.

"I'd like to ask a small favor," said Father. "No, nothing illegal, and nothing that will spark the ire of Chief Billowack. It's a simple thing, really."

I didn't get to hear what it was, because at that point I realized I had forgotten to bring a cup. Mumbling something about brain cells, I exited the room.

91

"MONSIGNOR ASPIC," SAID FATHER as the now not-so-perky nor self-confident archdiocesan consultant with two degrees in management efficiency and one in organizational psychology slinked into the study, guided by Millie's tired but firm hand. "I appreciate your coming, especially at a time like this."

"You said it was important on the phone," said our favorite Jonas, stuffing his hands into his pants' pockets but finding no change to jingle there.

"Will you be needing anything, Father?" yawned Millie from the doorway. It was a rare moment, one to savor, during which there was more fury in her heart than usual—you could see it in her eyes—but her puffy eyelids were almost swollen shut from lack of sleep.

"Only that you take a much-deserved nap," said Father. "Martin and I will fend for ourselves for lunch."

"But Sergeant Wickes—"

"I insist," said Father. "The sergeant is a bachelor. He knows his way around a refrigerator. It's ten now, and I don't want to see you again until at least four this afternoon—five would be better."

The fact that she acquiesced to that arrangement shows you how little sleep she and Veronika had managed to get during their vigil. With all that was going on, Jonathan hadn't arrived at the hospital to relieve them until almost three in the morning.

Of course, Father Baptist didn't get a single wink. After dismissing the Tumblars, he continued to discuss matters with Bishop Pip until five-thirty. Then he said morning Mass. All the while, Lieutenant Taper lay in a stupor on Father's bed.

This was going to be a long day for ol' Slap-Happy-Bappy.

For me, too, since wherever he went, I went.

GARDENING TIPS: "Slap-Happy-Bappy": another TEK
reference. I said this would be a challenge.
                                                     —M.F.

"Please be seated," said Father to Conrad Jonas Aspic.

"Sure," said the monsignor, settling into my favorite chair's twin. He didn't acknowledge my presence, and I returned the compliment. "But I'm afraid I haven't given the matter of your bill a thought in days."

"Neither have I," said Father Baptist. "I have asked you to come because there is something I want you to do for me."

"What could I possibly do for you?"

"I would like you to perform a priestly function."

"What's that?"

"A priestly function?" asked Father.

"No," scowled Aspic. "I mean: what's the priestly function you want me to perform?"

Father made his fingers into a steeple. "I want you to pay a visit to Mr. Thurgood T. Turnbuckle."

"What?"

"I took the liberty of having Sybil Wexler make an appointment for you to see him and his son, Biltmore, at their home at eleven-thirty."

"Who's Sybil Wexler?"

"A voice Mr. Turnbuckle wouldn't recognize."

"And why do you want me to go there?"

"Well," said Father, "I could say it's because Thurgood and Biltmore could use some attention right now, spiritual guidance, that sort of thing, but after some of what you've said to me recently, you're hardly the man for that job."

"I didn't come here to be insulted," said Aspic.

"That wasn't intended as an insult," said Father. "It was a simple statement of fact. For a priest who doesn't believe in the Resurrection—"

"I was being philosophical," snapped the monsignor.

"One of the great problems of our day," countered Father, "has been the divorce of philosophy from metaphysics, and theology from sanctity—but that discussion will have to wait for another time."

"Insufferable," said Aspic.

"Yes it is," said Father.

"So what do you want me to do?"

Father's finger steeple collapsed. "I want you to make sure that Mr. Turnbuckle and his son stay at their home until, say, two o'clock."

"What the devil for?"

"'What the devil' is right. I simply have to be sure where they are, that's all."

"Why?"

"That I can't tell you. Not now, anyway. It is better that you don't know."

The monsignor scowled at the last bit. "And how am I supposed to keep them there?"

"Heavens," said Father, "you ask that? Talking is your business, Monsignor. Cajoling, winking, nudging, tasting expensive wines, sampling the private chef's favorite dishes, even begging for donations for some fund no one's ever heard of—these should come easy for a man of your talents."

"And what if they have other plans?"

"See that they don't."

"And what if they leave anyway?"

"You won't let that happen."

"Why not?"

"Because, my dear Monsignor, you have noticed, haven't you, that news of the string of murders your brother committed while you were a guest in his house has not seen the light of day in the media. Hasn't that fact caught your attention?"

"Well, yes," admitted Aspic. "It has indeed. I've been waiting to hear all sorts of abysmal details on the car radio or splashed across the headlines—"

"But the police have kept the lid on," said Father, "and my sources tell me that they fully intend to continue to do so. I also understand that two of the owners of 'The House of Illusions' are city councilmen. Surely they don't want word of these murders getting around. Bad for business." Father leaned back in his chair. "And I further understand that Our Lord Archbishop, Morley Fulbright, Cardinal of Los Angeles, is likewise concerned—financially, I mean."

"Oh, that," said Aspic, sighing nervously.

"Yes, that," said Father. "Am I far afield if I surmise that it was you who suggested such an investment to His Eminence?"

"Among other things, yes." The monsignor rolled his next thought around in his mouth like a bit of food left over from breakfast. "Are you going to tell him about Surewood?"

"Being your brother? No. No doubt the cardinal has been informed that the killer has been run to ground, and that his name was Surewood Forst. As for the connection with you, I sense that the police intend to be discreet on all fronts. You'd be surprised how many gruesome murders go unpublicized even when solved. They feed the press some crimes, while withholding others. Some details they release, others they keep to themselves. It's a game I know well. I used to play it."

"Then what has that got to do with me?"

"Everything," said Father. "It only takes one phone call to a single reporter who's hungry for a scoop, and soon everyone from the lowest parish liturgical coordinator to the cardinal himself will know your connection with these crimes."

Aspic's jaw fell. "But I didn't—! You wouldn't—"

"No, I wouldn't," agreed Father. "I'd get someone else to do it, of course. Mr. Feeney, here, for example. And you know what? You can get a lot of mileage out of denial."

"'I swear to you, the men and women of the press, on my word of honor,'" I piped, hands folded fervently, eyebrows arched in rainbows of sincerity. "'Monsignor Aspic had *nothing whatsoever* to do with these horrible crimes that were committed under his very nose, and with teeth he himself fashioned for his psychotic brother. Furthermore, I categorically deny that he had any suspicion that the confidential information he gleaned while working as the cardinal's consultant, and which he inappropriately passed on to said brother, would in any way be put to use in the commission of unspeakable crimes against humanity—'"

"That will be enough, Martin," said Father.

"I see your point," said Monsignor Aspic coldly, eyes aimed at me, lips at Father Baptist. "Very well, I will make every effort to keep Mr. Turnbuckle—"

"And his son, Biltmore," said Father.

"—and his son, Biltmore, occupied at their home until—what time did you say?"

"Two o'clock."

"Is there any place in particular that you don't want them to go? I mean, is this ploy to keep them away from the Chancery?—or the bank?—or whatever? You understand, they may just want to go for a drive. If I can't keep them home, where is it that you don't want them to be?"

"Here," said Father Baptist. "They must not come within a mile of St. Philomena's."

"I see."

"See that you do."

92

"IF VOMIT YOU DO, I CARE NOT," rumbled Bishop Xandaronolopolis. "No disgrace is there in this.   Faint if you must, choke, scream—normal reactions are these. That you look, and that you see, this is what you all must do. As the one who made thee Knights, I command it."

Father Baptist, Father Nicanor, Monsignor Havermeyer, the Tumblars, and one quivering gardener were gathered around the unmarked grave of Buckminster Turnbuckle.

> GARDENING TIPS: The grave was unmarked because a
> stone had yet to be delivered. In my experience,
> they usually wait a few months for the ground to
> settle over a new grave before installing heavy
> stone markers to avoid subsidence.
>   --M.F.

Pierre Bontemps had arrived wearing a morning coat and cravat—whether for form or to get out of digging detail I don't know. Both worked.

Arthur was wearing a jacket and tie, but off they flew, and rolled-up became his shirtsleeves the moment shovels were handed around.

The others had come in jeans and denim shirts, ready for toil.

Toil of this sort I was not able to do, so I wore my usual clothes while looking on sagaciously. In addition to this negligible task, I was pluckily prepared to comply with the bishop's list of choices: to faint, choke, scream, or vomit as the situation required.

Monsignor Havermeyer was wearing his ill-fitting cassock. Fathers Baptist and Nicanor were wearing white surplices over theirs, with purple stoles draped around their necks and fastened in place with purple cinctures. The bishop was accoutered in the vestments of the Traditional Latin Requiem—black chasuble, stole, cincture, and maniple.

On the ground nearby was a vessel of holy water. Next to it was a hammer and a two-foot wooden stake, filed to a sharp point, which Joel had fashioned from an old aspen curtain rod.

"A matter of courage this is not, but of knowledge," said the bishop as the pile next to the rectangular hole grew. "For revealing to the children at Fatima a vision of Hell, some modern clerics have criticized the Blessed Virgin. How silly! How dangerous! How shortsighted are the fools that so reprove the Mother of God! For a great blessing was this! What greater deterrent to a wicked life could there be? A similar blessing you fine gentlemen are about to receive, for after this day the Face of Evil you will know—a glimpse of Hell you will have seen. From now on, a concept Evil will no longer be—no mere temptation with a pretty lady, or a creative untruth of the tongue, no—but know Evil you will as a cold, hard, living Reality. God in His Mercy was preparing you for this when in your hearts He placed the desire for Knighthood."

"Lulled you gentlemen have been," said Father Nicanor, "along with everyone in your culture, into a gentle coma with respect to Evil. Your movies and television shows equate 'good' and 'bad' with 'convenience' and 'unkindness'—with behavior, not morality."

"Excuse me, Your Lordship, if I may ask a less philosophical question," said Arthur, pausing for a moment to wipe the sweat from his brow with his forearm. "Is it true that vampires can change their shape?"

"Like into the bat, you ask?" asked the bishop.

"Or a wolf," said Joel.

"Or dust particles floating in the moonlight," said Pierre—though I suspected that in his mind the image was more like bubbles rising in champagne.

"Or a mist," said Arthur.

"The mist, yes," said the bishop. "How else could this fiend open the coffin lid with six feet of dirt on top, let alone claw its way through the earth? Like the boiling water through the coffee grounds, it seeped through."

"Not the other night," said Edward. "Tuesday, I mean, when we heard him—it—pounding the inside of its coffin."

"Or Wednesday night," said the gardener, "when the pounding woke Millie up."

"Even last night," said Jonathan. "We all heard it. But that time it got out."

"Change its shape the vampire can," said the bishop. "But how much, into what, is a matter of the talent and power of the demon. Not all the same powers do all vampires have."

"Nor the experience," said Father Nicanor. "For two nights this one thrashed around in its coffin before learning how to dissolve into a mist. The demon learns, and each vampire progresses according to its skill, and according to the obstacles it comes up against."

"So we don't know what we'll find down here," said Arthur.

"Not precisely," agreed the bishop.

Several pairs of eyes turned to Father Baptist for a word, a phrase, a hint of consolation, relief, or sympathy, but none was forthcoming. He stared upon us with penetrating eyes that seemed to whisper, determined but fearfully, "Considering all that has happened, gentlemen, and is soon to transpire, do you really expect me to offer any comfort other than the same sufferings for which I admonished you to prepare?" But all he said was, "Nearly there."

Soon they were really there. The scraping sound of their shovels suddenly changed, and the lid of the coffin emerged from the deep, dark soil.

"Perhaps this isn't the best time to bring this up," said Monsignor Havermeyer, who had remained silent through these proceedings. "But isn't it illegal to dig up a grave like this?"

"Without a court order, very," said Father Baptist. "But I can't imagine any judge in this county granting us official permission to exhume and exterminate a vampire—can you?"

"No," nodded the monsignor, "but surely your friends Taper and Wickes will find out."

"No doubt," said Father. "I think I'll be able to convince them that sometimes the civil law is beneath the moral, that what is right and necessary doesn't always conform to what is legal."

"I hope so," said Pierre, "seeing as how we're all accessories."

"Taper would be easier to convince than Wickes," said the gardener, "even if he hadn't met it face-to-face."

"In any case," said Father, "we can't let this thing reside in our backyard for fear of a county ordinance."

"Should we open it down here?" called up Joel, "or heave the whole thing up onto the level ground?"

"It is better that it be up here," said the bishop, producing a tattered leather book from somewhere under his black chasuble.

Accompanied by much grunting and heaving, the soil-stained box slid to a stop with a hollow groan at the bishop's feet.

"Whose honor shall it be," he asked sternly, "to open it?"

"Mine," said Pierre, stepping forth, crowbar in hand. Okay, he was at least willing to get his hands dirty. There he had one up on me.

It took some doing—modern caskets being a bit more complicated than the simple boxes in old movies—but Pierre managed to defeat the seals. The lid was already buckled and splintered in places, evidence that something inside had been struggling to get out.

"This is not going to be your typical graveside service," whispered the gardener. "I wish Chief Billowack and Pastor McIntosh were here to see this—"

"If here they were meant to be," said the bishop, "then here they would be."

"Mother of God," gasped Father Baptist as the lid creaked open.

Everyone crossed themselves.

"'Circumdederunt me gemitus mortis,'" intoned the bishop, "'dolores inferni circumdederunt me ...'"

I recognized it as the Introit from Septuagesima Sunday, taken from Psalm Seventeen:

> The groans of death surrounded me, the sorrows of Hell encompassed me: and in my affliction I called upon the Lord, and He heard my voice from His holy temple. I will love thee, O Lord, my strength: the Lord is my firmament, and my refuge, and my deliverer.

Buckminster Turnbuckle looked, well, not much like the young man who had occasionally attended Mass with his dad when he needed money—and not at all like Bucky Buckle as I'd seen him on the stage at the "House of Illusions." The thing in the coffin was emaciated, shriveled, horrible. Its skin was white but coarse, like hunks of freshly quarried chalk. The hair was matted and oily. The morticians had done their best to plaster-up and powder-over the gaping bullet wound in the left temple, but a good part of the right side of the skull where the missile had exited was gone and the undertaker's putty-filler had fallen away.

But that was the least of it.

A pair of long fangs protruded from its leathery lips, frozen in a putrefied snarl. The hands, which had no doubt been folded in repose by the morticians, were now parted—misshapen fingers, almost twice as lengthy as in life, were clutched against the chest, the nails splintered and bloody. The satin lining inside the arched lid had been shredded, no doubt during the vampire's first desperate attempts to leave its grave.

The body's chest was not moving up and down. It was certainly dead.

All this I took in through waves of syrupy nausea and swirling dizziness. The bishop's suggestions about fainting, choking, screaming, and vomiting suddenly all made perfect sense.

"Nothing remotely glamorous here," sniffed Pierre.

"Why does he look so ... *so?*" asked Jonathan, shaking his head slowly.

"'For the life of all flesh is in the blood,'" quoted the bishop from the seventeenth chapter of Leviticus. "This demon, it has not yet feasted. Its purloined flesh, it is thirsty—very thirsty."

"Hold on," said Father, stooping close to the casket.

"No, Father Baptist," warned the bishop. "The vampire you must not touch, not without much preparation and prayer."

"Hand me that crowbar then, Pierre," said Father.

"What are you doing?" asked the Tumblars severally.

"Checking a hunch," said Father, gingerly slipping the end of the tool into a tear in the body's dress shirt and pulling the cloth further apart.

"Find something, Father?" asked Monsignor Havermeyer.

"Martin," said Father, "you'd better look at this."

"You really think so?" I asked.

"Yes, Martin."

As I stooped to look at what was so important, and which I surely didn't want to see, Arthur was asking the bishop another practical question.

"Your Lordship, isn't a vampire supposed to crumble into dust or something if he's—it's—exposed to direct sunlight?"

"Sir Arthur," answered the bishop, raising his hands toward the sky, "see you any of this 'direct sunlight'? The 'Vampire's Shroud,' it is the demon's protection, like the ink of the squid. Of course, if the 'Shroud,' it should disperse, then yes, my friend, the sunlight, it will destroy the vampire."

All this theory going on over my head, and I was bent-over getting seriously vertiginous—and at the same time, morbidly fascinated.

The flesh of the vampire's abdomen was shriveled into tight, hard curds, like cottage cheese that had been left outside the refrigerator since last Sunday's picnic. The skin had an eerie translucence about it, the veins visible beneath the surface like branches and twigs in a frozen lake. And the smell, the fetid odor wafting up from the decaying skin—well, let's just say I'd rather bathe in Conrad J. Aspic's mouth-wash any day.

All that was gross, but curiously, the one detail that struck me the hardest, and really made my own abdomen contract with revulsion, was the black smear of caked blood on the mottled skin:

"This, I'll grant you," I whispered to Father, "is no 'accidental smudge.'"

"Father," gulped Pierre, looking over my shoulder, "how can this be?"

The others chimed in as they gathered around to look.

"How, I do not know," said Father, rising to his feet. "Why, is even more puzzling. But now is not the time to figure it all out. We have another task that is pressing in the immediate."

Father tossed the crowbar into the casket beside the body, knowing it should never be touched by human hand or put to useful purpose again.

"The Good Lord commands that we practice Charity," said the bishop at last. "This applies only to our fellow human beings. When with the minions of Hell we are dealing, hatred vile and ferocity unbridled are required. No sympathy do these fiends deserve, for adversaries they are of all that is right, just, and innocent. On them compassion has no effect because they were judged and their doom sealed before the Fall of Adam. Which of you men understands this enough to be the one to send this enemy of Christ back to Damnation?"

All eyes went to Pierre, but as he was in formal attire, and he had already performed his appointed labor, he declined with a slow shake of his head.

The eyes then went around the circle: Edward? No. Arthur? Nope. Jonathan? The desire but not the will—no. Joel? Almost, but not quite—maybe next time. Monsignor Havermeyer? Not no way, not no how. Father Nicanor? Well, possibly, but—

"I will do it," said Father Baptist.

No one argued.

With slow, measured movements, Father gathered up the necessary implements and knelt on the bare earth beside the coffin. Pausing for a brief and silent prayer, he summoned his courage, positioned the stake directly over the heart, and took a deep breath. Slowly, he raised the hammer and then, exhaling loudly, he brought the bludgeon down.

Once, twice, thrice.

The little cemetery behind St. Philomena's trembled with the scream that burst from the coffin.

Something gooey and black like tar gushed around the point of penetration. The thing's eyes popped open, glaring hatefully at the mortal whose hands had sealed its doom anew. White foam flecked with green erupted from its mouth, weirdly wiggling as the snakelike tongue thrashed within. Bones cracked and sinews snapped as the animating spirit separated from the physical fabric of the writhing monstrosity. Like an explosion in reverse, the body suddenly collapsed inward upon itself. A gust of molten air rose from the devastated corpse, coalesced into a nebulous shape without form or detail a few feet above the open box, and then dissolved in the tepid breeze. It drifted limply away in the direction of the back parking lot, and was gone.

Nothing remained in the coffin but a thin layer of shifting ashes and a warped crowbar that had been straight a moment before. Even the stake had been annihilated.

Loyalty to my fellow Knights prevents my revealing the one that retched, and the two that fainted on the spot. As for the gardener, he did both.

93

"HEY, WHAT'S GOING ON?" Sergeant Wickes came strolling across the cemetery, big as you please. Timing is everything.

Luckily, the two fainted Tumblars had revived, the pile of earth had been replaced in the grave, and the topsoil had been raked into a general semblance of its former lonely state. Nonetheless, with the exception of the clergy and Pierre, the rest of our company were streaked and caked with earth. I was dirty from my fall, and my shirt was stained with an embarrassing bit of something else.

Father Baptist was bending beside a faucet near the church wall, trying with limited success to get that sticky black stuff off his hands. "Sergeant Wickes," he said, shutting off the spigot, "I had hoped you'd arrive sooner—though no, on second thought, this worked out best."

"For what?" asked the sergeant, coming to a standstill in our midst. He looked around suspiciously. "You guys performing some secret ritual or something? Pierre, you look about normal. But Martin, you look terrible."

"And my looks are my happiest part," I said, leaning a couple of shovels against the nearest tree.

"So what gives?" persisted Wickes. Then he caught sight of the bishop in his grim vestments, looking like a character that had just stepped out of a Tarot card. "And who are you?"

"May I present Bishop Xandaronolopolis," said Father, wiping his hands on his cassock as he approached. "Your Lordship, this is Sergeant Wickes."

"Oh?" said the bishop, extending his hand to the sergeant. "This is the homicide detective you were speaking of this morning, Father Baptist. The apostate."

"The what?" blinked Wickes.

"A fallen-away Catholic," explained Father.

"Now I see what you mean," said the bishop.

"What do you mean?" asked Wickes, turning to face Father.

"I mean: you've lost your Faith."

"Is this not true?" asked the bishop.

"Well," hedged Wickes, "I suppose so."

"Suppose?" sighed the bishop. "There is either belief or disbelief. No in-between is there, Mr. Wickes, in the realm of Faith."

"Well," gulped Wickes. "Well, that is ..."

"Forgive us our candor, Sergeant," said Father. "It's been one of those days. Are you late because something has come up regarding the case?"

"Oh," said Wickes. "Yes—ahem—something has happened. Two employees of the 'House of Illusions'—two women—are missing."

"Sancte Michael Archangele," said Father Nicanor, crossing himself.

"You mean," said Father Baptist, "since Wednesday?"

"We don't know what happened to them," said Wickes with a nervous nod. "We don't even know if these disappearances are connected to the case. Is Lieutenant Taper still here? He hasn't reported in. Chief Billowack is having fits."

"Chief Billowack," observed the gardener, "is always having fits. He's having trouble, you see, getting in touch with his 'feminine side.'"

"We'll go see," said Father, taking the sergeant's arm and turning him in the direction of the rectory, "if Larry is awake yet."

"He's been sleeping?" squeaked Wickes. "I mean, you said he'd had a rough night—"

"He was nearly touched," said the bishop, following, "by the Hand of Evil."

"Oh," said Wickes, "the ol' 'Mano di Diablo,' eh? I've heard of it. Some new liqueur from south of the border—"

"More I see," sighed the bishop, "what you meant this morning, Father Baptist."

As we came to the rectory, Father halted and turned to the Tumblars. "Gentlemen: you have done well, and I'm proud of you. Much as I'd like to discuss events, I suggest that you all go home and get some rest."

"Rest?" asked Jonathan. "Who can rest?"

"Try," said Father. "Remember, you'll be taking turns watching Stella during the night."

"I suggest," said Pierre, "that before we retire for sleep, we retire to Darby's and have some sustenance."

"You mean champagne," said Arthur.

"Is there any other kind?" asked Pierre.

"Perhaps we should change," said Joel, looking down at himself.

"No," said Pierre, locking arms with his comrades as they headed down the brick path, "this is an after-battle celebration. We shall go as we are—in the armor that we wore in battle."

"That's easy for you to say," said Jonathan. "Look at your armor."

"Battle?" asked Wickes. "What armor?"

"It's a Tumblar thing," whispered the gardener to the sergeant.

"Yes," said Edward to Pierre, "about your armor—"

Thus the Tumblars went their way, to drink and fight another day.

As for Fathers Baptist and Nicanor, Monsignor Havermeyer, Bishop Pip, Sergeant Wickes and yours truly, we had business within.

94

"LARRY, YOU AWAKE?" asked the sergeant, nudging the unostentatious bed in Father Baptist's sparse room.

"Huh?" yawned Lieutenant Taper, blinking and rubbing his eyes. "Where am I? What's happened?" It came out more like "Harg? Wor'm by? Wart's hominy?" but since he's a policeman and protector of the common welfare, I'll clean up his act.

"Permit me," said the bishop, shouldering his way to the bed. "Look at him I must."

"Who are you?" asked Taper, taking his fists away from his eyes and blinking up at the bishop.

"You don't remember Bishop Xandaronolopolis?" asked Father Baptist, taking the lieutenant's pulse.

"No," moaned the lieutenant. "How could I forget a name like that?"

"Easily," said the gardener, "if you'd never learned to pronounce it in the first place."

"What do you remember," said Father to Taper, "about last night?"

"Hm," said the lieutenant, shoveling out the inside of his mouth with his tongue. It was gooey work. "I came here—didn't I?—with some lab results from John Holtsclaw."

"Heavens," said Father. "I'd forgotten about those reports. Martin, do you remember what I did with them?"

"You left them in the sacristy," I said, "but your *useful* gardener, model of efficiency that he is and upon whom you peculiarly rely, suspecting their importance, transferred them to the desk in your study."

"Good man," said Father. "I don't know what I'd do without you." Then to Lieutenant Taper: "Larry, do you remember walking up to the kitchen door?"

"What? Oh, yes. I think so. Then there was some kind of horrible sound. It seemed to come from the cemetery ..."

"And then?"

"Nothing," groaned Taper, rolling his head on the pillow. "Just darkness, and ... nightmares."

"Hmm," hmmed the bishop. "The mind, it is merciful. You were touched, my friend, not by the Hand of Evil, but only by the Breath. You were fortunate."

"This is crazy," said Wickes to all of us. "You mean to tell me he just fainted? And he's been asleep all this time?"

"What time is it?" asked Taper, shifting up onto his elbows.

"Half past lunch," said the gardener.

"You mean I've been out since last night?" gasped Taper. "Oh great. The chief is going to be furious."

"Already is," said Wickes.

"He's predictable that way," said the gardener.

"That's why I'm here," said Wickes. "Father Baptist called early this morning and said you'd had a 'rough time,' so naturally I assumed—"

"What's that you say, Sergeant?" asked Taper warily. "You assumed what?"

Wickes gulped. "I thought maybe you'd had too much to drink. That's what I told the chief."

"Swell," said Taper, sliding his legs off the edge of the bed and rising to a tilted sitting position. "That's all I need, for him to think I went on a binge."

"Actually," said Father, "that's probably the best explanation—for the present."

"And what about the future," groaned Taper, "that is, if I have one?"

"If the need arises," said Father, "I'll handle Montgomery Billowack. Don't forget, I was his superior officer for years. Now Sergeant, you must tell us about the disappearances."

"Disappearances?" asked Taper. "What have I missed?"

"Apparently," said Father Nicanor, r's rolling, "much."

"Two women," said Wickes, consulting his handy notebook. "Employees of the 'House of Illusions.'"

"That place again," said the gardener.

"Tamara Grafan, twenty-eight, and her partner and sister, Marla, twenty-six, didn't show up for work yesterday evening. Mr. Graves called us this morning, concerned."

"The Toolmaster," interjected the gardener.

"Right," said Wickes. "Sort of a general fix-it man and technical wizard for the magicians. We met him last Saturday."

"We know him," said Father. "Martin and I have spoken with him since then. Wednesday, I believe."

Wickes flipped a page. "He said the sisters have always been punctual and reliable, though it's possible that, with all the weirdness going on at the place, they just upped and quit."

"You said they were partners," said Father. "A stage act, you mean?"

"No," said the gardener, as some rather bad poetry floated to the surface of his memory, "a reef and a whirlpool."

> *"Be forewarned, who enter here."*
> *"Danger lurks 'neath every stair."*
> *"All who enter must needs take care ..."*
> *"Not to tarry, but beware."*
> *"And who are you?"* I had asked, noticing the nose ring clipped
> to the nostrils on the left. *"Scylla and Charybdis?"*
> *"I am Tamara."*
> *"And I am Marla."*
> *"We're life-force sentinels."*

"They're the two 'sensitives,'" I explained, "who stand guard in the tunnel between the entrance anteroom and the bar."

"Stand guard against what?" asked Taper, who must have missed them the night he and Wickes had come through, flashing their badges.

"Psychic vampires," I answered. "Those who siphon off the life-energy of others, and apparently don't even know they're doing it."

"You're joking," said Monsignor Havermeyer.

I shrugged. "That's what they said. It's their job. And, come to think of it, I may have seen Marla Grafan yesterday."

"Where?" asked Father.

"Here, or rather in the church, while you were in the confessional, Father. She came in through the front door and asked for you. I recognized the ring in her nose, but didn't put it together until just now. When I told her where you were, she ran away. I understand the sentiment, but—"

"She asked for me?"

"You, Father," I said.

"This is most puzzling," he said.

"No puzzle," I said. "The severity of your penances is legendary, though she assured me she wasn't a Catholic."

"You're sure it was her?"

"Pretty sure."

"Let us hope," said Father, "that instead of a 'psychic vampire,' the poor woman, unprepared, did not meet up with a real one."

"What was that?" asked Wickes, incredulous.

Father shook his head sadly. "Lives and souls, Martin. Lives and souls."

"Did you say 'real vampire'?" persisted Wickes.

"Martin," said Father, ignoring Wickes, "what was it you said yesterday morning at the hospital—when we found the blood smear on Stella Billowack?"

"Me?" I said. "I said a lot of things."

"Blood smear?" asked Wickes.

"You said," said Father to me, "'The countdown continues.'"

"It was just one of those things I say," I said. "You know, I have this uncontrollable tongue, and the words just sort of popped out."

"Countdown?" asked Wickes.

"Out of the mouths of gardeners," said Father.

"True," I agreed, "whatever comes. But need I point out that there was a break in the sequence? If there was a countdown, it's been botched."

"How so?" asked Father.

"Break in what sequence?" asked Wickes.

"Babbette Starr was 'minus ten,' or 'dash ten,' or 'whatever,'" I said, counting on my fingers. "Her body was found on Sunday. Then Stella Billowack was attacked on Monday, and her number was 'nine.' Then she came up 'seven' on Thursday morning—or was it Wednesday evening? Hope I'm getting this right."

"The chief's daughter?" asked Wickes. "A 'seven'?"

I understood his astonishment. I, too, would have rated her a "ten."

"But then," I said, holding up my finger as if the next words out of my mouth were going to be significant, "Bucky Buckle turned up with an 'eight' on his stomach—"

"Wait a minute," barked Wickes. "Wait one darn minute. If you mean Buckminster Turnbuckle, he died last week. I saw his body, and I assure you there was no 'eight' on his abdomen."

I shrugged. "There was today."

"Today?" gawked Wickes.

Lieutenant Taper winced, then began rubbing his temples.

"Yes, today," I answered. "So the sequence is broken."

"Nonetheless," said Father, "out of the mouths of gardeners."

"What the hell are you talking about?" cried Wickes.

"Patience, Sergeant," said Father. "Patience."

95

"IN THE DARKEST PAGES of the malign supernatural ..." Father Baptist was reading aloud in the study from a stained copy of *The Vampire: His Kith and Kin:*

> ... there is no more terrible tradition than that of the Vampire, a pariah even among demons. Foul are his ravages; gruesome and seemingly barbaric are the ancient and approved methods by which folk must rid themselves of this hideous pest. Even today ...

"Hm." Father Baptist paused to look at the copyright date. "Let's see: Montague Summers wrote this in 1928, which in the scheme of things is not that long ago." He regained his place and continued:

> Even today in certain quarters of the world, in remoter districts of Europe itself, Transylvania, Slavonia, the isles and mountains of Greece, the peasant will take the law into his own hands and utterly destroy the carrion who—as it is yet firmly believed—at night will issue from his unhallowed grave to spread the infection of vampirism throughout the countryside...

The phone rang.

"St. Philomena's parish," I answered, glancing at the clock.

"This is Sheriff Gilbert in Hemmet," said a gruff voice into my ear. "I'm returnin' a call to a Father Bathtub. Is this some kind of joke?"

"That's Father *Baptist,*" I smiled. "Father John Baptist, and he's no joke."

"Really," said the sheriff. "Gosh darn if I can't read Maggie's handwritin'. No offense, you understand."

"None taken," I laughed. "Father Baptist is right here." I handed him the phone across the desk. "Father Bathtub, it's for you."

Father flashed me a withering glance with his eyes while his mouth said jovially, "Sheriff Gilbert? Yes, yes, an understandable mistake. No problem."

He covered the receiver with his hand and addressed Lieutenant Taper and Sergeant Wickes: "A parish matter—only take a second."

Then back to the phone: "You might remember me, Sheriff. I used to go by the name of Jack Lombard. Yes, that's right: the Dickerson case. Homicide. That was a long time ago. Yes, things certainly *have* changed for me in the interim."

Lieutenant Taper and Sergeant Wickes exchanged glances.

I don't think I mentioned that Bishop Xandaronolopolis and Father Nicanor had left a short while before. They had confessions to hear at St. Basil's. Monsignor Havermeyer had retired to his camper to continue his study of rubrics.

It was almost five o'clock in the afternoon, and dinner was in the works. Millie, refreshed from a long nap, was bashing and clanging pots and pans in the kitchen. The sound of her culinary fury came echoing down the hallway. Lieutenant Taper and Sergeant Wickes had opted to brave Chief Billowack's wrath and stick around. The inevitable result of Millie's frenzied cooking contentions was always worth it. Besides, she had slept right through lunch, and the added component of guilt was goading her to greatness.

"Anyway, Sheriff," Father was saying, "the reason I called was to see if you've seen anything of our Mrs. Magillicuddy down your way—a sweet old woman, though a tad eccentric. She said she was going to visit her sister, Abigail. Oh, really, you know Abigail?"

"Know her!?" squawked the sheriff so loud I could hear him from my chair. "Why, I'll have you know—"

"It really is amazing," said Lieutenant Taper, softly so as not to interfere with Father's phone conversation.

"What is?" I asked.

"How in the midst of everything else, Jack finds time to watch after the forgotten people, his parishioners."

"You've got it backwards," I commented. "It's amazing that he finds time to help you guys find murderers. You forget, this parish is his real work."

"I'm learning," said Taper. "I'm learning."

"Well," Father was saying, "you have certainly eased my mind. Please say 'hello' to Mrs. Magillicuddy for me, won't you? Tell her we miss her, and we're praying for her safe return. Thank-you, Sheriff Gilbert. Good-bye."

"What's Mrs. Magillicuddy up to?" I asked as he set down the receiver.

"Later," said Father, "over dinner. Let's stick to the matter at hand."

"Which is?" asked Taper, sickly.

"Vampires, of course," said Father, regaining his place in the book from which he had been reading:

> ... Assyria knew the vampire long ago, and he lurked amid the primeval forests of Mexico before Cortez came. He is feared by the Chinese, by the Indian, and the Malay alike; whilst Arabian story tells us again and again of the ghouls who haunt ill-omened sepulchres and lonely cross-ways to attack and devour the unhappy traveller—

"Hm?" said Father, looking up from the page. "Larry—?

It was Lieutenant Taper's turn to bolt for the bathroom down the hall.

96

"FRIDAY DINNER JUST ISN'T THE SAME," mused Father Baptist, "without a visit from Mrs. Magillicuddy." He looked wistfully at the French window, the one near his elbow which depicted a golden Chalice with a Dove perched on its rim.

"My water glass isn't the same," agreed the gardener around a final mouthful of Millie's exquisite tuna casserole, "without one of her uprooted plants murking it up. I take it that Sheriff Gilbert knows her sister."

"Abigail," nodded Father, setting down his fork, "is known around Hemmet as 'Aunt Elfie of Mariposa Pass.' He said she's almost a legend in those parts. Talks to trees and wee folk that no one else can see. Apparently some of the townspeople prefer her herbal remedies to the prescriptions of the local doctors—"

"Who wouldn't?" growled Millie, grinding an aluminum saucepan against an iron soup kettle for no reason I could see other than the soothing effect the squeal of metal seemed to have on her nerves. "Have you seen the price of medicine these days? And none of it works. Ask Mrs. Cladusky."

"I don't mean to press the point," pressed Sergeant Wickes, leaning toward Father, "but are you going to explain what that, that—whoever he was—what he was saying about evil hands and bad breath?"

"You mean His Lordship Bishop Xandaronolopolis," said Father, "about vampires?"

"Yes," said Wickes.

"He's a Maronite," snorted Millie, adding a stainless steel frying pan to her metallic concerto. Then she added, "They must be doing well. Father Nicanor's housekeeper has an automatic dishwasher."

"Yes, Jack," said Taper, wiggling his pinkie in his left ear. "My memory's still a blur, but now I seem to have a personal stake in this vampire business."

"Good pun," commented the gardener. "'Personal stake.' Can I use that?"

"Whatever," said Taper, waving weakly. "Jack, for the record—"

"Will you please get to the vampires?" pressed Wickes.

"I'd rather talk about dragons first," said Father.

"Flagons?" yelled Millie over her shoulder. "You should see the set
of fine drinking cups they have over at St. Basil's—not to mention
dishes that actually match!"

"Dragons?" coughed Wickes. "What does that have to do with anything?"

"Oh, dragons," huffed Millie, flinging a spatula up in the air without
missing a scrape of the pans. "A fine thing to discuss over a quiet dinner."

"Quite a bit," said Father, casting a questioning glance at our beloved
housekeeper. Then he turned back to Wickes. "You'll recall, Sergeant,
that I asked you several days ago for your opinion regarding St.
George."

"Not again," moaned Wickes. "I do wish you'd get to the point."

"That's exactly what I'm doing," said Father. "I am like the 'man
building a house, who digged deep, and laid the foundation upon a rock.
And when a flood came, the stream beat vehemently upon that house,
and it could not shake it.'"

"Luke six," interjected the gardener, "verse forty-eight."

"No," said Wickes, slamming down his fork. "No more 'foundations.' Get to the point."

"Don't knock 'foundations,' Sergeant," said Father, "or you will be
like the man who built his house upon loose earth. When the storm
came, the house fell, and 'the ruin of that house was great.'"

"Verse forty-nine," I added, reaching for the salt.

"I don't get you," said Wickes.

"He said," intruded Millie, splaying coffee in all directions, every
drop, as usual, landing in our cups, "'when the storm came, the ruin of
the house was great.'" She slammed the pot down on the table. "Do
you have any idea how the roof is going to hold up around here when
that storm that's hanging over our heads finally lets loose?"

"N-n-no," said Wickes, looking up at her guiltily.

"You got any buckets?" she snarled. "We're gonna need 'em."

"The forces we're dealing with," said Father Baptist, keeping his
composure, "are insidious, powerful, and ancient. To combat them will
take great courage. But before you can engage them, you must believe
that they exist. That, Sergeant, is your weakness. I do not expect you
to suddenly embrace all that I believe, but to send you into battle without an explicit understanding of what you're dealing with would be a
gross dereliction of duty on my part."

"I don't follow you," said Wickes, eyeing Millie as she charged back
to the stove to engage in the next movement of her cacophonous symphony.

"Then try," said Father. "When I asked you about St. George, you
said that maybe the man existed, but certainly not the beast—that there

may have been a historical figure by the name of George, but the monster he killed was of necessity a myth."

"I don't think I said all that," said Wickes.

"But essentially you agree with what I've just presented," said Father.

"... Okay."

"Next I asked you about the Loch Ness monster, and on the basis of books that you've read, all of which contain blurred photographs and conflicting anecdotal accounts by locals, you said you think that something—something unspecified but something nonetheless—dwells in that deep Scottish lake."

"Uh, yes."

"And then, having expressed suspicion over the resurrection of Lazarus, you admitted some knowledge of his sister, Martha's, encounter with Jesus Christ, but nothing of their subsequent activities in France."

"You asked if I'd heard of a dragon in connection with her," said Wickes.

"And you hadn't."

"That's correct."

"Back to dragons," harrumphed Millie, rubbing the rims of two saucepan lids together like cymbals.

"And you wouldn't be likely to believe in such," said Father, "would you, preferring to relegate it to Christian mythology, stories to impress ignorant peasants, that sort of thing?"

"Not my words," said Wickes, "but yes."

"You believe in the Loch Ness monster, but you discount these tales of Saints battling similar things."

Wickes scrunched his lips. "But that was back when, you know, when myths and legends were believed, when science hadn't developed to the point of disproving such things."

"Like the Loch Ness monster," said Father.

"But that's different," countered Wickes. "There are witnesses."

"And there weren't before?" said Father. "Sergeant Wickes, are you even aware of in what country St. George lived?"

"That's easy," said Wickes, picking up a spoon to stir his coffee. "England."

"No," said Father. "Persia."

Wickes set his spoon down abruptly. "Persia?"

"St. George never set foot in the British Isles," said Father. "Because he was a soldier, his fame spread through the Roman ranks. The Romans eventually embraced the Faith, and as their armies were sent throughout Europe, devotion to St. George found a special abode in England where he was declared the Patron Saint of England and of Chivalry. But St. George lived in Persia centuries before that."

"Really," said Wickes, who never seemed to tire of revealing how little he knew.

"Yes," said Father. "He was a native of Cappadocia, and held the military rank of tribune in the Roman army. It was in that capacity that he went to the city of Silena in the province of Libya. Near the town was a lake, and in the lake dwelled a monster which the populace had been unable to kill or drive away."

The sergeant was opening and closing his fingers. "I suppose you're going to say next that this monster breathed fire."

"No, not fire," said Father. "Pestilence. When the beast approached the city walls, people were struck dead by its breath. Whether the agent was a noxious poison or a deadly bacteria is not known, since they did not in those times have the tools to discern these things."

"Aha," sniffed Wickes. "Science."

"But certainly there were many witnesses," said Father, "both to the dragon and St. George's victory over it. The people had taken to offering their children to feed the beast—"

"As is the tendency of all advanced societies," quipped the gardener, "including our own."

"—and the king was particularly grateful," continued Father, "since his own daughter was the next to be sacrificed. St. George's intervention was met with much celebration, and the king built a magnificent church in honor of the event."

"Oh really," scoffed Wickes.

"Afterwards, St. George was imprisoned for his Faith, and later executed by the prefect, Dacian, during the reign of Diocletian and Maximian."

"Hrmph."

"Interesting, isn't it," mused Father, "that the city is known, the characters are remembered in the chronicles of the time, and even the prison still stands where St. George awaited his execution, but the dragon—Heavens!—the dragon can't possibly be true."

"Like I said," said Wickes, "that was a long time ago."

"Oh," said Father, smiling, "time is the culprit? Then you certainly wouldn't believe that there is a city in France called Tarascon which was named after a dragon—"

"Excuse me, Father," said the gardener who had produced a book from somewhere under the mysterious folds of his napkin, "may I?"

"Of course," said Father.

I cleared my throat and read a passage from a tattered copy of *The Golden Legend: Readings on the Saints* by Jacobus de Voragine:

> At that time, in the forest along the Rhone between Arles and Avignon, there was a dragon that was half animal and half fish, larger than an ox, longer than a horse, with teeth as sharp as horns and a pair of bucklers on either side of his body. This beast lurked in the river, killing all those who tried to sail by and sinking their

vessels. The dragon had come from Galatia in Asia, begotten of Leviathan, an extremely ferocious water-serpent, and Onachus, an animal bred in the region of Galatia, which shoots its dung like darts at pursuers within the space of an acre: whatever this touches is burned up as by fire. The people asked Martha for help, and she went after the dragon. She found him in the forest in the act of devouring a man, sprinkled him with blessed water, and had a cross held up in front of him. The brute was subdued at once and stood still like a sheep while Martha tied him up with her girdle, and the people killed him then and there with stones and lances. The inhabitants called the dragon *Tarasconus,* and in memory of this event the place is still called Tarascon, though previously it had been called Nerluc, i.e., black place, because the forest thereabouts was dark and shadowy.

"And what's that prove?" asked Wickes, glaring.

"That there were witnesses," said the gardener, closing the book. "True, a whole city's worth of people agreeing to rename the town doesn't stand up to a few blurred photographs, but I find the evidence compelling nonetheless."

"What was Martha doing in France, anyway?" asked Wickes, and then added, "Supposedly."

"What does anybody do in France?" grumbled Millie. "Eat their meals in peace, one would hope."

"There's obviously much you don't know about her," said Father, eyes on Wickes. "For example, in spite of the poor hovel depicted in virtually all the 'life of Christ' movies, Martha was actually a wealthy woman. Her father, Syrus, was the governor of Syria; and her mother, Eucharia, bequeathed to her daughter three whole towns: Magdalum, from which her sister, Mary, derived her name, two cities named Bethany, and even a hefty section of Jerusalem."

"But if that's so," said Wickes, "what was she doing waiting on Jesus?"

"If you don't understand that," interjected the gardener, "you don't understand the Gospels."

"Well, I don't," said Wickes.

"Agreed," said Father, folding his hands. "You might be surprised that historians of the early Church wrote copiously of the dispersion of the disciples of Jesus after His Ascension. Martha, with her brother Lazarus, and her sister Mary Magdalene, as well as several others, were set upon by the Jews who were persecuting the Christians. They were put aboard a ship without sails, oars, or rudder, and no food—set adrift to perish on the open sea. By God's Providence, they landed safely at Marseilles—"

"They drifted all the way to France?" scoffed Wickes.

"—and set about the conversion of the people living there," said Father. "Lazarus—*Saint* Lazarus—was made Bishop of Marseilles. *Saint* Mary Magdalene retired to a life of contemplation in a cave, which is still preserved to this day. *Saint* Martha, the most famous housekeeper in history, went on to become the most forgotten of dragon-slayers."

"Why do you keep emphasizing the word 'Saint'?" objected Wickes.

"To reinforce a point," explained Father, "that these people were real, and are real, that they continue to intercede on behalf of believers to this day."

"But you were talking about dragons," dodged Wickes.

Father sighed. "Would venerable Saints in Heaven permit myths to be propagated about themselves?"

Wickes scrunched his lips again. "I don't know. What could they do about it? They're dead."

"If you think a man's life ends when he dies," said Father, "then you don't have any grasp of the soul's reality. And for Saints to have untruths attached to their lives would be to kiss the Enemy."

"So you say. I still don't believe in dragons."

"Even though the last one in England was killed in 1416, in a place called St. Leonard's Forest, just south of London?"

"No—I mean, yes."

"And until the 16th century, towns in the Rhineland were still reporting attacks of such beasts, almost always associated with lakes and rivers? If these beasts were not dragons, then what were they?"

"I don't know," said Wickes, adjusting his lapels.

"Even today in the South Pacific island of Kimodo," said Father, "tourists flock to see the famous Kimodo dragons, which are only tiny cousins of the gigantic creatures that used to dwell there."

"Now that's something I know about," cheered Wickes, coming out of his chair.

"Only with the essentials," whispered the gardener, "does our man Wickes fill his mind."

"Those Kimodo dragons are just big lizards," aha-ed Wickes.

"Whose saliva is so thick with bacteria," countered Father, "that the slightest bite is inevitably fatal from infection for which there is no known cure. You scoff at a dragon that breathed pestilence, while believing with ease that giant lizards crawl the earth today that are no less deadly."

"Hrmph," hrmphed Wickes.

Father smiled. "It was long ago, but Psalm Ninety speaks of dragons—"

"But that's symbolic," interjected Wickes.

"—in the same passage quoted by Satan when he tempted Christ:

> If thou be the Son of God, cast thyself down, for it is written:
> That he hath given his angels charge over thee, and in their hands
> shall they bear thee up, lest perhaps thou dash thy foot against the
> stone.

"St. Matthew chapter four, in reference to Psalm Ninety," quipped the
gardener who, you will recall, had been reviewing that same passage the
previous Sunday evening. I quoted aloud:

> For he hath given his angels charge over thee: to keep thee in
> all thy ways.
> In their hands they shall bear thee up: lest thou dash thy foot
> against a stone.
> Thou shalt walk upon the asp and the basilisk: and thou shalt
> trample under foot the lion and the dragon.

"Poetic symbolism," said Wickes.

"The lion and the dragon?" asked Father. "Spoken in the same
breath? Is the lion also a myth? Is therefore Christ a myth, of whom
this prophecy was spoken?"

"Remember that loose soil Father was warning you about," said
yours truly, obliging as usual. "The storm is coming."

"Yes," spat Millie, twirling a huge skillet over her head. "Bring
buckets."

Father folded his hands. "And the things killed by St. George and St.
Martha, what were those?"

"I don't know," said Wickes. "But even if all this is true—and I haven't admitted that it is—I don't see what possible connection there is
between dragons and vampires—and that's what we were supposed to be
talking about, remember?"

"My dear Sergeant Wickes," said Father. "You are a hard nut to
crack. But so be it. Your persistent doubt presents a consuming challenge that I hope to overthrow some day. But you're right, it's vampires we need to discuss. And the most famous vampire of all, fictional
though he may be, is Count Dracula."

"Right."

Father planted his elbows on the edge of the table. "And what, pray
tell, do you think is the derivation of the name 'Dracula'?"

"Oh no," said Wickes.

"Oh yes," said the gardener.

"Dragon," said Father Baptist and I together, sort of like a Greek cho-
rus.

97

"THE NEXT PROBLEM WHICH presents itself," said Father as Millie snatched away the dishes, "is a matter of a little crow-eating on my part."

"Oh?" said Wickes.

"Yes," said Father.

"Eating crow," tisked the gardener, "and on a Friday."

"Speaking of eating," interrupted Millie. "I don't suppose we'll ever get us a regular set of silverware, eh Father?"

"Whatever do you mean?" asked he.

"Well," she said, holding up an assortment of eating implements, "look at what I have to deal with when I wash the dishes. No two forks alike, spoons every size, knives of every conceivable shape. I can't get any speed when I'm scrubbing these things, not if I don't want to bloody my hands."

"I see your point," said the gardener, handing her a cleaver that he'd been using as a butter knife.

"As you know," said Father to Millie, "all these things have been donated over the years."

"Yes," puffed Millie, "one fork per family. Whenever someone gets a new set of tableware, they donate their discards to the rectory. And look at these plates—"

"That's parish life, I'm afraid," said Father, eyeing the clattering mismatched disks in her muscular hands. "No two diameters are equal."

"And since a dishwasher is out of the question—" said Millie, strutting toward the sink.

"It is," said Father.

"Well," she said, tossing the whole shebang into the basin with a resounding clatter, "I suppose I'll just have to make do."

"As all Faithful Catholics always have," said Father.

"Right," huffed Millie, squirting in the detergent and cranking the tap. "Sure. Unless they switch Rites and attend St. Basil's."

Father sighed.

"What was that about 'crow,' Jack?" asked Taper.

"And the consumption thereof?" prodded the gardener.

"Well," said Father, smiling, then frowning, "Sergeant, Lieutenant, you'll recall Martin's reference from Chesterton's Father Brown—"

"'Well,'" I quoted helpfully, "'I do believe some things, of course, and therefore I don't believe other things.'"

"The very one," said Father. "In the beginning of this investigation, I assured you that since certain elements of the evidence pointed to a perpetrator who couldn't possibly be a real vampire —"

"Sodium monofluorophosphate," commented the gardener, also helpfully, "calcium carbonate, propolis, carrageenan, parsley bits—"

"Martin," said Father.

"—and allicin," concluded the gardener, wilting as helpfully as he was able.

"In other words," said Father, "I surmised that what we were dealing with was a man—a madman, to be sure—but a mortal man nonetheless."

"True," said Wickes.

"Surewood Forst," said Taper.

"You're not suggesting he's not our man," said Wickes. "The evidence was conclusive."

"Indeed," said Father. "And evidence continues to come in. He was certainly our man ... up to a point."

"What point is that?" asked Taper. "The second attack on Stella Billowack?"

"It's easier to explain," said Father, producing several creased sheets of acrid-smelling paper from the mysterious folds of his cassock, "if I show you. I have here some topographic scans, courtesy of John Holtsclaw."

"Space-age stuff," said Taper. "The test results I brought by last night."

"Yes," said Father. "Unlike normal photographs, which are subject to, shall we say, subtle and misleading interpretations due to variants in tone and shadow, topographic scans reveal every nuance of an object's complex surface. I understand they're using this technology to make detailed maps of the landscape of Venus."

"The space age comes to the coroner's office," mused Taper.

"Exactly," said Father. "In an attached note, John explained that the originals of these images are eight-by-tens, so he reduced them for my immediate perusal, having a pretty good idea what I was looking for. Now, gentlemen, attend."

I pointed my chin to stretch my jaw sideways, looked at the images spread on the table between Father's hands, and melted silently back into my chair.

1. Kelly, Patricia   2. Stevens, Shelly   3. Alverez, Alicia

"As you can see," said Father, these are the bite impressions of the first three victims. Notice that in the case of Patricia Kelly, there were actually two sets of superimposed teeth marks. I suspect Mr. Forst was clumsy in his first attempt."

"But practice made perfect after that," said Taper a bit greenly, rubbing his temples vigorously.

"The next three victims are similar," said Father.

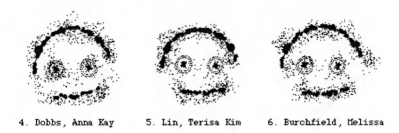

4. Dobbs, Anna Kay   5. Lin, Terisa Kim   6. Burchfield, Melissa

"Very similar," agreed the lieutenant, lips drawn tight.

"And here," said Father, "are Elizabeth Unger, Tiara Stockwell, and the unfortunate little girl, Patricia Marie Nealy. Between number eight and number nine, we have a distinct change in impression."

"Right," said Wickes. "The fangs are where they're supposed to be."

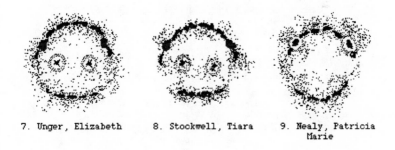

7. Unger, Elizabeth   8. Stockwell, Tiara   9. Nealy, Patricia
                                                            Marie

"There is our point of departure," said Father. "In the case of the Nealy girl, and Babbette Starr, and then Stella Billowack who fortunately survived, the puncture wounds are from canines."

"So Forst had a better set of teeth made," said Wickes.

10. Starr, Babbette   11. Billowack, Stella   12. Cushions, Nannette

"But," said Taper, looking closely, "Nannette Cushions' wounds are like the earlier ones—before the Nealy girl."

"Maybe he lost them again," said Wickes.

"They weren't found on him, or what was left of him," said Taper. "In fact, remember, he denied knowing anything about them, or having killed the Nealy girl or Babbette Starr."

At that moment, this gardener's mind went into overdrive. It cost me:

> *"Now I really don't know what you're talking about,"* Surewood had protested. *"Writing in blood? Nonsense. And I only have one set of fangs. I've even got them on me here somewhere. As for the little girl, I didn't—"*
>
> That's when he stopped in his tracks.
>
> *"Yes,"* sneered Sergeant Wickes, *"tell us about the little girl."*
>
> *"No,"* gasped Surewood, *"I didn't—"*
>
> *"What about Babbette Starr?"* drilled Lieutenant Taper.
>
> *"Babbette?"* said Surewood, growing agitated. *"No. I swear I didn't kill her."*
>
> *"And surely you haven't forgotten Nannette Cushions?"* said Taper.
>
> *"Nannette, well …"* That's when Surewood's face started twitching.
>
> *"Bad enough,"* said Taper, *"that you killed all those women, but that crippled little girl—"*
>
> *"That's one you can't pin on me,"* screamed Surewood, leaping from his chair. *"I had nothing to do with that. Babbette neither. That was ow—oof!"*

"What?" asked Sergeant Wickes.

I realized with a start they were all looking at me. "What?"

"You made a sound, Mr. Feeney," said Millie, pausing in her clatter.

"It sounded like 'Owl,' or 'Alf,' or something," said Taper.

"Sorry," I ahemed. "It must've been something I ate."

"Right!" snarled Millie, resuming her commotion. "After all my hard work—!"

"Maybe someone else has gotten a hold of those new dentures," said Wickes, dismissing me.

"Possibly," said Father, "if they *are* new dentures."

"How could they not be?" asked Taper.

"How can anything be anything around here?" barked Millie, dumping some more liquid soap into the sink. "This place is driving me bonkers."

"Indeed," said Father, glancing toward Millie and then back to Taper, "how could they not? I have here photos of the bite wounds on Elizabeth Unger's and Patricia Marie Nealy's throats. No enhancements, just ordinary photographs."

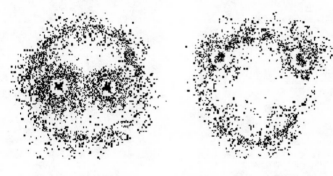

Unger, Elizabeth   Nealy, Patricia Marie

"I remember," said Taper, greener than before. He was going to rub holes into his skull.

"In addition," said Father, "I asked Mr. Holtsclaw if he could do some cross-sections of these bites. I had assumed this would be done by taking tissue samples, but he came up with a process called Magnetic Resonance Imaging."

"I know about that first-hand," I said, rubbing my spine. "Unlike X-rays which are good for studying bones, MRIs show soft tissue. They can slice up your whole body without touching you. Why, they showed me a cross-section of me right about here—"

"Right," said Father. "I'd forgotten you'd had that done, Martin. Well, this is what the assistant coroner came up with."

MAGNETIC RESONANCE SCANS

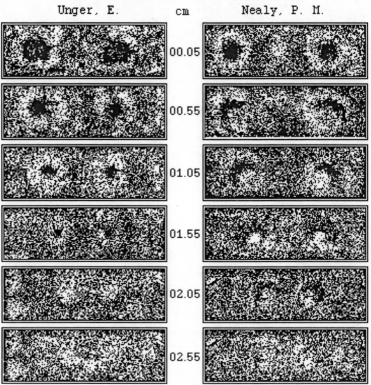

"I don't see anything but blurs," said Wickes, his forehead all twisted into pretzels.

"Ah," said the gardener. "The Loch Ness monster strikes again."

"Neither do I, much," admitted Father. "But the formidable Mr. Holtsclaw, with the assistance of the able Sybil Wexler, also worked up this computer projection. It's much easier to read."

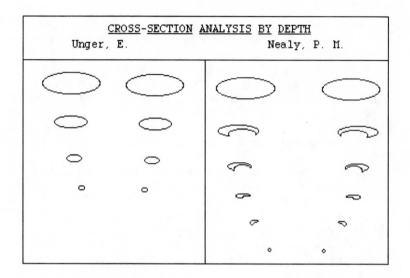

CROSS-SECTION ANALYSIS BY DEPTH
Unger, E.   Nealy, P. M.

"I still don't understand," said Wickes.

"Then I'll explain," said Father. "The fake incisors used by Mr. Forst, which he obviously wore as a bridge over his own front teeth, were conical in shape. When he punctured the jugular vein of his victim with them, they acted as plugs in the wound. He had to pull them out again to allow blood to flow. Then he had to remove them from his mouth so he could press his own lips and teeth against the neck."

"Erg," said Taper, holding his tummy.

"Erg is right," snapped Millie. "Such talk, and in my kitchen, such as it is, which isn't much, but what do you expect—?"

"The teeth that penetrated poor Patricia," said Father, "were round at the gums, but became crescent-shaped as they went deeper, then rounded again at the point. This allowed for the jugular to be punctured, and blood to flow up into the murderer's mouth along the back of the canines. All the murderer had to do was take one bite, then suck with the teeth still inserted."

"Jack," said Taper, wavering like Buzz Sawr in Elza's Sitting Room. "Where's this getting us?"

"To the fact," said Father, "that these new fangs were designed to do the job better than if they were hollow needles. I would suspect, judging from their apparent length, that they are retractable—folding up against the roof of the mouth when the lower jaw is closed."

"So what are you saying?" asked Wickes, eyes wide.

"I'm saying," said Father patiently eating his crow, "that in the deaths of Patricia Marie Nealy and Babbette Starr, we're dealing with a new predator—a genuine vampire."

"You can't mean that," said Wickes, eyes even wider.

"I can and do," said Father seriously. "Events of last night and today, which neither of you witnessed—or remember, in the case of Lieutenant Taper—bear this out."

"The graveyard," said Wickes. "You and your Tumblar pals, and that guy in the costume." His eyes narrowed. "What were you doing out there?"

"Killing a vampire," said Father, almost but not quite nonchalantly.

"Not Buckminster Turnbuckle," glared Wickes.

"Bucky Buckle," winked the gardener. "The same."

"You mean you, you, you just dug him up?" cried Wickes. "Right out there? No permit, no court order, no—?"

"I really didn't see that we had much choice," said Father. "No judge would believe us. It had already attacked Larry, and we couldn't risk letting it get out again."

"But what if the boy's father should, you know—?"

"Exume the body?" asked Father. "Well, it would certainly raise questions, like how did the body crumble completely into dust, including the bones—"

"This is madness," said Wickes.

"No!" roared Millie, wiping her hands on her apron and strutting across the linoleum floor toward us. She pointed to herself, "This, sirs, is mad-ness!" With that, she stomped out of the kitchen and thundered down the hall.

Father looked after her, gulped, then returned his attention to the discussion at hand. "As I was saying a moment ago, Patricia Marie Nealy and Babbette Starr fell victim to a genuine vampire—the teeth marks bear this out. But then Nannette Cushions was murdered by Mr. Forst, the fake vampire, throwing my growing suspicions into confusion. But the fog is now dispersed. The fiend who attacked Stella Billowack, both at the 'House of Illusions' and in the hospital, was not Surewood Forst, but the new enemy."

"Bucky Buckle?" gasped Wickes incredulously.

"No," said Father. "I have every assurance that young Turnbuckle never got the chance to kill anyone."

"So you're saying there's another one?" asked Taper, fingers pressed deeply into his temples, almost penetrating his brain.

"Indeed," said Father. "Gentlemen, we have a real vampire in our midst with which we must now contend. Since this is a direct reversal of my previous suspicion, I went to this extra trouble to convince you of my current conclusion. The first eight murders were committed by

Surewood Forst. After that, with the exception of Nannette Cushions, the real thing took over."

"You're nuts," said Wickes.

"Welcome to the dragon hunt," said Father.

"Should I call our contact at the Griffith Park Stables?" I asked helpfully. "We'll be needing that white stallion."

"As a last resort," said Father. "I want to try some more direct methods, first."

98

"SO WHAT'RE WE SUPPOSED TO DO?" asked Sergeant Wickes as we settled down in Father's study again, mismatched coffee cups full and steaming. "Not that I'm agreeing with you on a single point, mind you—but what do you propose that we do?"

"I don't know about you," said Father, sinking wearily into his chair and picking up his pipe. "I haven't had any sleep since ... I don't recall."

"What about you?" said Wickes, turning to his partner. "You believe all this stuff?"

"About dragons," sighed Taper, "who knows? I'm prepared to take a few things on Faith. As for vampires, I just wish I could remember what happened last night. I keep getting these glimpses, and then—poof!—gone."

"Too little sleep, too much sleep," said the gardener. "No rest for the weary either way."

"And what do you think?" said Sergeant Wickes, shifting his skeptical eyes in my direction. "You believe in vampires?"

"Sergeant," I sighed, "if you spent less time assuming, and more time reading—and not just that popular tripe you pour into your mind, but real thoughts penned by men with a concern for Truth rather than self-aggrandizement—you wouldn't have to ask everyone around you. You'd know yourself."

"Know what?"

I heard a small thump. Father Baptist's pipe had slipped from his hands.

"He's asleep," whispered Taper.

"Maybe we'd better go," said Wickes.

"Where?" asked Taper, sinking down in his chair. "I don't have the strength to move."

"Brother," said Wickes, looking helplessly at me.

"Don't look at me," I said. "I'm as tired as they are, and no, I don't like to play chess."

99

IT WAS JUST BEFORE MIDNIGHT when the phone rang.

"Whub?" I drooled into the receiver.

"This is Jonathan," said the voice in my ear.

"Hm-mmmm," I drifted.

"Martin! Wake up!"

"Wha—? Oh, Jonathan, what is it?" I looked around. Father Baptist and Lieutenant Taper hadn't moved. Sergeant Wickes wasn't there, but I could hear him rummaging around in the kitchen, bachelor that he was.

"Is Father Baptist there?" asked Jonathan. "Oh, my head."

"Yes—he's asleep," I yawned. "Do you know what time it is?"

"Yes. You've got to get down here right away."

"Here? You mean the hospital?"

"Yeah. It's an emergency. Stella's been, been—"

"What, again?"

"Yeah."

"Is she—?"

"She's alive, but ... Look, just get down here—you and Father—right away!"

Saturday, October Twenty-eighth

Feast Day of Saints Simon and Jude,
brothers, Apostles, and Martyrs (67 AD)

100

"I DON'T LIKE THE LOOK OF THIS," said Father Baptist as we came down the corridor toward Stella Billowack's room.   Two policemen were patting the cheeks of another one who was slumped on a chair in the hallway. A nurse was standing nearby struggling to liberate something supposedly helpful from its uncooperative antiseptic plastic sheath.

"Come on, Fred," one was saying. "Snap out of it."

"Hruminuminum?" mumbled Officer Fred, his face lolling from side to side. "Whud hid me?"

"Oh, Jack — I mean, Father Baptist," said one, jumping up as Father Baptist, Lieutenant Taper, Sergeant Wickes, and I arrived.

"Chuck," said Father to the officer. "What happened?"

"That's what I'd like to know," said Officer Charles Martel.   His nameplate shimmered under the sterile hospital overheads.   "Fred here was assigned to guard the door. Chief Billowack's gonna have a cow."

That, thought the gardener, I'd like to see.

"Father Baptist," said Jonathan from the doorway. He was holding onto the frame, zonked. "That nurse ... the coffee ... Stella ... help ..."

Lieutenant Taper caught Jonathan as he slid toward the floor. "Easy," he said. "Easy."

Without another word, Father entered the room with me right behind.

Our attention went first to Stella, who seemed deep in sleep and very pale on the bed. A doctor was at her side, busily attending a plastic pouch of blood that was dripping dark fluid into a tube connected to her arm. I could just make out the gentle hiss of her breathing, shallow and quick. The bandage around her throat had been pulled away, and a fresh trickle of blood from the familiar punctures on her neck was dribbling onto the pillow.

"I need you to check something," said Father to the doctor. "Look at her abdomen."

"What for?" asked the doc.

"If it's there, you'll know."

"If you insist," clucked the doctor, gently and modestly—this was a priest in a cassock, after all!—adjusting her gown until her navel came into view. "My word," he gasped.

The smear was still glistening and sticky.

"Now that," said Wickes, "I'll grant you, was no accidental smear."

"Out of sequence again," I noted. "Skipped six."

"How is she?" asked Father.

The doctor, who had been listening to her heart, removed the stethoscope from his ears. "She's alive but unconscious. Heart racing, pulse shallow. I don't know, she's lost more blood—but with this transfusion, I think she'll be all right." He looked at the oozing wound on her neck. "How in the world—?"

"Pierre," said Father, turning to the Tumblar sprawled on the floor next to the window. He knelt down beside the lad and touched his face.

"Never, on my honor," mumbled Pierre, "has anything fermented of grain or grape ever hit me like that."

"Like what?" asked Father.

"That coffee."

"What coffee?"

"The nurse—she brought us all a fresh pot."

Father reached up and grabbed the hospital-issue plastic pitcher. He sniffed it and set it back on the nightstand.

"Drugged?" asked the gardener.

"I guess so," said Pierre. "One minute we were toasting the American Martyrs, and the next thing I knew—"

"The officer outside, too?" asked Father.

"Yes," gulped Pierre. "She came with a tray of Styrofoam cups. He got one as well."

"You okay for a moment?"

"Of course. I'm on the floor. I'm not going anywhere."

Father rose to his feet and scanned the room again. "It's gone."

"What's gone?" I asked.

"The reliquary. I told Jonathan to keep it on the nightstand."

We looked, stumbling around one another.

"Nope," I said at last. "It's not here."

"And the Rosary," gasped Jonathan, still supported by Lieutenant Taper in the doorway. "It was pinned to her pillow—"

"Also gone," I said.

"Can you describe this nurse?" asked Father Baptist to Pierre, who had managed to claw his way up to a sitting position against the wall.

"Tall," said the wavering Tumblar. "Shapely. Olive skin."

"Was she the kind of person," asked the gardener, "who'd look at home in a garment called a 'djellaba'?"

"I suppose so," said Pierre. "She'd look good in just about anything."

"Marla Grafan," I ventured. "She was tall and beautiful—and would be in just about anything."

"I thought the ring in her nose a bit out of place for a nurse," said Pierre, running his fingers through his hair, "but I figured these days—"

"Yup," I agreed, "these days—"

"Perhaps," said Father. "This does not bode well. Our vampire couldn't enter this room, not with holy objects present—nor guarded by two men protected with scapulars and blessed medals. This means he has enlisted the help of a mortal woman to come in here, drug all three men standing guard, and take the objects elsewhere."

"Is this what you mean, Father?" asked a nurse from the doorway, holding up the little golden vessel. Her name tag said MARIA PILAR ORTEGA SANCHEZ. "I thought I'd seen it in here."

"Where did you find it?" asked Father, walking over to her and accepting the object with due reverence.

"Sitting on the counter at the nurses' station," she said. "I am a Catholic, Father. I remember things like this from when I was little. It looks valuable."

"More than you know," said Father. "Was there a Rosary with it?"

"No," she said, eyes on the vessel in Father's hand, "just that beautiful reliquary, and a pile of garlic."

"How long have you been on duty?"

"My shift began at ten o'clock," she said, glancing around the room.

"Did you see a tall nurse on the floor," asked Father, "dark complexion, with a nose ring?"

"No," she said, thinking hard. "But I've been very busy with several of the other patients."

"I'll have to speak with the other nurses who were on duty," said Father, looking again at the wound on Stella Billowack's neck. "This is unconscionable."

"You said it, Jack," growled another voice. Maria Pilar Ortega Sanchez wilted as the shadow of Chief Billowack filled the doorway. He looked around with those round, deep-set, fatty eyes. His ire came to rest on Jonathan and Pierre. "A lot of good you guys did."

"A lot of good your guard outside did," snapped Jonathan. "Sir."

"Really, Monty," said Father, "no one was expecting a ploy like this." He stroked a strand of limp hair from Stella's forehead. "We must take better precautions."

"Hrmph," grunted Billowack, strings of wiggling phlegm dangling from his jowls. "Officer Fred Staplewhite, you're on report. Officer Martel, you take his place. Taper, Wickes, I want this floor sealed off. No one comes, no one goes."

"Except us," said Father, including me with a wave of his hand. "After I speak with the other nurses, I have to get back to the parish for morning Mass."

"Sure," spat Billowack, "you do that."

101

"SO CAN YOU DO IT?" Father was asking Joel as I came into the kitchen a few minutes before breakfast.

Joel was looking at something Father had sketched on a legal-sized sheet of college-ruled paper. "Sure, I can do it," he said after a moment's hesitation, "but why would you want me to?"

"That can keep," said Father. "The main thing is that you go to the hardware store and get whatever you require. Tell Mr. Wheeler I'll settle the bill this afternoon. I'm sure he'll agree to that. If not, have him call me."

"I'll need some help with all this," said Joel.

"That's what Tumblars are for," said Father, "to assist in time of need."

"I could use some help," said Millie, turning up one of the burners on the stove. "But why waste my breath?"

"The carpet you can pick up from Vinnie Ng," continued Father, glancing at Millie. "He's remodeling the back of his shop—and he'll also provide you with a roll of dry-cleaner's plastic, the kind he packs suits in when they're ready for pickup."

"Sure," said Joel, folding up the sheet four times.

"What's that all about, Father?" I asked, pointing to the instructions Joel was stuffing into this shirt pocket.

"Later, Martin," said Father.

"Are you two staying for breakfast?" barked Millie, suddenly towering in our midst, glaring at Joel and his grandfather, Josef, who was standing beside the dining table, hands in pockets.

"Do," said Father, indicating the empty chairs.

"And what about that sneaky monsignor?" huffed Millie, folding her muscular arms angrily.

"Monsignor Mike's not—" began Joel, but caught himself in mid-protest. "I think I saw him heading across the street."

"Fine," said Millie, fists moving to her hips. "That'll be you, him, him, and Father."

I guess that made me the second "him."

Like a flash, Millie was back at the stove, lifting the lid off a steaming cast-iron pot and slamming it down on the counter where it rolled around a while before slowing to a stop. "There ain't no eggs," she huffed, stirring the contents with a long-handled ladle. "Not with all the festivities and feasting going on around here the last few days. So I'm making 'left-over surprise.'"

"Ah," said Father, "your famous vegetable beef soup. That is a nice surprise for breakfast."

"Especially when there's no beef, either," snarled Millie, dropping the ladle into a bowl and turning her attention to another large vessel in the sink, this one made of aluminum with splayed handles.

"Oh boy," said Father, a hint of anxiety in his voice. "I can't wait."

Just then the phone rang. I snatched it up as Joel and Josef seated themselves clumsily, eyes riveted on our sweet-tempered housekeeper.

"St. Philomena's rectory," I chimed into the receiver.

"I'm only calling a few people," said an old, cracking voice. "Just those I thought I should warn."

"Keep it short," snapped Millie over her shoulder.

"Mrs. Foghatter," I said melodiously. "How nice to hear from you. It's been a while."

"The comet is coming," scraped her sand-papery voice into my ear, "Fanny Mae Wiggings has had another vision."

"Really," I said, watching as Millie squeezed a mighty squirt of liquid detergent into the aluminum pot in the sink. "Has she?"

"She saw it clearly," said Mrs. Foghatter in determined tones. "It's as big as the moon, flames spurting every-which-way, and with a fiery tail as wide as Jupiter. It will land in the Pacific Ocean, and boil it all away."

"What's up?" asked Father.

"Fanny Mae Wiggings has had another vision," I whispered, cupping the mouthpiece with my hand. "A comet this time."

"Oh," said Father, unfolding his napkin.

Mrs. Falkenella Foghatter wasn't actually a member of our parish. She was more of an archdiocesen-wide panic-promoting telephonic prophecy disseminator. Her specialty was doomsday predictions, and her private channel to the future was Fanny Mae Wiggings, though sometimes she relied on other "undisclosed" sources.

I removed my hand from the receiver. "When did Fanny Mae say it would hit?"

"Sometime around noon," shuddered Mrs. Foghatter. "Give or take ten minutes."

"That soon," I said as Millie cranked the hot water spigot. A billowing head of snowy, steaming soapsuds rose within the aluminum pot. "Funny the astronomers haven't noticed its approach. You'd think a sighting like that would make the news."

"Bah!" she spat into my ear. I could almost feel the wet. "What do they know with their telescopes? They can't even guess which way to look."

"Indeed," I nodded. "But you'd think there'd be someone somewhere who happened to have their telescope aimed at the—"

"Potatoes," barked Millie, grabbing a bowl of russets as she whirled away from the sink, letting the water rush and the suds mushroom on their own. Unceremoniously, she dumped the roly-poly tubers into yet another pot—this one stainless steel—in which water was boiling merrily on one of the back burners. "This'll save time," she smirked: "a week's worth of that meddlesome monsignor's meals in one shot."

"Joel," Father was saying to our youngest Tumblar. "I've been meaning to talk to you, about Josef."

"Grampa?" asked Joel.

"Yah," nodded the old man, his angular Adam's apple wobbling up and down like a lopsided yo-yo. "Grampa."

"Yes," said Father. "I'm concerned about him."

"Grampa?" asked Joel again.

"Yah," grinned Josef. "Grampa."

"He may be ninety-three," said Joel, "but he's tough as nails."

"No doubt," smiled Father, "but with all that's been going on around here—"

"The soup!" cried Millie, tossing the empty potato bowl onto the counter with a clang and snatching up the ladle again. "Almost forgot to stir it. Mustn't let it stick."

"Fanny Mae says the steam will cover most of the earth," said Mrs. Foghatter with ever-intensifying syllabic emphasis. "The South Pole will melt, and all the ice will shift north to the Arctic Circle."

"That's going to be some comet," I nodded gravely. "What are we to do?"

"Do you still have the blessed cranberries?" asked Mrs. Foghatter.

"You mean from the last time?" I asked. "The poisonous cloud that the earth was going to pass through, the cloud that erupted from a volcano on Mars?"

"The same," said she, almost gleefully. "You had Father Baptist bless them, like I told you?"

"I'll have to check to see if they're still around," I said, watching Millie throw down the ladle as the rising soapsuds in the aluminum pot overflowed into the sink. "If I remember correctly, they had to be stored in a jar made of green glass. Isn't that right?"

"No," huffed Mrs. Foghatter. "The green jar was for the blessed camphor balls."

"Oh," I said, slapping my forehead. "Silly me. That was for the mutant moth swarm that was going to spawn in the Amazon jungle and eat all our clothes last May."

"No," harrumphed Mrs. Foghatter, her patience slipping. "That was the blue jar. The green jar was for the—"

"Eek!" squeaked Millie, counter-cranking the hot water spigot. The alarming growth of the mound of suds ceased. "Almost lost it."

"Things have taken a dangerous turn," Father was saying to Joel, "now that we know we're dealing with a real vampire."

"Ah," glowered the old man between them, Adam's apple turning sideways. "'Wampyr!'"

"Grampa doesn't speak much English—" said Joel.

"Yah," said Josef, smiling again, A's A bobbing. "Grampa."

"—but he knows what's going on."

"Then surely," said Father, "we should consider keeping him out of harm's way."

"Away from here?" gawked Joel. "No way. Trust me, Father. Grampa wouldn't miss this for the world."

"Yah," nodded Josef. "Mist dah vorld."

"There's one thing I don't understand, Mrs. Foghatter," I was saying into the phone as Millie gripped the handles of the foaming aluminum pot and lifted it out of the sink.

"What's not to understand?" said the voice on the phone. "Anyone with blessed cranberries in their house will be left unscathed."

"It's not that," I said, watching Millie turn her head this way and that, looking around confused. "It's—"

"The potatoes," Millie snarled, "the soup, this soap—"

"You're sure," said Father to Joel. "I couldn't live with myself if any harm befell your grandfather."

"Grampa," smiled the old man. "Yah."

"He and I have already discussed this," said Joel. "He's in. You couldn't drag him away with a herd of wild bulls."

"Are you saying," said Father, "that he fully understands that we're dealing with a vampire?"

"'Wampyr,'" scowled Josef, picking between his front teeth with his thumbnail. "'Bad.'"

"You see?" said Joel. "He hates them."

"'Vrykolakas,'" spat the old man, a piece of thumbnail landing on the table. "We kill, no?"

"I hope so," said Father to Josef, then to Joel: "Okay, it's against my better judgment, but he's in. Be sure he's wearing his scapular."

"Grampa hasn't taken his off in forty years," said Joel.

"Yah," said Josef, grinning again. "Grampa."

"The soup!" cried Millie, turning toward the stove, soapsuds from the pot in her hands slopping all over herself. She looked down as little bubbly trails meandered down her ankles. "Oh dear."

"Maybe Millie needs help," said Joel, starting to rise.

"You stay put!" yelled Millie, more suds slopping. "This is my kitchen! I don't need anybody's help!"

"Sorry," said Joel, settling back down nervously.

"What was that?" squawked the voice in my ear.

"Nothing, Mrs. Foghatter," I answered sweetly. "As I was saying, it's my understanding that comets are made of ice."

"Ice? Ice! Young man, ice doesn't burn!"

"Exactly," I said. "Nothing burns in space. It's so cold, you see, and there's no oxygen. Comets are just big hunks of ice."

"What about the fiery tail? Fanny Mae says it's huge, big as Neptune, and hot enough to vaporize the earth's oceans."

"Jupiter," I corrected her. "You said the tail is as big as—"

"Whatever," creaked Mrs. Foghatter. "So if you're so smart, how can a fiery tail not be a fiery tail?"

"Well," I said, summoning knowledge from a book I'd read years ago, "as I said before, a comet is basically a big chunk of ice. The tail forms as frozen particles are swept back from the head by the solar wind as the comet approaches the sun."

"What are you talking about, Martin?" asked Father.

"Doomsday," I said, checking my watch. "Around noon."

"Solar wind?" wailed Mrs. Foghatter. "What solar wind is that?"

"*The* solar wind," I assured her.

"The soup!" cried Millie, hoisting the pot in her hands until the sloshing soapsuds were even with her eyes. "It's going to stick!"

"No, Millie," I suddenly cried, dropping the phone and leaping from my chair. Well, it wasn't really a leap—more of a maladroit lunge. Okay, a belly-flop. In any case, it was a valiant attempt. A failed valiant attempt, I'll admit, but at least I tried. "Noooo!"

Time downshifted into a crawl as I skidded across the floor—hands outstretched, trying to stop her. As my hair fluttered slowly in the wind, I watched, mesmerized, as Millie poured the pot's contents—soapsuds and all—into the bubbling cauldron of "left-over surprise."

The unappetizing mixture in the cauldron steamed, swelled, heaved itself over the rim, and gushed down the sides. The pooling goop extinguished the gas flames, belched pungent gases as heretofore unacquainted chemicals formed unprecedented exotic compounds, and then scattered into lumpy rivulets which flowed down the front of the stove and spread like lava on the linoleum floor.

I squirmed this way and that as I slid toward the seething stew, hands and feet squealing against the freshly waxed linoleum. Closer, closer, closer. The law of inertia was doing me no favors at that moment. Closer … closer … slower … slower …

Thank Heavens, I finally ground to a stop, my fingers just inches away from the welcoming shores of Millie's "left-over-plus-suds surprise."

"Well," said Millie setting the pot on the counter as time jumped back into overdrive, wiping her hands on her apron as if nothing was amiss, "at least it didn't stick."

"At least," I agreed, crawling back toward my chair, every bone in my body expressing its pain in its own unique way.

"I should have known better than to call someone like you," squawked an enraged electronic voice nearby as the telephone receiver swung back and forth at the end of its wire.

Joel and Grampa Josef maintained a stoic silence as I heaved myself back up into my seat. I looked from them to Father Baptist, who seemed lost in thought, absorbed by the sight of all that nugget-rich ooze spreading across the kitchen floor.

"Leviticus chapter fifteen, verse nineteen?" I whispered.

Father glanced at me and shrugged.

"Well," huffed Millie, sidestepping the catastrophe, snatching up some clean mitts, and grabbing the pot of boiling water from the back burner. "I guess it's potatoes for everybody this morning."

"Yah," grinned Josef, rubbing his hands ravenously together. "Tatos."

"I'm scratching you off my list," roared the prophetic voice of Mrs. Falkenella Foghatter from the phone as I reached for the swinging receiver and set it down in its cradle. "See if I don't care if you don't survive! Ice my eye, do you hear me? Ice my—"

102

"ARE YOU SURE THAT'S WHERE you put it?" asked Father as I threw another armful of stuff out onto my bedroom floor. There was plenty more where that came from. My closet was commodious, and my ability to accumulate debris infamous.

"Has to be," I said over my shoulder. "It's certainly not anywhere else."

One of my quirks, you see, is to keep all the flotsam and jetsam in my closet, while presenting to the rest of the world a bedroom at once clean, simple, and functional. The fact that I was born in late May under the sign of Gemini has nothing whatsoever to do with it. I suspect my great-great-etcetera-grandpapa, Fényi György Szédülök Márton, married a Prussian girl, thus splicing the German compulsion for meticulous file-keeping onto the free-wheelin' ramblin' Gypsy attitude against accumulation of unnecessary accouterments. All that, blended with the fascination all Magyars have for stark, raving insanity—not to mention my birth on the Feast of St. Philip Neri, the "Laughing Saint"—and you've got me, Fényi Márton: Gardener, Chronicler, and Custodian of the Feeney Museum of Disjecta Membra.

My bedroom was unique among the other living quarters in the rectory in that its only door opened to the outside. Situated at the far corner of the building, my quarters provided privacy and a curious but cozy sense of detachment—not to mention a nice new view of the old cemetery. Swell.

Between my bedroom and Millie's kitchen there were three locked and mainly unused rooms, also with doors that opened only to the outside. Closest to my corner, and one of the largest rooms in the rectory, was the old parish library. Much as Father Baptist wanted to reorganize this treasure, he hadn't yet found the time nor the funds to refurbish those moldy old volumes which had been sitting virtually untouched since 1965. That was the year when the pastor, then-Monsignor now-deceased Auxiliary Bishop Eugene Brassorie, forbade his flock to read any book whatsoever published prior to 1962, feeling as he did that anything written before was "unenlightened." That included the Bible, by the way, except for the most progressive translations.

Next came an old windowless storage room where, half a century ago before the Great Coma, they used to store the banners, statues, poles, and everything else connected with the festivals and processions that at one time had been a regular part of Catholic parish life. The same late Monsignor Brassorie, Father Baptist's predecessor, managed to gut this room of its contents without finding any other use for it. It had remained empty ever since. Incidentally, this storage room was directly beneath "Wrecked Room Number Three." It would be put to useful purpose in this story, but that's still coming. Patience.

The third room, closest to the kitchen, was sort of a utility cubicle in which Joel's cousin Ernst had installed a new water heater to accommodate all the rooms upstairs that Joel and his grandfather were currently rewiring—this in addition to the old and somewhat senile basement water heater already in use.

"Almost to it, I think," I grunted, tossing another bundle of unnecessaries over my shoulder.

"Courage, my son," said Father, feigning patience. He glanced around my private domain, scrutinizing every form and shadow: my bed, my nightstand, my aspirin bottle and toenail clippers atop a four-drawer dresser, the bathroom door, my armchair and reading lamp, an old roll-top desk which couldn't be closed because Dad's portable Underwood was in the way. All in all, not much to write home about.

As I said, normally the bedroom part of my life was neat and sparse, except for days such as today when I was gutting my closet and needed to throw all that junk somewhere.

"Aha!" I announced, burrowing like a clumsy gopher. "I can see the tops of the bottles now. Just another couple of layers—"

Amidst the flutter and thuds of flying and landing debris I heard a stiff, spaced, cranking sound. My heart stopped. Father was examining the page I'd left in the typewriter carriage!

> "'And the Light shineth in darkness,'" read Father Baptist from the stained and tattered Bible in his lap as I rounded the patch of gardenias bobbing around the feet of the statue of St. Joseph. A gust of hot, humid air fluttered the edges of the page under Father's hand. "'And,'" he concluded ominously, rolling the covers of the flimsy book closed against the wind, "'the darkness did not comprehend it.'"
>
> It was late in the afternoon, and the sky looked gloomy and threatening. He was seated on the wooden bench in the garden between the church and the rectory, the hem of his threadbare cassock flapping in the sultry breeze ...

"Martin—?" I heard Father say as I extricated the top-heavy cardboard carton from the closet, bottles rattling, and whirled around to dump the bulging, heavy thing onto my bed.

"Yes, Father?" I panted from the effort.

"—you're not writing another book about me, are you?" He was running his hand self-consciously down the front of his somewhat threadbare cassock.

"No indeed," I gulped, engrossing myself in the task of removing the top layer of papers from the carton and arranging them chaotically on the bedspread. "I wouldn't dream of such a thing."

"No?"

"Typing is so much quicker," I assured him, setting the liquor bottles on my pillow for safe keeping. "Besides, agents won't accept handwritten manuscripts anymore."

"I see," said Father. "Are you still shopping your last effort?"

"Yes."

"Any responses?"

"All rejections."

He cranked the page up a little further, and read aloud:

```
     "In this sentence," said Father, hefting the
book in both hands as if it contained the weight
of the world, "is distilled the crux of our situa-
tion.  The Truth has presented itself.  Indeed, it
has intruded into history and is burning fiercely
like a beacon from shore during a ferocious storm,
seeking to penetrate the gloom of our bad will."
```

"This cassock, I admit, is in need of repair," he said, straightening. "But am I really so prolix?"

"Heavens no, Father," I reassured him as I dug deeper into the carton. "The priest described on that page is merely a fictional contrivance. The fact that he talks like you is completely coincidental."

"Then I do talk like this?"

"Oh no, Father. You talk like you."

"Hmm."

"Say," I said, holding out something for him to examine. "Remember this?"

He pondered the words of wisdom in a cheap copper frame that he himself had fashioned the previous June in commemoration of his being ordered by then-Archbishop-now-Cardinal-to-boot Morley Fulbright to add criminal investigation to his duties as a priest.

"I'd forgotten about that," he said presently. "Perhaps it belongs back on my desk in the study. As I recall, Millie didn't like it on the refrigerator door."

> As a dog that returneth to his vomit, so is the fool that repeateth
> his folly.
> —Proverbs XXVI: 11

"Or perhaps," I added as I foraged deeper into the carton's secrets, "it would look good above my antique roll-top desk."

"You mean centered over the typewriter?" asked Father. "Are we both fools?"

"Heavens, no," I smiled. "One of us will do. I don't know why I bother, but it's in me to do so do it I must. I figure that if God didn't want me to keep at it, He wouldn't have preserved Dad's Underwood and given me arthritis to keep me awake at night."

"Utilizing the talents God gave you," he said, holding the plaque above the typewriter to see how it looked, "that's hardly folly."

"Neither is Holy Obedience," I reminded him. "I define talent as 'what comes easy.'"

"Even when we have no idea where our efforts will take us," he sighed, shaking his head and slipping the plaque within the mysterious folds of his cassock, "we both do what we have to do, I suppose."

"I suppose," I said together with him, then added, "It's just that you have your favorite vomit, and I have— Hold everything! Here it is."

Just the feel of the envelope, slightly thicker and heavier than standard stock, and more so the moldy scent as I opened the flap, brought back a conversation held one Thursday morning four months before in the breakfast nook while Father and I perused the morning mail. I had just opened this same envelope, noting the flared, somewhat ornate penmanship executed in reddish-brown ink ...

"*'My dear Father Baptist,'*" I had read aloud, "*'I have been watching your exploits. I have no doubt that you will catch this insufferable murderer within the week. In fact, on my ancestors, I predict it. The time has come for you to meet a worthy adversary. Savor the moment. Expect me for Samhain.'*"

"*'Saw-win,'*" Father had corrected me.

"S-A-M," I spelled it for him, " H-A-I-N."

"*I know,*" he explained patiently. "*It's pronounced 'Saw-win'—the old Celtic feast of the dead ... And how does our ominous friend sign his name?*"

"He doesn't. There's just a wax seal here. Some sort of crest. See?"

"*Hmm. Where was it mailed?*"

"*Better and better,*" I said, turning my attention to the envelope. "*Would you believe Transylvania?*"

"*You're joking.*"

"*No, it's right here on the postmark. 'Transylvania, HY'—that's got to be Hungary.*"

"*Transylvania's not in Hungary, it's in Romania. Let me see that.*"

"Here."

"*That's not H-Y for Hungary. It's K-Y—Kentucky.*"

"*Transylvania, Kentucky?*"

"*Of course. There's a university there.*"

I waved my hands, oblivious. "*Of course.*"

"*No doubt some sort of prank,*" said Father pensively.

"*No doubt,*" I nodded. "*Indubitably. Should I throw it out?*"

"*Never throw anything out until the file is closed,*" he said sternly, "*and even then it's a good idea to keep it a while longer. You never know what may have a bearing on the case, or where the fallout may drift. For all I know, Larry Taper wrote this letter as a joke and sent it to one of his relatives in Kentucky to mail from that post office. But just in case, we'll hold on to it till we're sure...*"

"Martin?" Father Baptist was asking. "Martin?"

"Huh?" I blinked. The letter from Transylvania had somehow moved to Father's hand. "What?"

"You do have a phone out here, don't you?"

"Uh, sure. On the nightstand."

"Which is where?"

"Under that pile there."

"Ah," said Father, shifting a dune of debris to the armchair. "Here it is." As he dialed the number—yes, it was one of those old rotary-type phones—I edged my way over to the writing desk.

"'House of Illusions'?" he said presently, "this is Father John Baptist. I'd like to speak to Mr. Anthony Graves. Oh? Of course, Mr. Graves, sorry I didn't recognize your voice. We met last week on the Farquar Terrace and again last Wednesday down in the— Yes, that's right. Oh, excuse me a moment, would you?" He placed his hand over the receiver. "Martin."

"What, Father?"

"Stop trying to slip that page out of the typewriter without my seeing you do it and pay attention."

"Ulp."

"Listen," he said, still to me, "I want you to go to my study, get out the parish registry, and see if we've got any travel agents among our parishioners. I never travel so we don't have an 'in lieu of' agent, but check the 'occupation' column."

"Why," I asked, "are you taking a trip?"

"No," he answered, "you are."

"Me?"

"You."

"Where?"

"We'll discuss it when I come in."

"When?"

"When I come in."

"No, I mean: when am I taking this trip?"

"We'll discuss that when I come in, too."

"And when will that be?"

"When will what be?"

"When will you be coming in?"

"In a couple of minutes. Now please get going."

Baffled, not to mention disconcerted, I snatched up my aspen cane with the dragon's head handle and lumbered toward the door.

"Sorry about that, Mr. Graves," Father was saying into the phone again. "The reason I'm calling is that last Saturday, when you were showing the police detectives and myself around your establishment, you mentioned a nightclub in Lexington. My assistant, Martin

Feeney, is going to be passing through that part of the country and I thought maybe ... That's right ..."

Oh, I thought to myself as I gripped the doorknob: Massachusetts is it? Lexington and Concord, the Boston Tea Party, one if by land and two if by sea, and all that.

As I swung the door open, my lightning-quick, drizzle-thick mind precipitated the following memory from the previous Saturday:

> *"How long has Portifoy been working here?"* Wickes had asked.
> *"He only started a few days ago,"* answered Anthony Graves, the Toolmaster. *" Tuesday, I think it was ... Portifoy's a weird fellow, but he's a good magician ... I've seen him before."*
> *"Where?"* asked Father.
> *"Back in Lexington when I was visiting the folks last spring. A place called the 'Now You Don't.'"*
> *"Lexington?"*
> *"Yup."*

Hmm, I thought to myself as I pulled the door shut behind me, I can't imagine what the connection is between Lucius T. Portifoy's stint at the "Now You Don't" and that curious letter from some nameless prankster with ancestors he swore by who knew the word "Samhain."

"But," I said aloud as I approached the kitchen door, "much as I hate to fly, if I have to go somewhere, surely there are worse places than Massachusetts."

103

"WHAT DO YOU MEAN, I'M GOING TO KENTUCKY?"

"I mean," said Father calmly as he settled into his chair in the study, "that you're going to Kentucky."

"When?" I planted the tip of my cane between my feet and remained standing.

"Tonight," he said, digging the vomit plaque out of his cassock and setting it gingerly next to the telephone. "Bishop Xandaronolopolis is leaving for Lebanon this evening. Edward is driving him to the airport. I assumed you'd want to go along for a farewell chat with the bishop. Well, you might as well keep on going. I'm going to try to get you booked on a flight to Kentucky around the same time."

"But why? What's Kentucky have to do with Massachusetts?"

"Massachusetts?" he blinked. "Who said anything about Massachusetts?"

"You were talking to that Graves fellow," I said, "about some night club in Lexington."

"Oh," laughed Father. "Now I see. You're thinking of Lexington, Massachusetts. You forget there's also a Lexington in Kentucky. Actually, the last time I looked, there were twenty-two cities of that name in the United States."

"Really. When was that, Father?"

"When was what, Martin?"

"The last time you looked."

"Two days ago, after our visit to the prison. You mentioned Samhain in the car on the way home. That got me thinking."

"I thought you were already thinking, Father."

"Well, it got me thinking even more."

"About Kentucky?" I asked, rolling my eyes. They needed their exercise.

"About a number of loose ends," said Father.

"Hrmph," I hrmphed. "So what am I supposed to do in Lexington, Kentucky? Check out the 'Now You Don't'?"

"That, and a few other things I'm going to write out for you."

"Swell."

"What's your problem?" he asked as he wrote the number "1" at the top of a sheet of paper, circled it, and then started scribbling instructions across and down the page.

"Aside from the fact that I hate to fly, everything."

"Oh?" he said, underlining something three times. "I didn't know you have an aversion to flying."

"You wouldn't," I said. "We've never gone anywhere that required leaving ol' terra firma. For the record, the thought of soaring four miles above the earth at several hundred miles an hour makes my teeth soft. Can you imagine stalling at that altitude? Why, by the time the plane hit the ground, it would be going twice that speed—"

"Martin," said Father, circling a "2" and starting another paragraph, "you're not afraid of flying, you're afraid of dying. It'll do you good to say the Rosary under those conditions. It gives the phrase 'now and at the hour of our death' a whole new dimension."

"Fine, make jokes," I huffed. "So I'll fly, and maybe I'll die, but that's not what really bothers me."

"And," said Father, putting down his pen and folding his hands, "you're about to tell me what that is?"

"I am."

"Proceed."

I leaned forward and rested my knuckles on the desk. This was not a comfortable position for my spine to assume, but I deemed it appropriate under the circs.

"Father, something awful is going down. This fiend, whoever he or it is, is getting closer and closer. Bishop Pip knows it, you know it, the Tumblars know it—heck, even Sergeant Wickes knows it, if he'd just stop insisting on acting contrary to his own common sense. Lieutenant Taper knows it even if he can't remember, and so do I. Now don't get me wrong: I'm so scared I can't think straight. For five years now I've never refused to do anything you've told me to do."

"Oh?" asked Father, leaning back in his chair. "Let's not go overboard."

"Mostly never," I corrected myself.

"Let us say, 'rarely,'" said Father, "and pray that lightning doesn't strike."

"Whatever," I said, "you know what I mean."

"Surely. You mean that you do what I say on those occasions when you don't refuse to do what I say."

"Close enough," I nodded.

"Fine," he nodded back. "Please continue."

"For five years now," I said, taking a deep breath, "I've been your chauffeur, your valet, your right-hand man, your chief cook and bottle-washer when Millie's away—"

"Not to mention my chronicler," said Father Baptist, now on guard against all prolixity.

"But now," I persisted, "as absurd as it may sound, I am also a Knight. No doubt everyone who ever took the Oath, from St. George to St. Thomas More, from King Arthur to Blessed Charlemagne, are splitting their sides in Heaven at the very thought. But, all mirth and astonishment aside, I am just as much a Knight as any of them."

"Yes," said Father. "I am aware of that."

"And you're also aware of the *Ten Commandments of Chivalry* to which I swore my assent only a few days ago."

"Indeed, along with the Tumblars."

I shoved myself up to a straight posture. My spine responded accordingly. "Then surely you remember article five: *Thou shalt not recoil from thine enemy.*"

"Of course I remember it," said Father. "I translated it from the Latin text myself, just for the occasion."

"Then don't you see?" I said earnestly. "If I go flying off on some errand just when the going gets tough—to Kentucky, of all places!—the others will see it as an act of cowardice."

"I don't agree," said Father.

"Yes, they will," I countered firmly. "They're fine lads, and I'd trust them with my life; but they're also young and prone to making snap judgments."

"Like the other night," he said, "with respect to your taking the pledge."

"Yes," I grimaced, still smarting from the thought.

"I confess that I'm surprised. What they might think, and what you and I know, are two different things."

"Not in this case," I corrected him. "The two become one thing: cowardice."

"They do?" asked Father. "If a job needs doing, and I ask you do it, and you comply even though the thought of flying terrifies you, where's the cowardice in that?"

"But the Tumblars—"

"Are half your age," said Father, "and not suffering from arthritis. Surely you don't doubt their opinion of you?"

"Well ..."

"Then you're being foolish. I can assure you that those young men regard you with the highest esteem. They gave you that cane, didn't they? They include you in their 'events,' eh?"

"And my ancestors?" I asked, drawing myself up a little taller. It hurt.

"No doubt they revere them as well."

"No, I mean Fényi Márton. What will he think?"

"No doubt he prays for you daily, wherever he is. As do I. If, as we surely hope, he is in Heaven, then he, too, will know the truth of the matter."

"But Father, why send me on some innocuous errand? Why not send Sergeant Wickes? Why not just call one of your police contacts? Why me, just when things start heating up?"

"First, Martin," said Father, picking up his pen again and circling a "3" on the next available line, "this isn't just an errand: it's a mission—a reconnaissance, if you will. If you know your military history, you'll recall that many men have lost their lives on such maneuvers. Whatever you may think, flying miles above the earth at several hundreds of miles per hour is as dangerous as anything you're likely to do around here for the next couple of days."

"But—"

"Second, this mission is anything but innocuous. That's the wrong use of the word anyway, but never mind. Let your editor correct it when you get your manuscript published. I need some information that's vital to solving the problem at hand. This mission is essential to our success."

"But—"

"Let me finish, Martin. Third, I cannot send Sergeant Wickes because he is not mine to command. I am acting as a consultant to the police, and though I can request lab tests and cajole a few clerks into slipping me information, I have no actual authority. Besides, even if I could pull the necessary strings, I wouldn't send Wickes. I need to send an agent upon whom I can rely."

"You can't trust Wickes?"

"Not for anything which impinges on matters of Faith, no."

"And what about this 'mission' intrudes upon the Faith?"

"Just about everything," said Father, scribbling away.

"Okay," I said, sinking into my chair. "How long will I be gone?"

"A couple of days."

"A couple, meaning 'two'?"

"You know I insist that words mean what they say," said Father. "Though in this case, it is possible that the term of your stay in Kentucky may fall under the fourth definition in the dictionary, namely 'an indefinite small number,' rather than the first, which is 'two.'"

"Okay, okay," I sighed, struggling to my feet. "I'd better start packing."

"Yes, you should," said Father, "but first, did you find out if we have a travel agent in our parish?"

"Judith Richards," I said. "That's her phone number on the pad by your vomit plaque."

"Good work," said Father, snatching up the receiver and dialing. "You can get a couple of suitcases out of the utility closet and start organizing your necessities."

"For 'an indefinite small number' of days?"

"Right," he said to me, then to the phone: "Oh, am I speaking with Judith Richards? Excellent, this is Father Baptist at St. Philomena's. Yes, thank-you, that was one of my better sermons—"

"Too prolix," I snorted as I stomped out of the room.

"—though perhaps, I've been told, a bit on the long side. Well, you know how some people are. Anyway, I want to arrange a flight, this evening if possible, for my assistant, Martin Feeney. That's right, the crotchety fellow with the cane. Yes. How do we get him to Lexington, Kentucky—? TWA would be fine. Uh-huh, uh-huh, stop-over in Dallas? Hmm. And how much will it cost?"

I didn't hear the rest.

104

"AH, FATHER BAPTIST," Bishop Xandaronolopolis was saying as I tossed my suitcases into the back compartment of Edward Strypes Wyndham's van, which was idling at the curb in front of the rectory. "Know you not how eventful my stay in your City of Angels has been?"

"I'm afraid your stay may have included more than you bargained for," apologized Father.

"Yes," said Father Nicanor to his superior, "you came to bestow Knighthood on some young gentlemen, and got involved in a vampire hunt."

"Nonsense," said the bishop. "Most stimulating, this has been."

"'Terrifying' would be my word," said the gardener who was not exaggerating. Fear was pervading my nervous system, upsetting all my physiological functions, and would continue to do so throughout the next several chapters.

"Martin, Martin," said the bishop, placing his hand on my arm. "This, the stuff of life is. Oh, if only you knew how much it is that I wish I could remain here in the land of cheeseburgers and the French fries to join in the hunt of the 'vurkolak.' Alas, my duty lies elsewhere."

"Mine, too, apparently," I grumbled, looking at Father. "According to the encyclopedia, I'm going to the land of horse racing, bourbon, and tobacco." The last I didn't mind, the middle I couldn't touch, and in the first I had no interest whatsoever.

"How are we on time?" asked Father, insensitive to my ire.

"Tons," said Edward, consulting his watch. "It's only eight o'clock. Why Martin insists on getting to the airport so early is beyond me."

"I've heard tales of airports," I said in my defense.

"And true all of them are," said the bishop. "Know this I do, from vast experience."

"Besides," I said, "isn't there a bar right in the middle of the airport that rotates once every hour? Sounds like a good place to tremble in style."

"Yes," said Father Baptist, "but I doubt they serve Saint Thomas, Salisbury."

"Yeah," said Edward, "I bet they don't serve ginger ale at all."

"Oh," I grimaced, "that bartender's trick."

"And what is that?" asked the bishop.

"My Lord," I explained, "some unscrupulous bartenders don't bother keeping a supply of ginger ale because it's not in great demand. When someone like me comes along and orders it, instead of saying, 'Sorry, I'm too cheap or short-sighted to have that in stock,' they just add a shot of Coca-Cola to a glass of Seven-Up."

"God in Heaven," said the bishop, wringing his tongue in disgust.

"Believe it or not," I added, "most people can't tell the difference."

"In these United States," he answered, "believe anything, I can."

"Excuse me," intruded a voice from the top of the steps.

"Millie!" said the bishop, turning and going up to her with his arms open wide.

In a flash I considered leaping up the stairs and throwing myself between them. Who could imagine what antisocial behavior our Millie was likely to exhibit at this tender moment—especially in light of her "suds-plus-left-overs surprise" a few hours before? Oh well, still aching from my last valiant attempt, I stayed put and watched as the bishop's outstretched arms engulfed our housekeeper in a warm, affectionate embrace. He was not met with grenades and explosions. In fact, she actually cowered a bit, unused as she was to such open affection. She even managed to smile—sort of.

"I just wanted to say thank-you, Your Lordship," she said, curtseying in the midst of his giant bear hug, "for the beautiful silver Crucifix, which I will cherish always by keeping it over the sink because that's where I spend most of my time."

"Dear woman," laughed the bishop, releasing her, "your kitchen is your shrine."

"Thank-you," she said a bit quizzically, not sure what he meant by that. "Oh, and Father Baptist, there's a phone call for you—someone at Police Headquarters."

"I'd better take that," said Father, bounding up the stairs and charging through the front door. "Thanks, Millie."

Edward and I continued rearranging the bishop's assortment of baggage in the back compartment of his van. No matter which way we stacked the suitcases, when mine were folded into the mixture, they didn't seem to want to fit.

Presently, we heard Father Baptist emerge from the rectory and descend the stairs. I could tell by the sound of his shoes that something was up.

"We're going to make a detour," said Father, "so we'd best get started."

"Where to?" asked Edward.

"'The House of Illusions,'" said Father. "There's been another murder."

"Who this time?" asked the gardener as Father Nicanor and I helped Bishop Pip into the van through the sliding side door. "Anyone we know?"

"Roland Reginold Ryan," said Father, getting into the front passenger seat. "Also known as Reginold the Reiterator. Mr. Graves found him in the basement. The police are also on their way there."

"Now that's a switch," said I, allowing Father Nicanor in before I attempted the procedure myself. "Another break in the pattern."

"How so?" asked Father Nicanor, generously taking the rear-most seat so that I would end up sitting beside his bishop on the middle bench.

"Barring poor Buckminster Turnbuckle, who took his own life, all the victims so far have been women."

"Indeed," said Father Nicanor. "Our vampire's tastes have changed."

105

ROLAND REGINOLD RYAN, also known as Reginold the Reiterator, even as he lay there on the basement floor, an ugly wound on his neck, still seemed to look down condescendingly at the world.

"Dead," I must have said without realizing it.

"Brilliant, Feeney," said Wickes, who was standing beside me, flashlight in hand.

The body was stretched out on the bare concrete near a locked cabinet marked CAUTION: ELECTRICAL HAZARD, a half-dozen turns from Mr. Graves' little hideaway.   Mr. Graves, who looked grave indeed, was standing a few feet away, explaining the discovery to Chief Billowack.

"That's right," the Toolmaster was saying.   "The parking valet informed me that Mr. Ryan's car—"

"Make?"

"Ford, I believe."

"Model?"

"I think it's a Thunderbird."

"Color?"

"Reddish."

"Red?"

"Okay, red. I don't see how this—"

"Just answer my questions," snorted the chief. "Then what?"

Mr. Graves sighed wearily and continued.   "The valet said that Reginold's car was missing from the parking lot.   Presuming it had been stolen, and, reluctant to leave his post at the front of the building, he—"

"He gotta name?" grunted Billowack.

"Miguel," said Mr. Graves. "I don't know his last name."

"Go on."

"He asked me—"

"Who asked you?"

"Miguel. He asked me to see if Mr. Ryan was still on the premises. His punch-card had not been clocked out, so I came looking."

"And you found him right here?"

"Yes."

"And you didn't touch anything?"

"No. I went straight up to the reception desk and phoned you."

"Hrmph," hrmphed Chief Billowack, brilliant interrogator.

"Odd," Lieutenant Taper was saying, kneeling beside the body, surgical gloves on his hands.

"What?" asked Father.

"He was hit on the back of the head, Jack.   Quite a gash, but not enough to kill him, I think."

"So he was struck from behind, and then drained of blood."

"Right."

"Hmm," said Father. "One more thing to check. Will you do the honors?"

Larry Taper, rubberized fingers squeaking, deftly undid first the buttons on the black vest, then the studs on the dress shirt beneath. Even before he peeled the white fabric back, I could see the outline of the gruesome number scrawled on the reiterator's stomach:

"'The countdown continues,'" said Father, quoting a certain gardener. "It's almost as if—"

"I don't like being played with," bellowed Billowack, towering over the scene like Reptilicus licking his chops at Copenhagen. "When we nail the guy who did this—"

Suddenly, the room exploded with a blinding flash.

"Got that?" asked Jacco Babs.

"Got it," said Ziggie Svelte.

"Got 'em?" barked Billowack five seconds later.

"Got them," answered Lieutenant Taper and Sergeant Wickes.

"You're under arrest," said Billowack, poking Jacco Babs in the stomach with his stubby finger.

"Not again," moaned Jacco.

"I told you," whined Ziggie, "we shouldn't't'a come here."

"Has it really been all of seventy-two hours since we arrested you last time?" asked Wickes.

"Less," said Ziggie. "They let us out a few hours early for good behavior."

"Too bad you guys didn't learn," said Wickes. Then to the chief: "Material witnesses again?"

"Yup," said Billowack. "Put 'em on ice."

"What about the body?" asked Father. "Who's going to examine it with Wong and Holtsclaw out of town?"

"Wong and Holtsclaw," said Billowack, "when they get back."

"That's crazy," said Father. "We need to get some tests run immediately—"

"That's the breaks, Jack," snarled the chief. "Those are the shots, and I'm not shootin' 'em."

"My camera," shouted Ziggie. "I mean, it's the paper's, not mine. It's the third one you've impounded this week."

"Yup," sneered Billowack. "We've got quite a collection."

"But they're gonna start taking it out of my pay," whined Ziggie.

"Too bad," said Billowack. "Get 'em outta here, will ya?"

"Martin," said Father, taking me aside, "we'll make our good-byes now. I'll have Larry drive me home later. The bishop has been waiting out front long enough, and you don't want to miss your flight."

"But Father—" I said.

"You've got the list of things I want you to check out?"

"Yes, but—"

"And your Rosary?"

"Yes, but—"

"Just remember, Martin: the landing is the most dangerous part of the flight."

"Thanks for reminding me, Father. Can I at least have your blessing before I go?"

"Indeed," said Father, making the Sign of the Cross on my forehead with his thumb. "Now get going, and keep me posted."

"Right," I grumbled as I headed for the stairs. "Sure."

"Now, Larry," Father was already saying to the lieutenant, "in lieu of an autopsy or blood tests, we at least need to check out ..."

I felt very lonely as I made my way through the winding hallways of the "House of Illusions," and without Elza's sweet piano-playing to guide me.

"Zan-dar ..." I mumbled to myself as I lumbered this way and that, hoping I'd eventually find my way to the front door, where waited Edward's van and a bishop within whose name I had yet to pronounce. "... oh-no ... lo-po ... lis.

"Zan ... darrow ... no-lo ... police.

"Zandar ... o-no-lo ... puh'lease.

"Zandaro ... no-lo-po ... lease.

"Zan ... darono ... lopolis.

"Zan-dar-ono-lopo-lis.

"Xandaronolopolis.

"Xandaronolopolis.

"Xandaronolopolis.

"Gottit."

106

"TARZAN-NO-DRANO-POLICE," I said confidently as I poked my head through the open side door of Edward's van, which was parked near the valet station and the space-egg phone booth.

"Nice try, Sir Martin," answered the bishop with a look most people reserve for the mentally impaired. "Stick with 'Bishop Pip' you should."

"Father Baptist sends his regrets," I said, turning over in my mind how the bishop's name had come rolling out of my mouth and realizing I'd botched it, "but his attention is now consumed with yet another murder. He has suggested that we go on to the airport without him."

"Ah," said Father Nicanor, sliding out of the lonely back-most seat, circling around me, and hopping up into the passenger seat in front. "Then I will ride, as you say, the 'shotgun.'"

"And I," said Edward, gunning the engine, "will whip the horses."

"And we," said the bishop, motioning for me to sit beside him, "will chat on the way."

I crawled in, and off we went.

"So, this murder," said the bishop, settling back on the bench seat. "Tell me."

"A great big fellow named Reginold," I said, biting my tongue on the name as Edward went over a speed bump. "Bitten on his neck, like the Nealy girl last weekend."

"This, in a mansion of magicians?"

"Yes. As you well know, parlor tricks don't work against vampires."

"Hm," said the bishop, looking up at the sky through the window. "The 'Shroud' above, it is still there. The 'vurkolak' still walks."

"Pardon my asking," I said, "but if and when Father Baptist gets this vampire, how soon will that 'Shroud' disperse?"

"Practically at once," he answered.

"Really," I said. "I mean, when you consider that this weather pattern is caused by several major storms colliding over our heads, you can't expect it to just — *Ffft!* — go away, can you?"

"The 'Vampire's Shroud,' it is not subject to the whims of your weathermen. Believe me, Sir Martin, when the 'vrykolakas' dies, the stars you will see."

"Right," I said. "Sure."

"Heavy your heart is, Sir Martin," said the bishop, his tone dropping half an octave.

"Yes, Your Lordship."

"But why is this? You are off, as you say, to the land of Kentucky. This is a place to which I have never been."

"Care to trade?" I winked.

"Alas, no. Duty, it calls. Dangerous missions are for the young."

"My mission is hardly what you'd call dangerous, My Lord."

"I repeat: Dangerous missions are for the young. Your fellow Knights, they are in for, as you say, a 'tough time.'"

"That they are," I agreed.

"And this troubles you. You are concerned for them."

"Well, yes."

"But also for yourself, I see."

"For myself? What's to be concerned about? I'm just checking out a few loose ends. I don't see the point."

"Father Baptist, he sends you to do this, to check out these loose ends?"

"Yes."

"Has he not said that to everything he does there is a point?"

"Yes."

"And now the point you do not see?"

"No, I mean yes."

"And so doubt him, now, do you?"

"Well ... that is ..."

"Ah," said Bishop Pip, "he sends you away, you think, out of danger's way?"

I heaved my shoulders. "I guess so."

"His love for you—in this you see no point?"

"Well, when you put it that way—"

"How better to put it?"

"I don't know."

He sighed deeply. "Sir Martin, you are troubled by that which should gladden your heart."

"I never said I was consistent."

"No," he agreed, "this you have never said."

We traveled in silence for a while.

"Of flying," he said presently, "of this you are afraid?"

"Very much," I admitted. "Though Father Baptist pointed out I'm more afraid of dying."

"Aren't we all?" chuckled the bishop. "Aren't we all?"

"You?"

He pointed to his chest with his thumb. "'The root of wisdom,' said the son of Sirach, 'is to fear the Lord.'"

"Ecclesiasticus," I agreed, "first chapter, verse twenty-five."

"You know the Bible well, Sir Martin."

"I try, My Lord. Anything to avoid servile work."

"Yes," he winked, "you are most trying. I wish my wisdom, born of fear, could be of service to you now. Have you ever thought of becoming a priest?"

"Yes, when I was young and foolish."

"And now that you are older and more foolish?"

"Naw," I shook my head. "Too much water under the bridge. I'm far too set in my ways, not to mention unworthy in my ways."

The airport was coming into view.

"We will be parting now," said the bishop, reaching into the folds of his robe. "A gift I have, a token of my high regard it is, for this gardener who is so 'grim' and 'dour.'"

I blinked. Where had he heard that? "Don't forget 'crotchety,'" I said.

"Never," he said, handing me something wrapped in a black cloth. "No, open it not until high up in the sky you are, above even the 'Shroud.'"

"My Lord," I said through a tight throat, "I don't know what to say."

"You know," he said, shifting his weight around on the seat, "Father Nicanor, wise as he is, experienced that he is, has never himself stalked and killed the 'wampyr.'"

"Really," I said, observing the shape of the back of Father Nicanor's head. "I kind of assumed he had."

"No," smiled the bishop. "And when I sent him here to the land of cheeseburgers and the French fries, dream I did not that it was for this purpose."

"Indeed," I said, realizing after I'd said it how much I had intoned the word as Father Baptist so often did.

"Never forget, Sir Martin," he said, "that a mighty Hand guides our lives. Go to this Kentucky, and do as Father Baptist has asked. Know you do not what will come of it, nor to what end God's Purpose is pushing you."

"I'll try to keep that in mind, My Lord."

Edward pulled the van up to the curb in front of the TWA terminal, and we busied ourselves with unloading, checking in our luggage, and examining display screens in search of gates. My last sight of Bishop Xandaronolopolis was his head disappearing amidst the throng under the sign that announced INTERNATIONAL DEPARTURES.

"And I never pronounced his name right," I sighed as I headed for my own gate. "Xandaronolopolis."

"What's that you said?" asked Edward, who had decided to come along and wave as I stumbled through the metal detectors.

"Nothing," I said, waving back. "Thanks for the lift. I'll see you in a few days."

"Right," he said, turning and weaving his way through the oncoming stampede of agitated travelers.

107

"THE SEAT BELT SIGN IS OFF," said the captain's voice over the inter-com, two and a half Rosaries later. "I apologize for the turbulence we encountered as we came up through that dense cloud cover over Los Angeles. Feel free to wander about the cabin, but be advised that we'll be in for some bumpy weather coming into Dallas. Air Traffic Control advises that Hurricane Sidney is still buffeting the Gulf Coast. We hope you'll enjoy your flight, and thank-you for traveling on TWA."

"Would you care for anything, sir?" asked the perky stewardess.

"I don't suppose you have ginger ale?" I asked.

"I'm sorry," she said. "But you know, I can mix a little Coca-Cola with Seven-Up and you'll never know the difference."

"Fine," I said wearily. "I'll have that."

My untouched drink bubbling in a plastic cup, the constant turbu-lence wobbling it around on the fold-down tray, I reached inside my jacket and pulled out the black bundle the bishop had given me en route to the airport. Slowly, I unraveled the cloth.

A small circular golden container emerged, along with a folded piece of stiff paper. How the vessel got through the airport's metal detectors was beyond me—whether by some malfunction in the scanners, some quality of the black cloth in which the vessel was wrapped, or a move-ment of that Hand the bishop had been talking about. In any case, it hadn't set off the buzzers.

I peered into the little glass window of the golden reliquary. Mounted in the center of a circle of red satin was something that looked like an insignificant wooden splinter. Beneath it was the abbreviation on a tiny white piece of parchment:

S. Coron. Spin. D. N. J. C.

Curious, I turned my attention to the unfolding of the piece of paper. It was a document, bordered in twirls, a seal impressed in the lower right corner:

POSTULATOR GENERALIS
CONGR. S.S. RED.

"'Ominibus has litteras inspecturis,'" I read in whispers, "'fidem facimus ac testamur, nos ab authenticus reliquiis particulam desumpsisse ...'"

"Would you like some more ginger ale?" asked the stewardess.

"What?" I said, distracted. "Oh, no thank-you."

"My," she said, leaning close, "that's an interesting souvenir. Is it something from Disneyland?"

"No, nothing like that."

"It's beautiful," she said. "And, I don't know, it makes me kind of sad for some reason."

"More than you know." I crossed myself with the reliquary and kissed its tiny window. "This is a chip from the Crown of Thorns that Jesus wore on Calvary."

"Really? You don't mean—?"

"Yes. *The* Crown of Thorns."

"But I thought, I mean, you don't really think—"

"This is the documentation," I said, holding up the certificate of authenticity. "It is genuine, I assure you."

"Golly, I didn't know they had it somewhere. I mean, I thought—"

"Indeed. Are you an 'ex'?"

"No," she smiled, "I'm too old to be one of the 'X Generation.' My youngest sister is, though."

"I mean, are you a fallen-away Catholic?"

"No, but my dad was."

"Ah, so you're an 'ex' of an 'ex,'" I observed. "An 'ex' once-removed."

"How can you be an 'ex' of something you never were?" she giggled. "Neither of my parents went to church, and they didn't force their beliefs on us kids. They said I could choose when I grew up."

"So did you?—choose, I mean."

"Sure. I'm into the 'Church of the Inner Mind.' I've found great peace there. We're all so ... *eternal* ... you know?"

"Yes," I said, clutching my Rosary a little harder, "I'm afraid so."

"So why'd you ask if I was a former Catholic?"

"Oh that. Well, until recently, I could usually spot 'em a mile away."

"Really? Are you psychic?"

"No," I said. "Practicing."

"You're practicing to be psychic?"

"No, I'm a practicing Catholic. Believe it or not, there are a few of us left."

"Really," she said, winking and straightening. "I didn't know that."

"Now you do," I said, wrapping up the bishop's precious gift.

"You want some pretzels?"

"I'll pass."

She moved on up the aisle as the plane heaved a metallic sigh and climbed into the night.

Sunday, October Twenty-ninth

Feast of Christ the King

Feast Day of Saint Narcissus,
Bishop of Jerusalem, Pastor of Souls,
who died at the age of 116 (222 AD)

108

WELL, WHAT CAN I SAY? I landed at Bluegrass Field Airport, five miles west of Lexington, around four in the morning—that's LA time, or 7 AM Eastern—something on the order of ten rounds of the fifteen-decade Rosary later. My cab went by one of the entrances of Transylvania University on the way to my motel, The Best Western Roundup, where I fell into bed and spiraled downward into a fitful and all too brief sleep.

Shortly before ten, Kentucky Fried Time, I got directions from the desk clerk to the nearest Catholic Church. The Mass was a full-blown Novus Ordo affair, complete with a five-woman Bob Dylan look-alike music ministry. I'll bypass the details.

Back at the motel, I made a few calls, summoned a cab, and went about my mission. The intricate details of my afternoon, without a projector and three carousels of slides, would just consume a lot of pages and not move the story along much.

I did call Father Baptist that afternoon. The conversation went like this:

"St. Philomena's."

"Yippie-tie-oh-tie-yay!"

"Martin? Is that you?"

"Yes, Father. I tried to time this call so you'd be finished with lunch."

"I am. In fact, I'm curled up here in my study with Parson's *Studies in Church History*. I'm up to Volume Three: the 15th and 16th centuries. How about you?"

"Kentucky Highlights," I said, travel brochure in hand. "Did you know that Kentucky was part of Virginia before the American Revolution, and that originally it was going to be called 'Transylvania' because it was the 'woods across' the Allegheny Mountains?"

"Is this what you called to tell me?"

"Yes. Well, no. I just wanted to know how you are ... and Millie, uh, is she, um, still 'Leviticus chapter fifteen verse nineteening'?"

"That I can't answer," said Father, "because I don't know if that's what's causing her ... flare-ups."

"Well, at least here in Kentucky there's more to eat than potatoes."

"Glad to hear it," said Father.

"Speaking of Transylvania, have there been any more, you know—?"

"No," said Father, "not since we found Mr. Ryan last night."

"That's good, I mean, not that he was found, but that no others have been found since."

"I knew what you meant, Martin."

"And the body hasn't been examined yet, I take it."

"No." A long, tired sigh filtered through the phone. "Wong and Holtsclaw have been notified, but they won't be arriving back in town until late tomorrow evening. Obviously, two city councilmen—not to mention our beloved cardinal—don't want anything to get leaked to the news media, so none of the regular staff forensic specialists have been allowed anywhere near the morgue since the ambulance caddies put the bodies on ice."

"That's what they told me to expect. Strange."

"Not really. I used to deal with this kind of grit in the machine all the time. I'm surprised, frankly, that the staff at the 'House of Illusions' haven't all declared a holiday."

"I doubt there's much work available," I said, "for out-of-work fakirs."

"There is that," said Father.

"And how is Stella doing?"

"She's holding her own. We've augmented our vigilance."

"And Daddy Billowack? Has he enhanced his belligerence?"

"What do you think?" Father chuckled, then cleared his throat. "Okay, chatter aside, are you making progress? Have you found out anything?"

I consulted some scribbled notes I'd made on my complimentary Best Western Roundup memo pad. "I had a lovely meeting with Irma Shrumpf, the guardian of the historical museum. She normally wouldn't have been in on a Sunday, but several of her staff are out with the flu. Anyway, she was enthused because in her youth she went to UCLA, and unlike most of the folks around here, she has a fondness for 'Everything LA,' even yours truly."

"Did she have access to the information?"

"There are these marvelous inventions called 'cornputers'—I mean, 'computers,' Father. Ever hear of them? They came in as the horse-and-buggy was on its way out. What Irma didn't find this afternoon, she swears she'll have printed out by tomorrow morning. She also mentioned that—*ahem!*—this information could have been accessed from a terminal much closer to home, like at the nearest branch library."

"But without the local color," said Father.

"Right," sniffed the gardener, "or the local smells."

"What else?"

"It turns out that Miss Shrumpf's nephew's half-brother, Earl Cooper, is a sheriff who got shot in the leg trying to catch a poacher last year, and—"

"Martin."

"—*and,* instead of retiring early, Earl got himself a desk job at the main station, mainly filing police reports. You gotta understand, Father, how everything and everyone's interconnected in these parts. Anyway, I showed him the pictures, and he had a few things to chaw about."

"To 'chaw' about? Martin, you're beginning to talk funny."

"It's catching," I admitted. "I already walk funny. Why, thunder 'n' tarnation, I'll be chewin' n' spittin' tabacky by dinner."

"Heavens," he said, "that's all I need when you get back: an altar server who speaks genuine Pig Latin."

"I'm having dinner, by the way," I went on, ignoring his concerns, "with Eustace P. Franklin at the 'Now You Don't.' He's the folk historian everyone points to when you ask where the skeletons are buried, and that's the magic club you wanted me to check out, and Mr. Franklin says the food is good, and I have to eat, so I'm going to kill three birds with one horseshoe—or was that four?"

"Good, good."

"And I have arranged to meet with Hezikiah Denning at County Records tomorrow morning. As it turns out, Irma is also his sister-in-law or I'd never have been able to reach him on a Sunday to set up the appointment."

"Excellent, Martin."

"If all goes well, I may be able to catch the noon flight back to LA tomorrow."

"Only if you've covered everything I sent you there to find out."

"Only then," I agreed. What did he take me for? "By the way, how did it go?"

"How did what go?"

"You know: the 'Weekly Just-After-Sunday-Mass Sacrificial Sacerdotal Barbecue.' Was your flock as hostile as they were last week?"

"Piece of cake," said Father. "Mr. Turnbuckle didn't show, so all his cohorts didn't have a vortex to gravitate around. Kahlúa Hummingbird made an appearance at the request of Pierre Bontemps, which sent the more traditional Traditionalists into a dither."

"Now *that* I wish I'd seen."

"It was amusing, and thankfully, diverting."

"Of course, of course. 'Suicide' as a 'fashion statement' is far more discussible than as a 'life decision.'"

"True," said Father. "Dr. Volman, however, did get a bit hot-headed."

"Dr. Kaylan Volman?" I asked. "Our 'in lieu of' dentist? Is he big on 'fashion statements'?"

"No, 'life decisions.' He was out of town last week, and all his information was secondhand. He got belligerent, in fact, over Buckminster Turnbuckle's burial in unconsecrated soil."

"If he only knew the half of it. And you said?"

"I reminded him of his son, Piter, the one who died in Vietnam. His unit was wiped out because a frightened corporal broke cover and revealed their position. I asked him: 'Kaylan, how would you feel if I were to bury that coward beside your son, with full military honors?'"

"And he said?"

"'Father, I would surely break your jaw.'"

"And you said?"

"Nothing. The point was made."

"Oh."

"And—you would have enjoyed this—Helga Feuchtwanger put in an appearance just as everyone was dispersing."

"Who?"

"Remember the lady who lives down the alley? She dropped by to say that whoever has been taking joyrides in her Volkswagen has finally stopped doing so. At least, he didn't take it last night, and we're hoping he's lost interest. She still thinks the culprit was one of ours."

"Sure," I said. "Trads and Bugs, they go together like moonshine and jugs. A bit of Kentucky humor, Father. No need to laugh."

"So, if you've nothing further to report?"

"Only that I was refused Communion this morning."

"Why?"

"I wouldn't receive in the hand. The priest, Father Fitspew or something, got kind of confrontational about it. He made a caustic remark about not wanting to get saliva on his fingers. I wiped my tongue with my sleeve, but the man wouldn't give in."

"I understand. It's comforting to know that modernism has made such headway in the green woods of Kentucky."

"I'd use another word."

"Well then, on that discomforting note, I'll say good-bye."

"Good-bye, Father."

I watched TV for a while, killing time until my big night out at the "Now You Don't" with Mr. Franklin. We don't have one—a TV, I mean—at St. Philomena's, and fifteen minutes was enough to remind me why.

109

"LET'S HAVE A BIG HAND," smiled the fringe-clad MC, waving his hands wildly in the blue-white spotlight, "fer the Amazin' Blazin' Brothers."

The hooting applause swelled and died down throughout the "Now You Don't."

I looked at the sawdust and peanut shells on the floor. Compared to the "House of Illusions," this place was a pigsty. In fact, according to my authoritative copy of *Kentucky Highlights,* it originally *was* a pigsty. To be a shadow of one's former self—now that's what I call progress.

"Ah don't s'pose, Mr. Feeney," drawled Mr. Eustace P. Franklin, fifteen-gallon cowboy hat side-swiping everything in sight that was yay-high to his ears, "you got anythang like this here out thar in Californee?"

"No, Mr. Franklin," I shouted over the *doong-dingie-dong-dingie-dingie-dong* music that the house band had just started kerpluckering, "we surely don't, and that's a fact."

"Ah hear them West Coast gals is real purty," he said, smiling like a goat chewing a milk carton.

"I haven't noticed."

"Yer joshin' me."

"No, sir. I spend all my time admiring fulcra."

"Fulcra? What's thayat?"

"Thayat's another story. It'll keep." Forgive my feigned accent, but when in Rome. I tapped the top page of my Best Western Roundup memo pad. "Right now I have to drill that thar brain of yoors for this here information."

"Thayat'll sure be a meyess if'n you strike oil." He guffawed so hard he almost swallowed his spurs on that one.

I opened my mouth and pretended to be equally amused while counting on the raucous *doong-dingie* din to cover my deficiency of genuine hilarity. Pretending to regain my composure, I continued. "You do remember what we were talkin' 'bout, don'tcha?"

"Oh sure, yayuh," he said, wiping his lips with his palm. Talk about saliva. Anyway, he looked up, then down, then this way and that. After giving his eyeballs this strenuous cowpoke workout, he

started to let the ol' oil gush out of his cranial cavity onto my notebook. "Wall," he began, "the best Ah kin recollect, the first gen'leman
of thayat name showed up here in Lexington 'round 1774. Come from
Boston. He was what they used to call one of them, uh, um … it
rhymes with 'huge ol' knot' … 'Hugo-naught,' thayat's it. He was a
Hugo-naught."

"The best *you* can recollect, Mr. Franklin?"

"Wall yayuh, of what my pappy an' his pappy an' his used to yack
'bout 'round the fire. Anyways, thayat was just b'fore the Revoloosheeyun, back when Kentucky was part of Virginee—"

"A Huguenot, you say."

"Yayuh, thayat Ah did."

"So he was a French Calvinist."

"Beats me," shrugged Mr. Franklin. "Ah'm a bathed-an'-saved
Southern Baptist, m'self. What're you, Son?"

"I'm a Roman Catholic."

"Oh." He dislodged something that was stuck between his front teeth
with his tongue and swallowed the result loudly. "One o' them. Anyways, as Ah was a-sayin'—"

"'Scuse me," said another voice. We looked up into the sparkling
eyes of the MC, fresh from his introductory moment on the stage. "Ah
understand one of you gents asked to speak with me—? Oh, hi there,
Eustace."

"Mo," nodded Mr. Franklin, pumping the MC's paw. "This here's
Martin Feeney from Californee. Mr. Feeney, this here is Moab Chester
Smith."

"Pleased to meecha," I said, indicating an empty seat at our table.
"Got a minute?"

"Sure thang," said M. C. Smith, MC, easing his bulk into the chair
with a ripple and flutter of multicolored fringes. I found the symmetry
of his name about as fascinating as the rabbit's foot sticking out of the
band of his cowboy hat. He folded his hands with a little circular space
between his palms, as if he were wishing he was holding a drink.
"What can Ah do yer fer?"

"Do you recognize this man?" I said, pulling a "House of Illusions"
flyer from my pocket and shoving it across the table. The likeness was
a little blurry, the flyer being itself a photocopy, and even the original
had just been an artist's drawing, but it was all I had with the little
runt's face on it.

"Easy," said M. C. the MC, snatching it up. "Thayat's Ol' Roy."

"Ol' Roy?" I asked, trying to combine the corncob name with the
snobby, caped little fellow in my mind. It didn't seem to fit.

"Robert Leroy Portifoy," smiled M. C. Smith. "Ah'd know thayat
moustache an' monocle anywheres, even on a raccoon. What'd he do?
Flange up a new act in Californee?"

"Sort of," I said, not sure how one "flanges up" an act. "When I met him recently he called himself Lucius T. Portifoy."

"You a cop?" asked Eustace P. Franklin.

"No," I said, "I'm a gardener. I caught Portifoy's act in Los Angeles and someone told me he came from here."

"Who was thayat?"

"Who was what?"

"Who told you thayat Ol' Roy was from 'round here?"

"Anthony Graves," I answered, "who also said he has family in these parts."

"Anthony Graves," said Moab Chester Smith, thoughtfully. "Don't sound familyer."

"Serious feller," I said, raising my arm, "about yay high next to me. Glasses." I made an "X" over my nose with my forefingers. "Eye-brows."

"Lee Moss had big eyebrows," said M.C. Smith, rubbing his chin.

"Lee Moss?" I asked.

"Yayuh," said M. C., "but he didn't wear no glasses, an' he didn't have no kin 'round here."

"An' his last name weren't Graves," noted Eustace P. Franklin, hooking his thumbs in his blue suspenders. "Now, Ah know a Jeremiah Graves. Him an' his wife, Cornelia, lives a few miles thataway over yonder. They grow tabacky, or is it cotton? Come from quite an extended family, too: all descended from slaves."

"No," I said, "the Anthony Graves I spoke with in Los Angeles is white."

"Couldn't be Jeremiah then," said Mr. Franklin. "B'sides, to the best of my knowledge, he's never been outta the county, let alone all the way to Californee."

"Now, Tony Tooms is kinda serious," said M.C., rubbing his chin. "They call him 'Tony the Bony Tooms.' Real serious. Nearsighted, too."

"But—?" I asked, wondering why I bothered.

"He don't have hardly no eyebrows," said M. C.

"An' his last name ain't Graves, neither," added Mr. Franklin.

"Tell me more about Ol' Roy," I said, clutching the edge of the table as if it were the Santa Maria perched precariously on the brink of the world. "He worked here?"

"Yayup," said M. C. Smith. "He an' thayat Lee Moss feller Ah just mentioned hired on here the same time as me."

"Really," I said. "When was that?"

"Spring, 'bout ten years back."

"What kind of an act did he have?"

"Ol' Roy Portifoy?" said the MC, puffing out his cheeks. "You name it, he done it. More of a jokester than a prankster, you might say. Kept the audience off guard with his endless remarks in thayat French-style accent of his'n. Ah was sad to see him leave, though to tell you the truth, some of the reg'lars 'round here didn't like him one bit. Got on thar nerves."

"Imagine that," I nodded, imagining that. "Why did he quit?"

"Beats me," said M.C. "Ol' Roy, he kept purty much to hisself. One night 'bout three weeks back—the tenth of this month, Ah think it was, yayuh—he just up an' hauled off an' announced his early retirement, turned his magic wand into a train ticket, an' left us in a lurch without a headlinin' act."

"Thayat was 'round the time when the fever passed," said Mr. Franklin.

"The fever?" I asked.

"'Sylvie's Mis'ry,' they calls it," said M. C. Smith. "You gits as tired as a pack o' burned-out mules, plus you gits welts on yer neck. It got pretty thick 'round here last summer, but it's been plaguin' these here parts on an' off fer goin' on two an' a half hunnert years."

"Somethin' gits in yer blood," said Mr. Franklin knowledgeably. "A fungus or vah-ris, maybe. Maybe it's jus' somethin' in the soil 'round these parts. My great-grand mammy used to say it only came durin' them long stretches of humidity we gits 'round here."

"'Bert's 'Brella' we call it," said M. C. "You should see it, Mr. Feeney. The sky gits all black an' blue, an' rumbles up a storm—"

"But it don't rain," said Mr. Franklin.

"Everyone's sweatin' like pigs, an' gittin' sick b'sides," said the MC.

"Been known to go on fer months an' months," said Mr. Franklin. "No wonder lots of folks started quittin' an' movin' on. You come at the right time, Mr. Feeney. Bert done folded up his 'Brella a few weeks back, sendin' Sylvie packin', an' the weather's been jus' fine ever since."

"Thayat's right," said M. C. Smith. "Mabye Ol' Roy shoulda stuck it out a little longer. Anyways, like Ah was sayin': Lee Moss, thayat other feller, he quits in June; an; a couple months b'fore thayat, a couple o' sisters quits, too. 'Clove an' Nutmeg,' they called theyselves. Clove an' Nutmeg Sole. Sole, as in 'filet of.' They didn't do much—sort of a 'mind-readin'' act—but what they was really good fer was standin' 'round lookin' purty. B'fore them there was a three-sister act, 'The Teasin' Tweezers,' but they moved on last January—"

"An' don't ferget Tony Tooms," said Eustace P. Franklin. "He left back in the chin end o' summer."

"Chin end?" asked the pilgrim gardener.

"You know," said Mr. Franklin, indicating his own dimpled jaw. "May 'r June."

"June it was," said Mr. Smith.

"You sure?" asked myself.

"This magic business," said M. C. Smith with an assertive nod, "has a high turnover. Ah'd move on, too, one o' these days, but Ah got kinfolk here 'bouts to consider."

"Did Portifoy?" I asked.

"Did Portifoy what?" asked Mr. Smith.

"Did he have family around here?"

"Wall, not exactly here," said Eustace P. Franklin. "Ah don't know 'bout yer Graves feller, but Roy Portifoy weren't from 'here,' meanin' Lexington."

"But I thought you said his family moved here in 1774."

"Thayat ain't so, Mr. Feeney," smiled Mr. Franklin. "What Ah said was, the first gen'leman o' thayat name come here from Boston 'round the time of the Revoloosheeyun, sure. Thayat was Lucius Robert Portifoy, Jr. He was 'parently a sickly man, an' a pipsqueak. They say runt-ism ran in his family. He died twenty years later, an' his son moved his business to Charleston, South Carolina."

"So where was Ol' Roy Portifoy from?" I asked.

"Yorktown, Virginee," said M.C. "Ah remember, 'cause when Ah hired on here he 'n' me got to talkin', an' it turns out we both got relations in Williamsburg, too."

"Thayat's the capitol o' Virginee," added Mr. Franklin.

"These Portifoys seemed to get around," I commented.

"Thayat they did, son," said Mr. Franklin. "Thayat they did. Why, you'll find Portifoys in graveyards all throughout the Colonies."

"Must've been quite a family," said the MC, rising from his chair. "Anyways, if yer back out LA-ways, an' you see Ol' Roy, or whatever he calls hisself out there, tell him to come on back here when he gits tired o' them big-city lights an' fast highways. Some folks 'round here miss the li'l guy, even if others wanna string the li'l twerp up by his toes."

I found it curious that in a city the size of Lexington these locals were unaware of their own lights and highways, but decided not to comment. As for some Kentucky folks missing the little guy, go figure.

"Nice feller," said Mr. Franklin as M.C. the MC strode away to make idle conversation with other patrons of the pigsty. "Moab Chester Smith. Ah don't know much 'bout his pappy's side, but his momma was Alberta Augusta Hancock. One of her great-great-grandpappies helped organize the Sons o' Liberty—yayuh, the guys thayat dumped all thayat thar tea into Boston Harbor."

"Really," I said, turning my attention back to the chronicler of colonial skeletons. "Tell me more."

And he did, long into the night. My Best Western Roundup notepad was clean filled up by the time I got back to the motel. I had to ask for another one from the desk clerk.   He handed me two, with his compliments.

Monday, October Thirtieth

Feast Day of Saint Alphonsus Rodriguez,
a lay brother of the Society of Jesus,
who died saying the Holy Name of Jesus (1617 AD)

110

MONDAY MORNING I FARED somewhat better. Father Fitspew's assistant, Father Spewspit, said Mass at the same local church—Novus Ordo, of course, but sans the Dylan look-alikes since it was only a weekday affair. Apparently Fr. Spewspit didn't share his pastor's aversion to saliva, and he did say the Words of Consecration accurately and with reverence, as though he really meant them. I stayed after Mass for twenty minutes, thanking the Lord for big favors.

As for my meeting with Hezikiah Denning at County Records: no need to repeat myself. I'll reveal all later on.

Mr. Denning's niece, Nancy Mae, turned out to be, among other stylish things, the calligraphy instructor in the Art Department at Transylvania U. She was extremely helpful, as was her memory.

I swung by the historical museum and picked up the promised stack of printouts from Mr. Denning's sister-in-law, Irma, and returned to the motel well before check-out time.

Suffice it to say that I did catch the 3:00 PM non-stop flight back to LA, which meant I landed at LAX just past five, even though the flight lasted five hours. Time zones—you gotta love 'em. Sir Edward Strypes Wyndham was waiting graciously beside his Wyndhammobile in front of the TWA terminal as I came lumbering out, hair disheveled and bags under my eyes.

"Mission accomplished?" he asked as I tossed my suitcases into the back and pulled myself up into the shotgun seat.

"Yayuh," I assured him, waving him on. "An' how's 'bout y'all?"

"We—the Tumblars—have all been busy," he said, gunning the accelerator. "You know about the little construction project Father Baptist gave Joel?"

"I think he mentioned it. Something about the upstairs room."

"Right," said Edward, nudging the van up to a cruising velocity just shy of the speed of sound. He took his hands off the steering wheel for a moment to show me the bumps and bruises all over his fingers. "I'm no good with a hammer, but I've been helping out. So have Arthur and Jonathan."

"What about Pierre?" I asked, grateful that he didn't forget to grab the wheel again.

"He's a klutz," smiled Edward, "but he's a good sport. We've all been taking turns, including Father Nicanor and his housekeeper, watching Stella at the hospital."

"How's she doing?"

"Much better. The doctors say she's out of the woods."

"She's stable then?"

"They're talking about releasing her on Wednesday or Thursday."

"That is good news."

"By the time this is over," said Edward, displaying his bruised hands again, "I'll need a doctor myself, and a good night's sleep."

"You have been busy," I said, allowing the G-forces to distribute my weight equally in my seat. It occurred to me that maybe I'd been assigned the better task after all. "Why is the upstairs room so important?"

"You'll see," said Edward, downshifting as we careened gracefully through an interchange.

"That I will," I agreed, adopting the philosophical stance that whatever was going to happen, I'd find out eventually.

The City of Angels rolled by, oblivious to my return.

"And," I ventured to ask presently, "how's our Millie?"

Edward shrugged. "Haven't seen much of her. She keeps the coffee coming at the hospital, since none of us trusts the nurses anymore. Other than that, Millie's been keeping pretty much to herself."

"Hmm," I hmmed to myself, wondering what that might portend.

It was quarter to six when the Wyndham Wagon screeched to a halt at the curb in front of St. Philomena's rectory. The sight of the place, so quiet and peaceful, on the outside at least, was profoundly reassuring to this gardener returning from his travels.

"Thanks," I said, sliding out onto the sidewalk.

"See you in a few," he said, tossing out my suitcases and roaring off.

Keys in hand, joints aching, mouth dry, I ascended the steps.

"Anybody home?" I called as I pushed the front door open.

Silence. Well, not exactly silence. A thumping sound came ricocheting down the stairs from somewhere on the second floor. Tired as I was, I decided not to investigate just then.

As I closed and locked the door behind me, I spied a letter addressed to me on the little tilting table in the hallway. It was from a literary agent. Quicker than greased lightning, I dropped my bags, tore the envelope open, and unfolded the single typed page:

```
Dear Mr. Feeney,
    Thank you for thinking of us regarding The End-
less Knot.  We're sorry to report that we simply
did not have enough enthusiasm for your project to
pursue it.
                        Sincerely yours,

                        Blah B. Blah-Blah
```

I didn't realize until that moment that all literary agents enroll in the same Rejection Etiquette Seminars.

Gathering up my things, I headed down the hallway. Peering into Father's study and finding it empty, I continued onward. Pots were bubbling on the stove, spurting plumes of thick steam cheerfully into the empty kitchen. There was even a little saucepan on the back burner in which a single potato rolled around cheerfully in its bath of boiling water.

Millie was nowhere to be seen.

So much for my grand homecoming. I would've thought that at least—well, no matter. I was too exhausted to feel neglected.

Exiting through the kitchen door to the outside, I made my way through the dark garden toward my personal private quarters. As I passed the empty storage room, I heard more thumps within. There was no window so I couldn't see who was working in there or why. Somehow at that moment I was losing interest.

I could see a light on in Monsignor Havermeyer's camper as I scurried on—well, my lurching version of "scurrying"—taking care not to glance in the direction of the cemetery.

The clock on my nightstand said "06:35" as my head, hair still wet from the steaming shower, hit the pillow. Sleep enveloped me in a matter of seconds.

111

THE SAME CLOCK SAID "07:05" when Father Baptist shook me awake.

"Martin!" he said, "I thought I heard you come in."

"Yup," I groaned, "it was me all right. Nice of you to check, Father." I can't even begin to try to tell you how that actually came out, my tongue lying sideways on the pillow and all. At that precise moment I knew it was going to be a long, long day.

I suddenly though blearily realized that the warm amber glow playing on his face, which I'd mistaken for a nanosecond as the light of dawn, was actually coming from the nightlight in the bathroom. It wasn't morning after all. I'd only been asleep for a half-hour. Okay, so it was going to be a long, long night.

That pounding—my poor head.

"Sorry to disturb your much-needed rest," said Father, "but it is essential that you to tell me what you learned about Portifoy."

"Now?" I asked, peeling my tongue off the pillow and stuffing it back into my mouth.

"Now, Martin. I'm sure he's the key to what's been going on. I'll explain—"

"I know, I know: later," I said, hefting myself up onto one elbow so I could reach for my jacket, which I vaguely remembered draping over the bedpost. Finding my trusty stack of complimentary Best Western Roundup memo pads in the side pocket, I collapsed back against the pillow.

"Well?" said Father, turning my rickety typewriter chair so he could sit facing me.

"Ah yes," I said, examining my illegible squiggles, "my mission."

Father folded his arms.

"One moment," I moaned, reaching up and flicking on the reading light. "That's better." I settled back down. "Mr. Graves was right: Portifoy did work at the 'Now You Don't' in Lexington—until a little less than a month ago when he quit. I'll get back to that."

"The family history," said Father.

"Right," I said, flipping a couple of pages. "According to Irma Shrumpf's computers, combined with a smidgen of Mr. Denning's file search at County Records, not to mention the tales Mr. Franklin's great-grand pappy used to drawl in front of the family fireplace—"

"Yes, yes," sighed Father.

"Well," I yawned, "the name 'Portifoy'—which is French for 'Port of Faith'—first showed up in the Virginia Colony in 1680. Jacques Robert Portifoy." I was careful to pronounce the middle name so that it rhymed with "contraire." Father didn't seem impressed. "Apparently," I continued, "he came over with the first wave of Huguenots from France."

"A Calvinist, then," said Father.

"Yes," I said. "A heretic of the first order. He settled in Manakin, Virginia, and together with a partner, Claude, established an importing company: Portifoy and Pulch."

"Claude Pulch?" asked Father.

"P-u-l-c-h," I spelled it out.

"That's a peculiar name. Doesn't sound French."

"No, but that's definitely it. Anyway, it seems that Jacques, or rather his son of the same name—Jacques Junior, in other words—moved the business to Williamsburg, Virginia upon his father's death in 1707."

"Claude Pulch, too?" asked Father.

"Claude's son, Denis," I answered, turning another page. "Then, upon the deaths of said Jacques Robert Junior and Denis Pulch—"

"They died the same year?"

I squinted at my squiggles. "Yes, 1732. Well, Jacques Junior, anyway. I couldn't find a death date for Denis Pulch, at least not in the Colonial Cemetery Registry; but there's no record of him after that year."

"Hmm," hmmed Father, assimilating the information. "Continue."

"The sons of Jacques and Denis—Robert Auguste-Maximillion Portifoy and Jean-Luc Pulch, to be precise—moved the biz to Charleston, South Carolina in the latter part of 1732. The next generation, Lucius Robert Portifoy and Georges Pulch, decided that insurrection was their thing, so they loaded up their truck and they moved to Boston, Massachusetts in 1757. Lucius R. was apparently active in spreading sedition against the King of England, and was even mentioned in some of John Hancock's personal correspondence. Perhaps he was too active, because in 1774, the year after the Boston Tea Party, the next litter of Portifoys and Pulches moved to Lexington, away from the action, into what is now Kentucky."

"So," calculated Father, "every twenty to twenty-five years or so, when the older generation died off, the next moved on to a new locale."

"Or revisited an old one," I said. "From there the Portifoy and Pulch boys moved back to Charleston, South Carolina in 1794; then up to New Paltz, New York in 1814; New York, New York in 1835; then out to Newport, Rhode Island, 1865; then down to Yorktown, Virginia in 1895; and on and on."

"Odd way to run a business," said Father, "especially in that part of the country where 'Established 1680' would be appreciated by customers."

"A flighty bunch, these Portifoys and Pulches," I agreed. "In almost every case, the Pulch son went on ahead to the next town and secured the property for the new business a few months before the old location was shut down. And there's more. I mentioned the Colonial Cemetery Registry a moment ago. That's the computerized answer to a recent upwelling of patriotic nostalgia combined with a growing popular interest in geneology. Both Irma Shrumpf and Hezikiah Denning assured me that all the markers in every known cemetery in the colonial states have been cataloged."

"And?" pressed Father.

"And," replied the gardener, "not only could I not find any trace of Denis Pulch or his father, Claude, in the CCR, I couldn't find the name 'Pulch' at all—not on a single tombstone, chapel crypt, or mausoleum plaque, nowhere—which is amazing when you consider how many generations of Pulches we're talking about here."

"That goes beyond peculiar," said Father. "Perhaps all the way to 'sinister.'"

"You're telling me. Another strange thing: when I showed the MC at the 'Now You Don't' a program from the 'House of Illusions,' he identified our Lucius T. as 'Ol' Roy Portifoy.' So the current Portifoy likes to shift stage names. Bad for business, I'd imagine, but it seems to be a family trait: change for the sake of change, one way or another."

"Possibly," said Father. "Is there currently a 'Portifoy and Pulch' in Lexington?"

"No. Robert Andre Portifoy and Bartholomew Pulch put the 'closed' sign on the front door of the last family shop in Yorktown, Virginia, in 1989. Their lease on the property expired the following day, and the partners left no forwarding address."

"Hmm," hmmed Father. "And no new place of business since?"

"Nope."

"Odd. Did you find out about the Graves family?"

"Not much. There are over a hundred graves marked 'Graves' in the CCR data base. But as for living relatives in Lexington, our Toolmaster, Mr. Anthony Graves, was either mistaken or lying. I asked around and got nowhere. You see, Lee Moss had big eyebrows but didn't wear glasses or have kin around there, and had a different last name anyway. Eustace P. Franklin, the local historian, knew of a Graves family, Jeremiah and Cornelia, but they and their whole clan were black. Moab Chester Smith, the current MC at the 'Now You Don't,' said that a feller named 'Tony the Bony Tooms' was very serious by nature and nearsighted to boot. But his name was Tooms, not Graves—though he might've just lied about that and shaved his eyebrows."

"What are you talking about?" asked Father, his own eyebrows colliding above his nose.

"My mission. Captivating, huh? Intriguing, stimulating, enticing—"

"None of those terms would have been mine," said Father.

"Nor mine," I assured him. "I was just spouting antonyms. Nonetheless, having reviewed these seemingly unrelated facts, I got what you might call a hunch."

"What kind of hunch?"

"Well, I figured if this Portifoy could change his name, so could anyone. I thought maybe our Mr. Anthony Graves might be 'Tony the Bony Tooms'—seeing how T-o-o-m-s is only one letter shy of T-o-m-b-s, and the word 'Tombs' is synonymous with 'Graves.'"

"An odd coincidence," agreed Father.

"Not to mention the fact," I winked, "that Tony Tooms quit the 'Now You Don't' back in the chin end of summer."

"Chin end?"

"Transylvanian for May or June, probably June. If he was in cahoots with Portifoy, I thought—sort of a late version of Denis and the other Pulches—it would fit the historical pattern for him to come ahead to Los Angeles and set up a new identity for his partner."

"And did it?"

"And did it what?"

"And did it fit the historical pattern?"

"It would have," I yawned, covering my mouth with my palm, "except Tony Tooms simply retired from the stage and opened a little magic shop across the street from the university campus. I know: I dropped in on my way to the airport. Nice feller, near-sighted, no eyebrows. No hair at all except in his ears and nostrils."

"And you mentioned someone named Moss?"

"Lee Moss," I nodded sleepily. "Eyebrows, no glasses, no kin, different name. He quit in June, too. His departure went by almost unnoticed in the wake of Clove and Nutmeg, who used to thrill audiences by passing secrets via brainwaves. Alas, they left a few months before him. Their last name was 'Sole,' which made them the 'Sole Sisters,' or perhaps two 'only childs.' Take your pick. If I'm beginning to ramble, it's because I'm so tired my brain is turning to jelly."

"Good work, Martin," said Father.

"Does the worker deserve his just wage?" I asked.

"Of course."

"Then will you please let me get some sleep?"

"I insist," said Father, rising from the chair. "Mind if I review your memo pads while you collect your pay?"

"Not at all," I said, clicking off the light.

I don't remember hearing him leave.

112

THE SAME CLOCK SAID "07:37" when Father Baptist shook me awake.

"Martin!" he said, "get up."

It took me a moment to realize that it was still the same day, and the evening was getting longer and longer.

"Hurry," he said.

"Why?" said I, heaving myself up onto my elbows.

"Lieutenant Taper just phoned."

"Another?" I drooled.

"Another," he confirmed.

"Who?"

"Lucius T. Portifoy."

"What—?!?!?"

"An unexpected development, I'll admit."

> GARDENING TIPS: I fly across the country and back,
> tracing this guy, climbing his jitter-bugging fam-
> ily tree, and that's all Father Baptist had to
> say? An unexpected development?!?! Well, I had
> much to spout in reply, but I only had the energy
> to form a single word . . .
>
> —M.F.

"Where?"

"In the basement at the 'House of Illusions.'"

"Dead?"

"Dead."

"Sucked dry?"

"No. Another break in the pattern."

"What's it this time, a kangaroo?"

"Martin," he said, lowering his tone ominously. "Mr. Graves called the police and reported finding Mr. Portifoy with a wooden stake driven through his heart."

I shook my head. It rattled. "You're joking."

"Hardly, Martin."

"A stake?" Reality chose that moment to shift gears again. You'll think me a cold, hard fellow, but you're not getting the messages my stomach was sending to my brain at that moment via my undernourished nervous system. "A steak, huh? What about dinner?"

"Monsignor Havermeyer finished his potato fifteen minutes ago."

"What about ours?"

"Ours will have to wait."

"Our potato?"

"Our dinner."

"But Millie—she'll fly into a rage if we're late."

"Not to worry," said Father. "With all the activity around here, Millie's taken to soups and stews. She keeps them going all day so we can grab meals when we can."

"Millie—? We are talking about Millie, aren't we?"

"The same," said Father.

Reality shifted again—this time skipping a gear. Our Dinner-on-Time-or-I'll-Dent-Your-Ugly-Face-with-a-Skillet Millie? The very thought of her kitchen without a Do-or-Die timetable cost me my appetite.

"Is she ill?" I asked.

"In this time of necessity, Martin, our Millie has shown herself to be a courageous, generous, and patient trooper."

"It's that serious?" I coughed. "She must be dying."

"We shall see. Come, we have work to do."

"Ulp," I groaned, rising to a sitting position. That Biblical sentiment about a dog returning to its vomit crossed my mind. "My head," I groaned, reaching for the aspirin bottle, then I thought I'd have to take an antacid to handle the aspirin. Then I thought better of the whole thing. My brain was obviously out of sync with my stomach.

"Is this jet lag?" I mumbled.

Then it dawned on me that the persistent pounding was coming from somewhere outside my head—from the wall. It was answered by another thump than seemed to emanate from the ceiling.

"What're they making?" I asked.

"The Tumblars?" said Father. "A trap."

"Oh," I said, struggling to my feet and grabbing my cane. "Must be one Hell of a mouse. I don't suppose you'd care to fill me in on it—this trap, I mean?"

"Later," said Father. "Here are your pants, Martin. You could use a shave, but there's no time."

"That's okay," I said, shoving one leg in, "I've gotten used to grunge. I left behind all pretense of social grace in Transylvania."

"Fine, whatever," huffed Father. "The other leg, Martin."

"What?"

"Pants work best when both legs are inside."

"Oh, yeah. My shirt?"

"Here. Your arms go into the long tubes."

"Gottit."

"You can tie your tie in the car."

"How will I steer?"

"By the Grace of God. Let's go."

113

"YAYUH," SAID THE GARDENER, summoning his wits after taking a long look inside the small, wooden, gold-leafed child-sized coffin next to the water heater in the basement. "That looks like a stake, all right."

"Brilliant again, Feeney," said Wickes, who was standing beside me, flashlight in hand.

There he was: Lucius T. Portifoy, stretched out in a small wooden coffin with the lid propped open. And there, sticking out of his munchkin chest, just inches below that pewter clasp that held his cape together, was the stumpy tail end of a roughly hewn stick of wood.

My reader has no doubt gathered that I did not much care for Mr. Portifoy. I found him to be arrogant, snide, and capable of personal cruelty as he had deftly demonstrated with respect to the unfortunate Bucky Buckle. Even so, I took no delight in seeing him skewered thus, blood saturating his elegant red vest. Stretched out in that small coffin, clad in tailcoat and cape, he did exude a vague sense of B-movie elegance, but—

"What's this coffin doing down here anyway?" barked Billowack, who had apparently come along with Sergeant Wickes and Lieutenant Taper.

"A good question," said Father Baptist. "Mr. Graves?"

"That's the one I've been using as a footlocker in my room," said Mr. Graves, scratching his head. "All the stuff that was in it is piled on my bed."

"You used this coffin for a hope chest?" slavered Billowack.

"It's just an old prop," explained the Toolmaster. "You and your men have been all over this basement. You know there's all kinds of weird stuff down here."

Father was kneeling beside the little coffin, examining Mr. Portifoy's left hand. "Hm," he said, "there's blood on his index finger."

"There's blood on most of him," said Billowack. "So what?"

"I don't know," said Father, rising. "There are also scrape marks here on the concrete floor. It would appear that this coffin was dragged to this spot from somewhere over there."

Flashlights waving, we followed the tracks to a locked utility closet. CAUTION: ELECTRICAL HAZARD, said a rusted metal sign on the door. Yes, this was the same place, the same half-dozen or so turns from Mr. Graves' little hidie hole, where Reginold the Reiterator met his untimely end two nights before.

"Mr. Graves?" asked Father, indicating the padlock hanging on the latch.

"Right here," said the Toolmaster, jiggling a large ring of keys. He selected a small brass key and inserted it into the lock. "Nothing in there but pipes and conduits—"

"Good Lord," said Lieutenant Taper as the door squeaked open.

"Tamara!" said Mr. Graves.

We all looked in and regretted it.

Running horizontally along the ceiling of the small cubicle were several old, black, four-inch sewage pipes. Hanging vertically from one of them was the sash of a diaphanous purple garment that I have previously called a "djellaba." The sash ended in a tightly-knotted noose, in which was stretched the neck of a once-beautiful "sensitive." Her

face—well, I won't go into that.   Tamara Grafan's complexion no
longer had any connection with an olive.   And of all the bodies this
gardener had seen in the last two weeks, this one had certainly not been
drained of blood.

"I don't understand," groaned Mr. Graves, gripping his lower jaw
with both hands.   "She was so beautiful. And now this."

"Do you know where her sister, Marla, might be?" asked Father.

"No," said Graves.   "Tamara and Marla didn't show up for work
Thursday evening. I called the police, but the girls hadn't been missing
long enough to file a missing persons report. Besides, a number of the
crew didn't come to work last night or for rehearsal this evening. What
with Reginold being murdered last Saturday on top of everything else,
well, people are getting really scared. And now—this."

"Tamara G-r-a-f-a-n," said Wickes as he wrote the name in his notebook. "What is that, French?"

"English or German, originally," said Graves, "though I think their
mother was Mexican and Syrian.   Their father was Grafan the
Great—quite a magician in his day. I've only been here a few months,
but I'd sort of developed a fatherly affection for those two—"

"What's this?" asked Billowack, indicating a stain on the woman's
garment.

"Let me, Chief," said Lieutenant Taper, snapping on a set of surgical
gloves and carefully parting the folds of cloth over the abdomen in that
fascinating way policemen have of handling things without touching
them.

"Good Heavens," said Father Baptist.

Chief Billowack said something less repeatable.

But there it was, smeared on the poor woman's stomach:

$$\text{I killeD my MasT3R}_{\text{,}}$$

"So she staked this Portifoy guy," said Billowack, "and then strung
herself up?"

"After locking the closet from the outside?" asked Father. "How?"

"Hrmph," hrmphed the chief. "Maybe someone else just came along
and happened to see the closet was unlocked and—"

"I doubt that very much," said Father.

"Good point, Jack," said Lieutenant Taper, slipping off the gloves with a rubbery smack. "We'll have to see if this is written in Portifoy's blood."

"This runt was her master?" grunted Billowack, massaging his jowls. "Mighty strange. How many employees have keys to this locker?"

"Besides me, I hope you mean," said Mr. Graves. "Two or three come to mind, but I couldn't say for sure."

"Find out," said Billowack to Taper.

"Of course," said the lieutenant.

"Have Wong and Holtsclaw returned from San Diego?" asked Father.

"They're en route," said Taper. "I notified them by car phone. If there are no traffic complications, they should get to the morgue about the same time we do."

"Then I suggest we let your photographers do their thing," said Father. "The sooner we get these bodies to the morgue, the sooner we'll have some answers."

"Any chance of getting a bite to eat upstairs?" asked the gardener.

"Kitchen's closed," said Mr. Graves, following us away from the scene as the police photographer started popping his bulbs.

Oh well, I thought, Millie's stew will keep.

The thought did not make my mouth water.

"By the way," said Graves to the gardener. "I understand you took a trip to Lexington."

"Briefly, yes," I said. "Just sort of passed through. If I'd known your folks' address, I would've looked them up."

"I'm not sure what you mean," said the Toolmaster. "My folks are dead, and they're buried in Yorktown, Virginia."

"Perhaps it's my mistake, Mr. Graves," said Father Baptist. "I thought I understood you to say, two Saturdays back, that you had gone back to Lexington to see your parents."

Not only did Father think he understood all that, but yours truly's memory was quite clear on the replay as well:

> *"Portifoy's a weird fellow,"* Mr. Graves had been saying, *"but he's a good magician ... That stuff you saw flying around the stage last night—the smoke and props—that was just wires and relays controlled by the crew. But give Portifoy a deck of cards and a handkerchief—trust me, he's good. I've seen him before."*
>
> *"Where?"* asked Father.
>
> *"Back in Lexington when I was visiting the folks last spring. A place called the 'Now You Don't.'"*

"Ah, I see," said Mr. Graves. "You didn't know me well enough to understand that every April I make a point of visiting the cemetery just south of town."

"Since when is Yorktown, Virginia south of Lexington, Kentucky?" I asked.

"You still don't understand," explained Mr. Graves, wiping his glasses on his shirt. "My family goes back to colonial times. I've got all sorts of kinfolk resting in cemeteries from Maine to the Carolinas. My great-great-great-great grandparents are buried in a secluded cemetery called Bradbury Ridge. You can look them up in the Colonial Cemetery Registry: Mortimer Packwood Graves and his beloved wife, Estelle Hilburn Graves."

"Ah," I said. "That explains it. So you know about the CCR?"

"Of course," said Graves. "That's been a big deal for years, especially after the Bicentennial. By the way, did you visit the 'Now You Don't'?"

"Yes, I did. Nice place if you like sawdust and peanut shells. Moab Chester Smith told me to give his regards to Ol' Roy Portifoy when I saw him, but ..."

114

"I DON'T KNOW IF MR. PORTIFOY was a vampire or not," I said as I steered the Jeep down the now-familiar serpentine driveway of the "House of Illusions." The wheels squealed as I turned left onto Franklin. "He certainly didn't crumble into dust like young Buckminster, and Bucky the Vampire was only three days old when you staked him. So I guess Portifoy was human after all, though Tamara Grafan suspected otherwise, or why would she have staked him? In any case, I have it on good authority: there's still a vampire on the loose."

"What was that?" asked Father Baptist, who had been pondering something out the passenger window.

"Bishop Pip," I explained, "told me that the moment the vampire dies, the 'Vampire's Shroud' disperses—*Ffft!*—as in instantly. Look around. I don't see any stars."

"No indeed," said Father. "We haven't seen any stars since—"
He stopped.

"Father?"

"I'm thinking, Martin."

"Not again."

"Yes, Martin."

"So you're just going to leave me hanging here—"

"Martin."

"Right," I said, flipping the turn signal and gunning the engine. "Sure."

115

"SO MUCH FOR TAMARA GRAFAN," said John Holtsclaw, peeling a pair of surgical gloves from his hands and depositing them in a flip-top wastebasket. "No puncture wounds, no apparent loss of blood. This was a hanging, pure and simple."

"What was that?" asked Father Baptist, who was over by the NEAR-ZERO STORAGE UNIT. He had pulled out the drawer containing Lucius T. Portifoy, still attired in his MC apparel, pewter clasp and all.

"Death by hanging," said Holtsclaw.

"Hmm," said Father, gingerly touching the butt of the stake which still protruded from Mr. Portifoy's chest. "Might I ask when you're going to perform an autopsy on this fellow?"

"I'm beat," said Holtsclaw. "He'll keep till tomorrow morning."

"Agreed," said Solomon. "I'm so exhausted my eyes won't focus. Next time I'm ordered to make a speech, I'm going to develop laryngitis."

"Besides, he's been staked," said Holtsclaw. "He's not going anywhere."

"True," said Father. "Whether he was human or a vampire."

"Wasn't he?" asked Solomon.

"Wasn't he what?" asked Father.

"You know," said Holtsclaw. "I mean, Sergeant Wickes told us that you told him that—"

"Too many people are telling too many things to too many people," said Father, examining Mr. Portifoy's pewter clasp. "What we need to determine is whether this woman committed suicide, or if she was murdered."

I was impressed by how Father could be looking at one thing while talking about another. Really. What impressed me more was how hungry I was, in spite of being in a morgue.

"Good question," said Holtsclaw.

"That we can't prove either way," said Solomon. "Though there was no stool or stepladder found in the cabinet, she could have climbed up on the plumbing fixtures on the wall and swung out from there."

"But is that what she did?" persisted Father, leaving Mr. Portifoy in peace and stepping over to the table on which Tamara Grafan resided. "Let me see that writing on her abdomen again."

"Sure," said Solomon, lifting the sheet.

I killeD my MasT3R,

"Martin," he said, motioning me to approach. "You're a writer."

"Well, sort of," I said, wishing my stomach wasn't growling so loudly. "More of a typist with imagination, actually."

"Close enough," said Father. "Do you see anything peculiar about this message? The way it's written, I mean."

"Hm, yes," I said, hands folded behind my back. "It reminds me of the scrawls on the little girl."

"Patricia Marie Nealy."

"Yes. A jumble of small and capital letters. No consistency. In 'killed' alone you have a small 'i' and a small 'e,' but the 'l's' and the 'd' are capitals. I'm not sure about the 'k.'"

"Is the Nealy girl still here?" asked Father of the coroners.

"Yes," said Solomon, "over her aunt's objections. Drawer eleven."

"Can't we just look at a photograph?" I suggested, not prepared to see the pathetic little corpse again..

"Yes," smirked Holtsclaw, digging around in the filing cabinet. "Here's one."

I AM CoME-!!

"Good memory, Martin," said Father. "You're right: capital 'a' and a small 'm' in 'am,' and a small 'e' in 'come' with all the other letters capitalized."

"It's almost as if a child wrote it," said the gardener.

"The same child?" asked Father. "Or the same adult pretending illiteracy?"

"I see your point," said Holtsclaw. "I can send photos up to a handwriting specialist tomorrow."

"Wait a minute," said Father, looking closely at the photograph. "Is there a magnifying glass handy?"

"Sure," said Solomon, holding up several. "Any particular strength?"

"Whatever," said Father, accepting an implement at random from Mr. Wong's offered assortment. He perused the photo, then bent to examine the smears on Tamara's corpse. "Martin," he said, "you're a genius."

"So I've always claimed," I said. "But why do you bring it up now?"

"Because it was you who said, 'The countdown continues.'"

"Yes, I did. I also withdrew the point when I realized the murders had occurred out of sequence. I'm not above refuting my own theories."

"Nonetheless," said Father, motioning me to look through the magnifying glass in his hand. "Look here."

"Two exclamation points," I observed. "The murderer was very excited. I felt the same way when I got off the plane here in LA after my wild weekend in Kentucky."

"Kentucky?" asked Holtsclaw.

"Never mind," I yawned.

"Two exclamation points, yes," said Father. "But also the number 'eleven,' or rather 'dash eleven' —"

"Or 'minus' eleven," said Solomon.

"I may be symbol-sensitive after the Farnsworth case," said Father, moving the magnifying glass two inches to the left. "The 'I' with a smudge after it. Could it possibly be made to look like a capital 'T,' as in 'T minus'?"

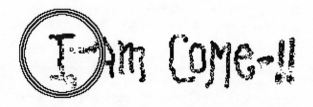

"You mean the way they used to call the countdowns at Cape Canaveral during the old Mercury days?" asked the gardener.

"'T' for 'take-off,'" said Holtsclaw. "I remember: 'T minus ten, nine, eight, seven, six …'"

"They never started," objected Solomon, "with 'T minus eleven.'"

"I don't know, Father," said yours truly, looking at the photograph
again. "You may be stretching it. Like you said, the Farnsworth case
may have gotten to you."

"Whether I am or not, or it has or not," said Father, "the pattern
starts here. This is the Nealy murder, the one where the MO suddenly
changed."

"Right," agreed Holtsclaw. "Different fangs, different means of dealing with the bodies—"

"And not actually murdering the victim," said Solomon, bumping a
rack of test tubes with his elbow, "as in the case of the chief's daughter,
and on several occasions."

The sound of the rattling glass tubes, the swirling of their contents,
and the sight of the coded labels sparked a fragmented memory in the
caverns of my cranium of a conversation over a week old:

> "Has the saliva been analyzed from around the Nealy girl's
> wound?" I had been asking someone.
> "The blood type is inconclusive," said that someone. "Some-
> how the lab tests got contaminated. It happens. Something to do
> with enzymes—ask Wong and Holtsclaw, not me. As for other
> residues—"

Who was that? I asked myself. Who's the "someone" I was talking
to?

My eyes went back to the labels on the test tubes—some yellow,
some white, some orange, all pieces of tape, peeling around the edges,
the tape—

"Taper," I said aloud.

"Larry?" asked Father. "What about him?"

"We were talking with him and Sergeant Wickes in your study," I
explained. "I think it was late Sunday, the day Patricia Marie Nealy's
body was found. The lieutenant said the test on the saliva from her
wound got botched. Enzymes or something."

"I remember informing Lieutenant Taper of that fact," said Holtsclaw,
snatching up his clipboard. "I ran the test. Contamination, it sometimes happens." He flipped a few pages. "Odd, though, the same problem happened with the test on Babbette Starr."

"Contamination?" asked Father.

"Yes," said Holtsclaw, reviewing his notes. "At least, I chalked it up
to contamination, but maybe it was something else."

"Like what?" I asked, feeling useful for once.

"Can't say," said the assistant coroner, tossing the clipboard onto a
countertop. "For some reason, the perpetrator's saliva in both cases
defied analysis."

"I wish I had thought to take a sample from Stella Billowack's throat in the hospital," said Father. "Of course, the doctors immediately dabbed the wound with disinfectants, so there really wasn't any opportunity."

"Could it be important?" I asked.

"I don't know," said Father.

"We'll see if we can do better with a sample from Mr. Ryan's throat," said Holtsclaw, snatching up the clipboard again and jotting a note to himself. "I'll be extra careful this time."

"Let's take a moment to review," said Father, changing the subject. He walked over to a "white board" on an easel, pulled the cap off a felt-tipped black marker, and said: "Solomon, John, the names of the victims from the start, in order please."

"Patricia Kelly was first," said Solomon, looking at the drawers in the NEAR-ZERO STORAGE UNIT as a memory aid. "Then Shelly Stevens, Alicia Alvarez, Anna Kay Dobbs—"

"Slower, please," said Father, writing the names on the board:

1.	Patricia Kelly
2.	Shelly Stevens
3.	Alicia Alvarez
4.	Anna Kay Dobbs
5.	Terisa Kim Lin
6.	Melissa Burchfield
7.	Elizabeth Unger
8.	Tiara Stockwell
9.	Patricia Marie Nealy

"The Nealy murder is where the pattern changed," said Father. "Let's see what happens if we make her number 'eleven' as well. Okay, then we have the countdown of numbers in blood."

9.	Patricia Marie Nealy	-11.
10.	Babbette Starr	-10.
11.	Stella Billowack	-9.

"The next victim was Nannette Cushions," said Solomon.

"But she wasn't marked with an 'eight,'" said Holtsclaw.

"Indeed," said Father. "She's a break in the new pattern—or rather, she's the last of the old."

"Come again?" asked Solomon.

"Properly placed in the sequence of events," said Father, making a sweep with the eraser, "Nannette Cushions is 'number nine' in the first series of murders, and should be properly placed after Tiara Stockwell. This is where the two sequences overlap. Let's see ... how shall I do this? Ah, I have it."

7.	Elizabeth Unger	
8.	Tiara Stockwell	
	Patricia Marie Nealy	-11.
	Babbette Starr	-10.
	Stella Billowack	-9.
9.	Nannette Cushions	
	--------	-8.

"Okay," said Solomon. "I see what you're saying: Nannette was the last of Surewood Forst's victims, while Patricia Marie Nealy was the first in the second killer's list."

"We still don't have a victim number 'minus eight,'" said Holtsclaw.

"Well ..." said the gardener.

"Agreed," said Father, flashing me a look that said, "Not now, Martin—Bucky Turnbuckle will require too much explanation at this juncture." He drew a dotted line. "Probably just hasn't turned up yet. Let's skip 'minus eight.' Then Stella Billowack was attacked again, but not killed. She was marked with a smudge that looked like 'minus seven.'"

"No 'six' either," said Holtsclaw.

"Okay," said Father, jotting another dotted line. "But then Stella Billowack was attacked a third time and marked with a 'minus five.'"

"Roland Reginold Ryan," said Solomon, looking over at the drawers, "was number 'four.'"

"But there's no 'three,'" said Holtsclaw. "Or at least, not yet."

"Don't be too sure," said Father, setting down the felt pen and going back to the woman's body on the table. He gathered the magnifying glass in his hand and motioned for the rest of us to look closely. "Tamara Grafan's so-called suicide note," he said. "Notice the backwards 'e' in 'Master.' See the little smudge in front of it?"

"'Minus three'?" said the gardener.

"I think so, yes," said Father. "It's that or a bizarre coincidence."

"Or you're symbol-sensitive, like you said," offered the gardener.

"Perhaps," said Father, setting down the magnifying glass and going back to the white board. "Perhaps not. And if I'm not, then our 'countdown' from Patricia Marie Nealy—disregarding Nannette Cushions as being part of the first sequence—has gone this far:"

Patricia Marie Nealy	-11.
Babbette Starr	-10.
Stella Billowack	-9.
--------*	-8.
Stella Billowack	-7.
--------**	-6.
Stella Billowack	-5.
R. R. Ryan	-4.
Tamara Grafan	-3.
?	-2.
?	-1.

GARDENING TIPS: Just to keep the record straight:
    (*)--You know and I know that "number 8" was
Buckminster Turnbuckle, recently turned vampire
and even more recently turned to dust.
    (**)--Just supposition at this point, but could
"number 6" be Surewood Forst? Hard to say, since
he had no abdomen left on which to leave messages,
after his encounter with the rolling machine.
    How Portifoy fit into the pattern--or even if he
did--is anybody's guess.
                                                    --M.F.

"But if Portifoy was the vampire," said Holtsclaw, "and this woman staked him, then we don't have to worry about 'two' and 'one.'"

"*If* Mr. Portifoy was our vampire," countered Father. "Otherwise, the countdown continues."

"If it's not him," asked Solomon, covering Tamara Grafan with a sheet, "then who?"

"Whoever it is," said the gardener, "he seems to have a marked liking for Stella Billowack. He's attacked her three times."

"You mean," said Father, "maybe he's playing with her—savoring her, perhaps—until the final blow?"

"I don't know. I just meant—"

"You're right, I think," said Father. "And even if you're not, I plan to move the chief's daughter to the rectory tomorrow."

"The chief won't like that," said the gardener.

"No," said Father, "but she'll be safer at St. Philomena's, I hope, than in a non-sectarian hospital. I plan to keep watch over her personally."

"I want to see this," said Solomon and Holtsclaw in unison.

"And well that you should," said Father. "Would you care to drop by my humble rectory tomorrow evening?"

"Sounds like a plan," said Solomon. "It beats waiting by my own front door with a bowl of candy for the creepy kids. It's Halloween, don't forget."

"That's right," said Holtsclaw. "It'll save a trip to the supermarket."

"Then we'll expect you when you arrive," said Father. He paused to rub his chin thoughtfully, eyes moving around the various objects in the lab, living, dead, and inanimate. "Are you sure you fellows aren't up to an autopsy of Mr. Portifoy now?"

"I'm so tired I can't see straight," said John Holtsclaw. Then to his boss: "How about you, Solomon?"

"No," said Mr. Wong, "my hands are shaking. Besides—you'll understand, I'm sure—I'd rather do the procedure in broad daylight."

"And," said Holtsclaw, "I'm not about to remove that stake before dawn."

"I do understand," said Father. "Martin, perhaps we should go home."

"No argument there," I said. "Millie's stew is beginning to sound better and better."

"Good night, gentlemen," said Father.

"Good night, Father," said the coroners.

The gardener, left out of the farewells, followed Father Baptist out of the room.

116

"SO TOMORROW IS HALLOWEEN," I mentioned as I steered the Jeep out of the morgue parking lot driveway and headed into the jungle of city lights.

"I know," said Father.

"Trick-or-treaters will be out in force."

"Indeed. Do you remember that song Pierre was singing in Elza's Sitting Room during our first visit there?"

"What song was that?"

"'Soul cakes, soul cakes,'" he hummed. It was unusual, in that car on that night, hearing Father Baptist singing: "'Meat nor drink nor money have I none. Still I will be merry anyhow ...'" He stopped. "That one."

"Yes," I said, taking up the next verse, "'One for Peter, two for Paul, three for Him Who made us all ...'" That's as far as I knew, so I ceased. "They play it a lot at Christmas time."

"Which is strange," said Father, "since it's really a Halloween song."

"How so?"

"Centuries ago, in the Age of Faith," said Father, "children used to go door to door, asking for soul cakes."

"Sort of the precursor to trick-or-treat," I surmised.

"Well, not exactly. Halloween is the eve of All Saints Day, November first, which is the day before the Feast of All Souls on November second."

"The Souls in Purgatory," I nodded, thinking of my ghostly friend, Elza.

"Right. The custom was for families to give the begging children a small cake for each member of the household who had died that year. In exchange, the children would pray for the dearly departed and eat the cakes on All Souls Day. The degeneration of such a beautiful practice into the greed of modern trick-or-treatery is a sad testimony to the times in which we live."

That being said, silence reigned in the Jeep for the next few miles.

"Speaking of tricks," I said presently, "you said something about a trap."

"I did."

"Joel and the Tumblars have been very busy. Are you going to tell me about it?"

"Not now, Martin, I'm thinking."

"Right. Are you thinking about the trap?"

"Martin."

"Right, you're thinking. About the trap?"

"Martin."

"Father."

Silence reigned for the rest of the trip home.

Millie's all-day stew, by the way, was quite good, as long as I kept my mind off dogs.

Tuesday, October Thirty-first

**Feast Day of Saint Wolfgang,
Missionary to the Magyars,
Bishop of Ratisbon,
tutor of Emperor Henry II,
and great benefactor of the Poor (994 AD)**

∞ All Hallows Eve ∞

[Samhain]

117

"BREAKFAST," ANNOUNCED MILLIE, dumping a pair of omelets on the table in front of Father Baptist and myself. "At least someone's staying put for a few minutes."

"Yum," said the gardener to show his stationary appreciation.

"What about you?" she said, whirling to face Joel who was standing beside the table, flanked by his grinning grandfather. "Going or coming?"

"Going," Joel gulped. "We'll grab a bite with Monsignor Havermeyer across the street."

"'Peanuts,'" nodded Josef. "Yah."

"Hrmph," she hrmphed, and headed back to the stove. "A man should mind the company he keeps."

"Monsignor Mike's not such a bad guy," said Joel uselessly to her back. "Once you get to know him."

"Monsignor Mike, is it?" snorted Millie. "HaaRRRRumph!"

Having paused to say Grace, Father hefted his fork. "You were saying, Joel?"

"Everything's ready," answered the lad. "We finished around ten last night. The only thing left is for Edward to pick up the garlic at the restaurant supplier this afternoon."

"Garlic," grinned Josef. "Whooh! Yah, goot."

"Bait for the trap?" I asked around a mouthful of hash browns.

"More like the noose," said Father. "I'll explain—"

"I know," I said, "later."

Joel left with Josef, leaving Father and myself to munch in relative peace—relative as in every other bite punctuated with resounding metallic clashes from Millie's direction. Presently, I asked a question:

"Why garlic, Father?"

"What's that?" said he, accepting a three-foot splosh from Millie's dive-bombing coffee pot. She doused my cup and headed back to the stove.

I was nudging a suspicious bubble in my omelet—nope, no suds. "Why is garlic repellent to vampires?"

"Hm," he said, savoring a long sip of the steaming brew, then setting down his cup. "That's an interesting question. According to ancient tradition, when Adam was driven from the Garden of Eden, he was allowed to take two plants with him. He chose onions and garlic."

"Adam had good taste, at least, considering all the havoc he and his wife caused," huffed Millie at the stove.

"Indeed," smiled Father.

"But of all the plants to choose from," I mused, "why two that stink so?"

"Perhaps," said Father, "it is a measure of our fallen nature that we don't perceive them as sweet."

"If you don't appreciate garlic," snorted Millie, shifting her pans around angrily, "you wouldn't have liked Paradise much, Mr. Feeney."

"But I do appreciate garlic," I protested. "Why, next to paprika, it's practically the Hungarian national flower."

"Hrmph," frowned Millie. "I'll show you a national flower."

"Historically," said Father, "garlic has always been used as a powerful medicinal agent."

"And where I come from," said Millie, dumping a frying pan into the sink under her favorite Crucifix, "it's used to counteract the effects of the Evil Eye."

"Really," said I.

"Yup," said she with authority. "It also repels the sin of Envy."

"Where are you from?" I asked, curious.

"None of your damned business," said Millie.

"Oh," I said. "Right."

"Which does make sense if you think about it," said Father. "St. Paul wrote in his Epistle to the Hebrews: 'And therefore we also having so great a cloud of witnesses over our heads, laying aside every weight and sin which surrounds us.'"

"First verse of chapter twelve," I nodded.

"A vampire," said Father, "is a demon who has been watching enviously the goings and comings of Man from that very cloud. Having been tortured for eons in the fires of Hell, it longs for the carnal existence we take for granted. For reasons and by methods about which we can only speculate, it condescends to don a jettisoned human shell, but alas it can never share fully in the Mystery of our humanity. It cannot love, so it cannot partake. It can never, for example, look upon the healing light of the Sun without being annihilated—which is why it often employs mortal humans to make its business and travel arrangements, humans which it uses for a while and then discards. And this is more crucial: it is part and parcel of the Angelic nature that its one-time choice to disobey God, in the beginning before Adam was created, transformed it into the pitiful thing that it is. Since Adam's expulsion from Paradise, it has watched with ravenous envy Man's ability to stumble, fall, and repent over and over."

"And garlic addresses all that," I said.

"Apparently so," said Father. "Vampires by nature are redolent with Envy. Garlic doesn't just repel them, it drains them of their physical strength and preternatural powers."

"You mean if you, let's say, managed to throw a vampire from a moving train, and he landed in a garlic field—?"

"He'd just lay there until the sun came up."

"That would be an interesting ending for a vampire movie. One more question."

"You promise?"

"I make no promises, Father, but I'd sure like to know: what about silver? It's not as precious as gold, yet you said vampires can't stand it."

"So the chroniclers of such things tell us," said Father. "Silver has always been associated by alchemists and metallurgists with the Moon. Our Blessed Mother is often portrayed standing upon the Moon, since She perfectly reflects the light of the Sun, Her Son, Christ Jesus."

"Where have you been, Mr. Feeney?" grumbled Millie, bowing at the mention of the name of Our Lord and Savior while rolling up her sleeves.

"I don't know," I admitted. "I must've fallen asleep when Sister Agatha was teaching us alchemy in the third grade."

"Silver," said Father, "is apparently imbued with those very properties which—"

The phone rang.

"St. Philomena's," I said sweetly into the receiver. "Sure, Mr. Holtsclaw. He's right here."

"Hello, John," said Father, accepting the phone from yours truly. His jaw suddenly dropped. "What's that—?"

"More trouble," grumbled Millie from the sink. "Why am I not surprised?"

"Repeat that," said Father, nodding and mumbling for a while. "Okay, Martin and I will be right over."

"What's wrong now?" I asked as Father handed me the phone and I tossed it into its cradle. "Another body?"

"The exact opposite," said Father, scowling to himself.

"What is the opposite of a body?" I asked.

"No body," said Father, and he wasn't kidding. "Lucius T. Portifoy is missing."

"You mean stolen?"

"I mean when Solomon and John went into the morgue to do the autopsy a short while ago, the body was not there. The police are scouring the lab for fingerprints as we speak. Apparently some of the blood samples in a locked refrigerator were also disturbed."

"Disturbed," I said. "How?"

"That's what we're going to find out," said Father. "Whatever happened, it occurred after we left last night."

"What about the other bodies," I asked, "in the NEAR-ZERO locker?"

"All present and accounted for," said Father.

"Halloween," grumbled Millie from her station at the sink. "It's always a bad day."

"Well," said Father, slapping his hands down on his knees. "Let's get our bodies over there."

"Funny way to put it," I said, grabbing my cane with the dragon's head handle.

118

"OKAY," SAID FATHER BAPTIST, having gone over with a magnifying glass every inch of the steel table that had been occupied the night before by Lucius T. Portifoy.

Yup, it was empty.

"Were the doors locked last night?" asked Father.

"Yes," said Solomon, "and the windows, which are barred besides. This is considered an 'evidence room.' High security."

"And there was no evidence of any of the locks being picked?" asked Father.

"Nope," said the coroners together.

"And you're absolutely certain," said Father, "that Lucius T. Portifoy was dead?—that there was no way he could have—?"

"No question," said Holtsclaw. "There was no pulse, no heartbeat, no skin conductivity other than what dead organic matter normally registers."

"Did you take any X-rays?" asked Father.

"Not last night," said Solomon. "That would have been our first procedure this morning."

"Did you check for brain waves?" asked Father.

"That's not something we're equipped to do in a morgue," said Holtsclaw testily. "We work on corpses, after all."

"For Heaven's sake, Father," said Solomon, even more testily, "the man had a stake through his chest."

"But only two weeks ago," said Father, looking grimly around the room, "you were both afraid that any of these bodies might get up and walk." There wasn't even a hint of facetiousness in his voice.

"Yes," admitted Holtsclaw, "but then you proved to our satisfaction that the vampire wasn't real—"

"But now," said Solomon, "you've been saying that it *is* real. Fine. So he was brought in with a stake through his heart. Even if he was a vampire, he couldn't survive that, right?"

"I don't know," said Father. "Until last night, I thought I knew more than I know now."

"Great," said Holtsclaw, hugging himself in a frustrated embrace. "If you're confused, where do you think that leaves us?"

"John," said Father, changing the subject, "you'd better show me the blood samples."

"Over here," said the assistant coroner, stomping toward a locked refrigerator. He gathered a bunch of keys from his pocket and opened the door. There were three shelves within, like in any ordinary household appliance, but this one was stocked with rows and rows of labeled, corked test tubes. "I almost didn't notice when I first checked them," he explained, calming down, "but I could swear the levels in some of these vials are low. They certainly didn't evaporate—not corked and chilled like that."

"Who would take a few drops of blood from each one?" asked Mr. Wong. "For what possible purpose?"

"These samples," said Father, scrutinizing them with the same magnifying glass. I was amused by the way it stretched his face as he looked back in our direction. "Were any of them connected with this case?"

"Some yes," said Solomon, "some no."

"Puzzling," said Father, closing the refrigerator door. "No prints I suppose."

"No," said Solomon. "Nothing other than our own."

"What are you going to do?" asked Holtsclaw.

"Gentlemen," said Father, stretching, "I'm going to make a quick visit over to the detention cells, and then I'm going home."

"To do what?" asked Holtsclaw.

"First to the holding cells to visit a couple of material witnesses," said Father. "Then I plan to spend the rest of the day in the church, praying."

"At last," whispered the gardener. "Some practical action."

119

"YOU WANT US TO WHAT?" scowled Jacco Babs, seated at the table in the familiar industrial-gray visitors' room.

"I'm inviting you to join us," said Father, seated opposite, "at St. Philomena's tonight for Halloween."

"What for?" asked Ziggie, seated beside his mentor and meal ticket, Mr. Babs.

"The story of your lives," said Father. "One which, I think, you will never print, but which you will forever be grateful that you witnessed."

"Sounds weird," said Jacco.

"Not if it doesn't land us back in here," said Ziggie.

"I don't think it will," said Father.

"Then I'm game," said Ziggie.

"I'll think about it," said Jacco.

"Fine," said Father, rising. "You do that."

"They'll be releasing us around dinner time," said Ziggie. "When should we come?"

"I can't say exactly when," said Father. "Men like you live by your instincts. Go with them."

"Sure thing, Padre," said Jacco.

"Surely something," said Father.

"And not fit to print," scowled Jacco. "What's the point?"

"You'll find out," said Father. "Martin, let's be off."

"Sure, Father," I said from my corner. "Anything you say."

120

"MAY I ASK," I VENTURED, setting down my fork after a wonderful lunch of bell peppers stuffed with seasoned rice, "why?"

"Why what?" asked Father, setting down his.

"Why invite those squirrels from the press?"

"More mouths to feed," growled Millie, grinding metal furiously. "I'd ask for a vacation, but I'd be too terrified at what I might find when I returned."

"Not just them," said Father. "I also phoned Taper and Wickes, Father Nicanor, and Monsignor Aspic just before lunch. The Tumblars, of course, are a given."

I took a deep slurp of coffee. "I repeat: why? Why have all these people around when you spring that trap you've been threatening to explain later? Isn't it going to be dangerous?"

"Yes," said Father. "But I want witnesses. There's more going on here than the unraveling of a sinister mystery. Don't forget, my sworn duty is to save souls."

"But—"

"Martin," said Father, resting his hands on the edge of the table, "there's no doubt in my mind that a countdown is in progress. At this point, I'm not sure what's what, but that letter you retrieved from your closet—"

"From Transylvania," I said, thinking of the piece of parchment that had booted me all the way to Kentucky and back.

"Right. Consider the wording." As he recited it from memory, I visualized it from mine:

> *My dear Father Baptist,*
> *I have been watching your exploits. I have no doubt that you will catch this insufferable murderer within the week. In fact, on my ancestors, I predict it. The time has come for you to meet a worthy adversary. Savor the moment. Expect me for Samhain.*

"Not just 'Dear,' but 'My dear Father Baptist,'" said Father. "A bit on the familiar side, don't you think?"

"A bit," I agreed. "Either that or he's old-fashioned and excessively gracious in a twisted, B-movie sort of way."

"'I have been watching your exploits'—meaning, of course, the Farnsworth murders. It sounds a little more imminent than reading a few newspaper clippings."

"What, like the guy has a crystal ball or something?"

"Perhaps. Vampires are demons, after all. As fallen Angels, perhaps they retain their gift of distant sight."

"Hmm."

"And I cook at the speed of fire," snarled Millie, fiendishly brandishing a spatula. Since lunch was over, I couldn't image what she was threatening to do with it.

Father continued: "'I have no doubt that you will catch this insufferable murderer within the week.' If I have my chronology right, this came true."

I rested my elbows on the table. "As if the writer had second sight, you mean."

"Perhaps," said Father. "'In fact, on my ancestors, I predict it.' The appeal to forefathers is interesting, in light of all you discovered on your trip to Kentucky."

"Maybe."

"'The time has come for you to meet a worthy adversary. Savor the moment.' If that isn't baiting, I don't know what is. We've all felt that we're being played along: descending numbers on the victims, messages with numbers in them, patterns shifting but nonetheless ongoing."

"Yeah, well—"

"'Expect me for Samhain.' That's the real clincher. Not only is 'Samhain' an uncommon word, an ancient word, but it denotes one of several days in the year when the membrane between the spiritual realm and the world of coarse matter grows thin. Your ancestors and mine understood this, and prepared themselves for it with fasting, prayer, liturgy, and ritual. They feared Samhain because they comprehended its implications. Rest assured, as the fabric of Reality weakens, the fiend who wrote that letter will come knocking this evening."

"I'll show him a thing or two," snarled Millie, slamming the spatula against a skillet. "Let him show his face in my kitchen—!"

"And for this you want witnesses," I gulped, looking from Millie back to Father.

"Perhaps," said Father, forming his fingers into a steeple, "we'll all catch a glimpse of Hell, and will therefore reconsider our lives more seriously. In matters such as the one which is set before us, that is invariably the point."

"Hmm," I answered.

"I'll tear him limb from limb," growled Millie, clawing her pots accordingly.

"And so," said Father calmly, "I want to spend some time before the Blessed Sacrament, preparing myself. And you, Martin?"

"Hmm," I hmmed. "I'll join you presently. With all the fuss that's been going on, I haven't checked on Monsignor Havermeyer's progress with the Rubrics."

"A splendid idea," said Father. "Preparation takes many forms."

"I guess I'll make a quick run to the market," said Millie, tossing down a towel, her rending demonstration completed. "Tonight's Halloween, and the trick-or-treaters will be knocking at our door." I thought she added, "Little Vermin," but I wasn't sure.

"All right," said Father, rising from his chair. "Let all go about our appointed tasks."

"Okay," I said, grabbing my cane.

"Right," growled Millie, untying her flowered apron.

121

"THE PALL," I SAID. "That's that small square of stiffened linen."

"This thing?" asked Monsignor Havermeyer.

"No, that's the Burse. The Pall is that white thing over there."

"You mean this."

"That's it."

Back in THE TORTOISE AND THE SPARE School of Rubrics, Martin Feeney presiding. Monsignor Havermeyer was bent over the little table, the accouterments of the Tridentine Mass set before him. A large red altar missal was propped up against a non-functional electric toaster. That was our practice Tabernacle.

"Okay," I directed, "you lift the Pall off the Chalice. Set it off to the right. You can't genuflect, since you're sitting, but that's what you would do if you could."

"Right," he said, eyes glancing every which way as he tried to remember what he was supposed to do next. He couldn't.

"Now, take the host in your right hand. Remember at this point it has already been consecrated, so only touch it with your thumb and forefinger."

He did so.

> GARDENING TIPS: Since this was only a prac-
> tice session--the priest's intent being
> lacking--the bread and wine were not, in
> fact, actually consecrated, which is why
> throughout this exercise I have not capi-
> talized the words "host" and "wine."
> —M.F.

"Pick up the Chalice with your left hand, remembering that you can't use the thumb and forefinger because they touched the host a few pages back during the Consecration."

"Awkward," he mumbled, trying to grip the Chalice stem with his third, fourth, and pinkie fingers.

"It's easier," I said, "if you keep your thumbs and index fingertips pressed together."

"How would you know? You're not even allowed to touch these things."

"In my youth as an altar boy, I watched closely. Now make the Sign of the Cross three times with the host over the Chalice while reading the next part."

I eyed the large, boldfaced, Latin words on the open page of the missal:

**Per [✠] ipsum, et cum [✠] ipso,
et in [✠] ipso ...**

"Good," I said. "Make the Sign of the Cross with the host between the Chalice and your chest."
"Here?"
"Yes."

**... est tibi Deo Patri [✠] omnipotenti,
in unitate Spiritus [✠] Sancti ...**

"Now lift the Chalice slightly," I said, "and hold the host above it."

... omnis honor et gloria.

"Set the Chalice down, put the host back on the Paten, and be sure to cover the Chalice again with the Pall before you genuflect."
"Why put the Pall back on the Chalice?" asked Havermeyer.
Remaining calm, I explained: "Because, My Senior, if you don't, a fly might happen along and land in the consecrated wine."
"You're joking."
"Not about this. During an actual Mass, every drop in that Chalice would contain the Blood, Body, Soul and Divinity of Christ. You are accountable for every drop. If a fly were to land in it, you'd be required to consume it."
"I see," said the monsignor, eyes a bit wider than usual. "So there's a practical reason for the Pall as well as a liturgical one."
"When it comes to the time-honored practices of Mother Church," I said, "that is usually the case. Okay, another genuflection, then you've got one more line to recite."

Per omnia sæcula sæculorum.   Amen.

"Very good, My Senior," I said. "And before we call it a day, what was it you just said?"

"You mean, translate this?"

"Go on, try."

He glared at the words on the page for several long seconds before speaking. As he did so, his gnarled hands made minute gestures as if going through the motions without touching the vessels; and his voice trembled with emotion.

**By [✠] him, and with [✠] him,
and in [✠] him
is to Thee, God the Father [✠] Almighty,
in the unity of the Holy [✠] Ghost,
all honor and glory.
For ever and ever. Amen.**

"Excellent," I said, placing my hand affectionately on his shoulder. Thinking better of it, I removed it immediately. "Well, that's enough for today, don't you think?"

"Yes," he sighed. "I tell you, Martin, I don't know how I'll keep all this straight. An old dog, you know."

"I'll be at your side when the time comes," I assured him. "Well, actually, a step behind and on my knees, but I'll be there. Hey, maybe there's a song in that."

He gave me a look that said he didn't think so.

Agreeing, I nodded good-bye and exited the camper.

My plan to join Father in the church was temporarily delayed by the sight of Roberto Guadalupe with his two companions coming across the cemetery with an empty wheelbarrow and a couple of shovels.

"Roberto," I greeted him. "What's up?"

"Oh, Señor Feeney," he said, setting down an aluminum spraying tank with a hollow clunk. "We were just planting some rosebushes over near the stone hut."

"Really," I said. "Father Baptist will be pleased."

"I also noticed the avocado trees—they are sick."

"I didn't know they were susceptible to the flu."

"No," laughed Duggo, his companion. "It is the bugs."

"Bugs?" I asked.

"Sí," said Spade, Roberto's other companion. "In the roots and branches."

"I wonder where they came from," I said.

"Well," said Roberto, "when we cleared the graveyard, we destroyed many homes. The little ones are simply trying to find new places to nest in. Maybe that's what killed the dichondra last week."

"Oh yeah," I said. "I'd almost forgotten. So you sprayed some poison."

"It is a last resort," said Duggo. "Insects, they are good, but only if they stay where they belong."

"Life is hard," I agreed. "Speaking of homes, did you ever get the door to that stone hut open?"

"No, Señor Feeney," said Roberto. "I tried, but even with the crowbar, it is still stuck. Maybe I will try the sledgehammer, and then build a new door."

"Like I said," I said, "life is hard. Well, adios, and muchas gracias."

"Someday I will teach you to speak the Spanish properly," smiled Roberto.

"I'll look forward to it," I said sincerely, moving away.

My plan to join Father Baptist was delayed further still by the sight of Joel Maruppa, his grandfather Josef, Jonathan Clubb, Edward Strypes Wyndham, and Arthur von Derschmidt coming through the garden carrying cartons marked WIDGEON'S PRODUCE: GARLIC FROM GILROY. Nodding a sweaty greeting, they disappeared into the old storage room two doors over from mine. Pierre, of course, was standing apart, directing.

It was odd to see them all again in work clothes—excluding Pierre, of course.

"Wow," I said. "What are you making in there? Garlic salsa?"

"The best," winked Pierre, immaculate in his business suit. "Only the best for Father Baptist."

"Sure thing," I said, moving right along.

122

"EXCUSE ME, FATHER, MARTIN," said Arthur in an almost inaudible whisper. "It's three-thirty. I think we should get started."

Father said nothing. Making the Sign of the Cross, he bowed to the Tabernacle that housed the Real Presence, rose to his feet, genuflected, and proceeded down the middle aisle of the church. His faithful gardener did the same things, but without the grace and style. The intent, though not the effect, was the same.

The Tumblars, still in work clothes—Pierre in suit—were lined up near the confessional, awaiting Absolution. I took up the rear.

That took about a half hour.

While awaiting my turn, I considered the propriety of fashioning a little budget escutcheon of my own to hang on the door to "The Box"—something once penned by that same Saint who is so good at helping me find misplaced things:

The demon can enter by the five senses, but only by the lips can he be rejected. Through many chambers does he have access to our conscience, but only through one door can he be expelled, that is: through the mouth, by confession.

—St. Anthony of Padua

Then Father led us all to the front of the church where the Tumblars received Holy Communion.   Having received the Holy Eucharist at Mass that morning, Father and I abstained.

"May the Lord God protect us all," said Father as he concluded the brief service. "In the Name of the Father, and of the Son, and of the Holy Ghost."

"Amen," said we all.

123

"GOSH," SAID STELLA BILLOWACK, trying to focus as Father, Jonathan, Joel, Edward, and yours truly gathered around her hospital bed. "What are all you doing here?"

"This is what is known as a 'jail break,'" winked Edward.

"Father Baptist," gasped Jonathan, nudging close and taking up her hand. "She's awake!"

"Of course she is," said a gruff female voice emerging from the tiny bathroom. "And dressed she is, under that blanket."

"Veronika," smiled Joel.

"Jonathan?" whispered Stella. "Is it true?"

"Is what true?" asked Jonathan.

"That you Baptized me?"

"Well, that is, uh ... yes."

"Not that I mind," she assured him with a finger squeeze. "I mean, I did so want Father Baptist to do it, but ... did I really almost ... you know ... die?"

"'Fraid so," said Jonathan.

"What else has Veronika told you?" asked Father.

"Only that I've been unconscious for almost a week," she said. "It's hard to believe."

"And how do you feel?" asked Father.

"Tired," said Stella, eyelids fluttering, "and terribly weak."

"Do you feel up to a little trip?" asked Jonathan.

"A trip? Where?"

"To St. Philomena's," said Father.

"Really?" she said, stirring under the covers. "So that's why this woman dressed me—Veronika, I mean. Father Nicanor came with her, and I know he's your friend, Father, so I went along with it."

"Where is Father Nicanor?" asked Father.

"He said he'd meet you at your rectory, Father," said Veronika, unrolling her sleeves. "He needed to fetch some tools or something."

"How will you get home?" asked the gardener.

"Oh, I'm coming with you," she beamed, buttoning her cuffs. Then she gathered her shawl around herself. "I wouldn't miss this for the world."

"There's always room for one more," said Edward.

"Yeah," I whispered, wondering who was going to sit on whose lap. I was already making plans to ride shotgun.

"I can't just walk out of here," said Stella.

"Of course not," said a voice from the doorway.

All eyes turned to the male nurse, all covered in hospital blues and wearing a surgical mask. He pulled a gurney behind him, which pulled behind it another similarly clad fellow.

"Your carriage awaits, Mademoiselle," said the first male nurse. Even before he spoke, I knew the eyes above the mask could belong to none other than Pierre Bontemps.

The other nurse's eyes were not so distinctive, but the ponytail draped down the back of his tunic could only belong to Arthur von Derschmidt. "We hope not to put your nerves to the test," he mumbled behind his mask, "but we've never driven one of these things before."

"I don't believe this," coughed Stella, weakly. "You guys are too much."

"Up you go," said Veronika, elbowing Jonathan aside and gripping Stella's arms. "Out of the way, gents."

With the swift whirl of a trained physical therapist, Veronika somehow scooped Stella out of the bed and whooshed her around onto the gurney. She made the maneuver seem effortless.

I looked on, from my cloud of arthritis, envious of her mobility and grace. Oh well, with all that garlic back at the rectory, Envy was one sin that wouldn't get much of a foothold this night.

"What fun," giggled Stella as Pierre and Arthur gripped the gurney for take-off.

"Shhhh," shushed Veronika, covering her with double layers of open-weave blankets. "Do you want us all to spend the night in jail?"

"Hurry," said Father to Pierre and Arthur.

They did.

And not a minute too soon.

Thirty seconds later, as the rest of us made ready to exit, none other than Montgomery "Bulldog" Billowack's gangrenous mass filled the doorway.

"What's goin' on here?" he bellowed, looking over our shoulders. "Where's my Stella?"

"Some orderlies were just here," explained Jonathan. "Sir."

"You again," said Billowack, glaring menacingly at his potential son-in-law. Ah, the Thanksgiving dinners they were going to enjoy together.

"They took her away," explained Edward.

"Away where?" bristled Billowack.

"One of them said something about a test," shrugged the gardener.

The cheerless chief swung his jowls in my direction.

Suddenly I understood what St. Martha and St. George felt when they faced their dragons—or perhaps what Dougle and Annie McHargue experienced one evening during a leisurely drive around a famous Scottish lake in their sporty Haggis Classic Roadster, when something dark, huge, and maybe even slightly blurred slithered out onto the road and looked hungrily into their oncoming headlights.

The slavering lips of my own personal dragon encounter parted for the next question.

"What kind of test?"

His pestilent breath wafted past me.

"A multi-syllabic test, no doubt," I said, smiling helpfully, eyes blinking against the heat.

"Idiot," he growled.

"Quite right," I nodded to my saurian nemesis, "which explains why I can't pronounce whatever-it-was they were going to do whenever they got her to wherever-it-was they were taking her."

"Jack," shouted Billowack, swinging his jowls toward Father Baptist, "if this is some trick—"

"Trick?" said Father, eyebrows arched innocently. "What kind of trick could we possibly be pulling here on the third floor of a major hospital?"

"I don't know," barked Billowack, "but I'm gonna find out."

"You big windbag," huffed Veronika, shouldering her way through us and standing before the malevolent chief. "Why don't you pick on someone your own size?"

"Like who?" sneered Billowack.

"Like me," she said in a tone that could have rendered liquid mercury into a frozen solid.

"Bah," bleated Billowack, turning away and stomping elephantine footprints into the linoleum all the way down the hallway. "If I find out anything's screwy around here, heads will roll. Even yours, Toots."

"Why of all the nerve," said Veronika, rolling up her right sleeve again.

"Not now," said Father, hand on her arm. He watched until the bull-dog was out of sight around the corner. "Okay everyone, let's get out of here."

As one we charged like a mighty stallion—well, it was really more like a strutting workhorse, followed closely by a lumbering street sweeper—but anyway, we made our way to the door marked STAIRS: NO ROOF ACCESS and rumbled our way down to the ground floor.

Stella had already been transferred from the gurney into the back of Edward's van, which was parked in one of the EMERGENCY slots.

As I'd planned, I managed to ride shotgun all the way home. I won't say who was on whose lap in the back. This was a moment of necessity.

124

"IN HERE?," ASKED STELLA as Father guided her into "Wrecked Room Number Three."

"In here," nodded Father, as the rest of us clamored in behind.

"What do you want me to do?" she asked.

"Nothing," said Father, indicating a lumpy couch which had been positioned against the far wall beneath the window. I noticed the small silver Crucifix, which Father usually kept on the nightstand in his bedroom, hanging from the ring of the window shade.

"With all the sawing and hammering I heard coming from up here," I commented, "I would have thought this place would look substantially different than before. Okay, so you did lay a new carpet, but the walls are still bare studs."

"The difference," said Pierre, still in his hospital clothes and mask, "is not obvious, but it is nonetheless here."

"Where?" I asked.

"Right before your eyes," said Pierre, winking over the mask.

"Will you take that thing off?" I asked.

"Anything you say, Fényi Márton."

"I want you to get some rest," said Father to Stella. He removed something from the folds of his threadbare cassock. "And I want you to keep this on you at all times tonight. Never let it go."

"Is this a relic?" she asked, accepting the small golden vessel. "I've never seen one up close."

"St. Philomena," said Father, folding her fingers around the reliquary. "She is the Patroness of this parish. Many are the times we have relied upon her help."

He motioned for Stella to lie down.

"Jonathan will stay with you until I return," said Father.

"Of course, Father," said Jonathan, brightening.

"Jonathan," said Father, "let her sleep."

"Sure," said Jonathan, dimming.

"The rest of us are going downstairs," said Father. "With all the cloud cover, it will be hard to tell precisely when the sun goes down. We must prepare."

"For what?" asked Stella sleepily.

"For Halloween," said Father, ushering the rest of us out of the room.

"Another one?" complained Millie as we came down the stairs.

Monsignor Conrad J. Aspic was standing nervously at the open front door.

"Oh well," cried Millie, martyr to the core, strutting down the hall-way toward the kitchen, "what's one more in a stampede? Veronika! Better break out the paper plates. No way I'm going to wash up after all this!"

125

"YOU WON'T SEE IT," SAID A SCRATCHY VOICE from the tiny transistor radio atop Millie's stove, "but the sun will go down at precisely three minutes after five o'clock."

"I was hoping the weatherman would say something about it," said Father, seated quietly in the little dining nook. He was scrutinizing the computer printouts I had brought back from Transylvania through a magnifying glass with a double-thick lens. "It's already so dark out-side, and it's only 4:45."

"Can I turn it off now, Father?" snarled Millie, whose tone was more cantankerous than usual—I would say at least five notches above aver-age on the angstometer.

"Yes," said Father, absently. "By all means."

"Thank God," she said, tossing the radio into her towel hamper.

I could see, from my vantage point, the sheet Father was reading. The outdated dot-matrix printer Irma Shrumpf used had been short on ink, and the font size small, hence Father's use of the glass.

WWW Project History to date:

001   March 1989--First project proposal (link is to later ver-
           sion) written and circulated for comment at CERN.
           Paper "HyperText and CERN" (in ASCII or WriteNow
           format) produced as background.

002   October 1990--Project proposal reformulated with en-
       couragement from CN and ECP divisional manage-
       ment. RC is co-author.

003   November 1990--Initial WorldWideWeb prototype de-
       veloped on the NeXT (TBL). Work begins on line-
       mode browser, also interface to CERNVM "FIND" in-
       dex running.

004   December 1990—Line-mode and NeXTSTep browsers
       demonstrable. Access is possible to hypertext
       files, CERNVM "FIND," and Internet news articles ...

Father had just circled the entry marked "003" with a pencil when Millie suddenly dumped a handful of cups and saucers into the sink with a crash. Whirling around to face us, she announced: "Now look, Fathers—"

By "Fathers" she was referring to Father Baptist, Father Nicanor, Monsignor Aspic, and I assume by association, myself. Monsignor Havermeyer, to avoid the humiliation of gulping down his single potato in front of the others again, had opted to eat across the street and hadn't yet returned. The Tumblars had gone out the back door to "take their stations" immediately after wolfing down double helpings of Millie's "Halloween Surprise Casserole." Veronika, standing at Millie's side with spatula in muscled hand, was apparently not included in the announcement.

GARDENING TIPS: If Millie ever tried marketing
that casserole, by law she would have to list the
contents on the package in order of magnitude.
The first three ingredients would be:

1) whole garlic
2) crushed garlic
3) all the juice from ingredient #2

Everything else would fall under the category of
"trace elements." I'm not kidding. No one who
dined at the rectory that night was kissable for
at least seventy-two hours--except if they wanted
to do so with each other, as in the case of Jonathan and Stella ... though of course they didn't
get a minute's peace anyway, once things got jumping.
                                        --M.F.

N.B. It being the vigil of a major holiday, Millie
had to make the "meatless" version. When I asked
her what kind of meat she used on other occasions,
she replied, "Onions."

"Now look, Fathers," Millie was saying, folding her arms in such a way that the sinews and veins collided to form something akin to dragon scales. "I've fed the lot of you, meaning we'll go without around here for the next few days. With Veronika's help, I'll clean up after you, which means staying up till all hours. With St. Martha as my witness, I don't begrudge the servile duties of a humble house-keeper."

Father Baptist glanced up from his printouts.

I met his eyes from my place beside the distilled water dispenser.

"But," said Millie, the worm turning, "under no condition what-so-bloody-ever am I going to go running to answer the doorbell every five minutes when those filthy, greedy, giggling little rat-runts come begging for treats at the front door."

"Suffer the little children do," I whispered, misquoting the nineteenth chapter of St. Matthew's Gospel, "who fall under the shadow of Millie's wrought-iron frying pan."

"Do I make myself clear?" screamed Millie, stomping her foot. The plates in the cupboards rattled.

Father Nicanor, for the first time since I'd known him, had no r's to roll, nor any other consonants to convolute. His eyes went to Monsignor Aspic, who looked like anything but the perky, rosy-cheeked, efficiency-managed psycho-reorganizer who first clip-clopped into our lives two weeks before. He looked at me, though why I can't guess. I was still busy looking at Father Baptist who had set down the magnifying glass and was searching around for something within the mysterious folds of his cassock.

"Ding-dong!" went the doorbell.

Timing is everything.

GARDENING TIPS: Timing is, indeed, everything. I
was awake when Sister Agatha taught us that. Actually, she woke me up just so I would feel included, and beat a rumba on my head by way of demonstration with her thirty-six inch ruler. Good
Heavens! I know people who abandoned their Faith
for less than that!
                                        --M.F.

Looks went around the room again. No one moved.

I could envision the ignited cannon fuse, brightly oxidizing as blinding white sparks spurted every which way, the consuming flame creeping inexorably toward the tightly-packed blend of potassium nitrate, charcoal, and sulfur which was loaded behind Millie's gun-barrel mouth.

"Ding-dong!" chimed the doorbell again, cheerfully, expectantly.

"You!" came the cannonball out of Millie's maw. We all watched it fly in a beeline for Monsignor Aspic. "Wake up, will you?"

"Me?" squeaked the not-so-perky archdiocesan consultant.

"You!" fired Millie at will. "Make yourself useful. Go answer it. There's a bowl full of teeth-rotting candies on the table by the front door."

Monsignor Aspic, unused to being addressed in this manner, shoved his hands deep into his pockets. Alas, poor fellow, he had no change to jingle. His shoes weren't shined, so he couldn't look down and admire his cherubic grimace. I reminded myself that he was in mourning, after all.

"And," said Millie, aiming an index finger that looked a bit too much like the barrel of a shotgun, "under no circumstances let any of those germ-spreading, nose-picking, goo-smearing rodents in to use the bathroom. They always miss!"

"Oh," gulped the monsignor, turning to go. "Okay, I guess I can manage that—"

"Hold on," said Father Baptist, rising from the dining nook. "Before you do, I want you to wear this."

"A Crucifix?" gasped Aspic, recoiling, stretching his face sideways to show his distaste, so much so that his nostrils ended up at odd diagonals. You'd've thought he was a vampire.

"Yes," said Father, holding up the black enamel sacramental with a golden Corpus on a stainless steel chain.

"I'd never wear such a thing," pleaded Aspic, arms out front, palms forward, fingers up—the stance of the average male seeing his bride without makeup for the first time the morning after the wedding—or that of the average female when she ... oh, never mind.

"You will tonight," said Father, sternly. "This Cross was blessed by Padre Pio."

"Never heard of him," said Aspic. "And I won't go around wearing the likeness of a, a, a dead man around my neck. It would be no different than wearing a pin on my lapel in the shape of a man hanged on the gallows."

"And you a monsignor!" glared Father Nicanor, r's rolling like the coffee in Millie's percolator. "Of the Crucifixion there is nothing to be ashamed except Man's woeful response to God! But even so, by this same Cross it is that Salvation comes, not the doily, not the creampuff, not the easy path—"

"Ding-dong!" rang the doorbell again, this time less cheerfully and more greedily.

"I don't know what you're talking about," said Conrad J-for-Jonas Aspic, eyes darting between Fathers Baptist and Nicanor, deftly avoiding the swaying Crucifix.

"Where did you find this apostate?" snarled Veronika. I wasn't clear on who she was asking. I got the impression she was just enjoying a good snarl.

"Fresh from the modern seminary," said Father Nicanor, r's purring like tigers rolling on their backs in a pile of catnip.

"Your collection-plate dollars at work," remarked the gardener, scratching his ear with the jagged teeth of his dragon-headed cane.

"Nonetheless," said Father Baptist to Monsignor Aspic, "you will wear this Crucifix as long as you are here on my property this evening, or I'll call a cab to take you elsewhere. Lieutenant Taper and Sergeant Wickes will be here soon, and they'll be glad to escort you—"

"All right, all right," Monsignor Aspic relented, allowing Father to maneuver the Crucifix over his head and drape it down the front of his cassock. "Great gravy, I don't know why I came here tonight in the first place."

"To learn something," said Father Baptist. "To learn that Jesus Christ, to whom you pretend some myopic level of allegiance, came down from Heaven and shed His Blood and died that we might live. The vampire, on the other hand, drinks the blood of the living, so that they die that he might live. The vampire is Satan's mockery of the Incarnation as well as the Resurrection."

"I already told you I don't believe in those myths," said Aspic.

"Most people," said Father, "don't believe in Hell, either. The worst thing they can imagine is death. So what do vampires in the monster movies bring upon their victims? Death. Lots of senseless, bloody, even sensuous death—much like the activities of your late brother, Surewood."

"Now see here—"

"But there are real vampires, Monsignor Aspic, as you will discover this night. Real vampires are but low-class demons possessing lifeless corpses. Their sole raison d'être is to populate Hell with human souls that have refused God's Grace."

"All of which is nonsense—"

"Vampires," persisted Father, "like priests, like you and me, are concerned with souls, not lives—the difference being that vampires seek to destroy them, whereas our job is to save them."

"Do you really think," countered Aspic, clutching the thing around his neck as though it were a boa constrictor—a very filthy, icky boa constrictor, "that wearing this provides protection against, against—?"

Father Baptist lowered his voice a half octave while taking a step closer. "My concern with respect to you, Monsignor, is not the mere preservation of your hide from harm, but the possibility of Salvation for your soul. Death may very well visit this rectory tonight, in which case—"

"Ding-dong!" intruded the doorbell, more imperative than ever.

"Are you just going to stand around talking theology?" screamed Millie, waving her skillet. "Somebody answer that blasted door or I'll—!"

Shrugging, I turned to comply.

"Not you!" barked Millie to me. "I said 'somebody.'" The fire in her eyes was directed at our favorite Jonas, God bless'im.

"One more thing," said Father to Aspic.

Millie let her skillet drop. It landed on the linoleum floor with a resounding thunk. Veronika stooped to fetch it, but Millie kicked it out of her reach. It skidded across the floor and slammed into the pantry door.

"Millie's right," said Father calmly. "Under no circumstances whatsoever, Monsignor Aspic—and this applies to everyone here present, so listen up: under no circumstances allow anyone into this house tonight without my say so. No one—man, woman, or even a child in desperate need of a bathroom. Not through any door, window, or other access. A vampire can only enter a house when it is invited by someone within. Got that?"

"Ding-dong!"

"Will—somebody—*get* that!" screeched Millie.

The rest of us "Fathers" listened as Monsignor Aspic, bewildered and befuddled as befit him, crept down the hallway to greet Millie's favorite rat-runts.

I turned to Millie. "Could I have a cup of—?"

"In your face or on your lap, Mr. Feeney?" she growled, snatching up the coffeepot from the stove.

I hesitated, taken aback by the intensity of the tone. What a mood she was in!

"Or you want I should just cram this whole thing," yelled Millie, brandishing the pot like some fiendish medieval instrument of torture, "down your throat?"

There was more than intensity in her tone. There was danger.

"Never mind, Millie," I said, backing away.

"Martin," said Father Baptist, who had managed to reseat himself in the dining nook in the interim. He had opened the French window usually used by Mrs. Magillicuddy for her Friday-night quasi-confessions, and was peering out at the garden. "Martin, it's getting so dark outside it's hard to see. Can you tell me what that is sitting on the ground near St. Thérèse's statue?"

I continued backing away from Millie, fearing to take my eyes off that deadly coffeepot, until I bumped Father's elbow.

"What did you ask, Father?"

"That thing on the ground, see it? Near the birdbath."

"Oh," I said, peering though the gathering gloom. "That looks like Roberto's tank—you know, for spraying insecticides. He must've forgotten it, or else he's going to use it again tomorrow."

"Where was he doing that?" asked Father.

"Where was he doing what?" I asked.

"Spraying?"

"Out in the new-old cemetery."

"When?"

"Today."

"Why?"

"Because when he and his men cleared away the jungle, they displaced a lot of insects and critters. The little buggers took up residence in the avocado trees in the far corner. He said that's probably why the dichondra died, too."

"What dichondra?"

"Didn't I tell you? I guess with all that's been going on it slipped my mind. Let's see, Roberto and his crew brought a truckload a week ago Monday—several hundred squares at least—and piled it up by the stone hut. But since that was the day we also buried Bucky Turnbuckle, they opted to leave the planting for another time. Then Wednesday it was when Roberto told me all the dichondra had died. Why, is it important?"

Father looked thoughtful. Then he looked pensive. Then he looked downright engrossed. It was quite a progression. Presently, he looked up at me.

"'Important,' you ask? Why, Martin, it flips my switch."

> GARDENING TIPS: Another TEK reference--
> prayerfully the last.
>
>   --M.F.

"I wish I'd known about this a few days ago," said Father, getting up from his chair, "but, come to think of it, I wouldn't have put it all together a moment before now anyway."

"Put what together?" I asked.

"Cheryl Farnsworth's vision," said Father, "and Helga Feuchtwanger's Volkswagen."

"Huh?"

"What time is it?" asked Father Baptist of anyone.

"Almost five o'clock," said Father Nicanor, consulting that triangular rectangular contraption with Arabic squiggles he called a watch. "Sundown any minute now."

"Martin," said Father Baptist. "Fetch a flashlight, will you? I hate to risk it, but you and I are going outside."

"Why?" I asked, fumbling in the drawer where Millie kept light bulbs and extension chords.

"Because we must," said Father Baptist. "Father Nicanor, please be so kind as to go upstairs and stay with Stella until I get back. Tell Jonathan to wipe that look off his face and join his comrades. Veronika, thank-you for helping Millie with her chores. Millie, I don't know what's eating you tonight, but please don't kill anyone. Martin, did you get that flashlight?"

"Right here," I said, not exactly enthused about another mission at that moment, especially outside. "See you soon, Millie, Veronika, Father Nicanor." I was gripped with the feeling that these good-byes might be final.

"Grrrrr!" growled Millie as Father and I opened the kitchen door and stepped outside. She cranked the spigots, flooding the enamel basin with steaming hot water. "Now for all this mismatched silverware. See if I don't cut myself!"

"Let me help, dear," said Veronika.

"You can dry," snarled Millie. "I'll take the dangerous detail."

On second thought, maybe outside with a vampire was safer than inside with Millie ... Naw, just kidding.

126

"FATHER, I D-D-D-DON'T SEE THE POINT," I stammered as we groped our way toward the cemetery, dank wind scattering leaves all around us, the beam of my flashlight sweeping this way and that. "This is not to say that I don't believe you have one, you understand, but I'm just pointing out that I don't see it."

"Nervous, Martin?" asked Father as we left the brick path and started traversing the bare dirt between the tombstones. They went by like crouching gnomes, picking their teeth and rubbing their tummies.

"P-p-puh-petrified would be my word, Father. I've always been a-f-f-fuh-fraid of dead things. You know that."

"What is the difference between a rock and a corpse?" asked Father as we passed the Turnbuckle grand memorial stone works—the biggest, meanest, block-headed troll in this disenchanted forest.

"The calcium content?" I ventured.

"Neither the rock nor the corpse is alive; but the corpse once was, while the rock has never been."

"Is that supposed to be consoling?"

"No. Clarifying."

"Thanks, I needed that."

A few steps more.

"So Father," I said, "what is the difference between a dream and an automobile?"

"What?"

"I haven't the faintest idea. I was hoping you'd tell me."

"Oh, you mean Cheryl Farnsworth's vision, and Helga Feuchtwanger's Volkswagen."

"Exactly."

"It's really very simple. Cheryl told you she was having some sort of contact—mental messages, whatever—with the vampire. Remember that?"

"Yes," I said, tripping.

> *"Fools, fools, fools,"* Cheryl had said, rubbing her arms. *"And there's the spiders."*
> *"Spiders?"*
> *"They catch flies."*
> *"Spiders and flies, spiders and flies ..."*

"And there's the hut," said Father as we entered the unconsecrated section where Bucky Turnbuckle lay twice dead. "The hut Roberto couldn't get into, that's somehow blocked from inside. If a substantial part of the displaced insect population attacked the trees, what percentage—the kind that like dark places—might seek refuge in this hut?"

"Why would Cheryl have visions about our stone hut?" I asked, wishing we weren't closing the distance to it.

"Why would living things start dying around it?" said Father, now less than ten feet away.

"Okay, I give," I said, considering my own living status. "Why?"

"We'll know that as soon as we get inside," said Father, stepping slowly up to the mysterious structure and gingerly placing his fingers upon the weatherworn wooden door. "I suspect it wasn't the insects that killed the dichondra."

"Do tell."

"First we have to figure out how to gain entrance when Roberto and his men could not." Father pushed against the door with his shoulder. Nothing. He felt around the narrow windowsills for loose stones. There were none. All the while I kept the flashlight trained on his movements.

"The far side of this hut is part of the outside wall, isn't it?" asked Father.

"Yes. It fronts the sidewalk."

"Let's go around and look out there."

"Sure."

Of course, that meant going back through the cemetery populated by brooding rectangular dwarves, out the back gate, through the parking lot past Monsignor Havermeyer's camper, down the alley to the street, then back up to the corner where the back side of the hut bordered the sidewalk.

"This is it?' asked Father as we reached the corner.

"It is," said the gardener, noting the withering avocado branches hanging over the stone wall along the sidewalk.

"The vampire is a consuming being," said Father ominously, eyeing the dead branches, "devouring all life within its reach."

"That's not Stoker," I observed.

"No," he answered. "Me."

"Oh."

"Let's see," said Father, stepping up to the wall. He began testing the stones, his fingers tracing every crack, every wedge, every gob of mortar on that corner. It didn't take long.

"Here we go," he said, giving a certain wobbly stone a sacerdotal yank.

Several large granite rocks came tumbling and rumbling out onto the sidewalk, revealing a gaping black hole, large enough for us to enter.

"Martin?" said Father.

"Father," said I.

"You have the flashlight."

"You have the courage."

"Age before beauty, eh?"

"Pearls before swine, Father."

"Let's go in together."

"Ah," I said, "pearls beside swine."

It only took a few seconds to explore the entire inside of the hut, since it was only twenty by fourteen feet, if that. But it contained a lot. Yes, there were lots of old tools hanging from nails, hooks, and rafters, most of which were partially if not totally rotted away. With so many things hanging every which way, it was a web-weaver's dream. Hence the place was crisscrossed and cross-thatched with spider webs, most of them inhabited by chubby little arachnids, fat with the blood of hundreds of flies that hung limply in silken shrouds.

"Spiders?"
"They catch flies."

Okay, Cheryl. I got that point.

But it was only the beginning.

Next, there was the immaculately polished wooden coffin on the dirt floor. It looked solid and heavy, and had been set with the foot end against the door, which was why the door couldn't be pushed inward from without. The lid of the coffin, left open, revealed a luscious layer of deep crimson satin, bearing a vaguely human-shaped impression in its soft, caressing folds. The material was mottled with dirt and twigs at the foot end, and there were bloodstains on the pillow where the head should go.

Coffins I'd seen before, even one occupied by a midget with a stake driven through his heart. I couldn't decide which was more unnerving: a coffin occupied by a corpse, or a coffin recently occupied by a corpse.

I'd also seen, just the previous evening, a pretty girl hanging from a sewage pipe. This night I got the chance to see her sister hanging from the central beam of the hut's ceiling.

"Marla," I gasped, focusing on the nose ring which was almost completely engulfed by the swollen tissues of her nostrils.

Death by hanging is never pretty, but in her case it was devastating. Marla, like her sister Tamara, had not been drained of blood. Her shimmering purple "djellaba" had been torn open savagely, shreds of cloth dangling from a ten-inch hole, revealing the chilling message:

I Killed my Sister

"What do you make of this, Martin?"

"Well," I paused, swallowing a wad of bile, "Marla came to see you last Friday. She seemed desperate about something."

"Yes."

"Not desperate enough to speak to you in the confessional, but obviously upset."

"Yes."

"Then she, posing as a nurse, drugged Jonathan, Pierre, and the policeman guarding Stella's room at the hospital."

"From which you surmise?"

"Perhaps someone—the vampire, maybe—was holding her sister hostage, threatening to harm her, forcing Marla to remove the reliquary and Rosary from Stella's room so it could go in there itself."

"Indeed," said Father, examining her right hand, which was clenched into a tight fist. "Aim the flashlight here, Martin. I thought this was a ring, but see? It's a loop of beads wrapped around her middle finger. The Rosary from Stella's pillow—she's still clenching it within her fist."

"So Marla, having helped the fiend, left the hospital with that Rosary," I shuddered. "Maybe she kept it for protection, but not being a Catholic, had no recourse to the Graces it could provide."

"I blessed this Rosary myself," said Father. "As a holy sacramental, it in and of itself could repel the fiend. But, not being Catholic, she wouldn't have known that."

"Most Catholics today wouldn't, either."

"True. And she wouldn't have known that its touch would be painful to the vampire, and so died clutching it in her hand." He closed his eyes for a moment. "So near, and yet so far."

"So," I continued, "Marla did the vampire's bidding at the hospital. But, instead of the deed buying her sister's release, she learned somehow that Tamara had staked Mr. Portifoy and hanged herself."

"We don't know that Tamara did that," said Father.

"But that's how it looked. Billowack certainly bought it, unless he was acting like it just to antagonize us. And if that's the story that got back to Marla, perhaps she came here to have it out with the fiend. Or, perhaps despairing—? No, that doesn't fit."

"No, it doesn't," agreed Father. "How could she have learned about her sister? The police have kept a lid on that. How did she gain access to this hut with the door blocked? I doubt the stone wall we came through could be reassembled from inside."

"Could she be part of the countdown?"

"Good question," said Father, fishing around in the folds of his cassock. He pulled out the magnifying glass he had been using back in the kitchen. "Funny that I brought this with me."

"Anything?" I asked, just to fill the silence as he examined the smears on Marla Grafan's abdomen.

"Indeed," said Father. "Look here, Martin. What do you see?"

"Similar mixture of capitals and small letters," I said, bending close while not wanting to, "as on the Nealy girl and Tamara Grafan. Same downward scrawl on the 'r' at the end."

"And the 'e' in 'killed'?"

"Looks suspiciously like a '2'?"

"Exactly."

"And the smudge through the second 'l' makes it 'minus two'?"

"Unless that's a coincidence, which would be one too many in too long a series of them."

My spine cracked as I straightened. "We'd better call Taper and Wickes," I suggested. The thought of the phone in Father's study in the safety of the rectory—or even the one within Millie's skillet range—seemed to beckon to me. This was not a place I cared to stay any longer than I had to.

"No need," said Father, still examining the writing on Marla's abdomen. "They'll be here any minute anyway. Please keep the light shining this way, Martin."

"Sure," I said, "but I'd like to keep my eye on that coffin, too, if you don't mind."

"It's empty," he reminded me.

"But how recently did it get that way?" I asked.

"I'm not sure," said Father, sighing with finality. His back cracked audibly as he stood up straight. Maybe a little of me was wearing off onto him. "Minutes, I suspect."

"Great." I swung the light around the room. *Spiders and flies.* "So how does Helga Feuchtwanger's Volkswagen fit into all this?"

"I think," said Father, folding his arms and rippling his fingers, "we've had an unwelcome guest here at St. Philomena's for the past two weeks—and I don't mean the mouse behind the altar."

"You mean," I swallowed loudly, "the vampire has been living here, or sleeping here, or dying here, or whatever it does—right in our own back yard?"

"Yes, Martin. This hut is built on unconsecrated soil, and up until two Wednesdays ago it was secreted in the most forgotten part of Los Angeles: our overgrown cemetery. Helga Feuchtwanger first approached us on Wednesday, October 18th, you'll recall, to complain that her Bug had been 'borrowed' the previous evening. This unexplained usage of her car continued until just a few nights ago. I think our guest moved its coffin in here on Tuesday, October 17—the day the 'Vampire's Shroud' rolled into the Los Angeles basin—and began using Mrs. Feuchtwanger's vehicle as a means of getting around that very night."

"Why didn't it just turn into a bat and fly wherever it wanted to go?" I asked.

"LA's a big city to traverse, I suppose, even for a large bat," he said, flicking a gnarly spider from his shoulder. "Why waste the energy? This being the twentieth century, the vampire used a current vehicle just as it would have procured an oxcart in an earlier era. Or, as Bishop

Xandaronolopolis explained, not all demons share the same talents. The one who stalked you up at the 'House of Illusions'—our same guest, I think—was able to surround itself in a veil of darkness. Perhaps darkness is its forte, not changing into bats."

"So it can drive," I mused, "and handle a stick-shift besides."

"Perhaps for a demon, who in its own realm lives outside the norms of time and matter," he said with a shrug, "the concept of 'timing' and 'coordination' have little or no meaning. Perhaps for such a creature, unused as it is to the restrictions of physical laws, a clutch and an accelerator pose a staggering challenge. Who knows?"

"Well, I'm impressed," said I, who in my own realm—a realm in which arthritis, inflammation, and fatigue prevail—sometimes find the concept of "getting out of bed" a challenge. "But you told me on the phone when I called from Lexington, and again just now, that the unauthorized borrowing of Mrs. Whatzit-wanger's car had stopped."

"Perhaps our guest found another means of getting around," said Father. "I'll suggest to the police that they check to see if there have been similar complaints in the neighborhood."

"Wait a minute," I said, scratching my nose with the handle of my cane. "Wasn't Reginold the Reiterator's reddish Thunderbird reported stolen the night he was murdered?"

"Yes," said Father.

"And isn't there one parked halfway down the block?"

We groped our way back to the hole in the wall and peered out.

"I'll bet that's it," I said, pointing with my cane to a car parked under the bright mercury-vapor street lamp. "I guess even a vampire can appreciate an automatic transmission."

"Check the license plate," said Father, stepping out onto the sidewalk and turning to look carefully at the hole he had just exited. "This explains how the coffin got into the hut. Setting the stones in place again must have been quite a chore. It had help."

"Do you think the vampire had to knock down and reassemble the wall every time it came and went?" I asked, squinting to catch the last two numbers on the plate.

"No," said Father. "Once our guest had secured its coffin within, it could seep in and out as a mist—assuming it enjoys that talent. Of course, the feat of moving the stones had to be repeated to get Marla Grafan's body inside. Do you have that license number?"

"Yup," I said tapping my temple. "Right here."

"Good," said Father. "Let's get back to the rectory."

"I was wondering when you were finally going to suggest that."

127

SOME SUGGESTION. At the risk of spoiling the tension, and with apologies to the Bard, whatever claim the rectory at St. Philomena's had as an oasis of safety in the storm was about to melt, thaw, and separate into a spew.

I know, I know. Shakespeare could have written this whole thing better, but I'm just an unpublished gardener, don't forget.

The sky, at this point, was the deepest, darkest, most threatening shade of purple I'd ever seen in my life. Thunder rumbled from one end of the horizon to the other, rippling the pulpy folds of the "Vampire's Shroud." The air was as hot and moist as it could possibly get, like the steaming ether in the shower when you turn off the water but haven't yet swiped the curtain. Only in this case, the neglected tiles in the stall were crawling with mildew, and the air was turning rank.

"Hmm," sniffed the gardener, lurching his way anxiously beside Father Baptist, yearning to toss his bones into his favorite chair, not realizing he'd soon be making a crash landing, but nowhere near Father's study.

Then, as we came through the garden, I saw something black coming toward us from the direction of the street in front.

"Nasty night," greeted Father.

"Lived in LA all my life," said Monsignor Havermeyer, who was the black thing coming toward us, "and I've never seen weather like this."

"I'm glad you're back, Monsignor," said Father. "Better that you should be inside with the rest of us."

"Had to eat," said Havermeyer with a pronounced shrug. "Unlike St. John Vianney, I just can't live on potatoes. I do wish Millie would stop holding that phone call to the cardinal against me. I really was trying to help, though I realized soon enough that I was out of line."

"I know," said Father Baptist. "I'll talk to her."

"Good luck," I said, looking toward her silhouette in the window as she stood washing dishes in the kitchen.

No, it wasn't quite a silhouette—more like a cloudy blur. The glass was thoroughly fogged over with steam rising from the scalding hot water in which she grappled with our mismatched eating ware. The fact that we could hear everything that was said in the kitchen while standing outside in the garden says a lot about how well-constructed was our rectory, and how insulation-free were its walls.

"Here are some more knives," said Veronika's blur sweetly as it came up beside Millie's blur from the direction of the dining nook. "I think that's the end of them."

"End?" roared Millie. "Do you really think that there will ever be an end?"

"Well, Sweetie," chuckled Veronika good-naturedly, her blur flutter-ing. "I guess I know what you mean. Father Nicanor sometimes in-vites over some rather strange people—"

"*Sometimes* invites strange people?" wailed Millie. "Why, St. Philomena's is a *magnet* for strange people. It's crawling with nut cases. I don't think the door's been darkened by a normal person in years. Why, if you ask me ..."

"... But not tonight," added Father.

"She does seem to be in a worse mood than usual," observed Monsi-gnor Havermeyer.

"Can I help with anything?" asked the browbeaten blur of Monsignor Aspic, entering the cloudy kitchen from the shadow of the hallway.

"No thank-you," bellowed Millie over her shoulder caustically. "You've caused enough damage."

"My dear woman—" began the Aspic blur.

"Don't you 'dear woman' me," spat Millie. "We saw you on televi-sion the other night while we were Stella-sittin' at the hospital."

"Um, oh, you must mean the talk show, 'Religion Revisted,'" said the monsignor, nodding. "Was that on again? A rerun, taped months ago when I was—"

"You said that all religions lead to Salvation," said Millie, blurs of fluffy suds dripping from her pointing finger, "that the Sacraments aren't really necessary to get to Heaven. You believe that?"

"Well, yes, actually I do," he sputtered.

"Then what do we need *you* for?" she screeched. "You faithless rat! Why don't you go get a *real* job?"

"Ouch." That was me. Even I flinched.

"She's in spectacular form," said Monsignor Havermeyer, beaming like a sportscaster. He was gracious enough to appreciate the intensity of Millie's current vehemence, and big-hearted enough to revel in the realization that the grudge she bore him was insignificant by compari-son. I imagine it also did the ol' boy some good to hear the same jab leveled at him by Father Baptist some ten days before hurled like a spear at our favorite Jonas by our beloved housekeeptrix. Real job, indeed.

"You said something about more knives?" barked Millie.

"Right here," said Veronika.

"Well don't just stand there, Woman," screamed Millie. "Dump them in."

There followed that peculiar, abrupt "chunk" that only happens when an apron-full of dissimilar not-necessarily-silver ware collides with an enamel surface under a foot of soapy water.

"Father," I said, "do you think it's possible that our Millie is having a Leviticus fifteen nineteen?"

"Gotcha," snarled Millie, lunging for the knives. "This is the job that separates the ma'ms from the marms."

"Or maybe," I reconsidered, "a fifteen twenty-five?"

Splash! Clatter! Sploosh! exclaimed the drawn-in sound effect balloons appearing around the kitchen window.

"No Martin," said Father. "I wouldn't be surprised if we have a full-scale Genesis, chapter eighteen verse eleven, in progress."

Clang! Slosh! Batter! Kabooosh!

"You may be right," I said knowingly. "Wow. A real eighteen eleven."

Bang! Bang! Bang!

"What the Hell are you two talking about?" asked Monsignor Havermeyer.

"We're trying to discuss Reality without violating propriety," I began to explain. "You see, Monsignor—"

"Ding-dong!"

"Great God in Heaven," cried the Millie blur. "Not again. Won't it ever stop?"

"They're just children, Honey" said Veronika soothingly "Just kids."

"They're alligator food!" yelled Millie.

"I'll get it," said the soppy, and-the-whale blur of Monsignor Aspic. "I'll get it."

"Do that," screamed Millie, suds flying as she threw up her hands. "Just once, make yourself useful."

Monsignor Aspic's blur receded. We could hear his footsteps exiting the kitchen and fading down the hallway.

"Here, Millie," said Veronika. "Let me help with that."

"Not on your life," countered Millie. "I wouldn't miss trying to get the crud off this butter knife for the whole, big, wide, disappointing world."

"No," giggled Veronika, "what I meant was—Oh!"

Just then there was a thunderous rumble, or a turbulent detonation, or whatever expression effectively conveys that the ground shook, the air itself pulsed, and the shutters rattled. It may have been an atmospheric discharge in the sky, a strike-slip fault releasing pressure deep in the mantle of the earth, or a herd of liturgical coordinators stampeding in utter terror at the reverent jingle of altar bells.

Whatever it was, it caught our attention.

What happened next took far less time than it's going to take to describe. Bear with me.

It began as a sudden change in the ambiance of the yellow incandescent light playing against the fogged window in which Millie's blur grumbled and growled as she attacked the knives in the sink with a scrubbing pad. A dark blackness seemed to billow into the room behind her. For a fraction of a second I thought the rectory's water heater had blown up, but that could not be because, as I explained before, the water heater for that part of the house was in the basement.

Before I could utter a sound, something swirling and black like smoke was nonetheless spreading throughout the kitchen.

A black nothingness I knew only too well.

"Queen of Heaven!" cried Veronika. "What—? Ooof!" She went flailing off to the right, flung aside like a rag doll. There was a thump as she collided with the pantry door and slipped out of sight.

"Aspic!" yelled the Millie blur, glancing over her shoulder. "I thought I told you not to let any of those weasels in!"

Then we all heard a voice, deep and dark and cavernous. What it said I could not tell, but it was abruptly cut off as Millie went into action.

"That does it!" she screamed at the top of her voice, pulling her hands out of the sink. Water splashed up against the window, clarifying a small area on the fogged glass. Through that little tunnel of clarity, I saw her left hand. In it was clutched the biggest, meanest-looking knife in our mismatched collection—the one I often used as a butter knife, but which could easily have been used to carve a roast. Her right hand reached up and grabbed something from above the window.

"I'll teach you—!" yelled Millie, turning to face what she thought was a trick-or-treater seeking emergency bathroom privileges.

Then we heard a scream.

GARDENING TIPS: The comic book balloon might be
rendered: "AAAAAAAAAAAARRRRRRRRRGGGGGGGGHHHHHHH!"
but I can't imagine how that might be pronounced.
Besides, it doesn't come close to capturing the
hatred, disdain, and utter violence of that hideous outcry.

                                        --M.F.

"Good Lord," gasped Monsignor Havermeyer.

"Martin," said Father Baptist, grabbing my arm and hauling me toward the kitchen door, a sudden blast of sultry air fluttering our clothing.

"Father," I said, lurching behind him.

The door flung open, Father and I plunged into the kitchen. It was like jumping into an open freezer—such skin-crystallizing cold! The darkness was receding back into the hallway, leaving behind wisps of gray smoke that curled and coiled like snakes in the frosty air. And the smell, the cloying smell of burned flesh—

"Millie!" said Father, rushing to her side.

"Did you—?" she whispered. "Did I—?"

In her right hand was the Crucifix Bishop Xandaronolopolis had given her, the one containing a splinter from the True Cross, the one she had kept in a place of honor above the sink. Her other hand held the knife, still smoking, a clod of sizzling, smoking flesh slithering down its gleaming edge. I watched, nauseous, as the organic chunk slipped from the blade and plopped onto the floor.

"I just wanted to frighten the rascal," gulped Millie, "the nasty little kid in that silly Dracula costume. I swung too hard and it touched his face ..." She looked down at the dripping blade, the gob of meat still sizzling on the floor, and then into Father Baptist's concerned eyes. "Was that —?"

"Yes," said Father. "It's here."

She waved the knife drunkenly in my direction. "Dessert, Mr. Feeney?" she gurgled. Then her eyes turned Heavenward as she collapsed into Father's arms. The knife landed point down, sticking itself into the floor.

"Perhaps the only piece of genuine silverware in the house," said the gardener, leaving it where it was.

"Monsignor," said Father, transferring her limp weight to Havermeyer's clumsy hands. "Look after her."

Meanwhile the gardener, repulsed by the thought of such a distasteful after-dinner morsel, was stepping backwards. My feet got entangled with those of Veronika, who was sprawled on the floor by the pantry door.

"Ulp!" I said as I stumbled back against the door, but managed to keep my balance.

"St. Maron preserve us," said Veronika, looking up at the carved dragon's head on my cane, waving above her face.

"Sorry," I said, gingerly stepping away from her and tucking the cane under my arm. I wanted to sink to a clumsy crouch and help her, but Father Baptist intercepted that impulse.

"Her, too," said he to Monsignor Havermeyer, pointing to Veronika who was rubbing the stars out of her eyes. "Martin, come with me."

The wisps of dissolving smoke swirled around him as he headed through the doorway into the hall.

"Place on my heart one drop of Thy Precious Blood, O Lord," I whispered, gathering my courage as my legs started churning after him, "that I may fear nothing." I didn't feel like a very courageous Knight at that juncture, but follow him I did down the hallway, curls of ill-smelling smoke parting as we hurried toward the front door, which was wide open.

Sitting on the floor, back against the little entry table, was Monsignor Conrad J. Aspic, holding the small Crucifix blessed by Padre Pio in both hands. The broken chain dangled from his trembling fingers. At our approach he looked up, eyelids twitching, tears spurting.

"What happened?" asked Father, staring down at him.

"I thought it was just a kid in a costume," said our Jonas through chattering teeth. "He looked so desperate, hopping from one foot to the other. I know Millie said not to, as did you, but I just couldn't say no. I'm a monsignor, after all, and this is a rectory, and I didn't want to seem uncharitable."

"So you invited him in," said Father.

"Well, yes. Then suddenly, it got so dark and cold. Those eyes—like something from a nightmare."

"And?" said Father.

"And I held up this," said Aspic, indicating the Crucifix, "and he seemed to ... well ... he seemed to explode."

"Explode?"

"I don't know how else to describe it. He flew every which way at once. The next thing I knew, I was here on the floor." He gulped loudly. "I never knew something like this could contain such power."

"Now you do," said Father, slamming the front door shut. "Come, Martin."

"Where?" I asked.

"Upstairs," he said, turning to the stairs. "Stella—the final blow."

"After you," I said, pointing with my cane.

"I didn't know," mumbled Monsignor Aspic, staring at the Crucifix in his hands as I lumbered past him. "I didn't know I had it in me—"

"Oh brother," said I, lunging up the stairs on Father's heels.

Suddenly he stopped, and I plowed into him from behind.

"What is it?" I gasped.

No answer. He dropped to a crouch beside the form of a man sprawled head-down near the top of the stairs.

"Father Nicanor," said Father Baptist, feeling around the throat for a pulse. "Father Nicanor?"

I have more than once described my impression of Father Nicanor as "something constantly-moving yet solidly stationary, like fine sand trickling through a ponderous hourglass." When I saw him draped on the stairs like that, I couldn't help but think of all the red corpuscles flowing toward his head, the hourglass having been overturned. I don't know why these things occur to me, and at the darn'dest times.

"Father Nicanor?"

"Lord have mercy," mumbled the Maronite priest, r's rolling a bit off-kilter—a few g's getting tangled in his tongue. He moved his limbs uselessly. "I heard a commotion downstairs, and I came to see—" He groped around for something on the stair beside him, a sprig of some dried flowering plant.

"Wolfsbane?" asked Father, helping him to shift into a sitting position.

"Yes," gasped Fr. Nicanor, holding up the curled-up cluster of brittle leaves and petals. "Bishop Xandaronolopolis said it has been known—"

"Did it?" asked Father.

"The thing just seemed to dissolve around me and continue on its way," said Father Nicanor. Then his eyes went wide. "Stella! She's alone!"

"Not for long," said Father. "Martin, come on."

The gardener complied, lumbering awkwardly past Father Nicanor.

"Hurry," said he, waving me by. "All right I'll be."

Achieving the landing, I followed Father Baptist down the upstairs hall past several closed doors. Our destination was the third on the right, and it was wide open. Clouds of that eerie blackness were puffing out into the hallway from the chamber within.

"No!" we heard Stella whimpering. "No, I won't. I won't!"

Arriving at the door, we looked into a swirling gyre of dim nothingness.

128

"STELLA," CALLED FATHER BAPTIST, standing in the doorway to Wrecked Room Number Three.

"I'm here," she cried from somewhere within the blackness.

"So am I," said another voice, a creepy, wraithlike whisper that seemed to come from every corner of the room at once.

"Help me, Father," called Stella.   "I haven't let go of St. Philomena."

"Good," said Father. "Hold on. I'm coming in."

"Good," said the voice, thicker now, substantial, resonating as if from the bottom of a gigantic chasm. "I've been expecting you."

I watched, paralyzed, as Father stepped into the charcoal fog and vanished from sight.

"Father Baptist," I gasped.

"Stay where you are, Martin," said Father's voice.

I heard the floorboards creaking as he traversed the carpeted floor.

"Father," Stella was whimpering. "I'm so afraid."

"Don't be," said Father. "I'm here now."

"Aha!" said the other voice, rolling around the room like ball bearings in a metal bathtub. "In that you are right, Pere Jean Baptiste Lombard! A minor point, no? But as in all things, we start with the simple, then progress to the complex."

At that moment it dawned on me that the Knights Tumblar—Knights not just in name any longer, but Knights in fact—were not here. The last I'd seen them, they went out the kitchen door after dinner, redolent with Millie's garlic casserole. Surely, I thought, they should be here, now, protecting Father in his time of need.

The thought vanished from my mind, which was suddenly consumed with another conundrum: the slowly swirling darkness in the room seemed to be condensing, shrinking. It's hard to describe because there were no details for the eyes to identify, no colors to compare and contrast, no distances to discern and measure. In fact, it was more of an inkling than a perception on my part. But I can say with absolute certainty, on my honor as a grumpy gardener and a not-so-courageous Knight, that it was happening.

"Don't move," said Father, I assumed to Stella because he surely couldn't see me. "Pray to the Blessed Mother for Her protection."

"I'm trying," said Stella. "Oh, what's happening?"

There. It wasn't just me. She saw it, or sensed it, too.

What Stella and I were seeing, or sensing—and I presume Father was, too, though he didn't make mention of it at the time—was that the darkness was gradually coalescing into a wavering human shape. Like a giant it seemed, the rippling head pressing against the ceiling, and the fingers on the widespread arms almost touching the walls on either side.

"Just one drop," I prayed in a whisper as the thing began to shrink, "that's all I ask, Lord."

Dwindle it did, hardening as it withered, twisted, and writhed in the center of the room. Wisps of black mist spun around and around, orbits collapsing, as every particle of darkness gathered together, adhering to the solidifying central form. And still it continued to decrease in size. Seven feet tall, six feet, five feet ... four ... until it finally resolved into a solid being whose weight sank into the deep pile carpet—a rather short solid being. In fact, a puny, impish, malformed dwarf I could recognize even from behind.

"Lucius T. Portifoy," said Father, whom I could now see, sitting comfortably on the tattered couch beside a visibly shaking Stella Billowack—at a respectable distance of an arm's length and a half. "I've been expecting you, too."

"Portifoy?" I gasped from the doorway. "But you ... the stake through your ...?"

Though Mr. Portifoy was facing away from me, the burning coals of his blood-red eyes seemed to turn around and look at me right through the back of his head. Now that was an unsettling sight, let me tell you.

"Humans are such fools," he said in Father's direction, but with an inflection that seemed to be aimed right at me. He held up a wooden stake in his right hand. "This little trick has served me well over the years. Permit me to demonstrate."

With that, he lifted the stake up to his chest, clutching it with both hands, and with a jerk and a grunt, pulled it into himself, thrusting it right through his ribcage. The point came bursting through the back of his cape.

"A magician's trick?" asked Father, the epitome of serenity.

"No," laughed Lucius T., holding up his empty hands as if to prove the point. "It really does go all the way through, unlike the phony magician's sword. This little body, it is not much, but it serves me well. Do you not know that within the twisted bodies of dwarves—the price some of your kind pay for the Fall—the internal organs are some-times—how do you say?—displaced? My heart, you see, is five inches to the right of where it should be. In a rib cage so small and warped, that is significant, no?"

He reached down and pulled out the stake. The point withdrew through the cape, the disrupted material swirling around the hole mo-mentarily, then condensing into what looked like ordinary cloth with no puncture. The concurrent scrape of wood against bone sent an electric shock through my teeth.

"This is my favorite stake," said Portifoy, secreting it away in some pocket or fold of his garments. "A spoke from a wheel of a cart that once carried ammunition for the North during the Civil War. Ah, what wonderful meals those battlefields provided. So many souls dying in despair. It was a demon's dream, no?"

"If you say so," said Father, crossing his legs and stretching his arms along the back of the couch. "So, what brings you to our neck of the woods, Mr. Portifoy?"

I marveled at Father's apparent nonchalance. My knees were knock-ing so hard you could have tenderized a rump roast between them.

"Hunger," said the imp. "I was resting in that morgue when you told the coroners you were going to bring this succulent appetizer here."

> Said Father: *"... I plan to move the chief's daughter to the rec-tory tomorrow."*
>
> *"The chief won't like that,"* said the gardener.
>
> *"No,"* said Father, *"but she'll be safer at St. Philomena's, I hope, than in a non-sectarian hospital. I plan to keep watch over her personally."*

"Hunger?" asked Father, indicating the woman beside him. "For Miss Billowack? Surely you know you'll have to go through me to get to her."

Stella's face went to pieces and reassembled itself at the way she was being talked about—succulent appetizer indeed!

"So sure of yourself, are you?" huffed Portifoy, dismissing the notion with a wave of his left hand. "Who wants her? One so recently Bap-tized, only a few venial sins on her soul. Why should I bother sending such a sweet morsel to Purgatory, only to be embraced by Heaven? She was merely part of the game, a plaything I used to taunt you."

"Really," said Father. "I expected as much."

A wave of anger seemed to ripple through the organic fabric of Lucius T. Portifoy. "You are the 'one.' It is you that I want, Pere Jean Baptiste, to send to Hell."

GARDENING TIPS: A few points of pronunciation I
might not have inserted earlier: "Pere" is pronounced sort of like "pair" and is French for "Father." "Jean" is French for "John," and "Baptiste" is pronounced "Bap-teest." I mention this
lest my provincially American readers say "Peer
Jeen Baptisty."
Don't mind me, I'm just interrupting.
                                          --M.F.

"You can see the condition of my soul?" asked Father seriously.

"I don't have to," said Portifoy. "You've been slipping, mon Pere. You're supposed to be saving souls, no?—and they've been trickling through your fingers like the melting snow."

"I see," said Father, uncrossing his legs. "Why me in particular?"

"This hole," said Portifoy, pointing as far as I could tell, to the center of his chest. "This hole, it was a gift from your grandsire, François Lombard."

"Indeed," said Father. "Was he the first to drive a stake through the place where your heart should have been?"

"No," said Portifoy. "A bullet. He shot me twice, actually, once with his own Matchlock—twenty-five pounds, what an awkward weapon!—and then again in the stomach with the gun of his fallen companion. It was Paris—long, long ago."

"August 24, 1572," said Father. "The so-called St. Bartholomew's Day Massacre."

"Oh?" squeaked Portifoy. "How did you know?"

"You alluded to it last Wednesday at the 'House of Illusions' when you said: 'Exidat illa dies œvo, nec postera credant sæcula.' Your Latin pronunciation is abysmal. It took me a moment to translate: 'Let this day be lost from time, and let posterity ignore the event.' I thought the phrase sounded familiar, so I looked it up in Parson's *Studies in Church History*. The line was attributed to Statius by Voltaire, though as usual, Voltaire's claims were suspect."

"Actually it was said by a man named de Thou, but no matter," said Portifoy. "You Catholics should bow your heads in shame at the slaughter of thirty thousand innocent Protestants."

"That was de Thou's claim," said Father. "A champion of the Huguenots. But when pressed for specifics regarding the deceased, he could only list seven hundred and eighty-six names. In any case, as has often occurred, the Catholics are left with undeserved guilt."

"Numbers," said Portifoy, shrugging. "Mere numbers. Who needs facts when there are feelings? Don't forget, mon Pere, I was there. I took on this very flesh less than a month before that glorious event at the command of my master, Balphegor. You may have heard the name?"

"I have," said Father.

"This shell, such as it is, was formally the vessel of one Robert Jacques Portifoy, a businessman, a financier, and a major supporter of the Huguenots—who, unfortunately, was also a poor chooser of friends and wives. Finding them more attached to each other than either to himself, and having studied the book, *Christianæ Religionis Institutio—*"

By John Calvin, thought the gardener.

"—and thereby convincing himself that, by virtue of his wealth, surely he was one of the elect, thus predestined for Heaven no matter the nature of his actions, he committed suicide by swallowing an inordinate amount of poison. You should have seen the look on his face when he woke up in Hell beside me, the demon who was waiting to take possession of his body. What a horrible taste I had in his mouth when I first opened these eyes! And there I was in Paris, just in time for the bloodbath. I give you this consolation: many Catholics went to Hell in that delicious confrontation, along with their Protestant victims."

"You know very well," countered Father, "that the Catholics were simply trying to prevent the overthrow of the French monarch, not to mention the wholesale slaughter of priests and nuns as had happened in Scotland and the Netherlands. Your new church—"

"L'eglise reformée de France," interjected Portifoy proudly.

"—was nothing more than a mob of terrorists."

"True," said Portifoy. "My favorite motto was, 'Que les rues soient inondeés avec le sang Catholique.' Let the streets run with Catholic blood."

"And for protecting themselves," said Father, "they were branded as murderers. How true it is that your sire is the Father of Lies. I don't know the circumstances, but frankly I'm glad François Lombard put two bullets through your undead carcass."

"It was on the steps of a house of a cousin of Le Duc de Guise," said Portifoy.

"One of the Catholic leaders," said Father.

What's this?!?! I thought ferociously, poised in the doorway, every muscle in my body trembling. A history lesson?

"François," continued Portifoy, "was ordered to guard Guillaume, the youngest of the household. I arrived with ten comrades. 'Small or no,' we cried, 'if he's the only Guise at home, we'll kill him!'"

"Did you?" asked Father.

"Unfortunately, no," said Portifoy. "As I said, your ancestor shot me twice. The second round devastated my gut—under normal circumstances my digestion would have been impaired for weeks!—and the cowards who claimed to be my friends scattered. They did not see me get up from the gutter and walk away. Nor did François, for that matter, since by then he had regained the doorway and was calling for more guards from within."

"And for this," said Father Baptist, "you came to Los Angeles, to avenge this act of bravery four centuries later? Why didn't you go after my grandfather, or his?"

"Ah," said the vampire, "your forefathers remained in France, and I had moved on to new adventures. Besides, my Angelic instincts told me that sooner or later one of François Lombard's descendants would take Holy Orders. That turned out to be you, Pere Jean Baptiste, the famous homicide detective, a most worthy adversary. As I told you at that decrepit 'House of Illusions,' I followed your exploits in the papers. But with my Angelic abilities, I was also close to you throughout those events of June last."

"And you hired a professional calligrapher to pen that letter you sent from Transylvania," said Father.

"My handwriting, it has never been so good."

"Indeed," agreed Father.

I grimaced from the doorway, thinking of the scrawls on the abdomens of all those victims—stomachs that had reminded Portifoy of that second bullet in his own.

"François Lombard," said Portifoy, "I did not like him, and I like you even less. So I have come."

"Surely not just for me," said Father. "What else brings you to the City of Angels?"

"Why, Hollywood, of course," said Portifoy. "I wanted to see if Tinseltown lives up to its reputation."

"Does it?"

"What can I say? Humans are fools everywhere."

"And when you arrived by train two weeks ago, you took up lodging in the stone hut out back."

"Ah, so you have visited my temporary dwelling. The idea, it was good, until those infernal caretakers removed the foliage from the graveyard. Spiders and flies I don't mind, but the earwigs—they're such nasty things, especially when you awaken from a good day's sleep with them making nests in your mouth."

The scene with Cheryl Farnsworth came back to me again:

"Spiders and flies," she kept saying, "spiders and flies ..." Then she looked me in the eye. *"What's an 'earwig'? Is that a bug, too?"*

Yes Cheryl, I thought, wishing I was sharing the relative safety of her cell at the moment: earwigs are bugs, too.

"Did you enjoy driving Mrs. Feuchtwanger's Volkswagen?" Father was asking.

"Ah, that," said Portifoy. "Well, it was—how do you say?—unostentatious. I have never mastered the batwings, unfortunately—fog and darkness being my 'thing,' you see. The Bug, it served its purpose, but Mr. Ryan's Thunderbird will be how I will drive away in style this night. The—how do you say it?—the automatic transmission is so much easier to deal with."

"'Drive away,' you say, to another coffin?"

"Oui. We vampires know that it is best to maintain several places of rest. It is a matter of common sense, no? You never know when unwanted intruders may come knocking. Grave robbers, too—is there no safety?"

"May I ask where?" said Father.

"Where?" asked the vampire.

"One in the stone hut. I suspect the child's casket at 'House of Illusions' in which you arranged to be discovered. Where is your third coffin?"

"In a forest. Oaks, mostly. Not many miles away."

"Ah," said Father, "the grounds of the Del Agua Mission."

"You are the clever one," said Portifoy. "Oui, that is the place. The Padres who built it, unfortunately, left many blessings behind. However, part of the woods was desecrated, as you know, by a coven of witches, so it is enchanted at cross-purposes. There were other beings who lived there as well. Things that exist between the realm of spirit and matter."

"Elves," said Father.

"That is one of your words for them. Flighty beings, mostly, easily dispersed."

Ah, thought the gardener, still standing in the doorway. Perhaps Mrs. Magillicuddy is not so mad after all.

There's other folks, she had told us the night she announced her plans to visit her sister, *that come out at night's, there is, now that the faeries has gone. The little people, they's more friendly than the faeries ever was, they is. They sings, and they plays their tiny drums and bagpipes, they do, but it's not the same ...*

"And Surewood Forst?" asked Father. "Where did he fit in?"

"That's just it," said Portifoy, throwing up his hands. "He did not 'fit in,' as you say. I came all this way to play my little game with you, and here he was confusing things with his silly false teeth. That farcical charade he put on for your benefit on that terrace—hanging from a string in an artificial fog, can you believe it? Embarrassing! Then he even let himself be seen by that deformed little girl when he was whisking the Unger woman away in that pathetic little excuse for a sportscar. Some vampire, no? Bad for the image."

"So you killed the Nealy girl," said Father. "As a favor to Mr. Forst."

"One has to start somewhere, no?" said Portifoy, twirling his mustache. "And as you say, a favor—both to Surewood, and to the hunchbacked girl. It is rich, no? I amaze myself sometimes. The whelp, Patricia, she missed her friend, and I told her if she let me in, I would take her to see 'Elibazeth.'"

"Elibazeth," I whispered from my ineffectual station at the doorway. The little girl missed her friend ...

> *"Here's her Crucifix,"* said Father, flicking the chain hanging from the bedpost. A hot breeze was buffeting the curtains as he stepped over to the window. *"It wasn't torn from her neck because she wasn't wearing it."*
>
> *"Mia Durham said it was odd,"* said the gardener, *"that the window was found open this morning. She said her niece insisted on keeping it closed at night to keep out the bugs."*

... and "Elibazeth" was the key by which this insidious, blood-sucking dwarf had gained entry into Patricia's bedroom:

> *"If you had heard a knock on your door,"* the bishop had said to Havermeyer, *"surely you would have opened it, no?"*
>
> *"Well,"* said the monsignor, *"I suppose—"*
>
> *"Only into the house where he is invited can the 'wampyr' enter."*

"So you revealed yourself to Surewood Forst," Father was saying.

"Oui," said Portifoy. "I befriended him, allowed him his amusements, rendered assistance, but—ah!—such ineptitude, such silliness! I swear to you, mon Pere: if the rolling machine had not killed him, I certainly would have. As it was, there was no place left to write 'minus six.'"

"But you did use him to entrap Mr. Feeney," said Father.

"That I did," nodded Portifoy. "Mr. Forst and I shared one mutual interest: the lust for blood—though my interest was, shall we say, 'professional,' while he remained a—how do you say?—ah, a 'rank amateur.' Even so, we struck a bargain. He supplied information which he gleaned from his brother, the 'doily monsignor'; he made the phone calls, proficient as he was in affecting voices—better, even, than myself; he delivered money and instructions to the cab company—you liked that touch, no?—the vampire who can hire cabs in broad daylight; and I breathed my enchanting breath upon that silly woman—"

"Nannette Cushions."

"—oui, her, and left her to be drained at his convenience."

"And Buckminster Turnbuckle?" asked Father. "Number eight?"

"Ah, that was luck, if you believe in such drivel."

"I do not."

"Neither do I. Let's call it 'circumstance' if you prefer. Or better yet: the 'action' which becomes the 'reaction.' One of my comrades in Hell, Gorphegor, wanted to try his hand at possessing a corpse, and I showed him how. Going about it in such a clumsy and obvious way, he didn't last long."

"No, he didn't."

"Tell me, Pere Jean Baptiste, does this line mean anything to you: 'He plays the fool who's playing the fool, while playing the fool'?"

"What if it does?" asked Father.

"Mr. Feeney?" asked Portifoy.

"Here," I answered.

"This sentence I have just said, it is familiar, no?"

"Kind of."

"'Kind of,'" he said with derision. "'Kind of'? This woman you visit in the prison tells you this, and to it your reaction is, 'Kind of'?"

"What are you driving at, Portifoy?" asked Father.

"That I'm playing the fool," said Portifoy, "who's playing the fool, and so on. Bucky Buckle was a tasty side dish to this delectable banquet. I caused his death, you know. In his brain I planted the germ of suicide, and then watered it, nurtured it, until—"

"He despaired," said Father.

"A vampire's fundamental food," said Portifoy, "is human souls. The blood, it is nice, but the soul is sublime. His demise was more of a 'devil thing' than a 'vampire thing,' I'll grant you. I had not intended to make him part of our game. But then I thought of Gorphegor rising from your own graveyard in this fool Bucky's body, and I just couldn't contain myself."

"Indeed," said Father.

"You and your pompous troop of young men, accompanied by that abominable bishop from Lebanon, made short work of him. So be it. In Gorphegor's defeat, I saw opportunity: to pull the young suicide onto our playing field. Your friend, Bishop the X—such a name even I cannot pronounce!—seeded the ground above Bucky's coffin with the garlic. But this I avoided by entering the soil within the hut, the hut you have since invaded. Moving through dirt, it is a distasteful thing, no? Seeping into his coffin as a mist to draw the number—now that was disgusting. But, as I obviously lack what you call 'class,' I managed the deed anyway."

"You're not above much," agreed Father.

"You must admit," said Portifoy, "that allowing myself to be found with the stake through my chest last night was a stroke of genius, not to mention something of a risk on my part."

"Yes and no," said Father. "Yes, I was taken aback—it threw my near-certainty into temporary confusion. I certainly had begun to suspect you, and was taking steps to substantiate my theory. Of course, in retrospect, you showed your hand the first night we met."

"Oh? How so?"

"When you introduced yourself to the Tumblars, they were wearing scapulars that I had recently blessed. You couldn't touch them in greeting, so you pulled your hand away."

"It was awkward, I'll admit," nodded Portifoy. "But I couldn't let you see my hand go up in smoke, now could I?"

"As to your claim of intellectual brilliance," said Father, "I'll let it pass. The risk you mentioned a moment ago: no, it was not that much of a risk, considering that you overheard our dinner conversation last Wednesday at the 'House of Illusions.' You knew that the coroners assigned to the case would be out of town, and were not likely to be up to performing an autopsy on their return Monday evening."

"Hrmph," hrmphed Portifoy. "Of course, if they had found the resolve to try, there would have been extra bodies in my countdown, and that would have thrown the game entirely out of whack, no?"

Whew! I thought. Wong and Holtsclaw have no idea how close they came:

> *"Are you sure you fellows aren't up to an autopsy of Mr. Portifoy now?"* Father had asked, no doubt anticipating the answer.
>
> *"I'm so tired I can't see straight,"* John Holtsclaw had said. *"How about you, Solomon?"*
>
> *"No,"* Mr. Wong had said, *"my hands are shaking. Besides—you'll understand, I'm sure—I'd rather do the procedure in broad daylight."*
>
> *"And,"* said Holtsclaw, *"I'm not about to remove that stake before dawn."*

"Of course," said Father. "But then there is the matter of Tamara and Marla Grafan—"

"Enough of this talk," said Portifoy. "I've come to fetch you to Hell, but no doubt you have a dozen relics hidden somewhere in that cassock of yours."

"No," said Father, gathering himself and rising to his feet. "The sacred radiance you sense is coming from the reliquary in this woman's hand. I knew it would come to this, and I am prepared to meet you unarmed."

"Then you are a fool," said Portifoy.

"Yes," said Father, taking a step forward. "That I am."

I, too, took a step forward. What in Heaven's name was Father Baptist up to? Having insisted that the rest of us be protected with holy objects, he was walking around unshielded?

"Stay back, Martin," ordered Father. "This is between it and me."

"'It'?" squeaked Portifoy. "To you I am a mere 'it'?"

"But Father—" I protested, not having the slightest clue what I could do to help him anyway.

"You heard me," said Father sternly. "Keep away."

"Patience," said Portifoy, looking at me over his shoulder for the first time, revealing the gash in the side of his face, courtesy of our dear angry Millie and the only piece of true silverware in our random knife collection. "I'll have you for dessert shortly, along with the rest of this household."

As Portifoy said this, his lips parted in a fiendish smile. Long white fangs slowly unfolded from the roof of his mouth and settled into position over his lower lip, dripping saliva. It was not a pretty sight.

"I think not," said Father, taking two broad steps closer to the vampire.

"I think so," said Portifoy, raising his arms threateningly.

"Think again," said Father, suddenly lunging forward.

I stepped into the room. I'm usually obedient when it suits me, and at that moment it didn't. Stupidly, I raised my cane to strike Portifoy from behind.

"Mother of God, protect me!" said Father as he stooped and grabbed the little imp, wrapping his arms around the creature. Hours of preparatory prayer apparently insulated Father from the poisonous effects of contact with the vampire. In fact, strands of gooey, pungent smoke squirted out from between them, along with a sickening sizzling sound that resonated with the fillings in my teeth. Portifoy squealed like a puppy, and began squirming and twisting in Father's grip. Cape and cassock whirled around as they grappled with each other.

"Now!" shouted Father.

"Now what?" I asked, stepping closer.

"Now!" shouted Father again, louder.

Not knowing what else to do, I lifted my cane a few inches higher.

"For the love of Heaven," screamed Father. "Now!"

As I brought the cane down, dragon's teeth flying as the handle made contact with Portifoy's lumpy little head, everything else went down, too. By that I mean the floor around Father Baptist and Lucius T. Portifoy suddenly subsided about a foot or so. The carpet was pulled into the depression by their weight, crimping itself into tight folds around their feet, pinning their legs together into a crushing tangle.

The movement of the carpet under my own feet caused me to lose my balance. For a moment I almost fell backwards, but with enough arm-flailing and chin-lurching I was able to regain my composure—just as the floor settled another foot or two, sending me flailing again.

"What in the name of Balphegor?" gasped Portifoy, struggling against Father.

"No," said Father, redoubling his grip. "In the Name of God."

"What the—?" I managed to say as the floor lurched again, this time to the sound of splitting timbers and snapping plastic, and Stella screaming over on the couch.

Luckily for her, the couch was resting on bare floorboards, beyond the edge of the grasping carpet.

A thick, almost sickening stench, familiar yet shockingly overpowering, suddenly billowed into the room, expelled from beneath the curling folds of the gathering carpet.

Then the floor—or at least an eight-foot square of it in the center of the room—gave completely away. Father Baptist and his adversary, along with the carpet around them, plunged downward into a gaping maw of darkness below.

Caught completely by surprise, I was thrown backward, landing on the edge of the carpet as it was sucked inexorably into the hole. Like a swimmer caught in a riptide, I made a grab for the rim of the hole, but to no avail. My fingers gouged by splinters, I couldn't get a grip. I felt myself slipping, sliding, tumbling, and finally dropping. Stella's prolonged scream receded as I plummeted downward, toward what, I didn't know.

"Well," I thought as the wind rushed by my ears, accompanied by angry flaps of the descending carpet, "I guess it's finally 'later.'"

129

BUMP, THUMP, *KERPLOP!*

Three falling bodies. The "kerplop," of course, was me.

I heard the carpet crumple off somewhere to my right as Father Baptist, Lucius T. Portifoy, and yours truly landed on something unexpectedly soft. Well, not really soft. It was rather a lot of small, roundish, hard but light-weight, paper-wrapped objects which had been heaped up into an enormous mound in the center of the storage room—the middle of the three abandoned rooms between my own quarters and Millie's kitchen—the one in which the Tumblars had been pounding and hammering the day before, and into which this afternoon they had been carrying boxes and boxes of—

"Garlic," I realized as the pile gave way beneath our weight.

Yes, an immense pile of garlic bulbs, perhaps six feet in height. I could not see it, the room being so dark, but I soon understood what I had been dumped upon. My legs and arms sank deeply into the rolling, rustling mass, which collapsed gently under our bulk, spreading outward as we subsided in its embrace. The smell, that familiar and overpowering stench, descended upon us, nauseating but surprisingly sweet.

"No," groaned Mr. Portifoy. I could hear him sliding down the pile to my right and rolling to a useless stop at the foot of the mound, paralyzed. "No, no, no ..."

I skidded to a slow standstill, flat on my back. There was light coming from above. I was looking up through a cloud of swirling particles, flakes from the protective garlic husks, that circled and whirled in the air like dry snow. There was a gaping rectangular hole in the ceiling through which we had fallen. Two wooden doors were still rocking back and forth on their hinges beneath it, as strands of clear plastic trailed lazily from their swinging, recently sawed edges.

"Plastic?" I whispered. It's funny what rivets one's attention at moments like that. But of course, the trapdoor had been sealed with plastic to keep the smell of the garlic contained in the room below. Otherwise, Portifoy, with a twitch of his pointed mustache, would have smelled the trap.

"Well done," said Father, rising to his feet off to my left.

A strange, momentary scraping sound emanated from all around in the dark as five matches flared as if on cue. As my eyes adjusted to the gloom I realized that the Tumblars were standing around the perimeter of the room. Each was dressed in formal attire, holding a thick altar candle in his right hand. A fine troop of Knights they were, standing at attention, awaiting orders from their leader.

My Knighthood, on the other hand, was proving to be a rather clumsy and awkward affair as I thrashed around, scattering bulbs in every direction. "My cane," I mumbled. "Where's my cane?"

"Yah," said Joel's grandfather, nodding somewhere in the gloom. "Yah."

"You all right, Father?" asked Arthur.

"Yes," said Father, ridding his cassock of the garlic remnants. "Though, I must admit, for a moment there—"

"Sorry about that, Father," said Joel from his post. "I guess we overdid the plastic. I underestimated its strength. It prevented the trapdoors from falling right away when we released the catches."

"I told you we needed to try it out first," said Edward.

"How?" said Joel. "You certainly didn't volunteer to take the plunge."

"Well, no matter," said Father, clapping the garlic flecks from his hands. "The trap worked. That's the important thing."

"Amazing," I said, struggling to get into a sitting position.

"As for you, Martin," said Father. "When are you going to learn to do as I say?"

"You said 'Now!'" I argued, slipping back to a prone position.

"I told you to stand back," said Father. "Now you're down here, when I wanted you up there."

"What happened?" asked a voice from above. Father Nicanor's penetrating eyes looked down at us through the hole. "Are you all right?"

"Yes, Father," called Father Baptist. "A bit of a tumble, but we survived. How's Stella?"

"She seems to have fainted."

"Just as well."

"Need anything, do you, down there?"

"No," said Father. "At least, I don't think so."

"Stay tuned," I called up, trying to sit up again, "for further details."

"That I will do, Martin," said Father Baptist. "And how is our guest?"

All eyes turned to the shape writhing where it had rolled to a standstill. Mr. Portifoy was on his side, squirming like a worm on a hot plate. "This is intolerable," it moaned.

"This is Justice," said Father, stepping over to the vampire and looking down at it with hardened eyes. Not in my wildest dreams could I have imagined such a look of utter disdain, determination, and even cruelty that appeared on his face. "It is your presence on this green Earth that is intolerable, Mr. Portifoy."

"Are you sure he—it—can't hurt us?" asked Jonathan.

"Let us hope not," said Father. "I suggest you keep your distance. And remember, all of you, your instructions. I am depending on you."

"The garlic," called Father Nicanor. "It is working?"

"Yes," said Father Baptist. "Seems to be."

"So much for old wolfsbane," said Father Nicanor, tossing down the sprig. It hit me on the forehead. Lucky for me it was as dry as one of Mrs. Magillicuddy's "periwinkies." Perhaps that was why it had lost its true potency—the juice being the life of a plant.

"Weren't you afraid up there, Father?" asked Joel. "I mean, grabbing this guy—this thing—like that?"

"Of course," said Father. "But it had to be done."

"You should have seen him," I mused, thinking of the picture on the wall in Patricia Marie Nealy's bedroom. "It was like Gandalf facing the Balrog."

"Hardly like that," said Father. "Gandalf had no idea what awaited him in the pit beneath the bridge in Moria. I, on the other hand, knew exactly what to expect. Choose your heroes with care—you won't find one here."

"Pfui!" I said. It wasn't meant as a nasty comeback, nor my impression of Nero Wolfe. I was merely spitting out garlic skins.

"Oh, that awful smell," whined Portifoy. "Will none of you help me?"

"You?" scowled Jonathan. "Why should we want to help you?"

"Ah," said Portifoy, managing to flop onto its back. "You'd be surprised how much I could teach you, the things I can show you—"

"Watch it," warned Pierre. "Its advice, even if true, is sure to be laced with lies."

"You say that," cried Portifoy. "You have brought me to this by trickery."

"Yes, let's talk about tricks," said Father. "A vampire doesn't survive for four centuries without learning a few, and practicing them with diligence. And survive you did, Mr. Portifoy. After your misdeeds in France, you came to the American Colonies."

"Even a vampire needs a change of scenery once in a while," sputtered Portifoy. "A fresh start, and fresh blood."

"So," I said, finally secure in a seated position. "Do we finish it off now?"

"Patience, Martin," said Father, casting me a stern glance.

"Patience?" I mumbled, more to myself than to him. "What the Hell for—?"

"It must have been a fascinating adventure," said Father, turning back to the vampire, "coming over with the first wave of Huguenots in 1680."

"A vain and superstitious lot," said Portifoy.

What's this? I huffed to myself. Another history lesson?

"Of course," said Father, as much to us, it seemed, as to the vampire at his feet, "you needed help. Your intolerance for sunlight forced you to enlist the help of a human being, someone willing to arrange your worldly affairs."

"There you are wrong," said Portifoy. "I need no one."

"Claude Pulch," said Father. "Together with him you started an import business, Portifoy and Pulch."

"You think you're clever, don't you?" scoffed Portifoy.

"It served as an excellent cover," continued Father, "bringing you into contact with all sorts of people—people who came and went, as is the nature of the merchant trade—people who disappeared from time to time without being missed for months, traveling extensively as they did, only making occasional stops in this or that town. One can only wonder how many colonists and traders met their end at your hands."

"Wouldn't you like to know."

"Of course, every twenty years or so—to avoid suspicion because you, unlike your partner, did not age—you had to move to a new location, posing as your own son, adopting a new identity to suit your needs. Meanwhile, the descendants of Claude Pulch carried on the tradition, each son scouting out the next city, buying the next business property, preparing for the arrival of the next Portifoy—but of course it was always the same Portifoy who came. I imagine that each partner, each Pulch that grew old and useless to you, ended up in a graveyard with a tombstone bearing the name of Portifoy for company."

"You think so?" said the vampire.

"Some reward," commented Arthur.

"Martin Feeney here," said Father, indicating yours truly, "made an extensive search of the colonial records, along with catalogs of tombstones. With so much interest in genealogy these days, it was a likely place to search for evidence of your passing. There are no records of any grave markers bearing the name of Pulch."

"Perhaps you are a tad clever," admitted Portifoy.

"Which also tells us that each Pulch generation sold themselves, body and soul, into bondage to you. After doing your bidding, each submitted to destruction. What did you do? Promise them eternity among the undead?"

"Patooey!" spat Portifoy, expelling garlic flakes. Nero Wolfe it was not.

"Imagine the mind of a man who would sell not just his own self, but his eldest son, to the likes of you. And the wives, daughters, and other children? Were they just successive courses in your ongoing banquet? Apparently they did not merit even a tombstone. No doubt they were discarded in back alleys or abandoned fields, to be listed as Jane Does."

"Pfffffut!" sputtered Portifoy.

"Your movements were not that hard to trace. From your first residence in Manakin, Virginia, you moved to Williamsburg, Virginia, then Charleston, South Carolina. I found it intriguing that every place you moved to—New Paltz, New York City, Newport, Yorktown, Lexington—these were all cities with high concentrations of Presbyterians and Huguenots."

"A man should be where he's comfortable," said Portifoy.

"But you are not a man," said Father.

"More than a man," said the vampire.

"And less," said Father. "I suspect that the years of your sojourn in Boston in the late 1700s were your most prosperous."

"That they were," said Portifoy, rallying a little. "In that you are right. Impressed would your young friends here be if they knew the names of the men I called 'friends.' The fellow who signed his name so large, thus breaking his oath of allegiance to the King."

"John Hancock," said Father.

"Him," nodded Portifoy, "and others. I tell you, mon Pere, and all you young whelps, that I was a frequent guest at the home of Apollos Rivoire."

"Who?" asked Jonathan.

"A silversmith of great renown," said Portifoy, "not to mention a devout Huguenot."

"No doubt," said Father.

"Apollos Rivoire," mused Pierre. "Wasn't he the father of Paul Revere?"

"Rivoire, Revere," I mused. "Another name-shifter."

"It was Apollos who made this clasp for me," said Portifoy, touching its medallion with weak, trembling fingers. "Being a silversmith, he of course wanted to fashion it out of the metal of his trade, but I told him pewter was more to my liking." Its hand dropped limply to its side.

"Fancy," said Joel. "A bit gaudy, but okay."

"Okay?" sniffed Pierre. "Where is your sense of taste, my friend? The garish thing lacks 'class.'"

"What would you know?" huffed Portifoy with much effort. Then a note of wistfulness entered its voice. "Apollos and I downed many a beer at the Green Dragon Tavern."

"Dracula, Dragon," I mused, struggling to my knees. "Why not?"

"Or rather he did," added Portifoy. "Naturally, I always poured mine into the flowerpots."

"A shame," said Pierre. "Four hundred years without a sip of alcohol—not even beer, let alone champagne. I tell you, lads, the thought rankles."

"The Green Dragon," said Arthur. "Wasn't that sort of a headquarters for the patriots?"

"Wo-ho!" laughed Portifoy. "Is that what you call them? 'Seditionists' would be more appropriate, no?"

"What do you mean?" glowered Joel.

GARDENING TIPS: Joel, like most children of the recently immigrated, regarded the United States as an almost holy nation, conceived in the Mind of God and forged by noble statesmen of the highest caliber. All of the Tumblars, to various degrees, had been raised to think so. While I was tangentially aware of some of what Portifoy was about to say, it nonetheless

```
gave me the heebie-jeebies to hear him speak
of it.
                                    --M.F.
```

"Aha!" said Portifoy.   "What plans we made!   What havoc we caused!   Why, did you know that John Hancock and Paul Revere were both Grand Masters of the Masonic Lodge?   I had access to all the lodges.   That's how I know.   You might say that I was one of the Higher Initiates.   In fact, I was one of the organizers of the Sons of Liberty."

"Give me a break," groaned Edward.

"No, truly," said Portifoy.   "Lying is my business, but even I couldn't come up with something like this.   Surely you don't think the dumping of all that tea into Boston Harbor was an act of patriotism, do you?"

"What're you saying?" interrupted Joel.   "'No taxation without repre-sentation.'   That's what it was all about."

"You keep believing that, young man," said Portifoy.   "It is best that you should."

"What do you mean?" growled Joel.   "Father—?"

"It means," said Father Baptist, "that, contrary to what you might have learned in school, the Boston Tea Party was—"

"Please, mon Pere," said Portifoy.   "I lived this part of what you call your history.   Let me tell the tale."

Father opened his mouth, but thinking better of it, allowed the vam-pire to continue.   I, meanwhile, hands on hips as I knelt there in the garlic sea, was wondering why we were wasting time.   Nostalgia did not seem the appropriate focus for the moment.

"The tea that went into the water," coughed Portifoy, "it was im-ported by the British East India Company, no?   But the Crown had just lifted the import tax on that very tea because the Company was hav-ing—how do you say?—'financial difficulties.'   I did have an import business, after all, and was privy to this information.   Mr. Hancock, whom you so admire, had made his fortune smuggling tea into the colonies from the West Indies."

"You're talking about *the* John Hancock," said Joel, skeptically.

"The one with the proud signature," nodded Portifoy.   "That's the one.   Until that moment, his tea had been cheaper.   Naturally, he did not want to be undersold, so he rallied those thugs we had been groom-ing for such travesties, known as the Sons of Liberty and—"

"By dumping the British tea into the harbor—" blinked Pierre.

"The colonists had to buy from Hancock," said Arthur, "and at his price."

"Now there's patriotism for you," winked Portifoy.

"This is insanity," I huffed to myself.   "What are we waiting for?"

"And every American looks to this man, Hancock, as a hero," mused Portifoy. "You wonder why I call humans fools. Mark my words, in four centuries your descendants will consider the German SS in a similar light."

"Never," said Joel."

"We shall see," said Portifoy.

"That we certainly won't live to see," said Father, "and neither will you. Pierre, where's the hammer?"

"Ah," I mumbled, getting up on wobbly legs. Without a cane or anything to hold on to for support, it was quite an ordeal. "At last we're getting on with it."

"Here," said Pierre.

"And the stake?" asked Father.

"Right here," said Arthur, holding up a sharpened piece of wood.

"But think of it, mon Pere," said Portifoy, voice rising to a shrill whistle. "If word of what happens here tonight should ever leak out, have no doubt that in a hundred years I'll be the hero of the story, and you'll be the fiend who killed the last of an endangered species."

"Are you implying that you're the last vampire?" asked Father, accepting the implements.

"Aha!" cackled the vampire, eyeing the tools in Father's hands, "that would be the cream of the jest if you believed that, no?"

"As I said," said Father, "we won't be around to find out, and neither will you."

"But wait," said Portifoy, voice wavering in desperation. "You, the great detective: you have not finished our game—the story."

"About you?"

"No, about the price of cucumbers in Japan." Portifoy made a clicking sound with its leathery lips. "Of course about me. The game, it is not over until the fat lady, whoever she is, she sings, no?"

"I'm not playing your game," said Father. "I never have been."

"But of course you were," coughed Portifoy. "From the moment you found that little girl, the hunchbacked whelp who unfortunately went to Heaven—but there was no help for it, no? Casualties of war, and all that. I needed to get your attention, Pere—and thus my little message."

Oh yes, I thought. Its little message, and so poorly executed:

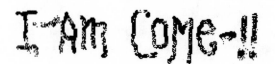

"From that moment, mon Pere," sneered the vampire, "you had joined the game. Jean Baptiste, the countdown had begun."

"T minus eleven," said Father.

"You watched too many old monsters-from-space movies," interjected the gardener.

Portifoy blinked and looked around. "What are you talking about, this 'T minus eleven'?"

"You mean you weren't thinking of a rocket taking off at Cape Canaveral?" I asked.

"Rocket?" squeaked Portifoy. "Cape Canaveral? Why should I concern myself with such things? And—pfffut!—whoever heard of counting down from eleven?"

"Okay, Martin," said Father. "Maybe I did read too much into it."

"Or he's lying," I said.

"A possibility," said Pierre.

"I am lying," said Portifoy, "every time I lie, like I am now."

"In any case," said Father, "you were saying that I had just joined in the game, Mr. Portifoy."

"Oui. That I did."

"Then do go on," said Father, gripping the hammer and stake. "I'm interested. You did say five inches to the right, did you not?"

"No," said Portifoy, "to the left—to the left, I said! You, a priest, and you do not know your Epistle side from your Gospel side?"

"It depends on which way you're facing, I suppose," said Pierre.

"East," said Arthur. "The Mass should always be celebrated facing east."

"They rarely are in this country," said Edward.

"Naturally," said Pierre with a sarcastic tone. "In a land whose discovery depended on the compass, rightful directional orientation means nothing."

"Let's see," said Father, hefting the implements. "We were talking about sides."

"No," said Portifoy, eyes darting this way and that. "We were talking about countdowns."

"Ah yes," said Father. "Countdowns."

"Ah me," I groaned. "More stalling. Father—?"

"Patience, Martin."

"Right."

"Countdowns," urged Arthur.

"T minus ten," said Pierre thoughtfully. "Babbette Starr. I turned her down. Perhaps if I had tried to tell her fortune, I could have warned her."

"Don't torture yourself," said Arthur.

"Don't kid yourself," said Jonathan.

"Still," said Pierre, "it's strange to think—"

"Don't," said Edward. "You'll hurt yourself."

"Pierre can't really tell fortunes," said Joel.

"So you say," sniffed Pierre. "It is said my family has the knack. What if it had worked?"

"Nothing concerning you," said Arthur, "will ever involve working."

"My true friends," said Pierre, sighing melodramatically.

"Each and every one," said Joel.

"Gentlemen," said Father, sternly. "Back to the matter at hand. Now, Mr. Portifoy, was that my Epistle side, or your Epistle side?"

"In the New Mass or the Old?" asked Portifoy.

"There is no Epistle or Gospel side in the New Mass," said Joel, the authority—after all, he was formerly a seminarian.

"Fancy that," said Father. "Now why should this be?"

"So we could waste time worrying about it now," I huffed.

"Martin," said Father.

"Father," said I.

"Stella," said Jonathan, suddenly shivering. "She was 'minus nine.'"

"And I might have been 'minus eight,'" said I, soberly. It was part of my immediate regimen for adopting "patience" as my primary intellectual exercise. What choice did I have, seeing that no one was in any particular hurry to get this dreadful business over with? "Yes," I said, cringing at the thought, "I might have been 'number eight,' if not for, well, never mind."

"And Nannette Cushions, Babbette's friend, could have been also," said Father. "But she ended up in an alley, courtesy of Mr. Portifoy, a gift for Surewood Forst."

"So," said I, my anxiety momentarily under control, "the dubious honor went to poor Buckminster Turnbuckle, known to all his anonymous fans as Bucky Buckle."

"Lucky eight," shuddered Portifoy, eyes riveted on the stake in Father's left hand. "A happenstance, a coincidence, a—"

"Vampire," said Pierre.

"This detail, I'll admit, was confusing," said Father, "because we didn't dig him up and see his number until Friday. By then, Stella had been attacked again in the hospital—"

"—and Surewood Forst had met his rather pressing end under a rolling machine. By Mr. Portifoy's own admission, it would have left a 'minus 6' on the body if there had been any place to draw it."

GARDENING TIPS: Since this was perhaps my only
correct supposition of the week, I proudly insert
a ghostly "might-have-been" kind of "minus 6"
here. I finally found a use for a gray crayon.
                                          --M.F.

"I don't think that's fair," said Joel. "Portifoy didn't even kill Mr. Forst. Why should he take credit for it?"

"It was 'murder by desire,'" said Pierre. "Modernist theologians have been tossing the idea around for years."

"It ranks up there," said Arthur, "with 'marriage by desire,' not to mention 'baptism of.'"

"And makes as much sense," said Joel.

"Be that as it may," said Father, "Mr. Forst was 'invincibly ignorant' of his peril—"

"Ouch!" said the gardener.

"—having been convinced that Mr. Portifoy here was his friend."

"Some friend," said Jonathan.

"Oh brother," I whispered, marveling at this new bit of meandering.

"Stella," said Jonathan coldly, back on track—good lad! "It attacked her in the hospital again. 'Minus five.'"

"It?" groaned Portifoy. "First you, Pere, and now this lovesick boy. Am I to be reduced to an 'it'? Jean Baptiste, you have studied the moral theology, no? You understand that disanthropomorphism is a means of dehumanizing the object of one's hatred, thereby rendering him easier to dispose of. No gender, no bothered conscience. This is also known as objectification. As a priest, you wouldn't want to disanthropomorphize me through dehumanizing objectification, would you?"

"As a vampire," said Father, "I should think you would welcome the attention. What do you think, Mr. Portifoy? I could just start punching holes in your chest—I'm bound to hit something vital to your incarnation eventually."

"Surely you jest," said Portifoy, feet pumping uselessly against the blanket of garlic bulbs.

"In any case," said Father, "Roland Reginold Ryan became 'minus 4,' at which point we had another shift in tactics."

"Perhaps I did not do it," said Portifoy. "Perhaps it was another vampire, one who loves the men, no? Perhaps one who is—how do you say?—"

"I suspect ..." said Father, then paused. "No, Mr. Ryan will keep for a moment. This brings us to the Grafan sisters."

"Yes," said Portifoy, struggling to slither away. "What about Tamara and Marla? So pretty, and yet so sad. Suicides, no?"

"How did they fit in?" asked Edward.

"Another diversion," said Father to the vampire. "Which, come to think of it, Mr. Portifoy, brings us back to your human partners in the import business. I found it interesting that the offices of Portifoy and Pulch closed its doors for the last time in 1989—just as the World Wide Web was in preparation, about to 'go on line' as they call it. With the advent of the Internet, you could no longer afford to have your movements so easily traced by computers."

"Indeed," said Portifoy. "I am impressed, Pere Jean Baptiste Lombard. Electricity is a necessary Evil, and it began to—how do you say?—backfire, no?"

"The name 'Pulch,' so unusual, was the key to that part of the mystery," said Father. "I suspect it comes from the French word, 'sepulchre,' a tomb."

"Bingo," said Portifoy.

It took me a second to figure that one out. S-e—P-U-L-C-H—r-e. Hm, a bit obscure, but it made sense.

"I have Martin Feeney to thank," said Father. "Though in a roundabout way. It was he who got me thinking about odd spellings, and words within words."

Actually, it had been rather brilliant of me, even if I was half-asleep at the time:

>"I thought maybe our Mr. Anthony Graves might be 'Tony the Bony Tooms,'" I had explained to Father, "seeing how T-o-o-m-s

is only one letter shy of T-o-m-b-s, and the word 'Tombs' is syn-
onymous with 'Graves.'"

"An odd coincidence," he had agreed.

"Not to mention the fact that Tony Tooms quit the 'Now You
Don't' six months ago. If he was in cahoots with Portifoy, I
thought—sort of a late version of Denis and the other Pulches—it
would fit the historical pattern for him to come ahead to Los Angeles and set up a new identity for his partner."

"While Martin played with 'Tony the Bony T-o-o-m-s,'" continued
Father, "and arrived at a dead end, I couldn't get my mind off the name
of 'G-r-a-v-e-s.' After all, it was the so-called Toolmaster's off-handed
remark about having seen you perform on stage before, Mr. Portifoy,
that resulted in Mr. Feeney's trip to Kentucky over this past weekend."

> *"Portifoy's a weird fellow, but he's a good magician ... I've seen*
> *him before."*
> *"Where?" asked Father.*
> *"Back in Lexington when I was visiting the folks last August.*
> *A place called the 'Now You Don't.'"*

"Last night, at the 'House of Illusions,'" continued Father, "Mr.
Graves explained he annually visited his colonial ancestors, Mortimer
Packwood Graves and Estelle Hilburn Graves, who died in 1792 and
1790 respectively. I called one of my contacts at the police department,
Miss Sybil Wexler, who, unlike me, is computer-literate. Using the
terminal in the crime lab, she 'linked-up' with the Colonial Cemetery
Registry Web Site, and verified the headstones at Bradbury Ridge. She
also confirmed what I had already suspected: that Mortimer and Estelle
Graves were interred in the plot right beside the ornate tomb of one
Lucius Robert Portifoy 1732—1794. Coincidence? Hardly."

"You've lost me," said Edward.

"Oui," said Portifoy. "You've even lost me."

"Mr. Graves was visiting an ancestor," said Father. "But not Mortimer and Estelle."

"How could a Portifoy be his ancestor?" asked Pierre. "Vampires
don't reproduce—at least, not that way."

"Let me get back to that," said Father.

"Ergg!" groaned the gardener.

"It dawned on me," smiled Father, "just a short while ago: Mausoleum—MOSS-oh-LEE-um—Lee Moss: the fellow who quit his job at
the 'Now You Don't' back in June, just about the time that Mr. Anthony Graves accepted the position of Toolmaster at the 'House of Illusions.'"

"Eyebrows," I had said while making an "X" over my nose with my forefingers

"Lee Moss had big eyebrows," M.C. Smith had said, rubbing his chin.

"Lee Moss?" I asked.

"Yayuh," said M. C., *"but he didn't wear no glasses, an' he didn't have no kin 'round here."*

"An' his last name weren't Graves," noted Eustace P. Franklin.

"So the mystery unravels, Mr. Portifoy," said Father. "In Lexington, Kentucky, Martin Feeney unknowingly uncovered your friendship with Lee Moss, who quit his job at the 'Now You Don't,' and left for Los Angeles in June. Here he adopted the name Anthony Graves, and procured the job of Toolmaster at the 'House of Illusions.' When Martin and I talked with him last Wednesday, he spoke of a job he planned to take in San Francisco, and mentioned a son, Henry, who is no doubt being groomed to be your next human servant—"

"Hey!"

Father's monologue was suddenly interrupted by a commotion from above.

"Yiiiiiiiii!" screamed a voice.

"Father Nicanor!" I yelled as the Maronite priest came hurling down, landing ungracefully on the heap of garlic bulbs. He rolled, tumbled, stalled, then sat up, shaking garlic flakes from his beard. I envied his grace and agility under such declivitous circumstances.

A new shadow filled his place at the hole above.

"Father Baptist," it said.

"Mr. Graves," said Father, "I've been expecting you."

130

"OH REALLY," SAID THE TOOLMASTER, eyebrows criss-crossed in amused derision—an' he weren't wearin' no glasses, neither. Yayuh. Apparently, the ones he'd been wearing lately were fakes.

"Of course," said Father, without skipping a beat. "I assumed Mr. Portifoy wasn't shoveling out the details of his sordid life just for our entertainment. He was stalling, waiting for your arrival, and we played along."

Oh, I thought, so *that's* why we've been exploring every conversational detour imaginable. Hrmph!

"Father Nicanor," said Arthur and Jonathan, helping our new arrival to his garlic-flecked feet, "are you okay?"

"Yes," sputtered the malleable Maronite. "My pride, it is stunningly purged."

"And now that you're here, Mr. Graves," said Father, "what do you intend to do?"

"This," said Mr. Graves.

There was a flash of light and a loud explosion.

The hammer flew out of Father Baptist's hand as the bullet penetrated his right shoulder. Dropping the stake, he reached over with his left hand and clutched the wound. Blood began trickling between his fingers.

"Father Baptist!" shouted the Tumblars, stepping forward.

"Stay where you are," ordered Father, teeth clenched.

"But Father—"

"I said stay put. Doesn't anyone around here understand simple orders? I'm all right."

"A sip," rasped Portifoy, eyeing the blood dripping from Father's hand. "Oh, for just one little sip—"

The Tumblars, visibly shaken, returned to their positions. Father Nicanor, swiping flakes from his cassock, straightened slowly and stood his ground a few feet to Father's right—if you could call that blanket of shifting garlic "ground."

"You've made your point, Mr. Graves," said Father, wincing.

"Yeah, I thought so," said the Toolmaster, pulling another shape into view. "And I've got another one right here." It was Monsignor Havermeyer. Mr. Graves—great-great-and-so-on-grandson of Claude Pulch, and recently known as Lee Moss—was holding a revolver to the monsignor's head.

"Father Baptist," gasped Havermeyer. "He said he was from the coroner's office. I didn't know—"

"Shut up," said Graves to the monsignor, then down at us: "Let's make this simple. You release Mr. Portifoy, and I'll let your friend here live. I'll let everybody down there live. In fact, I'll throw in your two housekeepers and that wimpy monsignor—Aspic is it?—for free."

"Where are they?" asked Father, straining to keep the anxiety out of his voice.

"In the pantry downstairs," said Mr. Graves. "A kitchen chair propped against the door. So, what do you say?"

"There's nothing to say," said Father Baptist. "If I let your master go, then untold hundreds of future deaths will be on my hands. This I cannot permit."

Monsignor Havermeyer's eyes went wide as Mr. Graves redoubled his grip on the gun. Perhaps the same conversation we had in the breakfast nook way back at the beginning of this story went through his mind as it did mine, this time with a whole new sense of immediacy:

> *"My vocation is to try to save souls, not lives,"* Father had said.
> *"There's a difference?"* Wickes had asked.
> *"I'm here, too, Father,"* Monsignor Havermeyer had reminded us. *"Don't forget that."* We wouldn't, and neither would he.
> *"Salad,"* was my final word during that conversation, though it came a page or two later. *"Hmmm, shallab."*

"Besides," continued Father, still talking to the Toolmaster, "how could I possibly trust a man like you? Not only have you willingly submitted your body and eternal soul to this fiend, you plan to persuade your son, Henry, to follow suit."

"He's already willing and waiting," said Graves.

"As are you, Mr. Graves," said Father, "but your time is up. You'll soon be joining your wife on Mr. Portifoy's plate. As soon as she birthed you a male after two daughters, you gave her to Portifoy. Leukemia, you said? I think not. The 'Vampire's Kiss' is what killed her. Then, if that wasn't enough, you sacrificed your own two daughters, besides."

"Hey?" asked the gardener. "Excuse me, Father. Where did you get all this?"

"'Grafan,'" said Father. "Tamara and Marla Grafan. 'Grafan' is an Old English word derived from the German 'graven'—'grave.'" He winked as if to say, "You do your digging, Martin, and I do mine."

"Ah," I nodded. Yes, it was all beginning to fit.

> *"… I've got a kid up at Berkeley,"* Mr. Graves had said.
> *"Really,"* said Father. *"Son or daughter?"*
> *"Son. Henry. He's twenty-three, majoring in Medieval History and Electrical Engineering, believe it or not. I've also got two older daughters, but they never got beyond high school."*
> *"So you're married?"*
> *"Was. The wife died of leukemia years ago. I've been living in bachelor pads like this ever since the kids left the roost, and to tell you the truth, I prefer it. Anyway, yes, I'm seriously considering a move to San Francisco or Oakland. I've heard it's a lot less stressful than life in LA."*

Yes, clearer and clearer. Just as "Se-PULCH-re" gave rise to "Claude Pulch" and his ilk, "MOSS-oh-LEE-um" begot "Lee Moss," which in turn begot "Anthony Graves," who had previously begotten "Clove and Nutmeg S-o-l-e" whose last name had been derived from "Mau-SOLE-eum" and who later became "Tamara and Marla Grafan" who never got beyond high school but who sure knew how to stand around:

"Ol' Roy, he kept purty much to hisself, " Moab Chester Smith had told me, *"One night 'bout three weeks back—the tenth of this month, Ah think it was, yayuh—he just up an' hauled off an' announced his early retirement, turned his magic wand into a train ticket, an' left us in a lurch without a headlinin' act."*

"Thayat was 'round the time when the fever passed," Mr. Franklin had added.

"'Sylvie's Mis'ry,' they calls it," said M. C. Smith. *"It got pretty thick 'round here last summer, but it's been plaguin' these here parts on an' off fer goin' on two an' a half hunnert years."*

"Somethin' gits in yer blood," said Mr. Franklin knowledgeably. *"A fungus or vah-ris, maybe. Maybe it's jus' somethin' in the soil 'round these parts."* He'd never know how close he came to the truth. *"My great-grand mammy used to say it only came during them long stretches of humidity we gits 'round here."*

"'Bert's 'Brella,'" the M. C. called it. *"The sky gits all black an' blue, an' rumbles up a storm ..."*

"You come at the right time, Mr. Feeney," Mr. Franklin had assured me. *"Bert done folded up his 'Brella a few weeks back, sendin' Sylvie packin', an' the weather's been jus' fine ever since."*

"Thayat's right," said M. C. Smith. *"Maybe Ol' Roy shoulda stuck it out a little longer. Anyways, like Ah was sayin': Lee Moss, thayat other feller, he quits in June; an' a couple months b'fore that, a couple o' sisters quits, too ... Clove and Nutmeg Sole ... They didn't do much—sort of a 'mind-readin'' act—but what they was really good fer was standin' 'round lookin' purty ..."*

"A few brief telephone calls this morning confirmed my suspicions," said Father. "Tamara and Marla began working at the 'House of Illusions' last April. Mr. Graves here arrived in June. Then, two weeks ago, his master arrived by train from the East. Portifoy befriended Surewood Forst, and the next bit you all know. Things went according to plan, until Martin's prayers for a Soul in Purgatory spoiled the party Portifoy had arranged that fateful Monday evening at the magic club. Stella and Jonathan had already been rendered unconscious by the 'Vampire's Breath.' When Martin arrived, Portifoy hunted him down but was ultimately foiled, driven from the premises by Divine Intervention—in this case, Elza Roundhead's ghost—which can only be described as the answer to Martin's prayer."

"Way to go," said Edward.

"Well done, Sir Martin," said Pierre.

Much as I enjoyed being the center of attention, if only for a moment, I couldn't help worrying that throughout all this yackety-yak Father Baptist was bleeding. Patience, I reminded myself, was the operating word for the evening. So, gathering my wits, such as they were, I opened my mouth and played along. "It was nothing."

"Oh, but it was indeed something," said Father. "We'll discuss it later in detail."

"If we live that long," added the gardener.

"But, to continue," said Father, "Martin was thus spared, and Stella ended up in the hospital. Portifoy was able to get to her there again, having decided not to finish her, but to use her as an ongoing source of blood—not to mention another piece in its nasty little puzzle."

"You're wasting time," said Graves.

"There's plenty before the sun comes up," said Father. "As your master has said, albeit before your arrival, let the detective tell the story."

"I don't want to hear it," said Graves.

"I wouldn't either, if I were in your shoes," said Father. "Portifoy knew that we would take precautions at the hospital lest it get to her again, and it needed a human dupe to get into Stella's room, drug Pierre and Jonathan and the guard, and remove the holy objects. Mr. Graves, you were known to the police by then and would have been recognized. Besides, you'd hardly make a convincing 'nurse.' So Portifoy demanded the use of your daughters who, I suspect, were unaware of their father's nefarious activities."

"That's enough," said Graves.

"No, it isn't," said Father.

"What're you doing, Father?" I hissed, losing my precious "patience" again. "Goading him into shooting you twice?"

"Hush," whispered Father in reply. Then, redoubling his grip on his hemorrhaging wound, he continued in a loud voice: "The vampire, Portifoy, revealed itself to Marla and convinced her that Tamara was being held prisoner. That was the lever it used to coerce Marla into playing the part of the nurse. Confused and desperate, she came to see me at the church while I was in the confessional."

"She did?" asked Graves, those colliding eyebrows of his disengaging in a moment of uncertainty.

"Yes," said Father, "but her aversion to all things Catholic overcame her anxiety for her sister and apparently her fear of Portifoy."

"You trained her well, Anthony," said Portifoy. "All the deeper into Hell you shall go!"

Mr. Graves' face snapped back into its original angry, smiling scowl.

"So she did the deed," said Father, "drugged these lads and the guard outside, removed the reliquary and Rosary, and left Stella Billowack at Portifoy's mercy. But Portifoy had no intention of releasing Marla's sister, Tamara, who was slated for death in Portifoy's 'game.' Tamara had been kept drugged—by a chemical agent or a dose of the 'Vampire's Breath' which Lieutenant Taper experienced last Thursday evening, it really doesn't matter—and was kept locked in one of the innumerable equipment closets in the basement of the 'House of Illusions.' And this was how Roland Reginald Ryan became the second unwitting male victim—"

"I'm lost," said Joel.

"After all," said Father, "it was Reginold the Reiterator who delivered to Martin and myself an invitation to the Farquar Terrace that first night we all visited 'House of Illusions.' A simple errand, and part of his job. He did not know who left the invitation at the front desk, but maybe he recognized the handwriting."

"Wasn't mine," said Mr. Portifoy.

"No indeed," said Father. "We know about that. No, you got Mr. Graves here to write it."

"You're sure of that," said Graves.

"Yes," said Father. "I recognized it myself when Martin and I visited your bedroom in the basement. You showed us the clipboard on which you keep the details of your activities. Portifoy, in order to seal a 'friendship' with Surewood Forst, ordered you to help with that silly demonstration on the Farquar Terrace. Forst couldn't have pulled it off himself."

"Sure he could," said Graves. "I told you, everything around there can be run by remote control."

That, he had:

> "Simple, really," Graves had told us. "Dry ice—frozen carbon dioxide—is dumped into a basin of water, and the resulting mist is blown through the conduits by remote-controlled whisper-fans."
>
> "Carbon dioxide?" I wheezed from exertion.
>
> "Remember how cold it got, Martin?" asked Father.
>
> "Dry ice?" I wheezed again. "Sure, that makes sense."
>
> "It also accounts for the crickets ceasing their music," said Father. "They were reacting to the change in temperature. Remote control, you say?"
>
> "Yep," said Mr. Graves. "Everything around here is triggered that way ..."

"Nonetheless," said Father, "someone had to run the fog machine for Mr. Forst since the remote control units only have a range of a few yards, and the fog began issuing out onto the terrace while he was several stories above us, preparing to lower himself with a winch."

Yup. I had to admit, that fit, too:

> "What would you say is the maximum range of one of these things?" Father had asked as he picked up a remote control unit.
>
> "Twenty feet," said Graves.
>
> "Doesn't seem very far."

> *"It can't be much more than that or one guy's trick is going to screw up another guy's in the next room."*
> *"Could one of these be adjusted to have a longer range?"*
> *"Not without upping the power,"* said Graves. *"And if I took that apart and showed you, you'd see there just ain't any more room for larger batteries inside."*

"In any case," said Father, "when Mr. Ryan came upon a work order, or something else with Mr. Graves' handwriting on it, he began to put two and two together—at least as far as the Toolmaster was concerned."

"I repeat," said Graves, an amused smirk on his face, "you sound sure of this."

"Well," said Father, "I do still have that invitation, and I did see your handwriting on the clipboard in your room, and if I could make the connection, so could Mr. Ryan. Little did he know, when he went snooping around in the basement, that he'd find Tamara locked in a closet, unconscious, and protected by a vampire—"

"That's enough," said Graves.

"—waiting to die at her father's own hands."

"No she wasn't," growled Mr. Graves. "And I didn't kill her. Portifoy did."

"But you did hit Reginold on the head," said Father, "rendering him, too, unconscious until your master rose from its grave at sunset."

"Go to Hell," spat Graves.

"What a feast to wake up to, no?" said Portifoy, licking its lips wistfully. "One large swig before the fast."

"The fast?" asked Pierre.

"It's what you might call a 'vampire thing," said Portifoy, "observing a day of rest while the priest wonders what's happening."

"Sunday," I mused. "A day of rest."

"Our staking of Gorphegor in Buckminster Turnbuckle's body," said Father, "had been a little too close for comfort, even if it did provide Mr. Portifoy with 'number eight,' so it spent the weekend at the 'House of Illusions'—the small coffin Mr. Graves used as a clothes chest—which is why Mrs. Feuchtwanger's car stayed put for once. Then Portifoy and Mr. Graves arranged the apparent death of Portifoy—"

"My favorite stake," said the vampire.

"—along with the hanging of the stupefied Tamara and the message in Portifoy's own blood."

I killed my Master,

"And me with so little to spare," mused Portifoy.

"That child's coffin," said Father, "which Mr. Graves claimed was just an old stage prop, was in reality one of Mr. Portifoy's spare abodes. No magician would have a solid mahogany casket, a genuine 1937 'Quimby & Qwimby' according to the plaque mounted in the lid. Even if one did, he wouldn't leave something so valuable behind."

"It couldn't have been a fake?" asked Edward.

"No," said Father, "you can't fake a 'Quimby & Qwimby.'"

"Why not?" asked Joel.

"It's a 'priest thing,'" said Father. "When you've said as many Requiems as I have, you come to recognize these things."

"Sure," said Arthur. "Sure."

"Yah," said Josef, back in the shadows. "'Priest t'ing.'"

Details, details. I remembered that when Mr. Graves had offered said QUIMBY & QWIMBY as a place to sit, Father had declined.

> *"Go ahead, have a sit,"* Mr. Graves had said. *"It won't bite you."*
>
> *"Splinters,"* said Father as he closed the lid, rubbing his thumbs and forefingers together. Apparently he'd had some suspicion about the coffin.
>
> *"Suit yourself,"* said Graves, puzzled or amused at something. It was hard to tell with those eyebrows. But of course his reaction was due to the fact that no genuine Q & Q would shed splinters, and he knew it. *"Mr. Feeney?"*
>
> "I'll stand, thank-you."

"I also found it significant," said Father, "that the child-sized coffin had been dragged along the basement floor, not from the direction of Mr. Graves' room, but from the closet where Tamara was hanged."

"You mean," said the gardener, "to lead us to her body."

"Right," said Father. "Then, these discoveries having been made according to plan, Portifoy spent an evening in the police morgue, sipping blood like aged port from test tubes in the refrigerator."

"Not much of a fast," said Pierre, disgustedly.

"So I have my weaknesses," shrugged Portifoy. "I am, after all—how do you say it?—less than human."

"And finally," concluded Father, "Mr. Graves retrieved a drugged Marla Grafan from wherever she had been secluded—perhaps another closet in the basement, I'm not sure. The police will no doubt sort out the details. He then drove Mr. Ryan's Thunderbird to the police morgue sometime last night or early this morning, picked up Portifoy, and brought them back to St. Philomena's. After reopening the stone hut from the sidewalk side, Marla was hanged from the rafter—"

I Killed my Sister

"—and Portifoy snuggled down for one final sleep less than a hundred yards from where we now stand. Mr. Graves replaced the stones and went his way."

"How did you learn about the hut?" asked Graves. "How did you know to look there?"

"A combination of things," said Father. "Plants dying around the place, and another intervention on Martin's part, one which falls more in the realm of the 'preternatural,' and which will require lengthy discussion at the next Tumblar meeting."

"If we should live so long," said I, thinking of Cheryl Farnsworth in her colorfully yet desperately decorated jail cell.

"Bravo," said Mr. Portifoy. "Pere Jean Baptiste, you are quite the detective."

"It was my prior vocation," said Father. "One I surely wish I could leave behind in the dust. I had hoped that this trap would bring this horrible chain of affairs to an end."

"Of course," I ahemed, "the trouble with this particular trap is that all the bait is caught inside."

"True," said Father. "Like I said before, Martin, I would have preferred that you be outside. In any case, you can see, Mr. Graves, why I cannot comply with your wishes. If we release your master, you'll just finish us all off. You'll have no choice, because we all know the details of your participation in Mr. Portifoy's game. If any of us survives, we will hunt you down."

"I can't argue with that," said Graves. "So I'll just have to kill you all, and as for Mr. Portifoy and myself, I am prepared to accept my fate—"

"Yeah?" roared an unexpected voice from above and somewhere behind Mr. Graves and Monsignor Havermeyer. "We'll just see about that."

Suddenly a fist came into view. It was huge, it was stubby, it was vicious, and it was accompanied by a spray of saliva. It belonged to none other than—

"Chief Billowack!" cheered the Tumblars.

Yes, cheers. Only events such as these could bring about something like that.

"Sir," added Jonathan.

The bulldog's fist made contact with Mr. Grave's face. The top of Grave's face went one way, and his lower jaw another. His eyebrows flew in opposite directions. The revolver spun out of his right hand, and Monsignor Havermeyer out of his left. The perplexed monsignor staggered, lost his footing, and fell over the edge. He came hurtling down, landing in a fluffy explosion of scattering garlic bulbs.

Flakes whirled anew.

"I don't like being toyed with," roared Billowack above, giving Mr. Graves the old one-two in the gut, in the chest, and then up to his face again. "And nobody messes with my little girl!" With one final punch, Mr. Graves followed Monsignor Havermeyer down into the heaving mound of garlic.

"That's that," said Billowack, wiping his hands on his pants. "And as for you, Jack-o, just wait'll I get my hands on you—kidnapping is a federal offense!"

"I await your arrest," said Father, "but do please consider—"

"Daddy," came a voice from above.

"Stella?" said Billowack, whirling. "Are you—?"

As Billowack spun on his heels, the wood cracked beneath his size-zillion wing-tipped shoes. Like an elephant executing a perfect pirouette, coattails splayed like a tutu, he spun all the way around and found himself toppling head-first over the edge.

We all threw up our arms as a wave of spinning garlic bulbs billowed all around us, accompanied by a roar that only Billowack could muster.

"You're all under arrest," sputtered Billowack, heaving his chest up from the sea of garlic with his tree trunk arms. His hands slipped out from under him, and he landed facedown in the prime ingredient of Millie's surprise casserole.

131

"SO," I SIGHED, "MR. PORTIFOY wasn't the only one who was stalling, eh, Father?"

"Indeed," answered Father. "It was only a matter of time before the chief figured out that Stella was not simply lost in hospital red tape."

"But you couldn't be sure," said Arthur.

"No," said Father. "But I had confidence that our combined prayers would be answered. As a priest, I have come to rely on Divine Intervention as a matter of course. And now we have one last duty to perform."

The Tumblars slowly shuffled through the garlic mounds, forming a circle around Mr. Portifoy. A shaken Monsignor Havermeyer, flakes clinging to his cassock, and a recovered Father Nicanor, too, joined us.

Chief Billowack, who was sloshing around like a whale in shallow water, continued to bellow and blather, but to no avail.

"Who shall do the honor?" said Father with a grimace, still clutching the wound on his right shoulder. "Alas, I cannot."

"Me," said Jonathan. "I have a personal interest in this."

"That is precisely why you should not," said Father.

"Then let it be me," said Pierre. "My ancestors would be proud."

"No doubt they are," said Father. "But I think the task should fall to Martin, son of Fényi Márton. Besides, he already has the most appropriate weapon."

"Me?" I squeaked. "What weapon?"

"Your cane," said Arthur. "It's made of aspen."

"And it has a silver dagger within," said Jonathan.

"But I've never figured out the catch," I said. "And I don't know where it is at the moment. I had it in my hand when I fell—"

"Cane, yah," nodded Josef, reaching down and picking up my walking stick from the surging tide of rolling garlic bulbs. No English my eye.

"Here," said Joel, accepting the stick from his grinning grandfather.

"But—" I stammered.

"I think I can figure it out," said Jonathan, taking the cane from Joel and struggling with a little button inside the dragon's mouth. "Whoops. It's jammed. It won't open."

"Better still," said Pierre, taking the stick from Jonathan. He ceremoniously snapped the shaft over his knee with a loud crack, thus breaking off the extremity with the rubber tip. Out of the splintered end gleamed a deadly point of metal. "A silver dagger inside an aspen shaft, a snarling dragon's head for a handle. What could be more fitting?"

"But really—" I mumbled as Pierre pressed the cane into my left hand, giving my shoulder a manly squeeze.

"Hammer," said Joel. "Where's the hammer?"

"I saw it fly over that way," said Jonathan, "when Father Baptist was shot."

"It was heavy," said Edward.

"Surely it sank," said Pierre.

"This stuff is still three feet deep in some places," said Jonathan.

"We're wasting time," said Father.

Oh, I thought, so now he's concerned about the time!

"Oh, Hell," said Arthur, leaning against the wall and lifting his foot. "Here, Sir Martin, use my shoe."

"Mighty neighborly," I said ungratefully, feeling the shoe pressed into my right hand. I hadn't realized that Arthur's feet were so huge. He and Billowack should hold a contest.

"Any time," said Arthur von Bigfoot.

I realized they were all looking at me, waiting.

"Well," I said.

"Well," said they.

"Martin," said Father. "You know you are the one who should end this thing."

"But I've never killed anyone," I said. "I don't know if I could—"

"Wait one minute there," huffed Billowack, clawing his way to a sitting position. "Feeney, don't even think what you're thinkin'!"

"This is not a man," said Father. "It is a devil. It is the enemy of Christ—and ours."

"It's murder," choked Billowack, spitting out a couple of garlic cloves. "Don't you dare—"

"We dare," said Father, "because we must."

"Les Prêtres sont les cochons!" spat Portifoy.

"The priests are pigs," translated Pierre.

"Most are," I nodded, gripping the cane and looking at Father Baptist, "but not this one."

Father Baptist returned my stare, and then drew my eyes with his to the vampire sprawled on the garlic heap. For some reason, as I looked down at the dwarf's chest, estimating where its ugly heart might be hiding inside that warped little rib cage, my eyes were drawn to that pewter medallion.

"That clasp," I said. "'Apollos' you explained, Mr. Portifoy, but who's 'Phegor'? And what I'd really like to know is: what's the 'B' stand for?"

"Ah, that," said Portifoy, sinking in defeat as its end loomed inevitable now. It could only prolong the outcome by a matter of moments. "Son of Fényi Márton, friend of Purgatory, it stands for my real name: Bobphegor. I am a minion of Balphegor."

"Balphegor," said Father Nicanor, grateful for the opportunity to roll his r's. "The Moabite god of licentiousness, as well as the demon of discoveries and ingenious inventions."

"That explains all the machinery entwined around the clasp," said Pierre.

"And," said Father, "if I remember correctly, Balphegor is closely connected with France, especially Paris."

"Correct," said Portifoy. "It was he who bid me to don this body and to take part in human affairs."

"Did he also bid you to come to America?" asked Pierre.

"No," shrugged Portifoy, "that was my idea."

"And your name is Bobphegor," I said.

"Did you not notice, Martin," said Father, "that every guise of Porti-foy throughout history included Robert in the name?"

"Except this one," I said. "Lucius T. Portifoy."

"I think I can explain that," said Father.

"You think you can explain everything," sputtered Portifoy.

"You asked him to," said Jonathan. "He's only complying."

"Okay," said Portifoy, trying to fold its arms protectively, but it couldn't find the strength to keep them up on its chest. They fell limply back to its sides with a dry plop.

"'T,' I suspect," said Father, "stands for 'Trebor.'"

"Trebor?" asked Jonathan and Joel in unison.

"What kind of a name is Trebor?" asked Edward and Arthur together.

Meanwhile, this gardener's cerebellum was experiencing what you might call a half of a nanosecond in overdrive. T-r-e-b-o-r-o-b-e-r-t, went the ol' gray matter. "It's 'Robert' backwards," said my mouth.

"Oui," said Portifoy.

"Bob?" I smiled.

"BOB?" laughed the Tumblars.

"Then," blinked Father Nicanor, snorting back an uproarious chuckle, "truly this is the Demon Bob."

"Who do you think they'd send to take over a dead body anyway?" pouted Portifoy. "It's not exactly—how do you say?—a 'big-draw job' in Hell, you know."

"You said the demon who took over Bucky's body was named Gor-phegor," I noted. "Is 'Phegor' a family name? It's there on your clasp as well."

"Well," said Portifoy, shrinking slightly, as if that were possible. "It's more like a mark of slavery."

"So you fled your master," said Pierre.

"The pay," said Portifoy, "it was not so good."

"Well," said Monsignor Havermeyer, still rubbing the sores from his ordeal with Mr. Graves, "you can tell your master, and all your fellow slaves down there, all about your fortunes in America."

"Ah," said Portifoy, "the legion of souls I have sent there before me. Surely—" It gulped worriedly. "—Balphegor will be appeased."

"But in your travels," said Father, "surely you have also encountered Saints. They have come and gone, gone to where you can never go, and to where you should have always been, where you were created to be. We humans, who you find to be so foolish, were made to fill the hole torn in the fabric of Heaven when a third of the Angels fell."

"You are wise," said Portifoy to Father. "Oui, I admit it. Heaven means much to you, no?"

"It means everything to me," agreed Father.

"Then listen! Listen: if you spare my measly existence, let me go about my business—we'll call it 'even,' no?—I will answer the deepest question on your heart."

"How would you know what that is?" asked Father.

"My Angelic sight tells me." Portifoy scrambled desperately, weakly, fawning pathetically at Father's feet. "I can tell you the answer! I know the eternal fate of your wife, Christine!"

"Wife?" gasped the Tumblars severally. "Father, what's it talking about?"

"Yes," said Father, eyes clouding as he looked around at his closest circle of friends. As far as I knew, I was the only one present privy to this specter from Father's past. He looked down, then around again at the ring of riveted eyes. "I was married, years ago. My dear wife, Christine, died of cancer. Amidst the turmoil of my life, and the terrors of my profession, it came as an awesome blow—one which threw my life into chaos, a chaos through which I ventured, a chaos which led me eventually, and by roads I hope you gentlemen never need travel, to the Catholic Faith and ultimately to my priesthood."

"I can set your mind at rest," said Portifoy. "Pere Jean Baptiste, formerly Jack Lombard the great detective: this I can do, for I know what became of her."

"You offer me this," said Father.

"Peace," said Portifoy. "I offer you peace. As an Angel, this I can give you."

"No," said Father sadly. "The peace that passes all understanding, the peace the Angels announced to men of Good Will on the night of Our Lord's Birth, the only peace that counts: by its very nature, it cannot be expressed, nor can it be provided by a mere cessation of worry. It is the peace a Saint encounters as he is tied to the pillar to be scourged and burned for his love of Christ. How dare you offer me a substitute?"

"Bah," scoffed Portifoy. "What do you—a mere human—know about peace?"

"More than you, Bobphegor," said Father, "for at least I can hope for it. All that is left you is eternal cacophony, the screams of human souls and fallen demons consumed with despair, denied the Beatific Vision forever."

"Father," I said, wanting to reach out to him, but feeling rather klutzy at the moment, brandishing a broken cane and a smelly shoe.

"Besides, Bobphegor," said Father, "I would never know if you were telling me the truth. The trouble with being the son of lies is that you come to believe them yourself. I could never trust your word, and my heart would only swell with more doubt in time. Martin, do your duty."

"Stay put, Feeney," bellowed Billowack, slipping again.

"You think I am cruel?" gasped Portifoy. "You do not know the meaning of the word. And look at you! Look at me! Where is your Christian Charity? Can you not see I'm in agony? This awful stench! Is this how you demonstrate this Love of God?"

"Christian Charity," said Father Baptist, "is reserved for human beings, not for demons."

"You mean we can do anything to it we want?" asked Jonathan, producing a flask from his jacket pocket. "I mean, after all it did to Stella—?"

"'Vengeance belongeth to me,'" said Portifoy, a hint of desperation in its voice, "'I will recompense, saith the Lord.'"

"You should know better," saith the gardener, growing angry, "than to quote the King James Bible to us."

"I am a Huguenot," said the vampire. "What do you expect?"

"Hebrews ten thirty," I went on, "is a reference to Deuteronomy thirty-two thirty-five: 'Revenge is mine, and I will repay them in due time, that their foot may slide—'"

I shifted my foot through the garlic bulbs for emphasis. "Is my foot sliding enough for you, Mr. Portifoy?"

"Good going," said Jonathan, sprinkling holy water on the vampire's head.

"Arrg!" it screamed, smoke spurting from its sizzling hair. "Not that!"

"But there's more to the verse," I said. "'The day of destruction is at hand, and the time makes haste to come.'"

"It should have known better," commented Arthur, "than to start a Scriptural argument with Martin Feeney."

"Gentlemen," said Father, "do you feel a 'day of destruction' coming on?"

"Indeed," said Pierre.

"I sure do," said Jonathan, emptying the flask on Portifoy's head. The vampire's skin hissed and burned. "It's useless to bless you, Demon Bob, but bless you I do!"

"Amen," said Arthur. "Let the destruction commence."

"You bet," said Edward.

"Not on your life!" bellowed Billowack, sprawling some more.

"Wait a minute," clamored the vampire, squirming maniacally, tendrils of smoke curling from its wagging forehead. "Let's not be hasty, dear fellows. There is much to discuss, much you can learn, much I can teach—"

Wincing, with the help of Arthur and Pierre, I managed to get onto my knees beside the vampire. With trembling hands, I counted five inches from the center of Portifoy's chest.

"Then I will give you another gift," panted Portifoy. "I will for once tell you the truth: everything you believe is a myth. I am eternal, but you are not. When you die, there is nothing! Nothing! Your religion is a sham, your hope is a lost cause, and your Faith is nothing but foolishness."

"The Cross is foolishness," said Father. "And by it I choose to live."

"So do we all," said the Tumblars.

"So do I," said Monsignor Havermeyer. "So do I."

"Martin?" said Father, calmly.

"One last thing," I said, staring down into Portifoy's hateful red eyes, "I want you to remember."

"Oh?" wheezed Portifoy. "What is that, Mortal Man?"

"Mortal that I am," I said, "it was to men such as I that Saint Paul wrote his First Letter to the Corinthians. I'm referring to the sixth chapter—"

"Bah! I hate that man Paul. He revealed too much!"

"—third verse: 'Know you not that we shall judge Angels?'"

"What's your point?" asked Pierre.

"It's just that right now, all we can do is consign this demon back to Hell," I said. "But some day, some of us—I pray we all make it to Heaven!—will be in a position to pass judgment on this devil."

"In other words?" said Arthur.

"It is we who will have the last laugh," I said.

"Martin," said Father.

"Yes, Father," I whispered, lifting the shoe with shaking hand. "Hail Mary, full of Grace ..."

"No, no, no!" whined Portifoy.

"Wait!" screamed Billowack, finally gaining his feet. "In the name of the LaaaaaAAAaaaaAAAAWWWW—!!" He landed face-down again in a plume of bulbs.

"'Circumdederunt me gemitus mortis,'" intoned Father, "'dolores inferni circumdederunt me ...'"

He was joined by Father Nicanor:

> The groans of death surrounded me, the sorrows of Hell encompassed me: and in my affliction I called upon the Lord, and He heard my voice from His holy temple. I will love thee, O Lord, my strength: the Lord is my firmament, and my refuge, and my deliverer.

As I brought Arthur's shoe smashing down on the forehead of my beloved aspen dragon, the sharp tip of my cane penetrated the chest of Lucius Trebor Bobphegor Portifoy. Whether it was some quality of the aspen wood, or the force of my blow—which I tend to doubt—or the final acceptance of the vampire, I do not know; but one blow was all it took to drive the cane through the body and into the dry blanket of pungent garlic beneath.

The fiend let out a terrible scream, a vaporous expulsion of terrible heat and fury and final despair. The hissing steam of its breath became a putrid plume of acrid dust, stinging my eyes and singeing my cheeks.

As I knelt there, nausea overtaking me, three marvelous things happened, so close together they might as well be described as simultaneous—though at that swirling moment, it was hard to say.

First, as I looked on, utterly horrorstruck, the flesh of Portifoy's face withered, cracked, pulverized, crumbled, and dissolved with a defeated sigh into a pile of fetid black dust. Even its pewter medallion erupted in metallic sores, blistering, then bubbling, then gurgling as the clasp liquefied and sank into the subsiding ashes. The only thing left, as the particles of the finally dead vampire sifted their way down through the garlic bulbs, was its aquamarine monocle.

Second, the clock in the old church steeple struck the midnight hour—twelve ominous, unevenly-spaced, deafeningly loud repercussions, the old steel clapper punching another series of gouges into the wooden beam where the huge bronze bell used to hang. Each hollow thunk caused the dust around my knees to churn and resettle among the garlic bulbs. No doubt the impression of my companions was that I was pounding the cane over and over again, but as I said, one stroke did the trick. Honest.

Third, amidst the resounding din, there was a blinding flash of light—three, actually, in quick succession, accented with the swift, shrill electric whines of a recharging photographer's strobe.

"Got that?" asked Jacco Babs, somewhere above my head.

"Bingo," said Ziggie, who must have checked out a more state-of-the-art camera than he'd been handing over to the police all week.

"Let's go!" barked Jacco, heaving himself away.

"Right-oh!" laughed Ziggie, chasing after him.

"What?" roared Billowack, rising and falling in the sea of garlic. "Taper! Wickes! Are you up there? Arrest them!"

"For what?" asked Wickes, looking down sheepishly over the rim of the hole.

"Material witnesses," bellowed Billowack.

"To what?" asked Taper, standing beside his junior partner. "Mr. Feeney driving his cane into a pile of dust with a shoe?"

Billowack's jowls slavered this way and that. "There must be something. Think of something." He raised his wobbly chins. "Anything!"

Just how long Taper and Wickes had been standing up there was anyone's guess, but apparently they witnessed the grand finale.

"Ptui," spat Josef, who had approached the spot where I was kneeling. His globular geriatric projectile landed squarely on that aquamarine lens. The monocle wobbled, tilted, and slipped down between the bulbs. "Yah," nodded the old man. "'Wampyr,' yah."

"They're gone, Chief," called down Wickes.

"I'll have your heads for this—!" screamed Billowack, losing his footing and landing on his mile-wide heinie.

"Oh Daddy," chided Stella, standing between Taper and Wickes. "Mellow out, will you?"

Wednesday, November First

∞ Feast Day of All Saints ∞

† Holy Day of Obligation †

132

"I HOPE THAT'LL HOLD," SAID JOHN HOLTSCLAW, pressing a final strip of white adhesive tape over the thick cotton gauze bandage on Father Baptist's bare right shoulder. "This isn't my usual line of work, you understand. My patients don't normally groan, or flinch, or move at all for that matter. Of course, I'll never be able to count on that again, will I? In any case, you really need to get yourself to a surgeon for some stitches."

"Will do," said Father, gritting his teeth as he pulled his open cassock back up over his shoulder with his left hand. "Right after morning Mass. With all of Monsignor Havermeyer's good intentions, he's not ready to handle that task."

"Sorry we didn't get here sooner," said Solomon Yung-sul Wong, attempting without success to fit the former contents of the standard police-issue first-aid kit back inside the plastic case. Funny, all those sterile emergency implements in their white paper wrappers and crackling plastic envelopes, now spread across the wide expanse of Father's desk in the study, had indeed emerged from that tiny little box a short while ago. "We got stuck in a horrendous traffic jam."

"Yeah," said Holtsclaw, handing Solomon the scissors and tape roll, as if these things would help solve the puzzle, "some rock band called 'Vampire Steaks' threw a big surprise Halloween concert downtown."

"Phooey," said Mr. Wong, overturning the box and trying again. "What a mess that caused."

"Nothing like the mess around here," said Lieutenant Taper, sticking his head into the doorway.

"No doubt," said Father, flexing his right hand and rolling his shoulder. "Whoa, the Elevation is going to be murder."

"You going on a vacation?" asked Wickes, who was right behind Taper.

"He means the Elevation of the Body and Blood during Mass," said the gardener, slumped in his favorite chair, utterly exhausted. He was cradling in his hands all that was left of his aspen cane: the dented and cracked dragon's head. The rest had disintegrated along with the vampire's depleted corpse.

"Did you catch Jacco Babs and Ziggie Svelte?" asked Father, eyelids fluttering with pain, as he eased himself down into his chair behind the desk.

"Didn't even try," smiled Wickes.

"They'll never be able to use those pictures," said Taper. "Not in the legitimate press, anyway."

"What charges will you bring against Anthony Graves?" asked Father, attempting to button up his cassock with his left hand.

"None," said Taper. "He broke his neck when he fell."

"Perhaps that's best," sighed Father, deciding he'd rather leave it open. "I can't imagine how the district attorney would go about prosecuting such a case. Our lives would be tangled up for months. And the television coverage! No, for us at least, it is a mercy."

"Excuse me, excuse me," came another voice, elbowing in between Taper and Wickes.

"What is it, Monsignor Aspic?" asked Father, leaning back wearily in his chair.

"I was wondering if I might possibly keep this," said our favorite Jonas, holding up the black Cross with the golden Corpus, stainless steel chain still broken and swinging. "You know, this Cross I used at the front door to ... the one that you said Padre Somebody blessed ... I don't know exactly what happened but ... you know?"

"Of course," said Father. "You may have it."

I was impressed, not by Conrad J. Aspic's sudden fascination with the Crucifix, but rather Father Baptist's generosity in giving away something that I knew had belonged to his dead wife, Christine.

"Father," I whispered. "Are you sure—?"

"It's okay," he said, waving me down. "I shouldn't be holding on to it anyway. Perhaps it will do the monsignor some good."

"Really appreciate it," said Monsignor Aspic, turning to leave, some sort of distant-shore lava-lamp activity glistening in his eyes.

"I don't suppose, Monsignor," said Father, "you could transmogrify your gratitude into the paying of my bill?"

"Oh that," said the monsignor vaguely. "I'll see to it directly."

"Thank-you," said Father, unconvinced. "As for my bill for subsequent services, it would be—"

"Amazing," mumbled Aspic as he stepped through the doorway into the hall, Crucifix in hand. His feet barely touched the carpet as he turned and drifted out of sight. "I didn't know I had it in me ..."

"Maybe you should include an instruction manual," I mumbled. "St. Alphonsus' meditations on the Crucifixion, perhaps. Monsignor Aspic doesn't even know which end is up."

"If there's any Good Will in him," said Father, "he'll learn."

"Begging your pardon," said Father Nicanor, whooshing into view between Taper and Wicke's shoulders in a flurry of rolling r's. "Veronika and I, we are leaving. I, like you, Father, have to say morning Mass, and for so splendid a feast day. A wire I will be sending to Bishop Xandaronolopolis shortly thereafterwards. Is there anything you wish me to tell him?"

"Just send him our deepest gratitude for all his help," said Father. "And Millie's, for her Crucifix. It saved her life."

"Of course," said Father Nicanor, bowing to Father.

"I'd like to add something," I said.

"Of course," said Father Nicanor, repeating the same bow to me. The effect was the same without being so. It's hard to explain.

"Would you be so kind," I said, "as to tell my good Friend and Lord, Bishop Pip, that he was right."

"Usually he is," agreed Father Nicanor. "It is his way. But about something in particular this is?"

"Tell him: 'Fényi Márton sees stars.'"

"Who's Fényi Márton?" asked Wickes.

"Me," said me.

"Stars?" asked Taper.

"Martin," tisked Father Nicanor. "Hit your head you did when you fell?"

"No," I said, holding up the dragon's head as if it were a puppet. Its aspen teeth were now missing, a jagged gash traversed the wooden skull, and the throat tapered to a charcoal stub. "Look outside," I said to it, cocking its head toward the window. "See? The 'Vampire's Shroud' is gone."

"Wow, Unca Marty," I said for it in strained falsetto, "I can see the Big Dipper and everything!"

"It is as I said," said Father Nicanor to Taper and Wickes, "poor fellow, his head, hit it he did."

"Ah, but which one?" squeaked the dragon's head, turning his splintered gums, chipped eyes, and dented scales in Father Nicanor's direction. "The big head here—the empty one with the moving lips—or me?"

"Brain damage," said Taper.

"No doubt about it," said Wicks.

"In any case," I said, dropping the useless but talkative handle into my lap, "the 'Shroud' is gone—vanished in a matter of minutes. I caught the news report on that transistor radio of Millie's a little while ago, and the weatherman's eating his charts."

"You know, he's right," said Taper, craning his neck toward the window. "I can see the Big Dipper."

"On the way to the airport," I explained, "the bishop told me: 'Sir Martin, when the 'vrykolakas' dies, the stars you will see.' He was right, that's all."

"Who's Sir Martin?" asked Wickes.

"Me," said me. "It's a long story, Sergeant."

"And who's your little friend?" asked Taper, pointing to the dragon's head in my lap.

"Impy," squeaked my little friend, popping awake. It tried to wink but its wooden eyelids wouldn't budge. "That's short for 'Imprimatur.'"

"Lord have mercy," whispered Father, massaging his shoulder.

"In other words," I said to Father Nicanor, slipping back into my gardener's voice, "please inform the bishop that Sir Fényi Márton sees the stars."

"Bishop Xandaronolopolis will be pleased," said Father Nicanor, bowing again like a palm tree in a storm. "I bid you good morning, and farewell."

"What're you going to do with all that garlic, Jack?" asked Lieutenant Taper, settling down into my chair's twin. "After that Portifoy fellow discombobulated himself into it, you surely don't want Millie to use it in her stew."

"Discom-BOB-ulated," I mused. "When Demon Bob came unglued."

"I'll have Roberto turn it into the topsoil in the cemetery," said Father. "The place will smell for a while, but at least we Children of Adam won't have to worry about vampires so close to home."

"I guess we'll be going," said John Holtsclaw, closing his valise and snapping the latches. "By the way, the saliva from the wound on Mr. Ryan's throat defied analysis again. There must be something in vampire spittle."

"Venom," said the gardener. "It's vampire venom. Type V."

"You were also correct," said Solomon, gathering his coat, "about Tamara Grafan being drugged. We ran the tests late yesterday afternoon. Some sort of narcotic. We'll know about Marla sometime this evening."

"Don't call," said Father as Wong and Holtsclaw headed out the door. "I plan to crawl into bed as soon as Mass is over."

"I plan to crawl to the nearest winery, myself," said Pierre Bontemps, passing between the exiting coroners. "Dom Perignon and I have some unfinished business."

"I'm for a glass of George Sandeman's Port," said Arthur von Der-schmidt, close behind.

"Harvey's Bristol Cream for me," said Edward Strypes Wyndham.

"Guinness Stout," said Joel Maruppa.

"After Mass, of course," said Pierre.

"Of course," said Father. "And before, I do suggest you all arrange a change of clothes ... the garlic."

"Inside as well as out," said Edward, burping a puff of Millie's casserole.

"Only one cure," said Arthur.

The Tumblars all looked at one another: "Cigars!"

"Outside, please," said Father. "More olfactory stimulus I don't need."

"What do you call incense?" asked Pierre.

"A breath of fresh air," said Father, "compared to the mushroom cloud you men are proposing. Go on. I'll be fully functional by the time of our Tumblar meeting tomorrow night."

"What about you, Sir Martin?" asked Joel.

"I already changed my clothes," I said, flapping the lapels of my jacket. "After a hot shower."

"We'll change our venue, for the nonce," said Pierre, clicking his pocket guillotine cigar clipper. "But we shall return."

"Hurrah," said the rest, stomping out of the room.

"Quite a bunch," observed Lieutenant Taper.

"I don't get it," said Wickes, who, I've observed on so many occasions, didn't get much. "Why do you encourage them?"

"The Tumblars?" asked Father. "Why, they're—"

"A fine bunch of young men," said Monsignor Havermeyer, strutting vigorously into the room. "I didn't understand at first, either. But as with so many things, I've learned, and have much to learn."

"What's that?" asked Father, indicating an old and tattered book under the monsignor's arm.

"I've been invading your bookshelves," said Havermeyer, hefting the volume, "when I'm not making inappropriate calls to Cardinal Fulbright or practicing my Rubrics. This caught my attention because I thought perhaps it had been misplaced, that it belonged on the 'To be forewarned' shelf. But as I said, I have much to learn."

"When did you borrow it?" asked Father.

"About an hour ago."

"And you're already finished?"

"I took a speed-reading course a few years back. At Latin, I'm a snail. But give me a book in English, and I'll finish it almost as fast as I can turn the pages. This took a bit longer because the print is so faded."

"And what did you learn from that particular book?" asked the gardener. *"The History of Magic* by Eliphas Levi is not standard reading in the modern seminary."

"It's better than most of what they consume there now," grunted Havermeyer, shoving the weighty volume into its niche. He placed a gnarled hand on his scarred forehead and quoted: "'After death the soul belongs to God and the body to the common mother, which is earth. Woe to those who dare to invade these asylums.' If I had read that before last night, I would have been more prepared to help."

"You've got that backwards," said Father. "It's because of the events of last night that you're able to take that book seriously. The lessons we have all learned are merely preparation for what lies ahead."

"Which is?" I asked.

"Who knows?" said Father, shrugging—then grimacing and grabbing his shoulder again.

"Well," said Havermeyer, "one thing I can say, and this with certainty: the best decision of my life was to come here to St. Philomena's. My priesthood finally seems to have a purpose."

"I'm glad you feel that way," said Father. "So do we."

"And," said the monsignor, "I think one of my first projects, once we get things cleaned up—which will take a while, I realize—but I want to get that old library next to Martin's room back into working order. There must be a wealth of information stored in those books out there."

"Indeed," said Father. "That's something I've been wanting to do since I got here, but the time and expense—"

"Are something I wish to assume," said Havermeyer. "I'll sponsor a fund drive. The parishioners should have access to useful books—not the heretical mishmash Fulbright and his Educational Committee are shoveling down everyone's throats."

"Down boy," I whispered.

"One thing at a time, Monsignor," smiled Father Baptist. "For now, let's get through morning Mass. It's a Holy Day of Obligation, so the church will be crowded."

"See you then, Father," said Havermeyer, starting to leave. Then he stopped, turned, and faced Father again. "I'm sorry I doubted you—about the Buckminster Turnbuckle affair, I mean."

"I'm sorry, too," said Father. "But let's set that behind us."

"Done," nodded Havermeyer, and was gone.

"I can see that you really have found your niche, Jack," said Lieutenant Taper. "When you first left the force, I thought you'd gone nuts. But now I see that you followed the right star."

"Mary, Star of the Sea," said the gardener.

"This is your rightful place," said Taper. "You belong here."

"Keep that in mind," smiled Father, "when the collection plate comes by. Will you be sending the 'all clear' to Lucille?"

"Already did," said Larry. "She'll be arriving at LAX just in time for dinner."

"Speaking of dinner," said Millie, huffing her way into the room, "or breakfast for that matter, the kitchen is crawling with your policeman cronies, Lieutenant. They won't let me in, and they're dousing the floor with chemicals—that meat on the floor!—the linoleum's ruined, I 'spect. And let me tell you, Father—"

"Millie, Millie, Millie," said Father, "you are anxious about many things. I suggest that, if I'm even awake by then, you and Martin and I go out for a fine meal at Darby's, to celebrate. Martin, make a note to call Alan Ross and reserve a table out on the patio. We could all do with an unimpeded view of the stars."

"On me," said Lieutenant Taper. "It's the least I can do, and I know my wife would love to sit down to a fine dinner after a long flight, and a week of her mother's cooking."

"Well," blinked Millie. "Well, I, that is, I, uh—"

Taper turned to his partner. "You too, Sergeant. You're looking pale."

"A thick slab of red meat will put the pink in your cheeks, young man," said Millie to Wickes.

"I've had enough blood for a while," said Wickes.

"Fish then," said the lieutenant. "In fact, a whole lobster sounds good."

"Or steamed crab," said Millie, licking her lips.

"Fine," said Father, throwing up his hands—then cringing for the trouble. "We'll make an evening of it."

"But no dragons, okay?" said Wickes, driving plesiosaurs in Scottish lakes out of his brain by giving the bridge of his nose a pliers-like squeeze. "I really don't want to talk about monsters tonight, real or imagined."

"No argument here," said Taper, massaging the dents he'd rubbed into his head the other night. "My receptivity quotient is about maxed out."

"Or here," snorted Millie, fists on hips. "I'm glad Halloween's over. I need a break."

"Done," said Father.

"Hey!" whined Impy. "What about mrhmmrrmrhm—?"

I cut off the little guy's objection by burying his aspen head deep within the not-so-mysterious folds of the lining of my jacket. I was a little tired of dragons myself.

"Oh, and Millie," said Father, ignoring me as best he could, "one more thing: don't you think it's about time to start serving Monsignor Havermeyer some regular food? I think he's been punished enough for his impropriety."

"Monsignor Mike?" said Millie. "Why, I thought he liked potatoes."

"Well," said the gardener, "break him in easy. A little crust of dry bread at one meal, a little soup the next—"

"Go on, Mr. Feeney," giggled Millie. Giggled! What was the world coming to? Then she grabbed her head and shrieked. "My dress! It needs ironing. And I'll need to wash my sweater, and, oh these nails, and ..." She exited, bemoaning her apparel shortcomings all the way down the hallway to her room.

"Genesis eighteen eleven, huh?" I mused. "Her moods are certainly swinging."

"I think so," said Father. "She'll get over it."

"What're you talking about?" asked Wickes.

"There's a Bible on the shelf," I said. "You look it up."

Wickes turned and glared at the hefty leather volume near his elbow, but his ingrained fallen-away aversion to all things Catholic overcame his anxiety about Millie's condition and apparently his fear of not knowing.

"Excuse us," said another voice from the doorway.

Jonathan came into view, and then Stella. They were holding hands.

"We want to thank you, Father," said Jonathan.

"For everything," said Stella. "And don't worry about Daddy—"

"I won't," said Father Baptist. "I'll leave that for Jonathan."

Jonathan didn't look all that pleased, but as his eyes wandered from us back to Stella, he didn't seem to care. And so it goes.

"Besides," said Stella, "he sprained his ankle."

"Badly," said Jonathan.

"I didn't realize," said Father. "When he fell through the trap door?"

"No," said Jonathan. "When Joel unlocked the door to the utility room, and we all went outside, Stella's father tripped and stumbled over the birdbath in the garden."

"He was chasing Jonathan at the time," smiled Stella, giving her gallant Knight an appreciative nudge.

"How sad," I said, thinking more of that little porous bird, the one that always falls off the rim, spending the night in the tangled ivy.

"He'll be all right," sparkled Stella. "We'll take care of him."

"You do that," said Father. "Good morning."

"We're not leaving," said Jonathan. "Mass is in less than an hour."

"Good Heavens," said Father, looking at that bent-up old watch of his. The face got another dent in the garlic trap. "You're right."

"Dent," said old Josef who had just materialized in the doorway, nodding and grinning. He looked at Father, and then down at Jonathan's and Stella's gently enfolded hands. His smile widened. "Yah."

"Ymm!" agreed a muffled voice inside my jacket. "YmrhMMM-hrmm!"

133

FATHER BAPTIST MADE IT through Mass with flying colors.

I meant that literally.

The Elevation of the Consecrated Host went well, though I could hear him suck in his breath abruptly as I rang the altar bells.

The Elevation of the Precious Blood was another matter. John Holtsclaw's make-shift dressing came undone, and suddenly a circle of red erupted through Father's white Alb. It continued to spread, much to the rising consternation of some members of the congregation. Whether their concern was for his injury or the cost of replacing a golden Chasuble—since it, too, was soon stained—I don't know. I imagine the split was somewhere between sixty-forty and fifty-fifty.

Of course, Father had no choice but to continue, it being a Mortal Sin for a priest to leave the sanctuary once Mass has begun.

Later, after Communion, as I was pouring the water during the Purification, a drop of Father's blood fell into the Chalice. Unperturbed, he swirled the mixture and drank it down. A drop of blood isn't a fly, after all, especially when it's your own blood.

And what Blood with which to mix it.

Thursday, November Second

∞ Feast of All Souls ∞

∞ Early Morning Epilogue ∞

134

"YOU'D BETTER NOT SIT ON THAT," warned Father Baptist, indicating the cement birdbath opposite the wooden bench on which he sat in his neat but threadbare cassock. "The Tumblars set it back up after Chief Billowack's unfortunate accident, but it's not secure in the ground."

"You're right," I said, testing it with my hand. It wobbled severely.

I had just finished hauling a large, heavy cardboard carton from Father's study to the closet in my quarters for storage. It cost me. All those lab reports, files, notes, and travel brochures were now safely tucked away under several layers of my own personal debris.

"It's sad," said Father.

"What is?" I asked, opting to rest my aching weight on the edge of the small stone platform that served as a base for Saint Thérèse's statue. My aspen cane now history, I had reverted to my original walking stick—plain, practical, and made of some generic mutt-wood that had no significant preternatural properties whatsoever. It kept me from keeling over, which was enough to ask from any cane. I rested its ordinary handle against St. Thérèse's delicate plaster feet.

"The little stone bird is gone," said Father.

"I know," I said, rubbing the small of my back. "I spent part of the afternoon fishing around in the ivy for that little guy, but—"

"Yes," sighed Father. "I was watching you out here, just before dark."

Now it was after dark. In fact, it was really dark. The porch light over the kitchen door was still burned out. The illuminated clock on Millie's stove said 12:07. I could see it through the kitchen window. The Feast of All Souls was only a few minutes old. The electric light in the dining nook warmed the stained-glass window from within, just as we hoped Mrs. Magillicuddy would warm it again from without one of these Fridays soon.

The previous evening, after a brief detour to the emergency room at the nearest hospital where a grumpy intern stitched-up Father's shoulder and scribbled him a prescription for some expensive antibiotic horse pills, we had feasted as planned at Darby's. Everyone had fish of one sort or another except the gardener, who chose rack of lamb. Millie ate enough dressed crab to inspire a Gothic horror novel. After a dessert of New York cheese cake and coffee, followed by a prolonged discussion on everything except things that go bump in the night, we made our farewells and dispersed: Lieutenant and Mrs. Taper to the warmth of their home; Sergeant Wickes to the vacuum of his thoughts; Monsignor Havermeyer to his top-heavy camper; and Millie, Father, and I to St. Philomena's rectory, which for the past two weeks had been anything but a haven of serenity.

"You seem nervous," said Father, gently kneading his right shoulder.

"Me?" I said, rippling my fingertips over and over again against my knees. "Yes, well, it's just that, after all that's come and gone ... that cemetery, this garden, the birdbath, the people connected with us, this whole place ... it will never be the same again."

"No place ever is," said Father. "All things change except God. How's the book coming?"

"I'm only up to page forty-three. This one will take a while. Not only was the plot complicated, but things got a bit prolix at the denouement."

"Did they?" smiled Father. "I guess that couldn't be helped. Got a title for it yet?"

"I'm toying with that passage from the Last Gospel about the Light: 'The Darkness Did Not Comprehend It.'"

"Too long," said Father.

"Yeah," I nodded. "Maybe I should lop off a couple of words."

We sat for a while in silence, taking in the refreshing early morning air, bathing in the dim but satisfying light from the canopy of tiny stars that danced their slow majestic waltz, guided so adroitly by agile Angels who—believe it or not—were more concerned with us down here than with their cosmic ballet up there in the Heavens.

"'And therefore we also,'" said Father thoughtfully, "'having so great a cloud of witnesses over our head ...'"

"Yes," I nodded. "We're down here playing the fools while playing the fools, and They're up there scratching their heads."

"You really think I was too prolix at the denouement?" asked Father presently.

"A bit," I said. "I'll have to edit it down, and even then it went on and on. But there's something I want to ask you."

"There always is," he sighed.

"Why didn't you tell me, about the 'trap,' I mean? It was always, 'Later, Martin, I'll explain it later.' Why should I be kept out of the loop? I'm your chauffeur, your valet, your right-hand man, your cook when Millie's away, your unpublished chronicler—"

"But you're not an actor," said Father. I could see the dim rectory lights glistening in his eyes through the gloom. "When we stood face-to-face with Portifoy—"

"Up in Wrecked Room Number Three," I interjected. "And I was face-to-back."

"—any hint of anticipation on your part, Martin, even a worried glance at the carpet, and the vampire might have sensed its peril."

"So you kept me in the dark," I pouted.

"To bring us all to the Light," said Father.

"Hm," I shrugged, still strumming my kneecaps with my fingers. "Or at least into the garlic patch."

"Something else on your mind, Martin?"

"Sure, Father. Always is. I was just thinking how, even though this was a battle against the supernatural, if you take away the smoke and fangs, it really boiled down to another tangle of more-or-less palpable, navigable, unravelable clues."

"You mean the case was solved by investigation and insight, rather than by leading an innocent boy atop a white stallion around the local graveyards."

"Yeah, sort of."

"That's because, when all is said and done, the spiritual realities in which we believe are more real and tangible than the coarse substance we take so much for granted. Would that more people recognized that Spirit is more 'here' than matter—if they would but reach out and grasp it."

"Can I quote you on that?"

"Could I stop you?"

The crickets made their sweet music for a while, passing their secret messages around us as we sat there in the garden, breathing in and out, in and out, as living things tend to do. In the background rumble of the city, cars and trucks sucked in oxygen and expelled fumes, as combustion machinery tends to do.

Something moved in the ivy, lunging this way and that, as predators tend to do.

"What's that?" asked Father.

"A cat, maybe," I said. "Or a lizard."

"No, I mean under your jacket. Are you still playing with that dragon's head?"

"Impy? No, I left him on my nightstand, right next to the relic of the Crown of Thorns that Bishop Pip gave me."

"A regal gift indeed. But I was referring to that bottle-shaped thing you've got cradled in your hand."

"What?" I asked, pulling it out. "You mean this bottle-shaped thing?"

"The same."

"Oh, it's just another souvenir from the closet."

"'Lacrimae Christi,'" said Father. "'The tears of Christ.' Are you perhaps suggesting that, as the membrane between the spiritual realm and the corporeal grows thick again—"

"And we close the closet door on another murder case."

"—that I suspend your pledge—"

"Temporarily, Father. The key word is 'temporarily.'"

"—for the purposes of a toast?"

"Well, yes."

He looked at me with those sparkling eyes that seemed to whisper, penetrating yet merrily, "Considering that an exception becomes the rule, Martin, you're not proposing to make this some sort of tradition, are you?" But, exhaling slowly while rummaging for something from within the mysterious folds of his cassock, what he finally said was, "I thought so."

"Are those wine glasses?" I blinked.

"Fluted glasses, actually. I assume you brought the corkscrew."

"Here," I said, pulling the implement out of my pocket.

The bottle opened with a welcoming *thoonk,* and an old but obliging scent touched my nostrils as I poured the wine into the offered glasses.

"To whom shall we toast?" said Father, raising his drink. "St. Martha?"

"St. George?" I said, lifting mine.

"Both," we nodded, pulling our hands back a little so we could clink our glasses in hearty, manly style.

That's when it happened, when our glasses were inches apart.

Clink!

We both turned to the cement birdbath, the one Chief Billowack had knocked over, the one upon which I had just opted not to sit.

"Martin," said Father.

"Father," I said. "Do you see what I see?"

"Indeed."

The little porous bird was sitting there in the dim starlight, perched on the pockmarked rim. If stone birds could wink and smile, this one was doing so, and right at us.

"Father."

"Martin, do you smell that?"

"You mean—? But that's ... that's ..."

"Blueberry brandy."

The unmistakable smell of that curiously sweet, dark, liquor which I had spilled all over myself at the magic club wafted past us, mingling with the light, slightly bitter scent of Lacrimae Christi. It seemed to swirl gently around us, dancing with the sounds of the morning. I could almost hear the swish of a shimmy dress.

"Martin," said Father, eyes reflecting the stars, "I think you have made another friend."

"A faithful companion," I said, looking around in wonder, "and a perpetual comforter in any weather."

"To Elza then," said Father as we clinked our fluted glasses.

"To Elza," I said. "May she dance in peace."

THE END

—March 20, 1997:
The Feast Day of the First Day of Creation
when God said, "Let there be Light";
and of St. Photina, the Samaritan woman Jesus met at the well,
who was later martyred for her Faith in the city of Carthage,
and whose name means "Light."
Rock Haven.

NOTES:

LaVergne, TN USA
03 February 2010
171982LV00002B/121/A